HUMAN BEHAVIOR AT WORK
ORGANIZATIONAL BEHAVIOR

McGRAW-HILL SERIES IN MANAGEMENT

Keith Davis and **Fred Luthans,** Consulting Editors

HUMAN BEHAVIOR AT WORK

ORGANIZATIONAL BEHAVIOR

Fifth Edition

Keith Davis, Ph.D.
Arizona State University

McGRAW-HILL BOOK COMPANY

New York   St. Louis   San Francisco   Auckland
Bogotá   Düsseldorf   Johannesburg   London   Madrid
Mexico   Montreal   New Delhi   Panama   Paris
São Paulo   Singapore   Sydney   Tokyo   Toronto

To Mary Sue

This book was set in Helvetica by Progressive Typographers.
The editors were William J. Kane and Annette Hall;
the designer was Nicholas Krenitsky;
the production supervisor was Robert C. Pedersen.
New drawings were done by J & R Services, Inc.
Von Hoffmann Press, Inc., was printer and binder.

Library of Congress Cataloging in Publication Data

Davis, Keith, date
    Human behavior at work.

    (McGraw-Hill series in management)
    First published in 1957 under title: Human relations
in business; 2d (1962)-3d (1967) editions under title:
Human relations at work.
    Includes bibliographical references and indexes.
    1. Industrial sociology. I. Title.
HD6955.D38 1977   301.5'5   76-18975
ISBN 0-07-015489-9

CONTENTS

CONTENTS

PREFACE

The subject of this book is people at work in all kinds of organizations and how they may be motivated to work together in greater harmony. This subject is called human relations, organizational behavior, or human behavior at work, and it is an integration of social sciences as they affect people at work. A subject as vast as this can be merely introduced in the space of one book. Management, labor, and others can take justifiable credit for excellent advances in organizational behavior during the last three decades, but there is a long way to go. Perhaps this book can suggest directions toward further improvement.

All people who work in organizations should find this book helpful. It is designed for use in university courses, management development programs, advanced supervisory training, adult education classes, and management self-study.

The book has been tested on the firing line in university classrooms and in work organizations for twenty years, and many ideas offered by earlier users have been incorporated into this latest edition. I have expanded features desired by readers, such as charts and real-life examples to illustrate ideas. Emphasis is given to content and substance with thorough citations to research, rather than elementary platitudes and notions. Further, in order to have a book both teachable and readable, I have tried to present material in an organized fashion that will enable the reader to integrate the various parts of this discipline into a whole philosophy of organizational behavior. Where possible, I have included different viewpoints in order to meet the desire to do one's own thinking on the subject, but I have attempted to screen out trivialities and fads.

Many scholars, managers, and students have contributed ideas to this book, and I am grateful for their aid. I am especially grateful to Dean Glenn D. Overman and Dr. Harold E. Fearon of Arizona State University for their administrative encouragement. Able clerical assistance was provided by Mrs. Patricia I. Welch. Most importantly, my wife Sue provided considerate cooperation.

Keith Davis

SECTION 1

FUNDAMENTALS OF ORGANIZATIONAL BEHAVIOR

CHAPTER 1
WORKING WITH PEOPLE

The human being is the center and yardstick of everything.
Ernesto Imbassahy de Mello[1]

If you dig very deeply into any problem, you will get "people."
J. Watson Wilson[2]

LEARNING OBJECTIVES

TO UNDERSTAND:
The meaning of organizational behavior
Some of the elements with which it is concerned
High points in its early history
Reasons behind its rapid growth
Distinctions between Theory X and Theory Y
Basic concepts of organizational behavior

Organizations are social systems. If one wishes either to work in them or to manage them, it is necessary to understand how they operate. Organizations combine science and people—technology and humanity. Technology is difficult enough by itself, but when you add people you get an immensely complex social system that almost defies understanding. However, society must understand organizations and use them well because they are necessary to achieve the benefits that technology makes possible. And they are necessary for world peace, successful school systems, and other desirable goals that people seek. Modern society depends on organizations for its survival.

Human behavior in organizations is rather unpredictable as we now see it. It is unpredictable because it arises from deep-seated needs and nebulous value systems of individually different people. However, it can be partially understood in terms of the frameworks of behavioral science, management, and other disciplines; and that is the objective to which this book is dedicated. There are no simple, cookbook formulas for working with people. There is no idealistic panacea for organizational problems. All that can be done at present is to increase understanding and skills so that human relationships at work can be upgraded. The goals are challenging and worthwhile.

We can work effectively with people if we are prepared to think about them in human terms. Consider the following situation in which a manager's motivation was increased after years of passive, minimum performance.

John Doe, age about fifty, worked as assistant manager of a branch bank in a large banking system. He had been an assistant manager for eleven years. His work was so ordinary that no branch manager wanted him. Usually his current manager arranged to move him out of the way by transferring him to a new branch that was just opening; so John had worked in eight branches in eleven years. When he became assistant manager at his ninth branch, his manager soon learned of his record. Although tempted to transfer John, the manager decided to try to motivate him. The manager learned that John had no economic needs because he had a comfortable inheritance and owned several apartment houses. His wife managed the apartments. His two children were college graduates and had good incomes. John was contented.

The manager made little headway with John and twice considered trying to fire him. Occasionally John developed drive for a few weeks, but then he lapsed into his old ways again. After a careful analysis of John's situation, the manager concluded that although John's needs for tangible goods were satisfied, he might respond to more recognition; so the manager started working in that direction. For example, on the branch's first birthday the manager held a party for all employees before the bank opened. He had a caterer prepare a large cake and write on top an important financial ratio which was under John's jurisdiction and which happened to be favorable at the moment. John was greatly moved by the recognition and the "kidding" which his associates gave him about the ratio. His behavior substantially changed thereafter, and within two years he became a successful manager of another branch. In this instance John's performance was improved because his manager carefully analyzed the situation and used behavioral skills to achieve a result beneficial to both parties. That is the essence of organizational behavior.

UNDERSTANDING BEHAVIOR IN ORGANIZATIONS

A FOCUS ON ORGANIZATIONAL BEHAVIOR. The term "organizational behavior" applies broadly to the interaction of people within all types of organizations, such as business, government, schools, and service organizations. Whenever people join together in some sort of formal structure to achieve an objective, an organization has been created. Generally the people also use some sort of technology to help achieve their objective, so there is an interaction of people, technology, and structure, as shown in Figure 1-1. All three of these elements are influenced by the external social system, and they in turn influence it. The resulting mix of four key elements describes the scope of organizational behavior. Most people tend to give more emphasis to the internal organizational elements, but the external social system cannot be ignored because it influences people's values and contains other influential organizations, such as labor unions and minority groups. Each of the four key elements will be considered briefly.

The *people* constitute the internal social system of the organization. They consist of individuals and groups, and large groups as well as small ones. There may be unofficial, informal groups or more official, formal ones. Groups are dynamic. They form, change, and disband. The human organization today is not the same as it was yesterday, or the day before. People are the living, thinking, feeling beings who created the organization. It exists to achieve their objectives. Organizations exist to serve people, rather than people existing to serve organizations.

Structure defines the role relationships of people in organizations. Different role relationships are required because labor must be divided so that people can perform different kinds of work. Not all people in an office can be accountants, and not all employees in a university can be professors. Work is complex, and many different duties must be performed. There are managers and employees, and accountants and assemblers. These people have to be related in some structural way so that the work may be coordinated effectively. The main structure relates to power and to duties. For example, one person may have authority to make decisions that affect the work of other people.

Technology provides the physical and economic conditions within which people work. They cannot accomplish much with their bare hands, so they build buildings, design machines, create work processes, and assemble resources. The nature of the technology that results has a significant influence on the working relationships of people. An assembly line is not the same as a research laboratory, and a steel mill does not have the same working conditions as a hospital. The great benefit of technology is that it allows people to work more effectively (i.e., with less wasted effort and resources), but technology also restricts people in various ways, so it has costs as well as benefits.

The *social system* provides the external environment within which an organization operates. A single organization does not exist alone. It is part of a larger social system that contains thousands of other organizations. All these organizations mutually influence each other in a complex system that becomes the life-style of the people. Individual organizations, such as a factory or a school, cannot escape being influenced by this external system. It influences the attitudes of people, affects working conditions, and provides competition for resources and power.[3] It must be considered in the study of human behavior in organizations.

Now that we have described certain key elements in the study of organizational behavior, we can define it. *Organizational behavior is the study and application of knowledge about human behavior in organizations as it relates to other system elements, such as structure, technology, and the external social system.* The purpose of studying organizational behavior usually is to improve relation-

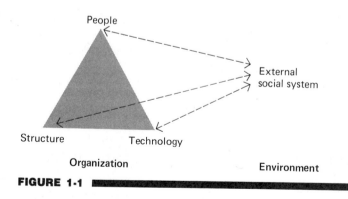

FIGURE 1-1 ■

Key elements in organizational behavior.

ships of people, structure, technology, and the external social system for better human results. Organizational behavior seeks to help people and organizations relate more effectively to each other. It is a human tool for human benefit.

THE ADMINISTRATIVE POINT OF VIEW. All people in organizations are concerned with improving organizational behavior. The janitor, the machinist, and the manager all have interactions with other people and thereby influence the behavioral quality of life within an organization. Managers, however, have a larger responsibility, because they are the ones who make decisions affecting many others in an organization. Essentially managers represent the *administrative system,* and in organizational behavior it is their role to integrate the *social system* (human system) with the *technical system* in order to improve people-organization relationships as shown in Figure 1-2. In this manner the organization can better accomplish the human benefits for which it was formed. From the administrative point of view *organizational behavior seeks to improve the people-organization relationship in such a way that people are motivated to develop teamwork that effectively fulfills their needs and achieves organizational objectives.*

The administrative view of organizational behavior contains a number of ideas. First, organizational behavior focuses primarily on people. Technical, economic, structural, and other elements are considered only as they relate to people. Second, these people are in an organizational environment, rather than in unorganized social contact. The principal focus of organizational behavior is to improve the people-organization relationship.

Third, a key activity in organizational behavior is developing an environment in which people are motivated. Managers are not trying to push or drive employ-

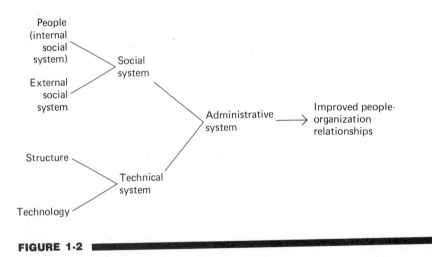

FIGURE 1-2

In organizational behavior the administrative system integrates the social system with the technical system in order to improve people-organization relationships.

ees; rather, they are trying to release inner drives that employees already have. People are the source of greatness in any organization. In the world of work all resources except human resources are restricted by the laws of mechanics, never having an output greater than their input. People alone through their creativity can produce outputs greater than the sum of their inputs.

Fourth, the direction of motivation is toward teamwork, which requires both coordination of the work and cooperation of the persons involved. *Coordination* refers to effective time and sequence in performing activities, while *cooperation* indicates the willingness of persons to work together toward objectives. The difference between these terms is illustrated by a team of five workers with sledge hammers driving a stake for a circus tent. All of them may want to drive the stake (i.e., cooperation), but unless their hammer blows are well coordinated, they will interfere with each other and produce only havoc, danger, and minimum results. This illustration shows that cooperation, or "goodwill," alone is not sufficient. On the other hand, cooperation is necessary for teamwork. Uncooperative letter-perfect obedience of rules and orders can be organizational sabotage. There is, for example, the story of the soldier who was ordered to "paint the whole truck." He did, including the motor, windshield, and seat cushions!

The fifth point is that organizational behavior seeks to fulfill both employee needs and organizational objectives. All people in organizations have needs that they seek to fulfill through organizational activities. They want economic, social, and psychological benefits. The organization's responsibility is to provide a behavioral climate in which people can gain need satisfaction while helping the organization reach its objectives. The desired goal is organizational success and employee satisfaction, not one or the other. In this way both parties benefit in the social transaction.

A sixth point about organizational behavior is that both employees and the organization seek results *effectively,* that is, with minimum costs in relation to benefits. Organizational behavior seeks to pay for itself both economically and psychologically by reducing wasteful activities and increasing effectiveness. In modern terms it reduces behavioral pollutants in the work environment and improves the quality of life.

HISTORICAL DEVELOPMENT OF ORGANIZATIONAL BEHAVIOR

HISTORICAL ORIGINS. Although human relationships have existed since the beginning of time, the art and science of trying to deal with them in complex organizations is relatively new. In the early days people worked alone or in such small groups that their work relationships were easily handled. It has been popular to assume that under these conditions people worked in a Utopia of happiness and fulfillment, but this assumption is largely a nostalgic reinterpretation of history. Actual conditions were brutal and backbreaking. People worked from dawn until dusk under intolerable conditions of disease, filth, danger, and scarcity of resources. They had to work this way to survive, so they had little time to try to improve behavioral satisfactions.

Then came the industrial revolution. In the beginning the condition of people did not improve, but at least the seed was planted for potential improvement, because industry was generating a surplus capital of goods and knowledge that eventually provided workers increased wages, shorter hours, and more work satisfaction. In this new industrial environment Robert Owen, a young Welsh factory owner, about the year 1800, was one of the first to emphasize human needs of employees. He refused to employ young children. He taught his workers cleanliness and temperance and improved their working conditions. This could hardly be called modern organizational behavior, but it was a beginning. He was called "the real father" of personnel administration by an early writer.[4]

Andrew Ure incorporated human factors into his *The Philosophy of Manufactures,* published in 1835.[5] He recognized the mechanical and commercial aspects of manufacturing, but he also added a third factor, which was the human factor. He illustrated how this factor was recognized by providing workers with hot tea, medical treatment, "a fan apparatus" for ventilation, and sickness payments. The ideas of Owen and Ure were accepted slowly or not at all, and in later practice they often degenerated into a paternalistic, do-good approach, rather than a genuine recognition of the importance of people at work.

EARLY DEVELOPMENT. Interest in people at work was awakened by F. W. Taylor in the United States in the early 1900s. He is often called "the father of scientific management," and the changes he wrought in management paved the way for subsequent development of organizational behavior. This is because he was the first to call attention to people in the work situation as important factors in the quest for efficiency in production. His work eventually led to improved recognition and productivity for industrial workers. He pointed out that just as there was a best machine for a job, so were there best ways for people to do their jobs. To be sure, the goal was still technical efficiency, but at least management was awakened to the importance of one of its hitherto-neglected resources.

Taylor's major work was published in 1911.[6] During that decade interest in human conditions at work was accelerated by World War I. The National Personnel Association was formed, and later, in 1923, it became the American Management Association, carrying the subtitle "Devoted Exclusively to the Consideration of the Human Factor in Commerce and Industry." During this period Whiting Williams was studying workers while working with them, and in 1920 he published a significant interpretation of his experiences, *What's on the Worker's Mind.*[7]

MAYO AND ROETHLISBERGER. In the 1920s and 1930s Elton Mayo and F. J. Roethlisberger at Harvard University gave academic stature to the study of human behavior at work. They applied keen insight, straight thinking, and sociological backgrounds to industrial experiments at the Western Electric Company, Hawthorne Plant. The result was the concept that an organization is a social system and the worker is indeed the most important element in it.[8] Their experiments showed that the worker is not a simple tool, but a complex personality interacting in a group situation that is hard to deal with and thoroughly misunderstood. Mayo pleaded that "collaboration . . . cannot be left to chance,"[9] and his colleague Roethlisberger added that "a human problem to be brought to a human solution requires human data and human tools."[10]

To Taylor and his contemporaries, human problems stood in the way of production, and so should be removed. To Mayo, human problems became a broad new field of study and an opportunity for progress. He is the father of what was then called human relations and later developed into the field of organizational behavior. Taylor increased production by rationalizing it. Mayo and his followers sought to increase production by humanizing it.

The Mayo-Roethlisberger research has been strongly criticized as being inadequately controlled and interpreted,[11] but its basic ideas, such as a social system within the work environment, have stood the test of time. The important point is that it was substantial research about human behavior at work, and its influence was widespread.

EXPANDING POPULARITY. The support of business leaders and academics led to a surge of interest in human behavior in organizations. By the 1950s the subject had become so popular that it had many of the characteristics of a fad. Some of the reasons for this heavy emphasis are as follows:

1. There was a cultural lag in understanding the human side of organizations so that heavy emphasis was needed to achieve development equivalent to that in engineering, production, sales, and finance. Management saw this imbalance and wanted to improve the situation.

2. A large amount of research followed the work of Mayo and Roethlisberger, giving managers new knowledge to work with in building a more effective organization.

3. Social forces brought increasing pressures for an improved human climate in organizations. Labor unions gained strength and pressed for a better working environment. Minority groups insisted upon a better climate for their members. Workers also were better educated and expected an improved, more human quality of leadership in organizations. Generally there was a change in social attitudes that required more social responsibility from organizations in dealing with all types of people, including their employees.

4. The work environment itself became more complex, requiring more attention from management to make it operate effectively. Increasing organization size compounded the complexity of work. Although it is relatively easy to get ten employees to work together effectively, it is more difficult to have a hundred employees do so, and very complicated to have a thousand employees working together. Increased specialization also contributed to the complexity of work. As organization size increased and technology advanced, more intense specialization developed, and employees became less able to understand the whole product or service that they helped produce.

The reasons discussed show that the emphasis given to behavior in organizations was a result of trends that had been developing over a long period of time. The new emphasis on people helped bring human values back into balance with other values at work. The unfortunate part of the situation, however, was that human relations grew so fast that much faddism and shallowness developed. Some practitioners began to emphasize the big smile, "being nice to people," and "keep 'em happy," while at the same time subtly trying to manipulate employees. This approach is illustrated by the cartoon in Figure 1-3. One humorist observed, "We have moved from the 'invisible hand' of Adam Smith's economics to the 'glad hand' of human relations." These practices led to well-deserved criticisms.[12] The term "human relations" gradually lost favor, although it continues to be used—especially at the operating level—because of its appropriateness. An example is the statement "The supervisor is effective with human relations." As the field became more mature and research-based, the new term that arose to describe it was "organizational behavior."

THEORY X AND THEORY Y. A powerful influence for maturity in organizational behavior was Douglas McGregor's Theory X and Theory Y, first published in 1957.[13] These two theories clearly distinguished traditional autocratic assumptions about people (Theory X) from more behaviorally based assumptions about people (Theory Y). The usefulness of the McGregor theories is his convincing argument that most management actions flow directly from whatever theory of human behavior managers hold. *Philosophy controls practice.* Management's personnel practices, decision making, operating practices, and even organization design flow from assumptions about human behavior. McGregor pointed out that Theory X was the set of assumptions held by most managers at that time. Even though they did not explicitly state their assumptions, they implicitly held them, because the kinds of actions they took could have derived only from Theory X.

Theory X implies an autocratic approach to managing. As shown in Figure 1-4, it assumes that most people dislike work and will try to avoid it if possible. They engage in various work restrictions because they are lazy and indolent. They have very little ambition and will avoid responsibility if at all possible. They are self-centered, indifferent to organizational needs, and resistant to change. The

PEANUTS ®   Charles M. Schulz

FIGURE 1-3

The cooperative approach can be overdone. (*Source:* United Features Syndicate, copyright © 1956. Used with permission.)

common rewards given by organizations are not enough to overcome their dislike for work, so the only way that management can secure high employee performance is to coerce, control, and threaten them. Though managers may deny that they have this view of people, their actions prove that Theory X is their typical assumption about employees.

Theory Y implies a humanistic and supportive approach to managing people. It assumes that people are not lazy and indolent. Any appearance they have of being that way is the result of their experiences with organizations, but if management will provide the proper environment to release their potential, work will become as natural to them as play or rest. They will exercise self-direction and self-control in the service of objectives to which they are committed. Management's role is to provide an environment in which the potential of people can be released at work.

McGregor's argument was that management had been ignoring the facts about people. It had been following an outmoded set of assumptions about people because it adhered to Theory X when the facts are that most people are closer to the Theory Y set of assumptions. There are important differences among people, so a few may come closer to Theory X, but nearly all employees have some Theory Y potential for growth. Managers had failed to recognize this potential; consequently, their policies and practices failed to develop it. The result was that many people regarded work as a curse on humankind instead of an opportunity for growth and fulfillment. Management's need was to change to a whole new theory of working with people: Theory Y.

THEORY X	THEORY Y
• The typical person dislikes work and will avoid it if possible.	• Work is as natural as play or rest.
• The typical person lacks responsibility, has little ambition, and seeks security above all.	• People are not inherently lazy. They have become that way as a result of experience.
• Most people must be coerced, controlled, and threatened with punishment to get them to work.	• People will exercise self-direction and self-control in the service of objectives to which they are committed.
	• People have potential. Under proper conditions they learn to accept and seek responsibility. They have imagination, ingenuity, and creativity that can be applied to work.
With these assumptions the managerial role is to coerce and control employees.	With these assumptions the managerial role is to develop the potential in employees and help them release that potential toward common objectives.

FIGURE 1-4

McGregor's Theory X and Theory Y, alternate assumptions about employees.

McGregor's ideas became a common subject in lecture halls, boardrooms, professional conferences, and business luncheons. They helped clarify direction for the new field of organizational behavior and move it toward the maturity that it needed. A large number of research projects were developed to test McGregor's ideas as well as other ideas, thereby giving a stronger research base to organizational behavior. Universities, such as Harvard, Ohio State, and Michigan State, and the Tavistock Institute in Britain made important contributions. By the 1960s the faddism of the 1950s had substantially vanished, and organizational behavior was becoming firmly established as an effective discipline.

FUNDAMENTAL CONCEPTS

Every field of social science (or even physical science) has a philosophical foundation of basic concepts that guide its development. In accounting, for example, a fundamental concept is that "for every debit there will be a credit." The entire system of double-entry accounting was built on this philosophy when it replaced single-entry bookkeeping many years ago. In physics, a basic philosophy is that elements of nature are uniform. The law of gravity is supposed to operate uniformly in Tokyo and London, and an atom of hydrogen is supposed to be identical in Moscow and Washington, D.C. But the same cannot be said for people.

Organizational behavior deals with a set of fundamental concepts, revolving around the nature of people and the nature of organizations. A summary of these ideas follows, and they are further developed in later chapters.

THE NATURE OF PEOPLE. With regard to people there are four basic assumptions: individual differences, a whole person, caused behavior (motivation), and value of the person (human dignity).

1. Individual differences. People have much in common (they become excited or they are grieved by the loss of a loved one), but each person in the world is also individually different. On the hills of Greenland lie billions of simple snowflakes; yet we are reasonably sure that each is different. On the planet Earth are billions of complex people who are likewise all different (and we expect that all who follow will be different)! Each one is different from all others, probably in millions of ways, just as each of their fingerprints is different, as far as we know. And these differences are usually substantial rather than meaningless. Think, for example, of a person's billion brain cells and the billions of possible combinations of connections and bits of experience that could be stored therein. All people are different. This is a fact supported by science.

The idea of individual differences comes originally from psychology. From the day of birth each person is unique, and individual experiences after birth make people even more different. Individual differences mean that management can get the greatest motivation among employees by treating them differently. If it were not for individual differences, some standard, across-the-board way of dealing with employees could be adopted, and minimum judgment would be required thereafter. Individual differences require that justice and rightness with employees shall be individual, not statistical.

Because of individual differences, organizational behavior philosophy, like democratic political philosophy, begins with the individual. Only a person can take responsibility and make decisions; a group by definition cannot do so. A group is powerless until individuals act therein.

2. A whole person. Although some organizations may occasionally wish they could employ only a person's skill or brain, all that can be employed is a whole person, rather than certain separate characteristics. Different human traits may be separately studied, but in the final analysis they are all part of one system making up a whole person. Skill does not exist separate from background or knowledge. Home life is not totally separable from work life, and emotional conditions are not separate from physical conditions. Each affects the others.

When management practices organizational behavior, it is trying to develop a better *employee,* but also it wants to develop a better *person* in terms of growth and fulfillment. Research suggests that jobs do shape people somewhat as they perform them, so management needs to be concerned about its effect on the whole person.[14] Employees belong to many organizations other than their employer, and they play many roles outside the firm. If the whole person can be improved, then benefits will accrue beyond the firm into the larger society in which each employee lives.

3. Caused behavior (motivation). From psychology we learn that normal behavior is caused by certain reasons. These reasons may relate to a person's needs and/or the consequences that result from acts. In the case of needs, people are motivated not by what we think they ought to have, but by what they themselves want. To an outside observer a person's needs may be illusory or unrealistic, but they are still controlling. This fact leaves management with two basic ways to motivate people. It can show them how certain actions will increase their need fulfillment, or it can threaten decreased need fulfillment unless they follow a required course of action.

Motivation is essential to the operation of organizations. No matter how much machinery and equipment an organization has, these things cannot be put to use until they are released and guided by people who have been motivated. Think for a minute in terms of a steam locomotive sitting in a railroad station. All the rails and equipment are in order; the schedule and routes are prepared; the objective is set; tickets are sold; and the passengers are on board. No matter how well all this preliminary work has been done, the train cannot move an inch toward the next station until the steam is usefully released—that is, until the motive power is supplied. Similarly, in an organization motivation turns on the steam to keep the organization going.

4. Value of the person (human dignity). This concept is of a different order from the other three because it is more an ethical philosophy than a scientific conclusion. It confirms that people are to be treated differently from other factors of production because they are of a higher order in the universe. It recognizes that because people are of a higher order, they want to be treated with respect and dignity—and should be treated this way. Every job, however simple, entitles the people who do it to proper respect and recognition of their unique aspirations and abilities. The concept of human dignity rejects the old idea of using employees as economic tools.

Ethical philosophy is reflected in the conscience of humankind and confirmed by the experience of people in all ages. It has to do with the consequences of our acts upon ourselves and others. It recognizes that life has an overall purpose and accepts the inner integrity of each individual. Since organizational behavior always involves people, ethical philosophy is involved in one way or another in each action.

THE NATURE OF ORGANIZATIONS. With regard to organizations, the key assumptions are that they are social systems and that they are formed on the basis of mutual interest.

1. Social systems. From sociology we learn that organizations are social systems; consequently, activities therein are governed by social laws as well as psychological laws. Just as people have psychological needs, they also have social roles and status. Their behavior is influenced by their group as well as by their individual drives. In fact, two types of social systems exist side by side in organizations. One is the formal (official) social system, and the other is the informal social system.

The existence of a social system implies that the organizational environment is one of dynamic change, rather than a static set of relations as pictured on an organization chart. All parts of the system are interdependent and subject to influence by any other part.

The idea of a social system makes the complexity of human behavior in organizations conceptually manageable. It provides a framework for considering and analyzing the variety of variables involved in any organizational situation.

2. Mutual interest. Mutual interest is represented by the statement "Organizations need people, but people also need organizations." Organization theory explains that organizations are formed and maintained on the basis of some mutuality of interest among their participants. People perceive organizations as a means to help them reach their goals, while at the same time organizations need people to help reach organizational objectives. If mutuality is totally lacking, it makes no sense to try to assemble a group and develop cooperation, because there is no base on which to build. Mutual interest provides a superordinate goal that unites the wide variety of needs that people bring to organizations. The result is that people are encouraged to attack organizational problems rather than each other!

BASIC APPROACHES TAKEN BY THIS BOOK

AN INTERDISCIPLINARY APPROACH. Organizational behavior integrates all the social sciences and other disciplines that can contribute to an understanding of people in organizations. It is neither psychology, nor sociology, nor organization theory; rather, it is all of these along with other disciplines. It integrates all of them in order to apply from each that which is appropriate when dealing with people at work. The field of organizational behavior is much like that of medicine, which integrates physical, biological, and social sciences into a workable practice.

The interest of various social sciences in people is sometimes expressed by the general term "behavioral science," which represents the systematized body of knowledge pertaining to why and how people behave as they do. This book especially seeks to integrate behavioral science with formal organizations. It has been said that the formal organization school sometimes speaks of "organizations without people," while behaviorists speak of "people without organizations." However, organizations must have people, and people working toward goals must have organizations; so it is desirable to treat the two as a working unit.

A HUMAN RESOURCES (SUPPORTIVE) APPROACH. The human resources approach is developmental. It is concerned with the growth and development of people toward higher levels of competency, creativity, and fulfillment, because people are the central resource in any organization. The nature of the human resources approach can be understood by comparing it with the traditional management approach in the early 1900s. In the traditional approach managers decided what should be done and then closely controlled employees to assure task performance. Management was directive and controlling. The human resources approach, on the other hand, is developmental and facilitative. It helps people grow in self-control, responsibility, and other abilities, and then tries to create a climate in which all employees may contribute to the limits of their improved abilities. It is assumed that expanded capabilities and opportunities for people will lead directly to improvements in operating effectiveness. Work satisfaction also will flow directly from employees making fuller use of their capabilities.[15] Essentially, the *human resources approach means that better people achieve better results.* It is similar to McGregor's Theory Y.

Another name for the human resources approach is the *supportive* approach, because the manager's role changes from control of employees to support of their growth and performance. Supportive managers may be compared to farmers. Farmers cannot tell plants how they should grow, but farmers can help provide the kind of climate in which plants grow to fulfill their potential. Similarly, supportive managers provide the type of organizational climate in which their employees can grow and be productive. The supportive model of organizational behavior is discussed in a later chapter.

A CONTINGENCY APPROACH. Traditional management relied on principles to provide a "one best way" of managing. There was a correct way to organize, to delegate, and to divide work. The correct way applied regardless of the type of organization or situation involved. Management principles were considered to be universal. As the field of organizational behavior developed, many of its followers also supported the concept of universality. Behavioral ideas were supposed to apply in any type of situation. For example, employee-oriented leadership should consistently be better than task-oriented leadership, whatever the circumstances. An occasional exception might be admitted, but the ideas were more or less universal.

15

Expanded behavioral research now shows that there are few across-the-board concepts that apply in all instances. Organizational situations are much more complex than first perceived, and the different variables in situations may require different behavioral approaches. The result is a *contingency approach to organizational behavior, which means that different organizational environments require different behavioral relationships for optimum effectiveness.*

No longer is there a one best way. Each situation must be analyzed carefully to determine the significant variables that exist in order to establish the kinds of behavioral practices that will be more effective. The strength of the contingency approach is that it encourages analysis of each situation prior to action, while at the same time discouraging habitual practice based on universal assumptions about people. The contingency approach is also more interdisciplinary, more system-oriented, and more research-oriented than the more traditional approach. Thus it helps to use in the most appropriate manner all the current knowledge about organizations. It is sometimes called the situational approach, because appropriate action depends on situational variables.

A SYSTEMS APPROACH. Conceptually a system implies that there are a multitude of variables in organizations and that each of them affects all the others in a complex relationship. An event that appears to affect one individual or one department actually may have significant influences elsewhere in the organization. This means that managers in taking actions must look beyond the immediate situation in order to determine effects on the larger system. Often negative effects as well as positive effects result from a behavioral action, so it is necessary to make a *cost-benefit analysis* to determine whether an action will produce a net positive or a net negative effect. No longer is it sufficient to look at benefits, because there may be costs in other parts of the system, as illustrated in the following experience of a supervisor.

In the upholstery department of a furniture factory a supervisor refused to allow an employee to take leave without pay to attend the funeral of a second cousin in a city 200 miles away. The employee claimed that special family relationships with this cousin required her attendance and took two days off without permission. When she returned, the supervisor disciplined her by giving her one day off without pay. Employees in other departments heard about the incident, and they felt that the discipline was unfair; so all plant employees walked off the job in a wildcat strike, threatening to remain off the job until the supervisor withdrew her penalty. The supervisor had failed to realize that actions in her department could have effects beyond that department in the larger factory system.

The systems approach applies especially to the social system discussed in the next chapter.

SUMMARY

Organizational behavior is the study and application of knowledge about human behavior in organizations as it relates to other system elements. Key elements are people, structure, technology, and the external social system. From the administrative point of view organizational behavior seeks to improve people-organization relationships in such a way that people are motivated to develop teamwork that effectively fulfills their needs and achieves organizational objectives. The administrative system integrates the social system with the technical system for improved human results.

From the 1930s to the 1960s organizational behavior was more commonly known as human relations, following the research of Mayo and Roethlisberger that began in the 1920s at the Western Electric Company. The maturation of organizational behavior was encouraged by widespread discussion of Douglas McGregor's Theory X and Theory Y, published in 1957, and by expansion of behavioral research.

Fundamental philosophical concepts of organizational behavior relate to the nature of people (individual differences, a whole person, caused behavior, and value of the person) and to the nature of organizations (social systems and mutual interest). Understanding is facilitated by the use of interdisciplinary, human resources, contingency, and systems approaches.

TERMS AND CONCEPTS FOR REVIEW

Organizational behavior

Human relations

Administrative system

F. W. Taylor

Elton Mayo and F. J. Roethlisberger

McGregor's Theory X and Theory Y

Individual differences

A whole person

Caused behavior (motivation)

Value of the person (human dignity)

Social systems

Mutual interest

Interdisciplinary approach

Human resources (supportive) approach

Contingency approach

Systems approach

REVIEW QUESTIONS

1. Define organizational behavior. What results do administrators seek when they practice organizational behavior?
2. Trace the early history of human relations and organizational behavior.
3. Describe McGregor's Theory X and Theory Y. Comment on the statement "Philosophy controls practice."
4. Comment on the statement "Organizations need people, but people also need organizations."
5. Discuss the basic philosophical concepts that form the foundation of organizational behavior. Is any one concept more important than the others?

CASE

THE TRANSFERRED SALES REPRESENTATIVE

Harold Burns served as district sales representative for an appliance firm. His district covered the central part of a Midwestern state, and it included about one hundred retail outlets. He had been with the company 20 years and in his present job and location for 5 years. During this time he had met his district sales quota each year.

One day Burns learned through local friends that the wife of a sales representative in another district was in town to try to rent a house. She told the real estate agency that her family would be moving there in a few days because her husband was replacing Burns. When Burns heard this, he refused to believe it.

Two days later, on January 28, he received an airmail letter, postmarked the previous day, from the Regional Sales Manager. The letter read:

Dear Harold:

Because of personnel vacancies we are requesting that you move to the Gunning District, effective February 1. Mr. George Dowd from the Parsons District will replace you. Will you please see that your inventory and property are properly transferred to him?

I know that you will like your new district. Congratulations!

Sincerely yours,

(Signature)

In the same mail he received his 20-year service pin. The accompanying letter from the Regional Sales Manager read:

Dear Harold:

I am happy to enclose your 20-year service pin. You have a long and excellent record with the company. We are honored to give you this recognition, and I hope you will wear it proudly.

Our company is proud to have many long-service employees. We want you to know that we take a personal interest in your welfare because people like you are the backbone of our company.

Sincerely yours,

(Signature)

Harold Burns checked his quarterly sales bulletin and found that sales for the Gunning District were running 10 percent below those in his present district.

QUESTION

1. Comment on the events in this case as they relate to organizational behavior. Was a human resources approach to people applied in this instance?

REFERENCES

1. Ernesto Imbassahy de Mello, "To Dignify the Human Being," *The Rotarian,* July 1975, p. 16.

2. J. Watson Wilson, "The Growth of a Company: A Psychological Case Study," *Advanced Management Journal,* January 1966, p. 43. Entire quotation italicized in the original.

3. For further discussion of the external social system, see Keith Davis and Robert L. Blomstrom, *Business and Society: Environment and Responsibility,* 3d ed., New York: McGraw-Hill Book Company, 1975.

4. Lee K. Frankel and Alexander Fleisher, *The Human Factor in Industry,* New York: The Macmillan Company, 1920, p. 8.

5. Andrew Ure, *The Philosophy of Manufacturers,* London: Charles Knight, 1835.

6. Frederick W. Taylor, *The Principles of Scientific Management,* New York: Harper & Brothers, 1911.

7. Whiting Williams, *What's on the Worker's Mind,* New York: Charles Scribner's Sons, 1920; and Whiting Williams, *Mainsprings of Men,* New York: Charles Scribner's Sons, 1925. A more recent related study is Studs Terkel, *Working: People Talk about What They Do All Day and How They Feel about What They Do,* New York: Pantheon Books, a division of Random House, 1974.

8. Elton Mayo, *The Human Problems of an Industrial Civilization,* Cambridge, Mass.: Harvard University Press, 1933; and F. J. Roethlisberger and W. J. Dickson, *Management and the Worker,* Cambridge, Mass.: Harvard University Press, 1939. The symposium on the fiftieth anniversary of the Western Electric Company, Hawthorne Studies, is reported in Eugene Louis Cass and Frederick G. Zimmer (eds.), *Man and Work in Society,* New York: Van Nostrand Reinhold Company, 1975.

9. Elton Mayo, Foreword to F. J. Roethlisberger, *Management and Morale,* Cambridge, Mass.: Harvard University Press, 1941, p. xix.

10. Roethlisberger, *op. cit.,* p. 9.

11. For example, see Alex Carey, "The Hawthorne Studies: A Radical Criticism," *American Sociological Review,* June 1967, pp. 403–416.

12. An example of the strong criticisms made is Malcolm P. McNair, "Thinking Ahead," *Harvard Business Review,* March–April 1957, pp. 15ff.

13. Theory X and Theory Y were first published in Douglas McGregor, "The Human Side of Enterprise," in *Proceedings of the Fifth Anniversary Convocation of the School of Industrial Management,* Cambridge, Mass.: Massachusetts Institute of Technology, Apr. 9, 1957. They were later popularized in Douglas McGregor, *The Human Side of Enterprise,* New York: McGraw-Hill Book Company, 1960.

14. Melvin L. Kohn and Carmi Schooler, "Occupational Experience and Psychological Functioning: An Assessment of Reciprocal Effects," *American Sociological Review,* February 1973, pp. 97–118.

15. Early emphasis on the human resources approach to organizational behavior was provided in Raymond E. Miles, "Human Relations or Human Resources?" *Harvard Business Review,* July–August 1965, pp. 148–163; and later presented in his book, *Theories of Management: Implications for Organizational Behavior and Development,* New York: McGraw-Hill Book Company, 1975.

CHAPTER 2
SOCIAL SYSTEMS

Organizations can be observed as a series of patterned interactions among actors.
J. Eugene Haas and Thomas E. Drabek[1]

We have ignored, for too long, the group nature of . . . organizations.
Fred H. Goldner[2]

LEARNING OBJECTIVES

TO UNDERSTAND:
How the social system works in an organization
The meaning of achievement motivation
The significance of the work ethic
How role and role conflict apply in organizations
Causes of status in organizations
How symbols of status affect work relationships

Stanley Pedalino graduated from the university in the top 10 percent of his graduating class. He decided that he needed some manual labor experience before entering his chosen profession of marketing, so he went to work as a construction laborer for a year. He found that his college education was of no value among his construction associates. Many of them looked down on college types, and some of them inquired what "a college dude" like Pedalino was doing working as a construction laborer. A year later, when Pedalino joined the sales research staff of a national firm, he found that his education was favorably received. Contrary to the construction crew, the sales research staff respected education and encouraged even further education.

Pedalino never stopped to analyze the situation, but what he was experiencing was a social system, and it was a significant influence on many parts of his job. It determined the attitudes and values surrounding the job, and it influenced the way that people interacted with each other. In this chapter we examine some of the ingredients of a social system, such as social equilibrium, culture, role, and status.

SOCIAL EQUILIBRIUM

CONCEPTUALIZING THE SOCIAL SYSTEM. A social system may be conceptualized as a complex set of human values and relationships mutually interacting in an infinite number of ways. Possible combinations of interaction appear to be as limitless as the physical universe with its billions of galaxies. Each small group is a subsystem within larger groups that are subsystems of even larger groups, and so

21

on, until the world's population is included. Within a single organization the social system is all the people in it, as they relate to each other and to the outside world.

The complex interactions in a system of this type may be illustrated by a chart, as shown in Figure 2-1.[3] The figure shows a box frame with objects A through E fastened to it by elastic bands 1 through 6. The objects are fastened to each other by bands 7 through 12. Suppose that elastic band 6 is moved toward point a. In this instance all five of the objects will be affected rather than just object E. They will move in location, and the tension on the bands will change. Consider object A. It will be affected by path 6-7, by path 6-11-12, and by path 6-11-10-9-8. At the same time all the other objects will be affected by various paths interacting together. If any of the other elastic bands are moved, all the other objects will be affected each time. This physical example illustrates the mutual interdependence of all parts of a social system. Simply stated, a change in one part of the system affects all other parts.

DEFINING EQUILIBRIUM. A system is said to be in *social equilibrium* when there is a dynamic working harmony among the interdependent parts of the system. Social equilibrium is a dynamic concept, not a static one. Movement is taking place all the time in a social organization, but the movement is done in a way that retains

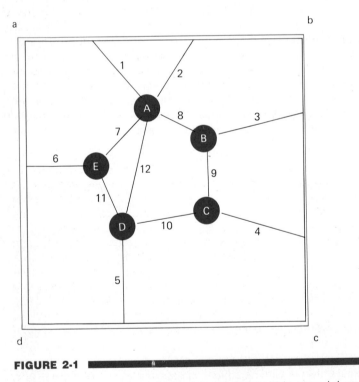

FIGURE 2-1

Illustration of the complex interdependence within a social system.

working harmony and balance in the system. The system is like an ocean, in which there is continuous motion but the basic character of the sea changes very little.

When minor changes occur in a social system, they are absorbed by adjustments within the system, and equilibrium is retained. On the other hand, major changes or a series of rapid changes may throw an organization out of equilibrium, seriously reducing its vigor and productivity, until it can reach a new equilibrium. In a sense, when it is in disequilibrium, its parts are working against one another instead of in harmony. Here is an example.

In a South American factory, accidents are high. The six native jefes, or supervisors, in the factory were not following management's instructions for accident prevention. They seemed agreeable but failed to "get the message" of accident prevention; consequently their employees were careless, too. This was disequilibrium, with groups working at cross-purposes.

Finally, management had papier-mâché heads of the six jefes molded and colored, with the idea that each week these heads would be arranged into a "totem pole" in the order of the weekly safety rank of each department. No jefe wanted to see himself as a low man on the safety totem pole; so the accident problem was quickly corrected.

A change such as the factory totem pole just mentioned is considered "functional" to the system when it reinforces or improves the system. When a change weakens the system it is "dysfunctional." One managerial responsibility is to appraise every contemplated change in terms of its possible functional or dysfunctional consequences on the social system. In order to do this, the manager must define the social systems that are most involved in the decision, because one decision could be functional to systems A and D but dysfunctional to system B. What is desirable for the whole may not be desirable for all parts of the whole. Further, decisions always will tend to be imperfect, because of our inability to understand the whole system and to foresee the future.

ADJUSTMENT OF INDIVIDUALS. Equilibrium in an organizational system does not imply that all the people in it are adjusted to it. They may or may not be. To the system, equilibrium is important; but to the person, *adjustment* is important. It is the employee's state of harmony with the system. Adjustment is dynamic rather than being achieved once and for all. People who have difficulty adjusting, or who adjust in a way not approved by society, are said to be maladjusted. Since all people are at times maladjusted, this condition becomes important only when a person rather frequently fails to adjust. Examples of the results of maladjustments at work are labor turnover, labor agitation, insubordination, absenteeism, and theft. For example, turnover studies consistently show that many new employees leave during their first few weeks of employment because of inability to adjust to their new situation. They get a poor first impression and never stay for the second impression. Others develop in the beginning certain maladjustments that later cause resignation or dismissal.

PSYCHOLOGICAL CONTRACT. What employees do when joining an organization is to make an unwritten *psychological contract* with it, although generally they do not recognize at a conscious level that a contract has been made. This contract is in addition to the economic contract for wages and working conditions. The psychological contract defines the conditions of each employee's psychological involvement with the system. Employees agree to give a certain amount of work and loyalty, but in return they demand more than economic rewards from the system. They seek security, treatment as human beings, rewarding relationships with people, and support in fulfilling expectations. If the organization honors only the economic contract and not the unwritten psychological contract, employees will tend to lose interest in their jobs.

Essentially the psychological contract is governed by *exchange theory,* which states that in order for people to join and remain with an organization, the benefits they receive must be more than their costs. Unless they feel that the exchange relationship is rewarding, they will tend to withdraw from it. The more rewarding it is, other things being equal, the more they will be attached to the organization and support it.

EQUITY THEORY.   Exchange theory relates to *equity theory,* which is concerned with each person's feelings of fairness about the rewards received from an organization. The rewards covered are all types, including psychological and social rewards along with economic rewards. The theory holds that employees tend to determine equity by considering their inputs and outcomes on the job compared with the inputs and outputs of selected comparison people. If the ratios of the two people are unequal, this condition creates a tension of inequity in the employee that motivates corrective action. What really occurs is a *cognitive dissonance* in which employee feelings of equity do not agree with the actual rewards received. There is a difference that the employee feels should be resolved to bring the employee's personal system back into balance. For example, in one organization, ledger clerks felt inequitably treated because their outcomes were too low in relation to their inputs when they compared their input-outcome ratio with the ratio for cash posters. When workers such as the ledger clerks perceive inequity in their social exchange with the organization, studies show that absences and turnover increase.[4]

As might be expected, when outcomes are low in relation to employee perceptions of equity, employees will be dissatisfied and will tend to reduce inputs to more nearly match outcomes. A less expected relationship that occurs is that when outcome ratios are high in relation to others, employees tend to reduce the inequity by *increasing* their inputs.[5] In other words, many people want to feel that in return for their rewards they are giving an appropriate contribution to their organization. They want to merit what they receive, because in this way their self-esteem is preserved.

CULTURE

Whenever people act in accordance with the expectations of others, their behavior is social, as in the case of an employee we will call Maria. Like all other workers, Maria grows to be an adult in a *culture,* which is her environment of human-created beliefs, customs, knowledge, and practices. Culture is the conventionalized behavior of her society, and it influences all her actions, although it seldom enters her conscious thoughts. Maria drives to work on the right side of the road or the left, depending on the culture of her society, but she seldom consciously stops to think of this. The car she drives, the drama she attends, the organization that employs her, and all other human-created items are evidence of her culture.

Culture changes slowly, and in doing so it gives stability and security to society. This is an advantage. However, there is a balancing disadvantage—the culture sometimes uselessly resists change. Employees, for example, often show cultural resistance to a technological change that management introduces. Managers, in turn, often resist changes in their management structure. The stable persistence of culture is shown by a comparison of industrial organization in Japan and in the United States. Both nations use the same technology, but Japan's factories are organized according to a different social logic.

Culture may interfere with rational production efficiency by requiring actions unnecessary or unrealistic from a rational point of view, but necessary from the cultural point of view. For instance, in the United States, construction of part of a large cathedral was once halted for several weeks because over a weekend birds had built a nest in one of the concrete forms. At a construction site in another nation construction could not begin until an appropriate ceremony had removed evil spirits from the site.

BASIC CULTURE AFFECTING WORK. Many aspects of life have a significant influence upon behavior; therefore, any understanding of employee behavior must be preceded by study and understanding of the culture in which they live. People meet in churches, schools, homes, and stores; they read books; they go to movies; and they engage in many other activities that cause them to develop a set of basic values long before they seek their first employment. In fact, basic values are so well ingrained that they are very difficult to change, even before a person finishes high school. They influence the amount of education one seeks, how hard one works on the job, and the way in which one cooperates with fellow workers and managers. The basic relationship is that culture off the job affects on-the-job performance.

MOTIVATIONAL PATTERNS. All parts of culture interact to develop in each person certain *motivational patterns*. These are configurations of many specific cultural influences that together determine the way individuals approach their jobs and even life in general. Motivational patterns develop especially from a person's family background, education, and national culture. Different countries, therefore, are likely to have one or two motivational patterns that predominate among their workers. Four motivational patterns that are especially significant are achievement, affiliation, competence, and power.

Achievement motivation is a desire to overcome challenges, advance, and grow. Much interest in it was generated by the research of David C. McClelland of Harvard University.[6] One of McClelland's studies covered a number of countries, comparing such items as the motivational pattern emphasized in stories in children's reading books with the actual motivational patterns of adults in the same country years later at the time the children would have been adults. He found much similarity in the two patterns. Generally the countries where achievement motivation predominates are those that have made the most socioeconomic progress. Achievement motivation leads to higher levels of aspiration, so the people work harder and make more progress.

Achievement-motivated persons are the best source of competent leadership in a nation's organizations, and those persons with more achievement motivation tend to rise the highest. Achievement-motivated persons seek accomplishment for its own sake. They are not strongly "money-hungry," although they may acquire wealth in their drives to achieve. They work because of the sense of challenge, accomplishment, and service to others that they feel. Monetary rewards are more a lure to people low in achievement motivation. The irony of all this is that the entrepreneurs and business leaders, since they are usually high in achievement drives,[7] turn out to be the ones who are not as money-motivated as many others are. It is estimated that about 10 percent of the people in the United States are highly achievement-motivated.[8]

Here is an example of achievement motivation in practice. During a heavy snowstorm the president and vice presidents of one company were able to get to their offices on time, but a number of lower managers were late or absent. The top executives undoubtedly were there because they felt an inner drive and sense of responsibility, factors which helped them climb to top leadership. On the other hand, some of the lower managers probably lacked this inner drive and felt no strong compulsion to brave blizzard conditions in order to get to work.

Affiliation motivation is a drive to relate to people. Comparisons of achievement-motivated employees with affiliation-motivated ones will illustrate how the different motivational patterns influence behavior. People with achievement motivation work harder when they have precise feedback about their successes and failures. But persons with affiliation motives work better when they are complimented for their favorable attitude and cooperation. Achievement-motivated persons select assistants who are competent, regardless of personal feelings about them; however, affiliation-motivated people select friends to surround them.

Competence motivation is a drive to do quality work. Competence-motivated employees often are so interested in technical aspects of their jobs that they are blind to the human factor at work. They seek job mastery and professional growth. *Power motivation* is a drive to be in control. Power-motivated persons tend to be somewhat higher risk-takers than others. They may use power constructively in building successful institutions, but they also may use it destructively in relation to institutions and people.

Additional motivational patterns are autonomy, security, and status. Motivational patterns are not mutually exclusive. The usual person has some of most motivational patterns, *but one or two patterns tend to predominate in job motivation.* McClelland believes that less developed nations need a substantial number of citizens with high achievement motivation in order to generate socioeconomic development. Fortunately achievement motivation can be developed. In India, which has a social climate deficient in achievement motivation, McClelland has been able to double the rate of entrepreneurial activity of persons having a course in achievement motivation. He asks, "Why have policy-makers been so slow to act on this knowledge to invest in programs that would develop people's motives rather than merely their opportunities for work?"[9]

Knowledge of motivational patterns helps management recognize those employees who are self-motivated, as distinguished from those who depend more on external incentives. Management can then deal with people differently according to their personal motivational patterns.

THE WORK ETHIC. For many years the culture of much of the Western world has emphasized work as a desirable and fulfilling activity. The result is that work is a central life interest to many persons.

One study was made of 331 first-through-third-level supervisors in six Michigan firms.[10] In a survey of the supervisors, 54 percent reported that work was a central life interest with them. Work interests tended to dominate their psychological life. There was no significant variation in percentage among the three levels. Higher-level supervisors were no more work-oriented than first-level ones. For comparative purposes, the proportion of industrial employees with work as a central life interest was 24 percent, as obtained in an earlier study.

The work ethic has its origin in both religious and secular values. From the religious point of view the work ethic was supported by Calvinism in the Protestant Reformation and by the Puritan way of life in the United States. Because of its religious origins it has been called the Protestant ethic. The religious view of the work ethic holds that work is a moral good in itself. Individuals become better persons by the act of working, and they also help build a better society to help fulfill God's plan. Human talents have been given to people by their Maker for the purpose of use, so hard work and frugality (lack of waste) become moral obligations. Studies show that religion has affected attitudes toward work, because people of different religious backgrounds do tend to vary in their work orientations.[11]

The secular origins of the work ethic are thought to have resulted from the hard necessities of pioneer life. People had to work hard to stay alive, and therefore they found reason to glorify work. It was a central fact of their environment. It also was their only possible path to improvement of their standard of living, so it was seen as a desired ideal by which each generation could contribute something to the generations that followed.

Research has provided interesting insights about the work ethic.[12] It appears that the work ethic may be deeply embedded in the drive to control one's environment. Experiments with small children, giving them opportunity to secure an equal number of marbles with or without work, showed that the majority wanted to work for their marbles. The researcher concluded, "The findings from this experiment revealed that children, regardless of their culture, sex, I.Q., and need-achievement, prefer to get their rewards by working."

The researcher concluded, "The important thing appears to be not that human beings get food, water, and shelter, but that they get these things in ways that convey to the individual the sense that he is important, that he does control

what happens to him." People have deep-seated drives to control their environ-
ment and to test and affirm their competence. Work is an important means to these
ends.

ROLE

The idea of role comes from sociology and is the *pattern of actions expected of a*
person in activities involving others. It includes both rights and obligations, both
power and responsibility. It arises as a result of the way each person's position is
viewed in the social system. In order to be able to interact with each other, people
need some way to anticipate others' behavior. Role performs this function in the
social system.

A person has roles both on the job and away from it, as shown in Figure 2-2.
One person performs the occupational role of worker, the family role of parent, the
social role of club president, and many others. In those various roles a person is
both buyer and seller, supervisor and subordinate, and giver and seeker of advice.
Each role calls for different types of behavior. Within the work environment alone,

FIGURE 2-2

Each employee performs many roles.

a worker may have more than one role, such as a worker in group A, a subordinate to supervisor B, a machinist, a member of a union, and a representative on the safety committee.

Undoubtedly role is the most complexly organized response pattern of which a human being is capable. Activities of managers and workers alike are guided by their *role perceptions,* that is, how they think they are supposed to act in a given situation. Since managers perform many different roles, they must be highly adaptive in order to change from one role to another quickly. Supervisors particularly need to be adaptable in working with the extremes of subordinate and superior and with technical and nontechnical activities.

A *role set* is the entire configuration of surrounding roles as they affect a particular role, such as the supervisor's role just described. That is, all the different persons with whom a supervisor interacts have *role expectations* concerning the way in which the supervisor should act, and these expectations collectively make up the role set for the job. This role set arises partly from the nature of the work itself, because managers in equivalent jobs but in different companies tend to perceive and play their roles in about the same way.[13]

The existence of role expectations means that a manager (or other person) interacting with someone else needs to perceive at least three role values, as shown in Figure 2-3. First there is the manager's role as required by the function being performed. Then there is the role of the person being contacted. Finally there is the manager's role as seen by the other person. Obviously one cannot meet the needs of others unless one can perceive what they expect. Research shows that

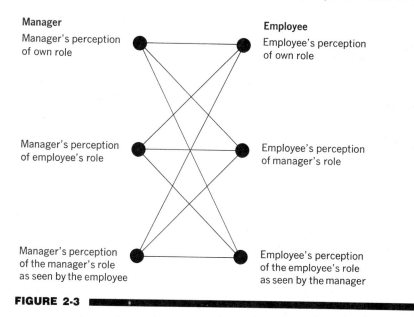

Manager	Employee
Manager's perception of own role	Employee's perception of own role
Manager's perception of employee's role	Employee's perception of manager's role
Manager's perception of the manager's role as seen by the employee	Employee's perception of the employee's role as seen by the manager

FIGURE 2-3

Role perceptions of a manager and an employee make a complex web as they interact.

where there is wide variance between a manager's role perception of the job and the employees' role expectations of that job, there tends to be poor motivation and inefficiency. They may even have difficulty communicating because they will not be talking about the same things in the same way. For example, difficulties may arise because a manager sees the best role as that of an autocrat, but employees expect a participative person.

When expectations of a role are materially different or opposite, a person tends to be in *role conflict* because there is no way to meet one expectation without rejecting the other. A president in one company faced role conflict, for example, when he learned that both the controller and the personnel director expected him to allocate the new organizational planning function to their departments.

Research shows that role conflict at work is fairly common. A national sample of wage and salary workers reported that 48 percent experienced role conflict from time to time, and 15 percent indicated that role conflict was a frequent and serious problem.[14] Role conflict was particularly difficult for employees who were required to interact outside the organization, because external expectations often differ considerably from internal expectations. When persons were classified according to the frequency of their job contacts outside their organization, those with negligible outside contacts had the least role conflict, and those with frequent contacts had the most conflict.

When role expectations are inadequately defined or are substantially unknown, *role ambiguity* exists, because people are not sure how they should act in situations of this type. Research consistently discloses that where role conflict and ambiguity exist, dysfunctional results occur. There is particularly a decline in job satisfaction and need fulfillment.[15] One study of professional employees in a research and development office, for example, reported that those with role conflict and ambiguity had significantly less job satisfaction.[16]

Employees generally are more satisfied with their jobs when expectations for performance are clearly defined. A fuller understanding of roles helps people know what others expect of them and how they should act. Human relationships also are helped by understanding the role of the persons with whom one is interacting, because then one has a better picture of why they are acting the way they are. Each person in an organization plays several roles, so the role that one is playing at a particular time must be understood for effective human relationships to develop. For example, in a factory an employee who was a union steward came to his supervisor for guidance on a work problem. His supervisor thought he was approaching in his role of union steward to challenge her authority, so a misunderstanding developed. In an office an older employee tried to play the role of adviser or helper with a new employee, but the new employee felt he was being "bossed" by someone who had no right to give him orders, so the relationship failed.

STATUS

The social rank of a person in comparison with others in a social system is referred to as *status*. Status may be either formal or informal. Formal status refers to the rank of people as designated by the authority structure of an organization. Informal status refers to the social rank accorded to people because of feelings toward them. It is the position that one has in an informal social system.

Status relationships require ranking and comparison, so two or more persons are required to make a status relationship. Individuals are bound together in *status systems,* or *status hierarchies,* which define their rank relative to others in the system. They sometimes will make a strong effort to achieve slightly more status. The term "lose face" is often used as a synonym for loss of status in personal interaction, and its seriousness is widely recognized. When people become seriously upset over their status and their inability to change it, they are said to have *status anxiety.*

Loss of status is a serious event for a typical person. People, therefore, become quite responsible in order to protect and develop their status. One of management's pioneers, Chester Barnard, stated, "The desire for improvement of status and especially the desire to protect status appears to be the basis of a sense of general responsibility."[17]

Since status is important to people, they will work hard to achieve it. Many will seek it for its own sake, even if it provides no additional pay or other tangible benefits. When status is attached to actions that further the company's goals, strong incentives are released toward their accomplishment.

By way of illustration, a laundry manager used to devote negative attention and reprimand (low status) to workers whom he found idle, even when they had finished their work and were waiting for more from another operator. He wanted them to help other operators, but he found that his approach simply caused them to work slower. Upon reexamination of his approach, he decided to try to build the status of his "idle" employees who finished their work ahead of others. He visited with them in a friendly way as he walked through his shop. He permitted them to go to any other work station to talk and visit, or to get soft drinks for themselves or others. The slow workers began to work faster to achieve this status, and the fast workers improved in order to preserve their relative position. As the fast workers visited other work stations, they developed friendships and did considerable informal training and helping of the slow workers. The manager later commented, "I am amazed by the changed attitudes of the workers and their increased productivity."

Status tends to be important only in the particular social group where the status is accorded, rather than being some general characteristic that goes wherever a person goes. One executive told how he worked hard for a promotion and the status it would bring him with his friends. The promotion finally came, but it required him to move to another city where he was unknown. He said that the promotion was hollow because in this new location his new friends were his peers and looked on him as "just another manager."

STATUS RELATIONSHIPS. Generally high-status persons in a group have more power and influence than those with low status. They also receive more privileges from their group as a result of their status. Other things being equal, those with high status tend to participate more in significant activities of the group. They also tend to interact more with their peers than with those of lower rank. Basically high status gives people an opportunity to play a more important role in an organization. As a result, lower-status members tend to feel isolated from the mainstream and to show more stress symptoms than higher-ranked members.[18]

Since status places people on different levels, which is contrary to equalitarian values in a democratic society, people sometimes perceive that any status is dysfunctional to the social system. This is not an accurate conclusion, however. Organized work requires that people perform different functions and levels of work, and these conditions cause status differences to develop. Status, therefore, provides a system by which people can relate to each other in group work. Without it they either would be a confused rabble or would spend most of their time trying to figure out how to relate to others in the system. Though status can be abused until it is dysfunctional, normally it contributes to the group because it enhances their ability to cooperate efficiently without an enormous waste of time.

Causes of status differences stretch almost to infinity because each situation is different. Some organizational causes of status are organizational level, type of work, skill used, working conditions, pay, and seniority.

OCCUPATIONAL PRESTIGE. As a result of various status influences, each occupation has a general prestige rating among the public. This rating is the one that an organization should expect in its jobs in that occupation, subject to some variation because of local factors.

Studies of occupational prestige in several nations show that it is especially related to education required and income received. Education generally gives people more job autonomy, ability to interpret and control their environment, and scarce knowledge that enables them to command the attention and respect of others. It also usually gives them jobs with better working conditions, such as pleasant surroundings and less arduous physical labor. For example, compare the working conditions of an accountant and a miner.

Occupational prestige is significant to human behavior in several ways. It often helps a counselor diagnose status problems and conflicts. It influences the kinds of promotions and transfers an employee will take. It helps determine who will be informal leader of a group composed of different occupations. It definitely serves as a motivation to those seeking to advance in the organization. Some persons are status seekers, wanting a job of high status regardless of its other conditions. These persons can be encouraged to qualify themselves for high-status jobs so that they can become better adjusted.

SYMBOLS OF STATUS. The status system reaches the ultimate of observable evidence with its *status symbols.* These are the visible, external trappings that attach to a person or workplace and serve as evidence of social rank. They exist in the office, shop, warehouse, refinery, or wherever work groups congregate. They are most in evidence among different levels of executives because each successive level usually has the authority to provide itself with surroundings just a little different from those of persons lower in the structure.

In one office, the type of wastebasket is a mark of distinction. In another, significant symbols are type of desk, stapling machines, and telephones. In the executive offices, such items of rank as rugs, bookcase, curtains, and pictures on the wall are important.

All this concern for symbols of status seems amusing, and at times it is, but at other times status symbols are a serious problem. They endanger job satisfaction because executives who do not have a certain symbol and think they should can become gloomy, nervous employees. Status symbols lead to conflict because executives vie with each other to get particular ones. And finally, symbols can affect the company budget if executives try to acquire too many of them.

Since symbols of status exist in every organization, a manager needs to be alert to them. They will serve as a disruptive force or as positive motivation, depending on the skill with which management handles them. When, for example, an employee gives unreasonable attention to status symbols, this is evidence of status anxiety that requires management attention.

What should be management's policy toward status symbols? Some managers go so far as to deny the existence of status symbols in their firms, but this is hardly realistic. Others allow symbols to develop as a part of tradition. It is understood that when a corner office becomes vacant the next person in line gets it, and so on, but nothing is put in writing. This policy works under conditions of stability, but a move to a new office building may so upset relationships that there has to be some codifying of the rules. Codification reduces friction, is the most efficient way to allocate space, and gives positive budget control over symbol purchases; but it also smacks of regimentation.

Regardless of which approach is used, the rule usually is that persons of equal rank in the same department receive approximately equal status symbols. There may be some variation between broad departments, such as production and sales, because work is distinctly different and rank is not so easily comparable. In any case, managers face the fact that status exists and must be dealt with. They do have the power to influence and control status relationships somewhat. The organization gives some status, and it can take some away!

SUMMARY

When people join a work group, they become part of that organization's social system. It is the medium by which they relate to the world of work. The variables in an organizational system operate in a degree of working harmony called social equilibrium. The individual's harmony with the system is called adjustment, and this is partially determined by the individual's psychological contract with the system. Relationships of the individual with the organization are governed by exchange theory and equity theory.

The environment that people create is their culture. Behavioral patterns that develop from cultural influences include achievement, affiliation, competence, and power motivation, and the work ethic.

Role is the pattern of action expected of a person in activities involving others. Related ideas are role perceptions, role set, role expectations, role conflict, and role ambiguity. Status refers to the social rank that a person has in comparison with others in a social system. Related ideas are status systems, status anxiety, and status symbols. Status symbols are sought like magical herbs because they may accord status to their possessor.

TERMS AND CONCEPTS FOR REVIEW

Social equilibrium
Functional and dysfunctional effects
Adjustment of the person
Psychological contract
Exchange theory
Equity theory
Culture
Motivational patterns
The work ethic

Role
Role set
Role conflict
Role ambiguity
Status
Status anxiety
Occupational prestige
Status symbols

REVIEW QUESTIONS ▬▬▬▬▬▬▬▬▬▬▬

1. Discuss how motivational patterns, role, and status influenced your interaction with others yesterday. What is your primary motivational pattern?
2. How does exchange theory operate to influence an individual's integration with an organization?
3. Discuss the work ethic as it applies to (a) you and (b) the members of your group.
4. Interview an office manager to determine what the manager believes to be the five principal status symbols in the office.
5. Prepare and administer in your class or other group a survey to determine the prestige of twenty occupations that you select. Interpret the results of your survey.

CASES

LIBERTY CONSTRUCTION COMPANY

Liberty Construction Company is a small construction company in Colorado. Over half of its revenue is derived from the installation of underground water and power lines, so much of its work is seasonal and there is high turnover among its employees.

Michael Federico, a college student, had been employed by Liberty as a backhoe operator for the last three summers. On his return to work for the fourth summer Federico was assigned the second newest of the company's five backhoes. The owner reasoned that Federico had nine months of work seniority, so according to strict seniority he should have the second backhoe. This action required the present operator of the backhoe, Pedro Alvarez, a regular employee who had been with the company seven months, to be reassigned to an older machine. Alvarez was strongly dissatisfied with being assigned an older machine, because he felt that as a regular employee he should have retained the newer machine, instead of having to give it to a temporary employee. The employees soon fell into two camps, one supporting Alvarez and one supporting Federico. Job conflicts arose, and each side seemed to delight in putting work impediments in the way of the other side. In less than a month Alvarez left the company.

QUESTION

1. Discuss this case in terms of the social system, equilibrium, the psychological contract, equity theory, role, status, and status symbols.

JAMES BOND

James Bond, an office clerk, has asked you, his supervisor, to issue a purchase order for a water bottle for his desk. He claims that his injured leg makes it difficult for him to get to the office water fountain about 50 feet away. You know that Bond does have a slight limp from a football injury ten years ago, but he moves about the office satisfactorily and has been going to the water fountain without complaint for five years. You know that Bond frequently seeks status symbols, and you judge that he really wants the water bottle to give his desk a more "executive look" than desks of the other clerks.

QUESTION

1. Bond is waiting for your response. What will you do?

THE GREEN CORPORATION

Jerry Blue is supervisor of purchasing for the Green Corporation, a manufacturer of a consumer product in a town of 5,000 persons. The company employs 350 persons. Reporting to Blue is one buyer, John James. James is an ambitious young community college graduate who is very intent on opportunity and advancement. His abilities have been recognized by higher management, and he is being considered for two different higher positions that may open within the next year. Blue, who is older and has only one year of college, is content in his present position.

James has a clerk-typist named Barbara Smith reporting to him. Recently Barbara Smith and her husband bought a new home in the same block in which the Blues live. Mr. and Mrs. Smith have since become close social friends of the Blue family.

As a result of this close friendship, recently Barbara has been going to Jerry Blue to get answers to her work problems, rather than to her immediate supervisor, John James. James feels bypassed in the chain of command, but he has said nothing to Blue or Smith about this. No one at the company knew about the problem until James's wife telephoned the personnel manager, explaining that James is so upset with the problem that he has had to seek medical attention.

QUESTIONS
1. Using the point of view of social systems, analyze the causes of this developing problem.
2. You are Jerry Blue, and the personnel manager has just told you about the telephone call. What will you do?

REFERENCES

1. Eugene Haas and Thomas E. Drabek, *Complex Organizations: A Sociological Perspective,* New York: The Macmillan Company, 1973, p. 8.

2. Fred H. Goldner, "Managers: An Improper Subject for the Study of Management," in Gerald G. Somers (ed.), *Proceedings of the Eighteenth Annual Winter Meeting,* Madison, Wis.: Industrial Relations Research Association, 1966, p. 82.

3. This manner of conceptualizing the social system was first brought to my attention in Lawrence J. Henderson, *Pareto's General Sociology: A Physiologist's Interpretation,* Cambridge, Mass.: Harvard University Press, 1935.

4. Charles S. Telly, Wendell L. French, and William G. Scott, "The Relationship of Inequity to Turnover among Hourly Workers," *Administrative Science Quarterly,* June 1971, pp. 164–172; and Martin Patchen, "Absence and Employee Feelings about Fair Treatment," *Personnel Psychology,* Autumn 1960, pp. 349–360.

5. J. Stacy Adams and William B. Rosenbaum, "The Relationship of Worker Productivity to Cognitive Dissonance about Wage Inequities," *Journal of Applied Psychology,* June 1962, pp. 161–164.

6. David C. McClelland, *The Achieving Society,* Princeton, N.J.: D. Van Nostrand Company, Inc., 1961. See also the relation of achievement and power motivation in David C. McClelland and David H. Burnham, "Power Is the Great Motivator," *Harvard Business Review,* March–April 1976, pp. 100–110.

7. See Paul F. Kaplan and Cynthia Hsien Huang, "Achievement Orientation of Small Industrial Entrepreneurs in the Philippines," *Human Organization,* Summer 1974, pp. 173–182.

8. Fred Luthans, *Organizational Behavior,* New York: McGraw-Hill Book Company, 1973, p. 402.

9. David C. McClelland, "Achievement Motivation Can Be Developed," *Harvard Business Review,* November–December 1965, p. 7; and David C. McClelland and David. G. Winter, *Motivating Economic Achievement,* New York: The Free Press, 1969.

10. John G. Maurer, "Work as a 'Central Life Interest' of Industrial Supervisors," *Academy of Management Journal,* September 1968, pp. 329–339. The Maurer article provides references to other studies of work as a central life interest. See also Robert Dubin, Joseph E. Champoux, and Lyman W. Porter, "Central Life Interests and Organizational Commitment of Blue-Collar and Clerical Workers," *Administrative Science Quarterly,* September 1975, pp. 411–421.

11. David L. Featherman, "The Socioeconomic Achievement of White Religio-Ethnic Subgroups: Social and Psychological Explanations," *American Sociological Review,* April 1971, pp. 207–222.

12. Devendra Singh, "The Pied Piper vs. the Protestant Ethic," *Psychology Today,* January 1972, pp. 53–56.

13. Henry A. Landsberger, "The Horizontal Dimension in Bureaucracy," *Administrative Science Quarterly,* December 1961, pp. 299–332, reporting research in three comparable companies.

14.   Robert L. Kahn and others, *Organizational Stress: Studies in Role Conflict and Ambiguity,* New York: John Wiley & Sons, Inc., 1964, pp. 56, 99–124.

15.   John R. Rizzo, Robert J. House, and Sidney I. Lirtzman, "Role Conflict and Ambiguity in Complex Organizations," *Administrative Science Quarterly,* June 1970, pp. 150–163; and Henry Tosi, "Organization Stress as a Moderator of the Relationship between Influence and Role Response," *Academy of Management Journal,* March 1971, p. 16.

16.   Robert T. Keller, "Role Conflict and Ambiguity: Correlates with Job Satisfaction and Values," *Personnel Psychology,* Spring 1975, pp. 57–64.

17.   Chester I. Barnard, "Functions and Pathology of Status Systems in Formal Organizations," in William F. Whyte (ed.), *Industry and Society,* New York: McGraw-Hill Book Company, 1946, p. 69.

18.   Allan Mazur, "A Cross-Species Comparison of Status in Small Established Groups," *American Sociological Review,* October 1973, pp. 513–514.

CHAPTER 3
MAINSPRINGS OF MOTIVATION

Motivation says do this because it's very meaningful for me to do it.
Frederick Herzberg[1]

If you are like a wheelbarrow, going no farther than you are pushed, then do not apply for work here.
Sign at Factory Employment Gate Many Years Ago

LEARNING OBJECTIVES

TO UNDERSTAND:
Types of needs that people have
How needs express themselves to affect action
The priority of different needs
The meaning of motivational and maintenance factors
The difference between intrinsic and extrinsic motivators

Assume that an employee called Mary Smith is employed as a computer programmer in a government office or in a business. Mary, an individual, enters the organization, an operating social system. She brings to her job certain needs that in her environment are translated into wants. Perhaps she wants to learn and advance, someday becoming controller of all financial activities, or perhaps she wants security and good working conditions. Within this situation the organization tries to provide a climate wherein Mary is *motivated* in a way that serves her and its interests.

In a way, this whole book is about Mary's situation; however, it is first necessary that certain psychological foundations be discussed, and this is the purpose of the next two chapters.

HUMAN NEEDS

When a machine malfunctions, people recognize that it needs something. Assume that a machine will not grind a piece of metal to a close enough tolerance. Perhaps it needs oil. Or maybe a nut is loose. First the operator tries to find the trouble. Then help is sought from the supervisor. Finally a maintenance mechanic is called, or an engineer, and so on, until the cause of the problem is found and the machine is put back into working order. All the people who tried to find the causes of the machine breakdown did so (or should have done so) in an analytical manner based upon their knowledge of the operations and needs of the machine. It would have been wasteful to begin haphazardly to tighten nuts and to oil gears with the hope that the trouble could be found. Such action might aggravate the malfunction.

Suppose that the machine operator malfunctions regularly by talking back to the supervisor in a way that borders on insubordination. The supervisor may want to reprimand the operator without analyzing the situation, but this would be no better than haphazard machine repair. Like the machine, the operator who malfunctions does so because of definite causes that may be related to particular needs. In the foregoing illustration, perhaps the operator felt insecure and was trying to gain reassurance through self-assertion. Motives are expressions of a person's needs; hence they are personal and internal. Incentives, on the other hand, are external to the person. They are something placed in the work environment by management to encourage workers to accomplish goals. For example, management offers salespersons a bonus as an incentive to channel in a productive way their needs for recognition and status.

Certain physiological functions occur without motivation, but nearly all conscious behavior is motivated, or caused. Growing hair requires no motivation, but getting a haircut does. Falling asleep will occur eventually without motivation (parents with young children may doubt this!), but going to bed is a conscious act requiring motivation. Management's job is to identify and activate employee motives constructively toward task performance. Diagramed very simply, the relation of needs to action is shown in Figure 3-1. Needs create tensions that are modified by one's culture to cause certain wants. These wants are interpreted in terms of positive and negative incentives and one's perception of the environment in order to produce a certain response, or action. To illustrate, need for food produces a tension of hunger. Since culture affects hunger, a South Seas native may want roast fish, while a Colorado rancher wants broiled steak.

TYPES OF NEEDS. There are various ways to classify needs. A simple but significant one is (1) basic physiological, or *primary,* needs, and (2) social and psychological needs, called *secondary* needs. Some of the physiological needs are food, water, sex, sleep, air to breathe, and satisfactory temperature. These needs arise out of the basic physiology of life and are important to survival and preservation of the species. They are, therefore, virtually universal among people, but they exist in different *intensity.* A child needs much more sleep than an older person. These needs also are conditioned by social practice. If it is customary to eat three meals a

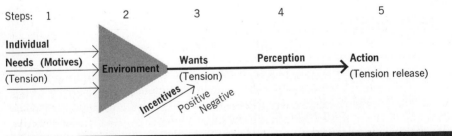

FIGURE 3-1

Conscious action arises from needs.

day, then the body comes to respond accordingly. It could exist on two or four meals. If a coffee hour is introduced in the morning, then that becomes a physical habit of appetite satisfaction, as well as a social one.

Secondary needs are more nebulous because they represent needs of the mind and spirit, rather than of the physical body. Many of these needs are developed as one matures. Examples are rivalry, self-esteem, sense of duty, self-assertion, giving, belonging, and receiving affection. The secondary needs are the ones that complicate the motivational efforts of managers. Nearly any action management takes will affect secondary needs; therefore, *management planning should consider the effect of any proposed action on the secondary needs of employees.*

Secondary needs vary among people much more than primary physiological needs. They may even exist as opposites in two different persons. One person has a need for self-assertion and is aggressive with people. A second person, on the other hand, seeks to be submissive and to yield to others' aggressions. Needs also change according to time and circumstance. Following is an example of how money assumed a different meaning for a man when he was promoted.

John Doe went to work for the Smith Company after he graduated from high school. He was intelligent, was hard-working, and made decisions effectively; consequently he was promoted rapidly within the company. Eventually he was promoted to vice president of production and at this time began to share in a liberal stock option plan. Rather quickly his whole attitude toward his job changed. The quality of his decisions deteriorated, and he could not make them objectively. Whenever a decision concerned money, he just could not emotionally bring himself to authorize the expenditure; however, during the twenty years before his promotion he had been able to make similar decisions easily. Something was wrong.

Soon he recognized that he had a problem and sought help to identify it. It was discovered that during his youth he had been very poor and had developed an emotional block against spending money. When he came under the stock option plan, he identified the company's money as his, and he could not bring himself to spend it. Earlier he had been spending the company's money, but now each expenditure seemed to be a drain on his own savings. When he finally saw his problem, he was able to face expenditures more objectively and become a top-quality manager again.

Secondary needs develop a variety of motives in each person. Analysis of behavior would be simple if a person's behavior at a given time were the result of one motive and one alone, but this is seldom the case. Motives of all types and intensities influence one another to accomplish a particular motivation. The result is that management, like Sherlock Holmes, is always looking for "the motive"! This is as hard to find as in detective work, because the same motive can cause different behavior at different times. Conversely, the *same behavior* can result from different motives. For example, the same behavior—absenteeism—can result from lack of interest in the job, conflict with a coworker, or for a variety of other reasons. Motives, however, do have limits, because they cannot immediately bring about a behavior for which one does not have the skill or competence, such as playing a violin or performing calculus. In the long run, of course, motives may encourage one to learn difficult behaviors.

CHARACTERISTICS OF SECONDARY NEEDS. Secondary needs are often hidden so that a person cannot recognize them. This fact alone makes psychological counseling quite difficult. Since secondary needs are so nebulous, dissatisfied workers usually attribute their dissatisfaction to something more tangible, such as wages. Many so-called wage disputes do not really concern wages, so meeting the wage request does not remove the basic dissatisfaction that existed.

In summary, secondary needs have the following characteristics:

1. They are strongly conditioned by experience.

2. They vary in type and intensity among people.

3. They change within any individual.

4. They work in groups rather than alone.

5. They are often hidden from conscious recognition.

6. They are nebulous feelings instead of tangible physical needs.

7. They influence behavior. It is said that "we are logical only to the extent our feelings let us be."

Although human needs have been classified as primary and secondary, this is for purposes of discussion only. In a particular human being they are inseparable. The state of the physical body affects the mind, and the state of mind can affect the physical body. In fact, medical research shows that body chemistry (a physical condition) affects the emotions and feelings. According to the renowned psychiatrist, Dr. William C. Menninger, "The psychiatrist believes that the mind and body are inseparable—the holistic concept. The former tendency to regard the mind and body as separate has been discarded. Now we study the physical, the chemical, the psychological, and the social factors of every individual who comes to us for help."[2]

MASLOW'S PRIORITY OF NEEDS

It is good to know what a person's primary and secondary needs are, but this does not answer the question of which ones are important at a particular time and place. Psychologists recognize that needs have a certain priority. As the more basic needs are satisfied, a person seeks the higher needs. If one's basic needs are not met, they claim priority, and efforts to satisfy the higher needs must be postponed. A need priority of five levels has been presented by A. H. Maslow and has gained wide attention.[3] These five needs are:

1. Basic physiological needs

2. Safety and security

3. Belonging and social needs

4. Esteem and status

5. Self-actualization and fulfillment

The important point about need levels is that usually they have a definite sequence of domination. Need Number 2 does not dominate until Need Number 1 is reasonably satisfied. Need Number 3 does not dominate until Needs Number 1 and 2 have been reasonably achieved, and so on, as illustrated in Figure 3-2.

LOWER-ORDER NEEDS. Need Number 1 is the basic survival need. In the typical work situation it rarely dominates because it is reasonably well satisfied. Only an occasional experience, such as two days without sleep or a crumb in one's windpipe, reminds us of the essential nature of basic physiological needs; however, in parts of the world where there is very low productivity, or famine, or disaster, the priority of survival needs is obvious. Under these conditions much of human conduct is dominated by physiological needs. Other needs do exist and influence conduct somewhat in times of crisis, but survival tends to dominate.

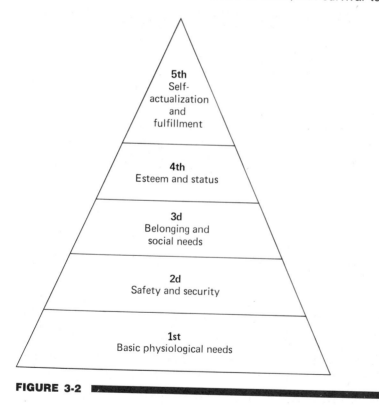

FIGURE 3-2

Order of priority of human needs according to Maslow.

People must work to satisfy their physiological needs, but when these are satisfied to some degree, it becomes their wish to satisfy other needs. The need that next tends to dominate is safety and security. It works somewhat as follows. Having met their basic physiological needs, people want some assurance that these needs will be met tomorrow and thereafter, and with less effort, pain, or worry, if possible. Having taken care of today, people want assurances for tomorrow. Accordingly they build walls around primitive cities, build granaries for food storage, or establish pension programs. They want bodily safety as well as economic security. Security essentially provides that physiological needs will be met tomorrow and as long thereafter as possible. In reality, then, Need Number 2 is still related to Need Number 1.

Because of individual differences, people seek different amounts of security, but virtually all people have some basic need for security. People also vary in the ways that they try to provide their security, as illustrated by the approaches of two sales representatives in an instrumentation sales office.

One of the men tried to provide his security by spending extra hours to write long reports on the analog control line to ensure that he would be considered so expert in this field that the company could not do without him. The other salesman reacted differently, going to school at night to learn about digital theory and application, which was a new product area with the company. He felt that he could best be secure by becoming knowledgeable in the new control equipment. Thus, two people reacted differently under the same circumstances and the same needs.

Physiological needs are essentially finite. People can be surfeited with them so that more of them actually will be harmful. One can have too much water, food, or warmth; and, in fact, we sometimes oversupply ourselves with them. We take too much for our own good. The same relationship appears to hold true for safety and security needs. We can be or feel so safe that we soon become careless or defenseless. We can feel so secure that our drives and independence fade away, until we become dependent on others. An ever-present dilemma is to determine how far to go in providing safety and security for people's development, but not enough to weaken them. The problem is faced alike by employer with personnel and by government with citizens.

HIGHER-ORDER NEEDS. Although physiological needs are essentially finite, needs at the third, fourth, and fifth levels are substantially infinite. Accordingly, these higher-order needs are likely to be the dominant ones in advanced civilizations. They are the ones that merit our attention and toward which this book is directed. These higher-order needs are social and self needs; however, we will continue Maslow's classification, which divides them into three priority levels. Need Number 3 concerns belonging, social involvement, and love. It is significant that this need does not dominate our energies until the first two have been partly met. It might be argued that Need Number 3 should be met mostly off the job; however, one-third to one-half of employee waking hours are spent at work. People work in a social environment, and some of their belonging needs must be met there as well as away from work.

Need Number 4 is esteem and status. We need to have, to receive, and to give these sentiments. We need to feel inside ourselves that we are worthy, to feel also that others think we are worthy (status), and to believe that they likewise are worthy. This particular need is especially recognized in the philosophy of "value of the person" presented in Chapter 1. It is an important need of modern society mostly because the first three basic needs are already partly satisfied in developed nations.

The fifth basic need is self-actualization, which means becoming all one is capable of becoming. This need is less apparent than others because many persons have not unleashed it. They are still busy with Needs Number 3 and 4. Though self-actualization dominates few people, it influences nearly all persons. They choose occupations that they like, and they get certain satisfactions from accomplishing their tasks. To the degree that the fifth need can be unleashed, people will find their work a challenge and an inner satisfaction, as illustrated by the following incident.

In August of 1963, in Seattle, Washington, I attended a meeting and listened to exciting comments by Jim Whittaker, who had just returned to the United States after being the first American to climb Mount Everest (May 1, 1963). This was a dangerous undertaking (one climber was killed) and an exhausting one (returning by the South Summit he could take only one step every five minutes when the oxygen supply became exhausted). One person in the group asked Jim why he dared the dangers of a climb to the top of Everest. His simple, straight answer came quickly, "Because it was there!" To him it was a challenge—something to do for self-actualization.

INTERPRETING THE PRIORITY OF NEEDS. Lower-order needs are primarily satisfied through economic behavior. People earn money as a medium of exchange to purchase satisfactions for physiological and security needs. Their higher-order needs, on the other hand, are primarily satisfied through symbolic behavior of psychological and social content. They attach meaning to their experiences and derive satisfactions from how they feel about their experiences. This is behavior of a different order from economic behavior, requiring different ways of thinking about people. Managers sometimes have felt that they could meet all need satisfactions by providing wages and letting employees then use the wages to acquire their own satisfactions. This economic approach does not hold up when analyzed in terms of the five basic needs, since money applies mostly to the first two of them. Sometimes it is difficult to get managers to drop their economic ideas of human behavior. A vice president described how he convinced two of his personnel as follows:

I once refuted two of my "money solves everything" associates in a nasty but effective way. I asked them to pick up their checks in my office. As they took them I remarked, "I wanted to tell you that you've been falling down in your work lately." In the shocked pause that followed, their own feelings were worth a thousand discussions. We are only beginning to realize that, besides proteins and vitamins, people must be nourished with feelings of security and friendship and dignity in order to function well.[4]

The five-way classification of needs is somewhat artificial because in a real situation all needs are interacting together within the whole person, as shown in Figure 3-3, but it does provide managers a convenient way of understanding which type of need is likely to dominate one's drives in a certain situation. It also gives some insight into history and future trends. Need priorities explain the emphasis on wages in nineteenth-century industry and the gradual development of new emphases in the twentieth century. Early in this century in the United States, the safety movement developed, until all states passed industrial safety laws. Later, in the 1920s and 1930s, security programs received predominant emphasis, continuing into the 1950s. Safety and security were second-priority needs, and—as these became moderately well met—there was increasing emphasis on third-priority social needs. This suggests that in the future the three higher-order needs, all of which heavily involve organizational behavior, will dominate employee relations.

The shift in need structure of the labor force in the United States from 1935 to its possible configuration in 1985, fifty years later, is represented by Figure 3-4. Assume that the distribution of the five Maslow needs in 1935 was as shown in the left side of the figure. Security needs dominated, followed by basic physiological needs. Very few people were at a level where self-actualization was their dominant need. Since 1935 need distribution has been shifting upward, and by 1985 we may assume that social and esteem needs will dominate, followed by self-actualization. Dominant physiological needs among employees should be rather rare by that date. Whether actual need distributions in 1985 look like the chart, the amount of change that has already taken place since 1935 represents a remarkable amount of progress up the need hierarchy. We are moving from economic to social to self-actualized persons.

It should not be assumed that once the labor force reaches need level five there is no further room for progress. Level five is a broad classification of needs, and it would be possible to reclassify it into five more steps for improvement. In fact, some researchers already have inserted "autonomy" as part of the need hierarchy between esteem and self-actualization.[5] Furthermore, needs can never be fully satisfied. People are perpetually wanting beings. The sports figure who makes

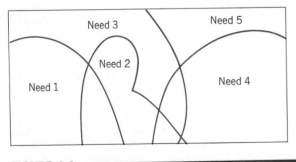

FIGURE 3-3

A diagram of five need levels interacting within a person, (*Source:* Kae H. Chung, "A Markov Chain Model of Human Needs: An Extension of Maslow's Need Theory," *Academy of Management Journal,* June 1969, p. 224. Used with permission.)

a million dollars has achieved all that was wanted when earnings were only a few thousand, but now wants have increased to 2 million or 5 million. The mountain climber who climbs a high mountain soon goes back for a higher or more challenging one. The conclusion that we must reach is that *need satisfaction is a continuous problem for organizations.* It cannot be permanently solved by satisfying a particular need today.

A conclusion that may be drawn from the changing distribution of need priorities is that organizations probably will be required to change their ways of operation to meet the changes in needs. Most organizational practices were established at a time when lower-order needs were dominant, so some of these practices may be outmoded as the need distribution changes. This suggests a contingency approach to organization practices. Appropriate organization practices are contingent upon the needs of the organization's labor force.

What the need-priority model essentially says is that gratified needs are not as strongly motivating as unmet needs. That is, *employees are enthusiastically motivated by what they are seeking, more than by what they already have.* They may react protectively to try to keep what they already have, but they move forward with enthusiasm only when they are seeking something else. In harsher terms, people work for bread alone only when there is no bread.

NEED PRIORITIES AT WORK. Assuming that the need-priority model applies to people in general, it is still appropriate to ask whether it applies to employees in organizations, because people satisfy many of their needs outside of organizations. Research shows that the model does apply, but not always. A major limitation is that needs are conditioned by environment, as was shown in Figure 3-1; so expression of what needs are important to people depends partly on the importance their social system attaches to different needs.

The model generally seems to apply to managers and professional employees in the United States and England. Studies show that their physiological and security needs are well met and they are seeking higher-order needs.[6]

The model also seems to apply to underdeveloped countries, where workers

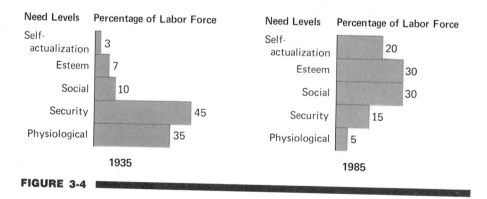

FIGURE 3-4

Possible change in distribution of dominant needs in the labor force, 1935–1985.

live under subsistence conditions. As would be expected, they emphasize basic physiological needs. A survey of 200 factory workers in India, for example, reports that they give top priority to job security, earnings, and personal benefits—all lower-order needs.[7]

Surveys in continental European countries and Japan (developed countries) show that the model does not apply as well to their managers. Unlike managers in the United States and England, their degree of satisfaction in needs does not necessarily vary according to the need-priority model. For example, managers in Spain and Belgium feel that their esteem needs are better satisfied than their security and social needs. Apparently cultural influences are an important cause of these differences.[8]

The need-priority model also does not seem to apply well to blue-collar occupations in the United States. Again, cultural values seem to be the prevailing influence. The predominant culture of blue-collar occupations seems to place high value on security and pay, even though blue-collar workers often have reached a level of affluence that should cause them to look toward higher-order needs, according to the need-priority model.

One study of blue-collar workers in two industries shows that they value most highly job security, good working conditions, and high wages in that order—all lower-order needs.[9] A study of government employees shows that blue-collar employees and supervisors emphasize security and belonging needs, while white-collar workers at comparable job levels focus on self-actualization needs. In other words, their blue-collar occupation controls their need expressions more than their level of accomplishment and affluence does.[10] Others have found that many employees seek higher-level needs even when lower-level needs are not gratified, which is contrary to Maslow's model.[11]

In summary, the need-priority model fits the responses of managers and professional employees in the United States and England and the responses of workers living under subsistence conditions. In other instances the model is less dependable, but is useful when interpreted in terms of environmental influences.

EMPLOYEE WANTS

WANTS ARE DERIVED FROM NEEDS. When needs are conditioned by environment, the result is a set of employee wants, as was shown in Figure 3-1. *Wants* are environmentally conditioned motivating forces or drives toward particular goals. Management achieves operational motivation by appealing to wants (and developing such favorable ones as it can). But the deeper foundations of its motivational program are always related to needs. Needs are the causes of action, but wants are the clues to the types of action likely to take place.

In trying to satisfy wants, a person does not always try to choose the best action but only a satisfactory one. Only in exceptional cases is there an effort to discover and choose the very best solution. In other words, a person "satisfices" rather than maximizes. Managers need to realize that employees working with a particular incentive are not likely to try to reach its maximum potential, but rather to seek a satisfactory return from it. ·

The long-run wants of a person at any given time are called one's *level of aspiration.* This represents hoped-for long-run goals as distinguished from practical short-run goals. As success, opportunity, and other factors vary up or down, the level of aspiration changes to keep always ahead of actual achievement and spur the person onward. If it is set beyond realistic opportunities, one will become frustrated. If it is set too low, one will reduce effort. Frequently the level of aspiration of college graduates is higher than it is for less educated persons. Since they view their jobs partly in terms of their higher aspirations, they are likely to be less satisfied with job conditions that are quite satisfactory to others. One study of first-level supervisors, for example, reported that those with college education were significantly less satisfied with their pay than those without college education. This relationship especially applies to younger employees.[12]

PERCEPTION. Reaction to employment is filtered through one's *perception,* which is the individual's own view of the world. People perceive their experiences in an organized framework that they have built out of their own experiences and values. Their own problems, own interests, and own backgrounds control their perception of each situation. Essentially, each individual is saying, "I behave according to the facts as I see them, not as you see them. My needs and wants are paramount, not yours; so I act on the basis of my perception of myself and the world in which I live. I react not to an objective world, but to a world seen from my own beliefs and values."

Since perceptions are strongly influenced by personal values, managers who motivate find it necessary to avoid excessive rationality. People insist on acting like human beings, rather than rational machines. We must accept them as the emotional beings they are and motivate them in their individual ways. We cannot easily change them to fit the motivational patterns we want them to have. Always we motivate people in terms of *their needs,* not ours.

The need for security provides an example of different perceptions of the same situation. Since security is largely psychological, a person may perceive relative security at a high level of real danger; or on the contrary, insecurity may be felt when real security is of the highest order. Thus, two passengers in a jet airplane face approximately equal chances of disaster, but one may feel much more secure from danger than the other. Observe that real, objective security is almost entirely independent of psychological security. Changes in actual security will not necessarily increase psychological security, which explains why many employee-security programs fail to improve security and why high employee insecurity still exists in our much-more-secure-than-before jobs. Advances in real security mean nothing if employees do not perceive them as advances (or if employee *expectations* of security rise an offsetting amount).

One of the difficulties with perception is *perceptual set;* that is, people tend to perceive what they previously have been led to believe they will perceive. If a new employee is told the supervisor is friendly, the employee will be more likely to see a friendly supervisor and respond in a friendly way. For this reason the entire organizational climate surrounding motivation is significant in creating a favorable perceptual set for it.

One supervisor's experience shows the tricks that perception can play. One of his machinists strongly wanted three days of vacation to go deer hunting. Since the department was so rushed it was working overtime every Saturday, the supervisor would not give him time off. The machinist also had a record of tardiness. One morning the machinist was thirty minutes late. The harassed supervisor, without giving much thought to his words, threatened the employee with three days off without pay if he was tardy again that month.

Guess who was tardy the next morning. You are correct. The machinist perceived the "threat" as an opportunity for his desired deer hunt. The supervisor saw no other choice than to give the machinist a disciplinary penalty of three days without pay. In this way management policies were upheld and the machinist reached his goal of deer hunting, but the needed work was not done.

MOTIVATIONAL AND MAINTENANCE FACTORS

A significant development in motivation was the distinction of motivational and maintenance factors in the job situation. The original research was based upon interviews of 200 engineers and accountants in the Pittsburgh area by Frederick Herzberg and associates.[13] Their approach was to ask the engineers and accountants to think of a time when they felt especially good about their jobs—and a time when they felt particularly bad about their jobs—and then to describe the conditions that led to those feelings. Herzberg found that employees named different types of conditions for good and bad feelings. That is, if a feeling of achievement led to a good feeling, the lack of achievement was rarely given as cause for bad job feelings. Instead, some other factor such as company policy was given as a cause of bad feelings.

Herzberg concluded that some job conditions operate primarily to dissatisfy employees when the conditions are absent, but their presence does not motivate employees in a strong way. Many of these factors traditionally are perceived by management as motivators, but the factors are really more potent as dissatisfiers. (Observe in this instance how the perceptions of management are not the same as the perceptions of employees.) These potent dissatisfiers are called *hygiene factors,* or *maintenance factors,* in the job, because they are necessary to maintain a reasonable level of satisfaction in employees.

Another set of job conditions operates primarily to build strong motivation and high job satisfaction, but their absence rarely proves strongly dissatisfying. These conditions are known as *motivational factors,* motivators, or satisfiers. For many years managers had been wondering why their fancy personnel policies and fringe benefits were not increasing employee motivation on the job. The distinction of motivational and maintenance factors helped answer their question, because fringe benefits and personnel policies were shown to be primarily maintenance factors.

The original Herzberg study included six motivational factors: achievement, recognition, advancement, work itself, possibility of growth, and responsibility. There were ten maintenance factors: company policy and administration, technical supervision, interpersonal relations with supervisors, interpersonal relations with peers, interpersonal relations with subordinates, salary, job security, personal life, working conditions, and status.

Motivational factors such as achievement and responsibility mostly are related directly to the job itself, the employee's performance on it, and the recognition and growth that is secured from it. Motivators are mostly job-centered; they relate to *job content.*

Maintenance factors mostly are related to the environment external to the job. This environment includes company policy and working conditions as well as interpersonal relations with others. Maintenance factors are mostly environment-centered; they relate to *job context.* This difference between job content and job context is a significant one. It shows that employees primarily are motivated strongly by what they do for themselves. When they handle responsibility or gain recognition through their own behavior, they are strongly motivated. If these conclusions are correct, then management's proper role becomes one of providing a proper environment for employee accomplishment. The employee performs the work, and management provides the supportive environment.

INTRINSIC AND EXTRINSIC FACTORS. The distinction between job content and job context is similar to the distinction between *intrinsic* and *extrinsic motivators* in the field of psychology. Intrinsic motivators are internal rewards that occur at the time of performance of the work, so there is a direct motivation to perform work because the act of performance is itself rewarding. An employee in this situation is self-motivated. Extrinsic motivators are external rewards that occur after or away from work, providing no direct satisfaction at the time the work is performed. Examples of extrinsic motivators are retirement plans, health insurance, and vacations, because none of them provides satisfactions during work.

Prior to Herzberg's research, organizational managers centered their attention on extrinsic maintenance factors, often with poor results. Now that they better understand the difference between these factors and the intrinsic motivational factors, they are giving more emphasis to intrinsic factors because of their superior possibilities for the employee, the organization, and society. Before Herzberg's research employees were paternalistically maintained too much and enthusiastically motivated too little.

INTERPRETING THE MOTIVATION-MAINTENANCE MODEL. The Herzberg model represents general tendencies only. Items that are designated as maintenance factors may serve as motivators to some people, and items that normally are motivators may be maintenance factors to other people. As with most other human information, only a tendency toward one direction exists. There is no absolute distinction; neither factor is wholly unidimensional in its influence.

A number of research projects have been completed on the motivation-maintenance model; and, as might be expected, they have both supported and rejected the model. On the support side the model has been shown to have wide application.[14] One interesting study that supported the model was in a cooperative group where salary could not be an influence on the results.[15] The model applies especially to managerial, professional, and white-collar employees, who seem to seek intrinsic job satisfactions. It applies less to blue-collar workers, where the work culture often emphasizes maintenance factors.

For example, some items normally considered as maintenance factors (such as pay and security) are frequently considered motivational factors by blue-collar workers. One study reported that both motivators and maintenance factors were positively related to job satisfaction of blue-collar workers. Another study showed that blue-collar workers gave much more emphasis to extrinsic job factors (primarily maintenance factors).[16]

Other work groups occasionally show exceptions to the model with regard to a particular factor. For example, one study showed that women emphasized interpersonal relations with peers as a motivational factor, although it is normally a maintenance factor.[17] Another study showed that New Zealand managers and salaried employees considered both interpersonal relations with peers and supervisory relationships to be motivational factors, apparently because of cultural differences from the United States.[18] These exceptions on individual items, however, do not invalidate the general ideas expressed by the model.

CRITICISMS OF THE MOTIVATION-MAINTENANCE MODEL. The motivation-maintenance model is known as the two-factor theory of motivation and job satisfaction because it suggests that job satisfiers and dissatisfiers are two qualitatively different factors. This two-factor idea has created much criticism by persons who report research that does not support the two-factor model.[19] These persons usually hold the view that job satisfaction and dissatisfaction are two opposite points on a single continuum.

Criticism of the model is reinforced by the fact that it is easiest to get results favorable to the model by using the method that Herzberg used. A number of other methods have failed to produce similar results.[20] Thus, it is contended that the model is "method-bound" to the Herzberg research method, a fact that gives it limited applicability for general use. It is reasoned that when the Herzberg method is applied and people are asked to report favorable job situations, their egos lead them to report things that *they* have done. When unfavorable situations are reported, then their egos lead them to report things that *others* have done, such as improper treatment from a supervisor.

Others have said that the model does not give sufficient emphasis to the motivating qualities of pay, status, and interpersonal relations. Admittedly these are important employee motivators; however, the motivation-maintenance model gives credit primarily to their maintenance capabilities.

In spite of all the criticism that this model has generated, it remains useful because of the significant distinction it draws between factors that motivate employees on the job and factors that primarily maintain employees ready to be motivated. In this manner the model provides new insights in organizational behavior. One major insight is the idea of *job enrichment.* According to Herzberg, jobs should be enriched by building more motivational factors into them. Job enrichment has become a significant organizational practice, so it is discussed extensively in a later chapter.

COMPARISON OF THE HERZBERG AND MASLOW MODELS. When the Herzberg and Maslow models are compared, it can be seen that they both emphasize the same set of relationships, as shown in Figure 3-5. Maslow centers on human needs of the psychological person at work or anywhere else. Herzberg focuses on that same person in terms of one's present state of needs. What the Herzberg motivation-maintenance model seems to say in general is that managerial and professional (and to some extent white-collar) workers have reached a stage of socioeconomic progress in modern society such that the two higher-order need levels tend to be the motivating ones. The three lower need levels are now minimally achieved so that they are no longer strong, driving forces for an employee. Rather, they are merely necessary for *maintenance* at one's current level of progress.

If this analysis is accurate, then blue-collar workers will not fit as well into the

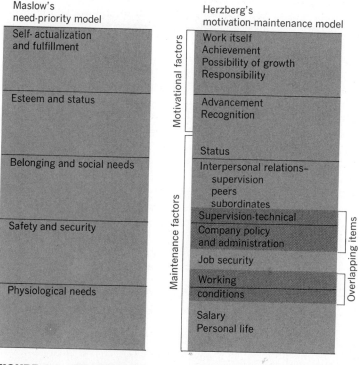

FIGURE 3-5

A comparison of Maslow's need-priority model with Herzberg's motivation-maintenance model.

motivation-maintenance model because they have not made the socioeconomic progress of others. This lack of fit to the Herzberg model was reported in earlier paragraphs. Similarly, it is likely that workers in less developed societies will designate some maintenance factors as motivators. Having made less socioeconomic progress, they are still motivated by what are now maintenance factors to major portions of the labor force in developed nations.

As we discuss the different needs of people in different environments, we essentially are discussing a contingency approach to organizational behavior. Contingency management recognizes that different persons have different needs and even the same person has different needs at different times, so motivation is contingent upon situational conditions at a particular time and place.

SUMMARY

When people join an organization, they bring with them certain needs that affect on-the-job performance. Some of these needs are physiological; others are related to psychological and social values. The latter are much more difficult to determine and satisfy, and individual differences in them are great. Maslow has proposed a priority of needs as follows: physiological, security, social, esteem, and self-actualization. Needs interact with environment to form on-the-job wants that management and employees try to satisfy. These wants vary from time to time, and an employee "satisfices" them, rather than maximizing them. Their long-run intensity is governed by a fluctuating level of aspiration.

Wants are given direction and vigor by maintenance and motivational factors, according to a model developed by Herzberg. Important motivational factors are the work itself, achievement, growth, responsibility, advancement, and recognition. These primarily are intrinsic motivators, rather than extrinsic. The Maslow and Herzberg models have many similarities, because they both focus on needs but from a somewhat different point of view.

TERMS AND CONCEPTS FOR REVIEW

Needs	Level of aspiration
Wants	Perception
Incentives	Perceptual set
Primary and secondary needs	Herzberg's model of motivational
Holistic concept	and maintenance factors
Maslow's model of need priority	Intrinsic and extrinsic motivators
Self-actualization	Two-factor theory
Lower-order and higher-order needs	Job enrichment

REVIEW QUESTIONS

1. Explain the sequence by which needs are translated into action in a work situation.
2. Explain Maslow's need-priority model and the extent to which it applies in organizations.
3. Explain Herzberg's motivation-maintenance model and discuss how well it applies in practice.
4. Discuss the difference between intrinsic and extrinsic rewards. Discuss how Herzberg's motivational factors are primarily intrinsic.
5. Compare the Maslow and Herzberg models with regard to similarities and differences.

CASE

THE PIANO BUILDER[21]

Mr. Waverly Bird builds pianos from scratch. His occupation is a piano consultant to a piano manufacturer. He is on call and works about one week a month, including some travel to solve problems of customers. He also rebuilds about a dozen grand pianos every year for special customers; but, according to Bird, the most satisfying part of his life is his hobby of building pianos from the beginning. "It's the part that keeps a man alive," he says. The challenge of the work is what lures Bird onward. He derives satisfaction from precision and quality, and he comments, "Details make the difference. When you cut a little corner here and a little corner there, you've cut a big hole. A piano is like the human body; all of the parts are important."

Bird has a substantial challenge in making a whole piano. His work requires skills in cabinetmaking, metalworking, and engineering, with knowledge of acoustics and a keen ear for music. It requires great precision, because a tiny misalignment would ruin a piano's tune. It also requires versatility, ranging from a keyboard that is balanced to respond to the touch of a finger all the way to the pinblock that must withstand up to twenty tons of pressure. Bird had to make many of his own piano construction tools.

Bird has built 40 pianos in his 34-year career. Though construction takes nearly a year, he sells his pianos at the modest price of a commercial piano. He is seeking not money but the challenge and the satisfaction. He says, "The whole business is a series of closed doors. You learn one thing, and there's another closed door waiting to be opened." Bird says his big dream is to build a grand piano; "It is the one thing I haven't done yet and want to do."

QUESTION

1. Discuss the nature of Bird's motivation in building pianos. Discuss whether an organization could build the same motivation in most of its employees.

REFERENCES

1. Frederick Herzberg, "Managers or Animal Trainers?" *Management Review,* July 1971, p. 9. The words *for me* are italicized in the original.

2. William C. Menninger, "What Makes an Effective Man?" American Management Association, *Personnel Series,* no. 152, 1953, p. 23.

3. A. H. Maslow, "A Theory of Human Motivation," *Psychological Review,* vol. 50, 1943, pp. 370–396; and A. H. Maslow, *Motivation and Personality,* New York: Harper and Row, Publishers, Incorporated, 1954. See also A. H. Maslow, *The Farther Reaches of Human Nature,* New York: The Viking Press, Inc., 1971.

4. Daniel Krakauer, "Worker Psychology: A Formula That Works," *Factory Management and Maintenance,* August 1953, p. 226.

5. Lyman W. Porter, "A Study of Perceived Need Satisfactions in Bottom and Middle Management," *Journal of Applied Psychology,* January 1961, pp. 1–10.

6. Mason Haire, Edwin E. Ghiselli, and Lyman W. Porter, "Cultural Patterns in the Role of the Manager," *Industrial Relations,* February 1963, p. 113, reporting a survey in eleven countries covering about twenty-eight hundred managers. Similar results are reported for Australia, see Alfred W. Clark and Sue McCabe, "The Motivation and Satisfaction of Australian Managers," *Personnel Psychology,* Winter 1972, pp. 625–638.

7. Paras Nath Singh and Robert J. Wherry, Sr., "Ranking of Job Factors by Factory Workers in India," *Personnel Psychology,* Spring 1963, pp. 29–33.

8. Haire, Ghiselli, and Porter, *op. cit.* See also R. A. Goodman, "On the Operationality of the Maslow Need Hierarchy," *British Journal of Industrial Relations,* vol. 6, no. 1, pp. 51–57.

9. M. Schwartz, E. Jenusaitis, and H. Stark, "A Comparison of the Perception of Job-related Needs in Two Industry Groups," *Personnel Psychology,* Summer 1966, p. 188. See also William E. Reif, "Intrinsic versus Extrinsic Rewards: Resolving the Controversy," *Human Resource Management,* Summer 1975, pp. 2–10.

10. Frank Friedlander, "Comparative Work Value Systems," *Personnel Psychology,* Spring 1965, pp. 1–20, reporting research on nearly fifteen hundred government workers. See also Michael Beer, "Needs and Need Satisfaction among Clerical Workers in Complex and Routine Jobs," *Personnel Psychology,* Summer 1968, pp. 209–222.

11. J. C. Wofford, "The Motivational Bases of Job Satisfaction and Job Performance," *Personnel Psychology,* Autumn 1971, pp. 501–518. Other rejections of the Maslow model are found in Edward E. Lawler III, and J. Lloyd Suttle, "A Causal Correlational Test of the Need Hierarchy Concept," *Organizational Behavior and Human Performance,* April 1972, pp. 265–287; and Mahmoud A. Wahba and Lawrence G. Bridwell, "Maslow Reconsidered: A Review of Research on the Need Hierarchy Theory," in Thad B. Green and Dennis F. Ray (eds.), *Academy of Management Proceedings, 1973,* State College, Miss.: Academy of Management, 1974, pp. 514–520.

12. S. M. Klein and J. R. Maher, "Education Level and Satisfaction with Pay," *Personnel Psychology,* Summer 1966, pp. 195–208, reporting a study of 727 first-level supervisors; and W. N. Penzer, "Education Level and Satisfaction with Pay: An Attempted Replication," *Personnel Psychology,* Summer 1969, pp. 185–199.

13. Frederick Herzberg, Bernard Mausner, and Barbara Synderman, *The Motivation to Work,* New York: John Wiley & Sons, Inc., 1959; and Frederick Herzberg, *Work and the Nature of Man,* Cleveland: The World Publishing Company, 1966.

14. Valerie M. Bockman, "The Herzberg Controversy," *Personnel Psychology,* Summer 1971, pp. 155–189. This article reports the first ten years of research on the model.

15. D. Macarov, "Work Patterns and Satisfactions in an Israeli Kibbutz: A Test of the Herzberg Hypothesis," *Personnel Psychology,* Autumn 1972, pp. 483–493.

16. In order of mention, the studies are Michael R. Malinovsky and John R. Barry, "Determinants of Work Attitudes," *Journal of Applied Psychology,* December 1965, pp. 446–451, covering 117 blue-collar workers; and Richard Centers and Daphne E. Bugental, "Intrinsic and Extrinsic Job Motivators among Different Segments of the Working Population," *Journal of Applied Psychology,* June 1966, p. 195. On the other hand, a study of a black blue-collar group strongly supported the Herzberg model. See H. B. Karp and Jack W. Nickson, Jr., "Motivator-Hygiene Deprivation as a Predictor of Job Turnover," *Personnel Psychology,* Autumn 1973, pp. 377–384.

17. Centers and Bugental, *op. cit.,* pp. 193–197.

18. George H. Hines, "Cross-cultural Differences in the Two-Factor Motivation Theory," *Journal of Applied Psychology,* December 1973, pp. 375–377.

19. Sample criticisms are Martin G. Evans, "Herzberg's Two-Factor Theory of Motivation: Some Problems and a Suggested Test," *Personnel Journal,* January 1970, pp. 32–35; and Charles L. Hulin and Patricia A. Smith, "An Empirical Investigation of Two Implications of the Two-Factor Theory of Job Satisfaction," *Journal of Applied Psychology,* October 1967, pp. 396–402. For a reconciliation of the one-factor theory and the two-factor theory, see Hanafi M. Soliman, "Motivation-Hygiene Theory of Job Attitudes: An Empirical Investigation and an Attempt to Reconcile Both the One- and the Two-Factor Theories of Job Attitudes," *Journal of Applied Psychology,* October 1970, pp. 452–461.

20. Following are examples of research projects that failed to support the Herzberg model when they used a different research method: Edwin A. Locke and Roman J. Whiting, "Sources of Satisfaction and Dissatisfaction among Solid Waste Management Employees," *Journal of Applied Psychology,* April 1974, pp. 145–156; and D. A. Ondrack, "Defense Mechanisms and the Herzberg Theory: An Alternate Test," *Personnel Psychology,* March 1974, pp. 79–89.

21. Liz Roman Gallese, "Stephen Jellen Builds Pianos Not for Money but for Satisfaction," *Wall Street Journal* (Pacific Coast Edition), Sept. 6, 1973, pp. 1, 12.

CHAPTER 4
MOTIVATING EMPLOYEES

Behavior is a function of its consequences
and can be changed through the management of those consequences.
Fred Luthans and Robert Kreitner[1]

I think I am doing all right,
because the boss hasn't criticized me in two or three months.
A Factory Worker

LEARNING OBJECTIVES

TO UNDERSTAND:
The expectancy model of motivation
The relation of valence and expectancy to motivation
How behavior modification is applied
Differences between expectancy theory and behavior modification
Whether punishment is a desirable reinforcement to use
Kinds of reinforcement that are most effective

Marsha Donner, a skilled advertising specialist, worked on special projects in the advertising office of a large department store chain. On one occasion her manager assigned her Project Symposium, which would require about one-third of her time for the next six months or more. The project required her to work with various business and service organizations in the region served by the department store. Donner felt that she should have been selected to handle Project Symposium, and she thought that the project would prove interesting; but she really was not motivated about it. She felt that it would interfere with some of her other duties that were more important.

Donner's supervisor recognized that she was not motivated and on various occasions discussed the project with her, hoping to motivate her. After several discussions he felt that he was making no progress, but one day he remarked to Donner, "Marsha, do you realize that Project Symposium will help you meet most community leaders in this region, and your acquaintance with these people would help you with Project Mainstream if we ever decide to go with it." Donner had developed the unique idea of Project Mainstream, and she strongly wanted it to be initiated. When she saw that her work with Project Symposium might help her with Project Mainstream, she immediately became motivated on Project Symposium. She worked hard at it for the next eight months, and both she and her supervisor were pleased with the results.

The situation with Marsha Donner concerns a problem of motivation. Although Donner was cooperative and interested in her work, she really was not motivated until she saw a connection between her present work and a future challenging project that she wished to initiate. She became motivated when her work was connected with something that was important *to her.* This relationship is the essence of motivation. *Motivated employees are those that see their work as helping them accomplish their important goals.* In this chapter we discuss two different motivational models. These are expectancy theory and behavior modification.

EXPECTANCY THEORY

A widely accepted model of motivation is *expectancy theory* as developed by Victor H. Vroom, based on earlier work by others.[2] This model has been expanded and refined by Porter and Lawler and others.[3] Vroom explains that motivation is a product of the values one seeks and one's estimation of the probability that a certain action will lead to those values. This relationship is expressed in the following formula:

Valence × expectancy = motivation

These ideas now will be discussed.

VALENCE. *Valence* refers to the strength of a person's preference for one outcome in relation to others. It is an expression of the amount of one's desire for a goal. For example, if an employee strongly wants a promotion, it is said that the promotion has high valence for the employee. The valence arises out of each employee's internal self as conditioned by experience, so it will vary substantially from person to person.

Since people may have positive or negative preferences for an outcome, valence may be negative as well as positive. When a person prefers not attaining an outcome compared with attaining it, then valence is a negative figure. If a person is indifferent to an outcome, then valence is zero.

Some employees will find intrinsic valence in the work itself, particularly if they have a strong work ethic. They derive satisfaction directly from their work through a sense of completion, of doing a task right, or of creating something. In this instance, outcomes are largely within the employees' own control, not subject to management's reward system.

EXPECTANCY. *Expectancy* is the strength of belief that a particular act will be followed by particular outcomes. It represents employee judgment of the probability that achieving one result will lead to another result. Since expectancy is an action-outcome association, it may range from zero to a value of one. If an employee sees no probability that an act will lead to a particular outcome, then expectancy is zero. At the other extreme, if the action-outcome relationship indicates certainty, then expectancy has a value of one. Normally employee expectancy is somewhere between these two extremes.

An important point with employees is that outcomes usually are under the control of someone else, so there is uncertainty about whether the outcomes will follow from the action. For example, if an employee is seeking a promotion that leads to higher pay and higher status, the promotion and higher pay are given at the discretion of management, and the higher status is given by one's associates. This second-party relationship often creates high uncertainty.

THE EXPECTANCY MODEL. *Motivation* in the expectancy model is defined as the strength of drive toward action. The model shows that a person's motivation toward an action at a particular time is determined by the anticipated values of all the outcomes (valence) of the action, multiplied by the strength of a person's expectation that the action will lead to the outcomes.

The expectancy model is further developed in Figure 4-1, which shows that motivation leads to increased effort. It is hoped that this increased effort will lead to outcomes that represent desired goals for which the employee had some valence. In turn, goal attainment should cause a more satisfied employee who is more likely to be motivated again.

If we accept the expectancy model, then it follows that in order to motivate a person to work we can do only two things. First, we can increase the positive value of outcomes through such means as better communication about their values and actually increasing them (i.e., increasing rewards). Second, we may increase expectancy that the work really will lead to the desired outcome; that is, we can strengthen the connection between the work and the outcome. We may do this through improved communication, or we may increase the actual probabilities of the outcome. Since expectancy depends entirely on the employee's view of the connection between work and outcome, often a simple, straightforward incentive is more motivating than a complex one. The complex one may provide so much uncertainty that the employee does not sufficiently connect effort with outcome. The simple incentive, on the other hand, provides a workable path that the employee can see and understand; therefore, its expectancy is higher.

An example of how the expectancy model works is the case of Marty Fulmer, age thirty-one, who works as a welder in a large factory. Fulmer has very strong de-

FIGURE 4-1

A diagram of the expectancy model.

sires (high valence) to be in white-collar work instead of his present job. He has wanted white-collar work since he was a child. He remembers how his father used to come home in the afternoon smelling like the factory where he worked, and Fulmer never did like that.

Fulmer, however, does not see how he can ever get into white-collar work (low expectancy). He does not like clerical work; and, since he has only a high school education, he sees no way to enter a profession. Because of Fulmer's low expectancy, he is not motivated to prepare for white-collar work. In this instance he strongly wants something, but because he sees no way to achieve it, he is not motivated to make any effort to reach it. Even though his wants are strong, he lacks drive for action because of low expectancy.

The expectancy model suggests that through experience people learn what kinds of rewards (outcomes) they value more highly than others. These outcomes may or may not be in the order of Maslow's need hierarchy, because there are many possible combinations of outcomes. Through experience people also develop estimates of the probability that a certain quality of performance will lead to certain outcomes. Based on a comparison of what outcomes they want (valence) and the possible connection between them and performance (expectancy), the employee develops a drive for action called motivation. In essence, the employee performs a type of cost-benefit analysis. If the estimated benefit is enough to justify the cost of more effort, then the employee is likely to apply more effort.

The valence-expectancy relationship may exist in an infinite number of combinations, but the most desirable combination is high valence and high expectancy. This produces the strongest motivation. If either valence or expectancy is low, then motivation will range in the moderate-to-low area. If both valence and expectancy are low, then there will be negligible motivation. If valence is negative, then the employee will seek to avoid the behavior entirely. The strength of avoidance behavior depends on the strength of valence and expectancy combined.

APPRAISING THE EXPECTANCY MODEL. The expectancy model is in an early stage of development and certainly does not provide a detailed understanding of all that happens in a real motivational situation.[4] The model, however, does provide a basic framework for interpreting work motivation. A number of studies have been made to test various parts of the expectancy model, and both support and lack of support have been reported.[5] Research projects show that the model is useful for explaining some of the motivational results in organizations, but not all of them. The model is only partially predictive, because there appear to be other important variables that are not included.

For example, one test of the model in two different companies found that it applied in one of them but was not effective in the other because of certain special conditions.[6] A study of 138 incentive workers in a steel fabricating plant showed that the expectancy model did apply, but the variances explained by parts of the theory were low.[7] Another study covered 76 women employees performing office work in a telephone company. The results clearly supported the general theory and the linkages that the theory predicts.[8] The model has been shown to apply in dif-

ferent cultures. One study of insurance sales representatives in Japan found that the model applied in approximately the same way that it does in the United States.[9]

The substantial testing of the expectancy model with office and factory workers, men and women employees, and employees of different national cultures gives some evidence that the model has general applicability to employees in work situations, even though its application at times may be weak.

BEHAVIOR MODIFICATION

The models of motivation that have been discussed up to this point are known as *cognitive theories of motivation* because they are based on thinking and feeling (i.e., cognition) within the individual. They relate to the internal psychological person and how that person views the world. For example, in Maslow's need hierarchy a person's internal state of needs determines behavior.

The major difficulty with cognitive models of motivation is that they are not subject to precise scientific measurement and observation. It is impossible, for example, to measure a person's esteem needs at any certain time. For this reason it is argued that more attention should be given to models that are more subject to scientific treatment. The principal model of this type is *behavior modification,* as evolved from the work of B. F. Skinner.[10] Its application in organizations may be called *organizational behavior modification,* or O. B. Mod.[11] Behavior modification is based on the idea that *behavior depends on its consequences.* This model is developed from learning theory. While cognitive theories argue that internal needs lead to behavior, behavior modification states that external consequences tend to determine behavior. The differences between the two approaches are substantial.

OPERANT CONDITIONING. Behavior modification is achieved through *operant conditioning.* Operant behavior is that which can be modified by its consequences. If the consequences of a certain behavior are favorable to the person (i.e., reinforcing to the person), the behavior will be strengthened. Conversely, if the consequences are unfavorable, the behavior will be weakened. In this manner operant conditioning occurs.

Operant conditioning differs from classical conditioning as represented by Pavlov's dogs. In that instance the ringing of a bell to indicate availability of food increased the dogs' flow of saliva. A stimulus led to a response. In operant conditioning, on the other hand, the consequences of a response lead to a repetition of that response.

The *Law of Effect* from learning theory explains the idea of operant conditioning. The law states that a person tends to repeat behavior that is accompanied by desirable consequences (reinforcement) and tends *not* to repeat behavior that is accompanied by undesirable consequences. Assume, for example, that an employee found that helping a trainee learn the job produced desirable consequences. The behavior would tend to be repeated with the next trainee. But if a helping effort produced only conflict and problems, then the employee would tend not to help the next trainee.

POSITIVE AND NEGATIVE REINFORCEMENT. Behavior primarily is encouraged through positive reinforcement. *Positive reinforcement* provides a favorable consequence that encourages repetition of a behavior. An employee, for example, may find that when high-quality work is done, the supervisor gives a reward of recognition. Since the employee likes recognition, behavior is reinforced, and the employee tends to want to do high-quality work again. The reinforcement always is contingent on the employee's correct behavior.

Negative reinforcement is the removal of something undesirable in the situation; therefore, it is not the same as punishment, which normally adds something undesirable. Consistent with the Law of Effect, behavior responsible for the removal of something undesirable is repeated when that undesirable state is again encountered. An example of negative reinforcement is a jet aircraft mechanic who learned that if she wore noise suppressors over her ears she could prevent undesirable jet engine noise, so reinforcement occurred to encourage her to wear the proper noise equipment.

An excellent example of positive reinforcement is the experience of Emery Air Freight with its containerized shipping operations.[12] The company's practice is to consolidate small packages into large containers in order to reduce handling and shipping costs. The standard is for 90 percent of small packages to be shipped in large containers, but an audit at various locations showed that actual use was about 45 percent. Further study showed that workers had been properly trained regarding use of the containers, so low performance was not a matter of workers being unable to perform better. They knew their jobs and were reasonably cooperative, but they still were not meeting the standard.

To improve performance a program of positive reinforcement was applied. Supervisors were trained in how to give performance feedback, recognition, and other rewards. A program was established to provide employees with regular, daily feedback about their performance, and supervisors were instructed to provide recognition on a regular basis. In the first test office, performance went to 95 percent the first day. As the program was applied in other offices, their performance also went to 90 percent or better, most of them increasing to standard within a single day. The effective results continued for the four years covered in the study. The regular feedback and recognition provided workers with consequences that strongly influenced behavior. In this instance positive reinforcement scored a notable success.

Shaping occurs when reinforcements are successively given as one comes closer to the desired behavior. Even though the correct behavior does not occur, it is further encouraged by giving reinforcement for behavior in the desired direction. Shaping is especially useful for teaching complex tasks.

An illustration of shaping is the training procedure of a supervisor in a retail store. The store was so small that it had no centralized training program for sales clerks, so all sales training was a responsibility of the supervisor. In the beginning a new sales clerk did not know how to deal with customers effectively, so the supervisor explained the proper sales procedure. The supervisor observed the clerk's behavior, and from time to time when there was improved behavior in the right direction in some part of the procedure, the supervisor expressed approval and encouraged the employee. This was favorable recognition in the employee's mind, so it served to shape behavior in the correct direction.

PUNISHMENT AND EXTINCTION. Punishment occurs when a consequence exists that discourages a certain behavior. Although punishment sometimes needs to be used to discourage an unusually undesirable behavior, it is not a very satisfactory practice because of certain disadvantages. A major one is that punishment only *discourages* an undesirable behavior; it does not encourage any kind of desirable behavior. Further, since the punisher is also the person who offers reinforcement at other times, the two roles become confused, which may reduce the punisher's effectiveness when offering future reinforcements. Also, persons being punished may become confused about what specific part of their behavior is being punished, so some desirable behaviors may be discouraged.

Extinction occurs when there are no significant consequences for a behavior. Learned behavior needs to be reinforced in order to occur in the future; if no reinforcement occurs, the behavior will tend to disappear. It is extinguished through lack of reinforcement, and it tends to be replaced by responses that are reinforced. In one instance an employee made three suggestions to her supervisor over a period of several weeks. The supervisor did not reject the suggestions, or accept them, or do anything else. The suggestions just disappeared in the bureaucratic maze. Needless to say, the employee's suggestion-making behavior was extinguished by these consequences.

SCHEDULES OF REINFORCEMENT. Reinforcement may be either continuous or partial. Continuous reinforcement occurs when a reinforcer follows each correct behavior made by an employee. In some instances this level of reinforcement may be desirable to encourage quick learning, but in the typical work situation it usually is not possible to reward an employee after every correct behavior. An example of continuous reinforcement is programmed instruction in a training session.

Partial reinforcement occurs when only part of the correct behaviors are reinforced. Learning is slower with partial reinforcement than with continuous reinforcement. However, a unique feature of partial reinforcement is that learning tends to be retained longer when it is secured under conditions of partial reinforcement.[13]

There are four types of partial reinforcement schedules: fixed interval, fixed ratio, variable interval, and variable ratio. Fixed interval schedules require that a certain period of time elapses between reinforcement. An excellent example of this type of reinforcement is a weekly paycheck. Fixed ratio schedules occur when there is a reinforcement after a certain number of desired responses. Some reinforcement is provided by fixed schedules, but it is not as strong and consistent as that provided by variable schedules.

Variable interval reinforcement occurs when a reinforcement is administered after a variety of time periods. Usually the variations are grouped around some target, or average, period of reinforcement. A variable ratio schedule occurs when the number of responses between reinforcements varies, such as reinforcement after 19, 15, 12, 24, and 17 responses. This type of reinforcement schedule provokes much interest and is the most powerful of all the reinforcement schedules. It is most likely to secure correct responses. An interesting fact is that slot machines and a number of other gambling devices operate on a variable ratio schedule, so gamblers experienced the power of this reinforcement schedule before it was isolated and studied by behavioral scientists.

Variable ratio reinforcement has been successfully used to reduce absenteeism. One project applied a lottery incentive system to 215 hourly employees in a manufacturing and distribution facility.[14] *Each day all employees who came to work on time were allowed to choose a card from a deck of playing cards. At the end of the week any employee who was on time every day had a normal poker hand of five cards. The highest hand won $20, and eight winners were allowed in the whole group. After this program was initiated absenteeism dropped 18 percent.*

Even though laboratory studies support the superiority of variable ratio schedules,[15] actual work situations have so many intervening conditions that the variable ratio may not work as well as it does under controlled conditions. In one instance marginal workers planting trees for a timber company were assigned to crews having continuous reinforcement or variable ratio reinforcement.[16] The crews having continuous reinforcement planted the most trees. The researchers concluded that a number of on-the-job interferences may have prevented the variable ratio schedule from working properly. Obviously the real work situation is not the same set of conditions as a controlled laboratory experiment.

APPLYING BEHAVIOR MODIFICATION. The major benefit of behavior modification is that it allows more scientific analysis than cognitive models, because it focuses on specific external consequences rather than intangible, internal human needs. It is, however, often difficult to apply. To initiate the process, it is necessary to identify behavioral events that are to be modified and then to determine what stimuli lead to them and how they are presently being reinforced. Based upon the facts uncovered by studying the work situation, an intervention strategy can be developed to encourage or discourage the behaviors along the lines shown in Figure 4-2. If the guidelines in Figure 4-2 can be applied to develop effective reinforcement, improvement often is substantial.

In a St. Louis hardware company a variable ratio schedule was used for the purpose of reducing absenteeism and tardiness.[17] *Employees who came to work on time for a month were eligible for a drawing at the end of the month, with one prize being awarded for each 25 eligible employees. At the end of six months, people with perfect attendance could draw for a television set. This plan reduced tardiness and absenteeism substantially, and sick leave costs declined an amazing 62 percent.*

Behavior modification was successful in training hardcore unemployed for a manufacturer of metal bed frames.[18] *The complex task was divided into eight parts,* and trainees were given reinforcement points convertible into money for correct performance of each step. The result was more accurate quality and faster learning.

CRITICISMS OF BEHAVIOR MODIFICATION. Although behavior modification has been effective in some situations, it also has major limitations. A frequent criticism is that it is an inherently autocratic method of management, because it involves manipulation of people.[19] Behavioral consequences are controlled in such a way that people find themselves forced to change their behavior. This approach is not consistent with humanistic models (for example, Maslow's need hierarchy), which assume that people are autonomous and self-actualizing, being motivated by their own internal needs. Behavior modification, on the other hand, assumes that the causes of behavior are outside the person and in the environment. The image of self-actualizing people is negated, and the question arises: Who will control the controllers?

Along this same line it has been said that behavior modification insults the intelligence of people. They are treated like rats in a training box, when in fact they are intelligent, self-controlled people capable of making their own choices.

A practical criticism of behavior modification is that the work environment is too complex for most of its ideas to apply. Much behavior modification research has been done under laboratory conditions, often with animals; therefore, it is not very applicable in complex, ongoing work situations. The problem is that many conflicting stimuli and reinforcements are presented in real work situations, so it is difficult to manipulate only one item independently. In short, behavior modification for organizational use is overrated.

INTERPRETING MOTIVATIONAL MODELS

Several motivational models have been presented in this chapter and earlier chapters. These include McGregor's Theory X and Theory Y, McClelland's achievement motivation, Maslow's need hierarchy, Herzberg's motivational and mainte-

---

GUIDELINES FOR APPLYING BEHAVIOR MODIFICATION IN ORGANIZATIONS

- Use positive reinforcement whenever possible.
- Use punishment only in unusual circumstances.
- Ignore undesirable behavior to allow its extinction.
- Use shaping procedures to develop correct complex behavior.
- Minimize the time between the correct response and reinforcement.
- Use variable ratio reinforcement schedules where possible.
- Provide reinforcement relatively frequently.

FIGURE 4-2

Some guidelines for applying behavior modification in organizations.

nance factors, Vroom's expectancy theory, and Skinner's behavior modification. All the models have strengths and weaknesses, supporters and detractors. No model is perfect; however, all of them have added something to our understanding of human behavior, and newer models being developed should add even more understanding.[20]

Cognitive models dominate present thinking about motivation. People are considered to have internal needs, and managers motivate people by providing a work situation that satisfies their inner needs while at the same time achieving objectives of the organization. Except for behavior modification, most of the motivational models are similar. They look at the same set of human needs, but with different approaches and interpretations. This similarity was shown by the comparison of Maslow's need hierarchy and Herzberg's motivational and maintenance factors in Chapter 3.

It seems likely that cognitive models will continue to dominate organizational practice for some time to come. They most nearly represent the human view of what leads to human behavior. Behavior modification will continue to provoke interest and will find special applications in organizations, but it will be held back by its limitations. Apparently there exists at this time a type of contingency relationship regarding motivation. Behavior modification will tend to be tried in stable situations with minimum complexity, where a direct connection can be made between behavior and its consequences. In more complex, dynamic situations where there are many interwoven variables, traditional cognitive models will tend to be used. In other words, the motivational approach attempted will be contingent on situational variables.

SUMMARY

Two distinctly different models of motivation are expectancy theory and behavior modification. Expectancy theory explains that motivation is a product of the values one seeks and one's estimation of the probability that a certain action will lead to those values. The formula is valence × expectancy = motivation. Valence is the strength of a person's preference for one outcome in relation to others. Expectancy is the strength of belief that a particular act will be followed by particular outcomes.

Behavior modification states that behavior depends on its consequences. It is achieved through operant conditioning. Various approaches that may be used are positive and negative reinforcement, shaping, and extinction. Punishment normally is not used. Reinforcement can be continuous or partial. There are four partial types: fixed interval, fixed ratio, variable interval, and variable ratio. Learning is faster with continuous reinforcement, but learning tends to be retained longer with partial reinforcement. Variable ratio reinforcement is the most powerful of the four partial types. Criticisms of behavior modification are that it manipulates people and that it does not apply very well in complex work environments.

TERMS AND CONCEPTS FOR REVIEW

Expectancy theory
Valence and expectancy
Cognitive theories of motivation
Behavior modification
O. B. Mod.
Positive reinforcement
Negative reinforcement

Shaping
Punishment
Extinction
Fixed interval reinforcement
Variable interval reinforcement
Fixed ratio reinforcement
Variable ratio reinforcement

REVIEW QUESTIONS

1. Explain how expectancy theory works.
2. Discuss whether the expectancy model applies to your own personal motivation.
3. Explain how behavior modification works.
4. What are the differences between expectancy theory and behavior modification?
5. Discuss the statement "Behavior modification in organizations is unacceptable because it manipulates people."

CASES

WESTSIDE DEPARTMENT STORE
Westside Department Store has a number of drivers who operate its delivery trucks. At the end of the day the drivers are required to complete a delivery report that takes 5–10 minutes. Preparation of this report has been a frequent source of conflict between management and the drivers. Drivers often fail to complete the report properly or delay completing it, which causes their supervisor to criticize and/or threaten them. The supervisor believes there must be a better way to motivate drivers to prepare reports properly, but he is not sure what approach to take.

QUESTION
1. Recommend to the supervisor a motivational model that might improve the drivers' behavior. Explain how it will apply to them.

JACOB ARNOLD
Jacob Arnold is an engineer in a large design engineering office. Jacob comes from a rural background in which his family had low income and stern rules. In order to earn his college degree he had to work to pay most of his own expenses.

Jacob is an intelligent and capable worker. His main fault is that he does not want to take risks. He hesitates to make decisions for himself, often bringing petty and routine problems to his supervisor or to other engineers for decision. Whenever he does a design job, he brings it in rough draft to his supervisor for approval before he finalizes it.

Since Jacob is a capable person, his supervisor wants to motivate him to be more independent in his work. The supervisor believes that this approach will improve Jacob's performance, relieve the supervisor from extra routine, and give Jacob more self-confidence. However, the supervisor is not sure how to go about motivating Jacob to improve his performance.

QUESTION
1. In the role of the supervisor, plan how you will motivate Jacob. Give reasons.

REFERENCES

1. Fred Luthans and Robert Kreitner, *Organizational Behavior Modification,* Glenview, Ill.: Scott, Foresman and Company, 1975, p. 16.

2. Victor H. Vroom, *Work and Motivation,* New York: John Wiley & Sons, Inc., 1964. See also J. W. Atkinson, *An Introduction to Motivation,* Princeton, N.J.: D. Van Nostrand Company, Inc., 1964; and K. Lewin, *The Conceptual Representation and the Measurement of Psychological Forces,* Durham, N.C.: The Duke University Press, 1938.

3. Lyman W. Porter and Edward E. Lawler III, *Managerial Attitudes and Performance,* Homewood, Ill.: The Dorsey Press and Richard D. Irwin, Inc., 1968. See also Robert J. House and Terence R. Mitchell, "Path-Goal Theory of Leadership," *Journal of Contemporary Business,* Autumn 1974, pp. 81–97.

4. There are even some questions about the decision-making assumptions on which expectancy theory rests. See Orlando Behling and Frederick A. Starke, "The Postulates of Expectancy Theory," *Academy of Management Journal,* September 1973, pp. 373–388.

5. Thirty-one early studies are reported in Robert J. House, H. Jack Shapiro, and Mahmoud A. Wahba, "Expectancy Theory as a Predictor of Work Behavior and Attitude: A Re-evaluation of Empirical Evidence," *Decision Sciences,* December 1974, pp. 54–77.

6. H. Peter Dachler and William H. Mobley, "Construct Validation of an Instrumentality–Expectancy–Task-Goal Model of Motivation: Some Theoretical Boundary Conditions," *Journal of Applied Psychology,* December 1973, pp. 397–418.

7. John E. Sheridan, John W. Slocum, Jr., and Byung Min, "Motivational Determinants of Job Performance," *Journal of Applied Psychology,* February 1975, pp. 119–121.

8. Gerald A. Kesselman, Eileen L. Hagen, and Robert J. Wherry, Sr., "A Factor Analytic Test of the Porter-Lawler Expectancy Model of Work Motivation," *Personnel Psychology,* Winter 1974, pp. 569–579.

9. Tamao Matsui and Toshitake Terai, "A Cross-cultural Study of the Validity of the Expectancy Theory of Work Motivation," *Journal of Applied Psychology,* April 1975, pp. 263–265.

10. B. F. Skinner, *Science and Human Behavior,* New York: The Macmillan Company (The Free Press), 1953; and B. F. Skinner, *Contingencies of Reinforcement,* New York: Appleton-Century-Crofts, Inc., 1969.

11. Luthans and Kreitner, *op. cit.,* p. 12. This book provides an extensive bibliography on behavior modification. Another extensive bibliography is in Craig Eric Schneier, "Behavior Modification in Management: A Review and Critique," *Academy of Management Journal,* September 1974, pp. 528–548.

12. "At Emery Air Freight: Positive Reinforcement Boosts Performance," *Organizational Dynamics,* Winter 1973, pp. 41–50.

13. W. Clay Hamner, "Reinforcement Theory and Contingency Management in Organizational Settings," in Henry L. Tosi and W. Clay Hamner, *Organizational Behavior and Management: A Contingency Approach,* Chicago: St. Clair Press, 1974, p. 100.

14. Ed Pedalino and Victor U. Gamboa, "Behavior Modification and Absenteeism: Intervention in One Industrial Setting," *Journal of Applied Psychology,* December 1974, pp. 694–698.

15. Gary Yukl, Kenneth N. Wexley, and James D. Seymore, "Effectiveness of Pay Incentives under Variable Ratio and Continuous Reinforcement Schedules," *Journal of Applied Psychology,* February 1972, pp. 19–23.

16. Gary A. Yukl and Gary P. Latham, "Consequences of Reinforcement Schedules and Incentive Magnitudes for Employee Performance: Problems Encountered in an Industrial Setting," *Journal of Applied Psychology,* June 1975, pp. 294–298.

17. Walter R. Nord, "Beyond the Teaching Machine: The Neglected Area of Operant Conditioning in the Theory and Practice of Management," *Organizational Behavior and Human Performance,* November 1969, pp. 375–401.

18. Craig Eric Schneier, "Behavior Modification: Training the Hard-Core Unemployed," *Personnel,* May–June 1973, pp. 65–69.

19. An example of criticism is Fred L. Fry, "Operant Conditioning in Organizational Settings: Of Mice or Men?" *Personnel,* July–August 1974, pp. 17–24. Fry comments on page 18, "Organizations are more complex than Skinner Boxes; men are more intelligent than mice; O. B. Mod. is simply behavioral Taylorism."

20. For example, see Korman's *consistency model* relating to self-image and self-esteem in Abraham K. Korman, "Hypothesis of Work Behavior Revisited and an Extension," *Academy of Management Review,* January 1976, pp. 50–63.

CHAPTER 5
JOB SATISFACTION

> Job satisfaction does seem to reduce
> absence, turnover, and perhaps accident rates.
>
> Robert L. Kahn[1]

TO UNDERSTAND:

The importance of job satisfaction

The relation of satisfaction and productivity

Other variables related to job satisfaction

The proportion of United States workers satisfied with their jobs

Benefits that result from job satisfaction study

How job satisfaction data are secured and applied

One of the surest signs of deteriorating conditions in an organization is low job satisfaction. In its more sinister forms it lurks behind wildcat strikes, slowdowns, absenteeism, and employee turnover. It also may be a part of grievances, low productivity, disciplinary problems, and other organizational difficulties.

One organization with declining job satisfaction faced a substantial rise in certain personnel problem indexes over a period of four years.[2] Absences rose 50 percent, and turnover rose 70 percent. Grievances increased 38 percent, and disciplinary layoffs climbed 44 percent. All these difficulties were traced primarily to workers' dissatisfaction with their jobs.

High job satisfaction, on the other hand, gladdens the hearts of administrators, because it tends to be connected with positive conditions that administrators want. Although high job satisfaction is the hallmark of a well-managed organization, it cannot be persuaded into existence or even bought. It is fundamentally the result of effective behavioral management. It furnishes a measure of the progress that has been made in developing a sound behavioral climate in an organization. Discussion in this chapter concerns the nature of job satisfaction, ways of securing job satisfaction information, and how to use this information effectively.

JOB SATISFACTION IN ORGANIZATIONS

WHAT IS JOB SATISFACTION? There are a number of different definitions of job satisfaction,[3] but the one we will use is that *job satisfaction* is the favorableness or unfavorableness with which employees view their work. It results when there is a fit between job characteristics and the wants of employees. It expresses the amount of congruence between one's expectations of the job and the rewards that the job provides. Since job satisfaction involves expectations compared with rewards, it relates to equity theory and the psychological contract discussed in Chapter 2.

Job satisfaction may refer to either a person or a group. An administrator can say either "Antonio Ortega has high job satisfaction" or "Department C has high job satisfaction." In addition, job satisfaction can apply to parts of an individual's job. For example, although Antonio Ortega's general job satisfaction may be high, he may be dissatisfied with his vacation plan. In the same way that health is important because it represents general physical conditions, job satisfaction is important because it represents general human conditions. It requires attention, diagnosis, and treatment, just as health does.

Job satisfaction can be more accurately interpreted in terms of the general emotional tone of employees. Some employees, for example, may be very satisfied with their home and community life, but they think their jobs are average. In this instance their job satisfaction is relatively low because it is below their other satisfactions. Other employees may be loaded with home and community dissatisfactions, but they also feel that their jobs are average. This means that their job satisfaction is relatively high. In order to relate general emotional tone specifically to job satisfaction, some organizations survey both job satisfaction and life satisfaction so that the two conditions may be compared. Job satisfaction and life satisfaction are often closely related. This is known as the *spillover effect,* meaning that one spills over to the other.[4] A different and less prevalent relationship is that people compensate for low job satisfaction by trying to achieve high life satisfactions. This is called the *compensatory effect.*

Another aid in interpreting job satisfaction is to determine how important each job satisfaction variable is to employees. Assume that employees answer "Below average" to one question about the company cafeteria and another about the company's fairness in making promotions. At this point their dissatisfaction seems equally important with each variable; but if each question has a second part asking how important each variable is to them, they may say "Unimportant" for the cafeteria question and "Very important" for the promotion question. Then management knows it should give first attention to promotions because problems there are more important.

Porter has developed an interesting approach to measuring job satisfaction.[5] He relates actual conditions to those perceived as ideal by the employee. A sample question from a Porter-type survey would read as follows:

The feeling of security in my job (circle one number):

(a) How much is there now?   (min.) 1 2 3 4 5 6 7 (max.)

(b) How much should there be?   (min.) 1 2 3 4 5 6 7 (max.)

(c) How important is this to me?   (min.) 1 2 3 4 5 6 7 (max.)

To determine satisfaction, the response to question *a* is subtracted from the response to question *b*. The lower the difference is, the higher the job satisfaction. Need importance is measured by the response to question *c*.

One point that is clear about job satisfaction is that it is dynamic. Administrators cannot establish high job satisfaction once and then forget about it for several years. It can leave as quickly as it came—usually more quickly—so it has to be carefully maintained week after week, month after month, year after year.

RELATION OF JOB SATISFACTION AND PRODUCTIVITY. Historically it was assumed that high job satisfaction led to high productivity, but later research indicated that this was an incorrect assumption. Satisfied workers may be high producers or low producers or only average producers. The satisfaction-productivity relationship is quite complex, being influenced by many intervening variables, such as the rewards that an employee receives.

Some correlations have been found between job satisfaction and performance, but these often are small and not statistically significant.[6] Further, there is a question whether job satisfaction leads to performance or performance leads to job satisfaction. Lawler and Porter have developed a model that suggests that productivity leads to satisfaction, as shown in Figure 5-1.[7] Performance leads to rewards; and if these are perceived to be equitable as explained by equity theory, employee satisfaction is the result.

Probably the most realistic assumption in terms of a system concept is that satisfaction and productivity are in a circular relationship in which each affects the other.[8] This model assumes that performance leads to rewards and satisfaction, which then lead to more effort because of high perceived expectancy (that is, perceived connection between performance and reward). The high effort leads to effective performance, which again leads to satisfaction in a circular relationship. Using this model, it can be said that high job satisfaction indicates a predisposition to be productive if effective leadership is provided.

The general relationship of job satisfaction and productivity is illustrated in Figure 5-2. The condition of high productivity and low job satisfaction is shown by line C of the chart. A supervisor of a paced production line can push primarily the techniques of scientific management, such as methods study, time study, and close supervision, and achieve the high productivity and low job satisfaction shown by line C. If, on the other hand, the supervisor thinks that effective organizational behavior means keeping workers happy regardless of the effects on organizational goals, the supervisor will achieve results similar to line A. There will be

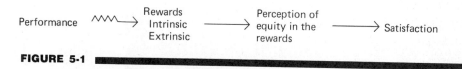

FIGURE 5-1

Model of performance leading to job satisfaction. (Adapted from Edward E. Lawler III and Lyman W. Porter, "The Effect of Performance on Job Satisfaction," *Industrial Relations,* October 1967, p. 23.)

much job satisfaction, but little work will be done. As one supervisor put it, ''My workers are so happy they don't feel like working.'' The most desirable arrangement—an integration of high satisfaction and high productivity—is shown in line B.

Although it is entirely possible to have high productivity with low job satisfaction, it is doubtful that extremes of this condition can be maintained in the long run. In a relatively free society, if a large enough group is affected, resistances and restrictions develop that lead eventually to lower productivity. People being what they are, they resist and avoid that which brings them dissatisfaction and lack of fulfillment.

RELATION OF JOB SATISFACTION TO OTHER VARIABLES. Job satisfaction tends to correlate with a number of other variables in organizations.

Turnover and absenteeism. As might be expected, job satisfaction consistently correlates with turnover. Those employees who have low job satisfaction are more likely to leave their employer.[9] The same relationship applies for absenteeism. If employees have low job satisfaction, they are likely to be absent from their jobs more often.[10]

Age. With regard to employee characteristics, research generally reports a positive correlation between age and job satisfaction.[11] As workers become older they

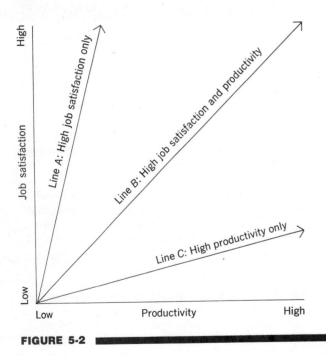

FIGURE 5-2 ▰▰▰▰▰▰▰▰▰▰▰▰▰▰▰▰▰▰▰▰▰▰

Relation of job satisfaction and productivity.

tend to become more satisfied with their jobs, probably because of increasing adaptation on the basis of experience. Younger workers, on the other hand, tend to have excessively high expectations of promotion and other job conditions; so when they first experience employment, they tend to be dissatisfied with it. The relation of job satisfaction to age has been shown to apply internationally. Studies in five nations report that older workers are more satisfied.[12]

Occupation. Studies of occupational groups have shown a consistent relationship between occupational level and job satisfaction.[13] Higher-level occupations report increased job satisfactions. One report of several surveys showed that the proportion of persons who would choose their same occupation again ranged from 82 to 91 percent for professional occupations, but from only 16 to 52 percent for unskilled-to-skilled workers. In another survey 55 percent of managers wanted to continue their work, but only 16 percent of unskilled workers wished to do so.[14] Following this line of reasoning, supervisors would be expected to have higher job satisfaction than their workers, but there are always exceptions to job satisfaction generalities.

The positive correlation between higher level work and higher job satisfaction also applies in other countries. Workers in Soviet Russia, the United States, Germany, Italy, Sweden, and Norway all report higher job satisfactions in the higher occupations. There were, however, wide variations. In the United States 72 percent of unskilled workers were satisfied, but only 23 percent of their unskilled counterparts in Russia were satisfied with their jobs. At the professional level there was less difference: 82 percent satisfied in the United States and 77 percent in Russia.[15]

Community conditions. One feature of job satisfaction is that it is influenced by community conditions. It might be reasoned that poor community conditions pull down job satisfaction, while better community conditions lift it, but this is not the case. What usually happens is that employees compare their job conditions with community conditions. If they have average job conditions surrounded by poor community conditions, these circumstances tend to lift their satisfactions because they see themselves relatively well off.

One research project covered 300 catalog order branches of a mail-order firm. All branches were very similar in job conditions, but there was wide variation in community conditions. The result was that more attractive community features led to lower satisfaction values, because workers evaluated job conditions in terms of other alternatives existing in the community. More slums and more business depression, for example, suggested that their job situation was better.[16]

It appears that workers also compare a job's "way of life" with the community's way of living, and they are most satisfied when these two value systems come reasonably close together. For example, does a job in a small town allow independence, variability, and a moderate pace? These are factors that would be consistent with the way of life in a town, compared with a large city. One intensive study found that town workers were more satisfied with jobs permitting autonomy, variety, interaction, and responsibility, but city workers were more satisfied with jobs low in these same factors.[17]

JOB SATISFACTION IN THE UNITED STATES. Studies show that most workers in the United States are satisfied with their jobs.[18] Considering the labor force as a whole, 90 percent respond that they are satisfied with their jobs, as shown in Figure 5-3. There has been an increase from 83 percent in 1962, and probably a substantial portion of it can be attributed to improvement in organizational behavior practices. As supervisors have learned more about organizational behavior, they have been able to apply improved job conditions and bring a direct benefit to workers.

All surveys asked essentially the same job satisfaction question, "Considering all factors, how satisfied are you with your job?" Employees who gave an answer in the area of "Very satisfied" and "Somewhat satisfied" were counted as satisfied. Those who indicated "Not too satisfied" or "Dissatisfied" were counted as dissatisfied. Both men and women were surveyed, and generally women have expressed about the same job satisfaction as men in the labor force. For the 1973 survey 89 percent of the women and 91 percent of the men expressed satisfaction.

The proportion of satisfied workers is large and to a certain extent refutes the pessimists who talk of dissatisfaction among workers. On the other hand, the 10

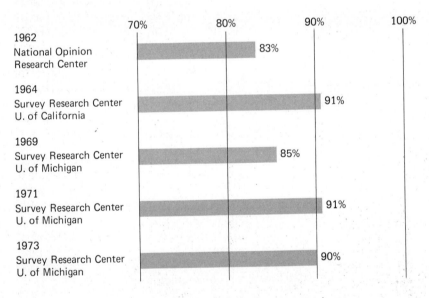

NOTE: "Don't know" answers were excluded from the percentage bases.

FIGURE 5-3 ▮▬▬▬▬▬▬▬▬▬▬▬▬▬▬▬▬▬▬▬▬

Percentage of satisfied workers in the United States, 1962–1973, based on five national surveys. (*Source:* U.S. Department of Labor, *Job Satisfaction: Is There a Trend?*, 1974, p. 4.)

percent dissatisfied represent approximately 10 million workers. This is a very large number of people who have not yet found job satisfaction, so it does indicate a major area for continued organizational behavior improvement. In addition, there is a need for those who are only somewhat satisfied to improve their satisfaction. This analysis leads to the conclusion that there continues to be a major need for improving job satisfaction in the United States.

SECURING JOB SATISFACTION INFORMATION

The importance of job satisfaction suggests that management needs to secure information about it in order to have sound information for making decisions that might affect it. This section discusses the benefits management can gain from the study of job satisfaction, what methods are available, and how they are used. A typical approach is a job satisfaction survey, also known as a morale, opinion, or attitude survey.[19]

BENEFITS OF JOB SATISFACTION STUDY. Several benefits accrue to management from job satisfaction study. One benefit is that it gives management an indication of the general levels of satisfaction in a company. This is done with reference to particular subjects such as employee services, and particular groups of employees such as the tool department or all employees over forty years of age. In other words, a survey tells how employees feel about their jobs, what parts of their jobs these feelings are focused upon, where these feelings are in terms of departments, and whose feelings are involved (such as supervisors, employees, and staff specialists). This means that the survey is a powerful diagnostic instrument for looking at employee problems. In one company, for example, major changes had been made in employee-relations policies, and the company wanted to check on employee reaction to the changes. Another company had recently doubled its work force, and it wished to determine how well new employees were being integrated into the firm.

Another benefit is the valuable communication brought on by a job satisfaction survey. Communication flows in all directions as people plan the survey, take it, and discuss its results. Upward communication is especially fruitful when employees are encouraged to comment about what is on their minds instead of merely answering questions about what is on management's mind.

One benefit, often unexpected, is improved attitudes. For some, the survey is a safety valve, an emotional release, a chance to get things off one's chest. For others, the survey is a tangible expression of management's interest in employee welfare, which gives the employee cause to feel better toward management.

Job satisfaction surveys are a useful way to determine certain training needs. Usually employees are given an opportunity to report how well they feel their supervisor performs certain parts of the job, such as delegating work and giving adequate job instructions, which in an indirect way indicates the kinds of training that different groups of supervisors need.

Surveys may also bring benefits to unions. As explained by one union officer, both management and union often argue about what the employees want, but really they do not know. The job satisfaction survey is one way to find out. At any rate, unions very rarely oppose surveys, and occasionally they give them support when they know they will share the results.

TYPES OF JOB SATISFACTION SURVEYS. Job satisfaction surveys, whether by questionnaire or by interview, are of three general types classified according to the form of question asked. *Objective surveys* present both a question and a choice of answers in such a way that employees merely mark the answer that is their choice. *Descriptive surveys* present questions but let employees answer in their own words. *Projective surveys* present abstract situations unrelated to job or company and require the worker to analyze and comment upon them. The typical questionnaire uses both objective and descriptive approaches.

Objective surveys. Looking first at objective surveys, there are a number of varieties. The most popular one uses multiple-choice questions. In this type of survey respondents read all the answers to each question and then mark the answer that is nearest to how they feel. Other types may be marked "True" or "False," or the employee may mark a numerical value along a horizontal scale of feelings. Regardless of the kind of objective survey used, its chief defect is that *management writes the answers.* The best that workers can do is check the answer nearest to how they feel, and this may be a grossly inaccurate expression of their real feelings. This approach really does not give them much chance to express themselves.

The chief advantage of objective surveys is that they are easy to administer and to analyze statistically. This permits much of the analysis to be performed on computers, which is an important cost consideration when thousands of employees are surveyed.

Descriptive surveys. In contrast to objective surveys, descriptive surveys get responses from employees in their own words. Responses are encouraged in either a directed or an undirected manner. The directed question focuses employee attention on a specific part of the job and asks questions about it. An example is: What do you think of the company's pension program? In this way, management in general determines the items that will be covered. The undirected question gives employees more leeway to discuss what comes to their minds at the moment. An example is: What are some of the things you like most about your job?

An interview survey is by its nature mostly descriptive rather than objective. A suitable interview usually takes from one to two hours for each interviewee; hence it is both time-consuming and expensive. In order to ensure that the same material is covered in a consistent manner with each employee, each interviewer usually is carefully trained and follows a standardized interviewer's guide that tells what material to cover and how to phrase questions.

Projective surveys. Projective techniques constitute a third way to interpret job satisfaction. These devices are personality probes developed by psychiatrists and psychologists for studying mental health. Projective devices are not used for general surveys, but they are mentioned here to show the full range of instruments that are available. On rare occasions they are used in professional counseling of individuals with special problems. The projective technique presents an abstraction that is incomplete or meaningless, which the employee must then project into completeness by describing what it means. The two main projective techniques are the Rorschach test using ink blots and the Thematic Apperception Test using pictures.

SURVEY PROCEDURES. Job satisfaction survey procedures are tricky and more complicated than they appear to be at first glance. It seems simple enough to go to employees, get their responses, and then interpret them, but experience has shown that careless procedural errors can seriously limit the validity and usefulness of a survey. Particular attention needs to be given to question construction, maintenance of anonymity for employees, and sampling procedures. No attempt is made here to cover the many details and pitfalls in survey procedures, but an overview is provided by describing how one organization made its survey.

Management determined its need for greater understanding of employee attitudes and called a consultant, who developed with management's assistance a set of objectives and written policies for the survey. These were approved by an executive committee with the company president in attendance. At this time the questionnaire method was chosen, and it was decided that all managers and workers were to be surveyed. Thereafter, the survey procedures were planned by the consultant, the personnel director, and a personnel specialist. A committee of seven middle managers was appointed by the president to help draft questions for the survey. The committee was guided by the consultant, who served as chairman. It also approved an official announcement of the survey (six weeks before it was given) and aided in grapevine publicity of the event.

The survey was given on three consecutive days. Somewhat different questionnaires were used for office, managerial, and operative employees. The questionnaires took about forty-five minutes to complete, so a new group of employees was convened every hour in a large conference room. The personnel director introduced the consultant and left the room, after which the consultant explained the survey and administered it. Replies were placed in a locked ballot box.

After the survey the consultant prepared a complete report for management and a condensed report that was distributed to employees. The consultant also advised the executive committee about its program of action following the survey.

USING EXISTING JOB SATISFACTION INDICATORS. A job satisfaction survey is similar to an annual accounting audit in the sense that it is merely a periodic activity; yet there is a day-by-day need for keeping up with job satisfaction just as there is a day-by-day need to keep up with the accounts. Management stays in daily touch with job satisfaction primarily through face-to-face contact and communication. This is its practical method of determining job satisfaction, but there are also a number of other satisfaction indicators already available in an organization, including the following ones:

1. Labor turnover

2. Productivity

3. Waste and scrap

4. Quality records

5. Absenteeism and tardiness

6. Reports from counselors

7. Grievances

8. Exit interviews

9. Accident reports

10. Medical records

11. Suggestions

12. Training records

Some of the records just mentioned are direct measures of job satisfaction, while others are indirect. Together they form a substantial body of knowledge about satisfaction in an organization. They are not as precise as a job satisfaction survey, but they are sound indicators of any major variation in satisfaction. Their chief advantages are that in most cases they are already available, they are easily kept because they are mostly objective, and they are a good measure of trends over a period of time.

APPRAISING AND USING JOB SATISFACTION INFORMATION

Once job satisfaction information is collected, the big question remaining is: What does all of this mean in terms of my organization and my employees? Although gathering satisfaction information is largely a technique, appraisal and use of this information require skilled managerial judgment. Accurate appraisal and action in terms of each organization's specific situation are important.

INTERPRETING JOB SATISFACTION DATA. The first step in using the information is to make it understandable and available to all key managers, rather than just to the specialists who conducted the survey. Even though the specialists know the weak spots, the managers who will make the changes want to see the evidence themselves. There are a number of ways to make the survey information meaningful. One way is to subdivide the data into categories that pinpoint different types of problems. Various graphic devices are also used when appropriate.

In larger organizations comparisons among departments are an effective way to encourage managers to sit up and take note of satisfaction data. Just as a lagging baseball team makes every effort to pass other teams in its league, managers whose departments do not show high job satisfaction will be spurred to improve their score by the time the next study is made. Comparisons of this type must be handled with skill so that the lower scorers will not feel intimidated.

If there is a chance of hurt feelings or personality clashes, it is wise to designate each department with letters such as A and B. Departmental managers are told privately which letter represents their own department. They can then compare their score with other departmental scores, but they cannot identify which score belongs to which department. Scores, however, must not be overemphasized in a way that makes "score-happy" managers. The real goal is to encourage desirable behavioral change, and a single score can only partially represent this complicated relationship. The score is a comparative tool, not a goal.

There are a number of useful comparisons besides departmental ones, such as age, seniority, marital status, formal education, company training received, sex, work shift, building worked in, and type of work done (e.g., scientific, clerical, or production). If earlier surveys have been made, trends over time can be plotted. More elaborate statistical comparisons and correlations can be made if the evidence looks promising. For example, do those who say their supervisor is a good manager say also that they have more pride in their organization as a place to work, compared with those who say their supervisor is a poor manager? Ultimately all the questions and job satisfaction categories can be compared with each other.

The managers' interests in job satisfaction statistics are heightened by asking them to predict ahead of time their subordinates' attitudes toward various items, and then to compare their predictions with actual survey results. Wherever their prediction misses its mark, they are forced to ask themselves why they were not aware of this condition. Even if a prediction is accurate, it may still encourage soul-searching. Consider the case of a department head who predicted his employees would report dissatisfaction with grievance handling. They did report dissatisfaction, which forced him to ask: "If I knew about this condition before the survey—and apparently I did—why haven't I done something about it?"

Although the foregoing discussion emphasizes statistics and scores, employee comments are useful, too. Comments can be scored and tabulated, but great value comes from organizing them into sub-groups, typing them, and then having appropriate members of management read them as the *employee wrote them*. In this way employees communicate directly with management in their own words. This information often makes a greater impression on management than scores, statistics, and charts do. Communicationwise, this gets through to them. Some comments are about very minor conditions, but they are nevertheless irritating to someone and are worthy of management's sincere attention. It is a mistake to correct only the big problems shown in a survey, while omitting many minor conditions that will add up to big problems.

ADMINISTRATIVE FOLLOW-UP. One way to get managers interested in introducing behavioral change is to set up working committees whose responsibility is to review the survey data and develop plans for corrective action.

In one company, for example, a special executive committee was appointed to recommend changes in overall behavioral policy, and supervisory committees were established in each department to discuss how the survey applied to local departmental problems. The supervisory committees worked out their own solutions on departmental matters, but if their proposed action affected other departments, it had to be forwarded to the executive committee for approval. The personnel director was chairman of each committee, which usually met monthly. At each meeting a separate part of the survey was discussed in some depth. Meetings continued for over a year, assuring a long-run follow-up of the information uncovered by the survey. This long-run approach kept executives thinking about the survey and gave it time to soak in.

The long-run approach to using job satisfaction information is important. Too many employers make the mistake of giving a survey immense publicity and interest for a few weeks and then forgetting about it until another survey is run. They shoot the works, giving their surveys all the fanfare of a Mardi Gras—but when Mardi Gras has passed, they return to their old way of living.

When corrective action is taken as the result of a survey, details of what was done should be shared with employees as soon as possible. Only in this way will people who participated feel that management listened to them and took action on the basis of their ideas. This also assures employees that their ideas really were wanted—and are wanted still. In fact, good publicity to managers and employees is essential from start to finish in a job satisfaction study—to explain what the study intends to accomplish, to report the information gathered, and to announce what corrective action has been taken.

One thing is sure: If a job satisfaction survey is made, management should be prepared to take action on the results. Employees feel that if they cooperate in stating their feelings, management should endeavor to make some of the worthwhile improvements they suggest. A sure way to close off future expressions of employee opinion is to fail to take action on the opinions already given. It should be remembered that management asked employees for their ideas; hence employees are justified in feeling that action will be taken on at least some ideas.

SUMMARY

High job satisfaction is an important ingredient of teamwork, which means that nearly all managers try to develop it in their employees. Job satisfaction and productivity sometimes are correlated with one another to a minor extent, apparently in a circular fashion, but the correlation is rarely statistically significant. High job satisfaction tends to be correlated with reduced turnover and absenteeism. Older people tend to have higher job satisfaction than younger ones, and higher occupational groups tend to have higher job satisfaction compared with lower occupational groups. Approximately 90 percent of the labor force in the United States report that they are satisfied with their jobs.

Job satisfaction information is secured by job satisfaction surveys. These may be objective, descriptive, or projective. Additional satisfaction information may be secured from existing personnel data. The ultimate test of job satisfaction information is the way it influences managers in their work. This means that it must be made available and understandable in terms of their environment. They must see the evidence in order to be encouraged to change their practices.

TERMS AND CONCEPTS FOR REVIEW

Job satisfaction	Compensatory effect
Spillover effect	Relation of job satisfaction and productivity

Job satisfaction survey

Objective survey

Descriptive survey

Projective survey

REVIEW QUESTIONS

1. What is job satisfaction? Why is it important? Do you think modern managers overemphasize or underemphasize it?
2. What is the relationship between job satisfaction and productivity?
3. Discuss the implications of the survey report that 90 percent of the United States labor force are satisfied with their jobs.
4. Join with an associate to make a job satisfaction survey of a small work team and report your results.
5. Prepare a plan for using job satisfaction survey results in a bank or an insurance office.

CASES

BARRY NILAND

Barry Niland, supervisor of a small sales department, noticed that one of his industrial sales representatives appeared to have low job satisfaction. Among other signs of low satisfaction, his sales had declined in the last six months, although most other sales representatives regularly were exceeding their quotas. Niland decided to try to boost his sales representative's satisfaction by reminding him of the many opportunities for satisfaction in a sales job.

Niland explained his actions as follows:

I pointed out that in his customer's eyes he alone is the company. He has the opportunity to help his customer. He has the opportunity to show his ability and knowledge to many types of people. He has the opportunity through his own efforts to help many types of people. He has the opportunity through his own efforts to help support the people who make our products, to reward the stockholders, and to control his financial return through his own know-how. He has the opportunity of testing his creative ideas, with immediate feedback about their value. He has the opportunity to meet constantly changing conditions, so there is no boredom in his job. There is no quicker way to achieve personal satisfaction than sales work.

QUESTION

1. Comment on Niland's approach in dealing with his sales representative.

THE MOONBEAM COMPANY

Following are the answers to one part of an objective job satisfaction survey made in the five regional offices of the Moonbeam Company. The part shown covers quality of supervision.

MORALE SURVEY DATA, QUALITY OF SUPERVISION
What is your opinion of the manager who supervises your work?

QUESTION ASKED	NUMBER ANSWERING				
	REGION 1	2	3	4	5
1. Does he pass the buck?					
a. Never	44	34	34	40	48
b. Seldom	40	27	17	25	33
c. Usually	9	10	10	18	9
d. Always	9	11	2	6	1
2. Does he keep his promises?					
a. Always	58	29	36	48	43
b. Usually	41	47	25	41	59
c. Seldom	4	6	4	4	2
d. Never	2	6	1	1	0
3. Does he welcome suggestions?					
a. Always	66	38	38	44	36
b. Usually	34	38	16	38	49
c. Seldom	4	8	7	7	14
d. Never	3	3	4	4	2
4. Is he a good teacher?					
a. Always	53	23	38	40	40
b. Usually	35	46	21	39	49
c. Seldom	6	8	5	10	7
d. Never	8	8	1	3	3
5. Is he friendly and easy to talk to?					
a. Always	70	59	49	61	74
b. Usually	31	26	11	26	27
c. Seldom	3	1	4	6	2
d. Never	3	2	3	1	2
6. Does he try to treat each worker fairly?					
a. Always	55	41	36	44	46
b. Usually	43	40	25	43	51
c. Seldom	4	4	2	3	1
d. Never	4	4	4	4	3
7. Does he give conflicting orders?					
a. Never	45	35	32	30	30
b. Seldom	48	39	22	44	62
c. Usually	11	9	5	14	4
d. Always	2	5	6	3	5
8. Does he control his temper?					
a. Always	48	40	36	34	27
b. Usually	48	41	28	49	70
c. Seldom	6	4	0	6	5
d. Never	2	2	4	5	2
9. Does he criticize you in front of others?					
a. Never	67	67	49	51	60
b. Seldom	28	17	13	32	33
c. Usually	6	1	4	4	5
d. Always	3	3	1	3	2

QUESTION

1. From the view of the general office manager, analyze these figures and discuss what they mean about the level of job satisfaction regarding supervision in the different offices.

REFERENCES

1. Robert L. Kahn, "The Work Module: A Tonic for Lunchpail Lassitude," *Psychology Today,* February 1973, p. 94.

2. "Low Productivity Gains Linked to Worker Morale at Recent AMA Briefing," *AMA Management News,* December 1972, p. 1.

3. Nine definitions of general job satisfaction are reviewed in John P. Wanous and Edward E. Lawler III, "Measurement and Meaning of Job Satisfaction," *Journal of Applied Psychology,* April 1972, pp. 95–105.

4. Benjamin Iris and Gerald V. Barrett, "Some Relations between Job and Life Satisfaction and Job Importance," *Journal of Applied Psychology,* August 1972, pp. 301–304.

5. Lyman W. Porter, "A Study of Perceived Need Satisfactions in Bottom and Middle Management," *Journal of Applied Psychology,* January 1961, pp. 1–10.

6. Examples of weak positive correlations are John P. Wanous, "A Causal-Correlational Analysis of the Job Satisfaction and Performance Relationship," *Journal of Applied Psychology,* April 1974, pp. 139–144; and Lawrence D. Prybil, "Job Satisfaction in Relation to Job Performance and Occupational Level," *Personnel Journal,* February 1973, pp. 94–100.

7. Edward E. Lawler III, and Lyman W. Porter, "The Effect of Performance on Job Satisfaction," *Industrial Relations,* October 1967, pp. 20–28. Research supporting the Lawler-Porter model is reported in Charles N. Greene, "Causal Connections among Managers' Merit Pay, Job Satisfaction, and Performance," *Journal of Applied Psychology,* August 1973, pp. 95–100.

8. Robert A. Sutermeister, "Employee Performance and Employee Need Satisfaction: Which Comes First?", *California Management Review,* Summer 1971, pp. 43–47.

9. Examples of this relationship are found in Benjamin Schneider and Robert A. Snyder, "Some Relationships between Job Satisfaction and Organizational Climate," *Journal of Applied Psychology,* June 1975, pp. 318–328; and Ray Wild, "Job Needs, Job Satisfaction, and Job Behavior of Women Manual Workers," *Journal of Applied Psychology,* April 1970, pp. 157–162. For a somewhat contrary opinion see W. W. Ronan, "Individual and Situational Variables Relating to Job Satisfaction," *Journal of Applied Psychology Monograph,* February 1970, pp. 1–31.

10. Lawrence G. Hrebiniak and Michael Roteman, "A Study of the Relationship between Need Satisfaction and Absenteeism among Managerial Personnel," *Journal of Applied Psychology,* December 1973, pp. 381–383.

11. Examples are U.S. Department of Labor, *Job Satisfaction: Is There a Trend?,* 1974, p. 7; and Michael R. Carrell and Norbert F. Elbert, "Some Personal and Organizational Determinants of Job Satisfaction of Postal Clerks," *Academy of Management Journal,* June 1974, pp. 368–373.

12. "'Inevitable Hierarchical Gap' Emerges in Study of Capitalist and Socialist Organizations," *ISR Newsletter* (Institute for Social Research, The University of Michigan), Autumn 1974, pp. 4–5.

13. U.S. Department of Labor, *op. cit.,* pp. 9–10; Edward A. Nicholson, Jr., and Roger D. Roderick, "A Multivariate Analysis of the Correlates of Job Satisfaction among Men Aged

45–59," in Vance F. Mitchell and others (eds.), *Proceedings of the 32nd Annual Meeting,* Minneapolis: The Academy of Management, 1973, pp. 221–224; and Kahn, *op. cit.,* pp. 39, 94.

14.   Robert Blauner, "Work Satisfaction and Industrial Trends in Modern Society," in Walter Galenson and S. M. Lipset (eds.), *Labor and Trade Unionism,* New York: John Wiley & Sons, Inc., 1960, pp. 339–360.

15.   Alex Inkeles, "Industrial Man: The Relation of Status to Experience, Perception, and Value," *American Journal of Sociology,* July 1960, p. 6.

16.   Charles L. Hulin, "Effects of Community Characteristics on Measures of Job Satisfaction," *Journal of Applied Psychology,* April 1966, pp. 185–192.

17.   Arthur N. Turner and Paul R. Lawrence, *Industrial Jobs and the Worker: An Investigation of Response to Task Attributes,* Boston: Harvard Graduate School of Business Administration, 1965, covering 470 workers on forty-seven jobs. See also Ray Wild and T. Kempner, "Influence of Community and Plant Characteristics on Job Attitudes of Manual Workers," *Journal of Applied Psychology,* April 1972, pp. 106–113.

18.   "Job Satisfaction Has Been High over 15-Year Period, Survey Findings Demonstrate," *ISR Newsletter* (Institute for Social Research, The University of Michigan), Summer 1974, p. 7; U.S. Department of Labor, *op. cit.,* pp. 47–54; and Robert J. Flanagan, George Strauss, and Lloyd Ulman, "Worker Discontent and Work Place Behavior," *Industrial Relations,* May 1974, pp. 101–123.

19.   An example of a company experience with an opinion survey is reported in Elizabeth D. Howe, "Opinion Surveys: Taking the Task Force Approach," *Personnel,* September–October 1974, pp. 16–23.

CHAPTER 6
DEVELOPING A SOUND ORGANIZATIONAL CLIMATE

Men employees are given one evening a week for courting and two if they go to prayer meeting. After 14 hours in the store, the leisure hours should be spent mostly in reading.[1]

LEARNING OBJECTIVES

TO UNDERSTAND:
The meaning of organizational climate
Climate's effect on motivation and productivity
How climate is developed in an organization
The meaning of allocative and incremental values
Different models of organizational behavior
The relation of models to Maslow's hierarchy of needs

If you board an airplane in Chicago on a cold winter day and fly to the warm sea breezes of Miami, the differences in weather climate will be apparent. There are similar differences in organizational climate. The introductory quotation and the factory rules of Amasa Whitney in Figure 6-1 indicate that organizational relationships have undergone tremendous changes during the last 150 years. Employers in early days had no program designated by the name "organizational behavior," but many of their rules concerned the subject as it is defined today. The old rules, measured by today's practices, are quaint and "out of this world." But before being critical of them, one should pause to wonder if someday a hundred years from now people will look back upon present-day factory rules and consider them quaint. This is the price, and the reward, of progress. One wonders what would be the reaction of employees today if their employer instructed them to spend their leisure hours in reading or attending prayer meeting.

Amasa Whitney's reference to employees as "hands" was a natural outgrowth of the concept that the employer purchased the commodity of labor, that is, the skill of the *hands* of employees. The words by which one refers to employees (such as "hands"), the attitudes of top management, company policies, and other matters all combine to establish the organizational climate in each institution.

Since this is the concluding chapter of the section on "Fundamentals of Organizational Behavior," it is appropriate to discuss how all behavioral factors combine to develop an effective organizational climate. In this chapter we discuss general conditions of an organizational climate, a basic organizational behavior system, and models of organizational behavior.

RULES & REGULATIONS
To Be Observed By All Persons
Employed In The Factory Of
A M A S A   W H I T N E Y

FIRST : The Mill will be put into operation 10 minutes before sunrise at all seasons of the year. The gate will be shut 10 minutes past sunset from the 20th of March to the 20th of September, at 30 minutes past 8 from the 20th of September to the 20th of March. Saturdays at sunset.

SECOND : It will be required of every person employed, that they be in the room in which they are employed, at the time mentioned above for the mill to be in operation.

THIRD : Hands are not allowed to leave the factory in working hours without the consent of their Overseer. If they do, they will be liable to have their time set off.

FOURTH : Anyone who by negligence or misconduct causes damage to the machinery, or impedes the progress of the work, will be liable to make good the damage for the same.

FIFTH : Anyone employed for a certain length of time, will be expected to make up their lost time, if required, before they will be entitled to their pay.

SIXTH : Any person employed for no certain length of time, will be required to give at least 4 weeks notice of their intention to leave (sickness excepted) or forfeit 4 weeks pay, unless by particular agreement.

SEVENTH : Anyone wishing to be absent any length of time, must get permisison of the Overseer.

EIGHTH : All who have leave of absence for any length of time will be expected to return in that time; and, in case they do not return in that time and do not give satisfactory reason, they will be liable to forfeit one week's work or less, if they commence work again. If they do not, they will be considered as one who leaves without giving any notice.

NINTH : Anything tending to impede the progress of manufacturing in working hours, such as unnecessary conversation, reading, eating fruit, &c.&c., must be avoided.

TENTH : While I shall endeavor to employ a judicious Overseer, the help will follow his direction in all cases.

ELEVENTH : No smoking will be allowed in the factory, as it is considered very unsafe, and particularly specified in the Insurance.

TWELFTH : In order to forward the work, job hands will follow the above regulations as well as those otherwise employed.

THIRTEENTH : It is intended that the bell be rung 5 minutes before the gate is hoisted, so that all persons may be ready to start their machines precisely at the time mentioned.

FOURTEENTH : All persons who cause damage to the machinery, break glass out of the windows, &c., will immediately inform the Overseer of the same.

FIFTEENTH : The hands will take breakfast, from the 1st of November to the last of March, before going to work—they will take supper from the 1st of May to the last of August, 30 minutes past 5 o'clock P.M.—from the 20th of September to the 20th of March between sundown and dark—25 minutes will be allowed for breakfast, 30 minutes for dinner, and 25 minutes for supper, and no more from the time the gate is shut till started again.

SIXTEENTH : The hands will leave the Factory so that the doors may be fastened within 10 minutes from the time of leaving off work.
AMASA WHITNEY
Winchendon, Mass. July 5, 1830.

FIGURE 6-1

Factory rules in 1830. (*Source:* Samuel H. Adams, *Sunrise to Sunset,* New York: Random House, Inc., 1950.)

ORGANIZATIONAL CLIMATE

Organizations, like fingerprints and snowflakes, are always unique. Each has its own culture, traditions, and methods of action, which in their totality constitute its climate for people. As new employees make their psychological contracts with their organization, they hope that it will have a supportive climate to help them meet their economic, social, and psychological wants.

Some organizations are bustling and efficient; others are easygoing. Some are quite human; others are hard and cold. An organization tends to attract and keep people who fit its climate, so that its patterns are to some extent perpetuated. Just as people move to a certain weather climate of sea, mountains, or desert, they will also choose an organizational climate. A certain manufacturing company serves as an illustration. Its management stresses seniority, centralized control, and cautious decisions. It has difficulty attracting and retaining young college graduates with promotion potential. What else could be expected? People of this background do not fit the company's pattern of living, its climate.

A sound climate is a long-run proposition. Managers need to take an assets approach to climate, meaning that they take the long-run view of climate as an organizational asset. Unwise discipline and putting pressures on people may temporarily get better productivity but at the cost of climatic assets, so the organization eventually will suffer from depleted assets.

INCREMENTAL VALUES ARE DIFFERENT. In one important respect human values are quite different from economic values in an organization. Economics deals with the allocation of scarce resources. If you have automobile A, I cannot have it; if you have budget B, those funds are not available to my department. Economic values are, therefore, mostly *allocative,* but human values are mostly *incremental.* They are self-generated, being created within a person. The difference is illustrated by a dollar bill and an idea. If I have dollar bill L95484272A and I give it to you, you have it and I do not. Either you or I can have it, but not both of us. However, if I have an idea and I give it to you, both you and I now have it. What was one unit is now two units; and though you have it, you took nothing of like kind away from me. You can give the idea away fifty times, but you do not lose it. All you do is spread it.

Human values, such as fulfillment and growth, are mostly of this incremental type. In order to build job satisfaction in employee A, it is not necessary to take it from employee B. In order to build satisfactions in department C, one does not have to take them from department D. Likewise, a climate of human dignity can be built without taking it from anywhere.

There are exceptions, of course, because organizational behavior is involved in all that goes on in an organization, much of which is allocative. In the main, however, organizational behavior is incremental. There is enough job satisfaction for everybody. In fact, some groups have achieved high cooperation and job satisfaction for every member; and, as indicated in the preceding chapter, about 90 percent of the labor force in the United States already report job satisfaction.

INTERPRETING ORGANIZATIONAL CLIMATE. Organizational climate can have a major influence on motivation, productivity, and job satisfaction. It does this by creating certain kinds of expectancies about what consequences will follow from different actions. Employees expect certain rewards, satisfactions, and frustrations, based upon their perception of the organization's climate. These expectations tend to lead to motivation, as explained by expectancy theory.

Climate exists in a contingency relationship with the organization, meaning that the type of climate that an organization seeks is contingent upon the type of employees it has, the type of technology, education of workers, and similar variables. A research department certainly would want to establish a climate different from that of a steel foundry.

Organizational climate represents the entire social system of a work group. It is clearly a system concept. Two important aspects of climate are the workplace itself and the treatment received from management. Employees feel that the climate is favorable when they are doing something useful that provides a sense of personal worth. One study, for example, found that challenging work that was intrinsically satisfying contributed to favorable organizational climate.[2] Many employees also want responsibility, as indicated in the motivation-maintenance model. In the area of treatment received from management they want to be listened to and treated as if they were someone of value. They want to be treated as if the organization really cared about their needs and problems.

One firm went out of its way to help an employee with home problems. Sara Burney was the sole support of her teenage diabetic son, who was confined to their home because he had to take four large doses of insulin daily. The doses were difficult to regulate, and he had been in the hospital on several occasions with insulin attacks. One day when she returned from work she found him in an insulin coma, and he did not regain consciousness until the next day in the hospital.

When Burney returned to work the second day, she was prepared to resign in order to remain at home to care for her son; but she found that company management was working on a plan to allow her to do her work at home. Her job was working with customer orders, using an electronic cathode-ray terminal. Management arranged for one of the complex terminals to be moved to her home, and cables were run from the factory to her home so that the equipment would be directly connected with factory records. An employee in the department brings her work to her each morning so that now she does not have to leave her home. The company's extensive human concern for her positively contributed to organizational climate.

MEASURES OF ORGANIZATIONAL CLIMATE. A number of instruments have been developed to measure organizational climate.[3] Generally the instruments try to measure the totality of the psychological environment in which the employee works. Litwin and Stringer have developed a climate questionnaire that covers nine characteristics of climate as follows: structure, responsibility, reward, risk, warmth, support, standards, conflict, and identity.[4] Using this questionnaire in organizational research, they concluded that different management approaches do create different organizational climates. They also determined that climate does affect motivation, performance, and job satisfaction.

Likert developed an instrument that focuses strongly on behavioral conditions and the management style used. The seven characteristics covered by the Likert scale are leadership processes used, motivational forces, communication, interaction-influence process, decision making, goal setting, and control.[5] Respondents to Likert's questionnaire check along a continuum for each item to indicate the degree to which the organization tends toward an autocratic, highly structured climate compared with a more participative, human-oriented climate. The steps along the continuum are called Systems 1, 2, 3, and 4. Likert's work generally concludes that the more human-oriented climate produces both higher productivity and job satisfaction.

By studying their climate, individual organizations can determine how effective it is and what elements they want to change.

One manufacturing organization decided to treat its employees more like adults.[6] The firm was not following any behavioral theory but simply wanted to remove conditions that were considered by employees as regimentation and counterproductive. Time clocks, buzzers, and bells were removed, and employees were put on salary instead of hourly wages. Rigid rules were eliminated, and routine disciplinary action was replaced with counseling. Employees were encouraged to participate in decisions affecting them personally.

As a result of this change in climate in a new plant compared with older plants, absenteeism was reduced about 50 percent, and turnover declined materially. Perhaps even more important, worker resistance to change declined substantially.

In summary of this section, three points may be made about organizational climate. First, it is a system concept. It relates to the whole system as a total lifestyle for the organization. Second, it should be supportive of employee needs. The human-oriented climate seems to be more effective. Third, climate is related to situational variables. Not all organizations want exactly the same climate. To be effective, they will tend to have different climates, contingent upon variables in their environment.

AN ORGANIZATIONAL BEHAVIOR SYSTEM

The climate of each organization is achieved through an organizational behavior system, as shown in Figure 6-2. Elements of this system will now be described.

ELEMENTS OF THE SYSTEM. The climate of an organization derives originally from the philosophy and goals of those who join together to create it. Persons bring their own psychological, social, and economic wants, which they express in both individual and group ways. All these different interests come together in a working social system.

Organizational behavior philosophy derives from both fact and value premises. Fact premises represent our view of how the world behaves. Accordingly, you would not jump from a ten-story building because you believe gravity will pull you downward and crush you on the earth. Value premises, on the other hand, represent our view of the desirability of certain goals. If you were so unhappy that you wanted to die, you might then choose to jump off the ten-story building. You still accepted the fact premise of gravity, but your value premises had changed. As this illustration shows, value premises are ultimately controlling and, consequently, more important.

The philosophy and goals of people are implemented by leadership (discussed in Section 2 of this book) working through formal and informal organizations (discussed in Section 3). Formal and informal organizations provide the structure to bind the institution together into a working team.

Referring again to Figure 6-2, observe that each institution is affected by other institutions with which it comes in contact. These constitute its social environment. In the figure these institutions are attached to the chart by a shaded line to show that they are distinct from the employing institution but may be very much involved with it. For example, union Local 3146 represents workers in companies A, B, and C. It is a separate legal organization but is very much involved in each of the three companies. This social environment is discussed primarily in Section 4 of this book.

All organizations influence their members by means of a control system that reflects the intermingling of formal organization, informal organization, and social

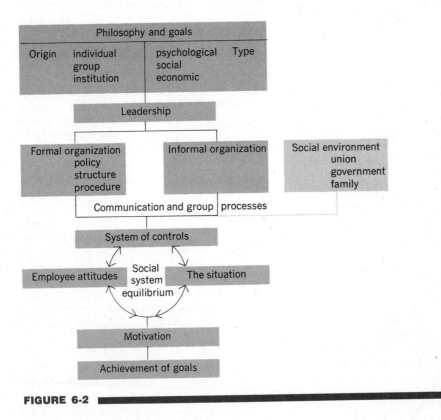

FIGURE 6-2

An organizational behavior system.

environment. This intermingling is made possible by communication and group processes, as described in Section 5 of the book. (Observe that the different sections of this book are organized according to the organizational behavior system.)

THE SOCIAL SYSTEM AT WORK. The system of controls in an organization interacts with a person's attitudes and with situational factors to produce a particular motivation for a designated person at a certain time. If any one of the three—controls, attitudes, or situations—is changed, the motivation will be different. The relationship is a contingency one. For example, if a control is tightened, but attitudes and the situation remain the same, motivation will change and produce different results. If controls and attitudes remain constant, but the situation changes, motivation will again be altered. Motivation is determined by the interaction of controls, attitudes, and the situation, all operating in equilibrium within the social system.

The result of an effective organizational behavior system is productive motivation. This kind of motivation should get above-average performance out of average people. It develops problem solvers out of problem makers. It builds two-way relationships, meaning that manager and employee are jointly influencing each other and jointly benefiting. This is power with people rather than power over them. There is no one-way manipulation of one party by the other. People are treated like people, nothing more and nothing less.

MODELS OF ORGANIZATIONAL BEHAVIOR

Organizations differ in the quality of organizational behavior that they develop. These differences are substantially caused by different *models of organizational behavior* that predominate in management thought in each organization. The model that a manager holds usually leads to certain assumptions about people and certain interpretations of events. Underlying theory, therefore, is an unconscious guide to managerial behavior. Managers tend to act as they think. Eventually this means that the underlying model that prevails in an organization's management determines the climate in that firm. For this reason, models of organizational behavior are significant.

We conclude this first section of the book with a discussion of three models that have found favor during the last century. They are the autocratic model, the custodial model, and finally the supportive model, which is the general theme of this book. (Earlier models of organizational behavior, such as feudalism and slavery, are bypassed.)

The three models are summarized in Figure 6-3. In the order mentioned they represent a historical evolution in management practice. The autocratic model predominated a hundred years ago. In the 1920s and 1930s it yielded ground to the more successful custodial model. In this generation the supportive model tends to dominate.

Although one model tends to predominate in the industrial life of a nation at one time, each of the other models finds acceptance in some organizations at the same time.

Just as organizations differ among themselves, so may one organization vary its practices among its departments or branches. The production department may work within a custodial model while the supportive model is being tried in the research department. And, of course, the practices of individual managers may differ from their organization's prevailing model because of their personal preferences or different environmental conditions in their department. The point is that one model of organizational behavior is not an adequate label to describe all that happens in an organization, but it is a convenient way to distinguish one prevailing way of life from another.

THE AUTOCRATIC MODEL. The autocratic model has its roots deep in history, and certainly it became the prevailing model of the industrial revolution. As shown in Figure 6-3, it depends on *power.* Those who are in command must have the power to demand. "You do this—or else," meaning that an employee who does not follow orders will be penalized. It is threatening, depending on negative motivation backed by power.

In an autocratic environment the managerial orientation is formal, official *authority.* This authority is delegated by right of command over the people to whom it applies. Management assumes that it knows what is best and that the employee's obligation is to follow orders without question and without interpretation. Management assumes that employees are passive and even resistant to organizational needs. They have to be persuaded and pushed into performance, and this is management's task. Management does the thinking; the employees obey the orders. This is the Theory X popularized by McGregor as the conventional view of management. This model leads to tight control of the employee at work.

Under autocratic conditions the employee orientation is *obedience* to a boss, not a manager. The psychological result for employees is *dependence* on their boss, whose power to hire, fire, and "perspire" them is almost absolute. The boss pays minimum wages because *minimum performance* is given by employees. They give minimum performance—sometimes reluctantly—because they must provide

	AUTOCRATIC	CUSTODIAL	SUPPORTIVE
Depends on:	Power	Economic resources	Leadership
Managerial orientation:	Authority	Money	Support
Employee orientation:	Obedience	Security	Job performance
Employee psychological result:	Dependence on boss	Dependence on organization	Participation
Employee needs met:	Subsistence	Maintenance	Higher-order
Performance result:	Minimum	Passive cooperation	Awakened drives

FIGURE 6-3

Three models of organizational behavior.

subsistence needs for themselves and their families. Some employees give higher performance because of internal achievement drives, because they personally like their boss, because the boss is "a natural-born leader," or because of some other fortuitous reason; but most of them give only minimum performance.

The autocratic model of organizational behavior is a useful way to accomplish work. Let us not condemn it completely. The picture of the autocratic model just presented has been an extreme one, but actually the model exists in all shades of gray from rather dark to rather light. This prevailing view of work built great railroad systems, operated giant steel mills, and generally produced the dynamic industrial civilization of the early 1900s. It does get results, but usually only moderate results. *Its principal weakness is its high human costs.*

The fundamental question we ask of the autocratic model must be: Is there a better way? Now that we have brought organizational conditions this far along, can we build on what we have in order to move one step higher on the ladder of progress? Note that the thought here is not to throw out power as undesirable, because power is needed to maintain internal unity in organizations. Rather, the thought is to build upon the foundation that exists. "Is there a better way?"

THE CUSTODIAL MODEL. As managers began to study their employees, they soon recognized that although autocratically managed employees did not talk back to their boss, they certainly "thought back." There were many things they wanted to say, and sometimes they did say them when they quit or lost their temper! Employees inside were a seething mass of insecurity, frustrations, and aggressions toward their boss. Since they could not vent these feelings directly, sometimes they went home and vented them on their families and neighbors; so the community did not gain much out of this relationship either.

It seemed rather obvious to progressive employers that there ought to be some way to develop employee satisfactions and security during production—and in fact this approach just might cause more productivity. If the insecurities, frustrations, and aggressions of employees could be dispelled, they might feel like working. At any rate the employer could sleep better, having a clearer conscience. Some employers were genuinely concerned with improving employment conditions and helping employees rise to greater opportunities, just as the employers themselves had risen in many instances.

To satisfy the security needs of employees, a number of companies in the United States began welfare programs in the 1890s and 1900s. In their worst form these welfare programs later became known as paternalism. In the 1930s welfare programs evolved into a host of fringe benefits to give the employee security. Employers—and unions and government—began caring for the security needs of workers. They were applying a custodial model of organizational behavior.

As shown in Figure 6-3, a successful custodial approach depends on *economic resources.* If an organization does not have the wealth to provide pensions and pay other benefits, it cannot follow a custodial approach. The resulting managerial orientation is toward *money* to pay the cost of benefits. Since employee physiological needs are already reasonably met, the employer looks to second-level *security* needs as a motivating force. (Observe that this progression follows Maslow's priority of needs, presented in Chapter 3.)

The custodial approach leads to employee *dependence on the organization.* Rather than being dependent on their boss for their weekly bread, employees now depend on organizations for their security and welfare. Pehaps more accurately stated, an organizational dependence is added to a reduced personal dependence on the boss. If employees have ten years of seniority under the union contract and a good pension program, they cannnot afford to quit even if the grass looks greener somewhere else!

It can be seen that the custodial model in practice emphasizes economic rewards and fringe benefits. The employee becomes psychologically preoccupied with the *maintenance* factors of the job, as described in Herzberg's motivation-maintenance model in Chapter 3. Maintenance factors are necessary to give security and contentment, but they are not themselves very strong motivators. In addition, the fringe benefits and other devices of the custodial model are mostly off-the-job, extrinsic rewards.

Employees working in a custodial environment are well maintained, happy, and contented, but they are not strongly motivated, so they give only *passive cooperation.* The result is that they do not produce much more vigorously than under the old autocratic approach.

The custodial model is described in its extreme in order to show its emphasis on material rewards, security, organizational dependence, and maintenance factors. In actual practice, the model has various shades of gray from dark to light. Its great benefit is that it brings security and satisfaction to workers, but it does have flaws. The most evident flaw is that most employees are not producing anywhere near their capacities, nor are they motivated to grow to the greater capacities of which they are capable. Though employees are happy, most of them really do not feel fulfilled or self-actualized. In confirmation of this condition, a series of studies at the University of Michigan in the 1940s and 1950s confirmed that "the happy employee is not necessarily the most productive employee."[7] Consequently, progressive managers and academic leaders in management started to ask again, "Is there a better way?"

The search for a better way is not a condemnation of the custodial model as a whole, but rather a condemnation of the assumption that this is "the final answer"—the one best way to motivate employees. The error in reasoning occurs when people perceive the custodial model as so desirable that there is no need to move beyond it to something better. A reasonable amount of the custodial model is desirable to provide security, just as a reasonable amount of power is needed in organizations. These conditions are the foundation for growth to the next step.

THE SUPPORTIVE MODEL. The supportive model of organizational behavior was originally stated as the "principle of supportive relationships" by Rensis Likert, who said: *"The leadership and other processes of the organization must be such as to ensure a maximum probability that in all interactions and all relationships with the organization each member will, in the light of his background, values, and expectations, view the experience as supportive and one which builds and maintains his sense of personal worth and importance."*[8] It is similar to McGregor's Theory Y and the human resources approach to people mentioned earlier.

The supportive model is summarized in the last column of Figure 6-3. It depends on *leadership* instead of power or money. Through leadership, management provides a climate to help employees grow and accomplish in the interests of the organization the things of which they are capable. The leader assumes that workers are not by nature passive and resistant to organizational needs, but that they are made so by an inadequately supportive climate at work. They will take responsibility, develop a drive to contribute, and improve themselves if management will give them half a chance. Management's orientation, therefore, is to *support* the employee's *job performance,* rather than simply supporting employee benefit payments as in the custodial approach.

Since performance is supported, the employees' orientation is toward it instead of mere obedience and security. They are responding to intrinsic motivations in their jobs. Their psychological result is a feeling of *participation* and task involvement in the organization. They may occasionally say "we" instead of always saying "they" when referring to their organization. They are more strongly motivated than by earlier models because their *higher-order* needs are better met. Thus, they have *awakened drives* for work.

Supportive behavior is not the kind of behavior that requires money. Rather, it is a part of management's life-style at work, reflected in the way that it deals with other people. The manager's role is one of helping employees solve their problems and accomplish their work. Following is an example of a supportive approach.

Juanita Salinas, a young divorcee with one child, had a record of frequent tardiness as an assembler in an electronic plant. Her supervisor, Helen Ferguson, scolded her several times about her tardiness, and each time Salinas improved for two or three weeks but then lapsed back into her normal habit pattern. At about this time Ferguson attended a company training program in organizational behavior for supervisors, so she decided to try the supportive approach with Salinas.

The next time Salinas was tardy, Ferguson approached her with concern about what might have caused her tardiness. Rather than scolding her, Ferguson showed a genuine interest in Salinas's problems, asking "How can I help?" and "Is there anything we can do at the company?" When the discussion focused on delays in getting a child ready for school early in the morning, Ferguson arranged for Salinas to talk with other mothers of children in the department. When Salinas talked about the distance she had to walk to catch a bus, Ferguson worked with the personnel department to get Salinas into a dependable car pool. Although the new car pool undoubtedly helped, an important point was that Salinas seemed to appreciate the recognition and concern that was expressed, so she was more motivated to come to work on time. She also was more cooperative and interested in her job. It was evident that the supportive approach and recognition given influenced Salinas's behavior. An important by-product was that Ferguson's job became easier because of Salinas's better performance.

Supportive approaches work well with both employees and managers. One study of 200 clerical workers, for example, reported that employees with high job satisfaction had supportive, Theory Y supervisors.[9] Another study of 200 managerial and professional employees reported that supportive supervision was correlated with organizational effectiveness and job satisfaction.[10] An additional study reported that supportive managers usually led to high motivation among their subordinate managers. Among those managers who were low in motivation, only 8 percent had supportive managers.[11]

The supportive model has been widely accepted by managers in the United States, particularly in the higher organizational levels. One survey of middle managers reported that 90 percent agreed with many of the basic ideas of a supportive, Theory Y approach to organizational behavior.[12] However, their agreement with supportive ideas does not mean that they practice these ideas regularly. The step from theory to practice is a difficult one.

The supportive model tends to be especially effective in nations with affluence and complex technology, because it appeals to higher-order needs and provides intrinsic motivational factors. It may not be the best model to apply in less developed nations, because their employees' need structures are often at lower levels and their social conditions are different.

INTERPRETING THE MODELS OF ORGANIZATIONAL BEHAVIOR. Several conclusions may be drawn about the three models of organizational behavior. The first is that change is the normal condition of these models. As our understanding of human behavior increases or as new social conditions develop, organizational behavior models are likely to change. It is a mistake to assume that one particular model is a "best" model that will endure for the long run. This mistake was made by some old-time managers about the autocratic model and by some humanists about the custodial model, with the result that they became psychologically locked into these models and had difficulty altering their practices when conditions demanded it. Eventually the supportive model may also fall to limited use. There is no permanently "one best model" of organizational behavior, because what is best is contingent on what is known about human behavior in whatever environment and with whatever priority of objectives exist at a particular time.

MODELS ARE RELATED TO HUMAN NEEDS. A second conclusion is that the models of organizational behavior that have developed seem to be sequentially related to a hierarchy of human needs. As society has climbed higher on the need hierarchy, new models of organizational behavior have been developed to serve the higher-order needs that became paramount at the time. Using Maslow's need hierarchy for comparison, the custodial model of organizational behavior is seen as an effort to serve employees' second-level security needs. It moved one step above the autocratic model, which was reasonably serving subsistence needs but was not effectively meeting needs for security. Similarly the supportive model is an effort to meet employees' higher-level needs, such as affiliation and esteem, which the custodial model was unable to serve.

A number of persons have assumed that emphasis on one model of organizational behavior was an automatic rejection of other models, but comparison with the need hierarchy *suggests that each model is built upon the accomplishments of the other.* For example, adoption of a supportive approach does not mean abandonment of custodial practices that serve necessary employee security needs. What it does mean is that custodial practices are given secondary emphasis, because employees have progressed up their need structure to a condition in which higher needs predominate. In other words, the supportive model is the appropriate model to use *because* subsistence and security needs are already reasonably met by a suitable power structure and security system. If a misdirected modern manager should abandon these basic organizational needs, the system would quickly revert to a quest for a workable power structure and security system in order to provide subsistence-maintenance needs for its people.

Each model of organizational behavior in a sense outmodes its predominance by gradually satisfying certain needs, thus opening up other needs that can be better served by a more advanced model. Thus each new model is built upon the success of its predecessor. The new model simply represents a more sophisticated way of maintaining earlier need satisfactions, while opening up the probability of satisfying still higher needs. Possible progress to future models is indicated by the collegial model in a later chapter. Maslow, using the classifications in this book, proposed before his death a Theory Z, which he felt was the next step above the collegial model.[13]

TENDENCY TOWARD MORE DEMOCRATIC MODELS.
A third conclusion suggests that the present tendency toward more democratic models of organizational behavior will continue for the longer run. In modern, complex organizations top managers cannot be authoritarian in the traditional sense and remain efficient, because they cannot know all that is happening in their organization. They must depend on other centers of power nearer to operating problems. In addition, modern workers are not readily motivated toward creative and intellectual duties by traditional, authoritarian orders. They require high-order need satisfactions that newer models of organizational behavior provide. Thus there does appear to be some inherent necessity for more democratic forms of organization in advanced societies.

DIFFERENT MODELS WILL REMAIN IN USE.
A fourth conclusion is that, though one model may predominate as most appropriate for general use at any point in time, some appropriate uses will remain for other models. Knowledge of human behavior and skills in applying that knowledge will vary among managers. Role expectations of employees will differ, depending upon cultural history. Policies and ways of life will vary among organizations. Perhaps more important, task conditions will vary. Some jobs may require routine, low-skilled, highly programmed work that will be mostly determined by higher authority and will provide mostly material rewards and security (autocratic and custodial conditions). Other jobs will be unprogrammed and intellectual, requiring teamwork and self-motivation and responding best to supportive or more advanced approaches. The best model in the situation will be contingent on all environmental conditions.

SUMMARY

Organizational climate represents an organization's way of life with its employees. It can have a major influence on motivation, productivity, and job satisfaction. Climate is derived from an organizational behavior system that includes philosophy and goals, leadership, formal and informal organization, and the social environment. These items converge in a system of controls that interacts with personal attitudes and situational factors to produce motivation in employees.

Three models of organizational behavior are the autocratic, custodial, and supportive models. The supportive model is more consistent with higher-order needs and intrinsic motivational factors. It provides a superior organizational climate, but even it probably will be outmoded as progress continues. The supportive model depends on leadership, which is the subject of the next section.

TERMS AND CONCEPTS FOR REVIEW

Organizational climate

Allocative value

Incremental values

Likert's Systems 1 through 4

Organizational behavior system

Autocratic model

Custodial model

Supportive model

REVIEW QUESTIONS ██████████████████████████████

1. What is organizational climate? Discuss its importance in an organization.
2. Distinguish between allocative and incremental values.
3. Discuss similarities and differences between the autocratic, custodial, and supportive models of organizational behavior.
4. Discuss why the supportive model of organizational behavior is considered an especially appropriate model to use in developed nations.
5. Discuss general conclusions about how the models of organizational behavior can be interpreted.

CASES

THE RAPID CORPORATION

The Rapid Corporation is a refrigeration service organization in a large city. It has about seventy employees, mostly refrigeration service representatives. For many years the company's policies have been dominated by its president and principal owner, who takes pride in being a "self-made man."

Recently the president attended a conference in which organizational behavior was discussed, so he decided that in order to develop a more effective organizational climate his firm needed a policy statement on organizational behavior. He instructed the general office manager to prepare a statement which will apply to all employees.

QUESTIONS
1. As the general office manager, prepare the policy statement, giving reasons for what you do.
2. Comment on the usefulness of a policy statement for changing the organizational climate in a firm of this type.

THE NEW PLANT MANAGER

Toby Butterfield worked his way upward in the Montclair Company until he became assistant plant manager in the Illinois plant. Finally his opportunity for a promotion came. The Houston plant was having difficulty meeting its budget and production quotas, so he was promoted to plant manager and transferred to the Houston plant with instructions to "straighten it out."

Butterfield was ambitious and somewhat power oriented. He believed that the best way to solve problems was to take control, make decisions, and use his authority to carry out his decisions. After preliminary study, he issued orders for each department to cut its budget 5 percent. A week later he instructed all departments to increase production 10 percent by the following month. He required several new reports and kept a close watch on operations. At the end of the second month he dismissed three supervisors who had failed to meet their production quotas. Five other supervisors resigned. Butterfield insisted that all rules and budgets should be followed, and he allowed no exceptions.

Butterfield's efforts produced remarkable results. Productivity quickly exceeded standard by 7 percent, and within five months the plant was within budget. His record was so outstanding that he was promoted to the New York home office near the end of his second year. Within a month after he left, productivity in the Houston plant collapsed to 15 percent below standard, and the budget again was in trouble.

QUESTIONS
1. Discuss the model of organizational behavior Butterfield used and the kind of organizational climate he created.
2. Discuss why productivity dropped when Butterfield left the Houston plant.
3. Knowing what you do, would you have promoted Butterfield? Discuss.

REFERENCES

1. "Store Rules" of a Chicago department store about 1850, *Advanced Management,* March 1954, p. 19.

2. Douglas T. Hall and Benjamin Schneider, "Correlates of Organizational Identification as a Function of Career Pattern and Organizational Type," *Administrative Science Quarterly,* September 1972, pp. 340–350.

3. Examples are John W. Hall, "A Comparison of Halpin and Croft's Organizational Climates and Likert and Likert's Organizational Systems," *Administrative Science Quarterly,* December 1972, pp. 586–590; Robert J. House and John R. Rizzo, "Toward the Measurement of Organizational Practices: Scale Development and Validation," *Journal of Applied Psychology,* October 1972, pp. 388–396; and Benjamin Schneider and C. J. Bartlett, "Individual Differences and Organizational Climate II: Measurement of Organizational Climate by the Multi-Trait, Multi-Rater Matrix," *Personnel Psychology,* Winter 1970, pp. 493–512. A discussion of organizational climate that provides extensive references is Don Hellriegel and John W. Slocum, Jr., "Organizational Climate: Measures, Research and Contingencies," *Academy of Management Journal,* June 1974, pp. 255–280.

4. George H. Litwin and Robert A. Stringer, Jr., *Motivation and Organizational Climate,* Boston: Harvard Graduate School of Business Administration, 1968, pp. 66–92.

5. Rensis Likert, *The Human Organization: Its Management and Value,* New York: McGraw-Hill Book Company, 1967, pp. 3–12.

6. "The Unregimented Workforce," *Management in Practice,* American Management Association, September 1974, pp. 1–2.

7. An example of this early research is a study of the Prudential Insurance Company in Daniel Katz, Nathan Maccoby, and Nancy C. Morse, *Productivity, Supervision and Morale in an Office Situation, Part I,* Ann Arbor, Mich.: Institute for Social Research, University of Michigan, 1950. The conclusion about job satisfaction and productivity is reported on page 63.

8. Rensis Likert, *New Patterns of Management,* New York: McGraw-Hill Book Company, 1961, pp. 102–103. Italics in original.

9. Byron G. Fiman, "An Investigation of the Relationships among Supervisory Attitudes, Behaviors, and Outputs: An Examination of McGregor's Theory Y," *Personnel Psychology,* Spring 1973, pp. 95–105.

10. Robert J. House and John R. Rizzo, "Role Conflict and Ambiguity as Critical Variables in a Model of Organizational Behavior," *Organizational Behavior and Human Performance,* June 1972, pp. 467–505.

11. M. Scott Myers, "Conditions for Manager Motivation," *Harvard Business Review,* January–February 1966, p. 61, covering 1,344 managers at Texas Instruments, Incorporated.

12. Joel K. Leidecker and James L. Hall, "The Impact of Management Development Programs on Attitude Formation," *Personnel Journal,* July 1974, pp. 507–512.

13. Abraham H. Maslow, *The Farther Reaches of Human Nature,* New York: The Viking Press, Inc., 1971, pp. 280–295.

SECTION 2

LEADERSHIP AND ITS DEVELOPMENT

CHAPTER 7
THE LEADERSHIP ROLE

Leadership is still an art despite the efforts
of social science researchers to make it a science.
James Owens[1]

LEARNING OBJECTIVES

TO UNDERSTAND:
The nature of leadership
Skills used in leadership
The path-goal theory of leadership
How positive and negative leaders differ
How autocratic and participative leaders differ
The meaning of structure and consideration
The contingency theory of leadership

Human beings are our most precious part of civilization. What responsibility could be more important than the leadership and development of people? Without leadership, an organization is only a confusion of people and machines. *Leadership* is the ability to persuade others to seek defined objectives enthusiastically. It is the human factor that binds a group together and motivates it toward goals. The leader's act of motivation is similar in its effect to the secret chemical that turns the insect pupa into the resplendent butterfly with all the beauty that was the pupa's potential. Leadership transforms potential into reality. It is the ultimate act that brings to success all the potential that is in an organization and its people.

Leadership is so important to group accomplishment that people have been concerned about it since the beginning of recorded history. Despite all this interest in leadership, we know surprisingly little about it. Much of what we do "know" is subject to disagreement. In this chapter we discuss the nature of leadership and how leadership is applied through different leadership styles.

THE NATURE OF LEADERSHIP

Leadership is a part of management, but not all of it. Managers are required to plan and organize, for example, but all we ask of leaders is that they influence others to follow. The fact that they influence others to follow is no guarantee that they are going in the right direction. This means that strong leaders can be weak managers, because they are weak in planning or some other managerial duty. Though they can get their group going, they just cannot get them going in directions that serve organizational objectives. The reverse is also possible. A manager can be a weak leader and still be an acceptable manager, especially if one happens to be managing people who have strong inner achievement drives. This combination of circumstances is less likely, and usually we expect an excellent manager also to have reasonably high leadership ability.

Even though leadership is something a person does, it should not be confused with mere activity. Aggressiveness and constant interaction with others will not necessarily develop leadership with a group. At times the appropriate leadership action is to stay in the background keeping pressures off the group, to keep quiet so that others may talk, to be calm in times of uproar, to hesitate, and to delay decisions.

We usually think of companies competing by means of their products, but they probably compete more by means of their leaders than their products. Better leaders develop better employees, and the two together develop better products; therefore, an employer who develops better leaders contributes more to society and gains a competitive advantage. Just as a company requires capital and modern physical facilities, it also requires a steady and continuous supply of competent leaders to fill vacancies caused by death, retirement, resignation, and so on. A growing company requires an even larger supply of leaders.

In the past a wide variety of approaches have been taken toward discovery of leadership talent. Graphology, the analysis of handwriting, was once popular with some people. Others thought that phrenology, a study of skull shapes, had potentialities. Even today astrology is occasionally depended upon. Biographical study of leaders possibly offers insight into the nature of leadership, or the leaders themselves may discuss what they think has made them successful. In reality none of these approaches has afforded much dependable evidence on the nature of leadership. A more scientific approach offering somewhat more promise is demographic studies of family background, education, and other vital statistics relating to leaders.[2] Even here the results have failed to give much insight into the causes of strong leadership.

PERSONAL TRAITS AS EVIDENCE OF LEADERSHIP ABILITY. The trait approach seeks to determine "what makes a successful leader" from the leader's own personal characteristics. From the beginnings of history people have referred to particular leaders as having certain useful traits that helped make them leaders, such as "strength of character" or "dominance"; so it was natural for early leadership research to point in this direction. The trait approach to leadership study was especially popular from 1930 to 1950. Lists of useful traits became longer and longer, but there was very little consensus among researchers. Generally trait study failed to produce clear-cut results.[3]

Trait study has not produced clear results because it does not consider the whole leadership environment. Personal traits are only one part of the whole environment. Though a certain trait exists, it will not become active until a certain group and situation calls for it; so there is no sure connection between traits and leadership acts.

Traits are also difficult to define and quantify in ways that will make them useful to managers. For example, fear of failure motivates some people to greater leadership, but too much fear will make them neurotics or tyrants. What is "too much"? As another example, good health is desirable in many leadership situations, but there are also successful leaders in other situations who do not enjoy good health. In fact, some are noted for the degree to which they "enjoy" their poor health! There are so many exceptions to any general statement about leadership traits that it hardly applies.

ROLE BEHAVIOR AS EVIDENCE OF LEADERSHIP ABILITY. As society has learned more about leadership, it has become increasingly evident that strong leadership is a result of effective role behavior. Leadership is shown by a person's acts more than by one's traits. Traits influence acts, but so do followers, goals, and the environment in which the acts occur. It follows that *organizational leadership is role behavior that unites and stimulates followers toward particular objectives in particular environments.* All four elements—leader, followers, goals, and environment—are variables that affect each other in determining suitable role behavior. The interdependence of these variables is illustrated by a hard-boiled superintendent who is still managing the way he was twenty years ago. This person thinks that leadership resides in himself alone, untouched by outside influences. He fails to realize that as his people and environment change, he needs to change his leadership. Though his style of leadership was acceptable twenty years ago, it is probably not today.

At this point it is apparent that leadership is a situational and contingency relationship. In one situation, A may be the best cluster of leadership acts, but in the next situation, B will be the best cluster. To try to have all an organization's leaders fit a standard pattern will stereotype its leadership and will be inefficient because many square pegs will be fitting round holes. Leaders function in a wide variety of complicated environments, and they succeed or fail for a variety of reasons. Leadership is part of a complex system, so there is no simple answer to the riddle "What makes a leader?"

Leadership acts may be viewed in two ways. Some acts are functional (favorable) to leadership, while others are dysfunctional. The dysfunctional acts are as important as the functional ones, because they serve to "demotivate" or "de-lead" the group. They interfere with the followers' natural desires to work together to accomplish something. In one study followers were asked to name important dysfunctional acts of their "poorest boss." The four acts most mentioned were inability to accept subordinates' ideas, poor human relations, display of emotional immaturity, and poor communication.[4] Clearly "de-leadership" acts merit attention if the potential power within the group is to be released.

The fact is sometimes overlooked that, with few exceptions, leaders within organizations are also *followers.* The supervisor works for a branch head, who works for a division manager, who works for the vice president of a department. A leader has to be able to wear both hats gracefully, to be able to relate both upward and downward. In formal organizations of several levels, followership ability is one of the first attributes of leadership. It is the key that unlocks the door to leadership opportunities and keeps the leader in balance with the rest of the organization.

SKILLS USED IN ROLE BEHAVIOR. The role behavior of a leader covers three different skills—technical, human, and conceptual.[5] Though they are interrelated in practice, they can be considered separately.

109

Technical skill refers to a person's knowledge of, and proficiency in, any type of process or technique. Examples are the skills learned by accountants, engineers, typists, and toolmakers in the practice of their specialties. This skill is the distinguishing feature of job performance at the operating level; but as employees are promoted to leadership responsibilities, their technical skills become proportionately less important, as shown in Figure 7-1. They increasingly depend on the technical skills of their subordinates and in many cases have never practiced some of the technical skills that they supervise.

One study of engineering managers, for example, showed that as they reached higher management levels, their technical orientation changed. The lowest management level saw itself as primarily involved in a technical engineering job, but successively higher levels were more oriented toward managerial and company activities. The highest managers were divorced from their technical specialties.[6]

Human skill is the ability to interact effectively with people and to build teamwork. No leader at any organizational level escapes the requirement for effective human skill. It is a major part of role behavior, as shown in Figure 7-1, and is discussed throughout this book.

Conceptual skill becomes increasingly important in higher managerial jobs, because these leaders are dealing more with long-range plans, broad relationships, and other abstractions. Conceptual skill deals with ideas, while human skill

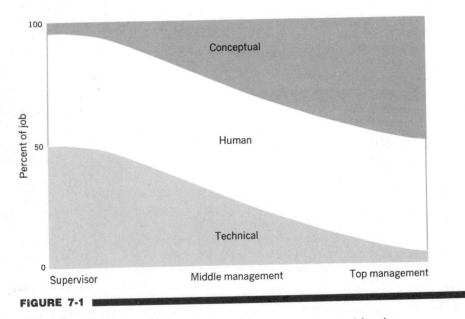

FIGURE 7-1

There is a variation in skills used at different management levels.

concerns people, and technical skill is with things. Conceptual skill enables a manager to deal successfully with abstractions, to set up models, and to devise plans.

Analysis of leadership skills helps to explain why an outstanding department head may make a poor vice president. He may be unable to provide the proper mixture of skills required for the higher-level job, particularly additional conceptual skill.

THE NEED FOR MEANINGFUL GOALS. A major responsibility of a leader is to encourage the group toward meaningful goals. Group members need to feel that they have something worthwhile to do and something that can be done with the resources and leadership available. Without goals, different members go in different directions. This difficulty will continue as long as there is no common understanding of the goals involved.

Managers often fail to establish meaningful goals. They believe their group should know the meaning of its work without having to be told. And so another group halfheartedly puts its nose to the grindstone, when it should with raised head be putting its shoulder to the wheel. Here is an example that made a dramatic impression on the leader involved.

A federal staff executive from Washington named Bailey appeared at a large federal regional office and called a meeting of its entire accounting staff of forty employees. When Bailey was introduced by the accounting chief, he immediately launched into an explanation of certain special work that all the staff would have to do quickly on overtime. The people were antagonistic and responded coldly. (Bailey commented later, "There was so much ice in that room that it cracked.") They objected strongly and started to ridicule Washington home-office leadership. Bailey perceived he was in trouble and tried to determine what was wrong.

He soon discovered that the staff did not know the purpose of the extra work. The accounting chief assumed Bailey would tell why the work was required, and Bailey assumed the staff already knew! As soon as Bailey explained why the work was needed, the group switched to an attitude of cooperation—and even enthusiasm. Bailey later reported, "That one incident taught me never to make assumptions about goals when I am motivating people."

Research shows that effective goal setting produces positive results. In one instance it was used with logging truck drivers to encourage them to carry nearer the legal capacity of their trucks.[7] Under instructions to "do your best" the drivers had been carrying about 60 percent of the legal limit. After goals were effectively set, performance increased to slightly over 90 percent of the legal limit, and this level continued for the twelve months covered by the study. Drivers were given no extra rewards for their higher production, except for recognition, but it is believed they also experienced a sense of achievement in meeting their goals and judging the loading of their trucks to the legal limit.

A PATH-GOAL THEORY OF LEADERSHIP. A useful way to perceive leadership acts is in terms of a path-goal theory of leadership.[8] Path-goal leadership derives from expectancy theory. Assuming that motivation is a result of valence ×

expectancy, as discussed in an earlier chapter, it becomes the leader's job to build both valence and expectancy for the employee. Leaders encourage development of valences that are in line with what the organization has to offer. In this manner employee goals are tied to organizational goals. Leaders also can increase payouts to employees for goal attainment, thereby increasing valence for the employee. With regard to expectancy, leaders structure the path toward goal attainment so that employees will see that their acts will lead to their goals. Leaders also make the path easier by training and direction and by removing barriers that stand in the way of the goal attainment. In essence, path-goal leaders become instrumental in helping employees achieve more success by performing better work. The theory suggests that a leader's behavior increases motivation and satisfaction to the extent that the behavior clarifies paths to goals and increases employee goal attainment.

According to the path-goal concept, in work of a high occupational level such as research and development, an emphasis on structure and task is well received because it helps clarify the ambiguities associated with those kinds of jobs. Paths toward the goal are clarified, so employees feel that the leader's task emphasis is supportive. For work at low occupational levels, such as factory work, the leader's focus on structure and task will tend to be considered an imposition of unneeded controls and will be unfavorably received. The work is already well structured, and employees know how to do it, so they need no further pressure or imposition from their supervisor. What they are likely to need is more social support and considerate behavior. These provide extrinsic social satisfactions for employees and make their paths toward their goals easier. There is some research support for these path-goal assumptions, although results are mixed.[9]

LEADERSHIP STYLES

Having discussed how leadership develops, we can now discuss how it is applied in practice as a part of different leadership styles. These styles describe a leader's predominant way of acting with the group.

MOTIVATIONAL STYLES: POSITIVE AND NEGATIVE LEADERS. There is a difference in the way leaders approach people to motivate them. If the approach emphasizes rewards—economic or otherwise—for followers, the leader uses positive leadership. If emphasis is on penalties, the leader is applying negative leadership. The stronger a penalty is, the more negative it is. The same reasoning applies to rewards, so what exists is a continuum ranging from strongly positive to strongly negative. Almost any manager uses both styles somewhere on the continuum every day, but the predominant style sets a tone within the group. Style is related to one's model of organizational behavior. The autocratic model tends to cause a negative style; the custodial model is somewhat positive; and the supportive model is clearly positive. Positive leadership generally achieves higher job satisfaction and performance.[10]

Negative leadership gets acceptable performance in many situations, but it has high human costs. Negative leaders act domineering and superior with people. To get work done, they hold over their personnel such penalties as loss of job, reprimand in the presence of others, and a few days off without pay. They display authority with the false belief that it frightens everyone into productivity. They are bosses more than leaders.

Under negative leadership subordinates tend to spend time "covering" (protecting themselves) for every move that they make. There is useless documentation of even trivial decisions, writing of needless memoranda, and keeping of unnecessary statistics and files that can be available for checking to prove that "it was somebody else's fault." Most of this unnecessary effort is incited by the fear that negative leaders instill in their employees.

Even the most competent leaders will at times have to fall back upon negative leadership, because they cannot always determine how to motivate an employee positively. Perfection can never be achieved, but the historical trend is that managers need more and more positive leadership skills in order to be rated "satisfactory." The days of the "boss" and "driver" are waning. Better employee education, greater independence, and other factors have made satisfactory employee motivation more dependent on positive leadership. The conclusion for management is that it needs to keep abreast of this trend by constantly reducing its negative leadership and increasing its positive leadership.

POWER STYLES: AUTOCRATIC, PARTICIPATIVE, AND FREE-REIN LEADERS.

The way in which a leader uses power also establishes a type of style. Each power style—autocratic, participative, and free-rein—has its benefits and limitations. A leader uses all three styles over a period of time, but one style tends to predominate as a normal way of using power. An illustration is a factory supervisor who is normally autocratic, but she is participative in determining vacation schedules, and she is free-rein in selecting a departmental representative for the safety committee. Although the following passages separate power use into three distinct styles, this is for discussion only. In actual use there are thousands of in-between shades of power than managers apply in their own ways. Power use exists along a continuum ranging from total power to no power use at all, and effective managers usually show some style flexibility along this continuum.

Autocratic leaders. Autocratic, or authoritarian, leaders centralize power and decision making in themselves, as shown in Figure 7-2. They structure the complete work situation for their employees, who do what they are told. The leaders take full authority and assume full responsibility. Leadership may be negative because followers are uninformed, insecure, and afraid of the leader's authority; but it also can be positive because the leader can use power to dispense rewards to the group. An autocratic leader whose motivational style is positive often is called a benevolent autocrat.

The benevolent autocrat achieves productivity and job satisfaction in some situations. Since people mature within a culture of many authorities, such as parents, teachers, and government bureaucrats, some employees have an expectation of autocratic leadership; so they derive security and satisfaction from working with an autocratic leader. Since this is their role expectation of their manager, they respond well to action in the expected role. This is particularly true in nations with more autocratic cultures. One study in Japan, for example, showed that authori-

113

tarian leaders were slightly more successful than highly democratic leaders.[11] Leaders also may feel more comfortable and effective when they are autocratic, because this gives them more security and confidence that they can take action.[12] Many persons are not as ready for participative approaches as some behavioral partisans would have us believe.

Some advantages of autocratic leadership are that it provides strong motivation and reward for the leader. It permits quick decision making, because only one person decides for all the group. Less competent submanagers probably can be used because their principal job is to carry out orders. They do negligible planning, organizing, or decision making, and they need little initiative.

The main disadvantage of autocratic leadership is that people dislike it, especially if it is extreme and the motivational style is negative. Frustration, low morale, and conflict develop easily in autocratic situations. Employees may feel that they are producing because they are required to do so, not because they are motivated to do so. They tend to work at "half-steam" because their drives and creativity are not released. One study, for example, reported that 50 percent of autocratic managers were rated by their subordinates as poor motivators and only 1 percent were rated as excellent motivators.[13]

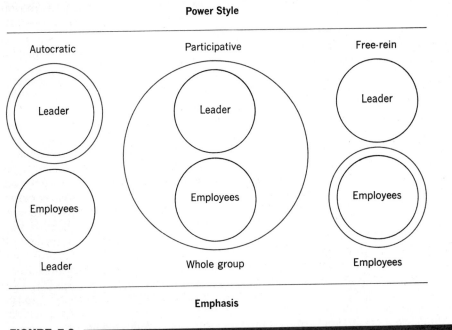

Power Style

FIGURE 7-2 ▬▬▬▬▬▬▬▬▬▬▬▬▬▬▬▬▬▬▬▬▬▬▬▬▬▬▬▬▬▬

Different emphasis (shown by colored lines) results from different leadership styles in use of power.

Participative leaders. Participative leadership decentralizes authority. Participative decisions are not unilateral, as with the autocrat, because they arise from consultation with followers and participation by them. The leader and group are acting as a social unit, as illustrated in Figure 7-2. Employees are broadly informed about conditions affecting their jobs, which encourages their ideas and suggestions. Whereas autocratic leaders control through the authority they possess, participative leaders exercise control mostly by using forces within the group.

Generally the trend is toward wider use of participative practices because they are consistent with the supportive model of organizational behavior. Autocratic use of power is not necessarily condemmed as "bad"; but rather, participative use of power is considered "better" for many situations where autocratic power was formerly used. Because of its importance participative management is discussed in a later chapter.

Free-rein leaders. Free-rein leaders avoid power. They depend largely upon the group to establish its own goals and work out its own problems. Group members train themselves and provide their own motivation. The leader exists primarily as a contact with outside persons to bring the group the information and resources it needs to accomplish its job. Free-rein leadership ignores the leader's contribution approximately in the same way that autocratic leadership ignores the group. As shown in Figure 7-2, it fails to give the group the advantages of leader-inspired motivation. It tends to permit different units of an organization to proceed at cross-purposes, and it can degenerate into chaos. For these reasons normally it is not used as a predominant power style, but it is used in certain situations where a leader can leave a choice entirely to the group.

ORIENTATION STYLES: CONSIDERATION AND INITIATING STRUCTURE. Two different leadership approaches to employees are *consideration* and *initiating structure,* also known as employee orientation and task orientation. There is consistent evidence that leaders secure somewhat higher productivity and job satisfaction if high consideration is their predominant leadership style. Considerate leaders are concerned about the human needs of their employees. They try to build teamwork and help employees with their problems. Structured, task-oriented leaders, on the other hand, believe that they achieve results by devising better methods, keeping people constantly busy, and urging them to produce.

The difference between the two orientations is illustrated by the reply of a mine superintendent in a Western mining town. A clerk brought him news about one of his truck drivers as follows: "John Jones just ran the truck off the road into Mile Deep Canyon." The superintendent's task-oriented reply was, "Get another truck out there right away and get that ore to the mill." (We wonder what happened to Jones.)

Consideration and initiating structure appear to be both somewhat related and somewhat independent of each other, so they should not be considered as always opposite ends on a continuum. A manager who becomes more considerate

does not necessarily become less structured. Each orientation is somewhat independent, so a manager may have both orientations in varying degrees.[14] Likewise it
is possible to have other orientations, such as social responsibility. If consideration
exists alone, production may be bypassed for superficial popularity and contentment; so it appears that the most successful managers are those who combine
relatively high consideration and structure, giving somewhat more emphasis to
consideration, as shown in Figure 7-3.[15] But attempts to be more considerate can
be misapplied, as illustrated by the cartoon in Figure 7-4.

How can it be that a leader is likely to get higher productivity by emphasizing
people more than the task? Primarily it is because the employees achieve the task,
instead of the reverse. In the production sequence, the producers precede the production. If they are not motivated to produce, production does not occur, regardless of the methods and materials available.

Early research on leadership style was done at the University of Michigan and
Ohio State University.[16] In several types of organizations, such as truck manufacturing, railroad construction, and insurance offices, the strongly considerate
leader achieved somewhat higher job satisfaction and productivity. Subsequent
studies confirm this general tendency and report desirable side effects, such as
lower grievance rates, lower turnover, and reduced stress within the group.[17] Further, the most successful managers, those who have risen to higher organizational

■ Consideration

■ Initiating structure

□ Other orientations

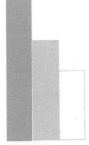

Leader A
Probably ineffective

Leader B
Probably effective

Leader C
Probably ineffective

Leader D
Probably effective

FIGURE 7-3

Some possible variations in leadership orientation.

levels, tend to have higher consideration than those below them.[18] The relationship between consideration or structure and other variables is somewhat mutual. For example, consideration may cause more job satisfaction, but also more satisfied employees may encourage supervisors to be more considerate.[19]

> *The general tendencies for beneficial results from consideration do not exist in all cases, even in the uniform culture of the United States. Looking at other cultures we might expect different results contingent upon different environments. A study of Peruvian white-collar and blue-collar workers shows that they prefer structured, task-oriented managers. The correlation of structure and satisfaction with supervisor was .39 for white-collar workers and .41 for blue-collar workers.*[20]

Although leaders have to be considerate and aware of the needs of others, they also have to be capable of saying "No" when the situation requires it. Leaders

"You idiot! Don't you know how to act when I'm using Theory Y on you?"

FIGURE 7-4

Misuse of consideration as a leadership style. (Reprinted by permission of the publisher from *Supervisory Management,* February 1973, p. 11. © 1973 by AMACOM, a division of American Management Association. Drawing by Al Hormel; text by T. Rendero.)

cannot be effective if they are overly sensitive to people. Research shows that the considerate, people-sensitive person is more vulnerable to role conflict on the job, especially when there are job pressures.[21]

A CONTINGENCY MODEL OF LEADERSHIP EFFECTIVENESS. In the past both consideration and structure have been observed to be effective under different conditions; so some sort of leadership model has been needed to explain this variability. Years of research by Fred E. Fiedler and his associates are beginning to clarify this relationship, and the result is a contingency model of leadership effectiveness.[22] Fiedler shows that the leader's effectiveness is determined by the interaction of employee orientation with three additional variables. The name of the model is derived from the fact that the leader's effectiveness is contingent upon the relationship among all these variables.

The three variables are leader-member relations, task structure, and leader position power. Leader-member relations are determined by the manner in which the leader is accepted by the group. If, for example, there is group friction with the leader, rejection of the leader, and reluctant compliance with orders, then leader-member relations are low. Task structure reflects the degree to which one specific way is required to do the job. "Leader position power" describes the organizational power that is provided for the position the leader occupies. Examples are power to hire and fire, status symbols provided, and power to give pay raises and promotions.

The relationship among these variables is shown in Figure 7-5. High and low employee orientation are shown on the vertical scale. Various combinations of the other three variables are shown in the horizontal scale, arranged from leader-favorable conditions to leader-unfavorable conditions. Each dot on the chart represents the data from a specific research project. The chart clearly shows that the considerate, employee-oriented manager is most successful in situations that have intermediate favorableness to the leader (the middle of the chart). At the chart's extremes, which represent conditions either quite favorable or quite unfavorable to the leader, the structured, task-oriented leader seems to be more effective.

For example, a military combat team has strong position power and a structured task, making it favorable to the leader; hence, the most appropriate type of leader to have, according to the contingency theory, is a structured one. Similarly, a structured leader is more effective in a position of weak power, low task structure, and poor leader-member relations. However, in intermediate conditions of favorableness, the considerate leader is the most effective; and these situations are probably the most common ones in work groups.

The conclusions of the Fiedler model may be rationalized in practice in the following manner. In highly unstructured situations the leader's structure and control are seen as removing ambiguity and the anxiety that results from it, so a structured approach from the leader may be preferred. At the other end of the continuum, in highly structured situations, structured leadership is perceived as appropriately fitting the situation. The remaining broad middle ground provides more of a cooperative, team situation where a more considerate, employee-oriented leader is effective.[23]

Fiedler has said that it is very difficult to train structured leaders to apply a considerate style. Rather than trying to change leaders' styles, Fiedler suggests matching existing leaders' styles with jobs calling for that type of leader. In other words, change the job assignment rather than trying to change the leader. Thus leadership style should and will vary among departments in a single organization, contingent upon different situations.

The contingency model is not a ready solution to all matters of leadership style. There are both strategic and procedural criticisms of the model,[24] and it accounts for only a portion of the variance in leadership effectiveness. However, the contingency model has helped to resolve confusion about optimum conditions for a considerate, people-oriented leader compared with a more structured, task-oriented leader.[25]

SUMMARY

Leadership is the ability to persuade others to seek defined objectives enthusiastically. Leadership is determined primarily by one's role behavior, not by one's personal traits. Leaders use technical, human, and conceptual skills, and they set

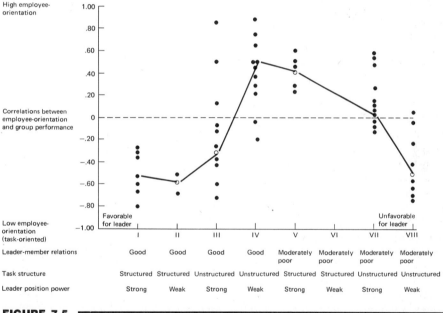

FIGURE 7-5

Research supporting the contingency model of leadership effectiveness. (Adapted from *A Theory of Leadership Effectiveness,* by Fred E. Fiedler, p. 146. Copyright © 1967 by McGraw-Hill, Inc. Used with permission of McGraw-Hill Book Company.)

meaningful goals for their groups. The leadership situation may be perceived in terms of a path-goal theory of leadership derived from expectancy theory.

Leaders use different leadership styles, and these tend to build different organizational climates. Motivational styles range along a continuum from strongly positive to strongly negative. Power styles range from autocratic through participative to free-rein. Orientation styles are consideration and initiating structure. Fiedler's contingency model of leadership is useful to determine optimum conditions for use of considerate and structured leaders.

TERMS AND CONCEPTS FOR REVIEW

Leadership

Technical, human, and conceptual skills

Path-goal theory of leadership

Positive and negative leaders

Autocratic, participative, and free-rein leaders

Benevolent autocrat

Consideration and structure

Employee-oriented and task-oriented leaders

Contingency model of leadership

REVIEW QUESTION ■■■■■■■■■■■■■■■■■■■■■■■■■■■■■■

1. What is leadership? What is its importance to an organization?
2. Discuss the path-goal theory of leadership.
3. Compare positive and negative leadership.
4. Discuss differences between autocratic and participative leaders.
5. Discuss how the contingency model of leadership applies to leadership styles.

CASE

WESTGATE COMMUNITY HOSPITAL

Manuel Martinez was the administrator of Westgate Community Hospital. The Controller, Sam Westin, reported to him and directed the financial affairs of the hospital. Westin's general attitude was to be a tight-fisted guardian of the dollar. He was rigid in attitude, not wanting to approve any action that was a departure from routine or a variance from policy. Martinez was the type that desired to take action, regardless of the restrictions of past practice or policy. The differing attitudes of the two men had led to conflict on past occasions, and on two occasions Martinez had warned, "If you can't follow my orders, Sam, I am going to have to fire you." Westin held his ground and usually won his arguments, contending that his approach was proper accounting practice and, therefore, not subject to challenge by Martinez.

One afternoon Martinez approached Westin and commented, "Sam, here's a merit wage increase that I just put through for Clara Nesbit. She's the best floor supervisor we have, and she deserves an increase. She threatened to leave unless we raised her. I promised this on her next pay check, so be sure to put it through at once."

Westin looked at the merit increase form and commented, "Manuel, you know I can't put this through. It is contrary to policy. She is already making the top rate allowed for her classification."

Martinez: "That doesn't make any difference. Put it through. I'm the administrator of this hospital, and when I say 'do it,' then put it through."

Westin: "I can't do it. It's against policy."

Martinez: "I'm the boss here, and I say do it."

Westin: I'm not going to violate policy."

Martinez, pointed his finger at Westin and talked so loudly that it attracted attention of others in the office: "Who's the boss here, Sam?"

Westin: "You are."

Martinez heatedly: "Then put through this raise."

Westin: "No."

A shouting match developed that diverted the attention of the whole office. Finally Martinez said, "Sam, I have had enough. You are fired."

Westin: "You can't fire me for that."

Martinez: "I just did it. You are through."

Martinez did not retract his action. Westin was removed from the payroll and left the hospital that afternoon.

QUESTION
1. Discuss the leadership style used by Martinez. Was it effective? Were Westin's needs being considered? What kind of organizational climate was being created?

ROLE-PLAYING SITUATION
1. Role-play an improved way for Martinez to deal with Westin when the merit raise is presented.

REFERENCES
1. James Owens, "The Uses of Leadership Theory," *Michigan Business Review,* January 1973, p. 19.

2.   Early studies of this relationship were Mabel Newcomer, *The Business Executive: The Factors That Made Him, 1900–1950,* New York: Columbia University Press, 1955; and W. Lloyd Warner and James C. Abegglen, *Big Business Leaders in America,* New York: Harper & Row, Publishers, Incorporated, 1955.

3.   For summaries of early research see Cecil E. Goode, "Significant Research on Leadership," *Personnel,* March 1951, pp. 342–350; and Ralph M. Stogdill, "Personal Factors Associated with Leadership: A Survey of the Literature," *The Journal of Psychology,* January 1948, pp. 35–71.

4.   David S. Brown, "Subordinates' Views of Ineffective Executive Behavior," *Academy of Management Journal,* December 1964, pp. 288–299, covering 103 business people and military officers.

5.   This three-way classification originally was proposed in Robert L. Katz, "Skills of an Effective Administrator," *Harvard Business Review,* January–February 1955, pp. 33–42. See also Katz's more recent comments on this article in Robert L. Katz, "Retrospective Commentary," *Harvard Business Review,* September–October 1974, pp. 101–102.

6.   Simon Marcson, "Role Concept of Engineering Managers," *IRE Transactions on Engineering Management,* March 1960, pp. 30–33.

7.   Gary P. Latham and J. James Baldes, "The 'Practical Significance' of Locke's Theory of Goal Setting," *Journal of Applied Psychology,* February 1975, pp. 122–124. See also Gary P. Latham and Gary A. Yukl, "A Review of Research on the Application of Goal Setting in Organizations," *Academy of Management Journal,* December 1975, pp. 824–845.

8.   Robert J. House, "A Path Goal Theory of Leader Effectiveness," *Administrative Science Quarterly,* September 1971, pp. 321–338; and Robert J. House and Terence R. Mitchell, "Path-Goal Theory of Leadership," *Journal of Contemporary Business,* Autumn 1974, pp. 81–97.

9.   John E. Stinson and Thomas W. Johnson, "The Path-Goal Theory of Leadership: A Partial Test and Suggested Refinement," *Academy of Management Journal,* June 1975, pp. 242–252; and Andrew D. Szilagyi and Henry P. Sims, Jr., "An Exploration of the Path-Goal Theory of Leadership in a Health Care Environment," *Academy of Management Journal,* December 1974, pp. 622–634.

10.   Henry P. Sims, Jr., and Andrew D. Szilagyi, "Leader Behavior and Subordinate Satisfaction and Performance," in Arthur G. Bedeian and others (eds.), *Proceedings, Academy of Management,* Auburn, Ala.: Auburn University, 1975, pp. 161–163.

11.   Edwin E. Ghiselli and Thomas A. Wyatt, "Need Satisfaction, Managerial Success, and Attitudes toward Leadership," *Personal Psychology,* Autumn 1972, pp. 413–420.

12.   For example, one study of 200 managers reported that younger managers tended to be more autocratic; see Craig C. Pinder and Patrick R. Pinto, "Demographic Correlates of Managerial Style," *Personnel Psychology,* Summer 1974, pp. 257–270. Perhaps the younger leaders had not yet gained confidence in organizational situations, so they tended to rely on authority when taking action.

13.   Scott Myers, "Conditions for Manager Motivation," *Harvard Business Review,* January–February 1966, p. 62, giving reports on 403 managers.

14.   Peter Weissenberg and Michael J. Kavanagh, "The Independence of Initiating Structure and Consideration: A Review of the Evidence," *Personnel Psychology,* Spring 1972, pp. 119–130.

15.   Edwin A. Fleishman and J. Simmons, "Relationship between Leadership Patterns and Effectiveness Ratings among Israeli Foremen," *Personnel Psychology,* Summer 1970, pp. 169–172. In some instances measures of consideration alone are adequate predictors of performance; see L. L. Larson, J. G. Hunt, and R. N. Osborn, "The Great Hi-Hi Leader Behavior

Myth: A Lesson from Occam's Razor," in Arthur G. Bedeian and others (eds.), *Proceedings, Academy of Management,* Auburn, Ala.: Auburn University, 1975, pp. 170–172.

16. Examples of early reports from each university are Daniel Katz and others, *Productivity, Supervision and Morale in an Office Situation,* Ann Arbor, Mich.: The University of Michigan Press, 1950; and E. A. Fleishman, *"Leadership Climate" and Supervisory Behavior,* Columbus, Ohio: Personnel Research Board, Ohio State University Press, 1951.

17. Steven Kerr and Chester Schriesheim, "Consideration, Initiating Structure, and Organizational Criteria: An Update of Korman's 1966 Review," *Personnel Psychology,* Winter 1974, pp. 555–568; Edwin A. Fleishman and Edwin F. Harris, "Patterns of Leadership Behavior to Employee Grievances and Turnover," *Personnel Psychology,* Spring 1962, pp. 43–56, studying fifty-seven production foremen and their work groups; and Harold Oaklander and Edwin A. Fleishman, "Patterns of Leadership Related to Organizational Stress in Hospital Settings," *Administrative Science Quarterly,* March 1964, pp. 520–532, covering 118 supervisors in three hospitals.

18. Guvenc G. Alpander, "Planning Management Training Programs for Organizational Development," *Personnel Journal,* January 1974, pp. 15–25.

19. Charles N. Greene, "The Reciprocal Nature of Influence between Leader and Subordinate," *Journal of Applied Psychology,* April 1975, pp. 187–193.

20. William Foote Whyte and Lawrence K. Williams, "Supervisory Leadership: An International Comparison," in *Proceedings, CIOS XIII International Management Congress,* New York: Council for International Progress in Management, Inc., 1963, pp. 481–488.

21. Robert L. Kahn and others, *Organizational Stress: Studies in Role Conflict and Ambiguity,* New York: John Wiley & Sons, Inc., 1964, p. 294.

22. Fred E. Fiedler, *A Theory of Leadership Effectiveness,* New York: McGraw-Hill Book Company, 1967; and Fred E. Fiedler and Martin M. Chemers, *Leadership and Effective Management,* Glenview, Ill.: Scott, Foresman and Company, 1974.

23. Training and experience could shift a leader to the left (more leader situational favorableness) on the Fiedler chart, so they could be dysfunctional if the shift were to quadrants I, II, or III at the extreme left. See Fred E. Fiedler, "The Effects of Leadership Training and Experience: A Contingency Model Interpretation," *Administrative Science Quarterly,* December 1972, pp. 453–470.

24. George Graen and others, "Contingency Model of Leadership Effectiveness: Antecedent and Evidential Results," *Psychological Bulletin,* vol. 74, no. 4, 1970, pp. 285–296.

25. Further interpretation of the contingency model in relation to other models is provided in "Leadership Symposium," *Organizational Dynamics,* Winter 1976, pp. 2–43.

CHAPTER 8
EFFECTIVE SUPERVISION

It is apparent that the supervisor's job is by no means as simple
as it often appears to be.
Aaron Q. Sartain and Alton W. Baker[1]

LEARNING OBJECTIVES ▬▬▬▬▬▬▬▬▬▬▬▬▬▬▬▬▬▬▬▬▬

TO UNDERSTAND:
The supervisor's unique organizational position
Different views of the supervisor's role
The keystone and linking pin concepts
Practices that improve supervision
Close supervision compared with general supervision
The clinical method

Marge Jones, age thirty-five, is a machinist in a small factory. She has been there for six months and is one of the few women machinists in the shop. She was not in the job market prior to training to become a machinist at a trade school a year ago.

Marge Jones's quality of work has been borderline during the last several weeks, so the supervisor decided to have a conference with her. After routine discussion of other matters, her supervisor asked her how she felt about the quality of her output during the last few weeks. Jones replied, "I know that I haven't been doing as good work as I should. I have thought about this a great deal; and, though I regret to tell you this, my conclusion is that you are the cause of my poor work! The problem is the way you talk to me and the others in this department. You talk to all of us so gruffly and in such a loud voice that I am upset all day long, and I can't keep my mind on my work."

The supervisor was visibly upset by Jones's comments, because he realized he was gruff and talked in a loud voice, but this was his normal personality.

The difficulties of supervision are legion, because supervisors are on the front lines. They are the point of direct contact with most of the people working in organizations. In this chapter we discuss the supervisor's role, different views of it, and some practices that make supervision more effective. The focus of this discussion is on the first-level supervisor.

THE SUPERVISOR'S ROLE

THE SUPERVISOR'S UNIQUE POSITION. A first-level supervisor's primary job is to manage workers at the operating level of an organization. It is sometimes assumed that supervisors are like other members of management, but actually both their function and their status are different, as illustrated in the following chain of command for an organization. The president directs a top-management family of vice presidents and assistants. Vice presidents manage a middle-management family, and superintendents have a management family consisting of supervisors. The supervisors, however, head a *nonmanagement family*—the workers.

A supervisor's job differs from that of other managers because the group supervised is different. This situation requires interaction in an authority relationship with *two groups:* (1) workers, who are subordinates, and (2) managers, who are superiors. Any manager who is not a supervisor interacts primarily with *two levels of only one group,* namely, managers, who are both superiors and subordinates. The result is that supervisors face decision situations that are somewhat different from those faced by other managers.[2]

With regard to status, all managers except supervisors are securely within the management group, because they have managers both above and below them in the structure; but supervisors are on the border. The usual case is that they once were workers and know that, as employment fluctuates, they may be workers again. This leaves them uncertain in their status, both formal and informal. Unusual problems arise, such as the supervisors who discovered that by accepting a supervisory job they lost their departmental seniority and if they later were returned to operating work in their department, they would start at the bottom of the seniority list—if a job was available. Only a few cases of the type just mentioned are enough to upset seriously the status of supervisors.

FIVE VIEWS OF THE SUPERVISOR'S ROLE. There are five traditional views of the supervisor's organizational role, as illustrated in Figure 8-1. Which one is the predominant practice today? Which should be predominant?

Key person in management. The traditional management interpretation of supervisors is that they are the key persons in management. They make decisions, control work, interpret policy, and generally are the key people in the process of accomplishing work. They represent management to the workers, and they also represent workers to management. Higher management knows its workers primarily through supervisors. They are an essential element because they sit astride the chains of authority and communication and can block anything going upward or downward. They are like the hub of a wheel: Everything revolves around them.

This key-person concept prevails in management literature and speeches. Management apparently believes it. Research, however, confirms that the step from belief to practice is quite difficult and that in practice many supervisors are less than key persons.

Supervisor in the middle. Supervisors according to the in-the-middle viewpoint are pressed between opposing social forces of management and workers. Management has one set of expectations for supervisors. It wants them to prevent waste, keep employees disciplined, control production, and otherwise carry out its plans. It demands loyalty and maximum effort. Its expectations are largely technical or production-centered. The pressures brought by workers are, on the other hand, largely matters of feeling. They want their supervisors "to be a good supervisor," to keep them out of trouble, to interpret their fears and wants to management, and to be loyal to them. In short, management expects one set of reactions from the supervisor, and workers expect another. The supervisor is caught between opposing forces, knowing that expectations of both cannot be met. All the supervisor can expect is frustration. In-the-middle supervisors are victims of the situation, not supervisors of it.

The view of supervisors in the middle was popularized in the 1940s at a time when management had inadequately defined the supervisory role,[3] but it still applies today in many situations. The result is that many supervisors find themselves

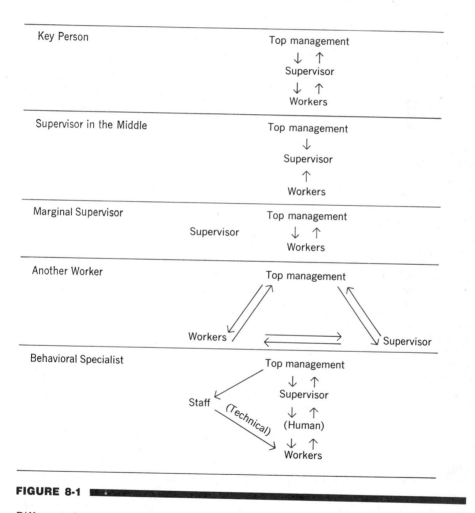

FIGURE 8-1

Different viewpoints of the supervisor's role.

in ambiguous situations in which they are not sure of the right course of action because of different expectations from different groups.

One survey, for example, asked supervisors and their managers for decisions with regard to a series of work incidents.[4] *Each one decided what would be the proper action to handle each incident, and the results showed that managers differed with supervisors in nearly 50 percent of their decisions. Clearly the supervisors had a different outlook from that of their managers.*

The marginal supervisor.   The marginal-supervisor concept is a sociological one referring to the fact that the supervisor is left out of, or on the margin of, the principal activities and influences that affect the department. Unaccepted by management, ignored by the staff, and not one of the workers, the supervisor is truly the one who walks alone. Top management has stockholders, other managers, and staff specialists supporting it. Workers have their union, their shop stewards, and their informal groups. But who supports the supervisor?

Though the picture of marginal supervisors is bleak indeed, they sometimes are found in organizations.[5] The fact that supervisors manage operative employees instead of other managers places them in a position to feel marginal in the beginning. Add to this the fact that various staff specialists make decisions and issue instructions that supervisors merely transmit, if they see them at all. Further, the supervisory role in labor relations is mostly a passive one. Others above the supervisors conduct labor negotiations, and any labor decisions the supervisors make are subject to review through the grievance procedure. They feel obligated to act like managers; yet they do not receive the reward of full participation in management. They are marginal persons.

Marginal supervisors exist in small organizations as well as large ones. In small ones an owner-manager or other officer can bypass supervisors just as effectively as they are bypassed by staff in larger companies. In either case the union can exclude them by working mostly with higher management. Marginal supervisors also are prevalent on night shifts because they are outside the mainstream of daytime activities.

Another worker.   A fourth view of supervisors is that only their title is changed, because they are still primarily employees. This was the viewpoint held by the National Labor Relations Board until 1947, when the law was changed to specify that supervisors are members of management. The "another-worker" viewpoint was predominant with thousands of supervisors who joined unions and organized the Foreman's Association of America during World War II.

Supervisors who look upon themselves as another type of worker do so for two basic reasons. First, they believe they lack authority. The center of decision making is elsewhere, and they are only an expediter who carries out these decisions. They do strictly operative work. They run errands, communicate, and make records. A second reason is that supervisors feel they are not a part of the management group. They lack management status, and their thought patterns are much closer to those of workers than to those of higher management. This means that supervisors often tend to interpret management policies and actions in a different way from that which management intended.

A behavioral specialist. Management in some situations looks upon the supervisor as primarily a behavioral specialist. According to this view, supervisors are specialists just like most of the staff people with whom they interact. They look after the human side of operations, and the staff handle its technical side. Supervisors are not marginal, because they are definitely a part of activities. Neither are they key persons; instead they are one of many specialists dealing with operating problems. Their specialty is human behavior. This viewpoint tends to be found in centralized, repetitive manufacturing, such as an assembly line.

Is the view of the supervisor as a behavioral specialist valid? It is partly, but only partly. As shown in the chart of management skills in the preceding chapter (Figure 7-1), human skills are a significant part of every manager's job, but other skills are also needed. Together these skills form a balanced package. No capable supervisor is just a specialist in one skill, such as human behavior.

Supervisors themselves tend to rate behavioral skills as most important for successful performance. When sixty-four manufacturing supervisors were asked to choose the eight most important factors (among twenty-eight choices) that cause best performance, the two factors most mentioned were behavioral factors: ability to get along with others and skill in obtaining cooperation of employees.[6]

WHAT IS THE SUPERVISOR'S ROLE? Different parts of the supervisory job may fit all five of the viewpoints just mentioned. Supervisors are partly marginal persons, just another worker, and so on. There are also substantial differences among jobs such as assembly-line supervisor, supervisor of toolmakers in a job-order shop, and supervisor of rate clerks in an insurance office. But there are also basic similarities that merit consideration and permit description of the supervisor's job in general terms.

Perhaps foremost, supervisors are management people. They direct the work of others. Since supervisors are management's point of contact with workers and vice versa, they certainly are key people in management; but also they bear pressures from both sides, similar to the in-the-middle concept; and they need to be behavioral specialists in dealing with their people. These three ideas can be reconciled by considering the supervisor as the *keystone,* not in management, but in the whole organization. As shown in Figure 8-2, the supervisor is like the keystone in an arch, which connects both sides and makes it possible for each to perform its function effectively. The sides are effectively joined only by using the keystone. It takes the pressures of both sides and uses them to strengthen, not weaken, the overall arch, and to make success possible for the organization.

To the extent that supervisors feel marginal, they are out of the arch and unable to serve in the keystone function. To the extent that they are like other workers, they are not in the keystone location. The marginal-supervisor and another-worker concepts have no place in the keystone model of the supervisor's role.

Another way of viewing supervisors is as *linking pins* in the organizational structure, as proposed by Rensis Likert and shown in Figure 8-3. There needs to be some structure that holds together the many parts of an organization so that they can become a whole that proceeds in one direction. This is done through each manager serving as a linking pin to connect the manager's group with the remainder of the organization. If all linking pin connections are strong, then the organization can operate as an integrated whole. Supervisors play a key role as linking pins, because they are the ones that connect workers with the entire management structure. If this linking pin connection is weak, then work cannot be done effectively.

WHAT MAKES AN EFFECTIVE SUPERVISOR?

The comments in the preceding chapter on leadership apply likewise to supervisors. Although leadership is a contingency relationship, generally leaders need to apply leadership styles that are positive, participative, and considerate; and they

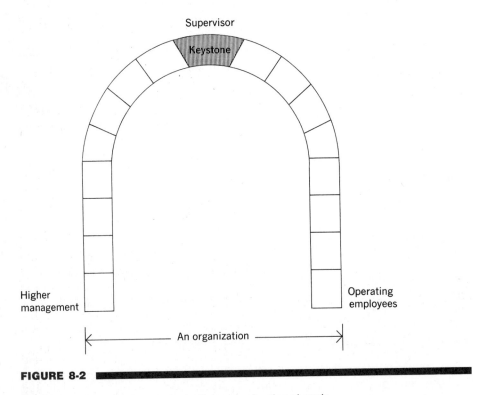

FIGURE 8-2

Supervisors are the keystone in the organizational arch.

need to provide path-goal conditions that give workers high expectancy that their acts will lead to desired rewards. There are also additional factors of special interest at the supervisory level. These will now be discussed.

SUPERVISORY EFFECTIVENESS IN RELATION TO SUPERVISION RECEIVED. Supervisory behavior is considerably affected by the kind of climate a department head provides for supervisors, because the department head sets a day-by-day example for them to follow. The conduct of the department head is a type of *behavior modeling* because it provides a model for supervisors to follow. Studies consistently show that supervisors tend to supervise as they themselves are supervised. If a department head is considerate and supportive in relation to supervisors, they are more likely to supervise in similar ways. It is natural for them to assume that the department head's practices reflect what top management wants and rewards. The obvious response is to try to learn and use some of those practices.

Even when supervisors do not consciously want to copy their department head, some of those practices are likely to creep subconsciously into their behavior patterns. It is consequently difficult for management to establish better behavioral practices only at the supervisory level. Though small improvements can be made, large gains depend on improving organizational behavior all the way up the chain of command. Management levels are interdependent insofar as behavioral improvements are concerned.

Another way that higher management affects supervisory performance is its control of the general environment in which supervisors work. It determines how

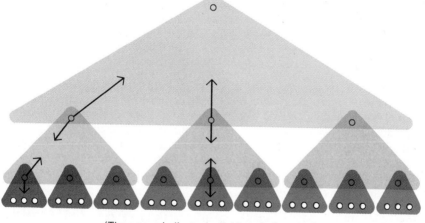

(The arrows indicate the linking pin function)

FIGURE 8-3

Likert's linking pin concept. (From *New Patterns of Management,* by Rensis Likert, p. 113. Copyright 1961 by McGraw-Hill Book Company. Used with permission of McGraw-Hill Book Company.)

much red tape they have to deal with, the type of staff they get, the overall communication patterns in the organization, and similar environmental factors. For example, a supervisor who is kept in the dark regarding plans and developments is thereby unable to communicate effectively with employees.

CLOSE SUPERVISION COMPARED WITH GENERAL SUPERVISION. *Close supervision* occurs when supervisors emphasize precise activities and follow up on every detail. *General supervision* occurs when supervisors establish broad work assignments and leave employees with some measure of discretion in their performance. Many jobs in modern society require worker discretion, so supervisors in these kinds of jobs who closely supervise their employees tend to reduce employee effectiveness and job satisfaction. Close supervision is inflexible and causes workers to feel that they have an inadequate range of freedom in decision making. When there is excessive checking up and adherence to rules, displacement of goals may occur so that a group works to live within the rules rather than to perform tasks toward goals. That is, the members spend their energies trying to get along with the system, rather than producing.

But low productivity and low job satisfaction do not always go with close supervision. Again the relationship is a contingency one. At the employee level some work requirements are more specific, requiring closer checking; and often the pace is faster, requiring more frequent follow-up. In addition, employees, as a result of their backgrounds and insecurities, may have role expectations of close supervision. The result is that close supervision will sometimes be effective at the employee level.

One study in manufacturing showed that close supervision was related to high productivity, provided the supervisor was considered a member of the work team and used a positive motivational style instead of a negative one. In this instance close checking was seen by the group as evidence of support.[7]

A study of Peruvian workers in the electric light and power industry showed that both blue-collar and white-collar workers were more satisfied with close supervision (correlations of about .20 for both). Apparently in this situation the role expectations of employees favored close supervision. For cross-cultural comparisons, the same study was duplicated in the same industry in the United States. Both blue-collar and white-collar workers reported they were less satisfied with close supervision (correlations of .23 and .17, respectively). Evidently cultural differences substantially caused these different responses in the two countries, since other conditions were about the same.[8]

Most other studies report negative results from close supervision.[9] Since the social system of the United States emphasizes employee independence and work autonomy, it is to be expected that usually general supervision will be more favorably received by employees. This relationship should especially apply in more sophisticated work groups, which are likely to need and expect more job independence.

THE NEED FOR EFFECTIVE COMMUNICATION. Supervisors are successful not only because of what they do but also because of how their acts are interpreted. Therefore, supervisors need to be able to tell, show, write, and listen so that they can convey to others what they are doing and want done. This communication job is a large one, taking from 60 to 90 percent of the working day, as shown by on-the-job observations.[10]

Since supervisors communicate with many different persons in a day, they need versatility in role behavior in order to deal with people in terms of their individual expectations. Different roles call for different communication behavior. Generally the effective supervisors, compared with ineffective ones, tend to spend more time making contacts with staff and service people outside their work group.[11] Apparently these outside contacts constitute a supportive act for a work group because the supervisor serves as intermediary with others to gain advantages for the group. (Or perhaps the group works better with the supervisor out of the way!)

POLITICS AND POWER. One way of interpreting outside contacts is that they assist supervisors in the practical politics of organizations. Political considerations are important in helping a supervisor keep on top of a situation and control conflict for constructive purposes. Politics concerns balances of power, saving face, horse trading, mending fences, adroit maneuvers in dynamic situations, ingenious compromises, and diplomacy. Minimum research has been done on organizational politics, but it is undeniable that politics is influential. It is the way supervisors gain organizational influence that they can use to accomplish their objectives. Supervisors who lack organizational power may want to do things for their group, but they are unable to do so because their power beyond the work group is insufficient. On the other hand, supervisors with power are able to accomplish actions such as a pay raise for their people, so their people are more motivated because their expectancy is improved. Politics does exist in organizations. Supervisors need to be aware of the political aspects of their environment.

SUPPORTIVE ROLE BEHAVIOR. Generally, what supervisors do to make themselves effective is to provide role behavior that is supportive of their group, according to the supportive model of organizational behavior. An essential step in being supportive is to try to remove any dysfunctional conditions that exist. When these exist, they block performance and result in employee discouragement and frustration. Consider the case of a supervisor who insisted upon high quality standards in her group, but she failed to provide adequate job training for many of her employees. The lack of training was a dysfunctional condition that needed removing. Other examples of dysfunctional conditions are insufficient authority, poor scheduling of materials, and inadequate tools to do the job.

Another essential step is for the supervisor to find out what the group's needs are. Action of this type requires empathy and social sensitivity. Much of a supervisor's communication time with people is spent trying to learn their needs, rather than trying to tell them what to do. When workers are trained and motivated, there is little need to tell them what to do. The primary need is for workers to tell supervisors what kinds of support are required in order for them to do a better job. This situation is almost a complete role reversal from earlier conceptions of a supervisor's job, and it is not an easy role to play.

Supervisors develop a supportive environment by wise use of social exchange theory. The supervisor wants employees to take certain actions, but in order to complete the social exchange the supervisor also must do something for them. Employees expect that the social exchange will be relatively equal, and if it is not, a psychological dissonance arises that interferes with cooperation. For example, a supervisor may give small unauthorized work breaks when work is slack. In turn, when the supervisor has a rush job, workers may be expected to reduce their rest break, thereby completing the social exchange.

THE CLINICAL METHOD. In trying to understand their situation, supervisors depend heavily on the *clinical method.* They take a clinical approach toward social systems in the same way that a physician takes a clinical approach toward biological systems. The clinical method is concerned with trying to understand the realities of a situation through observing, listening, seeing how one part is related to another, assessing the role of emotions, and recognizing one's own influence in the situation. It focuses understanding on a specific problem, rather than giving generalities about people. Through greater understanding it permits a supervisor to operate in terms of each person's individual needs, thereby supporting that person's identity and integrity.

Let us take an example. Just as a physician knows in general that penicillin is an effective medicine, so does a supervisor know in general that communication is a desirable practice. But neither penicillin nor communication is desirable in every case. The true question is: Will it be helpful with this particular person in this individual situation? The clinical method helps provide an answer.

The clincial method requires supervisors to be aware of their own roles and of the impact they have on the behavior of others. They accept and deal with others as they are. "As they are" means to understand and accept the feelings in a situation as well as its logical content.

Some years ago I saw how easily feelings in a situation can be a blind spot to an otherwise-intelligent administrator. I participated in an effort to help the general manager of an industrial research unit become more understanding of people. He was a gifted Ph.D., very capable in practical science as well as the theoretical side. He was friendly and warm as a person. He had proved himself capable in the technical side of management (planning, organizing, and controlling), but his job was in jeopardy because he could not comprehend the human side. Since he was capable, higher management wanted to keep him; so it made a substantial investment in developing him.

His blind spot was that his scientific training led him to accept only the logical content of a situation, not the feelings. Even after he had a year of special training, he changed very little. I can remember sitting in his office in the presence of the president and other top managers as we discussed certain feelings of lower management, and hearing him say again and again, "But that's not true. There's no need for concern about that because it's just not true. It's not true." Ironically, he was correct. What we were talking about was not true logically. His failure was his inability to understand that, from the point of view of feelings, "What's true to them is true—to them."

SUMMARY

The first-level supervisor occupies a unique position as the only member of management who supervises primarily nonmanagement persons. The supervisor may be viewed as a key person, supervisor in the middle, marginal supervisor, another worker, or behavioral specialist. A balanced interpretation considers the supervisor as the keystone in the organizational arch and as a linking pin joining higher managers and workers into a functional whole.

Effective supervisors are supportive of their work group. Although supervision is a contingency relationship, supervisors typically use positive, participative, and considerate leadership styles. They favor general supervision, develop communication contacts outside their work group, deal realistically with politics and power, and use the clinical method. Supervisors are likely to be more effective if their managers provide behavior modeling through practices similar to those just mentioned.

TERMS AND CONCEPTS FOR REVIEW

Key person in management

Supervisor in the middle

Marginal supervisor

Keystone role of supervisor

Linking pin concept

Behavior modeling

Close and general supervision

Clinical method

REVIEW QUESTIONS ■

1. How does a supervisor differ from other management persons?
2. Discuss differences among the five views of the supervisor's role. Relate these five views to the keystone and linking pin concepts.
3. Discuss what types of behavior make an effective supervisor.
4. In what ways can higher management affect supervisory performance?
5. Of what use to supervisors is the clinical method?

CASES

THE WORK ASSIGNMENT

Effie Pardini supervised eleven accounting clerks in the budget and planning department of a large computer manufacturer. None of the clerks had accounting degrees, but all were skilled in handling records and figures. They primarily prepared budgetary plans and analyses for operating departments. Data inputs were secured from the departments and from company records. Pardini assigned projects to the clerks based upon their interests and skills. Some projects were more desirable than others because of their prestige, challenge, contacts required, or other factors; so there were occasional conflicts over which clerk received a desirable project. One clerk who seemed especially sensitive and regularly complained about this issue was Sonia Prosser.

On one occasion Pardini received a desirable project and assigned it to a clerk by the name of Madden. Prosser was particularly distressed because she felt she should have had the assignment. She was so distressed that she retaliated by gathering up her present assignment and putting it away in her desk. Then she took a book from her desk and started reading it. Since all clerks were together in the same office, most of them observed her actions. She announced to one in a voice loud enough to be heard by others, "Nobody around here ever gives me a good assignment." Pardini overheard this comment and looked up from her desk, noting what was happening. Pardini was angered, but she sat at her desk for five minutes wondering what to do. Meanwhile Prosser continued reading her book.

QUESTIONS

1. What are the behavioral issues raised in this incident?
2. Discuss what action Pardini should take.

WILLIE LOMAX

Willie Lomax is a commission sales representative for a manufacturer of industrial supplies. He earns a small base salary plus a commission on all supplies he sells. During the last eight years Lomax has been strongly motivated to earn commissions in order to help his only daughter through medical school. Recently his daughter completed her internship and became a physician in a clinic, so she is financially independent. At about this time Lomax's job motivation declined drastically, and his sales declined proportionately. His sales supervisor does not know if the two events are connected.

QUESTIONS

1. In the role of Lomax's sales supervisor, explain the steps you will take to solve this problem. What supervisory practices and motivational models might be useful in this situation?
2. Role-play a meeting with Lomax on this problem.

MARTIN FORBUSHER

Martin Forbusher is supervisor in the lathe department of a manufacturing plant. Because of the complex production process, there is an equally complex organization; so Forbusher's department is serviced by about a dozen staff groups. Recently Forbusher's superintendent came to his department several times to see him and found him out of the department in other areas of the plant. The superintendent wonders whether he should talk to Forbusher about being away from his department so often. Although Forbusher's department has good productivity at the present time, the superintendent is concerned that Forbusher's frequent absences will harm productivity.

QUESTIONS
1. What behavioral issues are raised by this situation?
2. What should the superintendent do?

REFERENCES

1. Aaron Q. Sartain and Alton W. Baker, *The Supervisor and His Job,* 2d ed., New York: McGraw-Hill Book Company, 1972, p. 35.

2. Frank T. Paine and Martin J. Gannon, "Job Attitudes of Supervisors and Managers," *Personnel Psychology,* Winter 1973, pp. 521–529.

3. For an example of an early article of this type see Burleigh B. Gardner and William F. Whyte, "The Man in the Middle: Position and Problems of the Foreman," *Applied Anthropology,* Spring 1945, pp. 1–28. See also the reprint of F. J. Roethlisberger's 1945 article, "The Foreman: Master and Victim of Doubletalk," in *Harvard Business Review,* September–October 1965, pp. 22ff.

4. Bradford B. Boyd and J. Michael Jensen, "Perceptions of the First-Line Supervisor's Authority: A Study of Superior-Subordinate Communication," *Academy of Management Journal,* September 1972, pp. 331–342.

5. An early article on this subject is Donald E. Wray, "Marginal Men of Industry: The Foremen," *American Journal of Sociology,* January 1949, pp. 298–301. See also Thomas H. Patten, Jr., *The Foreman: Forgotten Man of Management,* New York: American Management Association, 1968.

6. Richard S. Schultz, "A Realistic Look at Supervisory Development," *Personnel Journal,* January 1964, p. 37.

7. Martin Patchen, "Supervisory Methods and Group Performance Norms," *Administrative Science Quarterly,* December 1962, pp. 275–294.

8. William F. Whyte and Lawrence K. Williams, "Supervisory Leadership: An International Comparison," in *Proceedings, CIOS XIII International Management Congress,* New York: Council for International Progress in Management, Inc., 1963, p. 485, covering 566 Peruvian and 907 United States employees.

9. Representative research reports on close supervision are Emanuel Kay and Herbert H. Meyer, "The Development of a Job Activity Questionnaire for Production Foremen," *Personnel Psychology,* Winter 1962, p. 416; and Treadway C. Parker, "The Psychological Environment and Work Group Behavior," *Personnel Administration,* September–October 1965, pp. 26–31.

10. E. T. Klemmer and F. W. Snyder, "Measurement of Time Spent Communicating," *The Journal of Communication,* June 1972, pp. 142–158; and John N. Yanouzas, "A Comparative Study of Work Organization and Supervisory Behavior," *Human Organization,* Fall 1964, p. 253.

11. Examples of early research on communication outside the work group are Quentin D. Ponder, "The Effective Manufacturing Foreman," *Proceedings of the Industrial Relations Research Association,* Madison, Wis., 1958, pp. 41–54; Frank J. Jasinski, "Foreman Relationships outside the Work Group," *Personnel,* September 1956, pp. 130–136; and Kay and Meyer, *loc. cit.* This type of research measures only the amount of time used for outside contacts, not how well it is used; but it is assumed that more time spent in this activity results in better performance of it, other things being equal.

CHAPTER 9
DEVELOPMENT OF PARTICIPATION

The fellow in the boat with you never bores a hole in it.
Anonymous

As a rule, participative management is more likely to produce high levels of satisfaction and motivation than an authoritarian management.
Edward E. Lawler III[1]

LEARNING OBJECTIVES

TO UNDERSTAND:
The idea of participation
The concept of social delegation
Prerequisites for effective participation
The practical usefulness of participation
Types of programs to build participation
The union role in participation
Limitations of participation

Supportive managers use participation to improve performance of their teams.
Participation has excellent potential for building teamwork, but it also has limitations. It is a difficult practice, and it can fail if poorly applied. When participation is
well done, two of its best results are acceptance of change and a favorable team
spirit.

*Observe in the experience of one organization how participation can improve
a situation. A large aircraft manufacturer employed from 5,000 to 20,000 shop
workers during a ten-year period. It used a safety committee system in which each
department was represented on the committee by one of its workers. During these
ten years not one person had a disabling injury while serving as safety committee
member. When people became safety committee members, they ceased having disabling injuries! This record occurred despite the fact that there were hundreds of
members during the decade, and sometimes "accident-prone" workers were appointed committee members in order to make them safety-conscious. The facts of
this situation show a significant difference between committee members and non-
members. Part of this difference surely came from the fact that the committee
members were responsible, participating persons with regard to safety.*

Let us now discuss what participation is, the kinds of experiences we have
had with it, management programs to develop it, and its ever-present limitations.

THE NATURE OF EMPLOYEE PARTICIPATION

WHAT IS PARTICIPATION? Participative managers consult with their followers, bringing them in on problems and decisions so that their groups act as social units in work performance. The managers are not autocrats, but neither are they free-rein managers who abandon their management responsibilities. Participative managers still retain ultimate responsibility for the operation of their units, but they have learned to share operating responsibility with those who perform the work. The result is that employees feel a sense of involvement in group goals. As shown earlier, in Figure 6-3, the "employee psychological result" of supportive management is "participation." It follows that *participation is defined as mental and emotional involvement of persons in group situations that encourage them to contribute to group goals and share responsibility for them.* There are three important ideas in this definition.

Mental and emotional involvement. First, and probably foremost, participation means mental and emotional involvement, rather than mere muscular activity. A person's *self* is involved, rather than just one's skill. This involvement is psychological, rather than physical. A person who participates is *ego-involved* instead of merely *task-involved.*[2] Some managers mistake task involvement for true participation. They go through the motions of participation, but nothing more. They hold meetings, ask opinions, and so on, but all the time it is perfectly clear to employees that their manager is an autocratic boss who wants no ideas. This is *busy work,* not participation. Employees fail to become ego-involved.

> The difference between ego-involved participation and task-involved activity is shown by a description of a part of a day for a worker named Joseph Carter. He wakens to the music of his clock-radio, interrupted occasionally by an announcer he does not know, cannot see, and cannot talk back to. After eating alone, since his family does not awake so early in the morning, his next personal interaction is with a bus driver whom he does not know and who works for some abstract transportation system that Carter does not understand and in which he has no control. At the plant he shows his badge to a guard, though he does not know the guard's name and does not really care when he asks, "How are you feeling this morning?" In fact, he is irked because the guard keeps asking to see his badge, though surely after three years the guard must know he is an employee. Going into the shop, he has to stop by the personnel office to sign an insurance paper which he cannot understand and which is thrust at him by an employee who acts as if she were selling soap in a grocery store. Finally, he enters his work area to be greeted by a supervisor whose name he does know, but that is about all, because the supervisor is only in the department temporarily for training to be sent somewhere else soon by "somebody upstairs." The supervisor's greeting is a gruff "Hello," because he is terribly busy on a rush order, but neither he nor Carter knows why it became "rush"! And so it goes throughout the day.

Though Joseph Carter has been furiously active all day, most of this was routine, impersonal activity that was imposed on him. How much was he ego-involved in his activity? How much did he participate?

Motivation to contribute. A second important idea in participation is that it motivates persons to contribute to the situation. They are given an opportunity to release their own resources of initiative and creativity toward the objectives of the organization. In this way participation differs from "consent."[3] The practice of consent uses only the creativity of the manager who brings ideas to the group for their consent. The consenters do not contribute; they merely approve. Participation is more than getting consent for something already decided. It is a *two-way* psychological and social relationship among people, rather than a procedure for imposing ideas from above. Its great value is that it uses the creativity of all employees.

Acceptance of responsibility. A third idea in participation is that it encourages people to accept responsibility in their group's activities. It is a social process by which people become self-involved in an organization and want to see it work successfully. When they talk about their organization, they begin to say "we," not "they." When they see a job problem, it is "ours," not "theirs." Participation helps them become responsible employee citizens, rather than nonresponsible, machine-like performers.

As individuals begin to accept responsibility for group activities, they begin to be interested in, and receptive to, teamwork, because they see in it a way to do what *they want* to do, i.e., to get a job done for which they feel responsible. This idea of getting the group to want teamwork is the key step in developing it into a successful work unit. When people *want* to do something, they will find a way. Under these conditions employees perceive managers as supportive contributors to the team. Employees are ready to work actively with managers, rather than reactively against them.

Participation is not a useless theory developed by someone looking for a new behavioral idea. There is ample evidence that it works in practice. It succeeds in a variety of jobs, such as forestry management and sewing operations. It applies to managers as well as employees.[4] And it applies with higher-level occupations as well as lower-level ones.

In one instance an insurance sales representative reported to friends that he had an outstanding new supervisor. The sales representative largely worked independently without supervision. He was highly skilled, possessing certificates as a Certified Life Underwriter and as a Certified Property and Casualty Underwriter. He was a member of the Million Dollar Club, meaning that he had sold over one million dollars worth of insurance in a year. Nevertheless he was pleased because his supervisor had sought his advice about what management could do to help him perform his job more effectively. He had worked for his organization eight years, but he said that never before had anyone sought his ideas. They were always trying to tell him what to do and urging him to do better.

The great benefit of participation is that it restores to people at work their birthright to be contributing members of the groups in which they work. It builds human values in organizations, because it serves the top four needs on the Maslow hierarchy. This improvement of human values at work is important for society as well as employees, because there is evidence that job experiences do affect the psychological functioning of people as citizens.[5]

141

SOCIAL DELEGATION THROUGH PARTICIPATION. Managers often ask, "If by means of participation I share authority and responsibility with my personnel, don't I lose some of my own authority? I can't afford to lose authority because I am responsible, and if I am responsible, I must have the authority." This is a perfectly normal worry of the executive who first considers the values of participation, but it is hardly a justifiable worry, because the participative manager still retains authority to decide. All that the manager does is make a *social delegation* so that the group can share in the decision-making process.

Social delegation in the behavioral domain is comparable to formal delegation in the organizational domain. Formal delegation does not weaken the organizational authority of managers; neither does social delegation weaken their authority. Modern managers do not object to formal delegation. In fact it is their stock-in-trade; it is the act that makes them managers. Likewise modern managers under normal conditions do not object to some social delegation through participation. It, too, is their stock-in-trade—that which makes them supportive managers.

INCREASED POWER AND INFLUENCE. Strange as it may seem, social delegation through participation actually may *increase* the power and influence of managers with their groups. This kind of statement sounds like double-talk, but it is a realistic conclusion from research.[6] Evidence is that the amount of influence in a social system is not a certain limited amount. Rather, influence is expandable just as the amount of savings in an economy is expandable. The process works like this. Managerial influence depends partly on such conditions as employee trust in management, feeling of teamwork, and sense of responsibility. Participation improves these conditions. Since employees feel more cooperative and responsible, they are likely to be more responsive to managers' attempts to influence them. In a sense what occurs is that managers make social transactions with their work groups that improve goodwill and responsibility. These conditions are similar to a savings deposit that managers can draw upon later when they need to apply their influence.

Here is an example of a manager's experience with social delegation. The manager of a computer operation having over fifty employees felt that some changes were needed. In the beginning she tried the usual autocratic approach, aided by a consultant. Desired changes were proposed, but the employees would not accept them. Finally the effort was abandoned.

The manager continued to think that changes were necessary, so a year later she decided to try again, using more participatory approaches. She discussed the need with her supervisors and several key employees. Then she set up committees to work on designated parts of a "self-examination study." The groups worked hard, and in a few months they submitted a capable report that recommended a number of important changes. In this instance the members felt a sense of pride and ownership in the report. It was theirs. They had created it. The result was that they made a genuine effort to implement it, and with the full support of the whole group some substantial changes were made. Social delegation had increased the manager's influence.

As a matter of fact, "old-fashioned" formal delegation of work to employees is the original participative practice. Delegation gets people ego-involved, motivates them to contribute, and encourages them to accept responsibility. It is the means by which the top person in an organization gets others to share in decision making when the task is too large to handle alone. If management can through formal delegation give employees a degree of autonomy over activities, there is little reason to talk about their "need to participate" in those activities where autonomy already exists. The existing autonomy is more than participation normally gives them. Therefore, when we talk about a "need for participation," we are typically referring to possibilities for participation in activities where autonomy is lacking, i.e., where formal delegation of decision-making authority does not exist.

PREREQUISITES FOR EFFECTIVE PARTICIPATION. The success of participation is directly related to how well certain prerequisite conditions are met. Some of these conditions occur in the participants; some exist in their environment. Taken together, these conditions mean that participation applies in a contingency relationship. It works better in some situations than in others—and in certain situations it works not at all. Major prerequisite conditions are as follows:[7]

1. There must be time to participate before action is required. Participation is hardly appropriate in emergency situations.

2. The financial cost of participation should not exceed the values, economic and otherwise, that come from it. Employees cannot spend all their time participating, to the exclusion of all other work.

3. The subject of participation must be relevant to the employee environment, else employees will look upon it merely as busy work.

4. The participants should have the ability, such as intelligence and knowledge, to participate. It is hardly advisable, for example, to ask janitors in a pharmaceutical laboratory to participate in deciding which of five chemical formulas deserves research priority; but they might participate in helping resolve other problems related to their work.

5. The participants must be able mutually to communicate—to talk each other's language—in order to be able to exchange ideas.

6. Neither party should feel that its position is threatened by participation. If workers think their status will be adversely affected, they will not participate. If managers feel that their authority is threatened, they will refuse participation or will be defensive.

7. Participation for deciding a course of action in an organization can take place only within the group's *area of job freedom.* Some degree of restriction on subunits is necessary in any organization in order to maintain internal unity. Each separate subunit cannot make decisions that violate policy, collective-bargaining agreements, legal requirements, and similar restraints. Likewise there are restraints in the physical environment (a flood closing the plant is an extreme example) and as a result of one's own limitations (such as not understanding electronics). The area of

job freedom for any department is its area of discretion after all restraints have been applied. In no organization is there complete freedom, even for the top executive.

Within the area of job freedom, participation exists along a continuum, as shown in Figure 9-1. Within a period of time a manager will practice participation at many points along the continuum. That is, a manager may seek the group's ideas before deciding vacation schedules, but the same manager decides overtime schedules independently. In spite of differences on individual decisions, each manager gradually becomes identified with some general style of participation as a usual practice.

The popular terms designated for amounts of participation along the continuum are representative of a broad area on the continuum instead of a certain point. Several of these terms are defined later in this chapter.

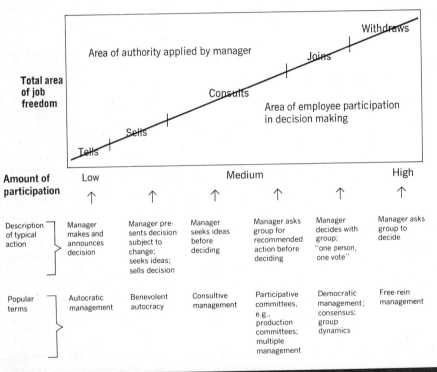

FIGURE 9-1

The amount of participation in a department exists along a continuum. (Adapted from Robert Tannenbaum and Warren H. Schmidt, "How to Choose a Leadership Pattern," *Harvard Business Review,* March–April 1958, p. 96.)

EXPERIENCES WITH PARTICIPATION

EARLY STUDIES OF PARTICIPATION. Although managers have for years recognized various benefits of participation, these benefits were first experimentally suggested in classic studies in industry by Roethlisberger, Bavelas, and Coch and French.

Roethlisberger. Roethlisberger and his associates originally sought to show the relationship of physical changes in environment and output.[8] In the course of their experiments new relationships, many of which involved participation, developed between (1) workers and supervisors, and (2) workers and experimenters. The results convincingly illustrated how these social changes improved both productivity and morale. Although participation was not the whole cause of these improvements, it seemed to be a significant cause.

Bavelas. Bavelas worked with a group of women on a sewing operation that was performed on a group incentive basis.[9] He chose for his experiment a superior group whose production averaged about seventy-four units, with a range of seventy to seventy-eight. He asked them if they would like to set their own production goal, which after considerable discussion they unanimously agreed should be eighty-four units hourly. Within five days this goal was exceeded, and another meeting was held to consider goal changes. A new goal of ninety-five was set, but it could not be met; so in a few days the women reduced the goal to the relatively permanent level of ninety units. During the next several months this group's output averaged about eighty-seven units, with a range of eighty to ninety-three. The net increase after participation was about thirteen units hourly.

Other methods were used to try to increase output in comparable groups, but negligible increases were made. In one instance the leader suggested higher goals, promising that rates would not be reduced if the women produced more, but improvements were insignificant. In another instance the leader held discussions with the women but did not suggest a new goal. The result was no improvement. Some years later Lawrence and Smith performed experiments similiar to those of Bavelas and reported substantially the same results; however, four of their eleven "discussion groups" showed substantial production increases (8 to 18 percent) in contrast to the lack of improvement in Bavelas's discussion group. All the eleven "goal-setting" groups increased their productivity. Bavelas's experiments, along with the follow-up by Lawrence and Smith,[10] suggest that participation can increase output, but that different degrees of participation tend to produce different results.

Coch and French. Coch and French worked also with sewing machine operators, introducing changes three different ways in matched groups.[11] In the first method, which they called nonparticipation, group members were told about the change, and any questions they had were answered. In the second method, they were told about the change and asked to select representatives to develop with management the work methods and piece rates involved. In the third procedure, called the total-participation method, all workers who were directly influenced by the change plus selected members of management met as a group and together made decisions about the change.

Results with the nonparticipation method consistently followed company experience. As shown in Figure 9-2, output dropped more than 20 percent and stayed down until the group was disbanded approximately thirty days later. There were grievances, restriction of production, and other forms of resistance. The group using the representation method fared much better, recovering original output in two weeks. Results with the total-participation method were best of all. They recovered their former speed of output in a few days and at the end of thirty days were about 15 percent better than their original standard. The nonparticipation group had 17 percent resignations, but neither the representation group nor the participation group had any resignations in forty days after the change.

These early experiments suggested the general proposition that, *especially in the introduction of changes, participation tends to improve output and general job satisfaction.* However, these experiments were made by skilled social scientists, so they offered no real evidence that managers with their limited social science backgrounds could make them work under the pressure of operating conditions. The step from experimentation to practice is a long one indeed.

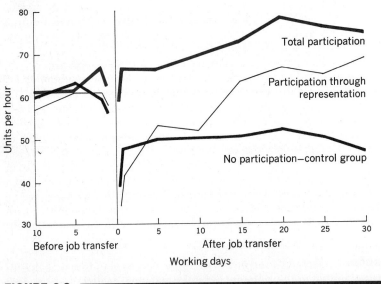

FIGURE 9-2

Employee participation in a job change in relation to productivity after the change. (*Source: Leadership Patterns and Organizational Effectiveness,* Ann Arbor, Mich.: Foundation for Research on Human Behavior, 1954, p. 4. From the experiment of Coch and French.)

PRACTICAL EXPERIENCE WITH PARTICIPATION. Application of participation in organizations generally has been successful, although there have been failures. One insurance company, for example, found that employee decision making became too independent. Some employees were duplicating prospects. Others were seeking only easy accounts, leaving the hard ones for someone else. Eventually the company had to restore some controls.

Improvements with participation tend to be moderate, in the range of 5 to 20 percent, but even this amount is important; and sometimes results are more dramatic. In various types of organizations under many different operating conditions, participation has contributed to one or more of the following conditions: higher productivity, improved motivation, greater job satisfaction, reduced stress, improved quality of work, better acceptance of change, more commitment to goals, reduced turnover, less absenteeism, and other benefits.[12] The results clearly show that participation is a broadly effective practice that favorably affects a variety of organizational outputs.

Participation is so involved with the whole social system that its application is contingent upon other conditions in the organization. One of these other variables is the structure of the organization itself, and structure likewise changes slowly. Participation and structure are complementary. A more flexible, human-oriented structure can make a participative practice more fruitful. This suggests that participation should be easier to develop by combining it with other related changes so that each reinforces the other in encouraging participation.

One manufacturer's program to increase participation involved company policy, organization structure, and a wide assortment of training and communication approaches. It used a team of social scientists, who spent up to eighteen months working with three departments in the organization. They were successful in developing effective employee participation. Employee productivity and satisfaction increased concurrently, and waste and absences decreased. We cannot say for sure that participation helped cause these favorable results, but at least it was positively associated with them.[13]

The system effects of participation are also illustrated by long-run experience with it. When participation has been used for several years, there is evidence that it affects the whole organizational system, including patterns of cooperation and employee attitudes. The organization as a whole becomes more humanly effective, and the organizational climate becomes more favorable. Follow-up in a clothing manufacturing operation after seven years showed that the improved results were durable.[14]

Participation is a flexible practice useful in many types of situations. There is some evidence that it works about as well when applied by an authoritarian personality as when used by a more permissive type of personality.[15] It also appears to work equally well with manual workers or office workers.

One experiment involved maintenance workers who participated in developing a pay incentive plan to reward good attendance on the job. These workers were part-time custodians who cleaned buildings in the evenings. One set of three cus-

todian groups participated in developing their own attendance incentive plans (Condition A). These plans were then imposed by management on other groups (Condition B). Two other groups served as control groups, not being changed at all (Condition C). Only Condition A produced a significant increase in attendance. Possible explanations offered by the researcher are as follows:

1. Those who participated were more committed to the plan. (This is one of the major advantages of participation.)
2. Those who participated were more knowledgeable of the plan.
3. Those who participated developed more trust in the good intentions of management with regard to the plan.[16]

An excellent example of participation by manual workers is the experience of an electronic manufacturer. When the company started production of a new navigation instrument, actual assembly time for the first few months was 138 hours, even though standard time was 100 hours. After three months of assembly experience the supervisor and the assemblers participated in a production improvement program that resulted in a goal of 86 hours for assembly. Within three months they had reduced production time to 75 hours, and at the end of nine months the time was only 41 hours.[17]

ORGANIZATIONAL PROGRAMS TO BUILD PARTICIPATION

We can further understand participation if we examine it in terms of a representative sample of management programs to develop it. These programs usually are clusters of practices that focus on some particular area of participation, such as employee suggestions. Success with participative programs depends on the quality of participation that actually develops, rather than on whether a certain technique is used.

CONSULTIVE MANAGEMENT. Consultive management is the kind of participation that managers can apply even though those above them do not apply it. No new policies are required, and existing authority-responsibility relationships are not affected. Consultive management, as the name implies, means that managers consult with their employees in order to encourage them to think about issues and contribute their own ideas before decisions are made. Managers do not consult on every issue, but they do set a climate of consultation. This approach requires managers to be genuinely receptive to employee ideas so that employees can perceive that their ideas may be useful. Managers applying consultive management must have the humility to admit that they do not know more than their employees and that managerial ideas are not always best. Managerial attitudes rather than procedures are the key ingredient, because employees will quickly perceive the superficiality of any procedure that is not underwritten by a genuine desire for employee ideas.

Consultive management does not weaken managerial authority because managers still retain the right to decide. It normally should strengthen managerial influence, because consultation with employees tends to increase their trust in what management is trying to do. Two major conveniences of consultive management are that managers can consult with their employees at any time without having to fit the straitjacket required by committee procedure, and that they can consult with any number of their employees ranging from one to the whole group. A manager who consults with the whole group has the option of talking to them either as a unit or one by one. In one instance, for example, a manufacturer encouraged informal discussions between supervisors and small groups of employees concerning cost reduction. Costs were reduced 1 percent, which resulted in a substantial saving of $10 million for the year. Small improvements can be large when applied to a whole organization.

DEMOCRATIC MANAGEMENT. Democratic management goes further than consultive management and releases considerable decision-making power to employees in appropriate areas of job freedom, as shown in Figure 9-1. The democratic manager brings to employees a sufficient number of decisional problems to cause them to feel that their creativity is being used and that they are fully involved in determining affairs that affect their work.

The main process by which democratic management occurs is group discussion, while consultive management can also be practiced on a person-to-person basis. Since democratic management emphasizes group discussion, it may be termed the group dynamics approach to participation. In its extreme form it operates according to consensus and equalitarian "one-person, one-vote" ideas, so it is possible for managers to lose control of whatever decisions they refer to their groups.[18] Normally, although managers let the group decide, they hold a rarely used veto power if group decisions are not consistent with the needs of the organization.

Democratic management is especially applicable in voluntary benefit groups and social organizations, where an easy pace and natural community of interests exist, but it is more difficult to apply in hierarchical, task-oriented situations.

One study of democratic management under operating conditions found that it did not provide adequate focus on organizational objectives. The study covered thirty-two geographically separate units of a nationally organized delivery company. Units with democratic management were not the high-performing ones. The researchers concluded, "While this pattern of control may lead to high rank-and-file morale, it does not appear to promote basic identification with organizational objectives and practices or motivated action leading to high performance. It appears that in this organization high rank-and-file control relative to the leaders may have the effect of members' acting simply in terms of their own self-interests and not accepting the contributions of the leaders."[19]

PRODUCTION COMMITTEES. Production committees are groups formally organized to consider work problems and composed jointly of worker and management representatives. They have been used for decades and on occasion have produced excellent results. They are applicable to both unionized and nonunionized organizations. In spite of their age, production committees have had a checkered record of success. In some industries they have been successful, but not in others. Some companies have used them for a while but then dropped them because they became burdened with red tape, lost continuity, or otherwise became ineffective. To be successful they require continuous interest by higher management, and the situation needs to be such that employees have the capacity to offer suggestions that are genuine improvements. Committees also are a successful part of profit-sharing and production-sharing plans, which will be discussed in a later chapter on economic incentives.

The Tennessee Valley Authority has had favorable results using a committee program with its power plant and engineering personnel. Employees are unionized, but committee members do not represent their union. Comparing those units where the committee program is active (i.e., high participation) and those where it is not active (i.e., low participation), the high-participating units have benefits which are statistically significant. There is stronger motivation, better acceptance of change, and higher employee support of the organization. These benefits apply even to employees who are low in general job satisfaction. The participative program works better with engineers than with nonprofessional power plant employees, apparently because engineers feel that participation is more legitimate in terms of their ability to contribute. The program also works best when employees can participate both at their work group level and at higher unit levels.[20]

Variations of the production committee idea include safety committees, task forces, and other types of committees and meetings that consider organizational problems. One company, for example, has "jobholder meetings" that are conducted annually with employees in a style similar to that of stockholder meetings. In this environment the jobholders have an opportunity to give their inputs directly to top management and to question management openly about any issue related to their organization.

SUGGESTION PROGRAMS. Suggestion programs are formal plans to encourage individual employees to recommend work improvements. Like production committees they need careful "feeding and watering" in order to flourish. One difficulty is that they exist primarily by written communication; hence the motivation that comes from face-to-face communication is lacking. In addition, some managers and staff specialists look upon suggestions in their area as criticisms of their ability. In a manufacturing plant, for example, the suggestion plan was nearly killed by an obstinate industrial engineering department that refused to accept the idea that employees could suggest improvements in the manufacturing processes that engineering had designed. Another problem with suggestions is that sometimes an employee is reluctant to make suggestions that affect the work of the other employees, because they may object to changes required by the suggestion.

Suggestion programs have a role in participative management, but their role is limited because of their narrow scope (suggestions only) and their emphasis on the written word. The suggestion rate for organizations that have suggestion programs in the United States tends to average about one suggestion for each two employees per year.

MULTIPLE MANAGEMENT. Multiple management is a participative practice started in 1932 at McCormick and Company primarily to develop participation by junior executives.[21] It uses formal advisory committees of junior executives for the purpose of creating ideas, screening ideas, developing executive skills, and broadening experience. Multiple management has been used successfully around the world in hundreds of companies, both unionized and nonunionized. Its central core is a junior board of directors that is given the opportunity to study any problem and to recommend courses of action. Employer information is made freely available to the board, and its meetings are unrestrained by the presence of any senior executives. Members set their own bylaws and rotate their membership.

Multiple management has proved itself as a participative practice for management, especially for the sometimes-overlooked middle managers. It is an excellent way to bring new blood into top management and to train employees as they move upward. It taps the reserve of creativity that middle managers sometimes are not using, and it encourages them to take responsibilities as rapidly as they are able. The result is a program that helps meet their age-old desire to participate and does so in a way that benefits managers, workers, owners, and customers alike. As with any program, there have been occasional failures.

THE LABOR UNION'S ROLE IN PARTICIPATION. A union is to some extent a participative instrument, because it gives workers a chance to participate in determining their conditions of work. A union, however, is a separate and independent organization, and it will be discussed in a later chapter. In this section we are talking about the labor union's role in management programs for participation. In responding to participative programs, unions make a distinction between (1) employee participation in the official role of union representative, and (2) participation by an individual employee, such as in a shop-safety committee. Unions are much more hesitant about the former because they are officially involved. They look more favorably upon the latter practice but still have some reservations.

Union leaders are sometimes fearful that participation will draw the loyalty of workers away from the union and closer to management, although there is no evidence that this result occurs. Since the union depends upon its membership for strength and growth, it is quite jealous of any social force that may threaten its members' loyalties to it. Union leaders have the ever-present problem of getting reelected; hence they are wary of any plan that might suggest they have "sold out to management." Participation, furthermore, takes a long time to show results, which means that it is not a very salable product to any union leader who must show short-run gains to support an annual reelection.

Some union leaders feel that if they participate in helping management decide courses of action, the union's ability to challenge those actions is thereby weakened. These union leaders would prefer to remain aloof, having complete freedom to express disagreement with management and challenge it at any time. The opposite point of view, held by other leaders, is that participation gives them an opportunity to get on the inside and to express their viewpoints *before* action is taken, which is superior to disagreement and protest *after* a decision is made. In practice most union viewpoints are somewhere between these two extremes; some types of participation are acceptable, but others are not.

151

LIMITATIONS OF PARTICIPATION. For several pages we have been speaking favorably of participation, so it is now appropriate to put the brakes on enthusiasm and toss a few brickbats. Participation does have its costs as well as gains. All the prerequisites discussed earlier are limitations to some extent, but there are others.

Technology and organizations today are so complex that specialized work roles are required, making it difficult for people to participate successfully if they go very far beyond their particular environment. This means that lower-level workers can participate successfully in operating matters, but they usually have difficulty participating in policy matters. After a thorough study of this subject internationally, one observer comments that, except for the personnel area where workers have a personal expertise, plans for worker participation *in management* have had minimum success.[22] With increased professionalization of management, workers can at best contribute only supplemental ideas, and these contributions are often not sufficient to sustain their interest.

Difficulties especially arise when workers make proposals in areas where they are not competent. Then when their idea is rejected, they refuse to support whatever course of action was adopted and become alienated. A related problem is that some workers develop a habit of expecting to be consulted on every issue, even those to which they cannot contribute. When they are not consulted, they become resentful and uncooperative.

Another issue is an employee's right *not* to participate. There is no evidence that participation is good for everybody. We have said only that participation is a useful means of building better relations in a group, and we have also said that people are all different. There is evidence that many persons do not want to be bothered with participation. Shall we, regardless, push them into its mold merely because we think it is good for them? Some persons want a minimum of interaction with their supervisor and/or associates. Sometimes a group can be kept participating only by pressure from above; and when that pressure is released, they revert to nonparticipation, apparently because it is more desirable to them under the circumstances. If autocratic means are used to impose participation, has anything really been gained?

Another difficulty with participation—as was the case with scientific management—is that practitioners become lost in the procedures of participation while overlooking its philosophy. The substance of participation does not automatically flow from its procedures; there is no such mechanistic connection. Procedures do not make participation; rather, when they are used at the right time and in the right circumstances, they make it possible for participation to develop in the minds of employees.

A serious issue with participation is that participative situations can be used covertly to manipulate employees. This manipulation is not necessarily by management. It may be by the union or by undercover cliques led by members skilled in group dynamics—the social engineers of consent. Too often groups are used to impose conformity on individualistic members. It is no wonder, then, that some employees prefer the open tyranny of an autocratic boss to the covert tyranny of a group.

CONCLUDING THOUGHTS. In spite of its numerous limitations, participation generally has achieved moderate success. It is not the answer to all organizational problems, but experience does show its general usefulness. The demand of employees to participate is not a passing fancy. It appears to be rooted deeply in the culture of free people around the world, and it is probably a basic drive in human beings. Because of its significance, participation is the kind of practice to which organizational leaders need to devote long-range efforts. It affords a means of building some of the human values needed at work. It has been so successful in practice that it has become widely accepted in more advanced nations.[23]

SUMMARY

Participation is an important contributor to organizational effectiveness. Participation is mental and emotional involvement of persons in group situations that encourage them to contribute to group goals and share responsibility for them. It is the employee psychological result of supportive management. It is a form of social delegation that serves as a supplement to formal delegation. It has numerous limitations, but when its prerequisites are met and the amount and type used reasonably fit the situation, it offers potential for higher productivity, higher job satisfaction, and other benefits. Some management programs to improve participation are consultive management, democratic management, production committees, suggestion programs, and multiple management.

TERMS AND CONCEPTS FOR REVIEW

Participation

Ego-involvement

Social delegation

Prerequisites for participation

Area of job freedom

Consultive management

Democratic management

Production committees

Suggestion programs

Multiple management

Limitations of participation

REVIEW QUESTIONS

1. What is meant by participation?
2. What sort of results have organizations had with participation?
3. What are the prerequisites for effective participation?
4. Explain the differences between:
   a. Ego-involvement and task involvement
   b. Social delegation and formal delegation
   c. Consultive management and democratic management

5. Appraise the comment "Managers have enough participation. They are on the 'inside' and make all the decisions, so they certainly do not need any participative aids such as multiple management."

CASE

JOE ADAMS

Joe Adams is supervisor in the final assembly department of an automobile body plant. Work in this department is not dependable, with temporary layoffs or short weeks occurring three or four times a year. The work is physically difficult, but the skill required is minimal; so most employees are high school graduates only. Some do not even have a high school education. About one-third of the work force comes from ethnic and racial minority groups. The work procedure and pace of work are tightly controlled by industrial engineers and other staff groups.

Adams attended a one-day conference of his Supervisors' Association recently and learned the many potential benefits of participation. In his own words, "This conference sold me on participation"; so now he wishes to establish it in his assembly department. Management feels that conditions on an assembly line are not suitable for participation. Further, it believes that the majority of workers employed have an autocratic role expectation of supervision. In addition, management has said that the production schedule will not allow time off for participation during the workday. This means that if Adams wants to hold any meetings about participation he will have to do so after work and on the workers' own time. Adams feels sure that his employees will not wish to remain after work on their own time, and he is not even sure that they would do so if he paid them overtime.

QUESTIONS
1. Recommend a course of action for Adams.
2. Would any ideas from the following be helpful in this case: McGregor, Herzberg, McClelland, Fiedler, and models of organizational behavior?

REFERENCES

1. Edward E. Lawler III, "For a More Effective Organization—Match the Job to the Man," *Organizational Dynamics,* Summer 1974, p. 27.

2. Gordon W. Allport, "The Psychology of Participation," *The Psychological Review,* May 1945, p. 122.

3. Mary P. Follett, "The Psychology of Consent and Participation," in Henry C. Metcalf and L. Urwick (eds.), *Dynamic Administration: The Collected Papers of Mary Parker Follett,* New York: Harper & Row, Publishers, Incorporated, 1941, pp. 210–212. From a paper presented in 1927.

4. Its usefulness to managers is described in Richard F. Powers and Gary W. Dickson, "MisProject Management: Myths, Opinions, and Reality," *California Management Review,* Spring 1973, pp. 147–156.

5. Melvin L. Kohn and Carmi Schooler, "Occupational Experience and Psychological

Functioning: An Assessment of Reciprocal Effects," *American Sociological Review,* February 1973, pp. 97–118.

6. M. Rosner and others, "Worker Participation and Influence in Five Countries," *Industrial Relations,* May 1973, pp. 200–212; Arnold S. Tannenbaum and Robert A. Cooke, "Control and Participation," *Journal of Contemporary Business,* Autumn 1974, pp. 35–46; and Rensis Likert, *New Patterns of Management,* New York: McGraw-Hill Book Company, 1961, pp. 130–134.

7. See Robert Tannenbaum, Irving R. Weschler, and Fred Massarik, *Leadership and Organization: A Behavioral Science Approach,* New York: McGraw-Hill Book Company, 1961, pp. 88–100.

8. F. J. Roethlisberger and W. J. Dickson, *Management and the Worker,* Cambridge, Mass.: Harvard University Press, 1939.

9. Norman R. F. Maier, *Psychology in Industry,* Boston: Houghton Mifflin Company, 1946, pp. 264–266.

10. Lois C. Lawrence and Patricia Cain Smith, "Group Decision and Employee Participation," *Journal of Applied Psychology,* October 1955, pp. 334–337.

11. Lester Coch and John R. P. French, Jr., "Overcoming Resistance to Change," *Human Relations,* vol. 1, no. 4, 1948, pp. 512–532; and John R. P. French, Jr., and Alvin Zander, "The Group Dynamics Approach," in Arthur Kornhauser (ed.), *Psychology of Labor-Management Relations,* Champaign, Ill.: Industrial Relations Research Association, 1949, pp. 73–75.

12. Examples of various types of improvements are reported in Gary P. Latham and Gary A. Yukl, "Assigned versus Participative Goal Setting with Educated and Uneducated Woods Workers," *Journal of Applied Psychology,* June 1975, pp. 299–302; J. Kenneth White and Robert A. Ruh, "Effects of Personal Values on the Relationship between Participation and Job Attitudes," *Administrative Science Quarterly,* December 1973, pp. 506–514; J. Timothy McMahon and G. W. Perritt, "Toward a Contingency Theory of Organizational Control," *Academy of Management Journal,* December 1973, pp. 624–635; and George H. Hines, "Sociocultural Influences in Employee Expectancy and Participative Management," *Academy of Management Journal,* June 1974, pp. 334–339. A general study of participation in the Tennessee Valley Authority is reported in Martin Patchen, *Participation, Achievement, and Involvement on the Job,* Englewood Cliffs, N.J.: Prentice-Hall, Inc., 1970. For a criticism showing that results are often small, see Charles Perrow, *Complex Organizations: A Critical Essay,* Glenview, Ill.: Scott, Foresman and Company, 1972, pp. 131–138.

13. Stanley E. Seashore and David G. Bowers, *Changing the Structure and Functioning of an Organization: Report on a Field Experiment,* Ann Arbor, Mich.: Survey Research Center, University of Michigan, 1963.

14. Stanley E. Seashore and David G. Bowers, "Durability of Organizational Change," *American Psychologist,* March 1970, pp. 227–233.

15. Henry Tosi, "A Reexamination of Personality as a Determinant of the Effects of Participation," *Personnel Psychology,* Spring 1970, pp. 91–99.

16. Edward E. Lawler III, and J. Richard Hackman, "Impact of Employee Participation in the Development of Pay Incentive Plans," *Journal of Applied Psychology,* December 1969, pp. 467–471.

17. Robert I. Dawson and Dorothy P. Carew, "Why Do Control Systems Fall Apart?" *Personnel,* May–June 1969, p. 13.

18. A discussion of consensus decision making within the management group of one organization is provided in Jack J. Holder, Jr., "Decision Making by Consensus," *Business Horizons,* April 1972, pp. 47–54.

19. Clagett G. Smith and Oguz N. Ari, "Organizational Control Structure and Member Consensus," *American Journal of Sociology,* May 1964, p. 638.

20. Martin Patchen, "Labor-Management Consultation at TVA: Its Impact on Employees," *Administrative Science Quarterly,* September 1965, pp. 149–174.

21. Charles P. McCormick, *Multiple Management,* New York: Harper & Row, Publishers, Incorporated, 1938; and K. Brantley Watson, "The Maturing of Multiple Management," *Management Review,* July 1974, pp. 4–14.

22. Milton Derber, "Worker Participation in Israeli Management," *Industrial Relations,* October 1963, pp. 51–72.

23. Wayne F. Cascio, "Functional Specialization, Culture, and Preference for Participative Management," *Personnel Psychology,* Winter 1974, pp. 593–603.

CHAPTER 10
MANAGING CHANGE

Cada hora tiene su verdad. (Translation: Each hour has its truth.)
Alejandro Casona[1]

He that complies against his will,
Is of his own opinion still.
Samuel Butler[2]

LEARNING OBJECTIVES

TO UNDERSTAND:
The nature of work change
The amount of change that exists
Resistance to change
The role of technical specialists in change
Basic frameworks for viewing the change process
The power of the group in affecting change
Ways to gain support for change

Change is a necessary way of life in most organizations. In fact, change is all around people—in the seasons, in their social environment, and in their own biological processes. Beginning with the first few moments of life, a person learns to meet change by being adaptive. A person's very first breath depends on ability to adapt from one environment to another. As indicated by the first quotation introducing this chapter, each hour is different, offering people new experiences. Since human beings are adaptive and used to change, how is it that in their work environment they tend to resist change? This question has troubled managers since the beginning of the industrial revolution. Even when managers use their most logical arguments to support a change, they frequently discover that workers are unconvinced of the need for it. Let us now examine the nature of change, resistance to it, and how to introduce it.

WORK CHANGE

THE NATURE OF WORK CHANGE. The term "work change" refers to any alteration that occurs in the overall work environment. Its effect is illustrated in an elementary way by an experiment using an air-filled balloon. When a finger (which represents change) is pressed against the exterior of the balloon (which represents the organization), the contour of the balloon visibly changes at the point of impact. Here an obvious pressure, representing change, has produced an obvious deviation at the point of pressure. What is not so obvious, however, is that the entire bal-

157

loon (the organization) has been affected and has stretched slightly. As shown by this comparison, the generalization is drawn *that the whole organization tends to be affected by change in any part of it.*

The molecules of air in the balloon represent a firm's employees. It is apparent that those at the spot of pressure must make drastic adjustment. Though the technical change has in no way made direct contact with the employees, it has affected them indirectly. Though none is fired (i.e., leaves the balloon), the employees are displaced and must adjust to a new location in the balloon. This comparison illustrates an additional generalization: *Technological change is a human problem as well as a technical problem.*

These two generalizations about change are illustrated by the reaction of workers in an electric utility which built a new power plant more automated than its other plants. The new plant was basically a technological change. It was also geographically distant from old plants and did not replace them, but workers in them were nevertheless affected. Their overtime work was reduced as the company came to depend more on its new lower-cost plant, and they developed job insecurity. In response to a survey, 87 percent of employees at the old plants felt they would have a layoff at their plant in case the company needed to reduce the work force, but only 14 percent of new-plant employees thought their plant would have a layoff. From the point of the total organization, the greater feeling of importance for new-plant workers was offset by the insecurity and lowered importance felt by workers at old plants. Thus, change in the form of a new plant affected employees in all plants; and although the change was technological, the feelings of employees were also involved.[3]

The comparison using a balloon may be carried further. Repeated pressure at a certain point may unnecessarily weaken the balloon at that point. So it is with an organization. Pressure and motion create friction and heat. Eventually a rupture occurs, causing an organizational breakdown.

Admittedly, the foregoing comparison is rough. An employing institution is not a balloon; a person is not a molecule; and people are not as free and flexible as air molecules in a balloon. What has been illustrated is a condition of molecular equilibrium. Organizations, too, tend to achieve an equilibrium in their social structure. This means that people develop an established set of relations with their environment. They learn how to deal with each other, how to perform their jobs, and what to expect next. Equilibrium exists; individuals are adjusted. When change comes along, it requires individuals to make new adjustments as the organization seeks a new equilibrium. When employees are unable to make adequate adjustments to changes that occur, the organization is then in a state of unbalance, or disequilibrium. *Management's general human objective regarding change is to restore and maintain the group equilibrium and personal adjustment that change upsets.*

ATTITUDES CONDITION RESPONSES TO CHANGE. Work change is further complicated by the fact that it does not produce a direct adjustment as in the case of air molecules, but instead it operates through each employee's attitudes to produce a response conditioned by feelings toward the change. This relationship was illustrated in a series of classic experiments by Roethlisberger and his associates. In one instance lighting was regularly improved according to the theory that better lighting would get greater productivity. As was expected, productivity did increase. Then lighting was decreased to illustrate the reverse effect—reduced productivity. Instead, productivity increased further! Lighting was again decreased. The result was still greater productivity! Finally, lighting was decreased to 0.06 of a foot-candle, which is approximately equivalent to moonlight. According to Roethlisberger, "Not until this point was reached was there any appreciable decline in the output rate."[4]

Obviously, better lighting was not by itself causing greater output. There was no direct connection between the change and the response. Some other intervening variable, later diagnosed as employee attitudes, had crept in to upset the expected pattern. Roethlisberger later illustrated the new pattern by means of the "X" Chart shown in Figure 10-1. Each change is interpreted by individuals according to their attitudes. The way that they feel about a change then determines how they will respond to it. These feelings are not the result of chance; they are caused. One cause is personal history, which refers to the biological processes of people, their backgrounds, and all their social experiences away from work. This is

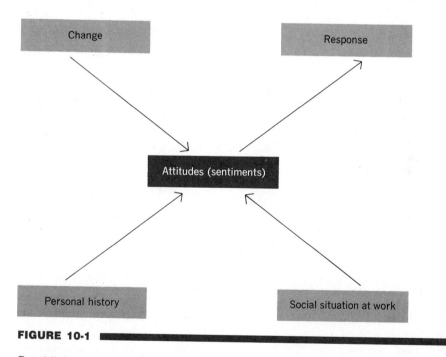

FIGURE 10-1

Roethlisberger's original "X" Chart. (From F. J. Roethlisberger, *Management and Morale*, Cambridge, Mass.: Harvard University Press, 1941, p. 21. Used with permission.)

what they bring to the workplace. A second cause is the work environment itself. It reflects the fact that workers are members of a group and are influenced by its codes, patterns, and norms.

One cause of favorable feelings in the groups studied by Roethlisberger was the interest shown by the researchers in the employees' problems. This phenomenon later was called the *Hawthorne effect,* named after the plant where the research took place. The Hawthorne effect refers to the spontaneous and unintended human effects that result from ongoing research in a group. These effects contaminate the research design, but normally they cannot be prevented.

Though people individually interpret change, they often show their attachment to the group by joining with it in some uniform response to the change, as shown in Figure 10-2. This phenomenon makes possible such seemingly illogical actions as walkouts when obviously only a few persons actually want to walk out. Other employees who are unhappy seize upon the walkout as a chance to vent their dissatisfaction and to affirm their cohesion to the group by joining with it in social action.

Since attitudes are so important in determining response to change, what are they like? In general they are slow to change, nebulous, and hidden. It is literally true that people sometimes do not know why they do or say something. They do not know their own feelings, much less someone else's. Feelings are a part of each

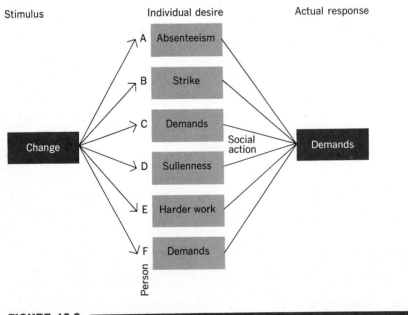

FIGURE 10-2

Different individual reactions to change are sometimes unified through social action.

individual's personal makeup and cannot be judged apart from the person who has them. People sometimes "believe" their feelings to the extent that they treat them as absolute facts and use them accordingly in making judgments. For example, an engineer who favors time study may accept the "fact" that it is desirable and think that all who oppose it either are illogical or do not understand it. The engineer is simply expressing feelings. For whom is it "desirable"? For what purpose?

Feelings are not a matter of logic. They are neither logical nor illogical, but are entirely different from logic. They are *nonlogical.* Feelings and logic are different, just as inches and pounds are different. For that reason, logic alone is an ineffective way to try to modify feelings because it does not get at them directly. Feelings are not much better refuted by logic than this book's length in inches or centimeters is refuted by its weight in pounds or kilograms!

THE SOCIAL SYSTEM AND CHANGE. As the preceding discussion illustrates, the dynamic force of change affects the whole social system. All elements of the social system are involved: its people, formal organization, informal organization, operating environment, communication patterns, decision making, and patterns of cooperation. Whether we are speaking of a department, branch plant, state government, or a whole society, the system is operating in some sort of equilibrium by which the parts are harmoniously related to each other. John Donne, the seventeenth-century English poet, beautifully stated the metaphysical aspects of this relationship as follows:

No man is an *Iland,* intire of it selfe;
every man is a peece of the *Continent,*
a part of the maine; if a *Clod* be washed away
by the *Sea,* Europe is the lesse, as well as if a
Promontorie were, as well as if a *Mannor* of thy friends
or of *thine owne* were; any mans *death* diminishes me,
because I am involved in *Mankinde:*
And therefore never send to know for whom the *bell* tolls;
It tolls for thee.[5]

In trying to maintain equilibrium, a group develops responses to return to its perceived best way of life whenever any change occurs. Each pressure, therefore, encourages a counterpressure within the group. The net result is a self-correcting mechanism by which energies are called up to restore balance whenever change threatens. This self-correcting characteristic of organizations is called *homeostasis;* that is, people act to establish a steady state of need fulfillment and to secure themselves from disturbance of that balance.

Viewed as a whole, the idea of social equilibrium implies (1) a system of interrelated parts, (2) a dynamic state of motion, rather than a static system, (3) an interdependence such that a change in one part affects all others, and (4) a homeostatic tendency to resist pressures and maintain a steady state (but not a static state). Equilibrium implies that some friction, jockeying, and trading among departments and groups is a normal condition of the organization, because its social system is in continuous motion. Social systems are never perfectly frictionless, and hence never reach an idyllic state of perfection having no conflicts or problems.

With the passage of time each social system develops programs of action that it can put into effect to accommodate change as it occurs. When a change is minor and within the scope of the correcting program, adjustment is fairly routine; but when a change is major or unusual, more serious upsets may occur.

A study of a naval research facility, for example, reported how a major change substantially disrupted that organization. The Navy revised facility objectives from "basic research" to "development." This meant that the development groups, originally established as service groups, became the primary function, while research became secondary, at least in size and emphasis. This was roughly equivalent to a change of development from staff (service) to line, concurrent with the change of research from line to staff. In this turnover, factions and conflicts arose. As the development group rose to power, a structural reorganization was accomplished to formalize their new strength. Conflict was so strong that the leaders and some members of defeated factions left the organization. Even some persons who gained increased status in the change left within the year to join organizations that promised less strain and conflict.[6]

HOW MUCH WORK CHANGE EXISTS? The tempo of technological and organizational change appears to be increasing in the United States and most of the rest of the world. There are openings and closings of plants and offices, job revisions, transfers, and promotions. Promotions, for example, are a frequent occurrence in large companies. In one giant corporation it was calculated that there was a promotion every ten working minutes. In a multiplant company the promotion of a higher manager led to the promotion of ten other people at lower levels as each moved up the line toward the top. Some of these promotions involved geographical moves to other locations, resulting in both employees and their families being uprooted and having to learn a new environment.

One study of transferred employees reports that over two-thirds of them were satisfied with their moves,[7] but problems do develop. Another study reports that 62 percent of those transferred were bothered by uncertainty about length of stay in one place.[8] They were less active in the community, made friends more slowly in their new location, and generally felt transient and temporary. Twenty-eight percent of them said they considered resigning at the time of their last transfer in order to remain in their community.

When spouses and children are considered, the results are much more negative. There is consistent evidence that they are upset and alienated by moves to new locations, especially if the moves are every two or three years.[9] The family's credentials do not transfer as easily as those of the employed person. The employee enters a community with an established position and status related to the job, but the spouse and children face a more difficult problem of having to start socially almost from the beginning. There are new schools to attend, new neighbors, and new social contacts to make. A number of spouses become bitter toward the organization that demands so much of them and their partner, and in frustration they may withdraw from the marriage partnership and from the community.

One study reported that 51 percent of wives of transferred husbands would react pessimistically if their husbands came home and announced a pending transfer. In addition, 36 percent were constantly concerned that their husbands might be asked to transfer. The result often is hesitancy to make community attachments, because 34 percent felt they had not made close friends in their new community.[10]

The issue with geographical transfers is the large social costs that result from their excessive use. For many people transfers are opportunities for growth, development, and new experiences; but when they are used excessively, dysfunctional social costs arise. People are forced to move at times when the move produces genuine hardship for them. Some would rather have the security that longtime friends and community stability provide. The basic issue is how much people shall be forced to fit the organization's needs, rather than adapting the organization to the needs of the people who work in it. A balance of interests is required so that excessive dysfunctional consequences will be avoided, while at the same time favorable consequences will be improved. If this is not done, increasing resistance to transfer will arise.

RESISTANCE TO CHANGE

SOURCES OF RESISTANCE TO CHANGE. As a result of homeostasis, social systems tend to resist change. Furthermore, individuals in the social system tend to resist many types of change because new habit patterns or sacrifices are required. This leads to the general proposition that *people and their social systems will often resist change in organizations.* This generalization applies to managers as well as employees. Though managerial culture in the United States is highly receptive to change, it is sometimes observed that the biggest barrier to introduction of change is resistance of *managers* to new methods of management. Resistance to change can be just as stubborn in a white collar as in a blue collar. It is no respecter of type of dress or job.

Although people tend to resist change, this tendency is offset by their desire for new experience and for the rewards that come with change. Not all changes are resisted. Some are wanted by employees. Other changes are so trivial and routine that resistance, if any, is too small to be evident. The lesson for management is that any change either can be successful or can develop into a behavioral problem, depending on how skillfully it is managed to minimize resistance.

Insecurity and change are an excellent illustration of the *chain-reaction phenomenon* in organizational behavior, by which a conflict with an intensity of 2x may affect others until it multiplies to an intensity of 95x or 195x. This is quite similar to an atomic chain reaction. For example, in one plant a routine dispute arose over the transfer of one man. Several of his fellow workers felt insecure about their transfer rights and supported him. Soon the department walked out, and shortly the entire factory of 4,000 persons was closed—all because of one person's transfer.

The fact that a group is intelligent does not necessarily mean that it will better understand and accept change. Often the opposite is true, because the group uses its extra intelligence to rationalize more reasons why a change should not be made. Intelligence can be used either for or against change, depending on how management motivates the group; therefore, intelligent high-level groups often cannot be sold new methods as easily as average groups can be sold.

One young executive, for example, supervised a group of unskilled laborers in a grocery warehouse. Higher management planned to install certain mechanized materials-handling equipment to reduce costs. Reasoning that his employees were of low intelligence and also somewhat ignorant of productivity and cost-cutting concepts, this executive worked hard to sell employees on the change and to involve them in it. The new system was installed with full employee cooperation. As he put it, "The change went through without a hitch."

Some years later this same executive had the job of installing a quality control system among a group of educated technical people. He reasoned that these employees were intelligent and alert and understood the company's problems; hence they could easily see reasons for the new program. They would not need the special selling effort that he had earlier applied to his warehouse laborers. This mistake in judgment cost him his job because his employees resisted the change until it was defeated, and shortly thereafter he was discharged. Though his employees had the intellectual potential to see reasons for the change, they chose not to do so.

COMPARISON OF COSTS AND BENEFITS. Opposition to change is not necessarily an undesirable human response, nor is change always a positive "good." A folklore has developed which assumes that change is always good and that the persons who introduce it—whether they are managers, specialists, or politicians—are the "good guys," while those who oppose it are the "bad guys." Experience shows that many changes introduced by managers and technical specialists (and politicians!) have been unwise changes, and people were correct in opposing those changes. Proposals for change are not inherently desirable. They require careful analysis to determine usefulness. Each change requires a detailed cost-benefit analysis. Unless changes can provide benefits above costs, there is no reason for the changes. It is illogical to emphasize benefits primarily while ignoring most of the costs, although change agents frequently take this approach. The organizational goal always is benefits greater than costs (B > C).

In determining benefits compared with costs, all types of each must be considered. It is useless to consider only economic benefits and costs, because even if there is a net economic benefit, the social or psychological costs may be too large. Although it is not very practical to reduce psychological and social costs to numbers, they must nevertheless be included in the decision-making process. Almost any change, for example, involves some psychological loss because of the strain that it imposes on people as they try to adjust.

TWO TYPES OF OPPOSITION TO CHANGE. The foregoing discussion suggests that two types of opposition to change may be distinguished. The first is *rational opposition to change* based on a reasonable analysis that determines costs greater than benefits. The second is *resistance to change,* which is based on emotionalism and selfish desires that ignore benefits to others, so it is less desirable in organizations. For example, labor union members because of vested interests may fight efforts to change a featherbedding practice that is dysfunctional to the organization and to customers. Sometimes it is difficult to distinguish between rational opposition to change and resistance to change, but usually there is strong evidence toward one or the other.

Even emotional resistance to change can have desirable consequences; so it cannot be classed wholly as a negative factor in organizations. One possible benefit is that it may cause change agents to clarify more sharply their reasons for wanting change and to define more precisely the desirable results they expect it to accomplish. They may also examine more carefully the negative side effects that accompany change in the same way that side effects accompany powerful antibiotic drugs. In some instances change agents will discover that they have an unwise plan that should be dropped. Emotional resistance may also identify pockets of low job satisfaction and poor motivation in the organization. It can pinpoint weaknesses in communication, because it frequently arises from inadequate communication about change. Finally, emotional resistance can cause change agents to give more attention to improved organizational behavior because they see that it is necessary for reducing resistance to change.

TECHNICAL SPECIALISTS AND CHANGE. Perhaps the people that have most overlooked the human and social problems of change are the technical specialists. It is normal that technical specialists have underemphasized the behavioral problems of change because their main job is some technical specialty, such as engineering, cost accounting, job analysis, or chemistry. Yet the more forward-thinking ones are deciding that, as long as specialists' work affects others, behavioral issues cannot be separated from their main job specialty. When specialists, such as industrial engineers, deal regularly with others, human skill is just as important a part of their specialty as is technical skill.

Technical specialists all too often have behavioral blind spots in dealing with people. Much of their work requires changes in the work of other persons, but they often do not recognize the social problems they cause. They are convinced that the technical part of their change is correct and, therefore, any opposition to it must come from bullheaded or ignorant people. When they talk to workers, they sometimes use jargon and theories that do not "make sense" to practical operating people. Further, they do not discuss; they tell. Convinced that their change is logical, they ignore the psychological!

The following situation is an example of the psychological myopia that technical specialists may develop. One specialist needed to make some routine studies of machine downtime in a manufacturing plant. Without explaining what his purpose was, he set up machine records to be kept by each machine operator to report the length, time of day, and cause of all machine downtime. The supervisor was told to require his employees to keep these records for thirty days. Both the supervisor and the employees stalled and complained and finally kept such inadequate records that they were not usable. The specialist concluded that the department was full of obstructionists who did not have the organization's interests at heart.

Closer examination revealed some human aspects of this routine technical requirement. Keeping records was more work for the employees, and some of them were not oriented toward paperwork. The machine work required them to have dirty hands, but they felt obligated to try to keep the downtime records clean. They also felt that the records pried into their activities, because some downtime was for personal reasons. They saw no direct benefit from the study, and some of them feared it would bring changes that would reduce their incentive earnings.

The supervisor likewise saw no direct benefit coming to him or his department from the study. He feared unknown changes in his department; and he disliked the chore of enforcing the record system, especially since his employees resented it. The result was that the supervisor and employees complained to the specialist and to one another. Soon everyone was obstructing rather than cooperating, and the specialist was wondering why there was so much commotion about "this little piece of paperwork." He was sure that a company with so many obstructionists would never be efficient. However—and here is a key point—one of the reasons the company had so many obstructionists was that it had technical specialists who did not understand human behavior and the social system at work. They were a cause of the problem, rather than a victim of it.

Though specialists are eager to propose changes in other departments, they often develop normal resistance when change applies to their own work. In research organizations the term "NIH," meaning "not invented here," has developed to refer to resistance that specialists have to ideas not originating within their own group or department. Since they did not develop the idea, they have difficulty giving it full emotional support. For example, the scientists in one product-development department rejected a sound design improvement suggested by a supervisor because they wanted to maintain their own image as the originators of ideas in this area. In another organization, a technically trained manager of a research department encountered the NIH factor so many times that she was moved to comment, "In all my research the most inert material I have observed is the human mind, with one exception—a *group* of human minds."

INTRODUCING CHANGE SUCCESSFULLY

Since management initiates most change, it has primary responsibility for handling it in such a way that there will be satisfactory adjustment. Though management is typically the change agent, the changees (employees) control the final decision to accept it, and they are the ones who actually make the changes. Under these conditions employee support becomes essential.

A FRAMEWORK FOR VIEWING THE CHANGE PROCESS. The state of equilibrium that exists in a group at any time is a dynamic balance of forces supporting and restraining change, as shown in Figure 10-3. The group operates within a field of forces both for and against a particular practice. There are, for example, pressures for and against high productivity that cause a particular norm of production within the group.

Administrators introduce change within a group by influencing either restraining forces or supporting forces, or both. These forces may be influenced in terms of their number and/or their strength. For example, increasing the number of inspections should be a supporting force for higher quality work, and increasing the strength of employee pride in work also should be a supporting force. A reduction of restraining forces in the same situation would be improved maintenance of machines so that better work could be done on them.

THREE DIMENSIONS OF CHANGE. Change has three dimensions, and administrators need to relate to employees in terms of each of these. There is the *logical* dimension based on the technical evidence of economics and science. This evidence needs to be presented to employees so that they can understand the technical and economic reasons for change. But there is also another dimension important to employees. That is the *psychological* dimension, meaning that the change is "logical" in terms of the human values and feelings in the situation.

A further dimension is the *sociological* one, meaning that the change is "logical" from the point of view of social values. Is the change consistent with norms of the group? Does it maintain group teamwork? These are the kinds of questions employees will have in their minds, and administrators need to show that change is favorable to these matters if they intend to deal successfully with the sociological dimension. Clearly all three dimensions must be effectively treated if employees

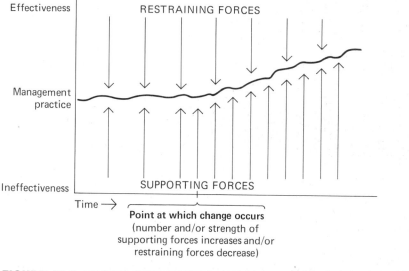

FIGURE 10-3

To produce change, supporting and/or restraining forces must be altered.

167

are to accept change enthusiastically. If administrators work with only the technical, logical dimension of change, they have failed in their human responsibilities.

It is recognized that in a typical operating group, full support cannot be gained for every change that is made. Some moderate support, weak support, and even opposition can be expected for various changes over a period of time. People are significantly different and cannot be expected to give identical support to each operating decision. What management seeks is a climate in which people feel that they can support most changes and therefore feel secure enough to tolerate other changes that they do not strongly support. When management cannot win support for change by any other method, it depends on formal authority to achieve change. It recognizes that authority sparingly used is a desirable way to get uniform progress toward goals; but if all actions depend on authority without any employee support, the authority will eventually become worthless.

ORGANIZATIONAL CHANGE FOCUSES ON THE GROUP. Most organizational change focuses on the group. Usually more than one person is involved, but more important is the fact that the group is an instrument for bringing strong forces on its members to change. A person's behavior is firmly grounded in the groups to which one belongs; hence a change in group forces will encourage a change in one's behavior. In this procedure the group is a *medium* for introducing change as well as the *target* of the proposed change. On occasion, the group also has a third function—*change agent*. That is, management goes beyond encouraging employees to "accept" change; it stimulates them to join in producing change. They recognize the need for it and initiate action toward management to formalize the desired change. When this kind of climate is built, the employees are true partners with management in seeking desired organizational change.

The power of a group to induce change in its members depends partly upon the strength of their attachment to it. The more attractive the group is to each member, the greater its influence can be for that person. Influence is further increased if members with top prestige in the group support the change.

Change should not disrupt the social system any more than is necessary. The social system is the hard core of opposition to change; and the unfortunate fact is that much of this disruption is unnecessary and not required by the change. It could be avoided if the persons making changes understood and considered the social relations of the work group. They need to recognize that any changes that require persons to deviate from the standards of their group will meet with resistance.

The ideal way to achieve planned change in organizations is to alter each person's entire role set to support a change. If an administrator works to change an employee alone, the employee is merely placed into role conflict because peers, service people, and others retain the same role expectations of the employee. A job change is fully supported only when the job's entire role set is revised to support the change.[11]

GAINING SUPPORT FOR CHANGE. Participation, discussed in an earlier chapter, is perhaps the best way to develop support for change, but there are many other ways. One of these is to establish various controls and pledges to protect employees from economic loss from change. Workers need to feel that they, personally, will not suffer. Some employers guarantee workers against reduced earnings from new machines or processes. Others offer retraining at employer expense or retard installation of laborsaving machinery until normal labor turnover can absorb displaced workers. Seniority rights, opportunities for advancement, and other benefits enjoyed by each worker are safeguarded when a change is made. Grievance systems give the employee a feeling of security that benefits will be protected and differences about them fairly resolved. All these practices help employees to feel economically secure in the presence of change.

Another approach is to permit workers to share in benefits that result from change. This approach uses positive motivation to counteract negative resistance. Profit-sharing and production-sharing plans are examples. Methods specialists are learning to use every opportunity to make the job easier and less exerting. Along with their methods changes they attempt to install employee comforts and conveniences, thereby showing that they are interested in the whole job situation, including the worker.

It is desirable for a change to pay off as directly and as soon as possible. From an employee's point of view, what's good in general is not necessarily good for the employee, and what's good for the long run may not be good for the short run. The changee's perception will be different from that of the change agent. This self-evident fact is all too often ignored by those who introduce change.

Management also increases support for change by preventing trivial and unnecessary change. It attempts to temper the specialist's eagerness to introduce change. Individuals can tolerate only so much change, and if they are bombarded with irritating small changes, they will be less apt to accept major changes. Management tries to maintain a neat balance between excessive change, resulting in an unstable organization, and negligible change which results in a static organization that is a poor competitor and no challenge to its employees.

Communication is essential in improving support for change. Even though a change will affect only one or two in a work group of ten persons, all of them need to know about the change in order to feel secure and maintain group cooperation. Management often does not realize that *activities that help get change accepted, such as communication, are usually themselves disrupted by change.* In other words, certain stabilizing social processes are weakest at the time they are needed most; therefore, management needs to make special effort to maintain them in times of change.

One retail establishment learned the hard way about the importance of maintaining communication during a change. Central management decided to change from manual to computer credit records in two branch offices. This was a technical decision in which the credit clerks did not participate. In the Oakhurst Branch the plan was to transfer and lay off twenty-three employees and retain five. In the Bay City Branch twenty-five were to be transferred or laid off and seven retained. In both branches most employees had an opportunity to transfer to other work, but major retraining was required in some cases. All employees who were to remain in the credit records activity would require substantial retraining.

The manager of the Oakhurst Branch informed all her employees about the

169

impending change, even those employees in other departments not affected by the change. As the change progressed, she continued to inform her employees and discuss operating details with them. The Bay City manager took a contrasting approach. She decided not to tell her employees about the change until the week of the changeover, because she did not want to upset them. She made elaborate precautions to keep information about the change tightly confined within the management group. When employees officially learned of the change, they were visibly upset.

Three months after the changeover management made an inspection of its success. In the Oakhurst Branch the change was progressing smoothly and most displaced employees had been transferred and retrained. In contrast, the Bay City Branch was in turmoil. Many displaced employees were so shocked or disillusioned that they had resigned. The employees retained in the credit activity were having difficulty adjusting, and billings were late. Cooperation had declined. Job satisfaction was low. The situation definitely had caused depreciation of the organization's human resources.

LEARNING DIFFICULTIES WITH CHANGE. Change requires *unlearning* old habits as well as learning new ones, and the unlearning may be really more difficult than the new learning. In the theory of change this process consists of *unfreezing, changing,* and *refreezing,* meaning that an employee unlearns old attitudes and practices, learns new ones, and then integrates them into habitual practice. Unless all three parts of the process are accomplished, employees may continue some of their old practices in a strange mixture with the newer practices so that little net benefit is accomplished from the change.

Organizations also have a learning problem with change. This is illustrated in Figure 10-4, which shows a learning curve for a cost-saving change. As shown in the chart, there are so many dislocations connected with change that immediately following its introduction the situation often becomes worse rather than better. Procedures are upset, employees have difficulty mastering the new skills, job satisfaction declines, and so on. The result is that whatever measure of performance is used, the situation often looks worse immediately after a change. During this transition period the change is particularly vulnerable to criticism and even failure, because it appears not to be working. Only after the passage of time, when teamwork and coordination are restored, is the change likely to produce the favorable results intended.

LEADERSHIP FOR CHANGE. Capable leadership reinforces a climate of psychological support for change. The leader presents change on the basis of the impersonal requirements of the situation, rather than on personal grounds. Leaders are asking for trouble when they introduce change with a comment such as "I have always felt you should not be able to leave the department during rest periods, and beginning tomorrow it will not be permitted." The natural responses are "It's not the supervisor's business where we go" and "Let's get together and figure out a way to beat the supervisor." Surely there must be some rational, impersonal reasons for the change, and, if so, they should be used. If not, maybe the intended change needs to be abandoned. Ordinary requests for change should be according to the objectives and rules of the organization. Only a strong personal leader can use personal reasons for change without arousing resistance.

Leaders have learned that when they have a new idea that may work, the idea is often better presented with the comment "Let's try this and see how it works," rather than saying, "Do this." People are more willing to accept an idea for trial, because it gives them a part in proving the idea's effectiveness. If there is an improvement, those affected are likely to be pleased. If the idea does not work, it can be dropped without either party "losing face." Of course, many problems must be decided officially without trial or experiment, but there are always cases where trial runs are helpful.

Change is more likely to be successful if the leaders introducing it have high expectations of success. In other words, expectations of change may be as important as the technology of change, as suggested earlier in this chapter by Roethlisberger's "X" Chart. For example, a manufacturer of clothing patterns had four almost identical plants. When a job enrichment and rotation program was introduced, managers in two of the plants were given inputs predicting that the program would increase productivity. Managers of the other two plants were told that the program would improve employee relations but not productivity.

During the next twelve months productivity did increase significantly in the two plants where the managers were expecting it. In the two plants where the managers were not expecting it, it did not increase. The results showed that high leader expectations were the key factor in making the change successful.[12]

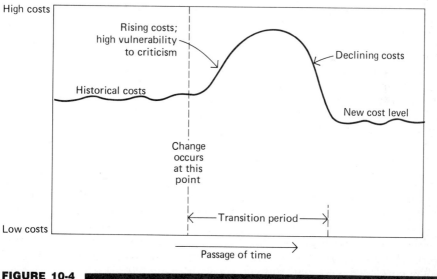

FIGURE 10-4

Typical organizational learning curve for a cost-saving change. (A similar curve applies to most other types of change.)

UNION RESPONSE TO MANAGEMENT CHANGE. Management in the performance of its function is primarily an instigator of change. The union, on the other hand, serves more as a restraint on management and a protector of security for its members; therefore it is frequently cast in the role of forestaller of change. These functional differences between management and unions tend to cause union-management conflict about change, but there are many exceptions. Unions sometimes support management in encouraging workers to accept change. Most unions as a matter of policy favor improvement through technological change and will approve a particular change that is carefully planned to protect member interests. Union approval does not ensure that there will be no opposition, because insecure workers sometimes resist changes even when their union pressures them not to do so.

There are historical reasons for union and worker opposition to change; so the management that improves its handling of change should not expect immediate improvement in union and worker responses. Workers have seen industries close and employees laid off because technological change made their work unnecessary. Sailmakers, glassblowers, and vacuum-tube specialists have seen declines in opportunity that required sacrifices on their part to learn new skills. But technological and social change will not be stopped. People in any industrial society cannot complacently expect serene conditions of work, but management in business and government can introduce change in such a way that employees at all levels will more easily assimilate it. Opposition can be decreased to the degree that employees can be helped to recognize the need for each change, to participate in it, and to gain from it. In summary, management's responsibility for change is fourfold:

1. Make only useful, necessary change. Change by evolution, not revolution.

2. Recognize the possible effects of change and introduce it with adequate attention to human needs.

3. Share the benefits of change with employees.

4. Diagnose the problems remaining after a change occurs and treat them.

Change when improperly handled manifests itself in slowdowns and showdowns.

SUMMARY

The work environment is quite dynamic. This disturbs social equilibrium and forces employees regularly to make adjustments. Response of employees to change depends on their attitudes, as shown by Roethlisberger's "X" Chart. This means that people react emotionally to change and are often not particularly influenced by the cold, hard logic for change. Though people react individually and differently to change, they sometimes unite through social action to make a uniform response, such as a slowdown or walkout.

Employees tend to resist change because it upsets their patterns of adjustment and threatens their security. Management overcomes resistance by altering the supporting and restraining forces affecting behavior. It also deals with the logical, psychological, and sociological dimensions of change. It uses group forces to support change. Management's behavioral objective regarding change is to restore and maintain the group equilibrium and personal adjustment that change upsets. A number of ways were discussed by which management discharges these responsibilities. Another major way of dealing with change, called organizational development, is discussed in the next chapter.

TERMS AND CONCEPTS FOR REVIEW

Roethlisberger's "X" Chart	Resistance to change
Hawthorne effect	Supporting and restraining forces
Homeostasis	Unfreezing and refreezing
Chain-reaction phenomenon	Learning curve for change

REVIEW QUESTIONS

1. Discuss how change affects an organization. How does it affect individual employees?
2. What is the meaning of homeostasis?
3. How may resistance to change have desirable consequences in an organization?
4. Discuss how equilibrium is maintained by a field of forces.
5. Discuss the meaning and usefulness of the organizational learning curve for change.

CASES

THE NEW SALES PROCEDURES

The Marin Company had more than 100 field sales representatives who sold a line of complex industrial products. Sales of these products required close work with buyers to determine their product needs; so nearly all sales representatives were college graduates in engineering and science. Other product lines of Marin Company, such as consumer products, were sold by a separate sales group.

Recently the firm established a new companywide control and report system using a larger computer. This system has doubled the amount of time the industrial field sales representatives spend filling out forms and supplying information that can be fed into the computer. They estimate that they now spend as much as two hours daily processing records, and they have started complaining that they have less time for sales effort. A field sales manager commented, "Morale has declined as a result of these new controls and reports. Sales is a rewarding, gratifying profession that is based on individual effort. Sales representatives are happy when they are making sales, since this directly affects their income and self-recognition. The more time they spend with reports, the less time they have to make sales. As a result they can see their income and recognition declining, and thus they find themselves resisting changes."

QUESTIONS
1. Comment on the sales manager's analysis.
2. What alternative approaches to this situation do you recommend? Give reasons.

THE INDUSTRIAL ENGINEERING CHANGE

An industrial engineer was assigned to an electronic assembly department to make some methods improvements. In one assembly operation he soon recognized that a new fixture might reduce labor costs by about 30 percent. He discussed the situation with the group leader and then the supervisor. The group leader was indifferent, but the supervisor was interested and offered additional suggestions.

Feeling that he had approval of the supervisor, the industrial engineer had the fixture made. With permission of the supervisor, he assigned a woman assembler to try the fixture. She was cooperative and enthusiastic and on the first day exceeded the expected improvement of 30 percent. When the group leader was shown the results at the end of the day, he claimed that this was one of the fastest workers in the department and that her results could not be generalized for the whole department.

The next day the industrial engineer asked the supervisor for another operator to help prove the fixture. At this point the supervisor noted that the fixture did not include her ideas fully. The industrial engineer explained that he had misunderstood but that he would include the other suggestions in the next fixture built. The supervisor, however, continued to be negative about the fixture.

When the industrial engineer attempted to instruct the second woman the way he had instructed the first one, her reaction was negative. In fact, when he stopped instructing her, it seemed that the woman deliberately stalled as she used the fixture. She also made some negative comments about the fixture and asked the industrial engineer if he felt he deserved his paycheck for this kind of effort. At the end of the day this woman's production was 10 percent below normal production by the old method.

QUESTION
1. Analyze the causes of this problem and recommend the course of action the industrial engineer should take. Role-play a meeting of the industrial engineer and the supervisor.

REFERENCES

1. Alejandro Casona, *La Dama del Alba*, edited by Juan Rodriquez-Castellano, New York: Charles Scribner's Sons, 1947, p. 93.

2. Samuel Butler, *Hudibras,* III, 1678.

3. Floyd C. Mann and L. Richard Hoffman, *Automation and the Worker,* New York: Holt, Rinehart and Winston, Inc., 1960, pp. 52–55.

4. F. J. Roethlisberger, *Management and Morale,* Cambridge, Mass.: Harvard University Press, 1941, p. 10. See also F. J. Roethlisberger and William J. Dickson, *Management and the Worker,* Cambridge, Mass.: Harvard University Press, 1939.

5. John Donne (1572–1631), *The Complete Poetry and Selected Prose of John Donne and the Complete Poetry of William Blake,* New York: Random House, Inc., 1941, p. 332. Italics in original.

6. Paula Brown and Clovis Shepherd, "Factionalism and Organizational Change in a Research Laboratory," *Social Problems,* April 1956, pp. 235–243.

7. William F. Glueck, "Managers, Mobility, and Morale," *Business Horizons,* December 1974, pp. 65–70.

8. Ronald J. Burke, "Quality of Organizational Life: The Effects of Personnel Job Transfers," in Vance F. Mitchell and others (eds.), *Proceedings of the Academy of Management, 1972,* Vancouver, B.C., Canada: University of British Columbia, 1973, pp. 242–245.

9. Robert Seidenberg, *Corporate Wives–Corporate Casualties?,* New York: Amacom, 1973; Jerome Steiner, "What Price Success?" *Harvard Business Review,* March–April 1972, pp. 69–74; and Lionel Tiger, "Is This Trip Necessary?: The Heavy Human Costs of Moving Executives Around," *Fortune,* September 1974, pp. 139ff. There is a correlation between the amount of change experienced and the incidence of physical illness; see Thomas H. Holmes and Minoru Masuda, "Psychosomatic Syndrome," *Psychology Today,* April 1972, pp. 71–72, 106.

10. Burke, *op. cit.,* pp. 242–245.

11. Robert L. Kahn and others, *Organizational Stress: Studies in Role Conflict and Ambiguity,* New York: John Wiley & Sons, Inc., 1964, pp. 396–397.

12. Albert S. King, "Expectation Effects in Organizational Change," *Administrative Science Quarterly,* June 1974, pp. 221–230.

CHAPTER 11
ORGANIZATIONAL DEVELOPMENT AND TRAINING

. . . A comprehensive O.D. effort constitutes the creation of a substantially new force field in the organization. . . .

Richard J. Selfridge and Stanley L. Sokolik[1]

LEARNING OBJECTIVES

TO UNDERSTAND:
The meaning of OD
What its characteristics are
The process by which it operates
Training methods used in OD
The usefulness of sensitivity training
Frameworks used in OD programs
The role of conventional training methods

In a large manufacturing plant, management decided on an organizational development program for its entire production group. This group had been having problems with quality and teamwork. The program consisted of six phases covering a period of fifteen months. At the end of the program the quality index had improved from an index of 71 to 92 for the day shift and 69 to 92 for the night shift. This was a significant improvement.[2] In a small manufacturing plant producing mirrors, an organizational development program was applied over a period of several years. During an eight-year period the production per unit of direct labor rose from an index of 100 to 149. About one-half of the gain was attributed to the organizational development program.[3] Improvements in the amounts just mentioned merit attention, because they bring benefits to society. Customers benefit from a better quality product having lower costs. Workers benefit from a more effective organizational climate, and the organization benefits because of its increased effectiveness.

In this chapter we discuss the concept of organizational development, how it works, possible benefits and problems, different types of programs, and also the effectiveness of more conventional types of training in organizational behavior.

UNDERSTANDING ORGANIZATIONAL DEVELOPMENT

In the 1960s a new, integrated type of training originated known as *organizational development* (OD). Organizational development is an intervention strategy that uses group processes to focus on the whole culture of an organization in order to bring about planned change. It seeks to change beliefs, attitudes, values, structures, and practices—in fact, the entire culture of the organization—so that the organization can better adapt to technology and live with the fast pace of change.

The origins of OD relate primarily to three causes. First is the fact that the reward structure on the job did not adequately reinforce training, so there was excessive loss of training momentum in the transition from a classroom to a work situation. Too many well-designed training and development programs substantially failed because the environment in the organization did not support the training. Under these conditions the reasonable next step is to try to change the entire organization so that it will support the training that is provided. This is exactly what OD tries to do.

A second reason is the fast pace of change itself, which requires that organizations be extremely effective in order to survive and prosper. OD attempts to develop the whole organization so that it can respond to change more uniformly and capably. It tries to "free up" communication by increasing the amount and candor of communication. It seeks to build problem-solving capability by improving group dynamics and problem confrontation. In short, it reaches into all aspects of organizational culture in order to make it more humanly responsive.

A third reason is the desire for more experiential learning processes in employee training, meaning that the trainees learn by actually experiencing in the training environment the kinds of behavioral problems they face on the job. Then they can discuss and analyze their own immediate experience, learning from it. This approach is shown to be superior to traditional lecture and discussion approaches in which people talk about abstract behavioral concepts.[4] Theory Y, Maslow's hierarchy, and other ideas are useful, but how does one apply them in a real situation? OD helps provide some of the answers. Participants work on real problems in real situations, and the experience helps to solidify, or refreeze, their new learning.

CHARACTERISTICS OF OD. OD may be understood in terms of a number of characteristics implied in its definition. One important characteristic is that OD focuses on a *whole organization* or major unit of it so that the environment around employees will tend to reinforce any learning that occurs in the program. More traditional training tends to focus on a certain job or small work group. An additional characteristic is that OD is *systems-oriented,* being concerned with interactions of various parts of the organization as they affect each other. It is concerned with intergroup relationships as well as interpersonal ones. It is concerned with structure and process as well as attitudes. The basic issue to which it is directed is: How do all these parts work together?

Another characteristic of OD is that it is *action research.* It works with ongoing conditions, not artificial ones. Action research is such a key characteristic that OD is sometimes defined as organizational improvement through action research. A related characteristic is that OD is *problem solving.* It seeks to solve problems, rather than to discuss them theoretically as in a classroom. These problems are happening at the time to the participants involved, so they are real, worthwhile, and interesting.

An important behavioral characteristic of OD is that it uses *group processes.* There are group discussion, intergroup conflict, confrontation, and team building. There is an effort to improve interpersonal relations, open communication channels, build trust, and encourage responsiveness to others. Another characteristic of OD is that it relies heavily on *feedback* to participants so that they will have concrete data on which to make decisions.

An example is a feedback exercise in one OD program. Participants were separated into two groups representing two different functions in the organization. Both groups were asked to develop answers to the following questions:

What characteristics best describe our group?

What characteristics best describe the other group?

How will the other group describe us?

After the separate groups had prepared their answers, they assembled and presented their answers to the other group. Here was concrete feedback about impressions each group had of the other, and there were major misunderstandings. In this presentation no arguments were allowed. Questions were accepted only to clarify what the other group was saying.
The groups again were separated to discuss two other questions:

How did these misunderstandings occur?

What can we do to correct them?

Based on this new feedback, the groups met together to develop specific plans of action for solving their misunderstandings. In each instance feedback about themselves was the basis for their activities.

The foregoing example illustrates another characteristic of OD. It provides *experiential learning.* As discussed earlier, there was a need for more experiential learning to help refreeze new behavior patterns, and OD tries to provide it. People experience behavioral concepts instead of having an expert present them. A further characteristic of OD is that it is situational and *contingency-oriented.* Traditional training efforts historically tended to point to a one best way, but OD is more flexible and pragmatic, adapting actions to fit particular needs.
A final characteristic of OD is that normally it uses a *change agent,* or consultant, for the participating group. Change agents are process consultants rather than expert consultants, meaning that their role is to guide groups toward more effective group processes. They help groups solve their own problems through their own internal processes, rather than playing the role of expert and telling them what to do.
In summary, by focusing on the whole rather than the parts, OD seeks to integrate the four elements of people, structure, technology, and social system into an effective unit, as discussed in Chapter 1. The result is improvement in organizational performance.

A criminal justice agency for a population area of 170,000 persons was in difficulty. There was conflict between staff and law enforcement personnel, poor community relations, arbitrary decision making, and high employee turnover. An OD program was developed to help the group achieve better teamwork. Definite improvements followed. Employee relations improved, and turnover declined from about 50 percent annually to less than 20 percent. Jail escapes declined from nine the first year to seven the next year, and then only one the following year.[5]

THE OD PROCESS. OD is a complicated process that tends to take a year or more in an organization and may continue indefinitely.[6] For a program of this magnitude top management support is essential. There are many different approaches to OD, but a typical complete program would include most of the following steps.

1. *Initial diagnosis:* Top management meets with the consultant to determine the type of OD program that is needed. The consultant could be either an external one or an internal service person skilled in OD. During this phase the consultant may seek inputs by means of interviews with various persons in the organization.

2. *Data collection:* Surveys may be made to determine organizational climate and behavioral problems in an organization. The consultant usually meets with groups away from the workplace to develop information from questions such as these:

What kinds of conditions contribute most to your job effectiveness?

What kinds of conditions interfere with your job effectiveness?

What would you most like to change in the way this organization functions?

3. *Data feedback and confrontation:* Work groups are assigned to review the data collected, to mediate among themselves areas of disagreement, and to establish priorities for change.

4. *Action planning and problem solving:* Groups use the data to develop specific recommendations for change. Discussion focuses on real problems in their organization. Plans are specific, including who is responsible and when the action should be completed.

5. *Team building:* During the entire period of the group meetings the consultant has been encouraging the groups to examine how they work together as groups. The consultant helps them see the value of open communication and trust as prerequisites for improved group functioning. Team building is further encouraged by meetings of the natural group of manager and immediate subordinates so that they can practice improved functioning with the guidance of the consultant.

6. *Intergroup development:* Following the development of natural teams, there may be development among larger groups comprising several teams.

7. *Appraisal and follow-up:* The consultant helps the organization appraise the results of its OD efforts and develop additional programs in areas where additional

results are needed. As an example of follow-up in one organization, the consultant asked managers to provide tapes of committee meetings that they chaired subsequent to the program. The consultant analyzed these tapes and used them to discuss with managers how well each was applying what was learned in the OD program.

The process just discussed obviously will vary with the type of organization and the culture of the society in which it is being applied. For example, in Europe trade unions are more political, and workers often are on managing boards. There is also more industry-government interaction. In this kind of environment the application of OD is more concerned with power and political implications of the action plans.[7]

When the OD process is well applied, it has potential for substantial results.

One successful program is that at Corning Glass Corporation.[8] Following OD in the glass shop, there was a productivity increase of 20 percent, and in the instrument department the increase was 17 percent. Two other gains were even more impressive in the instrument department. The quality increase was about 50 percent, and absenteeism was reduced 50 percent. While not all the improvement may be the result of OD, at least a substantial part of it appeared to be.

TRAINING METHODS USED IN OD. OD programs use conventional training methods, such as discussion, films, and presentations; however, the approach emphasized in OD is *laboratory training.* Laboratory training is the basis for experiential learning. It provides situations in which the trainees themselves experience through their own interactions some of the conditions they are talking about. In this way they more or less experiment on themselves. Causing trainees to experience certain human relationships under laboratory conditions tends to have a greater impact on them than conventional training methods. The following laboratory methods will be discussed: role playing, gaming, and sensitivity training.

ROLE PLAYING. Role playing is a laboratory method that can be used rather easily as a supplement to conventional training methods, as well as in OD. It is spontaneous acting of a realistic situation involving two or more persons under classroom conditions. Dialogue spontaneously grows out of the situation as it is developed by the trainees assigned to it. Other trainees in the group serve as observers and critics. Role playing is often considered a substitute for experience. In a sense it is more than experience because it permits techniques of observation, discussion, and emphasis that are not customarily a part of experience.

Since people take roles every day, they are somewhat experienced in the art, and with a certain amount of imagination they can project themselves into roles other than their own. This idea is not new, because dramatics is as old as recorded history. In role playing trainees can broaden their experience by trying different approaches, while in actual situations they often have only one chance. Persons may in two hours in a role-playing group observe as many different approaches to a problem as they would in two years of normal experience. By evaluating these different ways of handling the same situation, they are able to see the strengths and weaknesses of each approach.

Sometimes the participants play roles without knowing it.

One day in a training course a substitute leader is introduced. He is nervous, is ill-prepared, and cannot get going. There are agonizing pauses. He fumbles endlessly with notes. To increase pressure it is noted that one or two top-management persons are present as observers. Members of the group try desperately to fill the leaderless vacuum. Suddenly, as if gaining courage, the leader starts telling everyone what to do, using the "I-want" approach. He has the conferees perform useless work and even has one of them get him a drink, which he nonchalantly enjoys in front of them. When the conferees reach the limit of their patience, he announces that this was all in fun! He was merely illustrating free-rein and autocratic management so that they could actually experience the employee role in each. He then invites discussion of their experiences, and this discussion itself illustrates participative management; so in one session they have experienced the employee role under three management styles. This is more than demonstration because the conferees are unknowingly role-involved.

Role playing also has weaknesses that partly offset its values. It is time-consuming and expensive. It requires experienced trainers because it can easily turn sour without effective direction. The trainees may resent it as a childish approach to serious problems unless it is introduced carefully. Some trainees are embarrassed and hesitate to take part. Conversely, other trainees may place more emphasis on acting and showing off than on the problems involved.

GAMING. While gaming is not used extensively in OD, it does have some application. In one instance a group of managers played a decision game in the fifth day of their OD program, and in the first quarter of the game they failed to apply many of the ideas they had learned. When this fact was pointed out to them, they overcompensated in the second quarter of the game, becoming so conscious of interpersonal factors that they were ineffective. After this fact was brought to their attention, they were able to stabilize in the second half of the game and apply some of their newly learned ideas.[9]

Gaming is a laboratory method in which role playing exists, but its difference is that it focuses on administrative problems, while role playing tends to emphasize mostly feeling and tone between people in interaction. Gaming, therefore, provides a better balance of both rational and emotional issues. It is more like a real job.

Gaming arose primarily to use the computer's enormous capacity for processing data for decisions, but some games have been created that are workable without computers. Gaming is essentially a group exercise in sequential decision making under simulated organizational conditions. There are many variations, but the participants usually work in small groups, each group being in competition with the others. Groups make decisions within a system model that has been created for them and is at least partly unknown to them. Decisions are processed through the computer according to the model, resulting in a feedback to guide subsequent decisions. Usually, but not always, time is compressed; that is, a quarter year for marketing may be covered in an hour.

Games and simulation exercises were originally developed for aspects of business and military training, such as inventory control, marketing action, and air defense; however, they soon showed potential for training in organizational behavior, because participants were working in teams in various types of environments. Under these conditions a game can show how leadership evolves, what kinds of communication are effective, the disastrous market results of internal group conflict, human factors influencing decisions, and the effect of success upon group cohesion. Different organizational systems can be tried to see how each affects the people involved. The fact that time can be compressed makes it possible for much "experience" with different practices to be gained in a short time. The learning process can be hastened through feedback and discussion with a trainer after each decision unit.

Perhaps more realistically than other training methods, games show the effect of stress on participants as they undergo the pressure of time and competition. Members become so intensely involved that they let their guard down and react to stress in their normal pattern. On the other hand, it is possible that there is such deep involvement that the participant "takes it for real" and is not receptive to the feedback and criticism necessary in a learning situation. In the heat of competition the learning atmosphere is lost.

A variation of gaming is the in-basket technique in which trainees respond to a manager's incoming communications on a typical day. In this way they deal with problems as a real manager receives them. Usually one trainee plays the role of manager, and other trainees play roles of people mentioned in the in-basket. Some trainees may play surprise roles that interrupt the manager and present two or more simultaneous problems more like real on-the-job pressures.

SENSITIVITY TRAINING. Sensitivity training is the most controversial laboratory training method. Some former participants denounce it, while others strongly support it. Sensitivity training is a frustrating, challenging type of training that has grown from the work of specialists in group dynamics and nondirective counseling, both of which are discussed in later chapters. In contrast to role playing and gaming, which are pleasant ways of training, sensitivity training frequently is not pleasant to its participants, at least until they are far along in their training. They report that sometimes they are tense, angry, frustrated, uncomfortable, or confused. They have called it a bloodbath and a psychological nudist colony in which people are stripped bare to their attitudes.

Basically, sensitivity training is small-group interaction under stress in an unstructured encounter group that requires people to become sensitive to one another's feelings in order to develop reasonable group activity. It has been given most emphasis by the National Training Laboratories at Bethel, Maine. The training groups themselves are called "T-groups" or encounter groups.

There is no role playing in sensitivity training because participants are acting their own true roles. They are themselves; however, their environment is so artificial that they find their ordinary social patterns are no longer workable. In this environment they are encouraged to examine their own self-concepts and to become more receptive to what others say and feel. In addition, they begin to perceive how a group interacts, recognize how culture affects it, and develop skills in working with others. In summary, therefore, the goals of sensitivity training are understanding of self, understanding of others, insight into group process, understanding the influence of culture, and developing behavioral skills.

Although there are many variations of sensitivity training, there are certain essential elements for effectiveness. It is process-oriented rather than content-oriented; that is, people learn by doing and feeling rather than by being told. The group is at least partly unstructured so that responsibility is placed on members for developing group process. Some frustration is essential to accomplish the deep examination of self that is required, and it is necessary for the group to be small so that there can be a high level of participation. Finally, there is an attempt to develop a very permissive atmosphere so that members feel free to talk even if they think they will appear impolite, selfish, or ridiculous.

Following are examples of problems that may arise in a training class. One member is upset because his ideas have been ignored for five successive meetings. Another member takes the initiative, becomes authoritarian, and fails because she inspires group resentment. Another's superior attitude is uncovered as being defensiveness about his weaknesses. In all this turmoil the trainer tries to remain relatively detached, keep some stability, create learning situations, and occasionally introduce ideas.

CRITICISMS OF SENSITIVITY TRAINING. Criticisms of sensitivity training revolve around several issues. The principal problem is the casualty rate, meaning those who are psychologically harmed by the experience. Sensitivity training is not an appropriate method for trainees who are neurotic and cannot withstand stress.

One research study of encounter groups and sensitivity training reported a casualty rate of about 10 percent. Casualties were defined as those who showed evidence of serious psychological harm six to eight months after the groups ended, and this harm could reasonably be attributed to the group experience.[10] *In addition, another 8 percent made negative emotional changes, while 32 percent made positive changes. The casualty rate and negative changes show that sensitivity training is a high-risk training method that organizations should use with great caution.*

The study was made in educational encounter groups, rather than organizational ones. In OD programs, encounter group experiences may be less stressful because they are connected with other problem-solving activities. Nevertheless, the high casualty potential does raise questions about whether sensitivity training in its stressful forms should be used in OD programs.

Sensitivity training also raises questions of invasion of privacy if employees are required to attend and bare their emotions unwillingly. There is a fine line between voluntary choice and coercive pressure. If sensitivity training becomes the route to special status and favors in an organization, and if people who lack it are bypassed for promotion, then they are being coerced to submit to what they perceive is an invasion of privacy.

Other trainees claim that trainers act as manipulative social engineers who autocratically impose democratic values on stripped-bare groups and try to indoctrinate them with the dogmatism of group action. Trainees point to the implicit assumption of consensus that is often imposed on T-groups. A group in which the parties understand one another and still disagree is implicitly considered a failure. However, does not this assumption lead to hypocrisy in people, because they will say they agree in order to support group process, but they really do not agree? Isn't it also unrealistic for dynamic organizational life, because real people hold different values?

A variation on sensitivity training is human potential training, pioneered by the Esalen Institute in California.[11] Human potential training has objectives and encounter groups similar to sensitivity training; however, the technique of physical encounter is emphasized along with verbal encounter. There is much feeling and touching. The purpose of this experience is to help people become more open and sensitive to the feelings of others. It has limited use in organizational settings.

In spite of the criticisms of sensitivity training, organizations do use it, although it is not high on their priority of training methods.[12] In its less stressful forms it is particularly used in confrontation sessions in OD. Research studies indicate a moderate proportion of improvements among sensitivity training participants.[13]

EXAMPLES OF OD PROGRAMS.   Now that we have discussed some of the training methods used in OD, it is appropriate to review selected OD programs. Following are brief comments about three of them. The discussion shows that each program is built around some type of framework that provides a vehicle for applying the group process that is necessary to OD. Many other OD programs are tailored individually to an organization's needs without using a standard framework.

The managerial grid.   Robert R. Blake and Jane S. Mouton of the University of Texas developed the managerial grid.[14] The full program consists of six phases, although organizations may not proceed through all the phases. Phase 1 is the presentation of a framework called the managerial grid, as shown in Figure 11-1. The grid is based on the management style dimensions of concern for people and concern for production, which essentially represent the dimensions of consideration and structure discussed in an earlier chapter. The grid clarifies how the two dimensions are related and establishes a uniform language and framework for communication about behavioral issues. The "1,9 managers" are high in concern for people but so low in concern for production that output is low. They are "country club managers." The "9,1 managers" are overly concerned with production. They tend to be authoritarian bosses. A more desirable balance of the two dimensions is from "5,5" to "9,9." Using the grid, the entire managerial job can be discussed, such as the "back-up style" of managers. The back-up style is the one managers tend to use when their normal style does not get results. It tends to be more autocratic and concerned for production.

Phase 2 of the program is concerned with team development, using the grid as a framework for discussion. Focus is upon a single team and the manager to whom they directly report. Phase 3 is concerned with intergroup development to reduce conflict among groups. This phase tries to reduce win-lose power struggles among groups by showing how cooperation can lead to benefits for all parties. Phase 4 develops an ideal organization model, phase 5 seeks to apply the model, and phase 6 provides evaluation of the program. Experience with the managerial grid shows that it often produces positive results.[15] It has been successful world-wide.

Systems 1 through 4. An OD framework using four systems of management was developed by Rensis Likert of the Institute for Social Research, University of Michigan.[16] The systems are numbered consecutively from Number 1, which is the most authoritarian, to Number 4, which is the most participative. The object of the OD program is to try to move an organization's practices as far as possible toward the participative system. By administering surveys the OD consultant can secure insights concerning the system used in the organization and the more ideal system

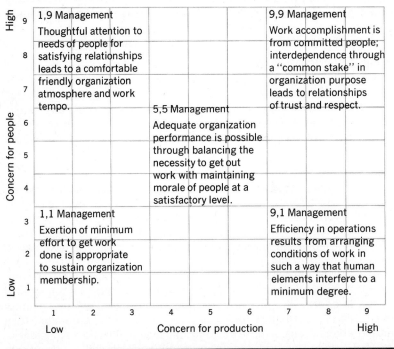

FIGURE 11-1

The managerial grid. (*Source:* Robert R. Blake and Jane S. Mouton, "Managerial Facades," *Advanced Management Journal,* July 1966, p. 31. Used with permission.)

that the participants have in their minds. The difference between the two represents the area of improvement that the OD program seeks to accomplish. Items on the survey form are organized around seven behavioral subjects as follows: leadership processes, motivation, communication, interaction, decision making, goal setting, and control.

The Likert system is known as the survey feedback method, because it makes heavy use of feedback to participants based on the surveys made. Programs of this type have produced effective results.[17]

3-D management. William J. Reddin of the University of New Brunswick has an OD program called 3-D management.[18] This program like the managerial grid, is organized around consideration and structure; however, it is also stated that these two orientations can be used in combination or they can be ignored by a manager, giving a choice of four styles. Since any of these four styles can be effective or ineffective, there are eight managerial style options available. The 3-D program is built around a study of these eight style options. When they are assembled into a chart, the result is a three-dimensional appearance, as shown in Figure 11-2. This is the origin of the term "3-D management."

The 3-D system is materially different from the other two systems mentioned because it assumes that there are four effective styles, while the other systems focus on only one, the considerate, participative approach. The 3-D system is therefore less ideologically bound than the other systems and is more realistic in

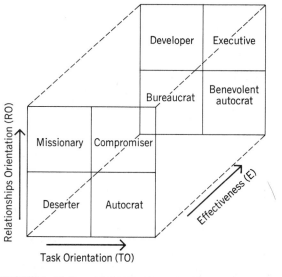

FIGURE 11-2

Chart of the 3-D system. (*Source:* William J. Reddin, *Managerial Effectiveness,* New York: McGraw-Hill Book Company, 1970, p. 238. Used with permission.)

terms of contingency concepts. The 3-D system carefully emphasizes that no one style is effective by itself. Its effectiveness depends on the situation in which it is used. Because of its flexibility the 3-D system has had international acceptance in different cultures.

BENEFITS AND LIMITATIONS OF OD. OD appears to move in the right direction. Its chief advantage is that it tries to deal with change in a whole organization or a major unit of it. In this manner it accomplishes more widely dispersed improvement. The principal improvements that occur are increased productivity, better quality of work, higher job satisfaction, improved teamwork, improved resolution of conflict, and reduced negative factors such as absences and turnover.

After an OD program in one organization, there were statistically significant improvements in trust, supportive environment, commitment to objectives, and other conditions of organizational climate. With regard to supervisory behavior there was improvement in listening, handling of conflict, relations with others, willingness to change, and other activities. With regard to performance, there were changes in quality level and profit that were attributable to the OD program. Clearly the effect of the program was widespread in the organization.[19]

As with any complex program, OD has problems and limitations. It is time-consuming and expensive. Some benefits have a long payoff period, and an organization may not be able to wait that long for potential benefits. Unless a professionally capable consultant is used, it may fall flat. There are questions of invasion of privacy in some of its methods. There are charges that participants sometimes are coerced toward group attitudes and conformity. There are other charges that excessive emphasis is given to behavioral processes rather than to job performance. Informal, interpersonal processes seem to be given precedence over needs of the formal organization.

In spite of its problems and limitations, OD generally seems to be a useful and successful practice. It has contributed to improved behavioral and organizational results.

CONVENTIONAL TRAINING METHODS

The success of OD does not imply that conventional training methods are ineffective in the area of organizational behavior. They continue to be successful, also. Coaching, lecture and discussion, conference training, and the case method are all useful training methods in organizational behavior. Conventional training methods are excellent for providing knowledge about behavior, and many employees need this kind of information. Studies show that these training methods also are useful in changing attitudes and performance. As indicated by one study, these improvements tend to persist. After eighteen months changes in the experimental group were higher than immediately after the program. In the control group, however, changes were negative.[20]

Following are three additional examples of improvement with conventional training methods.

Bank supervisors were given a course in human behavior using conventional instructional methods. Before and after the course they were given a standard test of supervisory judgment. The second test showed improvement significant to the .001 level.[21]

A number of nursing supervisors throughout a state were given a course using conventional training methods. The training sessions consisted of eighteen days of training for two groups on four separate occasions during the year. Standardized tests were given before and after the program. The tests showed knowledge increases significant to the .01 level, and a more democratic attitude orientation significant to the .01 level. There was also an improvement in job performance in one group significant to the .05 level, but not in the other group.[22]

Another study examined changes in the influence structure of a job following a training course in human behavior. Information on changes in influence was provided by trainees, their subordinates, and their superiors. Results showed that the influence structure changed to become more participative after the training.[23]

The principal need of conventional training programs is to build more reinforcement for them back on the job. Even the best of training will be ineffective if obstacles at the workplace discourage the trainee from using what has been learned. If people return to their jobs and find that their first cautious efforts to change are rejected or discouraged, then the Law of Effect operates to discourage repetition of that behavior. The result is that new practices tend to wither away. What is needed is reinforcement from superiors and peers. As discussed earlier, OD tends to provide a better reinforcement climate than conventional training; however, this advantage is partly offset by higher costs.

SUMMARY

Organizational development is an intervention strategy that uses group processes to focus on the whole culture of an organization in order to bring about planned change. Some characteristics are a focus on the whole organization, systems orientation, action research, group processes, feedback, experiential learning, contingency orientation, and use of change agents. The process covers such steps as diagnosis, data collection, feedback and confrontation, action planning, team building, intergroup development, and follow-up. It makes heavy use of laboratory training approaches, such as role playing, gaming, and sensitivity training. Typical programs are the managerial grid, Systems 1 through 4, and 3-D management.

Although OD has limitations, it is an excellent practice for introducing change and self-renewal in organizations. More conventional training methods are an effective supplement to it.

TERMS AND CONCEPTS FOR REVIEW

Organizational development (OD)

Action research

Experiential learning

Team building

Laboratory training

Role playing

Sensitivity training

The managerial grid

Systems 1 through 4

3-D management

REVIEW QUESTIONS ■■■

1. What are the advantages of OD compared with more conventional training methods?
2. Discuss the different phases by which an OD program develops.
3. Discuss the weaknesses and strengths of sensitivity training.
4. What is the principal difference between 3-D management and the managerial grid?
5. Explain how the reward structure on the job may not reinforce training.

CASE

THE T-GROUP

Mary Sorrel is an executive with a producer of women's clothing. This firm has embarked on an OD program that it wishes all its managers to attend. The primary training method that will be used is sensitivity training. Mary says that she welcomes the opportunity to participate in all phases of the OD program except sensitivity training, in which she refuses to participate. She says that she has a friend who was "emotionally damaged" by a sensitivity program and she believes this kind of training is an invasion of privacy; therefore, she will not participate. All the other executives have agreed to participate.

QUESTIONS

1. You are the vice president who is directing the program in the company. What course of action do you recommend and why?

REFERENCES

1. Richard J. Selfridge and Stanley L. Sokolik, "A Comprehensive View of Organization Development," *MSU Business Topics*, Winter 1975, p. 60.

2. Warren R. Nielsen and John R. Kimberly, "The Impact of Organizational Development on the Quality of Organizational Output." in Thad B. Green and Dennis F. Ray (eds.), *Academy of Management Proceedings, 1973*, State College, Miss.: The Academy of Management, 1974, pp. 527–534.

3. Harold M. F. Rush, *Organization Development: A Reconnaissance,* New York: The Conference Board, Inc., 1973, pp. 42–50.

4. Joseph Zacker and Morton Bard, "Effects of Conflict Management Training on Police Performance," *Journal of Applied Psychology,* October 1973, pp. 202–208.

5. R. Wayne Boss, "The Not-so-Peaceful Incident at Peaceful Valley: A Confrontation Design in a Criminal Justice Agency," in Arthur G. Bedeian and others (eds.), *Academy of Management Proceedings, 1975,* Auburn, Ala.: Auburn University, 1975, pp. 357–359.

6. For a more extensive discussion of the OD process see Edgar F. Huse, *Organization Development and Change,* St. Paul, Minn.: West Publishing Company, 1974; and Newton Margulies and Anthony P. Raia, *Organizational Development: Values, Process, and Technology,* New York: McGraw-Hill Book Company, 1972.

7. Noel M. Tichy, "Current Trends in Organizational Change," *Columbia Journal of World Business,* Spring 1974, pp. 98–111.

8. Edgar F. Huse and Michael Beer, "Eclectic Approach to Organizational Development," *Harvard Business Review,* September–October 1971, pp. 103–112; and William F. Dowling, "To Move an Organization: The Corning Approach to Organization Development," *Organizational Dynamics,* Spring 1975, pp. 16–34.

9. George Strauss, "Organizational Development: Credits and Debits," *Organizational Dynamics,* Winter 1973, pp. 2–19.

10. Morton A. Lieberman, Irvin D. Yalom, and Matthew B. Miles, "Encounter: The Leader Makes the Difference," *Psychology Today,* March 1973, pp. 69–76; and Morton A. Lieberman, Irvin D. Yalom, and Matthew B. Miles, *Encounter Groups: First Facts,* New York: Basic Books, Inc., Publishers, 1973. See also Kurt W. Back, *Beyond Words: The Story of Sensitivity Training and the Encounter Movement,* Baltimore: Penguin Books, Inc., 1973; and Clayton P. Alderfer, "Understanding Laboratory Education: An Overview," *Monthly Labor Review,* December 1970, pp. 18–27.

11. Jane Howard, *Please Touch: A Guided Tour of the Human Potential Movement,* New York: McGraw-Hill Book Company, 1970.

12. William J. Kearney and Desmond D. Martin, "Sensitivity Training: An Established Management Tool?" *Academy of Management Journal,* December 1974, pp. 755–760.

13. For details see John P. Campbell and Marvin D. Dunnette, "Effectiveness of T-Group Experiences in Managerial Training and Development," *Psychological Bulletin,* vol. 70, no. 2, 1968, pp. 73–104; and C. L. Cooper and I. L. Mangham, *T-Groups: A Survey of Research,* London: Wiley-Interscience, 1971.

14. Robert R. Blake and Jane S. Mouton, *The Managerial Grid,* Houston: Gulf Publishing Company, 1964; and Robert R. Blake and Jane S. Mouton, *Building a Dynamic Corporation through Grid Organization Development,* Reading, Mass.: Addison-Wesley Publishing Company, Inc., 1969.

15. Howard A. Hart, "The Grid Appraised—Phases 1 and 2," *Personnel,* September–October 1974, pp. 44–59; and "Using the Managerial Grid to Ensure MBO," *Organizational Dynamics,* Spring 1974, pp. 54–65. Questions are raised about grid effectiveness in H. John Bernardin and Kenneth M. Alvares, "The Managerial Grid as a Predictor of Conflict Resolution Method and Managerial Effectiveness," *Administrative Science Quarterly,* March 1976, pp. 84–91.

16. Rensis Likert, *The Human Organization: Its Management and Value,* New York: McGraw-Hill Book Company, 1967. See also Rensis Likert, *New Patterns of Management,* New York: McGraw-Hill Book Company, 1961.

17. Robert T. Golembiewski and Robert Munzenrider, "Persistence and Change: A Note on

the Long-Term Effects of an Organization Development Program," *Academy of Management Journal,* March 1973, pp. 149–153; and David G. Bowers and Jerome L. Franklin, "Survey-guided Development: Using Human Resources Measurement in Organizational Change," *Journal of Contemporary Business,* Summer 1972, pp. 43–55.

18.   William J. Reddin, *Managerial Effectiveness,* New York: McGraw-Hill Book Company, 1970.

19.   John R. Kimberly and Warren R. Nielsen, "Organizational Development and Change in Organizational Performance," *Administrative Science Quarterly,* June 1975, pp. 191–206.

20.   Herbert H. Hand, Max D. Richards, and John W. Slocum, Jr., "Organizational Climate and the Effectiveness of a Human Relations Training Program," *Academy of Management Journal,* June 1973, pp. 185–195.

21.   Joseph C. White, "Improving Supervisory Judgment through Training," *Personnel Journal,* December 1963, pp. 570–572, covering sixty-one trainees in three separate courses.

22.   S. Dale McLemore and Richard J. Hill, *Management-training Effectiveness: A Study of Nurse Managers,* Austin, Tex.: Bureau of Business Research, The University of Texas, 1965, covering 640 trainees.

23.   Bernard H. Baum, Peter F. Sorensen, Jr., and William S. Place, "Organizational Effect of Supervisory Human Relations Training: An Evaluative Technique," *Personnel Journal,* March 1966, pp. 148–152.

SECTION 3

ORGANIZATIONAL ENVIRONMENT

CHAPTER 12
ORGANIZATIONAL STRUCTURE AND DESIGN

An institution is like a tune; it is not constituted by individual sounds
but by the relations between them
Peter F. Drucker[1]

The findings indicate that job satisfaction decreases as the bureaucraticness of the
organization increases.
Nicholas Dimarco and Steven Norton[2]

LEARNING OBJECTIVES

TO UNDERSTAND:
Classical organization theory
Human effects of functionalization
The usefulness of classical organization theory
Human effects of centralization and decentralization
Human effects of tall and flat organizations
The effects of organization size on employees
Contingency organizational design

Modern civilization requires large aggregations of people working together to produce its goods and services efficiently. Organizations are the grand strategies created to bring order out of chaos when groups work together. As indicated by the first quotation introducing this chapter, things that are unorganized are indeed like individual sounds; they must be set in a suitable relationship to get a pleasant tune. Organization sets the relationship among people, work, and resources. Wherever groups of people exist in a common effort, organization must be employed to get productive results. The necessity for organization—and the havoc of disorganization—are illustrated by disorganizing a short sentence "riirggnagesnotztlsuse." In this form it is nonsense. Now let us reorganize it substantially: "organizinggetsresults." In this condition it is workable, but difficult. By the slight change of converting to a capital O and adding two spaces, it reads: "Organizing gets results." Yes, organizing of people and things is essential for coordinated work.

In this chapter we discuss classical organization theory, decentralization, the span of management, organization size, and contingency organizational design as these matters relate to organizational behavior.

CLASSICAL ORGANIZATION THEORY

Most organizations depend heavily upon classical organization theory in building their structures because it deals with essential elements in an institution, such as power, responsibility, division of labor, specialization, and interdependence of parts. Modern developments are amending classical theory, but its essential elements remain and must be understood in order to work with people in organizations. Organizational structure is significant because it partly determines the power of people in organizations and their perceptions of their roles.

The organizing process can be perceived in two ways. It may be considered as a process of construction in which a great number of small work units are built into jobs, departments, divisions, and finally a whole institution. A second approach is to view organization as a process of analysis by which a particular area or work is subdivided into divisions, departments, and finally jobs assigned to particular persons. This latter approach is more appropriate when organizing a work group because one starts with the total amount of work to be done. Viewed in this way, organizing is achieved by means of division of work and delegation.

DIVISION OF WORK. The manner by which work is divided can be illustrated by considering that a small triangle represents an area of work that a department must achieve. There are sixteen persons, including the department head, available to do

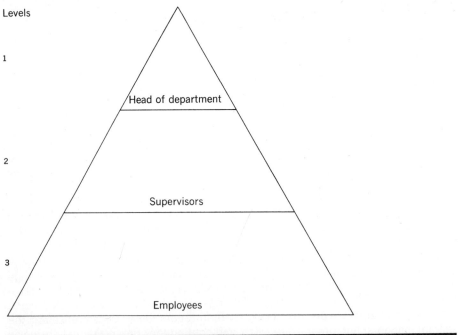

FIGURE 12-1 ███████████████████████████████████████

The scalar process: division of work into levels.

the work. The department head must subdivide the department's work so that a coordinated, effective group will develop. This is done by dividing work into levels and functions and then assigning people and resources to the jobs that result. Division into levels is represented by Figure 12-1. It is called the *scalar process* because it provides a scale, or grading, of duties according to degrees of authority and responsibility. The scalar process is virtually universal. Wherever there are two persons existing in a supervisor-subordinate relationship, this is a scalar relationship. It is apparent that this type of relationship has many behavioral dimensions. One is that influence processes tend to flow downward in organizations more than upward.[3]

Concurrently with division into levels, the work must be divided into different kinds of duties. This is *functionalization*. It is distinguished from the scalar process, which determines grades of duties. To use an illustration, the difference between vice presidents and supervisors is scalar. The difference between a foundry supervisor and a machine shop supervisor is functional. Scalar and functional divisions are superimposed on each other to form a framework such as that shown in Figure 12-2. By a simple two-way partition of duties, all the work to be done (as represented by the area of the triangle) is now assigned. Assuming that organizing is done perfectly, there are no unassigned areas and no overlaps of assignments.

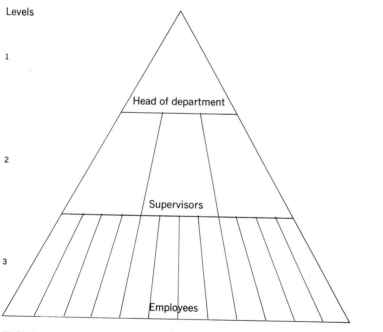

FIGURE 12-2

Division of work for sixteen persons by means of the scalar process and functionalization.

There is an intricate web of relationships among people that links them all together.

ILLUSTRATIONS OF FUNCTIONALIZATION. A farm situation will further illustrate functionalization. If fifty workers are hoeing corn, each doing the same work, the only division of labor is that the work has been broken into human units, i.e., an amount that one person can perform. If the work is reorganized and forty-nine workers hoe while the fiftieth sharpens the hoes and keeps the water jug filled, division of labor *of a different kind* has taken place. This is functionalization. In the course of time, the fiftieth worker will become more adept at sharpening hoes than the forty-nine are, and they will be more adept at hoeing than the sharpener is. This is because each is *specializing* as a natural result of functionalization.

Functionalization brings great benefits to a work group. Modern industrial society could not exist without it, because it permits people to develop specialized skill and knowledge and to produce more of their wants. It is one of the really fundamental ideas of civilization. Adam Smith in 1776 recognized its significance and picturesquely described it as it applied to manufacturing pins.

> To take an example, therefore, from a very trifling manufacture, but one in which the division of labour has been very often taken notice of, the trade of the pin-maker; a workman not educated to this business (which the division of labour has rendered a distinct trade), not acquainted with the use of the machinery employed in it (to the invention of which the same division of labour has probably given occasion), could scarce, perhaps, with his utmost industry, make one pin in a day, and certainly could not make twenty. But in the way in which this business is now carried on, not only the whole work is a peculiar trade, but it is divided into a number of branches, of which the greater part are likewise peculiar trades. One man draws out the wire, another straights it, a third cuts it, a fourth points it, a fifth grinds it at the top for receiving the head; to make the head requires two or three distinct operations! to put it on, is a peculiar business, to whiten the pins is another; it is even a trade by itself to put them into the paper; and the important business of making a pin is in this manner, divided into about eighteen distinct operations, which in some manufactories, are all performed by distinct hands, though in others the same man will sometimes perform two or three of them. I have seen a small manufactory of this kind where ten men only were employed, and where some of them consequently performed two or three distinct operations. But though they were very poor, and therefore but indifferently accommodated with the necessary machinery, they could, when they exerted themselves, make among them about twelve pounds of pins in a day. There are in a pound upwards of four thousand pins of a middling size. Those ten persons, therefore, could make among them upwards of forty-eight thousand pins in a day. Each person, therefore, making a tenth part of forty-eight thousand, might be considered as making four thousand eight hundred pins in a day. But if they had all wrought separately and independently, and without any of them having been educated to this peculiar business, they certainly could not each of them have made twenty; perhaps not one pin in a day; that is, cer-

tainly, not the two hundred and fortieth, perhaps not the four thousand eight hundredth part of what they are at present capable of performing, in consequence of a proper division and combination of their different operations.[4]

Like other benefits to society, functionalization brings disadvantages that must be weighed against all its benefits. Let us return to our fifty fieldworkers to illustrate some of these disadvantages as portrayed in this simple situation. The one worker who is sharpening hoes may not sharpen them to please one of the forty-nine, who always complains about a dull hoe. On another occasion a worker chips a hoe on a rock and wants it sharpened right away, but the hoe sharpener is busy getting water and cannot give immediate service. The chopper is forced to continue with a dull hoe. When the soil is rocky, the sharpener has too much to do, and hoes go dull. When the soil is soft, the sharpener sits idle. One day when the sharpener is absent because of illness, the workers bicker about who will sharpen that day. The worker selected is clumsy and delays the work. And so the trouble goes, day after day. The functionalized group is more complex and difficult to coordinate than the original group of fifty workers all doing the same work.

The fact eventually dawns on the fifty workers that the productivity gains of functionalization (assuming they exist in this illustration) can be achieved only if sound human relationships and coordination can be maintained. This problem of the fifty farm workers can now be translated into a general statement applying to functionalization in its current stage of development: *The benefits of functionalization are largely economic and technical, but its disadvantages are primarily human.* This inverse relationship creates an unfortunate imbalance between the quality of technology and of human relationships in organizations. More of the former tends to provide less of the latter, unless positive steps are taken to offset the disadvantages that arise. Functional conflicts tend to develop, as humorously shown in Figure 12-3. However, functionalization is the essence of advanced social systems. Whatever problems it causes must be weighed against its vast benefits.

DELEGATION. The relationships and duties determined by division of work are communicated and assigned to persons by means of *delegation,* which is defined as the assignment of duties, authority, and responsibility to others. If they accept the assignment, then they become a manager's "delegate" and are responsible for the assignment. If there is no acceptance, delegation has merely been attempted. Delegation permits managers to extend their influence beyond the limits of their own personal time, energy, and knowledge.

Poor delegation is a primary cause of managerial failure. Some managers feel that delegation is giving away something, so they cannot psychologically bring themselves to do it for fear it will weaken them. Others are such perfectionists that they have no confidence in letting others do work for which they are responsible. However, all need to realize that delegation is the act that initiates management. If there is no delegation to others, there is no one to be managed.

THE ACCEPTANCE THEORY OF AUTHORITY. The power of managerial authority depends on willingness of employees to accept it. This is known as their "zone of acceptance" and results in an *acceptance theory of authority.* Although authority gives persons power to act officially within the scope of their delegation, this power becomes somewhat meaningless unless those affected accept it and respond to it. In most cases when delegation is made, a subordinate is left free to make response choices within a certain range of behavior. But even when an employee is told to perform one certain act, the employee still has the choice of doing it or not doing it and taking the consequences. It is, therefore, the subordinate who always controls the response to authority. Managers cannot afford to overlook this human fact when they use authority. Accordingly, authority is really an institutional right to initiate decisions affecting others in the institution. Its operation is substantially the same in business, government, or other groups, although its source may be different in each. Thus an accounting department manager in a factory and one in a state office wield the same type of institutional authority.

OPERATING AND ULTIMATE AUTHORITY AND RESPONSIBILITY. Managers can redelegate to others, but this in no way releases them from the original delegation they received. Let us take responsibility as an illustration. In reality, responsibility is divided into two parts at the time of delegation, and the employee

"Hah! Accounting tried to walk all over me!"

FIGURE 12-3 ▬▬▬

Functionalization may cause conflicts between different activities.

assumes only the *operating* responsibility for the task. The manager retains *ultimate* responsibility for getting the job done, but emphasis is now upon getting the job done through someone else. If the employee fails to perform the job (operating responsibility), the manager is held responsible for this failure (ultimate responsibility). Ultimate responsibility operates somewhat like the fable of the magic pitcher in which the water level always remained the same no matter how much water was poured out. This relationship is shown in Figure 12-4. Even though the supervisor delegates many duties to two clerks, the supervisor is still responsible for the entire activity represented by the large rectangle. It is clear that in classical organization theory "to delegate" does not mean "to give away."

Duties need to be delegated so that no more than one person supervises another person. This idea of a single supervisor is known as *unity of command.* Studies show that when there is a violation of unity of command the organization has less effective performance, less satisfied employees, poorer use of time, and other dysfunctional results.[5]

Middle managers have a particularly difficult time in organizations. One thorough study of managerial roles shows that maximum role conflict and organizational stress occur at the upper middle-management levels. There is a curvilinear relationship in which role conflict is lower among supervisors and top

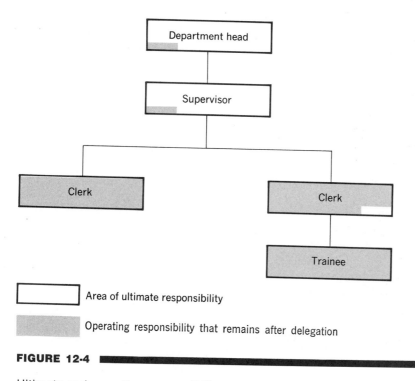

Department head

Supervisor

Clerk

Clerk

Trainee

☐ Area of ultimate responsibility

▨ Operating responsibility that remains after delegation

FIGURE 12-4 ▬▬▬▬▬▬▬▬▬▬▬▬▬▬▬

Ultimate and operating responsibility.

managers, and higher among middle managers.[6] Because of their ambiguous position, middle managers depend heavily on lateral communication, negotiation, and informal relationships to get their job done.

Generally there is a linear relationship between organizational level and job satisfaction.[7] Upper-level managers are probably more satisfied because of their greater autonomy and more challenging type of work.

BUREAUCRACY. When organizational structures, rules, and procedures are rigidly followed, a condition known as bureaucracy develops. *Bureaucracy* is characterized by a large, complex administrative apparatus operating with impersonal detachment from people. There are elaborate rules, detailed controls, a rigid hierarchy, and highly specialized functions performed by experts. Lower and middle managers are impersonal rule followers more than managers. As long as they follow rules and do not rock the boat, they have job security in the system. Managerial action is slow and paperwork is elaborate as people try to protect themselves by getting any proposed action approved by several persons at several levels. Generally the voices of individuality and originality are stifled. We can summarize by saying that bureaucracy's four main characteristics are high specialization, a rigid hierarchy of authority, elaborate rules and controls, and impersonality.

Bureaucracy has its advantages, such as stability and unified focus on objectives. The difficulty arises when there is too rigid adherence to the system. Then there is a tendency for psychological costs to increase and effectiveness to decline. There is evidence that as organizations approach the bureaucratic ideals of strong centralization and formalization, employees tend to become less satisfied and more alienated.[8]

INTERPRETING CLASSICAL ORGANIZATION THEORY. Classical organization theory has its strengths as well as its weaknesses. For example, organizational structure can support people as well as suppress them. Classical structure provides much task support, such as specialized assistance, aggregates of resources focused on a particular problem, security, and fairly dependable conditions of work. On the other hand, although classical structure is strong in task support, *it is weak in psychological support.* What is needed is organizational systems that provide both task and psychological support.

The modern approach is to be flexible with organizational systems, varying them in a contingency relationship with their environment. There is, for example, evidence that highly programmed jobs respond well to classical systems benevolently applied. Where the technology requires closely interwoven work, as on an assembly line, the use of a less precise structure with ambiguous lines of authority often adds to task confusion and employee frustration. The open structure provides neither task nor psychological support in these conditions.

On the other hand, open, ambiguous structures may be more efficient where work is less interwoven and task requirements are more variable, requiring more employee judgment and consultation. This kind of task condition requires open communication and personal contacts across chains of command. Here the human interaction is interwoven more than the task is. With jobs less programmed in this way, more flexible structures and fewer administrative bonds are desired.

Rules are less rigid, and the behavioral climate is more considerate. We would expect to find this condition in a research department. Between the extremes of research department and assembly line, there are different shades of conditions requiring different shades of structure.

Without a doubt, there is a decline in the use of hierarchy in modern organizations. One reason is changing social values, but it is also evident that lateral relations between chains of command are more important for effectiveness than was formerly realized. Supervisory influence with peers, service people, and other chains of command is becoming more significant. The pace and complexity of work today make lateral action more necessary. In the classical factory when a machine broke down, the worker called the supervisor, who called the superintendent, who called the production vice president, who started another chain of action downward to initiate repairs. Today's complex systems require a structure that gives the operating employee at the point of the problem the power and confidence to take more direct action with service people. The service specialists, knowing more about the situation than the superintendent, have an authority of operating knowledge that further chips away at the idea of hierarchy.

DECENTRALIZATION OF AUTHORITY

One way that structure is related to people is through decentralization of authority. As one manager put it, "I want a job that gives me a chance to accomplish something—to use my talents, whatever they are." Managers want a feeling of significance and attainment; but centralization and bigness in organizations often give managers a sense of powerlessness and loss of significance.[9] They feel that they are merely order takers and paper shufflers without much authority and responsibility. Decentralization is one of management's most effective measures to combat this feeling of nonresponsibility. *Decentralization* is defined as wide distribution of authority and responsibility to the smallest-sized unit that is practical throughout an organization. In essence, it is an advanced form of delegation to operating units.

Decentralization is both a philosophy of management and a technique. As a philosophy it refers to top management's belief that all employees should have maximum opportunity to develop and use their talents as responsible people and, therefore, that they should be given the necessary support from higher levels to get the job done. As a technique decentralization is a way of organizing which distributes authority to semi-independent decision units, but which exercises carefully devised controls to make sure that all separate decision units are working toward mutual goals. It increases the number of centers of initiative and reduces rigidity by permitting many independent decisions and, consequently, many different approaches to operating problems. (With full centralization there is but one decision, and if it happens to be a poor one, the whole organization is carried with it.) Since decentralization requires more decision centers, it also requires more managers of better quality. Some organizations have found that they could not move toward decentralization because they lacked sufficient qualified managers.

Decentralization takes time to understand and establish. In the beginning higher managers are concerned about the cost of mistakes by junior executives as they acquire experience in decision making; however, this reason often fades away upon close examination.[10]

In one company, for example, the chief executive was worried by the fact that a purchasing specialist, if given more authority, could make costly mistakes. Closer examination revealed that the costliest error he could make would involve only $100,000, but that it cost $142,000 annually in executive time, forms to fill out, and other precautions to insure against his error. There were further possible losses as a result of delayed purchasing decisions. Was the possible loss from independent decision making great enough to require the certain expense and possible loss of the checkup procedure?

Probably the major reason for managerial resistance to decentralization is hesitancy to give up authority. Most people hesitate to give up any authority, once it is gained. Executives are no exception. Authority sticks to them like glue, and considerable motivation is required to get it delegated. They need to be shown how decentralization helps the things they are interested in—how it helps their work and makes them more successful. If decentralization can help in this way—and it appears able to do so in many situations—it will be used.

The two most important human benefits of managerial decentralization are employee development and improved feelings of significance. Because employees are on their own, they are more strongly motivated to develop, and they feel a greater sense of accomplishment.

Decentralization is a useful practice, because decentralized organizations tend to be more successful than centralized ones,[11] but decentralization is a contingency relationship. It is not a sure bet, not always the correct move. Some organizations have tried it and had to retrace their steps at least part of the way. It can lead to lack of cooperation among departments, diversion from objectives, and excessive growth of service groups. Somewhere along a continuum connecting the two extremes of centralization and decentralization is the most desirable arrangement for each organization. Generally, the more complex and fast-changing the organization and its environment are, the more decentralization of operating decisions is required for effectiveness. In fast-changing situations centralized decision makers simply are unable to respond fast enough and with enough knowledge of operating problems to be effective. They may, however, continue to determine policy and broad controls.

USING THE SPAN OF MANAGEMENT

THE SPAN OF MANAGEMENT. A useful idea about organizations is the *span of management* (or span of supervision), which refers to the number of persons a manager directly manages. Classical theory placed limits on the span, because managers have limited amounts of knowledge, energy, and so on. The idea of a limited span developed from experience. It has always been a problem. The Holy Bible tells how Moses had to reduce his span of management.[12]

. . . Moses sat to judge the people, and the people stood about Moses from morning till evening. When Moses' father-in-law saw all that he was doing for the people, he said, . . . "What you are doing is not good. You and the people with you will wear yourselves out; for the thing is too heavy for you; you are not able to perform it alone. . . ."

So Moses gave heed to the voice of his father-in-law and did all that he had said. Moses chose able men out of all Israel, and made them heads over the people, rulers of thousands, of hundreds, of fifties, and of tens. And they judged the people at all times; hard cases they brought to Moses, but any small matter they decided themselves.

Napoleon, as well as other military leaders, recognized that the span of management is limited. In 1933 V. A. Graicunas explained it mathematically by showing how the total number of possible relationships among managers and their personnel increases geometrically as each new subordinate is added. For example, if a manager has four subordinates, there are forty-four interrelationships computed according to Graicunas's formula.[13] If another person is added to make five, the relationships increase to 100. And as each additional person is added, the relationships more than double.

A formula of the type just described is useful to show proportions, but it should not be taken literally. The span of management actually is a contingency relationship. Many factors determine the number of employees that one person can effectively manage. Some of these are capacity and skill of the manager, complexity of the work supervised, capacity and skill of the employees managed, stability of operations, contacts with other chains of command, contacts outside the organization, and geographic proximity of subordinates.

The differences in spans of management are illustrated by one study of the first-level supervisor's span in manufacturing. The study showed a wide variation in spans of management. In three types of production technology, as defined later in this chapter, the average span of management varied as follows:[14]

Unit or small batch production	*23 persons*
Mass production and assembly line	*49 persons*
Process and continuous production	*13 persons*

Assuming that the three types of production are listed from the simplest technology to the most complex, the data show a curvilinear relationship between technology and span of management; that is, the largest span is associated with medium technology, and lower spans are associated with both high and low technology. The differences are substantial, because one type of technology had a span more than three times as large as another type.

TALL AND FLAT ORGANIZATIONS. A small span throughout an organization causes a tall structure, and a large span causes a flat structure, as shown in Figure

12-5. Each structure has its advantages and limitations. In the tall structure closer coordination and control are permitted because each manager works with fewer people; but communication lines are longer, providing more opportunities for misinterpretation and editing.

The flat structure has a shorter, simpler communication chain, but managers have so many persons to direct that they cannot spend much time face-to-face with any one member of their group.

In an electronics company, for example, the president attempted to use a large span of management, resulting in a communications bottleneck at his office. When his subordinates were unable to gain access to him, they developed their own system of cross-communication within their group so that their activities could be properly coordinated. This permitted them to work effectively in spite of the bottleneck in the front office.

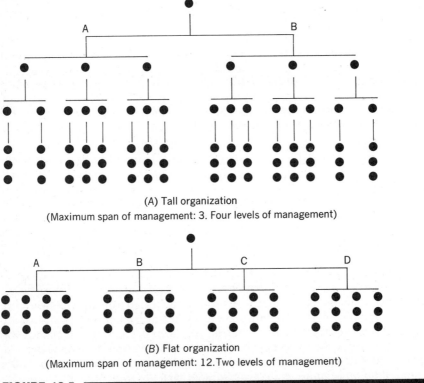

(A) Tall organization
(Maximum span of management: 3. Four levels of management)

(B) Flat organization
(Maximum span of management: 12. Two levels of management)

FIGURE 12-5

Organizational differences caused by different spans of management for the same number of operating employees (forty-eight).

In the tall organization employees tend to be more "boss-oriented." Since their superior is interacting with them regularly day by day, the employees tend to spend much time trying to please their superior.

Since a flat structure is more free of hierarchical controls, operative employees tend to prefer it. They like its freedom from close supervision. One study of sales representatives, for example, reported that those in flat organizations have more job satisfaction, less stress, and better production than those in tall organizations.[15]

The relation of tall and flat structures to managers tends to be complex. Studies in fourteen nations report that a flat structure is associated with greater managerial satisfaction in companies with under five thousand employees, but the trend is reversed in larger companies. In larger companies in the United States the tall structure actually provides more need satisfaction than the flat structure.[16] The reasoning appears to be that in large companies coordination and communication are more severe problems; hence, subordinate managers need to have ready access to their superior in order to maintain involvement with their organization. Under these conditions they perceive a tall structure as providing support for their needs.

In smaller organizations, on the other hand, problems of coordination and control are not as severe, and the organization is small enough for a managerial subordinate to feel directly involved through normal contacts. In this case, the frequent availability of one's superior is seen as interference, close supervision, and tighter control, which provide employees less satisfaction. These differences provide further evidence of a contingency relationship. Arguments for or against tall or flat structures need to take into account other organizational variables.

ORGANIZATION SIZE

Organization size often has an effect on behavioral variables. Generally the effect appears to be negative rather than positive. It should be made clear that size as discussed here refers to an operating unit of people working together in one coordinated group. It does not refer to the entire legal company or government employer; hence, a large manufacturer could operate with thirty decentralized units, all of small size.

Increasing size of operations introduces what may be called a *behemoth syndrome,* by which increasing size develops a series of interrelated symptoms and problems. For example, larger size is associated with lower employee satisfaction, which tends to increase absenteeism. Absenteeism, in turn, complicates coordination because most jobs are highly interdependent. Less coordination increases job frustration and probably reduces productivity. Less coordination and reduced productivity, in turn, lead to new work pressures, rules, and problems, thereby making the system self-regenerating in its depressing effects on people. The result is a syndrome of interrelated depressing variables dependent on organization size. Large size definitely is associated with absenteeism, turnover, and lower job satisfaction.[17] Following is an example of a job satisfaction study.

In the United States a general index of employee satisfaction was developed for each of ninety-three companies that used a standardized job satisfaction survey for their employees. When these indexes were compared with organization size, there was a definite tendency for the larger organizations to have lower employee satisfaction, as shown in Figure 12-6. The statistical correlation was significant at the .05 level of confidence. Further study of the data showed that only those satisfaction areas likely to be influenced by size were in fact reduced. For example, wages are not reduced with size; hence, satisfaction with wages should not decrease as an organization grows. Accordingly, this study showed no significant decrease in satisfaction with material rewards in the larger organizations, but there was a significant decrease in satisfaction with the company, supervision, fellow employees, and the job.

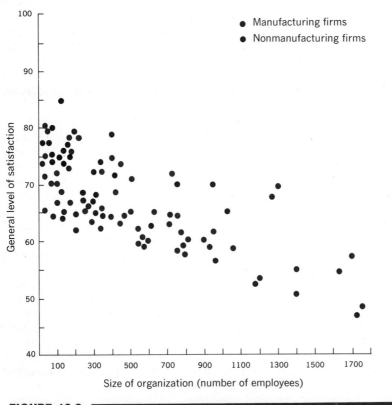

FIGURE 12-6

Scatter diagram of different organizations classified by size and corresponding level of employee satisfaction. (*Source:* Sergio Talacchi, "Organization Size, Individual Attitudes and Behavior: An Empirical Study," *Administrative Science Quarterly*, December 1960, p. 410. Used with permission.)

Evidence of the behemoth syndrome is too strong to ignore; however, most studies report that *some* large units do have high favorable results contrary to the general tendency. This shows that large units can avoid the behemoth effect by corrective action. Without corrective action large operating units tend to overwhelm people, disrupting supportive processes such as communication, coordination, and involvement. In turn, employees feel more alienated and constrained by the system, so they react negatively to their job experience.

CONTINGENCY ORGANIZATIONAL DESIGN

The large number of variables in organizations suggests that there is no one best organizational structure to fit all situations. This is the essence of *contingency organizational design,* which recognizes that different organizational structures and processes are required for optimum effectiveness in different kinds of environments. What is an appropriate organizational design in one environment may not be in another. Since environments change, there is even a need for flexible organizational designs so that they can be changed gradually to keep a best fit with the changing environment. The contingency point of view requires a fundamental change in philosophy compared with the traditional view that there is a one best way of organizing. Following are discussions of major research pointing the way toward more effective contingency design.

MECHANISTIC AND ORGANIC PATTERNS OF ORGANIZING. Some of the earliest research on contingency design was by Burns and Stalker in Britain.[18] They distinguished between *mechanistic* and *organic* (sometimes called *organismic*) organizations. The mechanistic form fits the traditional hierarchical way of organizing. People are specialized into many activities that are supervised by layers of supervision. Each higher level has more power and influence until the top is reached, where central direction of the whole organization takes place. Work is carefully scheduled, tasks are certain, roles are strictly defined, and most formal communication flows along the lines of the hierarchy. The whole structure is organized like a well-designed machine.

Organic organizations are more flexible and open. Tasks are more uncertain. Roles are less rigidly defined, allowing people to redefine them to adjust to situational requirements of the work. Communication is more multidirectional, particularly lateral. It consists more of information and advice, rather than instructions and decisions. Authority and influence flow more directly from the person who has the ability to handle the problem at hand. Decision making is more decentralized, being shared by several levels and different functions. The organization also is more open to its environment.

Burns and Stalker showed that mechanistic forms are more effective than organic forms in certain situations. If tasks are stable and well defined, changing very little from month to month and year to year, a mechanistic form tends to be superior. If changes in the technology, market, and other parts of the environment are minimal, then a mechanistic structure seems to be more effective. Worker attitudes also are a contingency factor. If workers prefer more routine tasks and desire direction from others, then a mechanistic form better meets their needs. If they are threatened by ambiguity and insecurity, then a mechanistic approach is better.

Organic forms are more effective than mechanistic forms in other situations, and these situations tend to be more typical in modern society. Organic forms work better if the environment is dynamic, requiring frequent changes within the organization. They also work better when the tasks are not well enough defined to become routine. If employees seek autonomy, openness, variety, change, and opportunities to try new approaches, then an organic form is better.

The conclusion is that mechanistic structures are more suited to stable, certain environments and employees who prefer stability. Organic structures are more suited to uncertain, unstable environments and employees who tolerate ambiguity and change. Even within the same organization, different departments may be organized differently in order to make a best fit with their environment. The research department may have an organic structure, and the production department may have a mechanistic structure.

TYPES OF PRODUCTION TECHNOLOGY. Research by Woodward with 100 firms in Britain shows that the most effective form of organization tends to vary with types of production technology.[19] Woodward classified firms into three types of technology, listed in increasing order of complexity.

- Unit and small batch production—produces one or a small number of a product, such as a locomotive, usually on the basis of an order.

- Mass and large batch production—produces a large number of a product in an assembly-type operation.

- Process production—produces in a continuous flow, such as an oil refinery or a nylon plant.

Woodward found that the most successful firms in each class of technology tended to group around a certain type of structure, while the less successful firms varied from the structure. The mass-production firms were more successful with mechanistic structures, while unit and process firms were more successful with organic structures. In essence, the most appropriate type of organization was contingent on the firm's type of technology. In relation to the amount of structure the relationship was curvilinear, with high structure required for the middle level of technology (mass production) and low structure required for either extreme of technology.

The curvilinear relationship has favorable implications for society, because it means that as technology advances, organizations will find it desirable to move toward more organic systems. Since organic systems are humanly oriented, people will benefit. The mechanistic trend of recent decades appears to be only a stage in the long-run advancement of humankind.

STABLE AND CHANGING ENVIRONMENTS. Lawrence and Lorsch in the United States studied industrial organizations, grouping them by amount of market and technological change.[20] Their work expanded and supported the research of

Burns and Stalker. They found that organizations in more changing environments required increasing differentiation in their structure. That is, they required many different sections, departments, occupational roles, and specialized patterns of thinking. These different parts enabled the firms to gain a variety of inputs that would allow them to react effectively to their uncertain environments. Because of differentiation, greater efforts toward integration were required. There was much coordination at lower levels, horizontal communication, interdisciplinary teams, and emphasis on flexibility. This system was similar to Burns and Stalker's concept of the organic organization. The firms with organic systems tended to function more successfully in changing environments.

Firms in more stable, certain environments required less differentiation. Standard rules and procedures provided sufficient integration in their stable environment, so they tended to be more hierarchical and centralized. The open systems and horizontal communication that were needed in the changing firms were not so necessary in the stable firms. Consequently, firms with mechanistic systems tended to be more successful in stable environments.

INTERPRETING CONTINGENCY ORGANIZATION. There is evidence that organizational systems need to be designed to fit their environments. Research is just beginning in this area, but the present state of the art suggests the following:

Mechanistic organizational systems are more effective when:

- The environment is relatively certain and stable.

- The technology is relatively unchanging.

- The production process is mass or large batch production.

- Employees have drives for security and stability.

Organic organizational systems are more effective when:

- The environment is dynamic.

- The technology is fast-changing.

- The production process is unit or continuous production.

- Employees have a tolerance for ambiguity and change.

The dynamic environment of modern society tends to require more organic systems in the typical organization, but many situations remain where mechanistic systems are effective.

SUMMARY

Classical organizational structure is established by functional and scalar division of work, and it is communicated to participants by means of delegation. Organization brings immense technical advantages that are offset by human costs. Essentially, classical structure is strong in task support but weak in psychological support. Highly structured organizations are known as bureaucracies.

Organizational structure tends to exist in a contingency relationship with other variables, but certain general tendencies are evident. Decentralized organizations tend to be more successful than centralized ones, particularly if they operate in a complex, fast-changing environment. Employees tend to have higher satisfaction in flat organizations compared with tall ones, and flat organizations are more flexible and innovative. Larger-sized organization units tend to have lower job satisfactions and higher absenteeism and turnover. This relationship of size to dysfunctional human results is known as the behemoth syndrome. Generally, mechanistic organization is more appropriate for stable, mass-production environments in which employees desire security. Organic organization is more appropriate in dynamic environments with unit or continuous production and flexible employees.

TERMS AND CONCEPTS FOR REVIEW

Scalar process	Decentralization
Functionalization	Span of management
Delegation	Tall and flat organizations
Acceptance theory of authority	Behemoth syndrome
Unity of command	Contingency organizational design
Bureaucracy	Mechanistic and organic organizations

REVIEW QUESTIONS

1. According to classical theory, how is an organization created?
2. How does bureaucracy relate to people in organizations?
3. How does decentralization of authority relate to people in organizations?
4. How does organization size relate to people in organizations?
5. Discuss contingency organizational design, including research about it.

CASES

THE SPLASHED ORANGE DRINK

In the Miller Company employees are allowed to take their morning break at their own discretion. After workers make a purchase from vending machines at the edge of the production floor, they are expected to consume it at their place of work. On his morning break Joe Kelly bought a bottle of orange drink and then stood near the vending machine to drink it. The machine was in the work area of supervisor William Gaines, who noticed Kelly and walked over to him saying, "You made your purchase; now get back to work."

Since Kelly worked for another supervisor rather than for Gaines, he continued to stand there sipping his drink.

Gaines came by again and spoke sharply, "I said get back to work. Now get going." Kelly was so upset that he waved the bottle forward and splashed orange drink into Gaines's face.

QUESTIONS
1. If you were Gaines, what would you do now? Why? If you were Kelly, what would you do now? Why?
2. How are organizational structure and authority related to the events in this case?
3. Role play the actions of Kelly and Gaines from the end of the case onward.

ROBBINS COMPANY

Robbins Company is a manufacturer of small appliances. Assembly operations are conducted on several assembly lines that require close coordination with other parts of the company, such as accounting, purchasing, materials management, and engineering. During a recession an accounting group that is studying expense reduction recommended that two branch plants of 300 employees each be combined with the main plant, thereby allowing the lay-off of 20 people working in jobs that would be duplicated when the plants are combined. The combined plant would employ 1,500 persons.

QUESTIONS
1. Why do you think the accounting group made this recommendation?
2. Give all the points you can both for and against the recommendation, and then explain whether you will accept it.

REFERENCES

1. Peter F. Drucker, *Concept of the Corporation,* New York: The John Day Company, Inc., 1946, p. 26.

2. Nicholas Dimarco and Steven Norton, "Life Style, Organization Structure, Congruity and Job Satisfaction," *Personnel Psychology,* Winter 1974, p. 589.

3. Jerome L. Franklin, "Down the Organization: Influence Processes across Levels of Hierarchy," *Administrative Science Quarterly,* June 1975, pp. 153–164.

4. Adam Smith, *The Wealth of Nations (1776),* New York: The Modern Library by Random House, Inc., 1937, pp. 4–5.

5. Martin J. Gannon and Frank T. Paine, "Unity of Command and Job Attitudes of Managers in a Bureaucratic Organization," *Journal of Applied Psychology,* June 1974, pp. 392–394; Robert J. House, "Role Conflict and Multiple Authority in Complex Organizations," *California Management Review,* Summer 1970, pp. 53–60; John R. Rizzo and others, "Role Conflict and Ambiguity in Complex Organizations," *Administrative Science Quarterly,* June 1970, pp. 150–163; and Richard E. Walton and others, "Organizational Context and Interdepartmental Conflict," *Administrative Science Quarterly,* December 1969, pp. 522–542.

6. Robert L. Kahn and others, *Organizational Stress: Studies in Role Conflict and Ambiguity,* New York: John Wiley & Sons, Inc., 1964, p. 382. See also Emanuel Kay, *The Crisis in Middle Management,* New York: AMACOM, 1974.

7. Denis Root and Henry Tosi, "Need Satisfaction of Domestic and Overseas Managers," in Thad B. Green and Dennis F. Ray (eds.), *Academy of Management Proceedings, 1973,* State College, Miss.: Mississippi State University, 1974, pp. 143–149.

8. Michael Aiken and Jerald Hage, "Organizational Alienation: A Comparative Analysis," *American Sociological Review,* vol. 31, pp. 497–507; and Dimarco and Norton, *op. cit.,* pp. 581–591. For a contrary opinion see Melvin L. Kohn, "Bureaucratic Man: A Portrait and an Interpretation," *American Sociological Review,* June 1971, pp. 461–474.

9. Valerie L. Sodano and Mahmoud A. Wahba, "Quality of Organizational Life: Organizational Structure, Climate, and Alienation," in William F. Glueck (ed.), *Academy of Management Proceedings, 1974,* Columbia, Mo.: University of Missouri, 1974, pp. 44–45.

10. Lawrence A. Appley, *Management in Action,* New York: American Management Association, 1956, pp. 278–279.

11. Bernard C. Reimann, "Dimensions of Structure in Effective Organizations: Some Empirical Evidence," *Academy of Management Journal,* December 1974, pp. 693–708.

12. The Holy Bible, Revised Standard Version, Exodus 18:13, 14, 17, 18, 24–26.

13. V. A. Graicunas, *Relationships in Organization,* Geneva: International Labor Office, 1933.

14. Joan Woodward, *Industrial Organization: Theory and Practice,* London: Oxford University Press, 1965, p. 69.

15. John M. Ivancevich and James H. Donnelly, Jr., "Relation of Organizational Structure to Job Satisfaction, Anxiety-Stress, and Performance," *Administrative Science Quarterly,* June 1975, pp. 272–280.

16. Lyman W. Porter and Jacob Siegel, "Relationships of Tall and Flat Organization Structures to the Satisfactions of Foreign Managers," *Personnel Psychology,* Winter 1965, pp. 379–392, covering nearly three thousand managers in thirteen countries; and Lyman W. Porter and Edward E. Lawler III, "The Effects of 'Tall' versus 'Flat' Organization Structures on Managerial Job Satisfaction," *Personal Psychology,* Summer 1964, pp. 135–148, covering over nineteen hundred managers in various types of companies throughout the United States.

17. Lyman W. Porter, Edward E. Lawler III, and J. Richard Hackman, *Behavior in Organizations,* New York: McGraw-Hill Book Company, 1975, pp. 248–252.

18. T. Burns and G. M. Stalker, *The Management of Innovation,* London: Tavistock Publications, 1961.

19. Joan Woodward, *op. cit.* Additional interpretations are provided in Peter M. Blau and others, "Technology and Organization in Manufacturing," *Administrative Science Quarterly,* March 1976, pp. 20–40.

20. Paul R. Lawrence and Jay W. Lorsch, *Organization and Environment: Managing Differentiation and Integration,* Boston: Harvard Graduate School of Business Administration, 1967; and Jay W. Lorsch and John J. Morse, *Organizations and Their Members: A Contingency Approach,* New York: Harper & Row, Publishers, Incorporated, 1974.

CHAPTER 13
INTEGRATING TECHNOLOGY
WITH PEOPLE:
SOCIOTECHNICAL SYSTEMS

In summary, it is not at all clear that designing jobs which are "efficient" from an engineering point of view—standardized, specialized, simplified—will result in higher productivity and higher profits.

Edward E. Lawler III, and J. Richard Hackman[1]

LEARNING OBJECTIVES

TO UNDERSTAND:
The operation of sociotechnical systems
Organizational effects of technology
Labor union attitudes toward technology
Effects of procedural initiation of action
Teamwork designs in work systems
Origins and effects of red tape
Alienation in organizations
Planning to introduce technology

Society has discovered that it needs to give more attention to the relationship of technology to people, because this relationship is a key one in the effectiveness of the system. This relationship of technology to people at work is known as *sociotechnical systems.* Consider the following rather simple technical-human interface.

> *Oil refineries are required to operate twenty-four hours a day because of the nature of the production process. One refinery established a central labor pool of skilled, versatile workers to be sent to other departments to replace persons absent. Before the pool was established, engineers and cost experts carefully proved that the idea was workable and would reduce costs by reducing overtime and/or regular standby workers in each department. However, after a year of effort by management the pool had to be abandoned, for two reasons. First, management could not keep workers in the pool. It lowered their status to be in the pool, and they objected to working for different supervisors on different jobs. They disliked being without a specific work station that they could count as theirs. Some employees chose to quit the company when transferred to the pool.*
> *Second, the pool increased labor costs instead of decreasing them. Since pool workers lacked interest and motivation, supervisors avoided them and started doubling shifts (working one of their own employees sixteen hours) instead of*

215

using pool workers. This left pool workers idle, further hurting their morale and increasing pool costs. It also increased department costs by requiring overtime.

In the next two chapters we examine the relationship of technology to people. In this chapter we discuss the social effects of technology, the relationship of work systems to people, and planning for technology. In the next chapter we discuss improved adjustment to technology through enriched jobs and sociotechnical work systems.

SOCIAL EFFECTS OF TECHNOLOGY

TWO FEATURES OF TECHNOLOGY. It is difficult to generalize about technology because each situation where it is used is different; however, we can say with some confidence that its overwhelming social features are change and integration. With regard to change, the price that technology exacts for the progress it brings is that people must change. The technological revolution produces, perhaps with a time lag, an associated social revolution. Technology is moving so fast that it is creating social problems long before society is able to develop solutions. At the workplace new forms of organization, new ways of supervision, new reward structures, and a host of other changes are being required in order to absorb technology. For adjustment to technology what is needed is more mobility—economic as well as social, occupational as well as geographic, managerial as well as employee.

With regard to integration, technology requires more of it. All the complex activities that technology requires must somehow be put back together to make a whole product, a whole organization, and a whole society. This integration is much more difficult in a high-technology society than in a low-technology one, because high technology tends to make a system more complex and make its parts more interdependent.

TECHNOLOGY AND OCCUPATIONS. Technology tends to require more professional, scientific, and other white-collar workers to keep the system supplied with resources and in operating condition. In most advanced installations the ratio of white-collar to blue-collar employees has increased. Since people by nature are not efficient machines, it seems appropriate to replace routine jobs with machine systems that can do the job faster and better, thus releasing people to do more advanced work, which usually is white-collar work.

As it moves workers into white-collar work, technology generally upgrades the skill and intellectual requirements of the total work force. The day laborer becomes a crane operator, the clerk becomes a computer programmer, and the laboratory technician becomes an electrical engineer working on new electronic marvels. Technology tends to require a higher level of skill both in production work and in supporting services. A generation ago the typical organization had a range of skills approaching curve *A* shown in Figure 13-1. This curve was shaped somewhat like the normal curve of abilities among people. Since the two curves were matched, an adequate supply of labor tended to develop.

In modern organizations the curve has moved toward the right, higher in skill, as shown in curve *B*. In many organizations the skill distribution has become bi-modal, as shown by the second top on the curve. Many scientific and professional people are needed to design, implement, and appraise the complex machines and work systems of technology, creating the secondary bulge toward the skilled end of the scale.

Curve *C* represents the skill distribution that is developing in firms especially oriented toward research, development, and government scientific contracting. Even though these firms manufacture products for sale, much of their effort is devoted to development and building prototypes. In some of these the number of scientific and professional people exceeds the total number of all other employees. Generally, a technologically advanced operation has a higher proportion of technical support groups and proportionately fewer direct production people. Even many of the production people are technically skilled knowledge workers operating electronic panels, rather than machine operators working with manual skill.

TECHNOLOGY AND EDUCATION. The modern need for higher skills means that a premium is put upon education in the labor market. More education and training of the work force becomes imperative in order to avoid a surplus of under-developed people and a shortage of highly developed people.

Most seriously displaced by technology are older workers[2] and those who lack the capacity for retraining. It is difficult to place them in other jobs in their organization, and often they are not qualified for other than unskilled jobs in the labor market. For example, when inefficient packing plants and assembly lines have been closed, from 30 to 50 percent of the labor force has been considered unsuitable for retraining for equivalent skills in the labor market. Some of these persons had to step down to less skilled jobs, and others found it necessary to

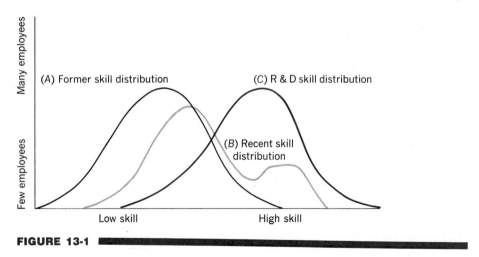

FIGURE 13-1 ■

Changes in skill distribution in an organization resulting from advances in technology.

move to service occupations.[3] Today's high school dropouts may not know it, but many have already set the limits of their own opportunity.

The need for an educated work force with high-level skills has sharply increased the demand for *biprofessional and multiprofessional employees.* These are persons who are trained in two or more professions or intellectual disciplines, such as engineering and law or accounting and science. Since these persons are competent in more than one discipline, they are able to perform some of the coordinative and integrative work required by modern complex work systems. The demand is especially high for multiprofessional managers who are qualified in some technical specialty in addition to management so that they can more easily manage technical work units such as a research function. A combination of physics and management is an example. The demand for multiprofessionals means that organizations will want to support in every way possible their ambitious employees who seek to develop a second intellectual capability. In future years those persons' biprofessional capabilities may be exactly the ones the organization comes to need.

TECHNOLOGY AND LABOR. In eighteenth-century England a band of workers known as Luddites challenged the industrial revolution by roaming the countryside, smashing machinery and burning factories. They believed that machinery threatened jobs. Laborers in the twentieth century have faced technology with more maturity but nevertheless with considerable anxiety. Some laborers and social analysts, like the Luddites, view technology with a *technophobia,* which is an emotional fear of all technology regardless of its consequences.

Workers especially seem to fear unemployment as a result of technology. In examining unemployment, it is necessary to distinguish a single employer from the economy as a whole. For the whole economic system the weight of evidence is that technology does not cause long-run unemployment.[4] Technology allows labor to be allocated to more efficient uses, but it does not destroy the need for labor. Throughout history, as productivity has risen from advancing technology, the number of jobs has not declined. From the international point of view, technology in one country may actually increase job opportunities because it reduces product costs in relation to costs in other countries, permitting more workers in the advancing country to be employed producing goods to sell internationally.

For a single employer technology nearly always causes job changes and employee retraining. Workers who think that technology will abolish the exact jobs they now have are probably correct. With technology moving as fast as it is, few jobs will remain static during an employee's working life. Technology does not destroy jobs for all time, but it does create different jobs that workers often are not prepared to fill. Therefore, it produces employee insecurity, stress, anxiety, and possible layoff, which management needs to handle most carefully in introducing technology.[5] Even when management is able to offer complete job and wage security with technological advances, workers still make sacrifices of their time and energy for retraining. Certainly they expect to make some sacrifices to advance productivity for their society, but this situation also obligates management to perform long-range planning to make the changeover as smooth as possible.

In spite of individual employee difficulties with technology, many union leaders have recognized that it is essential to long-run employee gains and have supported it in theory. In practice, they have sometimes opposed it as being too sudden, too broad in coverage, or inappropriate to the circumstances. They have also insisted upon retraining rights, severance pay, and other benefits that soften dislocations caused by technology. Practices differ among unions because technology affects their members differently and because unions have different philosophies.

THE RELATIONSHIP OF WORK SYSTEMS AND PEOPLE

There are two basic ways in which work is organized. The first relates to the flow of authority and is known as *organizational structure* or merely organization. The second relates to the flow of work itself from one operation to another and is known as *procedure.* Synonyms are method, system, and work flow. Alert managers usually recognize the behavioral aspects of organization structure because of the superior-subordinate relationship that it establishes, but more often than not they ignore or overlook the behavioral aspects of work flow. They reason that work flow and the layout over which it flows are *engineering* factors, which are to be distinguished from *human* factors. In the usual case, however, work flow has many behavioral aspects because it sets people in interaction as they perform their work.

One of management's most fundamental ideas is systems and methods improvement, by which it seeks to make optimum use of division of labor and specialization and to achieve order and balance in the performance of work. However, workers do not like to be "engineered" in methods improvement. They perceive that improvement is measured in technical terms and that the human dissatisfactions caused by the "improvement" are generally overlooked. The goal of methods improvement is greater productivity, but sometimes it brings human complications that reduce effectiveness and offset the technical advantages gained.

INITIATION OF ACTION. One important aspect of work flow is that it determines who will "initiate" an activity and who will "receive" it. At each point in the flow of work one person gives material to the next person who will work on it. Along the way, staff experts give ideas and instructions. This process of sending work to another is an *initiation of action* on another person. When an initiation results from work flow, it is called a *procedural initiation* to distinguish it from an *authority initiation,* which comes from formal authority of a superior, and *informal initiation,* which arises through the consent of the informal group. Receivers of any initiation are psychologically secondary, but receivers of a procedural initiation are especially so because they may receive from a worker who is neither a supervisor nor an informal leader—from someone who "just shouldn't be pushing them around." In one plant, for example, operator B was a fast worker and caused work to pile up at the next work station controlled by operator C. Considerable resentment was shown by C, who thought B made C look like a laggard.

When procedural initiation comes from someone of distinctly less skill, someone much younger, or someone inferior by any measure of status, human problems can become serious. These problems tend to be compounded if the relationship involves pressure on the receiver, as in the following example from an early study of restaurants.[6]

Large restaurants sometimes used teenagers as runners to communicate the needs of the serving pantry to the kitchen. This placed the runner in the position of "telling" the cooks to prepare and send particular types of food. The result was that teenagers initiated action on high-status cooks. In essence, they were telling cooks what to do. This relationship often was a trouble spot in the restaurants studied. Cooks resented the control exercised on them by teenagers of inferior restaurant status. Practical solutions included (1) using a mechanical voice system that eliminated face-to-face contact and (2) changing the initiator to someone of more status.

Further problems tend to arise when a procedural initiation affects "sensitive" areas such as how much work employees do (e.g., time study) and their rates of pay (e.g., job evaluation). Research is sufficient to support the general conclusion that *procedural initiations that are from low-status to high-status persons, that place heavy pressures on the receiver, or that affect sensitive parts of the receiver's work tend to be trouble spots.* Management's responsibility is to discover these situations in its work processes and, if they cannot be avoided, to plan them carefully.

Procedural, authority, and informal initiations of action come from persons; however, not all work initiations are identifiable as coming directly from some other person or group. Many activities arise directly out of the work itself, wherein people respond to cues implicit in the operating situation. For example, a ceramic glaze has finished its baking cycle and the operator acts to remove it from the furnace, or the cellophane ribbon creases on a cellophane machine and workers act as a team to correct it. In these instances, one cannot determine who initiates an event because it arises from the work itself. This kind of initiation not identifiable with persons is called an *impersonal, or situational, initiation of action.* Employees are more prone to accept this kind of initiation compared with procedural and authority initiations. The main reason appears to be that workers are less likely to resent and feel subordinate to the impersonal requirements of the work itself.

SYSTEM DESIGN FOR BETTER TEAMWORK. Another important aspect of work procedure is that it should permit people to work together as a team whenever the work flow requires it. Teamwork can be engineered out of a work situation by means of layouts and job assignments that separate people so that it is impractical for them to work together, even though the work flow requires teamwork. In one instance two operators, functionally interdependent, were unnecessarily on separate shifts, which prevented the operators from coordinating their work. In another instance, one operator fed parts to two separate lines that were in competition, and each line regularly claimed that the operator favored the other. In another situation the operator of a continuous bottle-forming machine was so far separated from the first inspection station on the line that there was no way to be sure whether the machine was producing satisfactory quality. The problem was solved by continuously reporting inspection results from the inspector to an information panel in front of the operator. This feedback helped the operator make proper machine adjustments.[7] One of the earliest illustrations of teamwork engineered out of a job was Rice's study of a textile mill in India.[8]

The mill was intensively reengineered according to basic industrial engineering procedures. Each job had carefully assigned work loads based on engineering study. In one room there were 224 looms operated and maintained by twelve occupational groups. Each weaver tended twenty-four or thirty-two looms, each battery filler served forty to fifty looms, and each smash hand served an average of seventy-five looms. The other nine occupations were service and maintenance, and each worker had either 112 or 224 looms.

Although the mill appeared to be superbly engineered, it failed to reach satisfactory output. Research disclosed that close teamwork of all twelve occupations was required to maintain production, yet work organization prevented this teamwork. Each battery filler served all looms of one weaver and part of the looms of a second weaver, which meant a weaver and battery filler were not a team unit, even though the nature of the process required it. In effect, a weaver tending twenty-four looms and using a battery filler serving forty looms, worked with three-fifths of a battery filler, while another weaver shared two-fifths of the filler. The situation was even more confused with smash hands who tended seventy-five looms.

Eventually work was reorganized so that a certain group of workers had responsibility for a definite number of machines. Workers then were able to set up interaction and teamwork that caused production to soar.

Work flow can also be set up in such a way that the job puts unreasonable stress on a person. In a series of similar offices the secretary of each was required to prepare technical correspondence for five to seven managers, answer the telephone, greet visitors, and serve as group leader of a few clerks. The result was high turnover and more than a normal amount of nervous disorders among the secretaries. Another example is that of a hotel food checker who inspected trays brought by food handlers on their way to dining rooms. The checker inspected two lines serving two separate dining rooms and also handled room-service orders on the telephone. Under conditions of this type it is useless to try to solve the problem by training the participants to understand each other better or to communicate better. The first requirement is to reorganize the work flow. Then interpersonal training may not be necessary.

COMMUNICATION PATTERNS. It is well known that plant layout and work flow have much to do with the opportunities that people have to talk with one another during work. In an insurance office, for example, the layout of desks was such that persons who needed to talk to coordinate their work were unnecessarily separated by a broad aisle. Employees met the problem by loudly calling across the aisle, but this eventually had to be stopped because of the disturbance. The end result was poor communication. In another company sewing machines were located so that talking was discouraged, but management soon discovered that another layout that permitted talking led to higher productivity because it relieved the monotony of routine work.

Managers often overlook the fact that layout can affect off-duty interaction of employees. Some years ago I visited a new factory that was a model of engineering efficiency. Although the lunchroom was spotless and efficiently designed, I ate an uneasy meal. I normally have an affinity for the factory environment, but this time it was too much—the cafeteria was located in the basement directly beneath stamping and light forging presses! Vibration was so terrific it stopped conversation. The floor and ceiling shook; the dishes rattled; there was no sound-deadening tile on the ceiling. The space beneath the presses apparently was not needed for other functions; so the cafeteria received it, but employee communication and relaxation were thereby excluded at mealtime. Lunch hours in the plant were staggered into four periods, which meant that the presses operated during the time most employees ate. When I asked my host "Why?" his answer was "The cafeteria is for eating only, and anyway the noise shouldn't bother anyone."

CONTROL OF RED TAPE. One aspect of procedure that is universally known and respected for its effect on people is red tape. It is the unnecessary procedure that delays and harasses people everywhere. The term originated from real red tape used to tie government documents, many of which have long been challenged as unnecessary by those who prepare them. No doubt some of the work in government—and in business as well—is true red tape, but some is in reality "fictitious red tape." It exists when those who perform the procedure do not know why they are doing it. They, consequently, *think* it is red tape, but from a broader viewpoint the work is both necessary and worthwhile. The remedy for fictitious red tape is improved communication and development of a broader perspective among those who perform the work.

Genuine red tape arises primarily because (1) managers are afraid to delegate and consequently set up all sorts of unnecessary approvals and checks, and (2) procedures, even though once useful, tend to persist long after their usefulness has passed. The first reason can be eliminated through good leadership, as discussed in earlier chapters, but the second reason deserves further attention at this point.

One cause of the "stickiness" of red tape is normal resistance to change. A procedure tends to become a habit, and people resist changing it. Since it was, in a sense, set up to eliminate thinking by giving its followers a routine to use without having to decide each step, they seldom think about changing it. They get "stuck in a rut." Another cause of useless procedure is that it is often determined by a higher authority who does not understand work problems, but employees hesitate to challenge the procedure because they did not participate in establishing it. In other cases, people do not know why they are performing a procedure; consequently they cannot know whether it is useless or not, and they do not dare to expose their "ignorance" by questioning a procedure that their boss may be able to prove essential beyond a shadow of a doubt. People do not like to get caught not knowing something about their work.

Another reason for useless procedures is that most of them cross lines of authority, jumping from one chain of command to another. Under these conditions, no one employee feels a personal responsibility to change the procedure. As one executive put it, "They know about this procedure, too—and it originates with them—so let them change it." An additional reason why procedures tend to outlive their usefulness is that the persons who created them are often supervisors who do not have to follow them; hence they tend to forget about them, letting them go on and on—and on.

The human problem with red tape is that it frustrates and irritates people and encourages worry and carelessness while they perform it. They do not like to do work that they think is useless. It challenges their human dignity and undermines their feeling that their work is worthwhile and necessary. In this way the apparently nonhuman activity called procedure can have a very definite effect on human behavior. This is simply further evidence that procedures of all types—necessary and unnecessary—are interwoven into the whole human fabric of an organization. Technical matters of procedure cannot be considered apart from the human environment in which they occur. Departments that are active in procedure creation, such as industrial engineering and accounting, need to give appropriate weight to the human dimensions of their procedures, because procedures that upset human relationships can do more harm than good. One sure way to raise the blood pressure of any group is to harness it with red tape.

The red tape of inflexible rules and procedures can result in injustice, as the following situation illustrates. A regional sales manager with a large firm insisted that reports of sales representatives' calls and their expense accounts for the week ending on a Friday be in his office on the following Monday, despite the fact that some of the offices had to mail their reports from distant cities. If a sales call report did not accompany the expense report, the sales manager would not pay the expenses for it.

While in most instances this rule was no problem, there was a case in a district office in which the sales representative mailed his expense account only, along with a note that he had been called to his parents' home in an emergency and that the sales call report would follow when he returned. The manager would make no exception, and withheld the sales representative's paycheck. Since the sales representative had no advance notice of this and no advance payment to cover his expenses, this was a real blow to him when he returned. Resentment was felt, not only by him and the other people in his district, but throughout the region because of the unfairness that they saw in the system and the way the manager interpreted it. A flexible system and a flexible manager would have produced better results.

ALIENATION. Alienation may result from poor design of sociotechnical systems. Since work systems are usually planned by someone other than the operators, often the operators do not understand why the system operates the way it does. In addition, division of labor lets each operator perform only a small portion of the total work to be done, so jobs begin to lose their social significance and appear meaningless. Workers no longer see where they fit into the scheme of things; no longer do they see the value of their efforts. When feelings of powerlessness and meaningless work become substantial, an employee may develop psychological problems. The general term describing these conditions is *alienation,* which is a feeling of powerlessness, lack of meaning, loneliness, disorientation, and lack of attachment to job, work group, or organization. When workers are performing an insignificant task, frustrated by red tape, isolated from communication with others, prevented from teamwork, and controlled by initiations of action from others, then alienation is bound to develop.

Alienated persons often tend to withdraw from realities and live in a detached world. The real world around them lacks meaning and satisfaction, and they feel estranged. In other instances they may feel antagonistic toward the system. From time to time all of us have these feelings during moments of frustration, but with some employees in some types of jobs the situation becomes more serious. Management then needs to take action such as job enrichment, mentioned in the next chapter, in order to overcome tendencies toward alienation.

Research shows that alienation tends to be low in high-technology process industries, compared with mechanized assembly-line operations. Using Woodward's classification, unit and process production are shown to have a low alienation, while mass production has high alienation.[9] The relationship is curvilinear, as shown in Figure 13-2. This relationship suggests that much of modern industry that is now in the mass-production stage will move toward less alienating conditions as technology advances. In this manner, advancing technology will be favorable to workers.

The relationship of alienation to technology is only a general one, because there are other causes of alienation. For example, an autocratic management may cause alienation, or alienation may be related to conditions external to the organization. Some alienation also may occur among managers and high-level professionals for a variety of reasons.

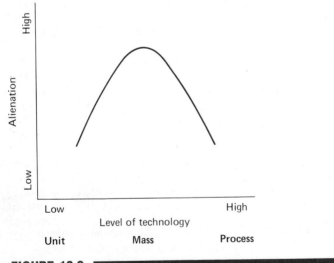

FIGURE 13-2

Relationship of alienation and level of technology.

EFFECTS OF WORK SYSTEMS.   The evidence is clear that work systems and layout have a substantial effect on human behavior. They do this by:

1.   Determining who initiates procedural action on whom, and some of the conditions in which the initiation occurs.

2.   Influencing the degree to which employees performing interdependent functions can work together as a team.

3.   Affecting the communication patterns of employees.

4.   Creating possibilities for unnecessary procedures, generally called red tape.

5.   Providing tasks that seem insignificant and powerless, thereby contributing to alienation.

    The general conclusion is that *relationships among workers in a system can be just as important as relationships of the work in that system.* In the design of any system it is folly to spend all one's time planning work relationships but ignoring worker relationships.

    From the social point of view we need to design systems that are as appropriate for people as possible, considering economic and other factors in the situation. Regardless of what kind of system is developed, workers and their supervisors will try to adjust to it. In nearly all cases they will adjust reasonably well, because people have a remarkable sense of adaptability. Following are two examples of employee adaptability.

    An air-conditioning manufacturer required three final assembly departments to complete a specific daily quota of air conditioners. Supervisors soon learned that the ordinary uncertainties of production caused them to produce over their quota on some days and under their quota on other days. However, management was quite insistent that they must meet the quota every day so that shipping schedules could be met. In response to this system established by management, the supervisors began their own "system." They started keeping a store of ten to fifty "almost-finished" air conditioners under a tarpaulin in each department. When they saw that they were running short for the day, they took from this store a nearly finished air conditioner and ran it through final assembly steps in order to meet the standard. Then, when they produced over the standard on another day, they worked some of their production back into the store.

    If one production line had a series of bad days, the other supervisors lent to it from their stores, if necessary, or they lent it an employee from their group to help catch up. In this way, management's needs for a standard output were met, and supervisors' needs for acceptance by management were met.

    A similar situation developed with the tool-grinding manager in another large plant. In this plant tool-grinding costs were under a very tight budget, but supervisory costs were more loosely budgeted. This manager used one of two tool supervisors on regular tool-grinding work four hours a day. This action kept grinding costs within the budget and gave no problem in the supervisory budget either. In this manner, formal requirements of the company were met, but one tool-grinding supervisor was unhappy doing operative work.

IMPROVING ADJUSTMENT TO TECHNOLOGY

The supportive model of organizational behavior suggests that what is most needed to help employees adjust to technology is supportive conduct by management. Employees need to feel that their interests in the work situation are being adequately considered and fully protected by management. They need confidence that in the long run they will gain from technology and that their employer will help them achieve these gains. When this supportive climate exists, they will be more receptive to the changes that technology is thrusting upon them. Earlier chapters, such as the ones on participation and change, are particularly applicable to technology; but some additional comments about planning and communicating are appropriate.

PLANNING FOR NEW TECHNOLOGY. A number of difficulties are caused by poor planning. Sometimes not enough time is allowed for a changeover to new technology, giving rise to much management pressure to make the system operative. Errors in planning can also lead to unexpected delays, or "bugs," thus increasing employee anxiety. Weak planning may lead to frantic, crisis installations, where every day produces a new emergency of some kind. In addition to technical planning, plans must be made for integration of all the human factors appropriately. If an organization has a long history of good employee relations, it will have a firm base on which to build its human plans.

A special area of deficiency is insufficient planning for transfers, reclassifications, and retraining. Employee changes of this magnitude require about as much lead time as technical parts of an installation require. However, management should not plan so absolutely that it commits itself irrevocably to some course of action that later proves impractical. Since the future cannot be foreseen accurately, flexibility is essential; and employees will rest easier with some of the setbacks during installation if they know that flexibility exists.

Another difficulty is that supplier representatives and others making the installation often deal poorly with the work group. Intent upon the technical complexities of their installation, they overlook its human complexities. The supplier has a natural tendency to emphasize hardware, because it is supplier machinery that is being installed, whereas the people are the employer's. Wanting to be certain that the product sold is technically perfect, the supplier has little compassion for the human element and may look upon the frailties of people as an impediment to better machine performance. Human problems are more or less bypassed, through no one's malicious intent but simply because those involved are concentrating on other matters.

If human problems are to get much hearing, the employer must consciously bring them in. In the very beginning top-management people need to make it clear that they are striving for a whole installation, rather than one only technically complete, and that they want human factors given equal billing with technical factors. And by follow-up they must show that they really do mean what they have said.

Deadlines and intermediate goals for both technical and human factors should be set so that employees have definite mileposts as they go along.

Since technology requires more supervisory competence and responsibility, long-range supervisory training must be started early. Supervisors need to be upgraded to handle their more complex duties before the equipment installation so that their full capacities are available during the difficult period of changeover. In too many cases, supervisors receive their training during installation, thus taking them away from their jobs when they are needed most, or after installation, when some of their special need for competence has passed. In new installations the supervisors clearly play their keystone role described in an earlier chapter.

The scientific matters of technology are likely to take care of themselves in the sense that adequate tangible evidence of their success or failure will be apparent in the operation of the equipment; however, human matters are more nebulous and may not disclose themselves unless they are consciously sought by specialists skilled in organizational behavior. Though less apparent, the human factor is more important because it is the operators and their supervisors who ultimately determine productivity of the system. The people operate the machines rather than the other way around. Machines are totally dependent on people for input and programming, and people can ensure system inefficiency by not "cooperating" with them, that is, by withholding data, giving input of poor quality, and so on. Technology is built on both scientific and human foundations, not on science alone.

THE NEED FOR COMMUNICATION. In spite of all its emphasis on communication, management sometimes has not communicated enough when technology comes on stage. Many employees are awed by the immense economic and technical complexities of technological systems and are ready to believe anything. In the absence of accurate, understandable information, they are prone to believe the worst. Studies have disclosed that often employees are dissatisfied with the amount and kind of information they receive. Management fails to sense the immense information void that it needs to fill. Conditions of change introduce many natural communication barriers that must be overcome. The greater the change, the greater the barriers are likely to be; and certainly technology is a change for both management and employees.

Communications about technology need to display both good intent and good judgment. They must agree with reality. For example, one company printed articles in its magazine stating that technology creates more jobs, but at the same time it was introducing new machinery that caused a few people to be laid off. Undoubtedly technology does create jobs but not necessarily for the particular people who have just been displaced by more efficient machinery. These articles undermined the integrity of communications by holding out glowing promises of what technology would do for people, some of whom were being laid off at approximately the same time! The whole picture was not presented.

It is essential for communications to reach all employees affected. In transfer situations the employees in the group receiving a transferred employee may be as upset as the transferred employee is, even though they will stay where they are. The fact that a new person is moving into their midst gives them cause for insecurity, as shown in the following example.

As a result of a new computer system, a bank planned to close a branch office and move it to the home office a few blocks away. The move was carefully planned and well organized. Knowing that branch employees would have cause for insecurity, management fully informed them of impending changes three months in advance and kept them informed as plans progressed. They knew what was expected of them during the move, what efforts management was taking to protect their interests, and what jobs they would be assigned in the home office. Their security was satisfactory, and morale was high.

The home office situation was opposite. Since these employees were "staying put," management overlooked communicating details of the move to them. But these employees were concerned about how their jobs would be affected, about the possibility of receiving incompatible members into existing groups, and about orienting and training the transferees. Many were insecure because they felt they might have to work for a new supervisor transferred from the branch. They wondered who would get the better job assignments, and so on. Their morale was low.

The result was an unusual situation regarding change. Communication and job satisfaction were definitely lacking in the home office but were abundant in the branch! Management was achieving sound results with its efforts but its efforts were improperly allocated—all to the transferees and none to the group receiving them.

SUMMARY

Technology is a powerful economic and social tool that can bring substantial benefits to society. Its effects are variable, but it tends to require higher worker skills, more white-collar work, and more multiprofessional employees. Labor unions generally accept technology as beneficial to society as a whole, but they want security provisions to protect individuals dislocated by it.

The flow of work especially affects people in organizations. It determines who initiates action on whom, influences the degree to which employees can work together as a team, affects communication patterns, creates possibilities of red tape, and may create powerlessness and low job significance. The results may be emotional problems such as frustration, a feeling of loneliness, stress, and alienation. The conclusion is that relationships of workers in a system can be just as important as relationships of the work in that system. For this reason, in the introduction of technology careful planning and communication are essential.

TERMS AND CONCEPTS FOR REVIEW

Sociotechnical systems	Initiation of action
Multiprofessional employees	Impersonal initiation of action
Luddites	Red tape
Technophobia	Alienation

REVIEW QUESTIONS

1. Explain how technology changes the skill distribution of workers in an organization. Prepare a chart to illustrate your discussion.
2. Discuss labor union attitudes toward introduction of technology in the United States. Interview union leaders to determine their personal views on this subject.
3. Discuss how initiation of action affects people at work.
4. Discuss possible technological causes of alienation and appropriate corrective actions that might be taken.
5. Prepare a thorough plan for handling human resources during introduction of a computer in an organization of your choice.

CASES

THE PLANT GUARDS

The Pemberton Company is building a new manufacturing plant, and management is trying to decide whether it should employ its own guards or use those provided by a separate security service. At its present plants the company uses its own guards, but it has been having difficulty recruiting them because the job is a dead-end one and most people hired feel it is a trivial, meaningless occupation at the plants. A person representing a security service says that its guards will demonstrate more expertness and pride in their work, because guard duty is the primary occupation of the security service. Furthermore, there are opportunities for advancement in the security service, rather than the dead-end job which the company offers its guards.

Analysis by company management shows that costs will be the same with either alternative, so the decision will be made on the basis of other than cost factors.

QUESTION

1. In the role of company management, appraise the noncost factors (the sociotechnical factors) in this situation and offer your decision with reasons.

TWO WORKERS

In a manufacturing plant a worker on one production line receives feedback about the quality of her work from an inspector who gives her an hourly report of the defective parts she has produced. On another production line a worker receives feedback about the quality of his work by means of a lighted control panel at his work station. The panel has two sections. One section tells the number of acceptable parts produced during the hour compared with standard for the hour. The other section gives cumulative acceptable parts for the day compared with standard production required.

QUESTION

1. Discuss differences between the sociotechnical systems for the two workers.

THE CENTRAL MOTOR POOL

A sales company established a central motor pool for its sales representatives, rather than allowing each representative to have an automobile. The pool was established to achieve estimated savings, because sales representatives spent about one-third of their time in the office and only two-thirds of their time visiting customers. Sales representatives complained bitterly about not having their own cars, and there was much squabbling regarding who would get which car. There was also careless handling of cars, because they felt no personal responsibility for the car assigned to them. Some of them reduced travel time, even though travel was necessary to make sales.

Because of difficulties with the pool, management finally decided that all sales representatives traveling over 1,000 miles a month could have an automobile. Then most of them started traveling that much, even when they did not need to do so.

QUESTION
1. Analyze the sociotechnical relationships in this situation and offer your recommendation.

REFERENCES

1. Edward E. Lawler III, and J. Richard Hackman, "Corporate Profits and Employee Satisfaction: Must They Be in Conflict?" *California Management Review*, Fall 1971, p. 49.

2. J. John Palen and Frank J. Fahey, "Unemployment and Reemployment Success: An Analysis of the Studebaker Shutdown," *Industrial and Labor Relations Review*, January 1968, pp. 234–250, reporting the relationship of age and unemployment to be significant to the .001 degree.

3. For an assembly-line example see "Auto Workers Learn New Skills," *Business Week*, July 29 1961, p. 74.

4. For example, the U.S. National Commission on Technology, Automation, and Economic Progress, in its *Technology and the American Economy*, vol. 1, 1966, p. 9, states flatly, "The persistence of a high general level of unemployment in the years following the Korean War was not the result of accelerated technological progress." Based on his study of employment statistics, the United States Commissioner of Labor Statistics, in his article "What Employment Statistics Show," *Automation*, April 1964, p. 55, concludes, "Technology as such does not result in a net loss of jobs in the economy."

5. For an example of the way technological change upsets employees see John Chadwick-Jones, *Automation and Behavior: A Social Psychological Study*, New York: John Wiley & Sons, Inc., 1970.

6. William F. Whyte, *Human Relations in the Restaurant Industry*, New York: McGraw-Hill Book Company, 1948, pp. 49–63.

7. For evidence that increased knowledge of performance brings better performance in routine work see P. S. Hundal, "Knowledge of Performance as an Incentive in Repetitive Industrial Work," *Journal of Applied Psychology*, June 1969, pp. 224–226.

8. A. K. Rice, "Productivity and Social Organization in an Indian Weaving Shed," *Human Relations*, vol. 6, no. 4, 1953, pp. 297–329.

9. Michael Fullan, "Industrial Technology and Worker Integration in the Organization," *American Sociological Review,* December 1970, pp. 1028–1039; and Jon M. Shepard, *Automation and Alienation: A Study of Office and Factory Workers,* Cambridge, Mass.: The M.I.T. Press, 1971. For a contrary opinion not supporting alienation of mass production workers see William H. Form, "Technology and Social Behavior of Workers in Four Countries: A Socio-technical Perspective," *American Sociological Review,* December 1972, pp. 727–738.

10. Geert Hofstede, "Alienation at the Top," *Organizational Dynamics,* Winter 1976, pp. 44–60.

CHAPTER 14
ENRICHING JOBS AND WORK SYSTEMS

When the work is right, employee attitudes are right.
That is the job enrichment strategy—get the work right.
Robert N. Ford[1]

Although job enrichment may, as a by-product, sometimes improve productivity,
it should really be thought of in terms of a responsibility
that employers have to workers and to society.
James O'Toole[2]

LEARNING OBJECTIVES

TO UNDERSTAND:
The complex nature of job design
Uses of job enrichment
Core dimensions of jobs
Natural work modules
Natural work teams
The contingency nature of job enrichment
Enriched sociotechnical work systems

An electric appliance manufacturer had an assembly line in which ten workers assembled about twenty parts into a product. Work was highly specialized and monotonous in the traditional manner of classical scientific management. Finally the job was redesigned to allow teams of two workers to assemble all twenty parts to produce the whole product. Now two people as a team felt responsible for each product produced. It was their own creation. The quality improvement that resulted was so large that field repair costs for the product were reduced by 25 percent, and you can imagine how much more pleased customers were when their product broke down less often. In addition, because the workers were more interested in their jobs, absenteeism fell by more than 50 percent.[3]

Traditional work design with its high functionalization and specialization has been successful in bringing benefits to society, but its disadvantage has been its high human costs. As times have changed, these human costs have become less acceptable, so organizations are giving more attention to work designs that provide effective human results along with their technical results. In this chapter we discuss approaches toward more human work design, including job design, job enrichment, and enriched sociotechnical work systems.

JOB DESIGN

Job design refers to specification of the content and relationships of jobs as they affect both people and organizational success. Classical job design as it developed from scientific management focused on specialization and efficiency in the performance of narrow tasks. As it evolved, it used full division of labor, rigid hierarchy, and standardization of labor to reach its objective of efficiency. The idea was to lower costs by using unskilled, repetitive labor that could be trained easily to do a small part of the job. Job performance was controlled by a large hierarchy that strictly enforced the one best way of work as defined by technical people.

Since classical design gave inadequate attention to human factors of work, many difficulties developed. There was excessive division of labor and overdependence on rules, procedures, and hierarchy. Specialized workers became socially isolated from their fellow workers, because their highly specialized work weakened their community of interest in the whole product. Many workers were so deskilled that they lost pride in their work. The result was higher turnover and absenteeism. Quality declined, and workers became alienated. Conflict arose as workers tried to improve their conditions. Management's response to this situation was to tighten controls, to increase supervision, and to organize more rigidly. These actions were calculated to improve the situation, but they only made it worse, because they further dehumanized the work. Management made a common error by treating the symptoms rather than the causes of the problems. The real cause was that in many instances the job itself simply was not satisfying. The odd condition developed for some employees that the more they worked, the *less* they were satisfied. Hence, the desire to work declined.[4]

A factor contributing to the problem was that the workers themselves were changing. They became more educated, more affluent (partly because of the technological effectiveness of classical job design), and more independent. They began reaching for higher-order needs, something more than merely earning their bread. Perhaps classical design was best for a poor, uneducated, often illiterate work force that lacked skills, but it was less appropriate for the new work force. Design of jobs and organizations had failed to keep up with widespread changes in worker aspirations and attitudes. Employers now had two reasons for redesigning jobs and organizations:

1. Classical design originally gave inadequate attention to human needs.

2. The needs and aspirations of workers themselves were changing.

OPTIONS AVAILABLE TO MANAGEMENT. Several options for job design problems were available to management.

1. Leave the job as it is, and employ only workers who like the rigid environment and routine specialization of classical design. Not all workers object to this form of work. Some may even relish it because of the security it provides.

2. Leave the job as it is, but pay workers more so that they will better accept the situation. Since classical design does produce economic gain, management can afford to share the gain with workers.

3.   Mechanize and automate routine jobs so that the labor that is unhappy with the job is no longer needed. Let machines do the routine work of people.

4.   Redesign jobs to have the attributes desired by people, and redesign organizations to have the environment desired by people.

Although all four options have usefulness in certain situations, the one that especially relates to organizational behavior is option Number 4. There is a need to give workers more of a challenge, more of a whole task, more opportunity to use advanced skills, more opportunity for growth, and more chance to contribute their ideas. The classical design of jobs was to construct them according to the technological imperative, that is, to design them according to the needs of technology and give little attention to other criteria. The new approach is to provide a careful balance of the human imperative and the technical imperative. *Jobs are required to fit people as well as technology.* This is a new set of values and a new way of thinking in job design.

HUMANIZED JOBS.   More humanized job design seeks to accomplish a number of goals. It attempts to serve the higher-order needs of workers as well as their more basic needs. It seeks to employ the higher skills that workers possess and to provide an environment that encourages them to improve their skills. The idea is that workers are human resources that are to be developed rather than simply used. Further, the work should not have excessive dysfunctional conditions. It should not put workers under undue stress. It should not damage or degrade their humanness. It should not be threatening or unduly dangerous. Finally, it should contribute to, or at least leave unimpaired, workers' abilities to perform in other life roles, such as citizen, spouse, and parent. That is, work should contribute to general social advancement.

The basic assumption of humanized work is that work is most advantageous when it provides a "best fit" among workers, jobs, technology, and the environment. Accordingly, the best design will be different to fit different arrangements of these variables. This is the essence of contingency job design. Since a design is required to fit the current situation, it is not a one-time thing to be established and retained indefinitely. Rather, there needs to be a regular readjustment among the factors just mentioned in order to maintain the best fit. Although design will be varied to fit environmental conditions, it is contended that for the typical modern job and worker a more humanized job design is needed.

One of the earliest controlled experiments with job design was in the 1950s in an appliance manufacturing plant.[5] In the preexisting job design each worker performed one of nine operations along an assembly line. In a revised design called the group design the conveyor and pacing were eliminated, and workers were rotated among the nine stations, using a batch method of assembly. In another revision called the individual design all operations including final inspection were combined into one complete assembly job performed by each worker.

In the group design the productivity index fell from 100 to 89, but quality improved from .72 percent defects to .49 percent. The individual design was the *successful one. Productivity was maintained and improved slightly, while quality improved from .72 percent defects to .18 percent. In addition, employee attitudes improved, and the production process was much more flexible because each worker was working independently.*

JOB ENRICHMENT

Modern efforts to humanize jobs are known as job enrichment. The phrase was coined by Frederick Herzberg based on his research with motivators and mainte- nance factors. Strictly speaking, *job enrichment* means that additional motivators are added to the job so that it is more rewarding, although the term has come to apply to any efforts to humanize jobs. The concept of job enrichment is an improvement on an earlier concept of *job enlargement* that sought to give workers a wider variety of duties to build their roles. The two terms often are used in- terchangeably, although the enrichment concept is more behaviorally sophisti- cated.

The result of job enrichment is really a role enrichment that encourages growth and self-actualization. The job is built in such a way that natural motivation is encouraged. Because motivation is increased, work performance should also improve, thus providing both a more human job and a more productive job. In this manner both the worker and society benefit. The worker performs better, has more job satisfaction, and is more self-actualized, thus being able to participate in all life roles more effectively. Society benefits from the more effectively functioning person as well as the more effective job performance. Following are examples of both quality and quantity improvements with job enrichment. Both an office and a factory situation have been chosen to illustrate its wide applicability.

In the Treasury Department of American Telephone and Telegraph Company, educated and intelligent employees handled correspondence with stockholders. They worked in a highly structured environment under close supervision in order to assure a suitable quality of correspondence. Under these conditions, quality of work was low and turnover was high.

Using a control group and a test group, the jobs of the test group were enriched as follows: (1) The employees were permitted to sign their own names to the letters they prepared; (2) they were held reponsible for the quality of their work; (3) they were encouraged to become experts in the kinds of problems that appealed to them; and (4) subject matter experts were provided for consultation regarding problems.

The control group remained unchanged after six months, but the test group improved by all measurements used. These measurements included turnover, pro- ductivity, absences, promotions from the group, costs, quality, and attitudes.[6]

Unusually high results were obtained with job enrichment in the assembly of electric hot plates in a manufacturing firm. Originally the employees worked on an assembly line, each worker performing a small part of the total assembly. Produc- tivity met the established expectations, Management decided on job enrichment, not because there was a problem, but because the task seemed appropriate for enrichment. *In the enriched procedure, each worker completed a whole hot plate, being personally responsible for its acceptability. The workers rapidly developed improved interest in their work. Controllable rejects dropped from 23 percent to 1 percent, and absenteeism fell from 8 percent to 1 percent. As shown in Figure 14-1, productivity improved as much as 84 percent within six months. Since no other changes were made in the department, most of these results appeared to be from job enrichment.*

APPLYING JOB ENRICHMENT. Viewed in terms of Herzberg's motivational factors, job enrichment occurs when the work itself is more challenging, when achievement is encouraged, when there is opportunity for growth, and when responsibility, advancement, and recognition are provided. In practical terms job enrichment occurs whenever employees feel that there is improvement in the content of the job. Always the improvement must be as viewed by employees, not as viewed by management. Employees are the final judges of what improves their jobs. All that management can do is make judgments about what tends to improve jobs and then try these to determine if employees feel they are improvements.

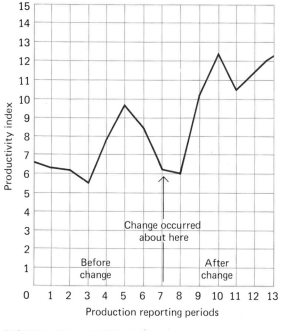

FIGURE 14-1

Productivity increases from job enrichment in hot plate assembly work. (*Source:* Edgar F. Huse and Michael Beer, "Eclectic Approach to Organizational Development," *Harvard Business Review,* September–October 1971, p. 106. Copyright 1971. Reprinted with permission.)

In trying to build motivational factors, management also gives attention to maintenance factors. It attempts to keep maintenance factors constant or higher as the motivational factors are increased. If maintenance factors are allowed to decline during an enrichment program, then employees may be less responsive to the enrichment program because of inadequate maintenance.

Since job enrichment must occur from each employee's personal viewpoint, not all employees will choose enriched jobs if they have an option. A contingency relationship exists in terms of different job needs, and some employees may prefer the simplicity and security of more routine jobs.

In one instance a manufacturer set up production in two different ways.[7] Employees were allowed to choose between work on a standard assembly line or at a bench where they individually assembled the entire product. In the beginning few employees chose to work the enriched jobs, but gradually about half of the workers chose them. For the other half, the more routine assembly operation seemed to fit their needs.

CORE DIMENSIONS OF JOBS.   Building on the work of Turner and Lawrence, Lawler and Hackman have identified five core dimensions that especially provide enrichment for jobs.[8] It is desirable that all five of these dimensions be provided. If one is missing, workers are psychologically deprived, and motivation tends to be reduced. The core dimensions tend to improve motivation, satisfaction, and quality of work, and to reduce turnover and absenteeism. Their effect on quantity of work is less dependable. Managerial and white-collar jobs, as well as blue-collar jobs, often are deficient in core dimensions. Admittedly there are large individual differences in how employees react to core dimensions, but the typical employee finds these to be basic for internal motivation.

Variety.   The first core dimension is *variety in the job*. Variety allows employees to perform different operations using several procedures and perhaps different equipment. It is illustrated by the following anecdote.

A tourist in Mexico stopped at a wood-carver's shop to inquire about the price of a chair that was hand-carved. The wood-carver replied, "Fifty pesos."
The tourist said that she liked the chair and wanted three more exactly like it. Hoping to receive a quantity discount, she asked, "How much for four chairs?"
The wood-carver replied, "Two hundred fifty pesos for four chairs."
Shocked that the price per unit for four chairs was more than for one chair, the tourist asked why. The wood-carver replied, "But, señorita, it is very boring to carve four chairs that are exactly alike."

Jobs that are high in variety are seen by employees as more challenging, because they are required to use a range of skills in performing their work. These jobs also relieve monotony that develops from any repetitive function. If the work is physical, different muscles are used so that one muscular area is not so overworked and tired at the end of the day. Variety gives employees a greater sense of competence, because they can perform different kinds of work in different ways.

One way that has been proposed to provide variety in terms of employee needs is to establish *natural work modules* that consist of a natural subunit of work on a product. Within the limits permitted by schedules, employees could then select one or more modules, depending upon their own desires and their job skills. In this manner each employee would have a personal, individual choice. Employees would be encouraged to acquire more skills so that they could perform other work modules, thereby providing personal growth and a potentially better employee. This type of arrangement would not be possible in many types of jobs, but it perhaps is feasible in others.

Task identity. A second core job dimension is *task identity,* which allows employees to perform a complete piece of the work. Many job enrichment efforts have been focused on this dimension, because in the past the scientific management movement led to overspecialization of routine jobs. Individual employees worked on such a small part of the whole that they were unable to identify any product with their efforts. They could not feel any sense of completion or feel any responsibility for the whole product. When tasks are broadened to produce a whole product or an identifiable part of it, then task identity has been established. This kind of whole job occurred in the assembly of the hot plates mentioned earlier in this chapter. Other examples are a radio factory where each worker assembles a pocket radio, and an office where a single employee prepares a major report rather than a part of it.

Task significance. A third core dimension is *task significance.* It refers to the amount of impact that the work has on other people, as perceived by the worker. The impact can be on others in the organization, such as performing a key step in the work process; or it may be on those outside the organization, such as helping make a lifesaving medical instrument. The key point is that workers believe they are doing something important in their organization or in the society in which they live. The story has been told many times of workers who were told to dig holes in various parts of a storage yard. Then the supervisor looked at the holes and told the workers to fill them and dig more holes in other places. Finally the workers revolted, because they saw no usefulness in their work. Only then did the supervisor tell them that they were digging the holes to try to locate a water pipe.

Autonomy. A fourth core dimension is *autonomy.* It is the job characteristic that gives employees some control over their own affairs, and it appears to be fundamental in building a sense of responsibility in workers. Although they are willing to work within the broad constraints of an organization, they also insist on a degree of freedom. You may remember that in the discussion of Maslow's need hierarchy in Chapter 3, autonomy was mentioned as a possible additional step on the need scale since it is so important to many people. A major study for the National Science Foundation concludes that in a work situation ". . . *autonomy/discretion alone is sufficient to account for positive attitudinal results."*[9] The popular practice of management by objectives (MBO) is one way of establishing more autonomy because it provides a greater role for workers in setting their own goals.

In an assembly operation a company established semiautonomous work teams.[10] *The teams were given responsibility for assembling the product according to whatever assembly procedure they chose. They also were permitted to schedule their own work and even stagger working hours according to needs of different employees as long as they met standard production. The improvements provided a substantial and significant increase in autonomy for the group. As a result, productivity climbed 15 percent.*

The idea of allowing employees to change their working hours to fit their own needs is a useful way to improve autonomy. This approach is known as *flexible working time,* flexitime, and gliding hours. It has developed faster in Europe than in the United States. With flexible time persons may adjust their work schedules to fit their own particular life-styles or to meet unusual needs, such as a visit to a physician. The idea is that, regardless of starting and stopping times, employees will work their full number of hours each day. Employees always work within the restraints of what hours the installation is open for business; and if a job requires teamwork, all employees on a team must flex their work together.

An office provides an example. The office is open from 7 A.M. to 7 P.M., and employees may work their eight hours anytime during that period. One employee is an early riser and prefers to arrive at work at 7 A.M., leaving at 3:30 P.M. in order to shop or engage in sports. Another employee is a late riser and prefers to come to work at 10 A.M., leaving at 6:30 P.M. Another employee arranges her work period to fit a commuter train schedule. Still another employee prefers to take two hours for lunch and occasional shopping. Each employee sets a schedule to fit personal needs. A certain percentage of workers must be at the office for certain hours in order to meet the public, but otherwise their schedule is relatively free.

An advantage to the employer is that tardiness is eliminated, since the employee works a full number of hours regardless of arrival time. Since employees are able to schedule outside activities such as appointments during their working day, they tend to have less one-day absences for these purposes. Perhaps the main benefit is that greater autonomy leads to greater job satisfaction.

Feedback. A fifth core dimension is feedback. *Feedback* refers to information that tells workers how well they are performing. The idea of feedback is a simple one, but it is of much significance to people in the performance of their work. Since they are investing a substantial part of their lives in their work, they want to know how well they are doing. Further, they need to know rather often because they recognize that their performance does vary, and the only way they can make adjustments to improve their performance is to know how they are doing now. Monthly output reports usually are inadequate, because the time lag is too great. Weekly and daily reports are much better, and hourly and continuous reporting may be better if the work process allows this type of feedback. For example, operators attending cigarette-making machines have automatic inspection that provides continuous feedback at panels on the machines so that they know at all times if the work is progressing satisfactorily. The same is also true for bottlers at bottling machines. One major study concluded, "Therefore, information/feedback appears to be the action lever with the single greatest impact on productivity."[11]

PROFILE CHARTS. Before undertaking job enrichment, organizations may study jobs to determine how high they are on each of the five core dimensions. Scales can be determined for each dimension, and then each job is rated according to where its characteristics fit on the scale. For example, on a scale of 1 through 10, variety may be given a rating of 6 and autonomy a rating of 4. In this way the weak dimensions of the job can be determined so that job enrichment needs can be pinpointed. A useful way to compare jobs is to place their dimensions on a profile chart, as shown in Figure 14-2. The chart shows that Job A has much less need for enrichment than Job B, except that Job A is weak in autonomy.

Once the profile of a job is determined, then the job can be studied in detail, giving particular attention to how the weak dimensions may be improved. Not all jobs can be made outstanding on all dimensions, but most jobs can have some enrichment. Compared with jobs that are low in the core dimensions, jobs that are high have been shown to have more motivated and satisfied workers, higher performance, and much less absenteeism. In one study jobs low in the core dimensions had a yearly average of seven days absent for each employee, but the high jobs averaged only three days of absence.[12] In another study workers in enriched jobs reported higher job satisfaction compared with workers *receiving equal pay* but working in unenriched jobs.[13]

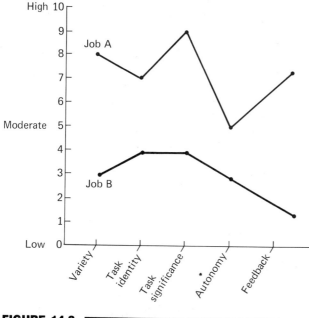

FIGURE 14-2 ■

Profile chart of core dimensions for two jobs.

The accounts section of a bank made major gains from improvements in core dimensions of clerical jobs.[14] Three dimensions were improved substantially, and the other two were improved indirectly. Task identity was improved by building a natural work unit for employees. The natural work unit also led to more task variety and significance. Autonomy was provided by giving the clerks power to approve the checks that they processed. Feedback was improved in several ways.

As a result of a greater sense of responsibility for approving checks, forgeries paid fell 56 percent. This provided a substantial saving for the bank. In addition, misfiled items decreased 19 percent, and complaints from branches decreased over 20 percent. The productivity index increased to 110 compared with a target level of 99.

NATURAL WORK TEAMS. It has been mentioned that natural work modules give an individual employee a sense of performing a whole piece of work. In a similar manner several employees may be arranged into a *natural work team* that performs an entire unit of work. In this way employees whose task requires them to work together are better able to learn each other's needs and develop teamwork. By attaching themselves to a larger team that performs a major task, those employees who are performing routine work are able to develop a greater sense of task significance. It is surprising how our desire to develop specialization often leads to separation of people that are needed to make natural work teams.

Consider the experience of a telephone company with its service order department.[15] Originally the service representatives and typists who prepared service orders were in separate areas of the office, and each took orders in rotation as they were received. Then different teams of representatives were assigned their own geographical region, and a few typists were moved to be with them, working only on their service orders. The employees now became a natural work team that could cooperate in performing a whole task. The result was that orders typed on time increased from 27 percent to between 90 and 100 percent, and service order accuracy exceeded the expected standard. Productivity also improved.

THE CONTINGENCY NATURE OF JOB ENRICHMENT. Although some would argue that job enrichment is universally desirable because it gives workers more important roles, evidence indicates that job enrichment is a contingency relationship. It is more appropriate for some situations than for others, and in certain situations it may not be appropriate at all. Some workers do not want increased responsibility, and other workers do not adapt to the group interaction that is sometimes required. In other words, enrichment is contingent on attitudes of employees and their capability to handle enriched tasks. It could be argued that employees should accept the "goodness" of job enrichment, but the approach that is more consistent with humanistic values is to recognize and respect individual differences of employees.

One survey of worker resistance to job enrichment showed that workers nearing retirement were more resistant, probably because they felt the costs of learning new ways prior to retirement were too great. Workers without a college

242

education also were more resistant, probably because they felt more threatened by the required change and less able to adapt. In total, about 40 percent of employees showed some resistance to job enrichment.[16]

Those planning job enrichment need to ask such questions as the following.

- Can the employee tolerate responsibility?
- What is the employee's attitude toward working with groups?
- Can the employee work with more complexity?
- How strong are the employee's drives for security and stability?
- Does the employee prefer supervisory authority compared with peer pressure?

In a similar manner, job enrichment does not apply to all types of situations. It appears to apply more easily to higher-level jobs, compared with lower-level ones, particularly if the lower-level jobs are dictated by the technological process. If the technology is stable and highly automated, the costs of job enrichment may be too great in relation to the rewards. Some organizations have such huge investments in equipment that they cannot afford to make substantial changes until the equipment is replaced. When difficult technological conditions are combined with negative employee attitudes toward job enrichment, then it becomes inappropriate until the environment for it can be changed.

Other limitations on job enrichment apply when it must be coordinated with other jobs, departments, or branches. For example, anticipated gains can be diminished because of effects on surrounding work systems. A projected enrichment in one organization assigned quality control to workers producing the product. Several highly paid quality-assurance people were put out of jobs, and the enrichment was delayed while their problems were resolved. In another organization job enrichment for operating employees reduced the supervisory role, so the program was not successful until the supervisors' jobs also were enriched.

Job enrichment also may upset pay relationships. In a branch operation a supervisor enriched jobs of sales clerks by allocating more responsibility to them. The clerks requested more pay, and the supervisor recommended it. The home office rejected the pay increase, thereby effectively rejecting the enrichment program. The home office was fearful that sales clerks in other branches would want similar pay, even if their jobs were not enriched. Either higher costs would occur, or lower morale would develop when raises were not given. The other alternative, enriching clerks' jobs in all branches, was not practical at the time.

An additional contingency factor is union attitudes. Job enrichment may upset existing job classifications, thereby causing union resistance. In some instances enrichment may create jurisdictional disputes between the territories of two unions. Likely places for this problem are maintenance work, construction work, and moving picture and stage productions. Distinctions between jobs are so narrow and rules are so rigid that unions sometimes will not tolerate changes. With the many contingencies that exist in job enrichment, the best strategy is to study the need for it carefully and then to try it in the most appropriate places first. As success is achieved, there can be a gradual move toward more applications. The organization that suddenly becomes sold on job enrichment and then takes a blanket approach to it is likely to generate more problems than it can handle.

ENRICHED SOCIOTECHNICAL WORK SYSTEMS

The next step above enriched jobs and natural work teams is *enriched sociotechnical work systems* in which a whole organization or a major portion of it is built into a balanced behavioral-technical system. This requires changes of a major magnitude, particularly in manufacturing that has been designed along specialized lines. The entire production process may require reengineering in order to integrate human needs, layouts may require changes to permit teamwork, and even entire buildings may require redesign. The fundamental objective is to design a layout and production process that serves needs of people as well as production requirements. Four of the most innovative and substantial experiments in design of sociotechnical systems have taken place at Saab-Scania and Volvo in Sweden and at General Foods and Non-Linear Systems in the United States. The Non-Linear Systems experiment has since been abandoned. The other three experiments were initiated in the late 1960s and early 1970s, so long-run experience with them is lacking, but they have provided some preliminary success.

SAAB-SCANIA. One of the earliest efforts toward integrated sociotechnical systems was at a Saab-Scania gasoline engine plant in the late 1960s.[17] Machine shop operations followed traditional patterns, but engine assembly was organized on a teamwork basis. Each team consisted of three employees who assembled an engine and were in total charge of their work. There was no assembly line. Workers used trolleys to bring an engine block to their work area when they were ready to work on it. The assembly arrangement allowed each team to work at its own pace. Since each team of three assembles a whole engine, members might gradually train themselves to perform all parts of the task as they rotated the work among themselves. Whatever the approach taken toward assembly, it was the team's choice, not management's. Following its innovations Saab-Scania reported increased satisfaction, and reduced turnover, absenteeism, and stoppages of production. Productivity and quality remained high. Experiments are continuing.

Compared with an assembly line, work teams of the Saab-Scania type are particularly useful in reducing the widespread effect of work delays. In an assembly line if there is a breakdown at some point, the whole line stops and many persons are idled. On the other hand, if a breakdown occurs in one team's operation, all the other teams can continue operation so that most of the production continues.

VOLVO. Volvo built a new car assembly plant in Kalmar, Sweden, in the early 1970s in which it attempted to incorporate technical, managerial, and social innovations that better served the needs of employees.[18] The design cost about 10 percent more than a comparable conventional plant, but Volvo took the risk because it hoped to secure increased satisfaction and productivity, and reduced turnover and absenteeism. The factory was designed to assemble 60,000 automobiles annually, using teams of fifteen to twenty-five workers for each major task. One team, for example, assembles electrical systems, while another assembles brakes. Each team has its own work area, and each is given substantial autonomy. The team is completely in charge of allocation of work among members and the rhythm of its work. There is no assembly line. Teams retrieve a car from a buffer zone when they want one, moving a car to their workplace on a trolley. When work is completed, the car is placed in the next buffer zone, a procedure that allows each team to work at its own pace as long as it can meet production requirements. Teams handle their own material procurement and manage their own inventory. The situation is much different from that of a traditional assembly line.

GENERAL FOODS. An ambitious, innovative sociotechnical system was built into a General Foods pet-food plant that opened in 1971[19] The plant was built to use work teams of seven to fourteen members. Careful attention was given even to such items as plant design to reduce traditional status symbols found in most plants. There was an open parking lot and a common entrance for plant and office people, and decor in the offices and locker rooms was similar. Distinctions between technical specialists and workers were reduced substantially because most specialized support activities were assigned to each operating work team. Examples of support activities substantially performed by each team within its own unit are maintenance, quality control, custodial work, and personnel activities such as helping screen and select new employees for one's team. Teams were given high autonomy over almost all activities for which they had capability. The role of supervisor changed to provide less direct supervision and more general management duties. Other innovations included:

- A single job classification for all operators, with pay increases geared to mastering additional jobs in the team and in the plant.

- Decision-making information for operators of the type that formerly only managers received.

- Enlarged jobs with most routine work mechanized.

- Team control of task redistribution when members are absent.

- Team counseling of members that fail to meet team standards.

Preliminary results have been favorable compared with other plants using traditional systems. Quality problems were reduced 90 percent, and absenteeism and turnover were less. Productivity increased, but this may have resulted from the technology of the new plant. A number of problems also developed. Employees objected to some team members earning more when they learned additional tasks. Some employees preferred traditional tasks without the required group work and added responsibility. Some team leaders showed traditional autocratic tendencies. Work teams sometimes became autocratic, exerting excessive peer pressure for conformity to group norms. Further, role confusion sometimes developed because people were not used to operating in these new kinds of roles.

NON-LINEAR SYSTEMS. The failure of the Non-Linear Systems experiment provides further evidence of the kinds of problems that develop in experiments with integrated sociotechnical work systems.[20] The firm manufactured digital electrical measuring instruments that were fairly complex, and it was the leader in its field. Much of the new program was initiated in 1960–1961.

In the new program traditional assembly lines were replaced by teams of three to twelve employees, each responsible for producing completed instruments from stockroom parts. Each team had a manager who provided consultation, advice, and minimum supervision, but work teams were relatively autonomous. They assembled, calibrated, inspected, and packed their own instruments. They determined among themselves whether instruments would be produced individually by each member, by small groups, or by the whole team. Work could be rotated, and the pace could be varied as they wished. Each group also dealt with its own problems of tardiness, absences, and conflict. Records were not required. Many other innovations existed so that the plant appeared to be almost the ideal of human relations and organizational behavior theory current at that time. The experiment was assisted and popularized by a number of leaders in organizational behavior.

Although early reports of the experiment were favorable, over a period of years the firm's product leadership declined, and productivity failed to keep pace with competitors. In 1965 the firm was forced to return to a more traditional work system. A number of other problems developed. Technical specialists were not adequately used, probably contributing to the decline in market leadership. The participative system proved cumbersome in responding to quickly needed changes. Wage costs in relation to output became a burden to the company. Job satisfaction of operating employees remained high, but it declined for technical employees and managers. Profits continued to deteriorate until losses were sustained. The firm failed to remain competitive, and the much-heralded creativity and innovation that was expected from the experiment failed to develop.

RESULTS OF COMPLEX SOCIOTECHNICAL SYSTEMS EXPERIMENTS.
Generally the Non-Linear Systems experiment shows that the design of complex organizational systems according to job enrichment and other behavioral principles is more difficult than many observers realize. There are many variables other than employee satisfaction that must be considered. One important variable is that the organization must be able to produce a product that customers will accept and at a price that they will pay. If a behaviorally oriented work system cannot remain innovative and productive, then it is unlikely to survive if customers have alternatives.

As other firms develop more experience with their experiments, they also may find increasing difficulties, or they may not. Only time will tell. Perhaps a type of Hawthorne effect is operating to make experiments successful during the exciting time of change, but allowing them to deteriorate as the glamor wears off. Many years and many types of experimentation will be required before answers are known with reasonable certainty.

SUMMARY

Job design refers to specification of the content and relationships of jobs as they affect both people and organizational success. Since people and the environment have changed, increased attention needs to be given to more human work design. Jobs are required to fit people as well as technology.

Job enrichment applies to any efforts to humanize jobs, particularly the addition of motivators to jobs. Core dimensions of jobs that especially provide enrichment are variety, task identity, task significance, autonomy, and feedback. It is especially helpful if natural work modules and natural work teams can be built. In spite of its desirability, job enrichment is a contingency relationship, being more applicable in some situations than others.

Enriched sociotechnical work systems provide a balanced behavioral-technical system for a whole organization or a substantial portion of it. Major experiments with these systems have been made at Saab-Scania and Volvo in Sweden, and at General Foods and Non-Linear Systems in the United States; and other firms are making similar experiments. Preliminary results are favorable, but many additional years of experimentation will be required to determine how effective these kinds of designs are.

TERMS AND CONCEPTS FOR REVIEW

Job design	Flexible working time
Job enrichment	Profile charts
Core dimensions of jobs	Natural work teams
Natural work modules	Enriched sociotechnical work systems

REVIEW QUESTIONS

1. How does job enrichment differ from traditional job design according to the concepts of scientific management?
2. What options are available to management in the design of jobs?
3. Discuss core dimensions of jobs and how providing more of them enriches jobs.
4. Discuss the contingency nature of job enrichment.
5. Discuss the successes and failures of efforts to develop enriched sociotechnical work systems.

CASE

VALLEY ELECTRONICS

Valley Electronics produces a line of electronic equipment, including a miniature tape recorder that can be held in one's hand. In the final assembly of the tape recorder fourteen employees work on an assembly line, using parts from parts bins. Each employee performs a different operation and then passes the assembly to the next person. The last two steps on the line are inspection and boxing. Inspection includes an operational test of each recorder. If a recorder fails inspection, it is placed at a bench where another employee reworks it. If the stack of recorders at the bench grows too large for the benchworker to handle, one of the regular assemblers is assigned overtime benchwork to reduce the backlog.

A recent job satisfaction survey showed that the assembly employees are reasonably satisfied. They have a friendly group, and the assembly design encourages conversation, because there are seven employees on each side of the line facing each other. Turnover and absenteeism are considered normal by management. The employees are organized by a national labor union, but none of them appears to be active in the union. In the group there are four racial minority members and several ethnic minorities.

QUESTION

1. Do you recommend any change in the job design for this assembly group? Discuss. If a change is recommended, discuss exactly what it will be.

REFERENCES

1. Robert N. Ford, "Job Enrichment Lessons from AT&T," *Harvard Business Review,* January–February 1973, p. 106.

2. James O'Toole, "Lordstown: Three Years Later," *Business and Society Review,* Spring 1975, p. 69.

3. "Job Enrichment: Two Heads Are Better Than Ten," *Management Review,* May 1972, p. 33.

4. A thorough discussion of work alienation is presented in W. E. Upjohn Institute for Employment Research, *Work in America* (Report of a Special Task Force to the Secretary of Health, Education, and Welfare), Cambridge, Mass.: The M.I.T. Press, 1973.

5. Louis E. Davis, "The Design of Jobs," *Industrial Relations,* October 1966, pp. 21–45.

6. Robert N. Ford, *Motivation through the Work Itself,* New York: American Management Association, 1969, pp. 20–44.

7. Edward E. Lawler III, "For a More Effective Organization—Match the Job to the Man," *Organizational Dynamics,* Summer 1974, pp. 19–29.

8. Edward E. Lawler III, and J. Richard Hackman, "Corporate Profits and Employee Satisfaction: Must They Be in Conflict?" *California Management Review,* Fall 1971, pp. 46–55; and J. Richard Hackman and others, "A New Strategy for Job Enrichment," *California Management Review,* Summer 1975, pp. 57–71.

9. T. G. Cummings, Edmond S. Molloy, and Roy H. Glen, "Intervention Strategies for Im-

proving Productivity and the Quality of Work Life," *Organizational Dynamics,* Summer 1975, p. 58. Italics in original.

10.   J. Carroll Swart, "The Worth of Humanistic Management: Some Contemporary Examples," *Business Horizons,* June 1973, pp. 41–50.

11.   Cummings, Molloy, and Glen, *loc. cit.*

12.   Hackman and others, *op. cit.,* p. 66.

13.   Harold L. Sheppard, "Task Enrichment and Wage Levels as Elements in Worker Attitudes," in Gerald G. Somers (ed.), *Proceedings of the Twenty-sixth Annual Winter Meeting,* Madison, Wis.: Industrial Relations Research Association, 1974, pp. 210–218.

14.   W. Philip Kraft and Kathleen L. Williams, "Job Redesign Improved Productivity," *Personnel Journal,* July 1975, pp. 393–397.

15.   Ford, *op. cit.,* pp. 96–106.

16.   Donald C. Collins and Robert R. Raubolt, "A Study of Employee Resistance to Job Enrichment," *Personnel Journal,* April 1975, pp. 232–235, 248. See also William E. Reif and Fred Luthans, "Does Job Enrichment Really Pay Off?" *California Management Review,* Fall 1972, pp. 30–37.

17.   *The Saab-Scania Report,* Stockholm: The Swedish Employers' Confederation, 1973; and Noel M. Tichy, "Organizational Innovations in Sweden," *The Columbia Journal of World Business,* Summer 1974, pp. 18–27.

18.   Tichy, *loc. cit.*

19.   Richard E. Walton, "How to Counter Alienation in the Plant," *Harvard Business Review,* November–December 1972, pp. 70–81; and "The Plant That Runs on Individual Initiative," *Management Review,* July 1972, pp. 20–25.

20.   Erwin L. Malone, "The Non-Linear Systems Experiment in Participative Management," *The Journal of Business,* January 1975, pp. 52–64.

CHAPTER 15
THE INDIVIDUAL
IN THE ORGANIZATION

The responsibility for improving the quality of individual-organization interactions rests with both the individual employee and the organization.
Lyman W. Porter, Edward E. Lawler III, and J. Richard Hackman[1]

LEARNING OBJECTIVES

TO UNDERSTAND:
Individual-organization relationships
Problems of conformity in organizations
How rights to privacy are interpreted
The ombudsman role
Dealing with drug abuse in organizations
Administration of disciplinary action
Individual responsibilities to organizations

When you read fiction and the social commentary of idealistic intellectuals, you find a common symbolic thread. It is that organizations are systems of medieval torture that suppress and subjugate their victim, the *individual*. Individuals live in helpless conformity, stripped of their self-esteem, in a phony and artificial environment. There is no challenge and no chance for psychological fulfillment. There is only dull security, if one will say "Yes" and smile and wear a gray flannel suit neatly. Individuals are too numb from all this to rebel, but they *should* rebel. In turn, the organization stands socially and morally condemned.

Throughout history there has been this view of people and organizations in perpetual conflict, but now we are beginning to realize that they live in some degree of mutual interest and harmony. Individuals use organizations as instruments to achieve their goals just as much as organizations use people to reach objectives. There is a mutual social transaction in which each benefits the other.

In this chapter we discuss some of the relationships of individuals to organizations, including conformity, rights of privacy, the individual and drug abuse, disciplinary action, and the individual's responsibilities to the organization.

CONFORMITY IN ORGANIZATIONS

THE INDIVIDUAL-ORGANIZATION CONFLICT. In 1956 William H. Whyte, Jr., published *The Organization Man,* which emphasized the struggle between the individual and the organization. He stated that social attitudes had developed to support excessive organizational demands for dedication and loyalty. As a result of broad acceptance of these ideas, people are "imprisoned in brotherhood." They "belong" to the organization. They are the ones "who have left home, spiritually as well as physically, to take the vows of organization life." The result is that individualism is unduly suppressed. The fault, however, is not in the organization itself but "in our worship of it." People's beliefs in the desirability of group values lead us to depend excessively on organized groups of all types.

Whyte's viewpoints apply to all types of organizations, not just business, and to various national cultures. Whyte says, "This conflict is certainly not a peculiarly American development," and he adds with a flourish:

> Blood brother to the business trainee off to join Du Pont is the seminary student who will end up in the church hierarchy, the doctor headed for the corporate clinic, the physics Ph.D. in a government laboratory, the intellectual on the foundation-sponsored team project, the engineering graduate in the huge drafting room at Lockheed, the young apprentice in a Wall Street law factory.[2]

Whyte's thesis is essentially an indictment of the custodial model of organizational behavior presented in Chapter 6. He sees the individual as cared for by organizations and overly dependent on them.

ARGYRIS'S INDIVIDUAL AND ORGANIZATION. In 1957 Chris Argyris published *Personality and Organization,* which further defined the conflict between the individual and the organization. Argyris particularly dealt with psychological problems of work, such as alienation, frustration, and suppression of self-actualization. He contended that there is a lack of congruence between the needs of psychologically mature employees and formal organization. They want independence; it wants dependence. The result of this conflict is frustration, sense of failure, and loss of self-esteem. The basic philosophy in Argyris's own words is as follows:

> An analysis of the basic properties of relatively mature human beings and formal organization leads to the conclusion that there is an inherent incongruency between the self-actualization of the two. The basic incongruency creates a situation of conflict, frustration, and failure for the participants. . . .[3]

In the Argyris thesis there is some recognition that not all persons are psychologically mature enough to want self-actualization, so they may prefer a way of life largely dependent on an organization. The viewpoint, however, is that self-actualization is a desirable human condition, and individuals should want it. This viewpoint raises philosophical questions about whether self-actualization is essential for psychological maturity. Perhaps some mature individuals do prefer high self-actualization, but other equally mature individuals may prefer substantial dependence on organizations.

INTERPRETING THE INDIVIDUAL-ORGANIZATION CONFLICT. The Whyte-Argyris thesis was a forerunner of the disenchantment with organizations that developed in the 1960s, particularly among youth. Without a doubt, there were many problems that needed correcting. In the 1950s the Whyte-Argyris thesis was quite appropriate in its application to the custodial model of organizational behavior, but as organizations have moved more toward a supportive model, the arguments are less applicable. Organizations have made much progress in working with people since the 1950s, even though many needs for improvement remain. As a matter of fact, organizational behavior practices such as are discussed in this book have done much to improve the ways that organizations serve individual needs.

Even though there is individual-organization conflict, that is only one side of the story. People and organizations also have strong mutual interests in their relationship. People need organizations. Without organizations, many modern social goals would be impossible to accomplish. Organizations make available resources and opportunities that an individual operating alone could not have, and they also provide psychological support for people. Organizations also need people, so both can gain in their mutual relationship.

The differences that exist between individual and organizational goals are not necessarily undesirable. An individual develops through facing problems and challenges, so some differences can be psychologically and socially healthful and creative. Reasonable differences, constructively handled, can lead to benefits for both the individual and the organization.

Sometimes the idea of individual-organization conflict is interpreted as an argument to abolish organizations as undesirable instruments. This interpretation is an erroneous extension of the concept. Neither Whyte nor Argyris argued that people should return to a primitive civilization to live without organizations. The conflict that exists is seen solely as a challenge that requires better resolution for better results. The idea is to have organizations serve people, rather than the other way around.

TO WHAT DOES ONE CONFORM? Implicit in the idea of an individual-organization conflict is the view that the individual is required to conform to the organization rather than the other way around. Conformity implies a dependence on the norms of others without independent thinking. To develop this point, it is necessary to recognize the different groups to which one conforms. First, there is an apparent conformity by which one conforms to the *technology.* That is, when the pot boils, take it off the fire; or when the batch in the furnace is ready, take it out. Some so-called conformity in organizations is actually a response to the technology; but this is not true conformity because it does not involve the norms of others. Furthermore, this "conformity" is the same in or out of an organization.

Looking at genuine conformity to group norms at work, there are three groups to which one conforms. One of these is the organization itself. Another is the informal work group, and the last is the external community. It is evident that the last two represent conformity *within* the organization instead of conformity *to* the organization. The organization does not impose these last two norms; they are simply there because the organization operates in a social system rather than a vacuum. Certainly there is some conformity to organizations, but much conformity arises from other than organizational causes. Business is particularly mentioned as a source of conformity, but these comments are usually supported more by example than by objective evidence. At least with regard to managers, research does not give strong support to the business-conformity thesis.

It is, for example, popularly considered that university professors are a prime example of a nonconforming group; therefore, they make a good group to compare with business executives. One study administered a psychological test on conformity to these two groups and found that the business managers were no more conforming than the professors. (And both were found to be less conforming than college students!) The study did find a wide range of conformity among both business managers and professors; so if one wanted to find examples of conformity in business, they could be found.[4]

Another study examined whether the reward structure in business tended to support conformity. Contrary to popular writing and opinion, the study found that those managers who scored lower in conformity were given higher ratings by their superiors.[5]

Another study showed that managers who were different (idosyncratic) were regarded as superior administrators.[6]

As a matter of fact, business organizations are known for their encouragement of initiative and differences, and have been among the strongest worldwide supporters of individuality. There is little evidence that conformity is a hallmark of business culture, compared with government, church, or labor unions.

LEGITIMACY OF ORGANIZATIONAL INFLUENCE. Every organization develops some conformity through its policies, systems, and rules in order to maintain unified action toward objectives. One way of examining the issue of conformity is to study how legitimate these requirements are perceived to be by other people. For example, would a woman employee perceive as legitimate a requirement that she not wear shorts to work in the office? What about a requirement that she not wear shorts as a spectator in the company ball park? Would either requirement also be considered legitimate by managers, union leaders, the general community, or other groups?

Figure 15-1 presents a chart of the legitimacy of organizational influence as typical employees might view it. The higher an item is in the system, the more probability there is that employees will question the legitimacy of management to influence them on that item. The system shows that routine coordinative requirements are the most readily accepted. We are all acquainted with the traffic light, which does require a sort of conformity, but whose purpose is to create sufficient order to permit all to proceed toward destinations of their own free choice and along routes freely chosen.

Substantive conformity may be either of action or of thought. If of action, it may be on the job or off the job, as shown in the chart. For off-the-job conduct, the organization can attempt to influence by means of educational programs and communications, but what about its right to use *disciplinary power* to enforce its desires? We can begin with the premise that it cannot use its disciplinary power to regulate employee conduct off the job; however, the line of separation is difficult to draw. What about a petroleum company employee living on a company pumping site and on twenty-four hour call? But even when an employee has departed from company property and is not on call, the boundaries of employer interest are still not fixed. Consider the employee who waited until his supervisor left the plant and then struck him several times in the presence of other employees. In cases of this type arbitrators have consistently upheld company disciplinary action because the violence was job-related. In the United States at least, the organization's jurisdictional line is clearly *functional,* related to the total job system and not to the property line.

Limited research shows that there is a reasonable amount of agreement con- cerning areas where organizational influence is considered legitimate. One study covered 812 labor leaders, managers who were students in management develop- ment courses, university students, and managers in companies. The survey re- ported general agreement on areas of legitimacy among all four groups, with rank- order correlations ranging from .88 to .98. However, managers as a group gave somewhat more support to legitimacy than labor leaders, with both groups of stu- dents ranking in the middle. The data as a whole support the chart of legitimacy

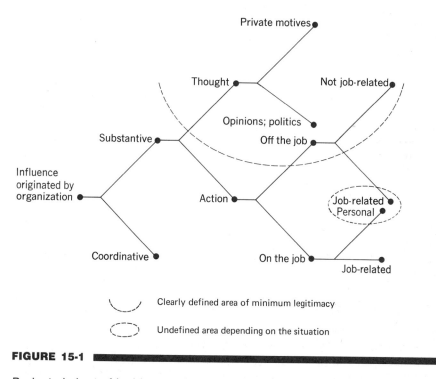

FIGURE 15-1 ▬▬▬▬▬▬▬▬▬▬▬▬▬▬▬▬▬▬▬▬

Projected chart of legitimacy of organizational influence with employees.

presented in Figure 15-1. High-legitimacy items related to work behavior or attitudes toward work and company. Items of low legitimacy primarily were non-job-related, such as family relationships, place of residence, and political and religious views.[7]

Using the same questionnaire, sixty members of the United States Air Force were surveyed, and their scale of legitimacy was approximately the same as in the original study just mentioned. Rank-order correlations with groups in the original study ranged from .88 to .97. Since these persons had lived a military life rather than a civilian life for years, and many had lived in other countries, their work experiences were distinctly different from those of the original sample. The high agreement among all groups suggests that either strong, general cultural influences are causing uniform views, or else the technology of the work itself rationally justifies areas of legitimacy to the respondents. Probably both influences apply.[8]

Data on legitimacy can be a useful guide to management. As long as there is agreement on legitimacy among the parties involved, they should be satisfied with their relationship. However, an attempt by management to influence employees in an area not considered legitimate probably will develop resentment. In the survey just reported, for example, 55 percent of company managers believed it was legitimate to influence a subordinate's participation in noncompany public activities, but only 10 percent of labor leaders thought so. If a company attempted action in this area, it probably would be opposed by labor leaders unless they clearly understood the company's rationalization in this particular case.

RIGHTS TO PRIVACY. Figure 15.1 shows that areas of least legitimacy are private thoughts, opinions, and motives. Privacy refers to the employee's private person or psyche as well as to private (noncompany) activities. Employees believe that their religious, political, and social beliefs are part of their own inner selves and should not be subject to snooping or analysis as a requirement for getting or keeping a job, unless these attitudes adversely affect job performance. The same view applies to personal conversations and to certain personal locations such as company rest rooms and private homes. Exceptions are permitted grudgingly, if at all, only when a job involvement is clearly proved, and burden of proof is on the organization.

THE POLYGRAPH. The polygraph is one instrument whose legitimacy is often questioned. We have learned that conscience usually causes physiological changes when a person tells a significant lie. Based on this information, the polygraph (lie detector) was developed. Used first in police work, it has now spread to public and private employment. Organizations use the polygraph primarily to control theft. It is estimated that employees steal several billion dollars a year from employers, so theft is a serious organizational problem. Employers argue that the polygraph would be less necessary if employees were more honest. Since the fact is that there is theft by a proportion of employees, the polygraph is used to control it.

In addition to protecting the organization, it is argued that polygraph tests also help protect employees. Dishonest employees may take property of other employees, cast suspicion on them in case of theft, or place them in compromising situations that would threaten their jobs. Especially in decentralized retail operations, such as drive-in grocery stores, routine polygraph tests permit a company to abolish various audits and controls that would otherwise be oppressive. This arrangement gives employees more freedom from surveillance and leaves them free to work in whatever manner is most productive.

Employees claim that polygraph tests sometimes are extended from job investigation to marital life and other nonjob subjects. Even when the polygraph is used only concerning the job, they tend to resent it because they consider their conscience personal, and they object to "being judged by a machine" over which they have no control. They especially object to having to prove themselves innocent, that is, having to take a test routinely even when no theft is known or no evidence points to them as thieves. They object less to a specific test about a specific known theft of major proportions. In this situation they may welcome a test to take the pressure of suspicion off them.

Regardless of the need for the polygraph, its intrusion upon the psyche is evident and is causing it to be more tightly controlled. Organized labor tends to oppose it, and several states have prohibited use of the polygraph in employment situations.

WORKING WITH PRIVACY ISSUES. Questions of infringement on individual privacy are complex and difficult. There are no simple answers. Each practice needs to be evaluated on its merits after careful study. Many individuals are sensitive about their privacy and will be quick to protest an infringement if they can find justification for protest.

Sometimes novel questions of privacy arise. Women employees in a major British company persuaded management to remove from their rest room a loudspeaker on the regular paging system. This was not a case of snooping. They simply claimed that they were shocked to hear a man's voice in their rest room, and they demanded privacy therefrom.

Some infringements on privacy may be justified for compelling job reasons, such as the polygraph for theft control. In those instances the employer should be certain that at the time the job is accepted the individual is fully informed of what is happening and why it is necessary. In the case of the polygraph, for example, employees often agree to its use as a condition of employment in a sensitive job.

If an organizational practice meets any of the following criteria, then questions of employee privacy are likely to arise:

- Invasion of the employee psyche, such as the polygraph.
- Secret observation, such as unknown surveillance.
- Observation of private acts or locations, such as prying in clothes lockers.

• Release of confidential personal information to unauthorized persons, such as careless handling of medical records.

Observations that are known to employees and have a compelling job reason usually are not considered to be undue infringements on privacy. Banks, for example, have hidden cameras for photographs during robberies. These photographs include employees, but this hardly infringes on the privacy of employees, provided use is confined to the original purpose.

An example of regular surveillance is a fast-food chain that installed a moving picture camera in a number of its stores. The camera photographed the cash register whenever it was open. Employees knew that it was there to control theft, although it also could photograph robberies. The camera worked effectively, providing an unexpected increase of about 10 percent in receipts.

USE OF AN INDEPENDENT ORGANIZATIONAL INVESTIGATOR. One way to help protect the individual in organizations is to use an independent organizational investigator, often called an *ombudsman* based on the Scandinavian origin of the role. In Scandinavia the ombudsman role developed as a check and balance on administrative decisions in the government bureaucracy. The ombudsman stands independent of the administrative hierarchy and has the power to investigate any administrative decision. Persons aggrieved by an administrative decision appeal to the office of the ombudsman for an impartial investigation and report. Ombudsmen can only recommend, persuade, appeal to reason, and publicly expose arbitrary decisions. They have no power to reverse decisions already made. Nevertheless, their informal powers often bring corrective action, and their presence discourages future arbitrary decisions. The goal is to provide justice in complex organizational situations.

The investigative role is an ambiguous one and is difficult to translate to private organizations. A few have experimented with it and have had mixed results. The investigative role is different from a grievance procedure, because the grievance procedure contains powers for changing the decision, while the investigator can only recommend.

THE INDIVIDUAL AND DRUG ABUSE

Individual-organization relationships are significantly affected when there is alcoholism or other drug abuses. These conditions present major medical and job problems, so employers need to develop responsible programs to deal with them without endangering rights of privacy.

ALCOHOLISM. It is estimated that between 4 and 8 percent of employees are alcoholics and that they cost employers about $10 billion annually in absenteeism, poor work, and related costs. Contrary to popular opinion, alcoholics are found in about the same proportion in all types of organizations, occupations, and job levels.[9]

Sometimes the job environment may contribute to an employee's alcoholism, but more often than not the employee's personal habits and problems are a major contributor to alcoholism. In some instances the employee is well on the road to alcoholism even before being hired. Regardless of the causes, an increasing number of firms are recognizing that they have responsibilities to help an alcoholic break the habit. Their responsibilities arise from three reasons. One is that the firm and employee already have an ongoing relationship on which they can build. A second is that any success with the employee will save both a valuable person for the company and a valuable citizen for society. A third reason is that the job appears to be the best environment for helping alcoholics recover, because the preservation of their jobs helps them retain their self-image as useful persons in society.

Successful corporate programs treat alcoholism as an illness, focus on job problems caused by alcoholism, and provide both medical help and psychological support for alcoholic employees. The organization shows alcoholics that it wants to help them and is willing to work with them over an extended period of time. A nonthreatening, no-job-loss atmosphere is provided; however, there is always the implied threat that alcohol-induced behavior cannot be tolerated indefinitely. For example, if alcoholic employees refuse treatment after their problem is discussed, then the employer has little choice but to dismiss them if their incompetent behavior continues.

Following is the way that one company operates. A supervisor notices that an employee has a record of tardiness and absenteeism, poor work, an exhausted appearance, and related symptoms that might indicate alcoholism or another serious problem. The supervisor discusses only the employee's job behavior with the employee, not referring to alcoholism unless the employee does so. Then the employee is given a period of time for self-correction. If correction is not forthcoming, the supervisor asks the employee for a joint meeting in the presence of a counselor. The supervisor presents the evidence of poor job behavior and then leaves the room so that the employee and counselor can discuss the situation privately.

In other instances medical examinations uncover alcoholism or an employee voluntarily asks for help. As soon as the problem is brought into the open, the treatment program is initiated in a supportive atmosphere. It may involve hospitalization to "dry out" the employee. Throughout the procedure the company is patient but firm. In one case, for example, a supervisor was allowed to refuse treatment for a year, although he was disciplined as a warning during that period. Finally he agreed to treatment, and the results were favorable.

Using the approach just described, the firm has achieved a recovery rate of over 50 percent.

DRUG ABUSE. Abuse of drugs other than alcohol, particularly hard drugs such as heroin, may cause severe problems for both employers and other employees. The seriousness of this problem is shown by a survey of ninety-five users of hard drugs, mostly heroin, who were employed at the time they used drugs.[10] Ninety-one of them reported that they had been under the influence of drugs during working hours, and forty said that they had used drugs in the lavatory at work. Even more serious from the point of view of other employees, forty-eight of the drug users admitted that they had sold drugs to other employees, and sixty-eight specified other types of on-the-job criminal activity. For example, twenty-eight reported thefts of cash or checks from the employer and/or employees, and thirty-seven admitted stealing company property and selling it to support their drug habit. These statistics make it evident that the pattern of behavior of hard-drug users is a serious threat to an ongoing organization.

Company programs for treatment of those who abuse drugs other than alcohol usually follow the same patterns as programs on alcoholism, except that hard-drug treatment may be more strictly controlled because of the hard-drug user's greater probability of criminal behavior on the job. Most organizations combine treatment of alcoholism, drug abuse, and related difficulties into one program for treatment of people with behavioral-medical problems. Normally the program focuses on both prevention and treatment.

Many firms are reluctant to employ former hard-drug users. Others recognize a social responsibility to provide jobs for persons who have recovered, and they are experimenting with carefully controlled employment programs. For example, one firm employed recovered heroin addicts with the employment condition that they regularly provide urine specimens for analysis to determine that they had not returned to heroin or certain other hard drugs. Is this an unwarranted invasion of privacy, or is it justified because of the danger of criminal behavior if the employees return to hard drugs?

DISCIPLINE AND DISCIPLINARY ACTION

The individual's adherence to organizational standards is maintained by discipline and disciplinary action, which will now be discussed.

DISCIPLINE. The quality of an organization's climate is reflected in the discipline of its employees. Discipline is employee self-control to meet organizational standards and objectives. It is the "taut ship" in navy jargon. It provides the self-control that underlies all genuine teamwork. Discipline relates to employee conduct, whereas morale relates to employee attitudes. Discipline is developed both by management and by the employee group. Employees themselves exert powerful influence on others in their group to toe the line, to keep up, and to "get with it." If these employee pressures can be guided to support organizational standards, then the group itself is a strong supportive force for discipline.

Management has responsibility for developing and maintaining discipline. In doing so, it must make its standards known and understood. If employees do not know what standards the organization expects, their conduct is likely to be erratic or misdirected. Employees will better support standards that they have helped create. They will also give more support to standards stated positively instead of negatively, such as "Safety first!" rather than "Don't be careless!" They usually want to know the reasons behind a standard so that it will make sense to them.

Management maintains discipline by applying standards in a consistent, fair, and flexible manner. Time and time again management has learned the hard way that it cannot turn a blind eye to infractions and then suddenly crack down on someone without warning. Here is an illustration.

Employees A and B disregarded a no-smoking rule on numerous occasions. Then employee C disregarded it and "the roof caved in." He was given a severe reprimand in front of others and three days off. To other employees and to C, this action was wholly inconsistent and unfair. Employees at this point did not know what management's real standard of conduct was, and discipline deteriorated. Originally they conducted themselves on the basis of how management enforced the sign (instead of what the sign said). When enforcement became erratic, they were both confused and resentful of injustice. It is evident in this example that consistent enforcement of standards is a key to discipline.

DISCIPLINARY ACTION. When standards are maintained by invoking a penalty against an employee who fails to meet them, this is disciplinary action. Its objectives are to reform the offender, to deter others, and to maintain the integrity of the organization. It is, therefore, educational and corrective, rather than punitive slapping back at an employee in the wrong.

Effective disciplinary action condemns the employee's wrongful act, not the employee as a person. There is a difference between invoking a penalty for a job not performed and calling an employee a lazy loafer.

The ultimate disciplinary action is discharge. It has been said that every employee discharge is evidence of management failure, but this view is not realistic. Neither managers nor employees are perfect; hence some problems cannot be solved. Sometimes it is better for an employee to go somewhere else. There are limits to how much effort an organization can devote to retain a poor employee. Furthermore, the effects of a poor worker on other employees must always be considered.

A manager of a school lunchroom had an autocratic, incompetent supervisor of food service whom he should have fired but decided to retain in order to help her. The next fall no employees returned to this department, and no students were on the part-time employment list. During the year he fired her, and the following fall, a normal amount of employees and students returned to this department. In other words, by retaining her originally, he lost all the other employees!

FLEXIBLE ENFORCEMENT RECOGNIZES THE INDIVIDUAL. One of the toughest problems management faces in taking disciplinary action is how to resolve the fundamental conflict between consistency and flexibility. Consistency is sought because it allows administrative simplicity and is expected by unions. Flexibility is necessary because people and situations are unique.

Certainly it can be argued that unequal treatment undermines teamwork and that a safe policy is never to yield an inch, make no concessions, and refuse to recognize extenuating circumstances. Labor unions, which presumably represent the best interests of their members, often take this stand in order to secure a more stable union-management relationship. They require the employer to make specific rules and to follow them without exception, and they bring management to task before an arbitrator when it varies its interpretations.

But something is lost with inflexible discipline of this kind. Unswerving adherence to the rules ignores the individual in the organization. Sameness of treatment breeds a type of mass conformity—a passive acceptance of things beyond the employee's control. It fails to motivate people toward positive attitudes and takes the heart out of disciplinary action. By bringing all people down to one level, regardless of their uniqueness, it subjects them to the same kind of treatment that we give to chairs or desks, thereby leaving nothing personal in the disciplinary relationship. Employees become the victims of a lifeless system, and actual injustice may result, as in the following case.

In a warehouse, two men came to blows in a fight and both were given a fifteen-day layoff by management. To both the fighters and the other employees this action appeared to be an injustice. Here are the facts. A known bully with a quick temper was the aggressor. The other man tried to get away from him several times, but each time was caught and a scuffle developed. Finally he was cornered and he knocked out the bully. Was equal disciplinary action in this case justified?

JUSTIFYING FLEXIBLE ENFORCEMENT. In disciplinary action long-seniority employees often are given special consideration because of their long service with the organization. When they have had a good record for many years, it seems unfair, for example, to dismiss them for a small rule infraction, even though a similar rule infraction might be serious enough to justify dismissal of a new employee who was not adjusting.

It is sometimes argued that minority employees with low seniority also should receive special consideration.[11] The key to their special consideration is their short experience with work values. The reasoning is that many of them come from marginal groups in society where they have not learned traditional social standards that are expected by organizations. For example, they may not have learned punctuality, so they are frequently late to work. Or, they may not have learned to be responsible for property, so they are careless with it. In these instances, they should be given a reasonable time to become familiar with work habits and conduct. The same reasoning may apply to ex-convicts who may lack familiarity with the work environment.[12]

Special consideration involves risks that it may not be understood and accepted by other employees, the union, or an arbitrator. In addition, it may be cited by a subsequently disciplined person as evidence of lax enforcement in the past. This means it should be applied only when fully justified, and the reasons should be documented so that the action taken is not interpreted as management's standard practice for that type of rule infraction.

Consider, for example, a supervisor who gives special consideration to a low-seniority minority employee without appropriate documentation. This action may place the disciplinary policy in jeopardy, because it provides evidence of lax enforcement. Later a nonminority employee in the department makes a similar rule infraction and is disciplined. The employee files a grievance claiming that the su-

pervisor's past practice shows that the rule was not enforced. The union supports the employee and wins the grievance on the basis of discriminatory discipline against the employee.

FLEXIBILITY WITHIN RULES. Since there are so many different interpretations of rules and pleas for special consideration, should organizations then go to the other extreme—avoid rules and leave disciplinary action solely to human judgement? Most likely neither extreme is the right one. The better solution will be a compromise between them that allows flexible interpretation of established standards of conduct. The flexible approach seems more in accord with behavioral research and concepts. It respects human dignity and individual differences because it allows for interpretation. It says: The employer is obligated to treat people alike insofar as they are alike, but the employer also is obligated to treat them differently to the extent that they are different and in different situations. In other words, the fair way to treat people is according to their individual situation. The appropriate disciplinary action is contingent upon the circumstances.

A flexible policy is also consistent with the basic aim of disciplinary action, which is to encourage future conduct within the rules rather than to punish. Since different people respond differently to the same treatment, different disciplinary actions are necessary to achieve what might be called equal results.

Take the case of Audrey, a responsible and conscientious employee who, because of a communication error at home and a chain of unfortunate circumstances, fails to notify her supervisor of her absence until three days have gone by. Bill, on the other hand, is the devil-may-care type who has openly declared that the reason for his absence is none of management's business. On the afternoon of the third day, Bill sends a telegram from Las Vegas saying, "Car broke down. Hope to return Monday."

Is it likely that exactly equal penalties in these cases will accomplish the objectives of disciplinary action? As a whole, it appears that the more mature organization will foster a more flexible disciplinary practice.[13]

THE COUNSELING APPROACH TO DISCIPLINARY ACTION. Most organizations use counseling in connection with disciplinary action, but a few firms have moved a step further and have taken a counseling approach to the entire procedure. In this approach an employee is counseled rather than progressively penalized for the first few breaches of organizational standards. Here is how the program works in one organization.[14]

The philosophy is that violations are employee malfunctions that can be constructively corrected without penalty. The first violation results in a private discussion with the supervisor. The second violation brings further discussion with the supervisor with a focus on correcting causes of the behavior. A third violation leads to counseling with the immediate supervisor and the shift supervisor to determine roots of the employee's malfunction. For example, does the employee not like the

*job and want a transfer? Is the employee prepared to abide by the standard? The re-
sult of the discussion is given to the employee in a letter.*

*A fourth infraction within a reasonable time, such as a year, results in final
counseling with the superintendent. The offender is released from duty with pay for
the remainder of the day to consider willingness to abide by standards. The offender is told that a further violation will regretfully result in termination, because
it shows that the employee is unable or unwilling to work within the standards of
the organization.*

*After a year the record is wiped clean, and any new violation starts at step
one. Certain serious offenses, such as theft and fighting, are exempted from the
procedure and may result in immediate termination.*

The focus of the counseling approach is fact finding and guidance to correct
causes of employee behavior, instead of using penalties to discourage errant
behavior. In this manner the employee's self-image and dignity are retained, and
the supervisory-employee relationship remains cooperative and constructive.

RESPONSIBILITIES OF THE INDIVIDUAL
TO THE ORGANIZATION

A discussion of the individual in the organization is incomplete if it covers only the
organization's obligations to the individual. The employment relationship is two-
way. Without question, the organization does have responsibilities to the individual, but also—and again without question—the individual has responsibilities to
the organization. Employment is a mutual social transaction. Each employee makes
certain membership investments in the organization and expects profitable payoffs
in return. The organization also invests in the individual, and it, too, expects profitable returns. A relationship is profitable for either party when benefits (outputs) are
larger than costs (inputs), measured in a total value system. In the usual organizational relationship both parties benefit, just as they do in the usual social relationship. Both parties benefit because the social transaction between them produces
new values that exceed the investment each makes.

The profitable relationship deteriorates if either party fails to act responsibly
toward the needs of the other. The employee can fail to act responsibly, just as the
organization can. Under these conditions if employees display shoddy responsibility toward organizations, they can expect organizations to respond by using
tight controls and investigative procedures to try to maintain a successful
operating system.

Consider the matter of theft, which was mentioned in connection with the
polygraph. Overlook for the moment the moral-ethical aspects of theft. From the
point of view of the organizational system only, theft interferes with work operations. It upsets schedules and budgets. It causes reorders. It calls for more controls. In sum, it reduces both the reliability and the productivity of the organizational system. This condition reduces output for the individual as well as for the
organization. In this situation the organization must act to protect other employees
as well as itself.

The social transaction called employment creates a mutual responsibility between the individual and the organization. In the same way that the organization becomes obligated to give support to the employee, the employee becomes obligated to support the operations of the organization. On the other hand, this obligation does not extend to support of illegal activities or those which seriously violate social standards or the employee's private conscience. All employees retain the right to their own private beliefs. Occasionally, when internal corrective action cannot be achieved, employees have chosen at their own risk to expose what they believe to be unconscionable practices of their own organization. This is called "blowing the whistle on the organization."[15]

SUMMARY

The concept of individual-organization conflict assumes a fundamental opposition between the needs of people and organizations. Conflict exists, but the individual and the organization also derive mutual benefits from their relationship. Some areas of possible conflict are conformity, legitimacy of organizational influence, privacy, and disciplinary action. An ombudsman is a possible arrangement for dealing with some individual-organization issues.

Disciplinary action is applied to individuals when they materially fail to meet standards. Fair disciplinary action is situationally flexible to respond to individual differences. Essentially the social transaction of employment is a two-way street with mutual responsibilities by both individual and organization.

TERMS AND CONCEPTS FOR REVIEW

Individual-organization conflict	Polygraph
Conformity	Ombudsman
Legitimacy of organizational influence	Discipline
Rights to privacy	Disciplinary action

REVIEW QUESTIONS ■■■■■■■■■■■■■■■■■■■■■

1. Discuss the concept of individual-organization conflict, including its limitations.
2. What are the different types of social norms to which a person may conform in an organization?
3. Discuss areas of strong and weak legitimacy of organizational influence.
4. Discuss employee rights to privacy, including the criteria that may be used to judge infringements on privacy.

5. Comment on the statement "The more mature organization will tend to provide a more situationally flexible disciplinary policy."

CASES

TWO ACCOUNTING CLERKS

Rosemary Janis and Mary Lopez were the only two clerks handling payments from customers in the office of Atlantic Plumbing Supply Company. They reported to the owner of the business. Janis had been employed for eighteen months and Lopez for fourteen months. Both were community college graduates about twenty-three years old and unmarried.

Through manipulation of the accounts in a rather ingenious way that would not normally be detected Janis was stealing from account payments as they were received. Lopez learned of Janis's thefts during Lopez's third month of employment, but she decided not to tell management, rationalizing that Janis's personal conduct was none of her business. Lopez did not benefit from Janis's thefts, and the two women were not close friends. Their duties allowed them to work rather independently of each other, each handling a different alphabetical portion of the accounts.

By the time the owner learned of Janis's thefts, she had stolen approximately $5,700. During investigation of the thefts the owner learned that Lopez had known about them for several months, because it was evident that the thefts could not have occurred for an extended period without Lopez's knowledge. At the time of employment both women had been instructed by the owner that they were handling money and strict honesty was required.

QUESTIONS

1. What issues are raised by these events? Discuss.
2. What disciplinary action, if any, do you recommend for each of the two women? Why?

PORTER MORROW

Porter Morrow is a custodian with eight months of seniority in a furniture and appliance warehouse in an urban area. He is a minority employee, aged twenty-eight. He was employed upon release from prison where he served time for burglary. As he left company property after work, the guard discovered that concealed in a handkerchief inside a folded newspaper he had a ball-point-pen desk set with the company emblem on it. Investigation disclosed that the desk set had been removed without authorization from the desk of a warehouse clerk who was absent that day. The value of the desk set was about $5. Morrow's employment record contained a memorandum that he had been told that, because of his criminal record, any act of theft would be sufficient cause for dismissal.

QUESTION

1. You are Morrow's supervisor and report to the warehouse manager. The next

day, after having secured the information mentioned above, what action would you take and why?

A WEIGHTY PROBLEM

Galaxy Airlines has certain weight standards in relation to height for its flight attendants. For example, a five-foot-five-inch attendant cannot weigh over 135 pounds. Attendants are weighed once a month. The first time they are overweight they are given a warning. The next month, if still overweight, they are suspended for fifteen days. In case they are overweight a third successive month, they are grounded until they can reach the proper weight and be reinstated to flight duty. No exceptions are made.

Galaxy states that the weight requirements are necessary because flight attendants need to be trim to maneuver adequately in narrow aircraft aisles and other working areas. Further, in case of accidents quick maneuverability might save lives. Galaxy does admit, however, that another reason for the standard is to present a trim and attractive public appearance that will give an image of a professionally operated airline and discourage passengers from straying to other airlines.

QUESTION

1. You are the supervisor of flight attendants. They are protesting the weight standards, so this policy has come to you for review. What analysis would you make, and what would be your decision? Some other airlines have similar standards.

PRIVILEGES FOR AN EMPLOYEE

Margie Wheeler, a divorcee with one child, is a bank clerk. She has had an excellent record for three years. In fact, she is so good that she has been given the added duty of instructing new employees in her department.

About three weeks ago management noticed a change in Margie's work attitude and habits. She became moody and irritable, seeming to have her mind on something else. She was absent from her work area for long periods during the day making telephone calls. She also left work early on several occasions. On two Mondays she took sick leave, reporting that she had influenza on one of the days. Her manager knew that she obviously had some sort of personal problem; so he let her take advantage of the rules by overstaying her coffee break and otherwise not performing her work. It was rumored around the office that she was dating a married man and had been taking long breaks in order to visit him in the office of another company in the building, but her manager had no proof of this rumor.

One morning a respected senior office clerk came to the manager and reported that other employees were resentful of Margie because they felt management was making exceptions for her that it would not make for other employees. The clerk added that Margie was not performing her work and that other employees were "at the point of revolt."

QUESTION

1. Assuming you are the manager, explain what you will do and why.

REFERENCES

1. Lyman W. Porter, Edward E. Lawler III, and J. Richard Hackman, *Behavior in Organizations,* New York: McGraw-Hill Book Company, 1975, p. 26.

2. William H. Whyte, Jr., *The Organization Man,* New York: Simon & Schuster, Inc., 1956, p. 3.

3. Chris Argyris, *Personality and Organization: The Conflict between the System and the Individual,* New York: Harper & Row, Publishers, Incorporated, 1957, p. 175. See also Chris Argyris, "Personality and Organization Theory Revisited," *Administrative Science Quarterly,* June 1973, pp. 141–167.

4. John B. Miner, "Conformity among University Professors and Business Executives," *Administrative Science Quarterly,* June 1962, pp. 96–109, reporting on forty-four executives and forty-one professors.

5. Edwin A. Fleishman and David R. Peters, "Interpersonal Values, Leadership Attitudes, and Managerial 'Success,'" *Personnel Psychology,* Summer 1962, pp. 127–143, covering thirty-nine managers in four soap manufacturing branches.

6. Edwin E. Ghiselli, "Individuality as a Factor in the Success of Management Personnel," *Personnel Psychology,* Spring 1960, pp. 1–10. An opposite view reports that business managers are more conforming than the general population, based on the Tomkins-Horn picture test. See Alfred W. Stoess, "Conformity Behavior of Managers and Their Wives," *Academy of Management Journal,* September 1973, pp. 433–441.

7. Edgar H. Schein and J. Steven Ott, "The Legitimacy of Organizational Influence," *American Journal of Sociology,* May 1962, pp. 682–689. Significant agreement on legitimacy also is reported between United States and German managers, but there are more areas of disagreement because of cultural differences; see Arthur G. Bedeian, "A Comparison and Analysis of German and United States Managerial Attitudes Toward the Legitimacy of Organizational Influence," *Academy of Management Journal,* December 1975, pp. 897–904.

8. Keith Davis, "Attitudes toward the Legitimacy of Management Efforts to Influence Employees," *Academy of Management Journal,* June 1968, pp. 153–162, based on research by Gerald R. Holladay.

9. "Business Dries Up Its Alcoholics," *Business Week,* Nov. 11, 1972, p. 168.

10. Stephen J. Levy, "Drug Abuse in Business: Telling It Like It Is," *Personnel,* September–October 1972, pp. 8–14.

11. Kenneth Jennings, "Arbitrators, Blacks and Discipline," *Personnel Journal,* January 1975, pp. 32–37, 64. However, the Supreme Court in *McDonald v. Santa Fe Trail Transportation Company* in 1976 held that special consideration may not be so extensive that it violates civil rights laws by discriminating against nonminority employees.

12. A discussion of employment of former convicts is reported in Marvin A. Jolson, "Are Ex-Offenders Successful Employees?" *California Management Review,* Spring 1975, pp. 65–73.

13. One study reports that less educated employees tend to interpret fair treatment as equal treatment for all, but better educated employees think fair treatment takes individual differences into account. See Philip Selznick and Howard M. Vollmer, "Rule of Law in Industry: Seniority Rights," *Industrial Relations,* May 1962, pp. 97–116.

14. John Huberman, "'Discipline without Punishment' Lives," *Harvard Business Review,* July–August 1975, pp. 6–8.

15. Kenneth D. Walters, "Your Employees' Right to Blow the Whistle," *Harvard Business Review,* July–August 1975, pp. 26ff.

SECTION 4

SOCIAL ENVIRONMENT

CHAPTER 16
INFORMAL ORGANIZATIONS

The number of informal social groups within an organization tends to be rather
large relative to the total number of individuals employed by it.

Lyman W. Porter, Edward E. Lawler III, and J. Richard Hackman[1]

LEARNING OBJECTIVES

TO UNDERSTAND:
The nature of informal organization
Benefits and disadvantages of informal systems
How informal groups encourage conformity
How informal organizations may be charted
The operation of organizational grapevines
How accurate the grapevine is
The nature of rumor and its control

When Bill Smith graduated from engineering school and joined the laboratory of a
large manufacturing company, he was assigned the task of supervising four laboratory technicians who checked production samples. In some ways he did supervise them, but in other ways he was restricted by the group itself, which was quite
frustrating to Bill. He soon found that each technician protected the others so that
it was difficult to fix responsibility for sloppy work. The group appeared to restrict
its work in such a way that about the same number of tests were made every day
regardless of his urging to speed up the work. Although Bill was the designated supervisor, he observed that many times his technicians, instead of coming to him,
took problems to an older technician across the aisle in another section.

Bill also observed that three of his technicians often had lunch together in
the cafeteria, but the fourth technician usually ate with friends in an adjoining
laboratory. Bill usually ate with other laboratory supervisors, and he learned much
about company events during these lunches. He soon began to realize that these
situations were evidence of an informal organization and that he had to work with
it as well as with the formal organization.

Beneath the cloak of formal relationships in every institution there exists a
more complex system of social relationships consisting of many informal organizations. Although there are many different informal groups, not one, we may refer to
them collectively as the informal organization. It is a powerful influence upon productivity and job satisfaction. Both the formal and the informal systems are necessary for group activity, just as two blades are essential to make a pair of scissors
workable. Together, formal and informal organizations constitute the social system
of work groups. This chapter presents a general overview of informal organizations
at work, including their communication system, popularly called the grapevine.

271

NATURE OF INFORMAL ORGANIZATION

INFORMAL ORGANIZATION ARISES FROM SOCIAL INTERACTION.
Widespread interest in informal organization developed as a result of the Western Electric studies in the 1930s, which concluded that it was an important part of the total work situation. These studies showed that informal organization is a network of personal and social relations not established or required by formal authority but arising spontaneously as people associate with one another. The emphasis within informal organization is on people and their relationships, whereas formal organization emphasizes positions in terms of authority and functions. Informal power, therefore, attaches to a *person,* while formal authority attaches to a *position* and a person wields it only when occupying that position. Informal power is personal, but formal authority is institutional.

Power in informal organization is earned or given permissively by group members, rather than delegated; therefore, it does not follow the official chain of command. It is more likely to come from peers than from superiors in the formal hierarchy; and it may cut across organizational lines into other departments. It is usually more unstable than formal authority, since it is subject to the sentiments of people. Because of its subjective nature, informal organization is not subject to management control in the way that formal organization is.

A manager typically holds some informal (personal) power along with formal (positional) power, but usually a manager does not have more informal power than anyone else in the group. This means that the manager and the informal leader are usually two different persons in work groups.

Managers sometimes wish they could order informal organization abolished with the stroke of a pen. Most of them would prefer to work with only formal organization, because this would make their jobs simpler. From their point of view informal organization is a disquieting force that regularly offers resistance to their formal orders, or amends them, or accomplishes them by a procedure different from the intended one. Regardless of how helpful or harmful it is, managers soon learn its first characteristic: It cannot be abolished. Managers can abolish any formal organization that they have established, but they did not create informal organization and they cannot abolish it. As long as there are people, there will be informal groups.

As a result of differences between formal and informal sources of power, formal organizations may grow to immense size, but informal organizations (at least the closely knit ones) tend to remain smaller in order to keep within the limits of personal relationships. The result is that a large organization tends to have hundreds of informal organizations operating throughout it. Some of them are wholly within the institution; others are partially external to it. Because of their naturally small size and instability, informal organizations are not a suitable substitute for the large formal aggregates of people and resources that are needed for modern institutions. Without formal organization the countless informal groups do not effectively pursue organizational objectives.

Workers recognize the different roles played by formal and informal organizations, including the more secondary role normally played by informal organizations. One study of workers reported that, although workers and managers saw the informal organization as influential and beneficial to their needs, they perceived the formal organization as more influential and beneficial.[2]

INFORMAL LEADERS. The leaders of informal groups arise for various reasons. Some of these reasons are age, seniority, technical competence, work location, freedom to move around the work area, and a responsive personality. The causes are numberless, because each leader arises under slightly different circumstances.

Informal groups overlap to the extent that one person may be a member of several different groups, which means that there is not just one leader but several of varying importance. The group may look to one employee on matters pertaining to wages and to another to lead recreational plans. In this way several persons in a department may be some type of informal leader. Perhaps there is an old-timer who is looked upon as the expert on job problems, a listener who serves as counselor, and a communicator who is depended upon to convey key problems to the manager. The general role of informal leaders is:

1.   To help the group reach its goals

2.   To maintain and enhance group life

In return for their services, leaders usually enjoy certain rewards and privileges. Perhaps the old-timer is permitted to punch the clock first, and so on. One significant reward is the esteem in which the leader is held.

Although several persons in a group may be informal leaders of various types, there is usually one primary leader who has more influence than others. Each manager needs to learn who the key informal leader is in any group and to work with that leader to encourage leadership that furthers rather than hinders organizational objectives. When an informal leader is working against an employer, the leader's widespread influence can undermine motivation and job satisfaction.

The informal organization is a desirable source of potential formal leaders, but it should be remembered that an informal leader does not always make the best formal manager. History is filled with examples of successful informal leaders who became arrogant bosses once they received formal authority. Some informal leaders fail as formal ones because they fear formal responsibility—something they do not have as informal leaders. They often criticize management for lacking initiative or for not daring to be different, but when they take a management job, they become even more conservative because they are afraid to make a mistake. Other informal leaders fail because their area of formal management authority is broader and more complex than the tiny area in which they had informal power. The fact that Joe is the leader in departmental social activities does not mean that he will be equally successful as the departmental manager.

FUNCTIONS OF INFORMAL GROUPS. Informal groups arise and persist because they perform desired functions for their members. One function is to perpetuate cultural values that the group holds dear. This function carries forward a particular life-style and helps preserve the unity and integrity of the group. A second

273

function is the provision of social satisfactions. Informal organizations give a person recognition, status, and further opportunity to relate to others.

In a large office, for example, an employee named Rose McVail may feel like only a payroll number, but her informal group gives her personal attachment and status. With them she is somebody, even though in the formal structure she is only one of a thousand clerks. She may not look forward to posting 750 accounts daily, but the informal group can give more meaning to her day. When she can think of meeting her friends, sharing their interests, and eating with them, her day takes on a new dimension that makes easier any disagreeableness or routine in her work. Of course, these conditions can apply in reverse: The group may not accept her, thereby making her work more disagreeable and driving her to transfer, absenteeism, or a resignation.

A third informal group function is communication. In order to meet wants and to keep its members informed of what is taking place that may affect them, the group develops systems and channels of communication. A fourth function is social control, by which the behavior of others is influenced and regulated.[3] Social control is both internal and external. Internal control is directed toward persuading members of the group to conform to its way of life. In an accounting office an employee wore a bow tie to work. Comments and razzing from other workers soon convinced him that a bow tie was not an accepted style in the group, so thereafter he did not wear it. External control is directed toward those outside the group, such as management, union leadership, or other informal groups.

DISADVANTAGES OF INFORMAL ORGANIZATION. Each of the four functions of informal organization causes disadvantages that require careful management attention. One major disadvantage related to each function will be mentioned.

Resistance to change. With regard to the first function, perpetuation of culture, there develops a tendency for the group to become overly protective of its life-style and to stand like a rock in the face of change. What has been good is good and shall be good! If, for example, job A has always had more status than job B, it must continue to have more status and more pay, even though conditions have changed to make job A now less difficult. If restriction of productivity was necessary in the past with an autocratic management, it is necessary now, even though the management is becoming participative. Although informal organizations are bound by no chart on the wall, they are bound by convention, custom, and culture.

Role conflict. With regard to the second function, provision of social satisfactions, the quest for group satisfactions may lead members away from organizational objectives. What is good for the employee is not always good for the organization. Coffee breaks may be desirable but if employees spend an extra fifteen minutes socializing in the morning and afternoon, productivity may be reduced to the disadvantage of both employer and general public. Essentially what occurs is a role conflict. Workers want to meet the requirements of both their group and their employer, but frequently these requirements are in conflict. Much of this role conflict can be avoided by carefully cultivating mutual interests with informal groups. The more the interests, goals, methods, and evaluation systems of formal and informal organizations can be integrated, the more productivity and satisfaction can be expected. However, there must always be some differences between formal and informal organizations. This is not an area where perfect harmony is feasible.

Rumor. The third function of informal organization—communication—leads to that well-known problem called rumor. It is discussed later in this chapter in connection with informal communication.

Conformity. The fourth function of informal organization—social control—exerts strong pressures for conformity. Although people normally think of the official management organization as the cause of conformity, the informal organization is also a significant cause of employee conformity. The informal side of organizations is so much a part of the everyday life of workers that they hardly realize it is there, so they usually are unaware of the powerful pressures it applies to persuade them to conform to its way of life. The closer they are attached to it, the stronger its influence is.

Informal group requirements for a uniform life-style are known as *norms,* and the group whose norms a person accepts is a *reference group.* Rewards and penalties that a group uses to induce persons to conform to its norms are *sanctions.* Informal norms and sanctions do induce conformity. They consistently guide opinion and wield power for or against the organization or the union. Nonconformers are pressured and harassed until they capitulate or leave.

Examples of harassment are interference with work such as hiding one of the offender's tools, ridicule, interference outside of work such as letting the air out of the offender's automobile tires, and isolation from the group. In Britain it is said that a person isolated from the group is "being sent to Coventry." [4] *In these instances the group refuses to talk with the offender for days or even weeks, and group members may even refuse to use any tool or machine the offender has used. Actions of this type can drive a worker from a job.*

BENEFITS OF INFORMAL ORGANIZATION. Although informal systems have their disadvantages, they also bring a number of benefits. Most important is the fact that they blend with formal systems to make an effective system for getting the work done. Formal plans and policies cannot meet every problem in a dynamic situation because they are preestablished and partly inflexible. Some requirements can be met better by informal relations, which can be flexible and spontaneous.

Dubin and Shartle were among the first to recognize the mutuality of formal and informal systems in accomplishing work. Dubin states, "Informal relations in the organization serve to preserve the organization from the self-destruction that would result from literal obedience to the formal policies, rules, regulations, and procedures." [5] Shartle, in reporting his field research on leadership, commented, "The informal structure is one index of the dynamics of getting work done, and it appears that for efficiency it will necessarily deviate from the formal structure." [6] If management accepts and respects this mutual existence of formal and informal systems and does not harass the informal, it will tend to secure better cooperation from informal systems. In this way it fulfills part of its psychological work contract with employees.

Another benefit of informal organization is to lighten the work load on management. When managers know that the informal organization is working with them, they feel less compelled to check on the workers frequently to be sure everything is shipshape. Managers are encouraged to delegate and decentralize because they are confident that employees will be cooperative. It follows that informal group support may cause a supervisor to exercise more general supervision (compared with close supervision), which in turn is associated with higher productivity in the United States, as discussed in an earlier chapter. These related conditions suggest that informal group support of a manager probably leads to higher productivity.

Along this same line of thought, informal organization may act to fill in gaps in a manager's abilities. If a manager is weak in planning ability, an employee may informally help with planning, through either suggestions or open action, so that the overall result is the same as if the manager planned effectively.

A significant benefit of informal organization is that it gives satisfaction and stability to work groups. It is the means by which workers achieve a sense of belonging and security. It gives workers a feeling that they have something worth remaining with, so turnover is reduced. An additional benefit is that informal organization can be a useful channel of employee communication. It provides the means for people to keep in touch, to learn more about their work, and to understand what is happening in their environment. For example, one survey of workers reported that if there were an important change, they would depend first on the informal organization for information about it.[7]

A significant benefit, often overlooked, is that the informal organization is a safety valve for employee frustrations and other emotional problems. Psychological research has shown that employees may relieve emotional pressures by discussing them with someone else in an open and friendly way, and one's associates in the informal group provide this type of environment.

Consider the case of Max Schultz, who became frustrated and angry with his supervisor, Frieda Schneider. He felt like striking her, but in the civilized culture of the organization that was not appropriate behavior. He wanted to tell her what he thought of her, using uncomplimentary words, but he might have been disciplined for that. His next alternative was to have lunch with a close friend, and to share with his friend exactly how he felt. Having vented his feelings, he was able to return to work and interact with Schneider in a more relaxed way.

A benefit of informal organization that is seldom recognized is that its presence encourages managers to plan and act more carefully than they would otherwise. Managers who understand its power know that it is a check and balance on their unlimited use of authority. They introduce changes into their groups only after careful planning because they know that informal groups can undermine an ill-conceived and shaky project. They want their projects to succeed because they will have to answer to formal authority if they fail.

CHARTING THE INFORMAL ORGANIZATION. Normally a manager does not attempt to chart an informal organization, but in research charting is sometimes necessary to get a better understanding of an informal system. A diagram of group attraction is called a *sociogram*. This study and measurement of feelings of group members toward one another was pioneered by J. L. Moreno in the 1930s and is called *sociometry*. Moreno classed feelings as attraction, repulsion, and indifference. To learn these feelings in a work group, he asked members to rank their choices of people with whom they would like to work or not to work. The person receiving the most votes is the star, or sociometric leader. This person is the one liked the most, but is not necessarily the true informal leader who motivates the group to take action. The star can make or break a social fad but may be secondary to someone else in leading the group toward a work goal. When the patterns of feelings are charted, the result is a sociogram.

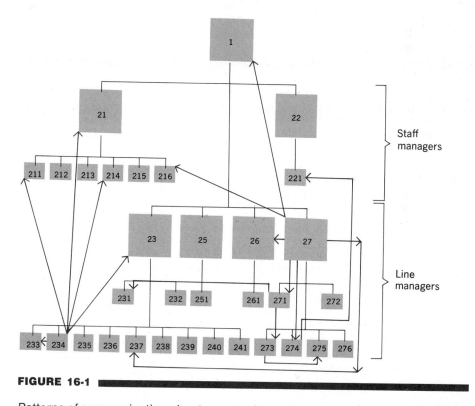

FIGURE 16-1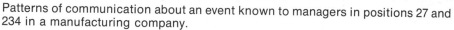

Patterns of communication about an event known to managers in positions 27 and 234 in a manufacturing company.

Another charting approach is to diagram the actual informal interactions of people, such as with whom an individual spends the most time and with whom one communicates informally. Charts of these relationships may be called interpersonal charts, interaction charts, informal organization charts, or grapevine charts. These interaction patterns may be superimposed on the formal organization chart in order to show variation between the two. This type of chart is illustrated by Figure 16-1, which is based on my own research. Superimposed on the formal chart are lines showing the patterns of communication that developed from an event known to the managers in positions 27 and 234. Most of these communications were outside formal chains of command, illustrating how the informal system is not bound by the official organizational structure. Discussion of informal communication continues in the next section.

INFORMAL COMMUNICATION

The informal grapevine coexists with management's formal communication system. The term "grapevine" arose during the War between the States. Intelligence telegraph lines were strung loosely from tree to tree in the manner of a grapevine. Since messages from the lines often were incorrect or confusing, any rumor was said to be from the grapevine. Today the term applies to all informal communication.

Though grapevine information tends to be oral, it may be written. Figure 16-2 is a copy of a grapevine communication sent by teletypewriter between company branches in two cities. During a period of months the two employees involved had developed an active interest in operations in the other branch. Though they never heard each other's voice, they frequently "talked" by teletype when the leased system was not in use. Observe that they were talking about their employer, and some of what they learned was undoubtedly passed along on the grapevine.

Since the grapevine arises from social interaction, it is as fickle, dynamic, and varied as people are. It is the expression of their natural motivation to communicate. It is the exercise of their freedom of speech and is a natural, normal activity. In fact, if employees are so uninterested in their work that they do not engage in shoptalk about it, they are probably maladjusted. If employees are so uninterested in their associates that they do not exchange talk about who will likely get the next promotion or who recently had a baby, they probably are abnormal. Employee interest in associates is illustrated by the experience of one company. The wife of a plant supervisor had a baby at 11 P.M., and a plant survey the next day at 2 P.M. showed that 46 percent of the management personnel knew of it through the grapevine.[8]

Since a grapevine cannot be held responsible for errors and is somewhat of an unknown, managers sometimes succumb to the wish that it would go away; but we have learned from experience and research that *"homicide" will not work with the grapevine*. It cannot be abolished, rubbed out, hidden under a basket, chopped down, tied up, or stopped. If we suppress it in one place, it will pop out in another. If we cut off one of its sources, it merely moves to another one—quite similarly to the way we change from one channel to another on a television set. It is as hard to kill

IS JOE* THERE GA[1]

YES

PUT HIM ON TELEX PLS[2] GA

THIS JOE

THIS SUE AND I AM A LITTLE CURIOUS ABOUT UR[3] TELEX YESTERDAY   COAST
CLEAR NOW   SO WHAT DO THEY ASK YOU GA

THE FIRST STUPID QUESTION WAS THEY WANTED TO KNOW WHAT HAPPENED TO
CERTAIN ITEMS THAT WERE ON THE INVENTORY ONE MONTH AND NOT ON THE NEXT
MONTH   I TOLD THEM IT WAS ONLY LOGICAL TO ASSUME THEY WERE SOLD   SO
THEY ASKED TO WHOM   TOLD THEM TO LOOK IT UP ON THEIR COPIES OF THE
DR'S[4] GA

UR ANSWER WAS PRETTY GOOD   UR RIGHT   THINGS LIKE THAT COME UP ALL THE
TIME BUT UNFORTUNATELY I HAVE TO FIGURE OUT MOSTLY FROM HERE   WHAT ELSE
JOE GA

THEY SAID MY INVENTORY WAS SHORT 25 TONS AND WANTED TO KNOW WHY   I
ASKED THEM FOR THE FIGURES THEY USED AND I CHECKED IT OUT ONLY TO FIND
THEY CANT EVEN COPY THE RIGHT FIGURES DOWN GA

WELL SOMETIMES I GUESS THEY MAKE BOBOS[5] LIKE THAT BUT UR LUCKY ONLY
BEING OFF 25 TONS   WE WERE OFF 400 TONS AND IT TOOK ME AWHILE TO FIND
IT   WHAT ELSE

THIS IS PROBABLY THE FUNNIEST   I PAY THE LOCAL PAPER HERE EVERY MONTH
FOR ADVERTISING AND WHEN OUR STATEMENTS COME HERE FROM CHICAGO THEY
NEVER HAVE ANYTHING CHARGED TO ADVERTISING WHICH AMOUNTS TO A FEW
THOUSAND A YEAR   I ASKED ABOUT IT AND THEY WERE SURPRISED   I GUESS
THEY DONT LOOK AT THE COPIES OF THE CHECKS THAT I MAKE OUT GA

WELL THEY SURE LOOK AT OURS BECAUSE THEY CONSTANTLY ASK US WHY AND TO
WHOM AND WHAT FOR WE PAID THIS AND THAT   THE ONLY ONE WHO KNOWS ABOUT
CHECK COPIES IS MAX SMITH AND I THINK HE KEEPS GOOD TRACK OF IT BUT U[6]
ARE RIGHT THAT IS FUNNY   OH GOOD GA

ANYWAY I REMEMBER GEORGE TELLING ME ABOUT UR PROBLEM AND I JUST WANTED
TO LET U KNOW U WERE NOT THE ONLY ONES THAT KEEP IN DAILY COMMUNICATION
WITH CHICAGO GA

I THINK IT WAS VERY NICE OF U AND AS FAR AS I CAN SEE I HAVE IT WORSE
THAN U SO MY COMPLIMENTS TO YOU AND THANKS AGAIN FOR UR CONCERN GA

THATS ABOUT ALL FROM HERE GA

OK JOE BIBI[7]

Key: *All names are disguised.
   [1]Go ahead.
   [2]Please.
   [3]"Your" or "you are," depending on the sentence.
   [4]Delivery receipts.
   [5]Errors; "boo-boos."
   [6]You.
   [7]Bye bye.

FIGURE 16-2 ▬▬▬▬▬▬▬▬▬▬▬▬▬▬▬▬▬▬▬▬▬▬▬▬▬

Actual transcript of a teletypewriter grapevine over a company private wire
between two warehouse clerks in separate cities.

as the mythical glass snake that, when struck, broke itself into fragments and grew a new snake out of each piece. In a sense, the grapevine is a human birthright, because whenever people congregate into groups, the grapevine is sure to develop. It may use smoke signals, jungle tom-toms, taps on the prison wall, ordinary conversation, or some other method, but it will always be there. Organizations cannot "fire" the grapevine because they did not hire it. It is simply there.

HOW ACCURATE IS THE GRAPEVINE? If we count the units of information in Figure 16-2 and then verify which are true and which are false, we will find that most of them are true. This is the way research on grapevine accuracy is done, and it shows that in normal work situations well over three-fourths of grapevine information is accurate.[9] People tend to think the grapevine is less accurate than it is because its errors are more dramatic and consequently more impressed on memory than its day-by-day routine accuracy. Moreover, the inaccurate parts are often more important.

On one grapevine, for example, a story about a welder marrying the general manager's daughter was true with regard to his getting married, the date, the location, and other details. The one detail wrong in this story having 90 percent accuracy was that the woman was not the general manager's daughter. She just happened to have the same last name, but this one wrong fact caused the whole communication to be wrong in general meaning, even though it was 90 percent accurate in detail.

It is also true that grapevine information is usually incomplete, so it may be seriously misinterpreted even though the details it does carry are accurate. That is, even though the grapevine tends to carry the truth, it rarely carries the whole truth. These cumulative inadequacies of the grapevine mean that in total it tends to produce more misunderstanding than its small percentage of wrong information suggests.

THE GRAPEVINE PATTERN. Managers occasionally get the impression that the grapevine operates like a long chain in which A tells B, who tells C, who then tells D, and so on, until twenty persons later, Y gets the information—very late and very incorrect. Sometimes the grapevine may operate this way, but research shows that it generally follows a different pattern, which works something like this: A tells three or four others (such as B, R, and F). Only one or two of these receivers will then pass on the information, and they will usually tell more than one person. Then as the information becomes older and the proportion of those knowing it gets larger, it gradually dies out because those who receive it do not repeat it. This network is a "cluster chain," because each link in the chain tends to inform a cluster of other people instead of only one person.

If we accept the idea that this cluster chain is predominant, it is reasonable to conclude that only a few persons are active communicators on the grapevine for any particular bit of information.[10] If, for example, eighty-seven clerks in an office know that Mabel was married secretly on Saturday, probably the word was spread to these eighty-seven by only ten or fifteen clerks. The remainder knew the information, but did not spread it. These persons who keep the grapevine active are called liaison individuals. For example, in one company that I studied, when a quality-control problem occurred, 68 percent of the executives knew about it, but only 20 percent of them spread the information. In another case, when a manager planned to resign, 81 percent of the executives knew about it, but only 11 percent passed the news on to others.

The grapevine is more a product of the situation than it is of the person. This means that *given the proper situation and motivation, any of us tends to become active on the grapevine.* Since people tend to be active on the grapevine when they have cause to be, they are acting partly in a predictable way. This element of cause and predictability is important, because it offers management a chance to influence the grapevine. What are some of these causes? One is that any group tends to be more active on the grapevine during periods of excitement and insecurity. Examples are a layoff or the installation of a computer in the office. At times like this, the grapevine is humming with activity, which means that managers need to watch it with extra care and "feed" it true information to keep it from getting out of hand.

People also are active on the grapevine when their friends and work associates are involved. This means that if Mary is to be promoted or Beatrice fired, employees need to know the full story as soon as possible. If they are not informed, they will fill in the gaps with their own conclusions; that is, people fill in missing signals according to their own perceptions.

People also are most active on the grapevine when they have news, as distinguished from stale information. Research shows that the greatest spread of information happens immediately after it is known; so it is important to get out the right story in the beginning.

The grapevine exists largely by word of mouth and by observation; hence, procedures that regularly bring people into contact will encourage them to be active on the grapevine. For example, in one company the chief link between two offices was the manager's secretary, who stopped by the other office right after lunch every day to pick up reports. In another office the link was an accounting clerk who every morning telephoned 300 yards across the company property to get some cost data. In a similar manner employees having nearby desks are likely to communicate more than two employees in separate buildings.

The foregoing examples show that the kind of job possessed by an employee has an important influence on that person's role on the grapevine. Some jobs give employees more opportunity to communicate than others, and some jobs provide employees with more news that might be worth communicating. The result is that certain employees are more active on the grapevine, not because of personality but because of their function in the organization. Their roles give them a strong basis for being key persons on the grapevine network. For example, one study showed that secretaries to managers were four times more likely to be key grapevine communicators, compared with other employees.[11]

Although type of job is an important grapevine influence, some employees are more active for personality reasons. Perhaps they like to talk about people, have a strong interest in what is happening in their organization, or have special communication abilities. Research, however, does not disclose any sex differences in grapevine activity. The grapevine is coeducational. Both women and men are equally active on the grapevine.[12]

FEATURES OF THE GRAPEVINE. The main feature of the grapevine is its tremendous capacity to carry information both helpful and harmful to the organization. To look at the positive side, the grapevine gives managers much feedback about employees and their work experiences, thereby increasing understanding of what actions are needed to be supportive. It also helps interpret management to the workers so that they may be more supportive. It especially helps translate management's formal orders into employee language, in this way making up for any management failures in communication. In several instances the grapevine carries information that the formal system does not wish to carry and purposely leaves unsaid. For example, a supervisor who is in a bad mood because of personal or job problems usually cannot announce this fact officially to employees. The better approach is to "put it on the grapevine" so that personnel are forewarned informally not to make requests that can be delayed. How often it is said, "Don't talk to the boss about a raise today."

Another grapevine feature is its fast pace. Being flexible and personal, it spreads information faster than most management communication systems. With the rapidity of a burning powder train, the grapevine filters out of the woodwork, past the manager's office, through the locker rooms, and along the corridors. Its speed makes it quite difficult for management to stop undesirable rumors or to release significant news in time to prevent rumor formation.

One company, when it signed its labor contract at 11 P.M., had to keep its publication staff busy all night in order to have a suitable bulletin ready for supervisors and employees when they came to work the next morning. This was the only way that it could match the grapevine's speed.

One study showed the speed of the grapevine in government. The study covered Canadian government engineers who had been transferred, and 32 percent reported that they first heard of their transfer on the grapevine.[13]

Another grapevine feature is its unusual ability to penetrate even the tightest company security screen because of its capacity for cutting across organizational lines and dealing directly with the people who know. The grapevine has long been known as the source of much information that the organization really did not want released.

All evidence shows that the grapevine is influential, either favorably or unfavorably. The grapevine accomplishes so much positively and so much negatively that it is difficult to determine whether its net effects are positive or negative. Undoubtedly its effects vary among different work groups and different organizations. Employees tend to remember its negative effects, such as the times that they were misinformed by the grapevine. One study of managers and white-collar employees reported that 53 percent of them viewed the grapevine as a negative factor in the organization. Only 27 percent viewed it as a positive factor, and 20 percent considered it as neutral.[14]

Regardless of the grapevine's net effects, it cannot be done away with, so the organization needs to adjust to it. Managers are coming to the realization that they need to learn who its leaders are, how it operates, and what information it carries. Though they used to ignore it, they now listen to it and study it. Many managers also try to influence the grapevine in various ways. Their object is to reduce negative effects and increase positive effects. They try to reduce anxiety, conflict, and misunderstanding so that the grapevine will have less cause to spread negative information. They also try to leak useful information to the grapevine so that it will have more positive information. Not all managers take this approach. Some prefer to ignore the grapevine and let it go its separate way, but this approach overlooks the important role it plays in organizations.

In any case, managers need to listen to the grapevine. It tells them what employees are excited about and what is important to them. It shows gaps in information and helps to pinpoint these with regard to certain departments or areas. It provides useful information to any manager who is trying to understand what is happening in the organization.

RUMOR. Probably the most undesirable feature of the grapevine—and the one that gives the grapevine its poor reputation—is rumor. The word "rumor" is sometimes used as a synonym for the whole grapevine, but technically there is an important difference between the two terms. *Rumor* is grapevine information that is communicated without secure standards of evidence being present. It is the unverified and untrue part of the grapevine. It could by chance be correct, but generally it is incorrect; so it is presumed to be undesirable. It probably has been a problem since the beginning of human history, as illustrated by Figure 16-3, an operatic aria of the early 1800s about rumor.

Allport's research in the 1940s showed that rumor is a product of interest times ambiguity in a situation.[15] If a subject has no interest to a person, then that person has no cause to rumor about it. In my own case, for example, I have never rumored about the coconut output on the island of Martinique for the preceding year. Similarly, if there is no ambiguity in a situation, a person has no cause for rumor because the correct facts are known. This means that both interest and ambiguity normally must be present both to begin and to maintain a rumor.

Since rumor largely depends on the interest and ambiguity perceived by each person, it tends to change as it passes from person to person. Its general theme can usually be maintained, but not its details. It is subject to *filtering* by which it is reduced to a few basic details that can conveniently be remembered and passed on to others. Generally persons choose details in the rumor to fit their particular interests and view of the world.

People also add new details, often making the story worse, in order to put in their own strong feelings and reasoning; this is *elaborating.*

For example, a worker heard a rumor that an employee in another department had been injured. When she passed the rumor to someone else, she elab-

orated by adding the implication that the injury was caused by the supervisor's poor machine maintenance. Apparently she made this elaboration because she did not like the supervisor, so she felt that if someone was injured, it must have been the supervisor's fault.

CONTROL OF RUMOR. Since rumor is generally incorrect, a major outbreak of it can be a devastating epidemic that sweeps through an organization as fast as a summer storm—and usually with as much damage. Rumor should be dealt with firmly and consistently, but how and what to attack must be known. It is a serious mistake to strike at the whole grapevine merely because it happens to be the agent that carries rumor; that approach would be as unwise as throwing away a typewriter because of a few misspelled words.

   The best approach in dealing with rumor is to get at its causes, rather than trying to kill it after it has already started. Getting at causes is wise use of the preventive approach, instead of a tardy curative approach. When people feel reasonably secure, understand the things that matter to them, and feel on the team, there are few rumors, because there is very little ambiguity in the situation. But when

"DON BASILIO'S SLANDER ARIA" from THE BARBER OF SEVILLE
English translation by Boris Goldovsky

Start a rumor, a mere invention,
Any story you'd care to mention.
Start it circulating lightly,
Oh so gently, oh so slightly.
Very soon it gets around all by itself.

Did you hear it? Most appalling . . . Just imagine! Quite enthralling. . .
Once it's born each idle rumor just keeps growing like a tumor,
No one knows where it has started, but he's anxious to repeat, to impart it.
And with every repetition it receives a fresh addition.
Is it fact or is it fiction? No one knows and no one cares.

There is no one to deny it; no one bothers to defy it,
Soon it blossoms like a flower, and begins to gain in power.
Now the tempest from the distance nearer grows with more insistence,
Rumbling louder, ever louder, till the storm is at it's worst.

Like a sudden flash of lightning, now the skies are rent asunder,
With an awful roar of thunder, and the rumor grows and fattens
Without reason, without rhyme.

There's no formal accusation, just a whispered intimation.
But the people are convinced that he's committed every crime.
He can give no explanation for his ruined reputation,
But the world has been aroused and will convict him every time.

FIGURE 16-3 ██

An operatic aria of the early 1800s about rumor. Copyright 1949 by Boris Goldovsky. Reprinted with permission of Boris Goldovsky, Goldovsky Opera Institute.

people are emotionally maladjusted or inadequately informed about their environment, they are likely to be rumormongers. This is a normal defensive reaction attempting to make their situation more meaningful and secure.

In spite of all that can be done, rumors do start. Then what? In general, not all rumors should be fought, for that would be a needless waste of organizational time. Most rumors are relatively harmless and soon die out. On the other hand, some rumors are serious enough to damage effectiveness or injure reputations. For example, when a rumor of a layoff developed in a factory, the amount of products coming off the end of the assembly line decreased a few percentage points. People appeared to be working just as hard, but the flow of products declined. In situations such a this, the rumor may be serious enough to require management action to try to stop it.

The best way to stop or weaken rumor is to release the facts. Ambiguity is reduced, so there is less reason for rumor, and the truth tends to prevail. Serious rumors should be attacked as early as possible because once the general theme of a rumor is known and accepted, employees distort future happenings to conform to the rumor. Thus, if employees accept the scuttlebutt that there are plans to move the firm's offices to a new building, every minor change thereafter will be interpreted as a confirmation of that rumor (even, for example, when an electrician comes to repair an electric outlet). If the rumor were dead, this same change could be made without any employee upset at all.

Usually, a face-to-face supply of facts is the most effective way because it helps answer the particular ambiguities in each individual's mind; but a word of warning is in order. The facts should be given directly without first mentioning the rumor, because when a rumor is repeated at this time, some people will hear it instead of the refutation. They then assume you have confirmed the rumor! Here is an example of a suitable approach.

In one company John Worker cut two fingers of his left hand at his machine one morning. He was sent to the medical office for first aid, and he returned to his job in about thirty minutes with his fingers bandaged. Meanwhile, word had spread through the shop that John had cut his fingers. The farther from John's department the story traveled, the more gruesome were his injuries, until finally the story had him losing his left hand. Alert supervisors soon observed the effect of this rumor on morale and investigated the facts. Management then announced over the public address system that the most serious injury treated that morning was two cut fingers of a machine operator who received treatment and returned to his job in Department 37. No mention was made of the rumor, but this announcement brought the rumor under control.

The communication of facts is more effective if it comes from a source that employees think is in a position to know the true facts. The source should also be a person who has a dependable communication record. Dependable informal leaders can help management stop a rumor if the facts are shared with them as soon as possible. Though face-to-face refutation is most effective, management may wish to reinforce the facts by confirming them in writing.

Managers sometimes ask help of the union in combating rumor. Although the union does not control the grapevine any more than management does, it does have influence. Since rumors are worst when management and labor are in conflict, any reduction of conflict should reduce rumors. Marked improvement frequently results in a department when the supervisor gains the union steward's cooperation in combating rumor, especially when the steward is a strong informal leader.

Regardless of the importance of a rumor, it should be listened to carefully because, even though untrue, it usually carries a message about employee feelings. Each manager needs to ask, "Why did that rumor originate? What does it mean?" In this way a manager gains insights into where ambiguities are and what the interests of employees are. It may seem unrealistic to listen to rumors that are untrue, but the usefulness of this approach can be illustrated with the case of the labor relations director who during a strike listened carefully to what the workers said management was going to do. He knew that these employee statements were rumors because management had not decided what to do. Nevertheless, he listened, because these rumors gave him insight into worker attitudes toward management and what kind of settlement they might make.

Many rumors are symbolic expressions of feelings and are not really offered by their communicators as fact or truth; hence, they must be interpreted symbolically. If, for example, an employee named Helen Morehouse tells a rumor showing how her supervisor is unfair, what she really is trying to express is this: I think that the supervisor is an unjust tyrant, and here is a story I have made up to illustrate what he would do if he had a chance to do it. The employee is merely using story details symbolically to express feelings, but the difficulty is that someone else along the rumor chain accepts the story as fact. Thus what was originally only a symbolic folktale gradually becomes represented as a fact. Managers can understand rumors better if they search for some symbolic meaning in them.

INFLUENCING INFORMAL ORGANIZATIONS

It has been noted that management did not establish informal organizations, and neither can management abolish them. Nor would it want to do so. But management can learn to live with them and have some measure of influence on them.[16] Mangement's job is:

1. To accept and understand informal organization.

2. To consider possible effects on informal systems when taking any action.

3. To integrate as far as possible the interests of informal groups with those of the formal organization.

4. To keep formal activities from unnecessarily threatening informal organization in general.

Care should be taken to make sure that informal systems remain secondary to formal ones, else long-run employer objectives may be lost in a maze of small-group interests. When the formal system is too weak to get the job done, the informal organization is often tempted to grow stronger in order to rush in to fill the void and hold the group together. As is said in some groups, "We get along here in spite of the supervisor." This arrangement may get passable productivity as long as informal systems support organizational objectives, but it can easily drift into take-it-easy practices or antimanagement attitudes. Since management is weak, it is unable to correct any deviant tendencies.

The situation is probably not much better if management tries to be strong and autocratic, while attempting to keep informal organizations suppressed. Under these conditions, informal organizations seem to gain strength as a strong counterforce in order to protect the group and make the work situation livable. The two opposing counterforces generate conflict. The result is only minimum productivity with negative side effects.

The most desirable combination of formal and informal organizations appears to be a predominant formal system to maintain unity toward objectives, along with a well-developed informal system to maintain group cohesiveness and teamwork. In other words, the informal organization needs to be strong enough to be supportive, but not strong enough to dominate.

SUMMARY

Informal social systems exist in all organizations because they arise naturally from the interaction of people. Informal organizations provide certain benefits in an operating organization, but they also present a number of disadvantages, such as resistance to change, role conflict, rumor, and conformity. Pressures are brought on employees by establishing norms and applying sanctions to those who violate the norms.

Informal communication, called the grapevine, develops in the form of a cluster chain. Its accuracy in normal situations tends to be above 75 percent, but there may be inaccurate key details, and the whole story is rarely communicated. The grapevine is fast and influential. Employees tend to depend on it for information, even though they often view it on the whole as a negative factor in the organization. Rumor is grapevine information communicated without secure standards of evidence. It results particularly from ambiguity and interest.

Management can have some influence on the grapevine, and its basic objective is to integrate interests of the formal and informal systems so that they can work together in better ways.

TERMS AND CONCEPTS FOR REVIEW

Informal organization

Norms

Reference group

Sanctions

Sociogram

Grapevine

Cluster chain

Rumor

Filtering

Elaborating

REVIEW QUESTIONS

1. What characteristics distinguish formal and informal organizations?
2. How do informal organizations encourage conformity?
3. Discuss both benefits and disadvantages of informal organizations.
4. What is the grapevine? Discuss its accuracy.
5. What is rumor? What can an organization do to prevent rumors and to reduce undesirable ones when they have started?

CASES

EXCELSIOR DEPARTMENT STORE

The Excelsior Department Store had a large shoe department that employed twelve salesclerks. Most of these clerks were loyal and faithful clerks who had worked in the department more than ten years. They formed a closely knit social group.

The store embarked on an expansion program requiring seven new shoe clerks to be hired in a period of six months. These newcomers soon learned that the old-timers took the desirable times for coffee breaks, leaving the most undesirable periods for newcomers. The old-time clerks also received priority from the old-time cashier, which required the newcomers to wait in line at the cash register until the old-timers had their sales recorded. A number of customers complained to store management about this practice.

In addition, the old-timers frequently instructed newcomers to straighten shoes in the stock room and to clean displays on the sales floor, although this work was just as much a responsibility of the old-timers. The result was that old-timers had more time to make sales and newcomers had less time. Since commissions were paid on sales, the newcomers complained to the department manager about this practice.

QUESTIONS

1. Discuss the source and meaning of the employee practices reported in this case.
2. As manager of the shoe department, what would you do about each of the practices? Discuss.

PEERLESS MINING COMPANY

A maintenance employee of Peerless Mining Company asked for a six-month leave of absence for personal reasons. The request was granted because it was in accord with company and union policy. A few weeks later the industrial relations manager of the mining company heard by the grapevine that the employee actually had taken his leave to work on a construction project in another part of the state. The report was that the employee needed some extra money, and he had taken this job in order to earn contract construction wages as a carpenter, because these wages were approximately twice those earned on this regular maintenance job. The act of taking leave for personal reasons, with the hidden purpose of working for another employer during the leave period was contrary to the labor contract, and the penalty for this could be dismissal. Accordingly, the industrial relations director prepared a "notice of hearing concerning dismissal action" to be mailed to the employee at his local address, since he had maintained his home where his wife and children remained. The letter of notice was dictated by the industrial relations director on Thursday morning.

Thursday night the employee called the industrial relations director at his home, saying that he had heard that the notice was being prepared, and that he felt that there was a misunderstanding. He said that he thought his action was acceptable under the contract, but if it was not acceptable, he wanted to return to the company immediately, because he did not want to give up his permanent job with the mining company. When the industrial relations director pressed him to learn how he knew about the pending dismissal notice, the employee said that his wife had called him that evening. He said that his wife had reported that another wife at a local grocery store had told her about the pending dismissal notice.

QUESTIONS

1. Is there any evidence in this case that both management and employees use the grapevine for their benefit? Discuss.
2. Assume grapevine facts are as follows: The industrial relations director's secretary told a fringe benefit clerk about the dismissal notice; the clerk, not realizing the information might be confidential, told some one else. If you were the industrial relations director, would you try to suppress grapevine leaks of this type? Discuss.
3. After the employee's telephone call, what action should the industrial relations director take?

REFERENCES

1. Lyman W. Porter, Edward E. Lawler III, and J. Richard Hackman, *Behavior in Organizations,* New York: McGraw-Hill Book Company, 1975, p. 77.

2. William E. Reif, Robert M. Monczka, and John W. Newstrom, "Perceptions of the Formal and Informal Organizations: Objective Measurement through the Semantic Differential Technique," *Academy of Management Journal,* September 1973, pp. 389–403.

3. Research by Warren shows that informal organization "is particularly decisive in achieving social control." See Donald I. Warren, "Power, Visibility, and Conformity in Formal Organizations," *American Sociological Review,* December 1968, p. 961.

4. The term "sent to Coventry" is derived from the citizens of Coventry who so disliked soldiers that persons seen talking to one were isolated from their social community, so the few people who felt like talking to soldiers did not dare do so. Hence, a soldier sent to Coventry was isolated from community interaction.

5. Robert Dubin, *Human Relations in Administration,* Englewood Cliffs, N.J.: Prentice-Hall, Inc., 1951, p. 68.

6. Carroll L. Shartle, "Leadership and Executive Performance," *Personnel,* March 1949, p. 378.

7. Eugene Walton, "How Efficient Is the Grapevine?" *Personnel* March–April 1961, pp. 45–49.

8.   Keith Davis, "Management Communication and the Grapevine," *Harvard Business Review*, September–October 1953, p. 44.

9.   One study found that the grapevine was 82 percent accurate for company information. See Walton, *op. cit.*, p. 48. My own research discloses an accuracy of 80 to 99 percent for noncontroversial company information. It is probable that accuracy is not so great for personal or highly emotional information.

10.   For research confirmation of this conclusion see Harold Sutton and Lyman W. Porter, "A Study of the Grapevine in a Governmental Organization," *Personnel Psychology,* Summer 1968, pp. 223–230.

11.   Keith Davis, "Grapevine Communication among Lower and Middle Managers," *Personnel Journal,* April 1969, pp. 269–272.

12.   Jay T. Knippen, "Grapevine Communication: Management and Employees," *Journal of Business Research,* January 1974, p. 55.

13.   Ronald J. Burke, "Quality of Organizational Life: The Effects of Personnel Job Transfers," in Vance F. Mitchell and others (eds.), *Proceedings of the Academy of Management,* Vancouver, B.C., Canada: University of British Columbia, 1973, p. 242.

14.   John W. Newstrom, Robert E. Monczka, and William E. Reif, "Perceptions of the Grapevine: Its Value and Influence," *Journal of Business Communication,* Spring 1974, pp. 12–20.

15.   Gordon W. Allport and Leo Postman, *The Psychology of Rumor,* New York: Holt, Rinehart and Winston, Inc., 1947, p. 33.

16.   For a research illustration of how management action may influence the informal organization, see Cecil L. French, "Some Structural Aspects of a Retail Sales Group," *Human Organization,* Summer 1963, pp. 146–151.

CHAPTER 17
WORKING WITH UNIONS

. . . We need to utilize existing techniques of conflict resolution developed by the behavioral sciences to minimize the negative consequences of win-lose power bargaining.
Irving Stern and Robert F. Pearse[1]

LEARNING OBJECTIVES

TO UNDERSTAND:
The nature of collective bargaining
Ideas of mediation and arbitration
The concept of integrative bargaining
How grievance systems operate
The need for effective judicial systems
Union response to individual employee needs
Third-party effects of union power

Not all employers deal with labor unions, but a number of them do. Union membership is high in some occupations, and it represents about one-fourth of the total labor force in the United States. Although one-fourth is not a large proportion, it does represent a powerful economic, social, and political force in the work environment. A union is a distinct organization separate from the employer. On the other hand, it is the closest of all external influences because its membership consists of employees, its interests concern conditions of employment, and its primary activity is representing worker interests to management. Observe in the following situation how readily the union becomes involved in work issues.

In an electrical company four employees worked at a table performing four identical skilled operations before passing parts to four other skilled workers at another table. Under these conditions they had a skilled artisan's pride in work and ample opportunity to engage in friendly conversation during the day. The work was then changed to assembly-line conditions where each employee was isolated along a conveyor belt and performed only a semiskilled fraction of the former skilled job. The result was unrest and constructive protest. When management failed to heed the protest, the employees appealed to their union, which made a strike issue of the incident and built union solidarity.

In this chapter we will examine the union's role in the work environment, collective bargaining, grievance systems, and behavioral issues that arise from union activity. Not all aspects of unions are discussed. Instead, we focus on those items which especially affect organizational behavior.

THE UNION'S ROLE IN AN ORGANIZATION

A labor union is an association of employees for the primary purpose of influencing their employer's decisions about their conditions of employment. It may also engage in fraternal activities, political action, and related activities. It is a social group, and it brings to the work environment a second formal organization, as shown in Figure 17-1. The union hierarchy sits alongside the management hierarchy, and the employee becomes a member of both. Sometimes this arrangement is beneficial to workers, because when their wants are not satisfied by management, they can turn to the union for help. At other times this arrangement is annoying, because each organization makes some conflicting demands on workers.

A second formal organization greatly increases the interaction relationships that can occur, some of which are shown by the lines in Figure 17-1. Looking only at the mathematics of the situation, the introduction of a second chain of command causes a geometric increase in relationships, which tremendously complicates human interaction. Although no more persons are added, most of them are now playing two formal roles, one as union member and one as company employee.

The union also introduces a second set of informal organizations. These informal groups are built around union interests and activities, and they are some-

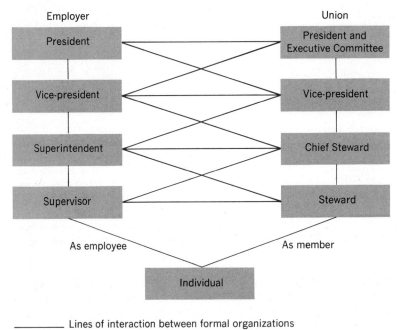

Employer   Union

President	President and Executive Committee
Vice-president	Vice-president
Superintendent	Chief Steward
Supervisor	Steward

As employee   As member

Individual

———————— Lines of interaction between formal organizations
———————— Lines of formal authority

FIGURE 17-1

The union adds a second formal organization to the employment relationship.

times as powerful as the union formal structure. Take an unauthorized strike as an example. Though union leadership joins with management in demanding a return to work, the demand is not always successful because of informal group pressures. Informal leaders have the group emotionally worked up and are so in control of the situation that formal union orders to return to work are ignored.

Since the combined union-management system is more complicated than a simple worker-employer relationship, it tends to require more sophisticated management skills to make it work effectively. For example, one study found that supervisors in unionized organizations felt less informed than supervisors in nonunionized organizations.[2] Consequently their effectiveness is likely to deteriorate unless better communication programs are developed for them. Further, when the complicated union-management system malfunctions, the results may be more disastrous than with the simple system. There is, therefore, more pressure to keep the complicated system working.

COLLECTIVE BARGAINING

Collective bargaining requires negotiations between representatives of management and labor to accomplish a written agreement covering terms and conditions of employment. It is essentially a compromise and balancing of opposing pressures of two social groups who have enough mutual interests and goals to reach a workable agreement voluntarily. (There are exceptions, of course.) Pressures at the bargaining table are usually framed in economic and technical terms; yet bargaining overall is a social process. The objective of collective bargaining is to work toward a new equilibrium of social forces and to make it easier to maintain this new equilibrium. To the extent that these pressures can be reconciled, conflict can be reduced. The following situation illustrates, however, that settlement of bargaining demands is only one part of the whole social situation.[3]

The president of a small, unorganized company believed in unions and was gratified when he was notified his employees were forming a union. Their negotiating committee submitted a list of demands in advance. The president studied them carefully and found them reasonable; so he decided to surprise his workers and grant all demands in full at the first meeting of the negotiating committee. This magnanimous attitude would, he thought, set a firm basis for good union relations. At the first meeting, he granted all demands as he had planned, but much to his own surprise, the union representatives were not at all pleased. The contract was duly signed, but relations deteriorated instead of improving.

What happened in this case? The union arose out of the employees' dissatisfactions and desires to assert themselves. Its members expected to have to fight to get what they wanted. Committee members took their task seriously and prepared long and hard. Their emotions were built up. When management conceded everything they wanted, they went away from negotiations with their pent-up emotions still awaiting expression. They were frustrated. They felt insufficient—if the president could grant these demands so easily, surely they had failed to demand enough. New emotions were piled atop the old ones still unexpressed. The employer made one major mistake in this case. He failed to recognize that bargaining deals in the *emotions* of people as well as in logic and economic interests. In fact, collective bargaining is a difficult human activity, requiring careful preparation and top-notch executive competence. It is not usually accomplished by some easy trick or gimmick.

Though it presents difficulties, collective bargaining is a useful practice to help preserve labor-management autonomy in a free society. If we require labor disputes to be settled by third parties, labor and management freedoms will be correspondingly reduced. Collective bargaining, therefore, serves long-run interests of a free society, as well as the interests of labor and management.

Bargaining is permitted for federal civil service employees and many local government employees, as well as employees in private organizations. Bargaining for government employees tends to be more limited since they are public servants, and it may not include the right to strike against government. Because of these limitations, government unions tend to rely more heavily on grievance machinery and political activity.

BARGAINING IS A CONTINUOUS PROCESS. People sometimes look upon collective bargaining as an affair that is conducted annually or less often, and then it is finished and forgotten until the next time for bargaining rolls around. This is the way they read about bargaining in the public press; and accordingly that is all there is to it. This viewpoint is shared by some managers. As one manager put it, "Thank goodness, bargaining is finished for this year. Now we can get down to business!"

Actually, this conception of periodic bargaining recognizes only a part of the whole cloth. From the behavioral point of view, *collective bargaining is a continuous process.* It is true that formal negotiations around a bargaining table take place only periodically; but after the contract is signed, a number of other parts of the bargaining process remain to be performed. The contract must be communicated to managers, employees, and union officers. After that, it must be interpreted. New situations, not exactly spelled out in the contract, are always cropping up, requiring management and union representatives to get together to try to interpret what the contract says or what they meant it to say. Decisions must be made concerning whether something is or is not covered by the contract.

All the while, as these interpretations are being made, both parties are watching for flaws in their contract so that they can introduce amendments at the next negotiation period. They are also studying local, industrywide, and nationwide labor relations developments to see how their own contract may be affected. This means that while the old contract is being interpreted (and according to the way that it is interpreted) plans for negotiating a new contract are under way. Truly, overall collective bargaining is a continuous process.

PLANNING FOR NEGOTIATIONS. In planning for negotiations, management first takes stock of the present state of its labor relations because each forthcoming bargaining period is built upon what has gone before. If labor relations are poor and the union is antagonistic, the next bargaining session will tend to be antagonistic also. However, if labor relations have matured to a state of active cooperation, bargaining should be reasonable and responsible. Mature union-management cooperation brings two important additions to the typical collective bargaining relationship: (1) a psychological atmosphere in which each party feels free to approach the other for cooperation without fear that this approach weakens its bargaining position, and (2) a problem-solving viewpoint and method rather than a balance-of-power outlook and method.

In appraising the current state of labor relations, management should not overlook conditions within the union. If there is trouble here, it may spill over into the bargaining sessions. Is the union leadership sound? Are there rivalries between two or more factions? Questions like these must be considered in order to predict what kinds of attitudes the employer will face across the bargaining table.

Regardless of the type of labor relations an organization has, in preparing for negotiations it needs to gain the participation of its supervisors and middle managers. These are the people who actually live with the current contract day by day, and they know much about where it is weak and strong. Furthermore, these are the people who will administer the new contract, and they will give the contract better support if they can participate in the changes that are made. If their voice is heard—and heard in advance—they should feel more responsible for making the contract work. Of equal importance, if top management comes to the bargaining table without its supervisors by its side, it will lack the realistic touch that the union has, because usually most union representatives are intimately acquainted with day-to-day problems.

DEVELOPING CONSTRUCTIVE ATTITUDES. Collective bargaining is a flexible, give-and-take group process. It depends upon both careful preparation and skillful maneuvering from a flexible position. If management takes extreme positions in its bargaining and consistently peppers the opposition with a categorical "No, we won't," it may have to waste much of its energy trying to withdraw itself from this unalterable position. Furthermore, this negative attitude sets the wrong emotional tone for bargaining sessions. Some employers attempt to build constructive attitudes by having prenegotiation conferences in which no direct bargaining confrontation takes place. The parties discuss mutual problems and try to obtain agreement on facts such as current wages and job classifications. In this way some agreement on the current situation is reached before agreement on new demands is sought.

Bargaining attitudes are important. If managers do not fully accept the union or if union leaders do not fully accept the organization, it is to be expected that sessions will be emotional and hard-fought. Each group will be defensive because it will feel that its survival is being challenged. In the same way that each group will be defensive about its institution, individuals will be defensive and emotional if they are personally challenged, and bargaining sessions will deteriorate into personal arguments.

In one company, for example, an international union negotiator stated to the company president, "What do you know about the needs of the workers in the shop? You never did any manual labor and you're too fat to do a day's work now if you had to!" The president replied that the union representative did not have enough education to understand business anyway, so why bother to bargain. At this point bargaining ceased and personal insults began to fly from both sides. No bargaining was accomplished until the next session several days later.

NEED FOR CLEAR BARGAINING PROCEDURES. Procedures for bargaining sessions have a significant influence on agreement, just as attitudes do. If bargaining procedures are not clear, each party never quite understands what the other is doing, and agreement becomes almost impossible until they can begin to communicate with each other. For example, what is the role of a lawyer at the bargaining table? Is the lawyer speaking as a bargaining representative of the employer, or only as a legal adviser? The same question can also be asked concerning an international union representative, if one is present. In fact, the overall question of who will attend the bargaining sessions is an important one. Each side will have a chief negotiator, but usually more than one person will speak across the bargaining table as a negotiator. However, it is wise to limit the size of the negotiating committee, because this reduces human relationships to a reasonable number. If the group is small, all active negotiators can get to know each other fairly well as negotiations develop.

It is common practice for both sides also to have present a number of non-negotiating advisers and observers. The advisers deal only with their own negotiators, rather than across the table. The observers usually listen only. The overall result is sometimes called "goldfish-bowl bargaining" because the active negotiators are constantly working in the presence of a large group of advisers and observers. Observers are often used as a means of communicating the current state of negotiations. Management, for example, may have its supervisors attend bargaining sessions on a rotating basis. In some cases the supervisors select their own delegates. The union may encourage stewards or rank-and-file members to attend in order to keep them informed and to assure them that their union leaders are working diligently and making no "sellout" to management.

BARGAINING TACTICS. One important tactical device is the *recess.* It is obviously useful when negotiators become fatigued, but more important, it is a means for the bargaining committee to discuss some point privately. If members of a committee show disagreement among themselves, this may indicate weakness to the other side; so when a knotty problem arises, some member may request a recess. This allows either party to thrash out the problem in private and return to the meeting with a united front. A recess, furthermore, gives one party time to work out of a difficult position. Just as a football team calls "Time out" when the going gets tough, a negotiating committee should recess to reconsider its position, assemble more information, or consult higher authority.

There are a number of other tactics that may make negotiations easier at the bargaining table. When some negotiators reach an especially troublesome issue that is delaying negotiations, they request that it be tabled and then taken up in later meetings. They hope that meanwhile the situation will change to make the issue more easily resolved. In some bargaining sessions there is mutual agreement to begin negotiations with the easy or minor problems, gradually working up to the more difficult ones. Subcommittees may be used to get a difficult problem out of the mainstream of bargaining into the quieter environment of a smaller group.

All negotiators use *counterproposals* in an effort to get the two sides closer together. To take an example, if the union asked for a 10-cent wage increase, management might (1) offer an 8-cent increase to skilled workers and 4 cents to all others, (2) offer a pension plan costing 6 cents in lieu of any wage increase, or (3) demand a management-rights clause along with the wage increase. Since the union typically does most of the asking during negotiations, management will be wise to introduce whatever elements it can to reverse this relationship and gain the initiative.

MEDIATION AND CONTRACT SETTLEMENT. If an agreement cannot be reached, the union may call a strike, or a *mediator* may be brought to the scene by one of the parties or by government. The mediator's role is that of an outside specialist who is free of the emotionalism in which the parties are involved. Mediators have wide experience and a fresh viewpoint, which may enable them to suggest settlements not previously considered. Mediators also help hold down emotionalism and use direct persuasion to try to get the parties to come to agreement. One comprehensive study reported that a mediator's two most important skills were intellectual ability and "tough" human relations.[4] From a human point of view an important function is that of confidential intermediary carrying messages and viewpoints from one party to the other. This enables the negotiators to sound out each other without formally committing themselves. Here is a simplified version of how this worked in one company.

Management hinted to the mediator that it might raise its wage offer to 12 cents if the union would drop the thorny union-security issue. The mediator scurried across the street to union headquarters and suggested that he might be able to get management to come up to 12 cents on its wage offer, but he didn't think management would budge on union security. The union officers hinted that they couldn't sell that kind of a package to the membership, but they might be able to sell a package that included a sixth holiday. After receiving that information, the mediator had another talk with management the next day, and so on.

When agreement is reached on any issue, it should be put in writing as clearly and concisely as possible, because people with different education, interests, and backgrounds will use it; and a clause is no good unless most readers can get the same meaning out of it. The contract is written to stabilize relationships rather than to confuse them. Legal terminology should be at a minimum because most of those who will use the contract are not lawyers. Though the contract must be legally correct, it also must command the emotional respect of the parties involved; and it will not do this if they cannot understand it. Contract clauses can be tested for meaning by having them read by supervisors and workers who have not attended negotiations and hence have only the written words to depend upon.

MAINTAINING THE CONTRACT. Signing the contract is only part of the job to be done. The next step is to communicate it to those who will work by it. Copies are usually printed for each supervisor and steward, and in many companies each worker gets a copy. When there are major contract changes, management may decide to hold meetings with supervisors to explain the new clauses. Union leaders may do the same for their stewards. Since employer and union goals in this instance are the same—better understanding of the contract—joint meetings are sometimes held. In this way supervisors and stewards get identical instruction and are shown that management and union have mutual interest in correctly interpreting the contract. Separate meetings, on the other hand, give the impression that there are separate management and union positions regarding the contract.

Although line managers will do most of the contract interpretation themselves, usually a staff agency is given responsibility for advising managers on difficult interpretations and following up to see that interpretations are consistent. This responsibility typically is assigned to a labor relations representative in the personnel office.

In the final analysis a collective-bargaining contract is merely a word symbol of the agreement that is in the minds of the parties. The same contract words can be interpreted and acted upon in many different ways depending on how people feel about them; so the wise manager tries to build sound overall union-management relations in order to get maximum effectiveness out of the contract.

INTEGRATIVE BARGAINING. A fundamental difficulty with the usual collective bargaining is that both management and labor approach it as a win-or-lose proposition; consequently, each girds itself to do battle with the other. This is *distributive bargaining,* or win-lose bargaining, because each party tries to win from the other party a favorable division of limited resources. Both parties come to the bargaining table ready to reject as unreasonable the other's demands. By expecting these things and preparing for them, each sets a tone of relationship that tends to bring about the conduct expected. Genuine collaboration becomes almost impossible. Since neither party wants to lose and both wish to win, either a bitter fight or a stalemate is likely to occur. If the fight gets too rough or the stalemate goes too long, the government is called in, thus restricting the combatants' freedom and making them more dependent on others. Under these conditions government control probably will continue to expand.

Though the situation described can be eased with various brakes and balms, the machinery of conflict is still there. What is needed is a different approach to bargaining. Behavioral science theory provides the framework for a better approach, already tried successfully by employers. This new approach recognizes union-management conflict as failures in problem solving; it attempts to help the group find the causes of its failures; and it directly treats these causes to restore mature relations. This is *integrative bargaining,* or problem-solving bargaining, because it takes a problem-solving approach to get joint gain for both parties through integrative action.[5]

In one small company the system worked as follows. All persons involved in the operation of a department met away from their work for a few days under the guidance of a behavioral scientist in order to discuss their perceptions of one an-

other, their goals, and finally their problems. Supervisor, workers, steward, and staff were included. They presented to management a statement of their problems with desirable solutions. Each department did this. Though the cost of these sessions was considerable, management and union for the first time had joint statements of needed changes from the work units themselves. These statements included items previously overlooked by both union and management. Note also that these items were developed in collaboration, not in bargaining. With this cooperative planning a problem-solving tone was set for the customary bargaining sessions, and a new and superior contract was readily agreed upon. This new contract had the support of the employees because it came from them and fitted their needs.

Experience with integrative bargaining has shown that useful innovations can be made—innovations that will help the participants solve their own problems instead of depending on outside force. The theory and techniques for integrative bargaining are now available and should be able to improve collective bargaining. Some conflict can be constructive, but it is questionable whether the whole bargaining process needs to have a conflict orientation, as it usually does in traditional win-lose bargaining.

GRIEVANCE SYSTEMS

A *grievance system,* or organizational appeal system, is a formal system by which disputes over working rules are expressed, processed, and judged in an organization. Grievance systems are used by both unionized and nonunionized organizations. The systems provide a means by which alleged wrongs may be reasonably and fairly resolved among organizational members. Disputes will arise in any organization, and appeal systems offer a socially acceptable way for persons to claim their perceived rights and occasionally to save face.

Studies show that appeal systems are found in all types of organizations—church, state, and business. Voluntary appeal systems (those not required by unions) occur more frequently in larger organizations. Greater complexities in large organizations seem to call for greater rationalization of procedures to protect member interests.[6]

GRIEVANCES. A grievance is defined as any real or imagined feeling of personal injustice that an employee has about the employment relationship. (In some unionized organizations, a grievance is narrowly limited to mean "any protested violation of the labor agreement.") This feeling does not have to be expressed to become a grievance. Neither does it have to be true or correct; a feeling that arises from imaginary conditions or from incorrect reasoning is still a grievance if it causes a feeling of injustice. Usually, but not always, the term "grievance" applies only to one's personal feeling of injustice. If Joe feels that Mary has been treated unjustly, Joe does not have a grievance. However, if Joe feels that both he and Mary have been treated unjustly on the same matter, procedures usually permit Joe to present his grievance both for himself and as an agent of all others similarly treated. In this way one dissatisfied person may present a grievance for one hundred others. When Joe formally expresses his grievance in the grievance system, it is said that he "files" a grievance. If he states it informally, it is often called a complaint or a gripe.

Quite often a distinction is made between a real grievance and a stated grievance. Employees sometimes do not know precisely what is making them dissatisfied. Their own feelings may set up mental blocks that prevent them from interpreting correctly what is happening. They may not have sufficient knowledge of human nature or of the many social forces affecting them. Not knowing their actual grievances but still feeling dissatisfied, they tend to file grievances about something else. When management corrects this "something else," both management and the worker find to their surprise that dissatisfaction still exists because of some real grievance yet uncovered. Even when the real grievance is known, a worker may disguise it out of fear that it will not make sense to management. Here is an example.

A semiskilled machine operator filed a grievance saying that he was not given an automatic seniority wage increase that was due him. Both the seniority and wage-increase systems were complicated, suggesting to management that there may have been a mistake or the operator could justifiably be confused. Careful investigation disclosed that the operator was not due an increase according to the labor contract, and management spent nearly an hour at two grievance levels trying to explain the rules to him. He did not seem convinced and kept answering, "Yes, but . . . ."

Finally an astute personnel clerk who was present concluded that there was something behind this stated grievance, because the operator kept referring to what "other workers" received. When the conversation was turned in this direction, the operator soon disclosed that a fellow worker who was hired the same day had said, "I got a 2-cent seniority increase on my last check. Did you?" This was the machine operator's real grievance, but he did not want to state it this way because it might embarrass his friend if it was untrue. As soon as the operator was assured that his friend did not get the raise, the operator's grievance vanished.

Many grievances are directed as much against other workers as they are against management. An example is a jurisdictional dispute.

In one factory semiskilled machinists claimed the right to operate certain new automated machines, but toolmakers said the machines were their responsibility. When management assigned the machines to the toolmakers, the machinists filed a grievance saying that the new machines required only semiskilled work which machinists were supposed to perform, even though they admitted that the new machine work was slightly more difficult than the work they had been doing.

GRIEVANCE RATES. A *grievance rate* usually is stated in terms of the number of written grievances for 100 employees in one year. So many factors affect grievances that a low rate is not necessarily desirable, because it may mean that grievances are suppressed. Neither is a high rate absolute evidence of poor labor relations. A typical industrial grievance rate is 5 to 20; however, well-managed organizations with mature labor relations have developed lower rates.

Employees of all types and at all levels develop grievances. They are not some headache brought about by unions. Some of the factors affecting grievance rates are management, unions, grievance procedures, job conditions, government rules, general social conditions, and the home environment. Management can alter some of these causes, but in other cases its job is to work out a reasonable accommodation to them.

International Harvester Company provides an example of how different factors affect grievance rates. Figure 17-2 shows how different combinations of consideration (employee orientation) and structure (task orientation) affect the grievance rate. Consideration shows itself to be a key factor in low grievance rates. A supervisor with high consideration could have any amount of structure and still retain a low grievance rate. On the other hand, with low consideration there was a high grievance rate regardless of the amount of structure. Note that the grievance rate of these supervisors was much above the typical grievance rate of 5 to 20 just mentioned.

Grievance procedures and the companywide behavioral climate also have a significant effect on grievance rates. For a number of reasons International Har-

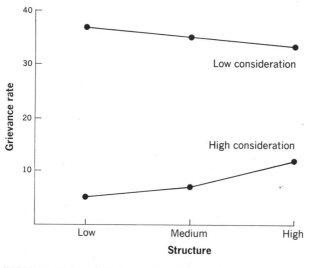

FIGURE 17-2 ■■■■■■■■■■■■■■■■■■■■■■■■■■■

Combinations of consideration (employee orientation) and structure (task orientation) related to grievance rate for fifty-seven supervisors and their work groups. (Adapted from Edwin A. Fleishman and Edwin F. Harris, "Patterns of Leadership Behavior Related to Employee Grievances and Turnover," *Personnel Psychology,* Spring 1962, p. 50.)

vester had a high grievance rate (27.5) during the 1950s, and a high proportion of grievances was going to the central level in preparation for arbitration. Between 1950 and 1962 over 100,000 grievances went to the central level! Recognizing a serious problem, top officials of both union and company worked hard to shift attitudes toward problem solving and to install a new program calling for settlement at the local level when the grievance was first presented orally. Local settlement was attempted even if this meant calling the superintendent, labor relations director, time-study specialist, and others to the workplace. People came to the problem, instead of having it sent in writing to them. The program was remarkably successful. Attitudes materially improved. More important, in the two years following the new program, not one grievance went to the central level, and fewer than ten were put into writing.[7]

Generally, effective contract administration tends to reduce grievances. Fair, open, and prompt treatment of problems that arise tends to reduce the misunderstandings that are the underlying causes of many grievances.[8] Increased participation is also an effective way to reduce grievances. When employees share in decision making about working conditions, they have fewer reasons to file grievances about their work.[9]

BENEFITS OF GRIEVANCE SYSTEMS. Probably the principal benefit of any grievance system is that it encourages human problems to be brought into the open so that management can learn about them and try corrective action. The social organization of a plant is much like a complicated machine in the shop. Both need constant attention and frequent adjustment. Grievances that are expressed, whether they are presented formally or informally, are symptoms that should be studied carefully by management to determine the real causes of this "human machine" breakdown. They signal to management that part of its human organization is not functioning properly and needs readjustment. It matters not that a grievance is invalid according to the technical terms of the labor contract; it is still a grievance and a symptom of social imbalance in some trouble spot somewhere. Any attempt to disregard it, smother it, or "throw it out of court" on some technicality will be largely ineffective because it still exists and will try to find expression in some other way.

Related to the foregoing benefit of grievance adjustment is the benefit of grievance prevention. Almost everyone agrees that it is better to prevent fires than to try stopping them after they start, and the same philosophy applies to grievances. As management begins to look behind grievances to the underlying problems that cause them, it can then try to correct these underlying problems and keep other grievances from arising.

Another benefit of grievance systems is that they help to catch and solve problems before they become serious. If problems are allowed to accumulate unsolved, their pressure may become large enough to cause a breakdown somewhere in labor-management relations. Or they may fester within an individual, becoming larger and more difficult to adjust with the passage of time. The aggrieved individual tends to communicate with others and thus spread the infection. An effective grievance system can prevent the developments just mentioned and keep social pressures within bounds.

A grievance system, like counseling, is a way of giving employees emotional release for their dissatisfactions. It provides a formalized means by which a frustrated and aggrieved employee can become aggressive and strike back at the various controls required by an organization. Emotional release often plays an important role in individual grievance cases. Union leaders sometimes carry a losing case higher in the grievance procedure "just to make the employee happy." They hope that as the case moves higher the employee's ill feelings will decline, and then the employee will settle down to the working relationship that union and management have specified in the labor contract. Even workers who do not use the grievance system for their own emotional release feel better because they know the system is there to use if needed. It builds within employees a sense of emotional security.

Another benefit of grievance systems is that they help establish and maintain a work culture or way of life. Each group has its own particular way of living together, and the grievance procedure helps develop this group culture. As problems are interpreted in the grievance procedure, the group learns how it is expected to respond to the policies that have been set up.

A further benefit of grievance systems—one that managers often fail to see—is the simple fact that the system's existence provides a check and balance upon arbitrary and capricious management action. Managers tend to give more care to the human aspects of their jobs when they know that some of these actions are subject to challenge and review in a grievance system. They are put on guard to make sound human decisions in each instance so that they are not placed in the embarrassing position of having to defend their poor judgment in the grievance system. They are encouraged to develop effective compromises and working relationships with their groups. Note, however, that the pendulum can swing too far. Supervisors may become so aware of the grievance system that they are afraid to make decisions and hesitate to direct and discipline employees. In this situation the supervisor's capability vanishes.

GRIEVANCE PROCEDURES. A grievance procedure is the method by which a grievance is filed and carried through different "steps" (decision levels) to an ultimate decision. Most procedures start with the supervisor and the grievant, have from three to six steps, and usually have arbitration as the last step. Other details vary greatly. As an illustration, here is a summary of the grievance steps in one organization:

1. Employee (and/or employee's representative) discusses grievance with supervisor.

2. If grievance is unsettled, employee presents grievance to supervisor in writing.

3. If it is still not settled, steward presents grievance to department head.

4. If it is still unsettled, union committee presents it to general manager, who is advised by the personnel manager.

5. If it is still unsettled, it is taken to an outside arbitrator for final and binding decision.

Most labor and management people agree that a grievance procedure should begin with the supervisor. Supervisors are the persons in direct contact with workers, and in many cases it is supervisory action that caused the grievance. In this connection reasonable speed in processing the grievance is important. Most procedures establish time limits at each step so that supervisors and others cannot use delays as subterfuges to prevent settlement. The supervisor who dillydallies with a grievance actually strengthens the grievant's cause, since the delay convinces the grievant that the grievance is a sound one that the supervisor is afraid to face.

The supervisor's attitude toward grievances is a long step toward their settlement. Many workers fear supervisory retaliation if they present a grievance, especially if they win it and thereby put their supervisor on the spot. The first step, therefore, is for supervisors to convince workers that they want to hear grievances and to settle them. Supervisors approach grievances in a problem-solving frame of mind, rather than with the idea "This is a fight—it's either them or me." The proper supervisory approach is discussion that moves rationally toward a mutual solution, instead of argument that emotionally seeks to provide a winner. All possible facts—including how people feel—should be gathered before making a decision.

ARBITRATION. As a grievance moves to higher steps, it becomes less a person-to-person discussion and more a group problem involving several union and management representatives. If the grievance is not settled at the highest company level, labor and management usually submit it to *arbitration,* which is final and binding decision by a third party or parties. The arbitrator's decision stands only until the next collective-bargaining negotiation, at which time the parties can negotiate any contract changes they wish. The arbitrator's role is merely to stabilize contract meaning during the life of the contract. This interpretation of what the existing contract means is called *grievance arbitration.* It is distinguished from arbitration to establish new contract terms, which is known as *contract arbitration.* The former is a method of grievance settlement, while the latter replaces collective bargaining. Management generally supports the former, but opposes the latter because it takes settlement power out of the hands of both management and union. In either case, if the parties mutually agree to arbitration, it is *voluntary.* If government forces one or both parties to accept arbitration, it is *compulsory.*

From the behavioral point of view, the chief values of arbitrators are that they are outsiders who bring a fresh perspective, they are not emotionally involved in the dispute, and they can render a final decision that usually is enforceable in the courts. Their decisions, however, can be painful to an inept management, as illustrated by the following situation.

A worker was discharged for smoking on a stair landing in a dangerous chemical operation. Discharge was clearly within the rules for this offense. When the case came to arbitration, however, he claimed that the company had discriminated against him, since many employees smoked on the landing and were still doing so. He challenged the arbitrator to count the cigarette butts on the floor. True enough, when the arbitrator and the representatives of both parties went there, they found cigarette butts all over the place. The worker was immediately reinstated with back pay.

The chief weaknesses of arbitrators are that they usually lack personal knowledge of the organization's way of life, which may cause them to make unrealistic decisions, and they tend to overlook human values and render a legalistic decision based on tangible, technical evidence. They also lack personal responsibility for the continuing labor-management relationship, because they often step out of the picture as soon as a decision is rendered. Some of these weaknesses are overcome by appointing a permanent arbitrator to arbitrate all issues for a period of time.

PROVISION FOR MANAGEMENT GRIEVANCES. The labor contract is a mutual document that imposes some obligations on the union; therefore it may be advisable to have a management-grievance procedure by which management can seek redress for union violation of the contract. One company has the following management-grievance clause in its contract:

> *In the event the Company has a grievance under the terms of this Agreement, it shall present such grievance in writing to the Business Manager of the Union, who shall immediately submit it to the Union Grievance Committee. The Committee shall promptly proceed to effect an adjustment, if possible; failing to do so, within five days (Saturdays, Sundays, and holidays excluded) the matter shall be referred for adjustment to the next regular meeting of the Union. If the grievance is not then satisfactorily adjusted within five days after such regular meeting, or in any event not later than thirty days after the grievance has been submitted to the Business Manager, it may be referred to a board of arbitration as provided in Article 10.*

IMPORTANCE OF JUSTICE IN GRIEVANCE SETTLEMENT. At this point it is appropriate to move the discussion from employer-grievance systems to an overall concept of grievance settlement. The basic objective of grievance settlement should be *justice,* which is defined as fairness according to established rules and relationships. Justice is a fundamental requirement in organizational behavior because it gives substance and meaning to human dignity. Throughout the history of the world justice has stood in the forefront of human ideas. It has made nations strong, or its lack has destroyed them. Kings have fallen because they abused it. Injustice in the hands of Pontius Pilate was the tragedy of the Crucifixion. Justice is a golden thread that binds together the different interests in a group. It provides the faith and confidence that are necessary for voluntary cooperation.

With all this emphasis upon justice it appears that employers have given rather minor attention to developing a sound judicial function in employee relations. Grievance systems were adopted rather late in the industrial revolution, and frequently they were established only when unions pressured them into existence. Even now there is considerable evidence that many managers look upon grievance systems as a necessary evil, rather than an organ for building employee relations.

Grievance systems, furthermore, concern mostly contract violations. What about the feelings of injustice not covered by the contract? Is there no place to treat them? How can management in its employee relations assure *equity,* meaning compliance with the spirit of the relationship in addition to the contractual obligations? Is not this problem important? (Note that in the English common law, courts of equity were established at an early date to deal with certain injustices not covered by law.)

A further difficulty is that most grievance systems are confined to unionized operating employees, but many nonunionized technical and managerial people also have grievances that merit resolution. Effective grievance systems are needed for them the same as for operating employees. One study of middle managers, for example, reported that 75 percent of them felt they should be allowed "to organize informal groups to discuss conditions of employment with top management."[10] However, few organizations have either a discussion procedure or a grievance procedure for their middle managers. The result is that many grievances probably remain unresolved.

Inadequately developed judicial systems appear to be a contributing cause of employee unrest. Early management leaders recognized the need for justice and equity in organizations. Harrington Emerson made "the fair deal" one of his twelve principles of efficiency,[11] and Henri Fayol made "equity" one of his fourteen principles of management.[12] Perhaps an organizational ombudsman, mentioned in an earlier chapter, is a step in the right direction; however, an ombudsman has only investigative powers, not settlement powers.

The involvement of justice in the whole social system is shown by a study I made some years ago. A statewide employer's association was losing an abnormally large number of hard-fought grievances in arbitration. To analyze this problem, grievances were classified into twelve possible causes. The classification revealed that nearly every grievance being lost related to only one of these twelve causes: equity, or fairness, in disciplinary action. An example of an equity grievance is an employee who was suspended for thirty days for an admitted breach of discipline. The contract permitted discipline in this case but stated no specific penalty, and the union claimed extenuating circumstances that made the thirty-day penalty unreasonable and inconsistent in this instance.

Not one equity grievance had been won within the twelve months covered by the study. Further investigation disclosed that one company had 80 percent of these equity-disciplinary cases. Out of approximately two hundred companies in the association, this one was the central trouble spot. It did have a tough union, but untrained and inconsistent management seemed to be the primary cause of the grievances. Within a year the company suffered financial reverses.

Should not a labor union also have an effective judicial system? Since it, like employers, is a formal organization applying controls to its members, each union needs a fair grievance system for members who are aggrieved with it. To the extent that it affects employees, it has as much obligation to distribute justice as does the employer. Furthermore, union member and company employee are the same person in different roles; hence, membership dissatisfactions with the union will spill over into the employee role.

In summary, there appear to be four principal elements in satisfactory grievance handling:

1. Policies and rules that are workable, just, and acceptable to both parties.

2. Attitudes of mutual interest and problem solving.

3. Procedures that are workable and equitable, including protection against retaliation, right of appeal, and so on.

4. Communication in order to understand each other's problems and feelings.

BEHAVIORAL ISSUES IN UNION REPRESENTATION

Unions have exerted a major influence on human relationships at work during the last half century, and it is certain that this influence will continue; however, certain behavioral issues arise from their presence. The following discussion focuses on two of several issues involving organizational behavior.

UNION RESPONSE TO INDIVIDUAL NEEDS. The union often has not served individual needs as well as it might. For example, the fundamental idea of individual differences has been effectively drowned by union demands for standardization, uniformity, and equal this-and-that for everyone. What can be done to make the inflexible procedure, the airtight contract, and the unionwide standard apply to individual situations? Growing pressure to think in global terms has caused issues to become symbolized in statistical norms and settled in central headquarters, leaving the *person* isolated on the sidelines. Union benefits are largely general, applying only to the group.

Closely related to individual differences is the issue of higher-order needs. Unions have been successful in dealing with economic issues and basic rights. Can they be equally successful in focusing on higher-order needs in a more affluent society? These higher needs are mostly job-related motivational factors that concern an individual employee's need structure. They are not easily served by nationwide norms. What is required is more emphasis on job enrichment, human resources, and human growth along channels that are personally desirable to each individual. Unionized workers appear to be aware of this union deficiency, because one study reports that 70 percent of blue-collar union workers feel that their unions should be doing more to improve their skills and help them merit promotions.[13]

UNION POWER. Another area of difficulty is union power, particularly as it may affect third parties not directly involved in a labor dispute. These third parties may be the general public or other employees who have no dispute with their employer and want to keep working during a strike. In a society that is becoming more complex, with greater interdependence among units in the social system, there will be less patience with strikes and similar practices that harm innocent bystanders. For example, at a school construction site a strike by plumbers caused the whole project to close, even though other workers had valid labor agreements and wanted to continue working. As another example, in a New York subway strike many employees could not get to work, some shopkeepers were put out of business, and many other inconveniences developed. Were the benefits from these union actions sufficient to offset the harm and inconvenience to other people in the social system?

To overcome third-party injury caused by strikes, a furniture company signed with its AFL-CIO union a strike-work agreement that provides for a nonstoppage strike. According to this agreement, when the union files a strike notice, the employees continue working. But from the moment of the notice, one-third of every worker's wage is set aside in a special fund, to which the employer contributes an equal amount. If agreement is reached in six weeks, all the money is returned. After six weeks only 75 percent is returned; then 50 percent after seven weeks, 25 percent after eight weeks, and not a penny after nine weeks. The amount that is not returned goes to local charities. Since "striking" employees keep working during this period, other employees and the general public are not inconvenienced. Only the principals to the dispute are penalized. The strike-work agreement is a constructive approach to third-party injury by strikes. In this company, however, after nine weeks the union may strike in the traditional manner.[14]

Union power over individual employees also is an important issue. One study covered seventy-two workers who suffered union-caused job discrimination and later "won" their cases before the National Labor Relations Board. Very often the victory was hollow. As stated by one employee, "When I won, the union did not surrender but just continued fighting me." The study concluded that existing federal law was "hardly adequate protection" for the individual employee.[15] When thinking about protecting individuals from the organization, we also need to think about protecting them from union organizations.

SUMMARY

The union introduces additional formal and informal organizations at work. Two major union-management activities are collective bargaining and grievance systems. Collective bargaining is negotiation between representatives of management and labor to accomplish a written agreement covering terms and conditions of employment. It is essentially a social process for balancing social pressures of two groups that have a mutual interest in employment conditions. Some important matters in negotiation are thorough preparation, constructive attitudes, clear bargaining procedures, bargaining tactics, mediation, and the problem-solving approach of integrative bargaining.

Grievance systems have as their goal the accomplishment of justice in employee relations. A grievance is any real or imagined feeling of personal injustice that an employee has about the employment relationship. Grievance systems help bring grievances into the open so that corrective action can be taken (1) to adjust a current grievance, and (2) to take action to prevent future grievances. It is questionable whether employers or unions have developed adequate internal grievance systems. There also are behavioral issues concerning union response to individual needs and union power.

TERMS AND CONCEPTS FOR REVIEW

Collective bargaining

Goldfish-bowl bargaining

Recess

Mediator

Distributive bargaining

Integrative bargaining

Grievance system

Grievance

Stated grievance

Grievance rate

Grievance arbitration

Contract arbitration

Nonstoppage strike

REVIEW QUESTIONS

1. In what way is collective bargaining a human problem, as distinguished from an economic and a technical problem? Discuss.
2. Discuss the idea that collective bargaining is a continuous process.
3. Do you think management should have a grievance system for presenting its grievances to the union? Discuss.
4. What suggestions can you offer for providing a suitable judicial system in both work organizations and unions?
5. Discuss issues of union response to individual needs and higher-order needs. How effective do unions tend to be in these areas?

CASE

(*Note:* The following case also relates especially to the two preceding chapters on the individual and on the informal organization. The case is a complete news article from an Australian daily newspaper.)

A VICTIM BACK FROM COVENTRY, BY ALEX HARRIS[16]
Keith Digney, a pressure welder at the State Electricity Commission's Muja power station at Collie, has become a victim of his own convictions.

Mr. Digney's beliefs came into conflict with his unionist working mates—and he was sent to Coventry and declared [unacceptable to the group].

Men he had worked with for nearly 10 years refused to speak to him on or off the job.

They refused to touch any equipment he touched, and raised demarcation issues over actions as simple as picking up a hammer.

After six weeks he decided to call it quits because, as he said yesterday, he did not like standing around doing nothing.

He is a Christadelphian and his beliefs prevent his joining a union or a political party. Six years ago he was granted exemption from union membership by the Industrial Commission.

He had been declared [unacceptable] before, but had battled it out and avoided trouble during strikes by taking leave without pay.

About two months ago, however, the issue of his beliefs arose again when he refused to subscribe to a Metal Trades Union's fighting fund—a so-called voluntary contribution which Mr. Digney claimed was not enforceable by law.

The Industrial Commission was called in to arbitrate and Mr. Digney agreed to pay an equivalent sum to a charity. But union representatives refused to compromise.

Mr. Digney said the word went out that he had to go. He is still puzzled why it took six years to decide his presence at the power house was intolerable.

He did not mind being sent to Coventry.

"What bothered me was standing 'round doing nothing all day," he said.

"I was getting paid for it but I have to work for my money; I don't like taking it under false pretences."

"The SEC didn't want me to leave and things were beginning to ease up a little at the power house but I knew they would not get better if I stayed."

"The same thing would have happened again so I got another job to make peace for all concerned."

The move cost Mr. Digney his 10 years' long service leave which would have come up this year.

"Of course I'll miss it but money is not my first concern," he said. "Money is not my god."

He and his wife do not feel bitter about the experience.

"We know what our beliefs are," Mr. Digney said.

"And men are the same everywhere."

"I suppose you could say it was a question of human rights and freedom of belief but I didn't expect these arguments to have any weight."

"If anything, I feel sorry for the men who took part in the ban. Sooner or later you reap what you sow."

QUESTIONS
1. Comment on the employment and union-power implications of this case.
2. Discuss the behavioral origins of the conduct described in this case.

REFERENCES

1. Irving Stern and Robert F. Pearse, "Collective Bargaining: A Union Program for Reducing Conflict," *Personnel,* May–June 1968, p. 63.

2. T. W. Bonham, "The Foreman in an Ambiguous Environment," *Personnel Journal,* November 1971, pp. 841–845.

3. Sidney Garfield and William F. Whyte, "The Collective Bargaining Process: A Human Relations Analysis," *Human Organization,* Summer 1950, p. 5.

4. Henry A. Landsberger, "The Behavior and Personality of the Labor Mediator: The Parties' Perception of Mediator Behavior," *Personnel Psychology,* Autumn 1960, pp. 329–347.

5. A thorough discussion of bargaining theories from the behavioral point of view is provided in Richard E. Walton and Robert B. McKersie, *A Behavioral Theory of Labor Negotia-

tions: An Analysis of a Social Interaction System, New York: McGraw-Hill Book Company, 1965. See also, by the same authors, "The Theory of Bargaining," *Industrial and Labor Relations Review,* April 1966, pp. 414–424.

6.   William G. Scott, *The Management of Conflict: Appeal Systems in Organizations,* Homewood, Ill.: Richard D. Irwin, Inc., 1965.

7.   Robert B. McKersie, "Avoiding Written Grievances by Problem-Solving: An Outside View," *Personnel Psychology,* Winter 1964, pp. 367–379.

8.   William B. Werther, Jr., "Reducing Grievances through Effective Contract Administration," *Labor Law Journal,* April 1974, pp. 211–216.

9.   Alan M. Glassman and James A. Belasco, "The Chapter Chairman and School Grievances," *Industrial Relations,* May 1975, pp. 233–241.

10.   Alfred T. DeMaria, Dale Tarnowieski, and Richard Gurman, *Manager Unions?* New York: American Management Association, 1972, p. 5.

11.   Harrington Emerson, *The Twelve Principles of Efficiency,* New York: The Engineering Magazine, 1912, pp. 167–201.

12.   Henri Fayol, *General and Industrial Management,* trans. by Constance Storrs, New York: Pitman Publishing Corporation, 1949, p. 38. Originally published in 1916.

13.   Harold L. Sheppard, "Some Selected Issues Surrounding the Subject of the Quality of Working Life," in Gerald G. Somers (ed.), *Proceedings of the Twenty-fifth Anniversary Meeting,* Madison, Wis.: Industrial Relations Research Association, 1973, pp. 137–153.

14.   "The Guys in the Middle," *Forbes,* Feb. 1, 1966, p. 5. See also Stephen H. Sosnick, "Nonstoppage Strikes: A New Approach," *Industrial and Labor Relations Review,* October 1964, pp. 73–80.

15.   Bernard Samoff, "The Impact of Taft-Hartley Job Discrimination Victories," *Industrial Relations,* May 1965, pp. 91, 94.

16.   Alex Harris, "A Victim Back from Coventry," Perth, Australia: *The West Australian,* Apr. 16, 1974, p. 1. Copyright 1974. Reprinted with permission of West Australian Newspapers, Limited.

CHAPTER 18
EMPLOYMENT DISCRIMINATION AND LESS-ADVANTAGED PERSONS

Men can keep their bus and train seats.
Just give us women more seats in the executive offices.
A Woman Manager

LEARNING OBJECTIVES

TO UNDERSTAND:
The nature of minority groups in the United States
Federal antidiscrimination laws
Affirmative action and proportional employment
Programs for equal employment opportunity
Employment of women and aged employees
Employment programs for the less-advantaged

Every organization likes to think that its employees are a cohesive group that is "one big, happy family." Employees are one family to the extent that they have mutual allegiance to the organization and believe in its objectives. On the other hand, employees in almost any organization are also divided into subgroups of different kinds. As discussed in earlier chapters, mutual similarities such as age, race, sex, type of work, rank in the organization, and social interests cause employees to relate themselves in all sorts of intricate subgroups. These are the "happy little families" that together constitute the "one big, happy family" about which employers dream.

Formation of employee groups is determined by two broad sets of conditions. First, *on-the-job* differences and similarities cause people to align themselves into groups. Throughout this text attention is given to these on-the-job conditions that cause separate interest groups such as line and staff people, incentive and nonincentive workers, and production and sales personnel. It is now appropriate to emphasize the second set of conditions—those arising *off the job*—because some of these lead to social interests and relationships that may result in employment discrimination.

In the first part of this chapter we will discuss discrimination and laws relating to it. Then we will examine how it applies to sex and age. We also discuss relationships with less-advantaged employees, many of whom are racial and ethnic minorities. The focus is on behavioral issues, leaving economic, legal, and other issues to special books on the subject.

EMPLOYER INVOLVEMENT IN DISCRIMINATION

MINORITY GROUPS. A *minority group* is one that has, or feels that it has, its employment status relative to other persons decreased in some important way by factors that do not concern job performance. The essential problem faced by a minority group is *discrimination,* which means that its employment opportunities are significantly decreased compared with others (1) of equal ability at the time of selection for the job, or (2) of equal performance when working on the job. Since ability and/or performance are equal by definition, discrimination apparently occurs for other reasons, normally social reasons. In most instances these reasons are not unique with the organization; it merely is reflecting some aspect of the culture of society.

From the behavioral point of view a feeling of discrimination is just as important as actual discrimination. If a group feels that it is subject to discrimination, it responds as if real discrimination exists and has many of the same human problems that persons have who actually suffer discrimination.

The term "minority group" does not arise from a group being a minority in number in an organization, because, for example, blacks might be the majority of employees in a firm and still be a minority group. Neither does it mean that a group is a minority in the population, because women are a majority of the population in the United States and most other nations and blacks are the population majority in many localities. What "minority" does imply is that these persons normally are a minority in the power structure of the organization, particularly in relation to their proportion in the labor force or the general population. The concern is that they may be subject to discrimination. Thus women and blacks may be called minority groups, because they often are not treated equally with others and are not proportionally represented in various jobs. However, white males could be a minority group in a female-dominated firm that was discriminating against them.

The United States society is composed of a coalition of many minority groups. It often is not realized that the minority groups covered by federal antidiscrimination laws *collectively make up a majority of the labor force.* As shown in Figure 18-1, just four groups covered by antidiscrimination laws constituted, at about the time the laws were passed, over 75 percent of the labor force in the United States. These figures leave less than 25 percent who could possibly be in the "majority"; and, as a matter of fact, many of these are members of smaller minority groups. Discrimination, therefore, is not a simple matter of domination of one or two small groups by one giant group. Instead it is competition among many minorities and coalitions of minorities. It is a means of controlling jobs and, in turn, allocating resources to the various minorities, none of which constitutes the majority. What exists is a state of *pluralism,* in which diverse groups maintain autonomous participation and influence in the social system.[1] Each minority participates in society with other minorities, and each influences the others. In pluralism there are many power centers, none completely independent unto itself, but each with some autonomy. When any group claims discrimination, it is claiming that it wants (and feels it should have) a better allocation of resources or power in the system.

As further evidence of pluralism in the United States, some comparisons of education and occupational rank of racial and national-origin groups may be

GROUP COVERED BY ANTIDISCRIMINATION LAW	NUMBER IN LABOR FORCE, 1968	PERCENT OF LABOR FORCE
Women	29,204,000	37.0
Nonwhite men	4,979,000	6.3
White men (40–64 years of age)	19,291,882	24.5
White men by religion (age 16–39 and over 65)*		
Catholic	5,987,122	7.6
Jewish	707,345	.8
Total	60,169,349	76.2

* Assumes that 6.3 percent of the members of each religion are nonwhite. Only two out of many minority religions are listed.

FIGURE 18-1

Four groups covered by antidiscrimination laws constituted over three-quarters of the civilian labor force in the United States at about the time the laws were passed. (Source: *The World Almanac, and Book of Facts, 1969,* New York: Newspaper Enterprise Association, 1969, pp. 219–220; and U.S. Bureau of the Census, *Statistical Abstract of the United States: 1969,* pp. 10, 211–213, 222–223.)

helpful. According to the United States census for 1960, the last census before passage of federal antidiscrimination laws, the Japanese were the people with the most education in the United States, rather than the group classified "white" in the census, and the gap between the two steadily increased from 1940 to 1960. The proportion of Japanese and Chinese men with a college degree was nearly 90 percent greater than it was for white men. This was a dramatic change for Chinese men, who ranked third in 1940 but first in 1960. With regard to occupational status for men, both Chinese and Japanese ranked higher than whites. Thus, whites at about the time federal antidiscrimination laws were passed, ranked approximately third in both education and job level.[2] These comparisons show that the social structure of the United States is fluid, rather than stratified and dominated by one particular group.

Figure 18-1 also illustrates that one person may be a member of several minority groups at one time, or in both minority groups and the majority group at the same time. Thus a woman (minority by sex) might be over forty (minority by age) and a Catholic (minority by religion), but she also might be Caucasian, which is considered in the majority by race in the United States. Furthermore, conditions that place a person in a minority group may be localized. A Caucasian waiter in a Chinese restaurant having nearly all Chinese employees will feel differently about employment opportunities than the waiter would in a restaurant with nearly all Caucasian employees.

EXTENT OF DISCRIMINATION. There is a difference between prejudice and discrimination. Prejudice is an attitude of mind, whereas discrimination is an action. One may occur without the other. Discrimination may occur as a social custom without prejudice, and likewise prejudice occurs without discrimination.

It is necessary to proceed with caution when judging that either prejudice or discrimination exists, because what we perceive as prejudice may actually appear this way only because *our own* prejudice distorts our perception. For example, when Mary thinks that a manager is discriminating against women for promotion, it may be because she perceives her friends as being better qualified than they really are.

Discrimination exists in both the formal and informal organizations of both employers and unions. Formal employer discrimination occurs, for example, when an older person is rejected for employment because of age. An example of informal union discrimination is harassment and threats by union members in such a way that a nonunion employee feels a lack of equal job opportunity. Actually, discrimination is by persons rather than the inanimate organization, but the organization is an instrument for accomplishing the act.

Although some persons think of only race, creed, sex, age, and national origin as areas of discrimination, actually the range of discrimination is much broader than that. Some other groups are minors, handicapped persons who are rejected for a handicap not affecting job performance, nonveterans in federal employment, nonunion employees confronting a union shop, and persons bypassed when relatives are promoted.

Even the honored institution of seniority is discrimination, because seniority is a criterion not based on quality of job performance. The longer-service employee is not necessarily the better performer; hence, a promotion by seniority discriminates against better producers in many cases. There are, of course, other reasons for using seniority, but its discriminatory nature should be recognized. Certainly when it is applied absolutely to suppress opportunities for superior performers while rewarding minimal performers, it is as much against the public interest as some other discriminations.

DISCRIMINATION AND THE LAW. We all have personal preferences of one sort or another, and these preferences are usually accepted and respected by others because they also have preferences that they wish accepted and respected. What we have in this instance is a social transaction in which there is a mutual benefit. People are mutually accepting each other's personal freedom to make choices. However, when any preference becomes a general employment practice, public issues of discrimination arise because job opportunities for that group are affected. Its members tend to band closer together and take positive action to better their condition. Pressures first are brought on the community for voluntary correction of practices, but if discrimination continues to be widespread, the group tends to appeal for legislative action on the basis that it is in the public interest for qualified people to have free choice of work. This was the case with the Federal Civil Rights Act of 1964 and subsequent amendments.

Title VII of the Civil Rights Act is entitled "Equal Employment Opportunity," and it requires employers, labor unions, and employment agencies to treat all persons without regard to race, color, religion, sex, or national origin in all phases of employment. This includes hiring, training, apprentice programs, promotions, job assignments, and other personnel actions. Certain exceptions are allowed, primarily with regard to religious organizations and "in those certain instances where religion, sex, or national origin is a bona fide occupational qualification reasonably necessary to the normal operation of that particular business or enterprise" (sections 702 and 703). An exemption is also provided to allow use of seniority for job choices. The law applies to employers and unions that affect interstate commerce and have fifteen or more employees.

The Age Discrimination in Employment Act of 1967 added age as a characteristic for which employment discrimination is prohibited. Ages forty through sixty-five are covered by the law, and it applies to employers and unions in the same manner as the Civil Rights Act.

Those typically perceived as minorities are not the only ones protected by the acts just mentioned. These acts apply to all persons. The essential purpose of the laws is that there shall be no employment discrimination against people because of race, color, religion, sex, national origin, or age.

Antidiscrimination legislation can contribute to improved human relationships at work. It should cause minority groups to find that they have more equal opportunity, thus reducing insecurities and defensiveness, and leaving them more free to give their full energies to improved job performance. By removing discriminatory practices, all groups should be able to work together in more harmony.

In order for discrimination to be seen in its full perspective, it should be recognized that not all discrimination is considered socially unacceptable. Only certain types of discrimination are specified in antidiscrimination laws. At other times discrimination is favored by legislative bodies in the public interest. Two examples are:

1. Preferential employment of veterans in the civil service. (Section 712 of the Civil Rights Act specifically provides an exemption for this practice.)

2. Employment rejection of young people at certain ages and for certain types of work (federal and state law).

THE EQUAL EMPLOYMENT OPPORTUNITY COMMISSION AND AFFIRMATIVE ACTION PROGRAMS

The Civil Rights Act established an *Equal Employment Opportunity Commission* (EEOC) to administer the equal employment provisions. Aggrieved employees take their complaints to the EEOC. The EEOC holds hearings and tries to settle valid complaints by conciliation and persuasion. If these measures fail, a complaint may be taken to a federal court for a court order requiring appropriate remedial action.

The chief weapons of the EEOC have been (1) detailed investigations that require employers to keep elaborate records about minorities in order to answer allegations, and (2) affirmative action programs. *Affirmative action programs* are employer programs for seeking, training, and promoting on an accelerated basis underrepresented minorities in an organization. The justification given is to require the employer to make up for alleged past practice that did not allow equal opportunity for employment. It is expected that employers will have timetables by which they will accomplish certain goals, particularly a representative proportion of minorities in various jobs and levels in the organization. It follows that as employers scramble to meet goals for higher proportions of minorities, these minorities have more-than-equal employment opportunity compared with others of equal ability. The result is *reverse discrimination,* by which there is an opposite discrimination designed to compensate for an alleged earlier discrimination; however, in 1976 the Supreme Court in *McDonald v. Santa Fe Trail Transportation Company* placed limitations on reverse discrimination. Following are examples of possible reverse discrimination:

For four years from the date of a court order a company was required to hire two blacks for every one white until the combined work force, production and clerical, was consistent with the black-white ratio in the 1970 U.S. census.[3]

A U.S. Court ruled in a consent decree that at least sixty percent of future promotions to management levels in a bank will be filled with women and minorities. By a stated future date the bank's managerial ranks must have at least nine percent blacks, fourteen percent Hispanic, and thirty-seven percent women.[4]

EEOC policy has created behavioral problems when nonminority employees suffer reverse discrimination, especially regarding promotions for which they have worked and prepared. They want equal employment opportunity, and they argue that the way to end discrimination against some is not to discriminate against others. Minorities reply that affirmative action is required to compensate for past discrimination in order to equalize present conditions. A basic long-run issue is whether proportional employment will be abandoned after acceptable equality in the work force is achieved, or whether it will become entrenched in law and custom, thereby making job structures rigid and reducing free job choice by workers.

PROGRAMS FOR EQUAL EMPLOYMENT OPPORTUNITY. To establish equal employment opportunity in an organization, the first requisite is a well-designed equal employment program. In large organizations an equal employment opportunity office is established to administer the program, and this office is placed at a high level so that it has sufficient power to secure results. Strong top management support is provided, and consultants and task forces may be used to provide additional support. In small organizations a key person is given the added duty of equal employment opportunity.

The next step is to gather data to identify problem areas. Information is sought about such items as seniority, salary, education, promotions, and employment level of different minorities. For example, a public school or a retail store may think that it has no discrimination problem regarding women because most of its employees are women. However, the data may show that the majority of managerial and better-paying professional jobs are held by men. In another organization the data may show that less pleasant and dirtier blue-collar jobs have been given to certain minorities, while women and nonminorities have been given more pleasant, higher-status, cleaner jobs. The purpose of the statistics is to help identify areas of discrimination, but it should not be assumed that every instance of unequal representation in jobs is proof of discrimination. There are many other reasons for unequal representation, such as education of employees. The data only provide a base for further investigation.

A further step is to identify and develop those minorities in the organization that have potential for promotion. An important point is to assure them that equal employment opportunity is available, because in the past they may have felt discriminated against, so they were discouraged from developing themselves and seeking promotion. In one office, for example, when equal employment became a reality, a number of women and blacks became interested in self-development plans for possible promotion. Prior to equal employment, they showed no interest in self-development.

An additional step is to be sure that there are equal recruitment activities for all types of people. Recruitment cannot be merely in familiar channels, or among friends, in a way that might perpetuate dominance of one sex, race, or ethnic group in certain jobs, such as that of engineer. Recruitment should be in ways that reach all types of minorities, and any advertising should portray equality in all types of jobs. For example, a telephone company attracted favorable attention with a recruiting advertisement showing a woman climbing a telephone pole as part of a telephone line crew. The EEOC as a matter of policy is encouraging both men and women to move into what is called *nontraditional employment,* such as a woman becoming a crane operator or a man becoming a secretary. The policy is to create an image of *unisex jobs* equally acceptable to men and women.

Following are some of the affirmative action recruitment efforts made by one employer trying to meet proportional employment goals expected by the EEOC.

1. *Selective recruiting in high schools having mostly minority students.*

2. *Selective recruiting in black and women's colleges.*

3. *Establishing a recruiting office in a minority neighborhood.*

4. *Selective advertising in minority newspapers.*

5. *Hiring minority recruiters.*

6. *Relaxing employment standards for minority applicants, particularly with regard to education, experience, and criminal records.*

7. *Special training programs for minorities lacking employable skills.*

Another step is communication within the organization to maintain constant awareness of the equal employment opportunity program and of the policies that exist to implement it. In many instances when a program begins, training sessions are held with all managers to explain the program to them. When there is a large influx of minorities, supervisors may be given special programs to make them more aware of different work attitudes and values of minorities.

A final step is appraisal and follow-up. If minority employment is important in an organization, then the managerial appraisal system must reflect this policy, because managers tend to emphasize the practices on which they are appraised. Follow-up also provides a basis for correcting deficiencies in the program, and it provides evidence for the EEOC and others that equal employment opportunity is being accomplished. When a program is well planned there is evidence that minorities and nonminorities are accepted with approximately equal success.[5]

EMPLOYING WOMEN

Women employees are the largest minority group included in the Civil Rights Act. They constitute about 40 percent of the employed labor force. Women are found in all business and nonbusiness occupations listed in the United States census, but in some occupations they are not as well accepted as men. As one woman in a moment of frustration stated, "The men expect me to look like a woman, think like a man, act like a lady, and work like a dog!"

Although employers tend to favor women for certain jobs, such as nurse and flight attendant, there has been employment discrimination against women in a number of other occupations. Historically many women have received less pay than men for equal jobs, although this kind of discrimination now is prohibited by the Federal Equal Pay Act of 1963 and state equal-pay acts. The primary discrimination has been lack of equal access to jobs, particularly higher professional and managerial jobs. Research using census data also suggests that women have fewer jobs that require substantial discretion, or decision making. Since challenging work contributes to job satisfaction, this lack of discretion suggests that women have less intrinsically satisfying jobs than men.[6]

At times discrimination against women can be subtle. For example, a large bank was feeling the effects of a recession, so it needed to reduce its corporate lending staff. Six women lending officers were transferred to positions with less prestige in other areas. More than seventy male corporate lending officers were left in the lending office. (Can you speculate about reasons for this action? Was the selection of six women merely a matter of chance, or was it intentional? Did the selecting executives think that male lending officers presented a better image to clients? Did the executives simply have more confidence in male friends that they knew better? What were the reasons?)

In spite of lower pay, less discretion, and lack of access to jobs, research using data collected by the U.S. Bureau of the Census reports that women hold jobs of equal occupational status with men. They have not been denied equal occupational prestige and status in the United States society. As stated by the researchers, ". . . Women and men work at jobs which, on the average, have virtually equal prestige."[7] One reason for the high occupational status of women is that they dominate in a number of high-status jobs such as nursing, teaching, and clerical work. These are more than sufficient to offset their participation in lower-status jobs.

JOB RESPONSES OF MEN AND WOMEN. Comparisons of men and women on the job show more similarities than differences. It should be recognized that comparisons of this type always represent statistical studies of groups, and that both women and men have wide individual variations in their behavior. Generally women approach jobs in the same way that men do. For example, men and women are equal in the importance they give to having jobs with high chances for promotion. They also are just as concerned as men with self-actualization on the job, and they equally like intellectually demanding jobs.[8] However, women with only a temporary interest in the job market often have different job expectations.[9] This situation may account for some of the alleged employment differences of men and women, since historically more women than men have entered job markets on a temporary basis.

Turning now to the supervisory level, men and women who occupy similar positions are shown to have similar patterns of leadership behavior. They also show similar levels of effectiveness.[10]

There are some job differences that primarily appear to result from different socialization of men and women. For example, studies show that women tend to give more emphasis to interpersonal relationships, especially with peers, and to desirable working conditions.[11] Some women with home responsibilities also develop role conflicts between job and home responsibilities.[12] These conflicts are a cause for many women temporarily entering the labor market, and they tend to contribute to higher separation rates for women in some jobs.[13] However, when job responses are viewed as a whole, there appear to be few male-female job differences. These can operate as advantages or disadvantages in various circumstances, so they are not sufficient to interfere with equal employment opportunity.

EQUAL EMPLOYMENT FOR WOMEN. Many of the impediments to equal employment are built into the social fabric of organizations as a result of historical differences in the roles of men and women, so they often are difficult to remove. For example, men often go to a business lunch together, not inviting a woman executive, because they feel more comfortable among themselves. The result is that she may be left off grapevine tidbits of useful information about what is happening in the organization and the business world. Having less opportunity for informal social interaction with male executives at lunch or golf, she may not understand their personality as well as she could, so she is handicapped in interpersonal relations with them about some job problem.

Rarely are women permitted to pick up the check at a small business luncheon, as men might do. Even when a woman is taking a client to lunch or dinner for business discussion, she finds that male clients insist on picking up the check, and they may become embarrassed or angry if not permitted to do so. On the other hand, a man entertaining a client could easily pick up the check.

Some firms are reluctant to send women on business trips alone or in the company of one male employee. Travel and business appointments alone may be particularly difficult in other nations where women in business are not as well accepted.

There are also many petty annoyances in some organizations, such as the expectation that a woman in a meeting will take notes and serve the coffee. Sometimes women are expected to do their own filing and other clerical chores, when a man in a similar job would not be expected to do so.

In seeking equal employment opportunity, firms can quickly remove many of the impediments and annoyances for women, but others imbedded in the external society probably will disappear more slowly. The only suitable approach for the organization is to include women naturally in all ongoing activities, such as committees, special assignments, travel, and undesirable chores. Women and men should be treated equally, but as individual persons, recognizing individual needs and problems among both sexes.

EMPLOYING OLDER WORKERS

Since older persons aged forty through sixty-five are protected by the Age Discrimination Act, employers cannot discriminate against them for reasons of age.

For example, it has been the practice of large employers to force out or place on early retirement older executives to make way for "new blood" in the form of younger executives. When this happened in one company, the older executives sued. The suit was ended at a cost to the company of about $2 million.

The selection of age forty as a dividing point between younger and older workers is an arbitrary division, because the age at which actual employment difficulties are faced depends upon the person's skill, union policies, the industry in which one works, and other factors. In terms of the employment market an assembler may be "old" at forty, while a toolmaker is still "young" at sixty.

SECURING EMPLOYMENT AFTER AGE FORTY. Following are some of the reasons older workers have had difficulty securing employment in the United States as industrialization advanced. These conditions in a general way apply to other advanced countries as well.

1. Decline in self-employment on farms and in small business. Over 80 percent of workers are employed by someone else; so the self-employment market for older workers is small.

2. Systematic seniority and promotion-from-within policies that protect the employed worker but make it more difficult for older persons to secure jobs, other than a low-paid entry job often below the older person's skill level.

3. Changes in older workers' needs, so that employment is more necessary. Now more older persons maintain separate households instead of living with relatives, and more household necessities are purchased rather than made at home.

4. Shifts in occupational structure, so that skills learned in youth are not now needed. One personnel officer said of an older worker, "This applicant is looking for a 1955 job in 1976."

5. Educational obsolescence because older persons do not have an educational level competitive with younger workers. Also, new technology demands education of types they do not have.

6.   Industrial migration from one area to another and declining industries, requiring more older workers to seek work because of layoff.

7.   Pension and retirement systems that require compulsory retirement and/or increase costs of hiring older workers.

8.   The failure of older workers to learn new skills and to change as employer needs change. Older workers often seek protection rather than opportunity, refuse retraining, become careless and sensitive, or resign imprudently over a small matter, thus putting themselves unprepared on the job market. In one organization, for example, a man aged fifty had worked for the same firm thirty years. When it introduced some technological changes, he was assured of continued employment at regular earnings, but he resented the changes and chose to resign. He found it difficult to secure new employment.

JOB ADJUSTMENT OF OLDER WORKERS.   As workers grow older, they have many adjustments to make. With regard to organizational behavior, older workers tend to develop gradually into a social group that is separate from younger workers. Their interests and even their day-to-day conversations are different. Older workers become less able to take part in active sports such as company softball. The important point is that these changes need to take place without causing older persons to feel socially isolated and insecure. Older employees need to be accepted and understood—to be respected for what they have to offer, rather than penalized for what they cannot help. Age comes alike to all persons, so management, unions, and work groups need to recognize their responsibility to build an organizational climate that does accept and integrate older workers.

Age also affects the performance characteristics of workers. Some workers become slower and less adaptable, but they try to compensate for these deficiencies by improving dependability, steadiness, quality of work, and attendance. Considered as a whole, job performance of older workers and younger workers is about the same.

There are, however, some older workers who want to keep working but who have some special infirmity of age that does not permit them to do a full day's work in their regular trade. They can be helped to keep their jobs by means of *job engineering* or *job reassignment.*

Job engineering revises job requirements so that the infirmities of age are no handicap in performance. Some helpful changes are installing power tools and hoists, arranging the job so that the employee can work sitting down, providing power feed of stock to machines, reducing the required reach or other motions, reducing the required pace of production, and providing a "bank" of parts so that pressure is not on the worker.

Job reassignment moves older workers from their regular jobs to others more suited to their age. In some instances these are jobs that have been engineered for older workers. In other instances the new assignments are simply jobs with different requirements elsewhere in the organization. One older employee, for example, was moved from a standing job to a sitting job, and sick leave declined from an excessive amount to zero for the next sixteen months.

In some factories certain jobs off the production line are reserved for older employees to work at a variable pace or even on a part-time schedule. Other factories report that older workers successfully train new workers, set up machines, and rework rejects from the production line. Job reassignment is especially necessary for older workers on fast-paced assembly lines and in other rigorous work.

For job placement of older workers some organizations use a procedure by which a profile of the employee's physical and mental capabilities is compared with a profile of the job's requirements in these areas, as shown in Figure 18-2. If the employee and job profiles reasonably match, then the employee is placed on the job. If there is a mismatch, in some instances the job can be altered to make a better match or an employee infirmity may be corrected, such as better eyeglasses for poor eyesight. In Figure 18-2 the employee shows favorable characteristics for placement on the job.

This approach is called the GULHEMP system, an acronym for the characteristics measured in the profile. With the aid of counseling for proper placement, this system has improved employment for unemployed older persons, and reduced absenteeism and sick leave for job incumbents.[14]

Another type of adjustment is required by older executives of limited ability who finally face the blunt realization that they have reached the end of the

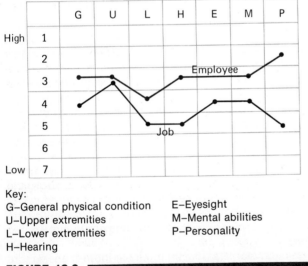

Key:
G–General physical condition   E–Eyesight
U–Upper extremities   M–Mental abilities
L–Lower extremities   P–Personality
H–Hearing

FIGURE 18-2 ▉

Profile comparison of an older employee with job requirements using the GULHEMP system. (Adapted from Michael D. Batten, "Application of a Unique Industrial Health System," *Industrial Gerontology,* Fall 1973, p. 41.)

line—that they have had their last promotion. As long as they saw the possibility of one more promotion ahead, it acted as a satisfying hope and powerful drive at work; but there are only a few top jobs, and most persons can climb only part of the way. Employees who have reached their limits in the organization face a readjustment of their level of aspiration to something different from one more promotion. Some older managers tend to decline in job satisfaction around the age of sixty, apparently because their opportunities for further growth and self-realization are partially blocked. One study shows that as a result of these blockages, older managers turn their attention more to *maintenance factors* on the job. Since motivational factors are harder to reach, managers avoid job dissonance by emphasizing the maintenance factors that come with the job. But because these factors do not provide intrinsic satisfactions, the manager who is sixty to sixty-five may be less satisifed and motivated.[15]

PLANNING FOR RETIREMENT. For those who reach it, retirement is a significant milestone, but it also requires one of life's greatest adjustments.

Consider the case of Mack McGuire, whose department is holding a retirement dinner for him. There he stands at the head of the table fiddling with the watch the company just gave him. He is choked with emotion and fishing for the right words to tell how he feels inside. A month ago he was willing and able to work, but now he is sixty-five and—according to a company and union agreement—unable to work. He knew retirement was coming, but he never did want to think about it before, because the subject was too painful. Suddenly he realizes that retirement is upon him, and he panics at the thought of it.

The case of Mack McGuire illustrates two important policy problems that arise concerning retirement: (1) Shall retirement be *fixed* according to chronological age or *variable* according to job-performance age? and (2) What kind of preretirement counseling should be given potential retirees? When retirement age is fixed, the typical age is sixty-five years, though some employers are extending the age upward or downward from this base. The age of sixty-five is more a social custom than a scientifically determined standard. The retirement age of sixty-five originally was selected by German Chancellor Otto von Bismarck in the 1880s for a public pension plan. In those days few persons lived to that age, which meant that the Chancellor had a good program from the political point of view at negligible cost. Years later insurance companies began to use age sixty-five in planning retirement and annuity programs. When the Federal Social Security Act was passed in 1935, age sixty-five was selected as a compromise between one group that wanted sixty years and another group that wanted seventy years. The typical retirement age varies among nations as well as organizations. In Japan more than half the firms that require compulsory retirement fix the age at fifty-five years, but a gradual upward movement of retirement age is taking place.[16]

When retirement is based on chronological age, it may create a haven for deadwood because there is a tendency not to retire an employee until that age is reached, regardless of one's deficiencies. Furthermore, many workers object to the idea that their employment is controlled by their age instead of their ability to do the job. The problem is not solved, however, by changing to a variable retirement age. With variable retirement, each case has to be decided on its own merits, and there is no simple way to decide when a person should retire. "Horse trading," prejudice, and errors in judgment are difficult to prevent, and it becomes difficult to sell a worker on a retirement date when it is selected. The result is that variable retirement causes as much difficulty as fixed retirement, or more; and unions tend to favor a fixed retirement age because there is less chance of arbitrary management action.

A workable compromise between fixed and variable retirement is a plan that makes retirement compulsory at age seventy, but permits either the employer or the worker to select retirement any time between age sixty-five and seventy. This gives some workers a chance to decide their own retirement date, rather than having their employer tell them when to retire. It also lets them schedule their retirement more to fit their personal needs and plans after retirement. Another compromise has a fixed retirement age but permits temporary rehiring on one-year contracts for as long as five years. This plan is quite workable with executive and technical specialists, since it gives more flexibility in replacing an employee. Another workable solution is part-time work on the temporary payroll after retirement. In some cases two retirees work half time to fill one job.

It is understandable that some persons do not wish to retire at age sixty-five. A job gives status to a person, a meaning to life, and a feeling of contribution to general welfare. Work also permits a person to keep active and energetic and have constructive social interaction with others. In one study, for example, employees were asked a number of questions indicating how important their recreation, education, church, and work were to their general feeling of satisfaction. Work was clearly more important than any of the nonwork factors.[17]

Regardless of the age at which retirement occurs, workers may need preparation through communication and counseling. They need to be informed about pension choices and insurance benefits after retirement. If they appear to have retirement anxiety, counseling may be provided, but it is not always popular. Some overzealous employers have started counseling five or more years before retirement, often with a negative effect because workers resent being reminded that early. Retirement, like one's own funeral, is something most people would rather not talk about.

EMPLOYING LESS-ADVANTAGED PERSONS

Less-advantaged persons are those whose background has deprived them of the capability to make normal behavioral responses in the society in which they live. In the employment area the term "less-advantaged persons" typically applies to those who have cultural deficiencies that limit their employability. This group includes a large number of racial and ethnic minorities. The Federal Civil Rights Act of 1964 prohibits discrimination against these people, but concern for the less-advantaged person "goes a second mile" and makes a positive effort through affirmative action to develop them and integrate them into a normal work force. It assumes that those persons who want work do have the potential to perform it and should be given the opportunity for it, regardless of their present conditions.

SOCIAL BENEFITS EXPECTED.　Some of the social gains that will result from employing and training less-advantaged persons are as follows:

1.　We create a useful member of society who is positively contributing to it.

2.　We improve the self-image and general development of a human being.

3.　We change a receiver of tax benefits into a payer of taxes.

4.　We reduce the heavy hand of government welfare and other paternalistic care programs in a person's life and perhaps in a whole family's life; that is, we improve the person's quality of life.

5.　We strengthen the role of business as an effective institution for solving social problems, along with its already established role of economic efficiency. Concurrently we should improve the image of business as a socially viable institution.

The social costs and benefits of a program for less-advantaged persons may be calculated. An example is an American Indian training program to improve skills through actual work experience. A researcher calculated that the social costs of the training amounted to $1,010 for each trainee, but social benefits for the first year amounted to $2,034. This social benefit was primarily the higher earnings, productivity, and taxes paid. It did not include such intangible social benefits as possible lower crime rates, reduced cost of welfare services, and similar benefits. When social benefits were considered over a period of years, it was shown that in five years benefits were nearly nine times costs and in ten years they were nearly fifteen times costs.[18]

UNDERSTANDING THE LESS-ADVANTAGED CULTURE.　Although less-advantaged persons may appear at first to lack the independence and drive that are traditional with other persons, these values may be only suppressed or undeveloped, and they can be developed with training and job experience. As stated by one ghetto dweller, "I can't be a father to my kids if you [welfare people] give them what they need. I can only be their father if I give to them."

In understanding less-advantaged persons it is important to realize that often they have developed in a deprived culture. They are likely to have a low self-image, and they may be school dropouts. They may have grown up in a situation in which they were criticized for failures but seldom encouraged when they achieved. Perhaps they lived in conditions of squalor and poor care. Often they are apathetic, frustrated, and angry. For example, one study of the hard-core unemployed reports that they distrust people, authority figures, and the organizational environment.[19]

Favorable attitudes toward work often are lacking among less-advantaged persons. One study reported that they are low in the work ethic and pride in work.[20] This means that they have less internal motivation to work. Often their outlook on time and rigid work schedules is different. They may have been living for the moment, seeking immediate gratification, rather than planning for the future. It may be difficult for them to understand long-range planning for self-development that will lead to pay raises and promotions. Similar undisciplined and short-range attitudes may exist concerning management of money, living according to organizational rules, interpersonal relationships, and other items. Even when they are highly motivated, their background may hinder proper channeling of their motivations.

As a result of their employment deficiencies, less-advantaged persons are likely to give poor performance unless they are thoroughly trained and developed so that their potential talents are released. Some of their probable performance deficiencies include the following:

1. Low productivity.

2. Inferior quality of work. Quality is so low that production costs become excessive.

3. High tardiness, absenteeism, and turnover. In one firm without a training program turnover was 50 percent during the first week, 67 percent by the end of the first month, and 90 percent in the first year!

4. Apprehension about supervision and work rules, and sometimes open hostility.

5. Poor work habits. The person is not used to performing in terms of the rigidities of a time schedule and work rules.

6. Slow improvement. Progress may not be at a normal pace because deficiencies hold back the person.

7. Job incidents such as fighting and loafing.

Research shows that typical cultural deficiencies can be overcome when less-advantaged persons become integrated and experienced on the job. One study covered Mexican-American and Anglo employees in several occupations. The study showed that when the two groups were matched for education, seniority, and other formal job qualifications there was no significant difference in their performance. The following measures of performance showed no statistically significant difference: efficiency ratings, promotion test scores, taking of annual leave, taking of sick leave, and accident rates. In other words, a less-advantaged cultural background did not prove significant for employees with the same formal qualifications; hence, purely cultural deficiency was not a job handicap for the integrated, experienced minority employee.[21]

EMPLOYMENT AND TRAINING PROGRAMS. Since purely cultural deficiency seems to be no handicap once a person has a job and has gained experience, a key step for less-advantaged persons is a successful employment and training program. There may be a need for training in attitudes toward work in order to overcome habits that constitute job deficiencies, such as the tendency to be tardy frequently. In addition, remedial education may be necessary to bring newcomers up to whatever standards are necessary, such as basic arithmetic. Next, there is a need for job skills training. This usually is the larger part of the training program and may last for months. Finally, supporting services are needed both during the training and after the employee is on the job. They include counseling, medical assistance, financial guidance, follow-up on absences, and other aids. Special tutoring and counseling have proved to be helpful, because they assist the trainee over many of the rough spots that develop during the first few months of employment.[22]

The work of David C. McClelland, discussed in an earlier chapter, demonstrates that attitude training is important. He shows that training in achievement motivation does make a difference. In one instance he trained black business people from Washington, D.C. The training focused on development of an "achievement syndrome," that is, how a person who is achievement-motivated thinks, talks, and acts. When the trainees were compared with an untrained group at the end of six months, 20 percent of the trainees had been promoted, but only 8 percent of the untrained group received a promotion. In addition, the trained group made eight new business starts, but there were no new business starts in the untrained group.[23]

Support of fellow workers is also necessary while less-advantaged employees are learning their jobs. If employees are not prepared to accept a certain minority, they need guidance in how to interact with the trainees and what to expect. It is important for them to be convinced of the organization's commitment to equal employment opportunity.

SUPERVISORY SUPPORT. Supervisory support is essential because supervisors are the point of daily contact with less-advantaged newcomers. Research shows that supervisory consideration contributes to job success, but excessive structure has an opposite effect.[24] On the other hand, the opposite extreme of a weak structure appears to be undesirable because it prevents establishment of the self-discipline that is necessary for effective group work. One study, for example, showed that softening of absence standards was self-defeating. It led to an increased separation rate by the trainees.[25]

Supervisory attitudes as well as performance will have a significant influence on job success of less-advantaged trainees.

One company discovered that its supervisors had a built-in expectation of failure for new less-advantaged employees. When this expectation came into contact with the newcomer's natural expectation of failure, the result was a high failure rate. The company's solution was to train its supervisors before it employed additional less-advantaged persons. Now all supervisors take a special three-day training course designed to improve their attitudes toward less-advantaged newcomers.

SUMMARY

A minority group is one that has, or feels that it has, its employment status relative to other persons decreased in some important way by factors that do not concern job performance. The essential problem faced by minority groups is employment discrimination. Title VII of the Civil Rights Act prohibits employment discrimination regarding race, color, religion, sex, or national origin. The Age Discrimination in Employment Act adds ages forty through sixty-five to these prohibitions. Taken together, the groups covered by antidiscriminatioh laws exceed 75 percent of the labor force. The purpose of these laws is equal employment opportunity for all persons.

Antidiscrimination laws are administered by the EEOC, which has established a policy of affirmative action for accelerated employment and promotion of minorities, often with goals for proportional employment representation. The result sometimes is reverse discrimination and internal organizational conflict. Equal employment opportunities for women, older persons, and less-advantaged persons were further discussed.

TERMS AND CONCEPTS FOR REVIEW

Minority group	Reverse discrimination
Discrimination	Proportional employment
Pluralism	Unisex jobs
Title VII of the Civil Rights Act	Job engineering
Age Discrimination in Employment Act	Job reassignment
Equal Employment Opportunity Commission	GULHEMP system
Affirmative action	Less-advantaged persons

REVIEW QUESTIONS ███████████████████████████

1. Do you think some discrimination is justified, such as denial of certain jobs to young people below certain ages, business owners hiring relatives, unions enforcing union shops, or the government giving job preference to veterans and their widows? If some is justified, how will that which is just be distinguished from that which is unjust?
2. Discuss current administration of antidiscrimination laws, including affirmative action, proportional employment representation, and reverse discrimination.
3. Prepare an appropriate affirmative action program for women in an organization of your choice.
4. Discuss the GULHEMP system for job assignment of older persons.
5. Discuss the kinds of activities that might improve job success of less-advantaged persons.

CASES

BORDER ELECTRONICS

Border Electronics is an electronic assembly plant in a community near the Mexican border. About 60 percent of employees are Mexican-Americans, and a few others are Mexican citizens. This firm had a rush order that required steady work from all employees and no leaves of absence. This order extended through September 16, the Independence Day of Mexico. This holiday and surrounding days are elaborately celebrated by the Mexican-American community; however, the company strongly needed full attendance of all employees during this period.

To ensure attendance, department superintendent Max Ways wrote a directive, as was his usual practice with employees, stating that no leave would be granted to anyone during the holiday period because the rush order was not completed.

Another superintendent, Arleigh Watkins, called his employees together in his usual way and explained the problem in detail in both English and Spanish. He stated that he could allow leaves only to a few persons who were on entertainment committees and had other special reasons for absence. He appealed for the cooperation of all employees to continue working because of the rush order.

QUESTION

1. Appraise the different ways in which the two superintendents approached their employees. Discuss the probable absence rates in the two departments during the holiday period.

MEREDITH INSURANCE COMPANY

Meredith Insurance Company is a life insurance company with its home office in Omaha, Nebraska, and regional offices in San Francisco, California, and Richmond, Virginia. Sales are handled by independent agents who are not employees of the company. Meredith Company is under pressure from Equal Employment Opportunity Commission representatives to develop a stronger affirmative action program to achieve a higher proportion of minorities in its jobs. The following options are being discussed.

1. The minority work force of each office should match local population percentages reported in Standard Metropolitan Statistical Area census data.

2. The work force in each major job level and category should match local population percentages.

3. Since the company operates nationally, its minority representation companywide should match national figures from the latest census.

4. National representation figures should be applied to each job level and category companywide.

5. Minorities should be represented in each major job level and category ac-

cording to their present proportions in the company, because this is the source of its talent for promotion from within, which is a major policy of the firm.

6. An exception should be made for jobs requiring college education, such as lawyer and actuary, and they should be represented only according to their graduation rate from universities, since that is all the supply that is available.

7. An exception should be made for women, using only the proportion in the *labor force* rather than in the population, since many women choose not to enter the labor force.

8. The percentages set should be minimums. If more of any minority applied and were qualified, they should be employed, even though this would require eventual reduction of nonminority representation to allow overrepresentation of minorities.

9. The company should increase its recruitment efforts among minorities, but should employ and promote the best persons who apply, without regard to proportional representation. As one manager said, "How would you like to be told that you cannot be promoted because we already have too many of your race, sex, or ethinic group in that job category?"

QUESTION
1. Develop an appropriate affirmative action plan for the company, discussing the advantages and disadvantages of each option presented. Develop other options if they are appropriate.

REFERENCES

1. For further discussion of pluralism and its implications, see Keith Davis and Robert L. Blomstrom, *Business and Society: Environment and Responsibility,* 3d ed., New York: McGraw-Hill Book Company, 1975.

2. Calvin F. Schmid and Charles E. Hobbs, "Socioeconomic Differences among Nonwhite Races," *American Sociological Review,* December 1965, pp. 909–922. In addition, the proportion of Chinese and Filipino women with a college education is more than double that of white women.

3. "Court-ordered Affirmative Action," *FEP Guidelines,* April 1974, p. 3.

4. "Company Performance Roundup," *Business and Society Review/Innovation,* Winter 1973–74, p. 86.

5. Allen I. Kraut, "The Entrance of Black Employees into Traditionally White Jobs," *Academy of Management Journal,* September 1975, pp. 610–615.

6. Julius S. Brown, "How Many Workers Enjoy Discretion on the Job?" *Industrial Relations,* May 1975, pp. 196–202.

7. Donald J. Treiman and Kermit Terrell, "Sex and the Process of Status Attainment: A Comparison of Working Women and Men," *American Sociological Review,* April 1975, pp. 174–200. See also McKee J. McClendon. "The Occupational Status Attainment Processes of Males and Females," *American Sociological Review,* February 1976, pp. 52–64.

8. "Facts and Fictions about Working Women Explored: Several Stereotypes Prove False in National Study," *ISR Newsletter* (Institute for Social Research, The University of Michigan), Autumn 1972, pp. 4–5.

9. Philip J. Manhardt, "Job Orientation of Male and Female College Graduates in Business," *Personnel Psychology,* Summer 1972, pp. 361–368.

10. David R. Day and Ralph M. Stogdill, "Leader Behavior of Male and Female Supervisors: A Comparative Study," *Personnel Psychology,* Summer 1972, pp. 353–360; and Kathryn M. Bartol and Max S. Wortman, "Male versus Female Leaders: Effects on Perceived Leader Behavior and Satisfaction in a Hospital," *Personnel Psychology,* Winter 1975, pp. 533–547.

11. Randall S. Schuler, "Sex, Organizational Level, and Outcome Importance: Where the Differences Are," *Personnel Psychology,* Autumn 1975, pp. 365–375; William E. Reif, John W. Newstrom, and Robert M. Monczka, "Exploding Some Myths about Women Managers," *California Management Review,* Summer 1975, pp. 72–79; and "Facts and Fictions . . . ," *loc. cit.*

12. Douglas T. Hall and Francine E. Gordon, "Career Choices of Married Women: Effects on Conflict, Role Behavior, and Satisfaction," *Journal of Applied Psychology,* August 1973, pp. 42.–48.

13. John J. Mathews, William F. Collins, and Bart B. Cobb, "A Sex Comparison of Reasons for Attrition in a Male-dominated Occupation," *Personnel Psychology,* Winter 1974, pp. 535–541.

14. Special issue on "Functional Capacity and Job Performance," *Industrial Gerontology,* Fall 1973, pp. 38–70.

15. Shoukry D. Saleh, "A Study of Attitude Change in the Preretirement Period," *Journal of Applied Psychology,* October 1964, pp. 310–312.

16. "The Compulsory Retirement Age Is Gradually Being Extended," *Japan Labor Bulletin,* November 1974, p. 2.

17. Frank Friedlander, "Importance of Work versus Nonwork among Socially and Occupationally Stratified Groups," *Journal of Applied Psychology,* December 1966, pp. 437–441, covering 1,468 civil service employees in one community.

18. Loren C. Scott, "The Economic Effectiveness of On-the-Job Training: The Experience of the Bureau of Indian Affairs in Oklahoma," *Industrial and Labor Relations Review,* January 1970, pp. 220–236.

19. Harry C. Triandis and others, "Ecosystem Distrust and the Hard-to-Employ," *Journal of Applied Psychology,* February 1975, pp. 44–56.

20. James G. Goodale, "Effects of Personal Background and Training on Work Values of the Hard-Core Unemployed," *Journal of Applied Psychology,* February 1973, pp. 1–9.

21. Charles N. Weaver and Norval D. Glenn, "Job Performance Comparisons: Mexican-American and Anglo Employees," *California Management Review,* Fall 1970, pp. 27–30.

22. David B. Lipsky, "Employer Role in Hard-Core Trainee Success," *Industrial Relations,* May 1973, pp. 125–136; and Paul Salipante, Jr., and Paul Goodman, "Training, Counseling, and Retention of the Hard-Core Unemployed," *Journal of Applied Psychology,* February 1976, pp. 1–11.

23. David C. McClelland, "Black Capitalism: Making It Work," *Think,* July–August 1969, pp. 6–11.

24. Richard W. Beatty, "Supervisory Behavior Related to Job Success of Hard-Core Unemployed over a Two-Year Period," *Journal of Applied Psychology,* February 1974, pp. 38–42.

25. Elchanan Cohn and Morgan V. Lewis, "Employers' Experience in Retaining Hard-Core Hires," *Industrial Relations,* February 1975, pp. 55–62.

CHAPTER 19
MANAGING SCIENTIFIC AND PROFESSIONAL EMPLOYEES

The best way to manage scientific and professional people is to give them an interesting, challenging job and then leave them alone.
Anonymous

LEARNING OBJECTIVES

TO UNDERSTAND:
Characteristics of scientific and professional employees
Differences between cosmopolitans and locals
Responses of scientists and professionals to unions
The collegial model of organizational behavior
The nature of organizational pluralism
Operation of matrix organization

John Reason was a top student at State University. When he received his master's degree in chemistry and joined a small manufacturing company, he looked forward to all the contributions he would make to society. Within a few months after he took his job, he proposed several elaborate ideas, but he discovered that management was cautious about his proposals, constantly asked questions about costs, and was not oriented toward chemistry. Most of his ideas were rejected; so he became dissatisfied with this environment and eighteen months later joined the development laboratories of a large, progressive chemical firm. He was unhappy to discover that this firm required him to prepare a large amount of paperwork to justify his research, and he commented to an associate that 35 percent of his time was wasted performing duties below his competence. Furthermore—and much to his surprise—he found that the senior scientists in this large laboratory already had vested interests in the laboratory's projects. They did not give him a key position on important projects and did not accord him the status and recognition that he wanted. They also talked about costs and budgets when he made elaborate proposals. He was frustrated and dissatisfied.

John's experience is perhaps extreme in the degree of dissatisfaction that developed, but it does illustrate a common occurrence with scientific and professional (S & P) employees as they try to adjust to modern organizations. The situation would be no different in a university laboratory or a government bureau. In the university John might object to a vice president with a degree in literature or business deciding whether he could have a large budget allocation for equipment for a

335

project in which he had a special interest. In the government laboratory he might object to the lack of travel funds and quantity of red tape. John's problem is essentially one of adjusting his highly specialized interests and way of life to the integrative way of life of an organization that brings together many specialized interests such as John's are.

In this chapter we discuss how S & P interests are somewhat different and how they may be better integrated into the organization.

UNDERSTANDING SCIENTIFIC AND PROFESSIONAL WORK

Scientific and professional workers constitute over 10 percent of the labor force, and they occupy many important organizational positions. The distinguishing features of S & P work are that it is intellectual in nature and focused on some particular specialty that requires intellectual preparation for proficiency. Usually education beyond high school is required because there are professional ways of work and a professional literature to learn. There are one or more professional associations that help maintain standards in the field and encourage development of members. Examples of S & P occupations are electrical engineering, accounting, physics, and medicine. There are other occupations that are semiprofessional in nature but are seeking full professional recognition, and often their members conduct themselves substantially the same way that members of established S & P occupations do.

Differences exist between scientific and professional work, but the two types of work are grouped together in this discussion because there is much in common in the job behavior of people who work in these areas. Essentially, scientific work is an area of specialized, rational knowledge, while professional work applies to practice. Thus, the occupation of physicist focuses on scientific knowledge, while the occupation of electrical engineer focuses on professional practice using knowledge of science. A professional occupation may also include practice outside of science, such as accounting or law.

SCIENTIFIC AND PROFESSIONAL EMPLOYEES. There are all types of persons in S & P work. On the other hand, further understanding of S & P work can be gained by generalizing about the outlooks and ways of action that predominate among S & P workers compared with other workers.

S & P employees usually are more intelligent and intellectually oriented than the majority of other employees. They are strongly achievement-motivated, particularly toward solution of problems in their areas of interest. They have an analytical turn of mind and are self-disciplined, depending as much on their own standards as on the standards of the organization. Because of their strong achievement drives, they require recognition, status, and opportunities for growth. Their task orientation means that they want involvement, responsibility, and self-actualization. Their strong drives and exacting nature mean that they can be sensitive, restless, and vulnerable to frustration. For example, an administrative block that prevents action really does not bother an employee who is not going anywhere; but an S & P employee may develop frustrations and defensive reactions to that same block, because it seriously hinders drives for achievement.[1]

Studies consistently show that scientists, as well as professional employees, want high autonomy, or job freedom. They want to have some choice about the kinds of projects on which they work and the ways that they approach problems. They prefer not to be bossed or commanded. There is evidence, however, that very high autonomy is not associated with high productivity. The optimal condition is one in which a scientist has considerable autonomy but frequent contact with the supervisor and others who can contribute to the job. Provided a scientist has considerable autonomy, contacts with the supervisor and others are usually perceived as being supportive. These contacts also help keep a scientist focused on organizational objectives. The amount of autonomy that is optimal for scientists depends somewhat on how strong their drive for autonomy is. This drive varies, and studies show that the higher a scientist's academic education is, the stronger is that scientist's drive for autonomy.[2]

Care should be taken to assure that a group of S & P employees does not develop into an independent unit whose members mutually judge their own work without effective control and appraisal from outside in terms of the whole organization. Full autonomy and self-isolation may lead to an attitude that the group's work exists for its own sake without any obligation to tie it to the larger organization.

S & P drives for achievement and autonomy are emphasized throughout much of the world. One major study covered over 2,500 professional workers in sixteen nations. Surveys were administered in the native language of the nation. The seven most important goals that were reported by these professionals all concerned drives for achievement and autonomy. (Earnings ranked eighth.) Clearly these professionals were seeking challenging, responsible work that would help them grow and that could be performed with some autonomy.[3]

S & P employees have a high investment in education and professional preparation. They expect to be rewarded accordingly, and if they are not rewarded to their satisfaction, they feel that their occupational membership permits them to secure jobs elsewhere at about the same level. Compared with other workers, they tend to be highly mobile, being willing to move elsewhere for new opportunities and new challenges.

One study of S & P turnover covered 437 scientists and engineers who had left a variety of organizations. Their most important reason for leaving was motivational factors (36 percent.). This category included such items as disliked nature of work, better opportunity to use skills, and lack of opportunity for advancement. Other reasons included significant organizational changes affecting work (16 percent), desire to live in a better geographic area (12 percent), and improved earnings (11 percent).[4] When this survey is compared with the international survey reported earlier, it confirms that for S & P employees earnings are a secondary goal and a secondary reason for termination. Higher-order needs tend to dominate their outlook.

COSMOPOLITANS AND LOCALS. An important distinction among employees is whether their occupational orientation is *cosmopolitan* (centered on occupational recognition, regardless of who employs them) or *local* (centered on recognition within their employing organization). In general, S & P employees have a stronger cosmopolitan orientation than most other employees. For example, a nationwide sample of scientists reported that 59 percent of those in business and over 75 percent of those in government and nonprofit organizations had a cosmopolitan orientation.[5]

Cosmopolitans are oriented beyond the organization to their occupation and to recognition in it. Their frame of reference for judging personal progress is not so much their rank in the organization (though this is important), but rather their rank in the professional community. They are as much interested in what their professional peers think of their work as what their manager thinks of it. Looking outward beyond their employer and having their own professional standards, cosmopolitans are more independent and resentful of close supervision, deadlines, and paperwork. The organization is merely the vehicle that permits them to pursue their professional goals. In the extreme example, we can say that cosmopolitans work on something they desire to do in any case, and luckily they find an employer willing to hire them to do this work.

Locals, on the other hand, focus their interests on the organization that employs them. Their loyalty is to their organization and its goals. They seek management approval and advancement within the ranks of their organization. Organizational rank and recognition tend to be more important to them than professional status and recognition. To the local, internal politics and developments are major issues; but to the cosmopolitan, they are of secondary interest unless they directly affect the cosmopolitan's professional work.

The importance of the cosmopolitan-local distinction is that cosmopolitans are motivated by different incentives than locals. For example, locals want a sense of belonging and the feeling that they have important jobs, while cosmopolitans are more motivated by an opportunity to contribute to the advancement of knowledge and by a feeling of autonomy from administrative trivia. Locals respond to status and recognition given internally. Cosmopolitans also respond to internal recognition; but in addition they are motivated by the opportunity to make a professional speech or do research that will result in a professional paper.

SCIENTIFIC EMPLOYEES ON THE JOB. A persistent trend in the study of scientists and engineers is that scientific output rises as they broaden and diversify their activities by spending less than full time on their scientific specialty. For example, scientists are more productive scientifically if they spend about one-fourth time in teaching, administration, or communication. They are also more productive if they work in more than one application of their specialty, such as both pure research and product improvement. More productivity also arises when scientists are qualified and interested in three or more areas of their field. In other words, an organization may be taking the wrong step if it tries to make its scientists narrow specialists working intensely on highly specialized subjects.

Apparently when scientists work outside their narrow field, the cross-fertilization of ideas reinforces their scientific productivity. This condition occurs even if the outside work is nonscientific, such as administrative work. In some cases more productive scientists naturally gravitate to doing a variety of duties, but it is also evident that variety of work encourages (causes) a scientist to be more productive.[6] Basic reasons for this relationship are that multiple roles tend (1) to increase the variety of a person's inputs, which should increase creative and decision-making abilities, and (2) to reinforce self-image and ego satisfactions, which should improve motivation.

S & P employees in modern organizations are rarely isolated individuals hidden in a laboratory and having little interaction with others. This is the exception rather than the usual condition. In real life S & P employees spend a large part of their time coordinating, learning what others are doing, keeping up with policies, and selling ideas—that is, communicating. One study of scientists and engineers in chemical research and development reported that they spent approximately 60 percent of their time communicating.[7]

When communicating with associates in the same occupation, S & P employees can use the elaborate terminology of their technical specialty; but when they communicate outside their field, the complex language of their subject is no longer appropriate. Instead, they need to use an understandable language common to people in various types of work. Communication ability is especially important when S & P employees serve as liaison persons between a technical group and nontechnical managers in the organization. If S & P employees cannot communicate scientific needs and accomplishments to management, they are unlikely to receive the kind of support they desire.

Though S & P employees often fail to sell ideas because of their complex language, studies show that they can be trained to use understandable language. One training course taught research chemists and engineers how to write readable progress reports to management. All nineteen trainees improved according to a standard index of readability, and some improved their index more than one-third.[8]

SCIENTIFIC AND PROFESSIONAL EMPLOYEES IN MANAGEMENT. S & P employees are a major source of talent for promotion into management. They have such desirable characteristics as achievement drives, dedication to work, education, intellectual ability, and an analytical mind. On the other hand, the transition to management is sometimes difficult, particularly if they lack management and behavioral training. Their orientations toward logic, the physical world, and/or the frameworks of their specialty, may result in narrow viewpoints and blind spots in such areas as interpersonal contacts on the job. Consider the following experience of an engineer.

Art Sneed was a field engineer with a construction company. In the field he proved to be an outstanding engineer whose work was invaluable to the company. In addition to being an outstanding engineer, he knew how to talk with construction workers and supervisors in one-to-one relationships on the job. Generally, he knew he was right, and he took a firm stand.

After a few years, in order to continue paying him what he was worth, the company "rewarded" him by moving him to the position of engineering supervisor in the firm's central office in a large office building. His new job required him to make horizontal contacts with other specialists such as urban planners, account-ants, and economists. He was uncomfortable in these horizontal contacts, and was autocratic with his subordinates. He always insisted he was right. Eventually he withdrew to himself and became an unhappy office recluse. He was ineffective, unable to make the transition to management.

Many scientists and professionals do not want to move into management. They prefer to advance their competence in their specialty, but as soon as they reach the professional level, they often find there are no further promotional opportunities unless they are willing to move to management. Since S & P employ-ees are achievement-oriented, frustration develops because they conclude: The only way to earn a promotion is to become a manager. The result may be that the employee will begin to look elsewhere for a job. One way to overcome this difficulty is to establish a *dual promotion ladder,* as shown in Figure 19-1.

In the dual ladder a professional has the choice of moving upward in rank and pay as a manager (becoming more general) or moving to similar levels of rank and pay within a professional specialty. In this way those persons so inclined may advance to an equivalent management level solely by improved technical compe-tence. Special designations are used for top ranks, such as corporate fellow, engi-neering fellow, or consulting scientist.

JOB SATISFACTION OF SCIENTIFIC AND PROFESSIONAL EMPLOYEES.
Scientific and professional employees receive more rewards than the typical employee, but their need structure is also more advanced. The net result is that as a group they are not much more satisfied than other employees. Since they do em-phasize higher-level needs, S & P employees respond favorably to motivational factors such as those proposed by Herzberg. These factors are achievement, recog-

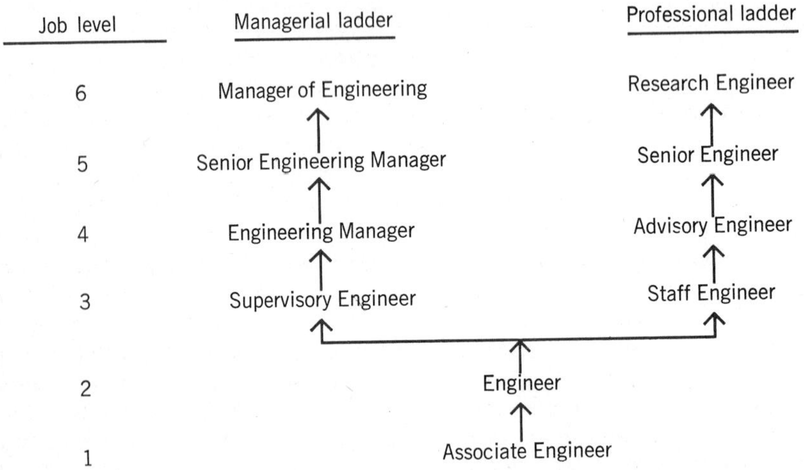

Job level	Managerial ladder	Professional ladder
6	Manager of Engineering	Research Engineer
5	Senior Engineering Manager	Senior Engineer
4	Engineering Manager	Advisory Engineer
3	Supervisory Engineer	Staff Engineer
2	Engineer	
1	Associate Engineer	

FIGURE 19-1

A dual promotion ladder for engineers.

nition, advancement, the work itself, possibility of growth, and responsibility. S & P employees have more job satisfaction when there is more challenge in their jobs.[9]

Because of the rather variable work environment of S & P employees compared with factory and office work, their dissatisfactions tend to vary considerably from job to job and industry to industry. Some of the complaints of S & P employees are lack of autonomy on the job, excessive administrative trivia, time spent beneath their capabilities, inadequate funding of their work, lack of assistance, and insufficient employer and community recognition.

A motivation–job satisfaction program for S & P employees is most successful when it specifically applies to their areas of need. If they are already well motivated and satisfied in a particular area because of their professional orientation or the nature of their work, then a program directed toward that area will provide some reinforcement, but it is unlikely to produce a major change.

For example, one company surveyed its hourly employees and salaried engineering personnel to determine their response to a zero-defects quality motivation program. Both groups expressed a favorable attitude toward the program; however, the hourly employees' feelings of job satisfaction and communication improvement were higher than the engineers' feelings by a statistically significant amount. In other words, the quality motivation program had less impact on the engineers because they were already quality-motivated, had effective communication, and had reasonable job satisfaction.[10]

RESPONSE OF SCIENTIFIC AND PROFESSIONAL EMPLOYEES TO UNIONS. Although unions have appealed to some professionals, they have had only moderate appeal to S & P employees as a whole, compared with factory employees. This is understandable for a number of reasons. Scientists and professionals feel closer to management and typically are closer in terms of communication chains and office location. More important from a behavioral point of view, much union philosophy has emphasized conflict (for example, bargaining and strikes) to wrest resources from others, while the philosophy of professionals is to be of service and to contribute more in order to be worth more. The latter approach appears to offer a better self-image and better self-motivation for creative and intellectual workers.

In addition, when S & P groups seek labor representation, scientists and professionals who are supervisors find that they must become relatively inactive in their local professional group, because it is now a bargaining agent. This leaves them isolated from their fellow professionals. Most scientists and professionals prefer a unified professional group in which even those who become managers can remain active. For example, accountants who are managers normally may remain active in their professional association, continue to develop their professional competence, and even hold office. There is unity among the entire group as professionals. On the other hand, machinists who become supervisors are separated from their machinist associates and continued growth in that occupation. Typically, if a machine-shop supervisor performs work on a machine, a union files a grievance. It claims that a supervisor cannot do "union work" because that will deprive some union member of employment.

INTEGRATING SCIENTIFIC AND PROFESSIONAL WORK INTO THE ORGANIZATION

Expanding S & P work in organizations has established it as another occupational area with its own set of claims on the organizations. Formerly management and labor were the principal occupational groups, but now those laborers who perform intellectual work are somewhat separated from those who use primarily manual skills. If an organization employs many S & P workers, and certainly if they are a major group in the organization, then it needs to make some adaptations in its way of life in order to integrate them effectively. In the following paragraphs we will discuss some of the adaptations that are being made.

THE COLLEGIAL MODEL OF ORGANIZATIONAL BEHAVIOR. A major adaptation to S & P work has been the gradual evolution of a collegial model of organizational behavior, as shown in Figure 19-2. This model is an extension of the supportive model discussed throughout this book, and it has been made feasible by expanding knowledge about people in organizations. The collegial model is being consciously followed in research laboratories and similar work environments, and it is gradually evolving in much S & P work. It readily adapts to the flexible, intellectual environment of S & P activities, and it effectively fulfills the work expectations of S & P employees.

Application of the collegial model in factory and office work is more limited. What exists is a contingency relationship in which use of the collegial model is contingent on conditions of unprogrammed work, intellectual environment, relative job autonomy, and similar variables of the type found in S & P work. In other environments other models are more appropriate. Even within a single large organization there are likely to be several approaches to people at work contingent on job circumstances and employee expectations. This is the essence of the contingency idea.

As shown in Figure 19-2, the collegial model depends on management's building a feeling of *partnership,* or mutual contribution, among participants in the

	COLLEGIAL
Depends on:	Partnership (mutual contribution)
Managerial orientation:	Teamwork
Employee orientation:	Responsibility
Employee psychological result:	Self-discipline
Employee needs met:	Self-actualization
Performance result:	Some enthusiasm

FIGURE 19-2 ▬▬▬▬▬▬▬▬▬▬▬▬▬▬▬▬

The collegial model of organizational behavior, a fourth model particularly used with scientific and professional employees. (For the first three models refer to Chapter 6.)

organization. Each employee feels a sense of contribution to the organization and feels needed. The employee feels that management and other specialties are contributing also, so it is easy to accept and respect their roles in the organization. Managers are seen as joint contributors, rather than overhead or bosses.

The managerial orientation, and consequently the role that management plays, is toward *teamwork.* Management is the coach that builds a better team. The employee response to this situation is *responsibility,* a feeling commonly found among S & P employees. For example, employees produce quality work not because management tells them to do so or because the inspector will catch them if they do not, but because they feel inside themselves an obligation to provide others with high quality. They also feel an obligation to uphold quality standards that will bring credit to their profession.

The employee psychological result of the collegial approach is *self-discipline.* Feeling responsible, employees discipline themselves for performance on the team in the same way that football team members discipline themselves to training standards and the rules of the game. In this kind of environment employees normally feel some degree of fulfillment, worthwhile contribution, and *self-actualization,* even though the amount may be modest in some situations. This self-actualization will lead to *some enthusiasm* in performance.

Emphasis on collegial approaches with S & P employees tends to produce improved results. One study covered scientists in three large research laboratories. Laboratories A and B were operated in a relatively traditional hierarchical manner. Laboratory C was operated in a more open, participative, collegial manner tending toward what Burns and Stalker called an organic approach. There were four measures of performance as perceived by the participants: esteem of fellow scientists, contribution to knowledge, sense of personal achievement, and contribution to management objectives. All four were higher in Laboratory C, and the first three were significantly higher. [11]

ORGANIZATIONAL PLURALISM. S & P interests and collegial practices are producing a sort of *organizational pluralism.* The organizational type of pluralism is much like its counterpart in the external social environment. Organizational pluralism means that within the organization there are many groups that operate somewhat independently according to their own internal standards, all working toward common organizational objectives. Professional groups with their self-government, cosmopolitan orientation, and authority through expertise do develop into rather independent units within the organization. Management's job is to integrate these diverse units, because it cannot wholly command them in the traditional hierarchical sense. It can, for example, do little about their professional standards of work and professional ethics. Those practices are always there to live with, so they must be integrated into the ongoing system.

Essentially, organizational pluralism leads to a wider distribution of power within an organization. This is accomplished through jointly narrowing the scope of command authority and widening the scope of authority through expertise. It also distributes status more widely because much status is acquired through one's profession regardless of one's rank in the organizational hierarchy.

Although organizational pluralism may conform to certain democratic ideals, it is not all favorable. It makes coordination among groups in a firm more difficult. It adds complexity and interdependence to the organization, increasing the probability and cost of breakdowns. It may make some decisions more sluggish because they will depend on consensus rather than unilateral decision making. Probably more attention will be diverted to internal politics as groups compete for power. Inevitable status rivalries between specialties will consume energies. Conditions such as status rivalries exist in traditional organizations, but organizational pluralism will probably intensify them.

Basically, organizational pluralism fractionates an organization somewhat, making coordination and integration more important functions in order to achieve the wholeness that all organizations need. Therefore, we can say that organizational pluralism is not necessarily something that management should actively seek. Rather it is something for management to deal with as it gradually develops with S & P employees in our highly technical society. It is the means by which S & P employees can be effectively brought onto the team.

MATRIX ORGANIZATION. Another adaptation to S & P work is *matrix organization,* also called program management and project management. In effect matrix organization is a second form of organizational pluralism that is overlaid on the professional type just discussed. Instead of separating people into professional groups, matrix organization separates some of the organization's activities into projects that then compete for allocations of the organization's people and resources. Professional groups are primarily a permanent commitment for an employee, but project groups are temporary up to several years. Employees are assigned to a project for its limited life or as long as their specialty is needed on the project. As one assignment is completed, employees move back to permanent assignments in traditional departments, or they are assigned to another project. In fact, an employee can be assigned part time to two or more projects at the same time. In each instance the temporary matrix organization overlays the permanent hierarchical organization.

In matrix organization a project manager is established to direct all work toward completion of a major project, such as development of a new rocket motor. Employees assigned to this project work under the coordinative command or direct command of this project manager.

A more simple example of matrix organization is an annual United Fund drive for contributions to community charities. It could be handled through the traditional hierarchy, but often it is assigned to a temporary hierarchy of employees as a part-time duty. They carry the assignment to completion and are then disbanded.

Employees assigned to a project may remain in their present location or they may move to a project location, in which case their situation is something like temporary duty in a military organization. As in a military situation, temporary rank in the matrix organization may be above one's rank in one's permanent assignment. For example, consider a physicist named Sally Ames, who is working at the fourth level in the permanent organization. She may operate at the second level in the matrix structure. In the permanent organization she may be an operating worker, but in the matrix structure she may be a consultant or a supervisor. In some instances her position in the matrix structure will permit her to call upon her permanent supervisor to perform certain services needed by the project.

Figure 19-3 portrays relationships of employees in Project Roger, a project in an electronics firm. It shows how ranks, peer relations, and supervisor-subordinate relationships vary between the permanent organization structure and the matrix structure. With regard to rank, employee DD is permanently attached to the fourth

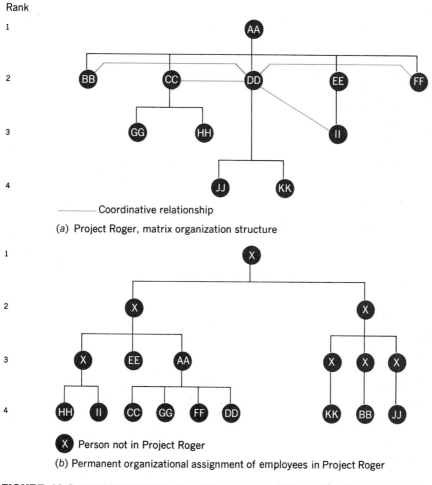

(a) Project Roger, matrix organization structure

(b) Permanent organizational assignment of employees in Project Roger

FIGURE 19-3 ■■■■■■■■■■■■■■■■■■■■■■■■

A comparison of the matrix structure and the permanent organizational assignment for employees in Project Roger.

level, but she has a key second-level rank in the matrix structure. With regard to peer relations, GG and HH work in separate departments in the permanent organization, but they work together in the matrix organization. Concerning supervisor-subordinate relationships, GG works for AA in the regular structure, but in the matrix structure he works for CC, who is his peer in the regular structure. In essence, matrix structure overlays one or more project structures simultaneously on the permanent organization.

Matrix structure is as confusing to operate as it is to describe. It requires multiple roles for people, and sometimes they get frustrated and insecure in these ambiguous roles. It dilutes authority and increases requirements for coordination and control. There is conflict, but it is "purposeful conflict" in the sense that it seeks to accomplish a significant task more effectively than the traditional functional organization can. In this kind of situation the participants depend heavily on problem-solving meetings to resolve issues as they arise.[12]

In order to overcome the confusion that arises from complexity and multiple roles, all persons involved with matrix organization need to understand the roles of project employees and the project manager. Understanding can be improved through both training and experience. A study of role perceptions in two electronics firms that had used matrix organization for several years showed that perceptions of the project manager's role were consistent within management ranks. There was general agreement about seven dimensions of the role as seen by higher managers in the permanent structure, the project manager personally, and lower managers in the matrix structure.[13]

Of all the people in the matrix structure, the project manager particularly needs to have role adaptability to interact with persons both within and without the structure. Project managers essentially occupy *boundary roles* that require an ability to interact with a variety of different groups in order to maintain their project as an ongoing operation. Each group has its own special language, values, and style of relationships, so project managers need to be sensitive and flexible in order to secure project needs from other occupational and organizational groups. Project managers often have relatively weak hierarchical authority in relation to the traditional hierarchy, so their mission is best accomplished by communication, developing challenging assignments, negotiation, and contributing through their own expertise.

One study covered project managers in electronic manufacturing. Their operating style was studied and then compared with their performance ratings. Those who used styles that emphasized challenging work and who contributed their expertise in a helpful way had high performance ratings. Those who used traditional authority to accomplish their project had low performance ratings. In addition, employees working under the authority style felt less project involvement.[14]

BENEFITS OF MATRIX ORGANIZATION. In spite of its complexity, matrix organization is widely used for a number of reasons. It effectively focuses resources on a single project, permitting better planning and control to meet deadlines. It is more open and flexible than a traditional functional hierarchy, thereby better absorbing the inevitable changes that occur as work progresses on advanced scientific projects. Its distribution of authority and status is more in agreement with democratic norms of S & P employees. For example, more emphasis is given to authority of knowledge that a specialist can contribute to a project, and less emphasis is given to rank in the permanent hierarchy. This kind of environment also allows frequent testing of the technical and managerial capabilities of promising S & P employees. It widens their scope of initiative when they are ready and able to contribute, thereby helping a specialized employee become more a generalist.

Provided it is working satisfactorily, matrix organization improves motivation because people can focus more directly on completion of one project than they can in the traditional functional organization. It also improves communication by encouraging direct contact and reducing the inhibitions that result from formal rank.

Summarizing the application of matrix structure, it focuses on adaptive short-run systems operated by relative strangers who contribute diverse organizational skills. The group is organized around a problem to be solved. Its manager is more a coordinator and boundary mediator between occupational groups, and less an absolute authority. The manager is familiar with the diverse language of different groups and has ability to relay information among groups. People are differentiated less vertically according to rank and more flexibly according to current contribution. Although matrix organization has limited application, where it does apply it is psychologically more advanced than traditional work hierarchies. Its use is contingent upon conditions such as the following:

• Special projects, particularly major ones

• Need for diverse occupational skills, particularly higher-level ones

• Conditions of change during project operation

• Complex issues of coordination, problem solving, and scheduling

• High needs for authority of knowledge and expertise, compared with existing functional authority

VENTURE TEAMS. Some organizations use *venture teams,* in which employees are organizationally separated to develop and test a new product or service. In this manner team members can have a feeling of independence and risk of failure associated with having one's own company. Employees who propose a new venture in some businesses are allowed to take an equity position in it in order to share in potential profits.

The New Ventures Program of an electronics firm encourages employees to develop detailed new venture proposals. If the proposal seems feasible, the firm finances extensive pilot tests. If the proposal passes final tests, a subsidiary is established, and the person or group that made the proposal is expected to make an equity investment in it of up to 10 percent. The subsidiary is operated by the parent firm using its depth of managerial, marketing, and financial resources, something that normally would not be available to employees as individual entrepreneurs. The investing employees retain their jobs during the venture, so their jobs are not risked by the venture.

After a certain period the firm buys back the equity investment, paying in proportion to retained earnings after taxes. For example, a 10 percent investment of $25,000 in a venture subsidiary with $250,000 capitalization would return $1 million if accumulated earnings were $10 million when the time came for the subsidiary to buy back the equity interest.

OTHER ADAPTATIONS FOR S & P EMPLOYEES.   Some organizations are experimenting with relatively unstructured S & P groups that are given only general objectives and allowed to develop their own structure and methods to accomplish those objectives. This approach is an adaptation of management by objectives.

Organizations also develop special programs to give status and recognition to S & P employees.

One firm has established an exclusive scientific and technical society open only to employees who have secured a patent for the company. The society holds an annual awards dinner at which time new members for the year are recognized and admitted. All persons are guests of the company, and the program is attended by both employee and spouse so that the spouse can share in the recognition. The program is chaired by an executive member of the board of directors and attended by other executives. In addition, all patent grantees have their names displayed in "Pride Hall," which is a hallway in the main building.

There is some evidence that S & P employees perform best when they are relatively free of organizational uncertainty, because they often are made uneasy by the complexity of organizational systems. Managers concerned about this problem are endeavoring to filter out organizational instabilities, enabling S & P employees to work in a less disruptive environment.[15]

Other adaptations being made for S & P employees are provision of technical libraries, support of professional seminars often including distinguished consultants as leaders, sponsoring membership in professional organizations, paying travel to professional meetings, and support of research peripheral to the job but leading to professional recognition and a professional paper. The general philosophy is to support S & P employees in their professional growth in the belief that in the long run the organization and the community will benefit.

SUMMARY

S & P employees perform work that is intellectual in nature and requires educational preparation for proficiency. They tend to be self-disciplined and achievement-oriented. They prefer considerable autonomy and are more productive when that autonomy is coupled with supportive contact with others. They tend to be cosmopolitans more than locals, and they are more productive when their interests and activities are diversified. Promotional opportunities for those who do not wish to move into management are provided by dual promotion ladders.

S & P norms and life-styles encourage organizational pluralism. Adaptations made to better integrate S & P employees are matrix organization, venture teams, unstructured groups, recognition, better protection from organizational uncertainty, and a more professional environment.

TERMS AND CONCEPTS FOR REVIEW

S & P employees

Cosmopolitans

Locals

Dual promotion ladder

Collegial model of organizational behavior

Organizational pluralism

Matrix organization

Boundary roles

Venture teams

REVIEW QUESTIONS

1. Explain the different characteristics of S & P employees that tend to set them apart from most other employees.
2. Discuss differences between cosmopolitans and locals.
3. Compare the collegial model of organizational behavior with the three models mentioned in earlier chapters.
4. Discuss the operation of pluralism in an organization.
5. Discuss matrix organization, its benefits and disadvantages, and how its use is contingent on certain conditions.

CASE

THE MOUNTAINSIDE COMPANY
The Mountainside Company, a large chemical firm, has its research and development laboratories in its home office in a large metropolitan center. The company has chemical plants throughout the United States and in several foreign nations. In general, the company has tried to assure that everyone gets the same treatment in the home office. Research and development employees have the same salary scale and receive the same benefits as other salaried personnel in the home office. They are also rated and promoted in the same way. They eat in the same cafeteria as other personnel, and they must sign out if they leave the building. Commuting time for most employees is about one hour and fifteen minutes each way, although employees who choose to live in new suburbs need to commute as much as one hour and forty-five minutes each way.

Recently the Mountainside Company has made a study of conditions among its 740 employees in its research and development laboratories. It learned that turnover of these employees is about 25 percent annually, compared with a desired maximum turnover of less than 10 percent. In addition, a job satisfaction survey reports low morale for the group.

QUESTION

1. Propose a program to improve morale and reduce turnover for the research and development laboratories of the Mountainside Company.

REFERENCES

1. For research evidence that job frustration reduces creative performance see Bernard L. Hinton, "Environmental Frustration and Creative Problem Solving," *Journal of Applied Psychology,* June 1968, pp. 211–217.

2. Mark Abrahamson, "The Integration of Industrial Scientists," *Administrative Science Quarterly,* September 1964, pp. 208–218.

3. Geert H. Hofstede, "The Color of Collars," *Columbia Journal of World Business,* September–October 1972, pp. 72–80.

4. Sherman Tingey and Gordon C. Inskeep, "Professional Turnover," *Chemtech,* November 1974, pp. 651–655. For a confirming study see Arthur Gerstenfeld and Gabriel Rosica, "Why Engineers Transfer," *Business Horizons,* April 1970, pp. 43–48.

5. Howard M. Vollmer, *Work Activities and Attitudes of Scientists and Research Managers: Data from a National Survey,* Menlo Park, Calif.: Stanford Research Institute, 1965, p. 84, covering 3,691 scientists.

6. Donald C. Pelz, "Conditions for Innovation," *Trans-action,* January–February, 1965, pp. 32–34, summarizing several studies at the Survey Research Center, University of Michigan; and Frank M. Andrews, "Scientific Performance as Related to Time Spent on Technical Work, Teaching, or Administration," *Administrative Science Quarterly,* September 1964, pp. 182–193.

7. John R. Hinrichs, "Communications Activity of Industrial Research Personnel," *Personnel Psychology,* Summer 1964, p. 199.

8. Theodore J. Carron, "Training the Professional-Technical Employee," *Journal of the American Society of Training Directors,* October 1962, pp. 8–9.

9. Douglas T. Hall and Edward E. Lawler III, "Job Characteristics and Pressures and the Organizational Integration of Professionals," *Administrative Science Quarterly,* September 1970, pp. 271–281.

10. Jerry L. Holman, "An Analysis of Employee Motivation," *AIIE Transactions, Industrial Engineering Research and Development,* June 1969, pp. 172–180.

11. Frank Harrison, "The Management of Scientists: Determinants of Perceived Role Performance," *Academy of Management Journal,* June 1974, pp. 234–241.

12. For further discussion of these issues and others in matrix organization see Andre Delbecq and Alan Filley, *Program and Project Management in a Matrix Organization: A Case Study,* Monograph No. 9, Madison, Wis.: Bureau of Business Research and Service, University of Wisconsin, 1974; and Clayton Reeser, "Some Potential Human Problems of the Project Form of Organization," *Academy of Management Journal,* December 1969, pp. 459–467.

13.   Keith Davis, "Mutuality in Understanding of the Program Manager's Management Role," *IEEE Transactions on Engineering Management,* December 1965, pp. 117–122, covering 144 managers.

14.   Hans J. Thamhain and Gary R. Gemmill, "Influence Styles of Project Managers: Some Project Performance Correlates," *Academy of Management Journal,* June 1974, pp. 216–224.

15.   Todd R. LaPorte, "Conditions of Strain and Accommodation in Industrial Research Organizations," *Administrative Science Quarterly,* June 1965, pp. 21–38.

CHAPTER 20
MANAGING EMPLOYEES
IN MULTINATIONAL
OPERATIONS

Any time you have industry come in anywhere it brings change.
Plant Manager in a Less Developed Area

LEARNING OBJECTIVES

TO UNDERSTAND:
How different cultures affect organizational behavior practices
The operation of ethnocentrism and cultural shock
Different behavioral environments in developed and developing nations
Different attitudes toward productivity
Integrating different cultures in multinational operations

Many organizations operate in more than one country, and these multinational operations add new dimensions to organizational behavior. Expansion beyond national boundaries is much more than a step across a geographical line. It is also a step into different social, political, and economic environments. Communication lines are lengthened, and control becomes more difficult. It is hard enough to operate an organization in one language and one culture, but when two, three, four, five—or twenty—languages and cultures are involved, difficulties are compounded. Complex organizations of this type push administrative skills to their limits. The best of intellectual capacities and goodwill are called upon in order to make these organizations workable. It proves easier to handle the technical factors of building a new plant than to handle the social factors of operating it thereafter. The following case illustrates the complexities that arise as different cultures are mixed in multinational operations. I learned about it from the consultant in the incident while we were both working on assignments in the nation involved.

In a South American nation a consultant from the United States was called to study why the West German machinery in a cellophane plant owned by South Americans was not operating properly. (This single preliminary sentence reveals that already three different cultures were involved in the incident.) When the consultant arrived, he studied the situation for several weeks. His conclusion was that there was nothing at all wrong with the machinery. It was of excellent quality and in perfect adjustment. The raw materials and other supporting factors were entirely satisfactory.
The real problem, in the consultant's opinion, was the supervisors who had a father image of the patriarchal mill manager and were unable to make operating

decisions without his approval. They deferred to him as their elder and superior. When something in the mill went wrong, they waited indefinitely for his decision before correcting the problem. Since he had other business interests and was frequently out of the mill for part of the day, or even for two or three days, they permitted the continuous-production machinery to produce scrap cellophane for hours or even days because of some minor maladjustment which they could have corrected. The mill manager tried to delegate decision making on these control matters to his supervisors, but neither he nor they were able to overcome this custom of deference to authority which existed in their culture. As the consultant finally summarized the situation, "The problem is the people, not the machines."

The cellophane machinery was built to operate in an advanced industrial culture, but in this instance it was required to operate in a less developed culture. Neither the machinery nor the supervisors could be quickly changed to meet this new situation. Reengineering of machinery would be costly and time-consuming, and, in this case, might reduce the machinery's productivity. Training of supervisors to change their culture, even if this were possible, would likewise be time-consuming. The solution offered by the consultant was an effective compromise. He advised the manager to appoint one person as "acting director" during his absence, give the acting director an imposing office, and work to build the acting director's image of authority with the supervisors. Then there would always be someone at the plant to make decisions quickly.

Discussion in this chapter will focus on conditions that develop when an advanced organization moves into a less developed culture. It is recognized that this situation presents extreme contrasts, but it is the predominant situation in modern times because much of the world is underdeveloped. In more advanced nations where cultural contrasts may be smaller, the issues raised in this chapter will be lesser in degree, but they continue to exist. Discussion is limited to issues affecting work behavior, leaving other aspects of multinational operations to other books. In this chapter we examine the nature of multinational operations, ways for an organization to integrate social systems, and ways to improve motivation in less developed cultures.

THE NATURE OF MULTINATIONAL OPERATIONS

The people of the world are organized into communities and nations, each in its own way according to its resources and cultural heritage. There are similarities among nations, but there are also significant differences. Some nations have a customer-oriented economy, while others have a centrally planned economy, and there are various shades of practice in between. Some are economically developed, but others are just now developing. Some are political dictatorships; others are more democratic. Some are socially advanced, while others have minimum literacy and social development. And in each case the conditions of work are different because of different expectations from participants. Let us examine certain key social, political, and economic conditions as they influence organizational behavior.

SOCIAL CONDITIONS. The overriding social condition of less developed countries is underdeveloped human resources. There are major shortages of managerial personnel, scientists, and technicians, and these deficiencies limit the ability to employ local labor productively. Needed skills must be temporarily imported, while vast training programs prepare local workers.

A Central American nation, for example, welcomed an electronic assembly plant to its capital city. The plant was labor intensive, so it provided many jobs to reduce the nation's high unemployment rate. Wages were above community standards, working conditions were good, and the plant was environmentally clean. In addition, the valuable and tiny product that was assembled provided needed foreign exchange, because it was shipped by air to assembly plants in other parts of the world.

Perhaps most important of all, the company's agreement with the nation provided that the company would provide a cadre of managers and technicians to train local employees in all phases of operating the plant. Locals would gradually become supervisors, superintendents, technicians, accountants, purchasing specialists, and so on, until at the end of five years the company could have only eight nonlocals in the plant, including the general manager, scientists, and auditing personnel. In this manner the labor force of the nation would be upgraded.

As a matter of fact, the lending of trained people to a nation for training local replacements may be of more lasting benefit to its development than the lending of capital, because of the *training multiplier effect* by which these people develop others. As soon as one group of local workers is trained, these persons become the nucleus for developing others in an ever-widening arc of self-development. Social and economic improvement are almost impossible unless human resources are developed concurrently, and the occupational areas whose development will provide the greatest return are scientific, professional, and managerial personnel. International studies show that per capita productivity tends to increase as the proportion of these occupations increases in the labor force.[1]

Another significant social condition is that the local culture is not oriented toward advanced technology or sophisticated organizational life. The background of local employees is usually agrarian, not familiar with machinery and the close tolerances of work that it requires. Achievement motivation often is low, sometimes even among managers.[2] Characteristics such as initiative and acceptance of responsibility are scarce.

Acceptance of responsibility is particularly difficult to develop, and it is often deeply involved with the social tradition of saving face. As explained by one manager, "We've been able to teach our local employees technical skills, but we can't seem to get anyone to accept responsibility." No one wants to take responsibility for making a change, correcting an error, or disciplining an employee. Persons wait indefinitely for someone else to decide, rather than making decisions themselves. The result is that work may slack off unless top managers are regularly checking operations at the worker level and are available to back up lower-level supervisors. Here is an example of how productivity is affected.[3]

A textile mill was installing some new looms in Java. By early afternoon of the first day the first loom was installed. The second loom went faster and was completed by the end of the day. During this period the general manager, his factory manager, and the technical assistant visited the installation several times to show that they were checking on its progress.

Work on the third loom began the next morning. That day the general manager was out of town; the factory manager was busy in conferences all morning and went home after lunch; and the technical assistant did not appear after lunch. When the general manager returned at 4 P.M., the third loom was not yet installed. Called to account, the local supervisor said that he had given orders just as before. In fact, he had tried a little harder; but because there was nobody there to back him up, he could not get the employees to work.

The Western nations over a period of two centuries have adapted their culture to an industrial and organizational way of life, but this is not so in many other nations. Punctuality, regularity, and job discipline may be very difficult for their people. In the Middle East, for example, a petroleum company hired 133 locals over a period of several months. Only four of them remained beyond two weeks. The work was not demanding in knowledge, skill, or physical effort, and the pay was above local rates; but the workers were unable to endure the punctuality, regularity, and discipline of the jobs.[4]

Fortunately, over a period of time workers tend to recognize the benefits of factory work and adjust better to it. Figure 20-1 shows the changing attitudes of factory workers toward their jobs over a period of ten years in a less developed area that was newly industrializing. In the beginning their view of factory work, compared with farming and shopkeeping, was only moderately favorable. After ten years, however, a strong majority favored factory work as the most desirable of the three occupations. There was a major favorable change toward "provides a better family life." One reason was that good pay provided more family necessities than earlier, and another reason was that steady pay gave workers some security that

	PERCENT OF WORKERS FAVORING FACTORY WORK	
FACTORY WORK:	**1958**	**1967**
Provides a better family life	29	58
Provides more security	46	58
Is more useful	46	60
Requires more education	49	72

FIGURE 20-1

Factory workers' perceptions of factory work, compared with farming and shopkeeping, following introduction of a factory into a less developed area newly industrializing. (*Source:* Cynthia A. Cone, "Perceptions of Occupations in a Newly Industrializing Region of Mexico," *Human Organization*, Summer 1973, p. 147.)

their family standard of living might be maintained. In addition, factory work provided shorter hours than farming and shopkeeping, so workers could spend more time participating in family life. They also recognized that factory work gave them more opportunities to improve themselves through education.

POLITICAL CONDITIONS. Political conditions that have a significant effect on organizational behavior are general political instability, nationalistic drives, and subordination of employers and labor to an authoritarian state. Instability spills over into organizations in the country, making them cautious and unstable. It leaves workers insecure and causes them to be acquiescent and low in initiative. They bring to the job an attitude of "What will be, will be; so why try to do anything about it."

In spite of instability, nationalistic drives are strong for locals to run their country by themselves without interference by foreign nationals. A foreign manager often is not welcome.

In Burma, for example, a visiting professor presented a case problem where there was conflict between a British shipmaster and a Burmese crew. Expecting a human relations discussion, the professor was surprised when his class focused on how to train Burmese to take over from the British master so that they would not have to deal with him.

Organized labor in many nations is not an independent force, but is mostly an arm of the authoritarian state. In other nations labor is somewhat independent, but it is socialistic, class-conscious, and oriented toward political action more than direct negotiation with employers. Employers find that the state tends to be involved in collective bargaining and many other practices affecting workers. In some nations, for example, employee layoffs are restricted by law and made costly by means of required dismissal pay. Even employee transfers may be restricted. Following is an incident that illustrates how different employment practices among nations may cause employee-employer frictions for multinational companies. In this instance, both nations were economically developed.

Air France, a major international airline, provides service to Japan. It employs a number of Japanese flight attendants who are stationed in Tokyo and serve flights to and from that city. In order to provide further international training and integration of its flight attendants, it transferred thirty Japanese stewardesses to Paris. The stewardesses refused to go, so the company threatened dismissal for refusal to transfer. The stewardesses sought relief through the courts, and the Tokyo High Court upheld a lower court injunction preventing Air France from dismissing the stewardesses. They could retain their Air France jobs in Tokyo, because transfer to Paris would: "(1) restrict their civil rights as Japanese citizens, (2) cause them the anxiety of living in a place where the language and customs are different, and (3) affect their marital situation."[5]

Several European nations have laws requiring *codetermination*, which provides for worker representation on the board of directors and sometimes other boards of major companies. The idea is to advance worker participation in higher management levels, giving them some voice in major policy and operating decisions. By expanding workers' control over their jobs, often called *industrial democracy,* the nations hope to increase labor understanding of higher managerial problems and reduce labor unrest. While codetermination may reduce unrest and improve labor responsibility, it also places additional restrictions on multinational operations. A local, job-protecting attitude of labor representatives particularly may interfere with broader strategic decisions involving plants in a number of nations.

ECONOMIC CONDITIONS. The most significant economic conditions in less developed nations are low per capita income and inflation. Many nations of the world exist in genuine poverty compared with the United States. A number of nations have per capita incomes under $600 annually. With their population also increasing, they are fortunate if they can increase their real per capita income 1 percent in a year. Assuming an annual income of $600, a 1 percent increase is $6, or slightly more than $30 in five years, which is not much motivation for an individual citizen.

A common economic condition in many underdeveloped countries is inflation. The United States has had moderate inflation reducing the value of its dollar substantially since 1940, but in other parts of the world their currency has been cut to one-hundredth or even one-thousandth of its value since 1940, as reflected by cost-of-living indexes. What used to cost one unit of currency now costs one thousand or more. In terms of dollar currency, a 10-cent ice cream cone now costs 10,000 cents, or $100!

Inflation makes the economic life of workers insecure. They must spend quickly lest their money lose its value. Savings payable in fixed currency units become meaningless because they lose their value; hence, workers often do not plan for their own security as in the United States. They develop more dependence and more anxiety, and they become more volatile with social unrest.

Looking at social, political, and economic conditions as a whole, we see that these conditions impede advanced technology and sophisticated organizational systems. They are deficient in the stability, security, and trained human resources that advanced organizations require to be productive. A new plant in a less developed country cannot expect to produce as efficiently as it would in a developed nation, because environmental conditions for the plant do not support high productivity. The unfortunate fact is that these traditional environmental conditions cannot be changed rapidly, because they are too well established and woven into the whole social fabric of a nation. High productivity is not achieved by such simple answers as a new plant or more capital. As explained by Peter Drucker, "A society is poor not because it has a problem, not because it has hookworm, but because it cannot organize its resources to do anything."[6]

INTEGRATING SOCIAL SYSTEMS

Multinational operations require a blending of various cultures and new adjustments by all persons involved. Managers and technicians who enter a developing nation to install an advanced organizational system will need to adjust their leadership styles, communication patterns, and other practices to fit their host country. In some instances these new employees are *parent-country nationals* from the nation where the home office is located, or they may be *third-country nationals* from some other nation. In either case their role is to provide a fusion of cultures in which both parties adjust to the new situation of seeking greater productivity for the benefit of both the organization and the citizens of the country in which it operates.

ADAPTATIONS TO A HOST COUNTRY. The dominant feature of all international operations is that they are conducted in a social system different from the one from which the organization came. This social system affects responses of all persons involved. Managers and technicians who come into a host country in order to get a new branch established naturally tend to judge conditions in a new country according to standards of their homeland. They are predisposed to think that their homeland conditions are best. This predisposition is known as a self-reference criterion, or *ethnocentrism.* Though this way of perceiving conditions is very human, it will interfere with understanding and productivity. In order to integrate the imported and local social systems, expatriate employees need cultural understanding of local conditions. Having this understanding, they must then be adaptable enough to integrate the community of interest of the two or more cultures involved.[7]

In spite of the evident need for expatriate employees to understand local culture and to be adaptable, they often arrive unprepared at their new posts. Their selection is typically based upon their performance in the home country, with little regard for the fact that they will be doing business with people whose traditional beliefs are different from their own. They may not know the local language and may have little interest in becoming a part of the community. Frequently they are not given cultural training before departure.[8] As one company stated the situation, "Our main concern is that they can do the technical job we send them to do"; however, cultural understanding is essential to avoid errors and misunderstandings that can be costly to an organization.

Many organizations try to hasten adjustment to a host nation by encouraging employees to learn the local language. They offer language training, and some even give pay differentials to expatriate employees who know the local language. The added language facility seems to be well worth its cost, because those who possess it can speak with local employees in their native tongue, thereby avoiding the social distance and misunderstanding that arise when communications have to be translated. However, language training is not a substitute for cultural training. Both are needed. Even when two parties speak the same language, if a communication is expressed in one cultural context and then interpreted in another, misunderstanding can occur.

Employees may experience additional need deficiencies when they transfer outside their home nation. This means that their need satisfactions are not as great as those of comparable employees who remain at home. Although a move to another nation may be an exciting opportunity, there are also difficulties, inconveniences, insecurities, and separation from relatives and friends. Thus, employees who are given assignments in other nations are often given extra pay and fringe benefits to compensate for need deficiencies that they may endure.

359

One study covered need deficiencies of United States managers in Europe.[9] *Looking first at need deficiencies of top-level executives (presidents and vice presidents), the study found that deficiencies for security, social, esteem, autonomy, and self-actualization needs were significantly greater (which means lower satisfaction) for the executives in Europe. In the following instances the deficiencies were significant to the .01 degree or more: opportunity for friendships, prestige outside company, and opportunity for independent thought and action. In addition, middle managers in Europe showed very low security need satisfactions, but their self-actualization need satisfactions were comparatively favorable.*

CULTURAL SHOCK. Entering another nation with or without training, employees and their families tend to suffer some *cultural shock* in which they feel insecure and upset by the strangeness of their new environment. There is the feeling of not knowing how to act and of losing face and self-confidence by responding incorrectly to strange stimuli. In severe cases their surroundings appear to be behavioral chaos. They become disoriented and retreat into isolation or return home on the next airplane. But a different culture is not behavioral chaos; it is a systematic structure of behavior patterns, probably as systematic as the culture in the employee's home country. It can be understood if employees have receptive attitudes. But it is different, and these differences are a strain on newcomers regardless of their adaptability.

Cultural shock is virtually universal. It happens even on a move from one advanced nation to another. For example, when Japanese or European employees move to the United States, they suffer cultural shock; and when United States employees move to Japan or Europe, they also suffer cultural shock.

Even more interesting is the fact that employees who are returned to their *home country* after working in another nation for some time tend to suffer cultural shock in their own homeland. This is sometimes called cultural shock in reverse.[10] Having become adjusted to the culture of another nation, they find some difficulty readjusting to the new surroundings of their home country. The situation is made more difficult by the multitude of changes that have occurred since they departed. Furthermore, in their host country they may have enjoyed higher status, better pay, and special privileges such as servants, but back home they are merely one of several employees with similar rank in the home office. Friends who remained at home may have been promoted, leaving returning employees with a feeling of being bypassed and losing opportunities.

TRANSCULTURAL MANAGERS AND TECHNICIANS. It is evident that careful attention should be given to cultural preparation of expatriate employees. Eventually a cadre of employees with cross-cultural adaptability can be developed in organizations with large international operations. These employees are *transcultural employees* because they operate effectively in several cultures. They are low in ethnocentrism and adapt readily to different cultures without major cultural shock. They usually can communicate in more than one language.

Transcultural employees are especially being sought by large, multinational firms that operate in a variety of national cultures. For a firm to be truly multinational in character, it should have ownership, operations, markets, and managers truly diversified without primary dominance of any one of these four items by any one nation. Its leaders look to the world as an economic and social unit; but they recognize each local culture, respect its integrity, acknowledge its benefits, and use its differences effectively in their organization. Note that these firms are not supranational in the sense that they try to operate free of national and cultural ties. Neither do their employees advocate only one standard culture or government. Rather, they relish the flavor that differences bring and, hence, adapt readily to them.

MANAGEMENT'S INTEGRATING ROLE IN A HOST COUNTRY. Once managers are on location in a host country, their attention needs to be directed toward integrating the advanced technological culture with the local culture. Where local practices that interfere with production cannot be changed, they can perhaps be bypassed temporarily or integrated into a modified production plan. If, for example, a one-hour siesta must be accepted, perhaps siesta hours can be staggered so that equipment can be kept operating. The job of international managers is to try to retain in their management practices the essential elements of both old and new cultures so that their employees may work with the security of some old practices, but also with greater productivity than the old culture has normally accomplished. As we have learned from both experience and research, technological change is also social change. The technological part of change usually can be solved by the logics of science, but the social part is dependent on effective leadership.

Managers as well as technicians need to restrain their tendency to set up complex administrative and production systems in the host country to match those in their own country. These systems are often beyond the capabilities of local people, and will be misunderstood and inefficiently operated. A simpler system will operate better.

In one instance a personnel specialist set up a complicated performance rating system having ten items just like the one used in the Chicago home plant. Local supervisors nodded their heads with an understanding "yes" as rating instructions were given, so the personnel specialist thought everything was shipshape. When the first ratings were received, all seven local supervisors rated each employee exactly alike on all ten items.

Investigation disclosed that the supervisors nodded "yes" because they wished not to offend the specialist, who was to them a guest and a superior, but they did not understand what the whole idea was about. Furthermore, they could not culturally accept the idea of judging their neighbors in writing because neither party in this kind of situation could save face.

In another instance a mill manager announced a grievance system and was amazed when workers interpreted grievances as external problems. Workers brought to the mill manager their problems about families, relatives, and finances, perceiving him in the role of a paternalistic autocrat who would care for them and resolve their personal disputes. They gave little thought to complaining about working conditions, because working conditions were above average, so complaints in this situation would be considered poor manners in their culture.

361

THE COMMUNITY ROLE OF EXPATRIATE MANAGERS. Expatriate managers need to consider what their roles will be in a local community. Although they are respected figures with considerable economic power, they are in a country as a guest and will not be readily absorbed into the social and power structures of a local community. Even if they speak the local language and live in a community for years, they still may not be fully accepted into its social structure. A study of North American managers in an Argentine community showed that they were well accepted in their limited roles of manager and guest within the country, but they were marginal to the extent that they were not accepted into the intimate social structure of the community. Surveys of these executives showed that, as a result of their marginal social role, they misinterpreted much of the community value structure. To illustrate, the North American managers ranked the military as the most influential institution in the society, but top local influentials ranked it fifth while ranking religion first. The North Americans ranked religion seventh in the community power structure. The findings further showed that, contrary to the charges of some critics, the North American managers clearly were not manipulating the local power structure. They were largely marginal to it, even though a large proportion of citizens in the community thought that they were key people in the power structure.[11]

Since managers are partly marginal to the intimate community social structure, they must be cautious not to overstep local customs by getting too familiar. The Spanish language and other languages, for example, have familiar pronouns and verb conjugations that are used only among close friends. One manager related the following experience on this subject.

> I was assigned to a country whose people spoke the Spanish language. I had been there two years, and since I speak the language fluently, I felt that I was working very well with the community. On one occasion I was particularly pleased when our top local manager asked me to his home to meet his grandmother, who was the family matriarch and revered by all of the family. When I was introduced to her in rather formal circumstances, without thinking I spoke to her in the familiar form of the verb. Immediately the room turned to ice, and my interview was hastily terminated. I still didn't know what had happened, but on my way home I asked our local manager, and he emotionally told me that this kind of familiarity is not accepted in his culture. It took me weeks to make the proper apologies through necessary intermediaries, and I felt I never did recover socially from this setback.

Though these kinds of cultural errors may seem minor to an outsider, they are not minor to a local citizen. Expatriate managers must not establish the image that they are callous to local culture or desire to overthrow it. They succeed by maintaining a balance of local culture and an advanced organizational system. If local culture is ignored, the resulting imbalance in the social system interferes with productivity. Likewise, if the organization acquiesces wholly to the culture of the less developed country, the resulting imbalance in the technological system will cause loss of efficiency. Both local culture and advanced technology must be integrated.

MOTIVATING EMPLOYEES IN A HOST COUNTRY

When motivating employees in less developed nations it is especially difficult to communicate the real meaning of productivity. The concept of productivity is not well understood in many cultures of the world. Many persons perceive productivity as simply more output, without any thought of input costs, but genuine productivity is an input-output relationship in which less inputs are needed to produce certain outputs. Therefore, *the lower the productivity, the greater the waste of a society's limited resources.* With limited worldwide resources, waste in any form usually is undesirable.

Communication among people of different cultures is difficult enough; but when one steps up to the level of abstraction involved in the idea of productivity, effective communication is additionally difficult. The image that an expatriate message sender transmits is not likely to be that which local receivers interpret, because they will see the image from their cultural point of view. Communication is made even more difficult by the fact that an expatriate manager's communication with workers is usually secondhand through local supervisors who may attach their own interpretations to what is being transmitted.

CULTURAL RESTRICTIONS ON PRODUCTIVITY. Even when employees accept the idea of productivity, it may not be sufficiently ingrained into their habits to be reflected in their day-to-day work. The following incident, which I observed in South America, shows how productivity is overlooked.

Seven men were unloading ½-inch steel rods from a flat-bed truck at a construction site. In normal circumstances, this job could have been accomplished in an hour or so, but in this case it took more than one day. On the truck bed, there were four men. Three men lifted the rods one by one and threw them to the ground. A fourth man on the bed counted the rods. On the ground, two men picked up the rods and moved them about five feet to a stack. A third man in a coat supervised the entire operation.

Of particular interest was the fact that one man on the truck bed always picked up a rod on its wrong side. Two men were on one side of the rod, and he was on the other; therefore, when they stepped to the edge of the truck bed to throw off the rod, his head always was in the way! At that point, he had to let go of the rod, stoop under it, and grasp it on the other side before it could be thrown off the truck. The supervisor watched this operation all day without offering any suggestion for improvement in productivity. Furthermore, the truck could have been driven adjacent to the stack so that the rods could be thrown onto the stack or skidded onto it. However, this was not done. It appears in this case that the supervisor as well as his men did not have an abiding interest in productivity; consequently, they were unable to discover means to improve their productivity as they worked.

The idea of productivity includes quality of output as well as quantity. Developing nations too often emphasize amount of output regardless of quality in order to make their record look favorable. The importance of quality was made evident to me when I visited a developing country's modern rayon plant. I noticed that each sheet of cellulose (the main raw material) was made in Canada, 9,000 miles away. I asked why local cellulose was not used, because I knew that this country had several cellulose plants and vast forest reserves. The reply was, "We haven't yet been able to get our workers to make cellulose of good enough quality to be used in this modern plant."

Sometimes employees understand productivity but choose not to give it priority over other cultural values that are inconsistent with it. An office in India had five secretary-typists who spent a great amount of time visiting, arriving late, leaving early, drinking tea, and otherwise wasting time. When a friend from the United States asked one of them why they wasted their time, the local citizen replied that if they put in a full day's work two persons could perform the job, leaving three persons out of a job. To him that answer was complete and rational.

Even government may support inefficient labor policies. The makers of Daisy air rifles worked with the State of Punjab, India, to build an air rifle plant 51 percent owned by the State of Punjab. Daisy officials were instructed to think in terms of an abundance of people when planning the plant. In one instance Daisy officials proposed forklift trucks for hauling, but the Indians told them to use people instead.[12]

UNDERSTANDING OF PRODUCTIVITY AMONG LOCAL MANAGERS. Even local managers often do not understand the idea of productivity; and if they are not fully capable with it, how can they communicate it to their supervisors and workers? One study of local managers in ten Latin-American countries reported that "only a minority of the managers interviewed had a reasonably clear concept of productivity."[13] The majority thought in terms of production (a net increase in output regardless of inputs), rather than in terms of productivity (an input-output measure of efficiency). My own experiences internationally confirm that many managers and workers in developing nations fail to see the full meaning of productivity, while in more advanced areas, such as much of Europe, the United States, and Japan, the idea is both understood and actively pursued. Although productivity attitudes are high among managers in the United States, one study reports that they are even higher in Japan.[14]

The gap in understanding productivity is made even worse by the fact that local managers often ignore rational methods of solving problems and making decisions.[15] They tend to treat management as a personal art, solving problems subjectively and impulsively without adequate attention to whether their decision will increase or decrease productivity. When decision habits are so firmly ingrained, it is difficult to change them regardless of the quality of communication and training programs. Further, these same managers seldom follow up their decisions with objective measures to try to determine whether productivity was in fact increased.

Productivity is the central idea that the people of a country need to absorb in order to develop the spirit to rise above poverty, inefficiency, and wasteful use of their resources. Without a devotion to productivity, new capital inputs are dissipated. Without a belief in productivity, more education merely increases the demand for wasteful personal aides, attendants, and helpers. Without productivity, achievement motivation merely increases competition for resources that are not growing. Since national resources are not expanding, whatever one gains is at the expense of others.

ADAPTATIONS REQUIRED OF EXPATRIATE MANAGERS. Expatriate managers who wish to motivate local employees in a host nation, rather than merely ordering them around, need to make some changes in themselves. Their success will depend on upgrading their knowledge of local needs, ways of thinking, and cultural idiosyncrasies. This strange environment actually requires managers to have greater understanding of local social systems than they would need in their own nation to accomplish equal results. They need to be alert, sensitive, and understanding so that they can react to local culture effectively.

Managers often need to make adjustments in their personal manners in dealing with people. In the United States it is the custom for people in face-to-face conversation to maintain some physical distance between them, perhaps a foot or two feet. In some cultures, however, it is the custom for people who talk face-to-face to do so quite closely, at perhaps six inches' distance. A manager from the United States may be uncomfortable in a conversation of this type. I observed one manager overseas who, by the end of a short conversation, had backed halfway across the room trying to increase the distance between himself and an employee who, of course, kept following him in order to keep the cultural distance of six to nine inches with which he was familiar. Under these conditions it is difficult to motivate employees because a manager appears uncomfortable in their presence.

LESS-ADVANCED NEED STRUCTURES OF LOCAL EMPLOYEES. Many workers in less developed nations are correspondingly less advanced in their need structures.[16] They are still seeking basic physiological and security needs; therefore, some of the sophisticated and elaborate motivational devices of modern management may not be appropriate in these countries. The needs of workers may be more simply reached by direct motivation. In some instances they have worked in economic systems that had little direct connection between how effectively they worked and how well their needs were satisfied. Therefore, they require management to show them simple, direct evidence that if they work more effectively, they will receive more. In other words, work must be interpreted in terms of their immediate needs, rather than waiting for indirect results through a complex economic or social system. Accordingly, actions that would be inappropriate in an advanced nation may be desirable in a developing nation.

Studies show, for example, that authoritarian management styles are not necessarily dysfunctional in many situations in developing nations. Employees may have strong security needs that are met by authoritarian, paternalistic leadership, and they may have role expectations for it, so it may be the correct approach in these conditions.[17] Essentially the correct management and organizational behavior practices are contingent upon local conditions in the host nation.

SUMMARY

The basic point of this chapter is that organizational practices of one country cannot be transferred directly to another, especially if the host country is less developed. Practices need to be adapted to the particular culture, level of development, and employee need structure that a host country has. In effect, neither the advanced nation's nor the host nation's traditional practices are used. Instead, a third set of practices contingent upon situational needs is developed that integrates the most workable ideas from both sets of traditional practices.

A less developed nation's social, political, and economic conditions are similarly less developed. There are various combinations of underdeveloped human resources, low organizational sophistication, instability, nationalistic government, inflation, low per capita income, misunderstanding of productivity, and less advanced need structures. Employees entering this kind of situation from another country need to be transcultural employees, low in ethnocentrism, in order to avoid cultural shock.

TERMS AND CONCEPTS FOR REVIEW

Training multiplier effect	Transcultural employees
Codetermination	Productivity
Ethnocentrism	Less advanced need structures
Cultural shock	

REVIEW QUESTIONS

1. Discuss key social, political, and economic conditions that influence organizational behavior in developing nations.
2. Discuss how cultural shock may affect the performance of employees as they transfer from one nation to another.
3. Discuss how managers may play an integrating role between the cultures of two nations, especially a developed one and a less developed host nation.
4. Discuss cultural restrictions on productivity, particularly as they apply to developing nations.
5. What is meant by the statement that "employees are likely to have less advanced need structures in less developed nations"?

CASE

THE PIEDMONT COMPANY
The Piedmont Company is a major multinational manufacturer with plants in several nations in Europe. Its home office is in the United States. The company recently completed a survey of its European and United States middle managers to determine their need deficiencies in their jobs. The result of their survey is reported in the following table:

AVERAGE NEED DEFICIENCY SCORES OF MIDDLE-LEVEL AMERICAN MANAGERS[1]
Europe versus United States

NEED CATEGORIES AND ITEMS	MANAGERS IN EUROPE (1968) N = 48	MANAGERS IN U.S. (1969) N = 201	LEVEL OF SIGNIFICANCE[1]
I. Security needs			
a. Security in job	1.06	.23	.01
II. Social needs			
a. Opportunity to help people	.96	.31	.01
b. Opportunity for friendships	.64	.29	.02
III. Esteem needs			
a. Feeling of self-esteem	.90	.70	.02
b. Prestige inside company	.63	.63	ns
c. Prestige outside company	.47	.44	ns
IV. Autonomy needs			
a. Opportunity for independent thought and action	.88	.59	.01
b. Authority in position	.92	.90	ns
c. Opportunity to participate in goal setting	.52	.88	.01
V. Self-actualization needs			
a. Opportunity for growth and development	.69	.92	.05
b. Feeling of self-fulfillment	.83	1.02	.05
c. Feeling of accomplishment	.92	1.13	.05

Note: The larger the average mean values, the less the perceived need satisfaction.

[1] Significant differences were determined by two-tailed *t*-test. (*Source:* John M. Ivancevich and James C. Baker, "A Comparative Study of the Satisfaction of Domestic United States Managers and Overseas United States Managers," *Academy of Management Journal,* March 1970, p. 74. Copyright 1970. Used with permission.)

QUESTIONS
1. Analyze the data and give your interpretation of the kinds of problems that exist.
2. Prepare a plan for innovations in home office policy that will improve the need satisfactions of European middle managers in their most deficient areas.

REFERENCES

1. P. R. G. Layard and J. C. Saigal, "Educational and Occupational Characteristics of Manpower: An International Comparison," *British Journal of Industrial Relations,* July 1966, pp. 222–266, especially fig. 1, reporting studies of census data in twenty nations.

2. Thomas W. Harrell, "Some Needs of Iran Managers," *Personnel Psychology,* Autumn 1971, pp. 477–479.

3.   Ann Ruth Willner, "Problems of Management and Authority in a Transitional Society: A Case Study of a Javanese Factory," *Human Organization,* Summer 1963, pp. 137–138.

4.   Howard D. Lowe, "Doing Business in the Developing Countries," *Business Horizons,* Fall 1965, p. 30.

5.   "Court Invalidates Airline's Policy for Transfers to Foreign Cities," *Japan Labor Bulletin,* Nov. 1, 1974, p. 7.

6.   Peter F. Drucker, "What Have We Learned about Economic and Social Development?" *Proceedings, Annual Conference on International Management,* New York: Council for International Progress in Management, 1966, p. 6.

7.   For a study of differences and similarities in employee wants in twenty-five nations, see David Sirota and J. Michael Greenwood, "Understand Your Overseas Work Force," *Harvard Business Review,* January–February 1971, pp. 53–60.

8.   James C. Baker and John M. Ivancevich, "The Assignment of American Executives Abroad: Systematic, Haphazard or Chaotic?" *California Management Review,* Spring 1971, pp. 39–44.

9.   John M. Ivancevich and James C. Baker, "A Comparative Study of the Satisfaction of Domestic United States Managers and Overseas United States Managers," *Academy of Management Journal,* March 1970, pp. 69–77.

10.   J. Alex Murray, "International Personnel Repatriation: Cultural Shock in Reverse," *MSU Business Topics,* Summer 1973, pp. 59–66.

11.   Delbert C. Miller, assisted by Eva Chamorro and Juan Carlos Agulla, "Community Power Perspectives and Role Definitions of North American Executives in an Argentine Community," *Administrative Science Quarterly,* December 1965, pp. 364–380.

12.   "Not Just Kid Stuff," *Business Week,* Jan. 25, 1964, p. 90.

13.   Albert Lauterbach, "Executive Training and Productivity: Managerial Views in Latin America," *Industrial and Labor Relations Review,* April 1964, p. 366.

14.   George W. England and Raymond Lee, "Organizational Goals and Expected Behavior among American, Japanese, and Korean Managers: A Comparative Study," *Academy of Management Journal,* December 1971, pp. 425–438.

15.   Anant R. Negandhi, "Comparative Management and Organization Theory: A Marriage Needed," *Academy of Management Journal,* June 1975, pp. 334–344.

16.   For example, see a study of workers in similar plants of the same firm in the United States and Mexico: John W. Slocum, Jr., Paul M. Topichak, and David G. Kuhn, "A Cross-cultural Study of Need Satisfaction and Need Importance for Operative Employees," *Personnel Psychology,* Autumn 1971, pp. 435–445.

17.   Negandhi, *loc. cit.*

SECTION 5

COMMUNICATION AND GROUP PROCESSES

CHAPTER 21
COMMUNICATING WITH EMPLOYEES

> . . . One of my fundamental assumptions is that the most important resource
> an organization has is valid information. . . .
>
> Chris Argyris[1]

LEARNING OBJECTIVES ▰▰▰▰▰▰▰▰▰▰▰▰▰▰▰▰▰▰▰

TO UNDERSTAND:
The communication process
The importance and effects of communication
Barriers to communication
The significance of nonverbal communication
Applications of readability
The role of listening in communication

A Hollywood movie company was filming a movie near a small Western town. The script involved some narrow-gauge-railway scenes; and a local resident, regularly a railroad engineer, had been selected as engineer of the narrow-gauge train. He was very proud of his assignment. One evening when both the Hollywood visitors and the engineer were in a local bar, the engineer walked over to the director of the movie company and asked, "John, how did I do with those train scenes today?"

The director, in a good mood, gave his most favorable Hollywood response, "Joe, you are doing one hell of a job."

Joe, not understanding the favorable meaning of this colloquialism, took it as a criticism and was immediately ruffled, replying, "Oh, I don't know about that. You couldn't do any better."

The director, still trying to communicate (but in terms of his own frame of reference), said, "That's what I said, Joe. You are doing one hell of a job."

At this point Joe became angry and an argument broke out, with Joe vowing that he wouldn't be talked to that way in front of friends. Eventually it was necessary to separate the two men to prevent a fight.

Whether one is working for a Hollywood movie company, the Jones Manufacturing Corporation, or the federal government, communication is an ever-present activity because it is the means by which people relate to one another in an organization. Communication is as necessary to an organization as the bloodstream is to a person. Just as persons develop arteriosclerosis, a hardening of the arteries that impairs their efficiency, so may an organization develop "infosclerosis," a hardening of the information arteries that produces similar impaired efficiency.

Because of its significance in organizational behavior, communication is discussed in the next three chapters. In this chapter we discuss the general concept of communication as it relates to management activities. The next chapter covers communication involving different organizational groups, such as managers and employees. In the third chapter we discuss counseling activities.

COMMUNICATION IN ORGANIZATIONS

Communication is defined as the *process of passing information and understanding from one person to another.* It is essentially a bridge of meaning between people. By using this bridge of meaning a person can safely cross the river of misunderstanding that separates all people.

A significant point about communication is that it always involves two people—a sender and a receiver. One person alone cannot communicate. Only a receiver can complete the communication act. This fact is obvious when one thinks of a person lost on an island calling for help when there is no one near enough to hear the call. The relationship is not so obvious to managers who send out bulletins. They tend to think that when their bulletins are sent, they have communicated, but the message transmission is only the beginning. A manager may send a hundred bulletins, but there is no communication until one of the bulletins is received and read.

THE COMMUNICATION PROCESS. The entire sequence of a sender communicating with a receiver requires a minimum of six steps, whether they talk, use hand signals, or have some other form of communication. This complete sequence is the *communication process,* shown in Figure 21-1. The first step is ideation by a sender, who must create an idea or choose a fact to communicate. This is the content of communication; it is the basis of a message. Senders must have something to say before they can "say." Certainly this first step is crucial, because further steps are rather fruitless without a message. A poor message will not be improved by glossy paper or a bigger loudspeaker. The motto for this step is "Don't start talking until you begin thinking," or "Be sure brain is engaged before putting mouth in gear."

In the next step, encoding, senders organize their ideas into a series of symbols that they feel will communicate to their intended receivers. Senders organize for rationality and coherence. In this step they also select an appropriate method of communication, because their encoding will be in relation to methods

		Barriers			
Ideation $\longrightarrow$	Encoding $\longrightarrow$	Transmission $\longrightarrow$	Receiving $\longrightarrow$	Decoding $\longrightarrow$	Action
(Sender has a message)	(e.g., idea to words)	(Over a channel)	(Tuned to transmitter)	(e.g., words to idea for understanding)	(e.g., storage)

FIGURE 21-1

The communication process.

as well as receivers. A telegram, for example, is usually worded differently from a book, and both are different from face-to-face conversation. The method or methods selected must be those which will reach the intended receivers and which they will heed. It does little good for the ramp attendant at an airport to yell to the pilot of a departing airplane. The attendant had better use hand signals or a two-way radio.

The third step is transmission of the message as encoded. Transmission confirms the method selected in the preceding step. Senders also choose certain channels, such as bypassing or not bypassing the superintendent; and they communicate with careful timing. Today may not be the right day to talk to one's manager about that pay raise. Senders also try to keep their communication channel free of barriers, or interference, as shown in Figure 21-1, so that their messages have a chance to reach receivers and hold their attention. In interviewing, for example, freedom from distraction is desirable.

In the fourth step initiative transfers to receivers, who tune to receive the message. If it is oral, they need to be good listeners, as will be discussed shortly. If the receiver does not function, the message is lost.

The fifth step is decoding, by which the receiver takes meaning from the symbols encoded by the sender. Understanding is the key to the decoding process. Senders want receivers to understand what was sent, which means that the receiver will take from the message the meaning intended by the sender. If the sender transmits the idea of a square, but the receiver sees a rectangle, then the communication is ineffective. Although some receivers may be uncooperative and may try to misunderstand, normally they make a genuine attempt to understand the intended message. Even with the best of intentions, a receiver may not understand *exactly* what the sender intended, because perceptions of the two people are different. The more realistic goal in most organizational situations is for understanding that is close enough for the communication to be called successful.

Understanding can occur only in a receiver's mind. A communicator may make others listen, but there is no way to make others understand. The receiver alone chooses whether to understand or not. Many employees overlook this fact when giving instructions or explanations. They think that telling someone is sufficient, but the communication is not truly successful until that which is received is also understood. This is popularly known as "getting through" to a person. Communicators should ask themselves every day: "Am I getting through to others?"

The encoding-decoding sequence is somewhat like the activity involved when a famous British castle was moved to the United States. The castle could not be moved in one piece; consequently, it had to be disassembled stone by stone, with each stone marked as to its proper location. This was similar to a sender who has an idea and encodes (dismantles) it into a series of words, each marked by location and other means to guide the receiver. In order to move it (transmit it), the sender had to take it apart by putting it into words. The reassembly of the castle stone by stone in the United States was similar to a receiver who takes words received and mentally reassembles them back into whole ideas.

The last step in the communication process is action. The receiver acts in response to the communication. The action may be to ignore it, to perform the task assigned, to store the information provided, or something else.

THE RULE OF FIVE IN COMMUNICATION.   Two additional receiver steps are desired by senders in organizational situations, but they are not essential to a completed communication. These steps are acceptance of the communication by the receiver and feedback to the sender regarding it. Senders in organizations usually want receivers to accept their communications so that cooperation and motivation will be improved. Similarly, senders want feedback because it establishes a basis for improved understanding. Although acceptance and feedback are not essential to complete a single communication, they are essential for an effective long-run working relationship. No organization can operate for long without these additional steps in the communication process.

When all the sender's expectations of the receiver in the communication process are considered, they are sometimes called the Rule of Five in Communication, which means that there is a sender goal for the receiver to (1) receive, (2) understand, (3) accept, (4) act, and (5) provide feedback. If a communication accomplishes these five steps with a receiver, it has been fully successful.

Senders always need to communicate with care, because communication is a potent form of self-revelation to others. It tells the kind of persons communicators are, the way they think, and what their values are. It is, therefore, basic in all interpersonal and group relationships.

PURPOSES OF COMMUNICATION.   Managers depend on communication to achieve organizational objectives. Since managers work through others, all their management acts must pass through the bottleneck of communication, as shown in Figure 21-2. Great management ideas are strictly armchair thoughts until a manager puts them into effect through communication. A person's plans may be the best in the world, but until they can be communicated they are worthless.

Communication has its limitations. It is merely the process by which a manager takes action, rather than being all that is necessary for successful management. The best communication will not compensate for poor plans. In fact, managers who are good communicators of poor plans merely hasten their groups toward failure. They are, let us say, "successful at failing." All managers, therefore, need to set communication in proper perspective as an important and essential process

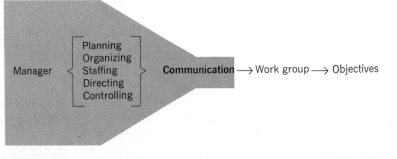

FIGURE 21-2

All management passes through the bottleneck of communication.

that does not substitute for good management ideas but does enable them to carry out whatever good ideas they can generate.

The relationship between communication and management can be explained in terms of a small group consisting of a manager and four employees. Assume in the beginning that each is surrounded by psychological and physical barriers that totally prevent communication among them. The barriers are so high that workers cannot even see their associates, because that would be a form of communication. It is obvious that under these conditions a manager cannot lead employees—nor can they follow. Workers have no way to know what their manager wants them to do. The manager cannot give orders and instructions. There is no way to motivate workers because the manager cannot know their needs and wants. When there is absolutely no communication, organized effort is impossible. Organizations cannot exist without communication.

Normally the barriers between people do not screen out all communications. Rather, they operate like filters to permit some communications but hold back others, thereby making communication inadequate. The result is misunderstanding, lack of motivation, insecurity, conflict, and inability to make effective decisions. This "halfway" communication gets "halfway" results.

If the barriers are substantially removed so that managers and employees can communicate, then they are able to work together. This fact makes it obvious that *one purpose of communication is to develop the information and understanding necessary for group effort.*

Although the members of a group can work together, will they? Whether they do depends on their attitude toward cooperation. It depends on how well management integrates employee interests with employer interests. This is another purpose of communication: *to provide the attitudes necessary for motivation, cooperation, and job satisfaction.* This second purpose is extremely important, because there is increasing evidence that modern work problems are related more to attitudes than to fundamental skills and job knowledge. These two purposes of communication are summarized in Figure 21-3 as "the skill to work" and "the will to

COMMUNICATION AS A MANAGEMENT ACTIVITY
The process by which managers take action

PURPOSES		RESULT
1. To provide the information and understanding necessary for group effort	2. To provide the attitudes necessary for motivation, cooperation, and job satisfaction	Better communication gets better job performance and more work satisfaction
The **skill** to work	+ The **will** to work	= **Teamwork**

FIGURE 21-3 ■■■■■■■■■■

Two purposes of communication as a management activity.

work.'' The result is the joint achievement of high productivity and high job satisfaction through teamwork.

EFFECTS OF COMMUNICATION.   Other things being equal, improved communication tends to encourage work and attitude improvement, although the relationship among these variables is complex and not always predictable. One study compared two manufacturing plants as nearly identical as possible. Both were represented by the same union and were located in similar towns. They were operated by the same company. The chief difference was that one of them, Plant X, had maintained an active communication program for nine years, while Plant Y had no such program.

The results were startlingly favorable to the use of a communication program. Workers' responses to three summary questions will show how the plants differed. When workers were asked, ''Does your company do a good job of telling you what's going on and what's being planned?'' in Plant X, 55 percent thought it did a ''very good job,'' but only 18 percent in Plant Y thought so. In Plant X, 62 percent felt they ''really'' were a part of the company, but only 29 percent felt so in Plant Y. Forty-five percent of Plant X thought their company was ''one of the very best'' to work for in the community, but only 20 percent of Plant Y thought so. For each of the three questions, the plant with the communication program had *more than twice* as many enthusiastic answers as the other plant.[2]

Another study compared twenty-seven branches of a package-delivery organization. All branches performed similar work, but there were wide variations in productivity. Communication data were secured by a survey of all 975 employees in the branches. Comparing productivity and communication data, the researchers concluded that high performance in branches tended to be positively associated with openness of communication channels between superiors and subordinates.[3]

Communication, properly done, can be surprisingly effective. One plant through communication persuaded its production employees to bring their own coffee and have coffee breaks at their machines, instead of taking a regular time-lost coffee break in the cafeteria. The company dealt directly and frankly. It presented to each employee in meetings a curve of electricity use for the plant showing how power use was less than half of normal for fifteen minutes before and after coffee break, plus the normal productivity loss during the break. The company made a sound case for the fact that this long period of inactivity and partial activity prevented profitable operation. The power-use charts were convincing, and employees readily accepted the coffee-break policy.

LABORATORY STUDIES.   Further evidence of the effect of communication is found in experimental laboratory studies of communication networks. Experiments of this type can isolate one particular variable to show its influence on communication; however, since a real organization is much more complex than laboratory conditions, conclusions from these experiments do not directly apply to operating organizations. The main value of these experiments is to show potential influence of any variable.

Early classical studies of simple communication networks showed that each caused different levels of job satisfaction, speed, and accuracy, as shown in Figure 21-4. The wheel and chain networks gave the best job performance, but they also had the lowest job satisfaction and showed low flexibility to changes.[4] On the other hand, experiments using more complex problems showed that the circle was faster and made fewer errors than the wheel.[5] These experiments appear to support the management idea that better results are accomplished by using various networks and media of communication, rather than one alone. In this way, some of the advantages of each are secured and both high productivity and high job satisfaction are possible.

Later refinements of these classical studies show that as variables are changed for experimental groups, they make efficient adaptations rather rapidly, using whatever ideas they have learned from earlier experiments. The point is that there is a natural tendency of groups to solve their assigned problem as efficiently as possible, that is, with as little expenditure of effort as they can develop.[6] These experiments seem to support the idea of management by objectives, allowing the group some leeway to make adaptations to reach assigned objectives in the most appropriate ways.

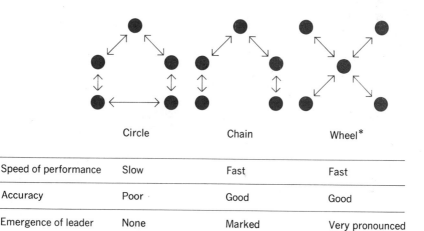

	Circle	Chain	Wheel*
Speed of performance	Slow	Fast	Fast
Accuracy	Poor	Good	Good
Emergence of leader	None	Marked	Very pronounced
Job satisfaction	Very good	Poor	Very poor
Flexibility to job change	Very fast	Slow	Slow

*Called a wheel because all communications pass through the center person, similar to the hub of a wheel.

FIGURE 21-4 ▬▬▬▬▬▬▬▬▬▬▬

Effect of different communication patterns on work performance under experimental conditions. (Adapted from Alex Bavelas and Dermot Barrett, "An Experimental Approach to Organizational Communication," *Personnel,* March 1951, pp. 370–371.)

Group adaptability may in the long run lead to substantially the same effectiveness regardless of network restrictions. One experiment compared an all-channel network (one in which any person could communicate with any other) with a modified chain network. All groups eventually reached the same level of performance regardless of structure or written-oral restrictions. The result was true for both simple problems and complex problems, although the all-channel group held the initial advantage on complex problems.[7]

RESPONSIBILITY FOR COMMUNICATION. It is generally agreed that the communication climate of an organization tends to reflect attitudes of its top management. If top managers establish sound information exchange with their associates and insist that their associates do likewise with others, this spirit of information sharing tends to cover the whole institution. A successful communication program, therefore, depends upon top management to initiate and spark it. But top management's ultimate responsibility does not relieve other management members of their basic communication obligation. No level or area of management can escape this responsibility because it is always a part of the management function. Managers may delegate a small part of their communication activities to specialists, but the major part cannot be delegated because their leadership takes effect through communication.

As a matter of fact, managers are doubly responsible for communication. Like everyone else, they are responsible for communicating with others, but they also are responsible for maintenance of good communication among their personnel.

Research shows that managers have difficulty accomplishing their communication responsibilities. When they were asked, "What causes you trouble with your job?" more of them (80 percent) mentioned communication than any other item. In another study managers had more desire for communication training than any other subject, with approximately 75 percent strongly wanting communication training.[8]

Communication also is a responsibility of every operating employee in an organization. Employees in any job must communicate with others—sometimes more, sometimes less—and they must be able to judge when, where, and how to communicate. Communication is a responsibility of every person in an organization.

SEMANTICS

Semantics is the science of meaning, as contrasted with phonetics, the science of sounds. Nearly all communication is symbolic; that is, it is achieved using *symbols* to suggest certain meanings. These symbols are merely a map that describes a territory, but they are not the real territory itself; hence, they must be interpreted. The word "dog" does not look like a dog, sound like a dog, or smell like a dog, but it means a dog because we have made it a symbol for a dog. This symbolic transfer of meaning is a very difficult, very personal process. The meaning that receivers take depends on their experience and attitudes—not the communicator's. If in a receiver's experience the symbol has meaning X, the communicator who insists on using the symbol with meaning Y will have difficulty getting through to the receiver. The key thought of this discussion is that transfer of meaning can be improved by communicating in terms of the receivers' backgrounds and attitudes.

BARRIERS TO COMMUNICATION. Communication is impeded by three broad types of barriers—physical, personal (social-psychological), and semantic. Physical barriers are environmental factors that prevent or reduce the sending and receiving of communications. They include physical distance, distracting noises, and similar interferences.

Personal barriers arise from the judgments, emotions, and social values of people. They cause a *psychological distance* between people similar to the physical distance just mentioned. Psychological distance may entirely prevent a communication, filter part of it out, or simply cause misinterpretation. Our emotions, for example, act as filters in nearly all our communications. We see and hear what we are emotionally "tuned" to see and hear; thus, communication cannot be separated from our personality.[9] We communicate our interpretation of reality instead of reality itself. Someone has said, "No matter what you say a thing is, it isn't," meaning that the sender is merely giving an emotionally filtered perception of it. Under these conditions, when the sender's and receiver's perceptual profiles are reasonably close together, their communication will be more accurate.

Semantic barriers arise from the limitations of the symbolic system itself. Symbols usually have a variety of meanings, and we have to choose one meaning from among many. An important distinction in these situations is to separate *inferences* from *facts*.

Suppose we see a person come out of a bar, enter a car, and drive from his parking place into a crash with another car. We may infer that he has been drinking alcoholic beverages in the bar, but we have no objective evidence to make this a fact. We may say it is a fact that he is driving his own car; however, it may not be his car, but his neighbor's. It appears to be a fact that two cars crashed and a person who walked out a door labeled "Bar" was driving one of the cars!

Inferences are an essential part of most communication. We cannot avoid them by waiting until all communication is factual before accepting it. However, since inferences can give a wrong signal, we need always to be aware of them and to appraise them carefully. When doubts arise, more feedback can be sought.

Symbols may reach a person's brain through any of the senses, such as feeling or hearing. Symbols may be classified as language, pictures, or action.

LANGUAGE. Words are the principal communication instrument of all employees, particularly managers. A large majority of this word communication is spoken, not written. Managers and many other employees live in a verbal environment and must have reasonable language capacity in order to do their jobs well. Normally the higher people go in management, the more they will need to use communication to perform their jobs.

379

A study of research managers, for example, reported that first-level supervisors spent 74 percent of their time communicating, second-level managers spent 81 percent, and third-level managers spent 87 percent. The same study showed that two groups of nonmanagement technical employees spent 57 and 60 percent of their time communicating. [10]

Another study covered over 3,000 employees, including office employees, in a research and development activity. It reported that they spent 69 percent of their time communicating. Other studies confirm this general relationship of communication dominating work time in most situations. [11]

A major difficulty with language is that nearly every common word has several meanings. Multiple meanings are necessary because we are trying to talk about an infinitely complex world while using only a limited number of words. Used in one sense, a word may be derogatory; but when used another way, it can be acceptable. For example, the term "dummy" in an argument at the office may be quite uncomplimentary, but its use to refer to the person serving as dummy in a game of bridge is acceptable.

The variety of word meanings often is surprising. A standard desk dictionary reports seventy-nine different meanings for the popular word "round." Many of the meanings are entirely different, as shown by six examples in Figure 21-5. A study of

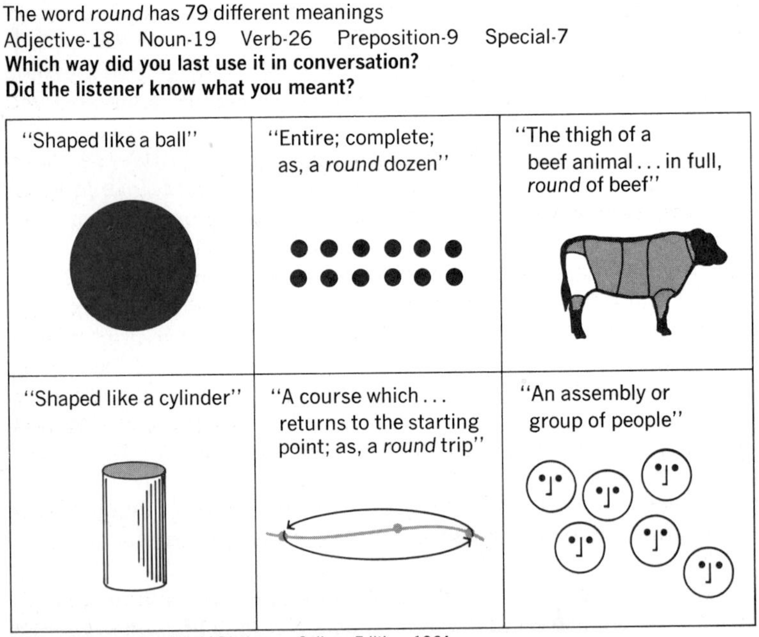

The word *round* has 79 different meanings
Adjective-18   Noun-19   Verb-26   Preposition-9   Special-7
Which way did you last use it in conversation?
Did the listener know what you meant?

| "Shaped like a ball" | "Entire; complete; as, a *round* dozen" | "The thigh of a beef animal . . . in full, *round* of beef" |
| "Shaped like a cylinder" | "A course which . . . returns to the starting point; as, a *round* trip" | "An assembly or group of people" |

Source: Webster's New World Dictionary, College Edition, 1964.

FIGURE 21-5

Example of the multiple meanings of a word.

a larger dictionary, the *Oxford Dictionary,* reports an average of twenty-eight separate meanings for each of the 500 most-used words in the English language.[12] No wonder we have trouble communicating with each other!

If words really have no certain meaning, how can we make sense with them—how can we communicate with other people? The answer is *context.* We use the word in a certain environment, such as the "dummy" example just given, and we surround the word with other words until meaning is narrowed to fairly certain limits. Individual words have so many meanings that they become meaningless until they are put into context. Consequently, effective communicators are idea-centered, rather than word-centered. They know that *words* do not mean—*people* mean.

The experience of a government personnel director illustrates the importance of context. There were nearly two thousand employees in clerical operations in an office. The entire activity was located in a converted warehouse on an abandoned Army base.

Several hundred employees held "temporary" rather than "permanent" civil service appointments. Because of variations in the work load at this installation, there were occasional layoffs of these temporary workers. Recently, when layoffs were necessary, the personnel director used the loudspeaker system to make an announcement somewhat like the following: "The following employees are requested to report to classroom 10 at 4 P.M. this afternoon." Then the names were announced over the loudspeaker.

When the employees arrived, they were told that this was their last day of temporary work, and they were given their separation papers. This procedure was followed with layoffs during a period of several weeks.

A few days later the personnel director had a training assignment for some employees who had "permanent" appointments; so he decided to call them to classroom 10 at the end of the day to tell them about the training program. He went to the loudspeaker in the afternoon and announced, "The following employees are requested to report to classroom 10 at 4 P.M.," and then the names were read.

As the names were read over the loudspeaker, several women started crying, assuming they also were being laid off. Soon a number of other women started crying in sympathy with the first group, upsetting the entire office. It took some time for supervisors to discover the cause of their weeping, to find the real reason for the call to the classroom, and to quiet the office force. All this difficulty was caused because the context of the communication was improper.

In summary, language with inadequate context is a semantic smog. Like a real smog, it irritates our senses and interferes with our perceptions.

PICTURES. A second type of symbol is pictures. They are used especially to aid and clarify word communication, which is their use in Figure 21-5. Organizations make extensive use of pictures, such as blueprints, charts, maps, films, three-dimensional models, and similar devices. There is a saying that "a picture can be worth a thousand words," which is certainly true when one observes a blueprint or sees a painting.

381

A shoe manufacturer, who was having trouble getting his workers to maintain quality, made good use of pictures to restore careful work. He placed finished-shoe rejects in a large room for several weeks and then brought representative employee groups into the room "to browse around and see for yourselves." Few words were spoken, but much meaning was imparted when employees saw the mountain of rejected shoes. This manager was using pictures effectively to supplement his language communication.

Pictures are, as the term implies, visual *aids,* and are most effective when used with well-chosen words and actions to tell the complete story.

ACTION (NONVERBAL COMMUNICATION). A third type of symbol is action, also known as nonverbal communication.[13] Often people forget that what they do is a means of communication to the extent that it is interpreted by others. For example, a handshake and a smile have meaning. A raise in pay or being late for an appointment also has meaning.

Two significant points about action sometimes are overlooked. One point is that *failure to act* is an important way of communication. A manager who fails to compliment someone for a job well done or fails to take a promised action is also communicating with that person. Since we communicate both by action and by lack of action, we communicate almost all the time at work, whether we intend to or not. Being at one's desk has meaning, but being away also has meaning.

A second point is that action speaks louder than words in the long run. People believe action more than they do words. Employees who say one thing but do another will soon find that others "listen" mostly to what they do. The amount of difference between what one says and what one does is that person's *communication credibility gap.* When an employee's credibility gap is large, dysfunctional human results are likely to follow, such as losing confidence in that person. The following illustration shows how a credibility gap works in practice.

The zone manager of a sales office gave considerable stress to the idea that he depended upon his employees to help him do a good job because, as he stated it, "You salespeople are the ones in direct contact with the customer, and you get much valuable information and useful suggestions." In most of his sales meetings he stressed the fact that he always welcomed their ideas and suggestions. But here is how he translated his words into action. In those same sales meetings the schedule was so tight that by the time he finished his pep talk there was no time for anyone to present problems or ask questions, and he would hardly tolerate an interruption during his talk because he claimed this destroyed its "punch."

If a salesperson tried to present a suggestion in the manager's office, the manager usually began with, "Fine, I'm glad you brought in your suggestion." Before long, however, he directed the conversation to some subject on his mind, or had to meet an appointment, or found some other reason for never quite getting to the suggestion. The few suggestions that did get through he rebuffed with, "Yeah, I thought of that a long time ago, but it won't work." The eventual result was that he received no suggestions. His actions spoke louder than his words. His credibility gap was too large for employees to overcome.

BODY LANGUAGE. An important part of nonverbal communication is *body language,* by which people communicate meaning to others with their bodies in interpersonal interaction. Studies of body language are providing evidence that it is an important supplement to verbal communication in most parts of the world.

The face and the hands are especially important sources of body language in work situations. Examples are eye contact, eye movement, smiles and frowns, touching, and a furrowed brow. In one instance a manager frowned when an employee brought a suggestion, and the employee interpreted the frown as a rejection when in fact it was a headache. In another instance a smile at an inappropriate time was interpreted as a derisive sneer, and an argument erupted. Other types of body language are closeness, hip movements, breathing rate, and odor. Consider how the body language of closeness applied to one manager in an office.

In interaction with visitors to her office the manager usually sat rigidly behind her desk, leaving the other person somewhat distant on the other side of the desk. This arrangement created a psychological distance and clearly established her as the leader and superior in the interaction. Then she rearranged her office so that a visitor sat beside her on the same side of her desk. This suggested more receptiveness and equality of interaction with visitors. It also had the additional advantage of providing a work area on her desk for mutual examination of appropriate documents. When she wished to establish a more informal relationship, particularly with subordinates, she came around the desk and sat at the front of the desk in a chair near the employee.

Of all communication symbols, probably the two most important in employee communication are face-to-face conversation and action. These communication symbols are not new, but management has much to learn about how to use them for improved communication. The printing press and typewriter are wonderful inventions, but they are no substitute for face-to-face communication at work. Face-to-face interaction provides multiple channels, including body language, thereby increasing the probability of better understanding. It also allows immediate feedback so that each party can adjust to the individual needs of the other. In sum, face-to-face communication tends to be more enriched with information than other forms of communication.

READABILITY. Since meaning is difficult to impart, a natural assumption is that if symbols can be simplified, the receiver will understand them more easily. Further, if symbols of the type receivers prefer are used, they will be more receptive. This is the thinking behind the concept of *readability,* which seeks to make writing and speech more understandable. Readability was popularized by Rudolf Flesch in *The Art of Plain Talk* and *The Art of Readable Writing,*[14] following considerable earlier research by Flesch and others. These researchers developed formulas that can be applied to magazines, bulletins, speeches, and other communications in order to determine their level of readability.

The Flesch formula is based upon a count of average sentence length and average number of syllables for each 100 words. These two averages are applied to a scale that gives the reading-ease score. For example, an average sentence length of fifteen to seventeen words, with 140 to 147 syllables for each 100 words, rates "standard" on the Flesch scale. Standard should be satisfactorily read and understood by at least 83 percent of adults in the United States.

Research shows that much organizational literature to employees is more difficult than standard readability. Bulletins, magazines, training manuals, employee handbooks, and collective-bargaining contracts consistently rate "difficult" and "very difficult," beyond the level of satisfactory reading for typical adults.[15] It is often observed that the typical employee communication appears to be written by college graduates for college graduates. Many readers do not understand such complicated writing unless they carefully study it, which they are seldom motivated to do. It follows that managers have not applied the idea of readability to adapt their words and style to fit the language level and ability of their receivers. Since the main purpose of communication is to be understood, there is a need to consider receivers and try to fit their needs.

Readability scales have been criticized on the basis that they degrade language to the level of first-grade primers, tend to destroy style, do not measure all the factors that determine readability, and contain similar weaknesses. These criticisms have merit, and readability certainly must not be overstressed. Nevertheless, readability is something that everyone needs to consider when communicating. Practice will develop a readable style, and readability is easy to test on most scales, once the knack is learned.

Following are some guides to readable writing. Their use is illustrated in Figure 21-6.

1. Use simple words and phrases, such as "improve" instead of "ameliorate," and "like" instead of "in a matter similar to that of."

2. Use short and familiar words, such as "darken" instead of "obfuscate."

3. Use personal pronouns, such as "you" and "them," if the style permits.

4. Use illustrations, examples, and charts. These techniques are even better when they are tied to the reader's experiences.

5. Use short sentences and paragraphs. If there were two reports on the same subject, one report labeled "reading time: ten minutes" and the other report labeled "reading time: ninety minutes," which one would likely be read first? Big words and thick reports may look impressive to people, but the communicator's job is to inform people, not impress them.

6. Use active verbs, such as "The manager said . . ." rather than "It was said by the manager that . . . ."

7. Economize on adjectives and language flourishes.

8. Arrange thoughts in logical, direct style—avoid "blunderbuss writing." A blunderbuss is an old-fashioned gun that scatters shot because the barrel flares out. A blunderbuss word or idea scatters meaning over a wide area. It is difficult to get the intended idea from blunderbuss writing.

9. Make every word work for you—avoid "deadhead words." In railroading "deadheading" refers to a passenger who occupies a seat but pays no fare. A deadhead word in a sentence adds nothing to it. For example, in the sentence "Bad weather conditions prevented my trip," the word "conditions" is an unnecessary, deadhead word. Say, "Bad weather prevented my trip."

LISTENING. Hearing is with the ears, but listening is with the mind. Effective listening helps receivers take exactly the idea a sender intended. They can then make better decisions because their information inputs are better. Good listeners also save time because they learn more within a given period of time; and they learn about the person talking, as well as what the person is saying. Good listening is also good manners; people think more of us when we listen to them attentively. Finally, our good listening encourages others to reciprocate by listening to what we have to say. It is a form of behavior modeling for them.

ORIGINAL PARAGRAPH

There is a remote possibility that in the future there may be somewhat more jobs available. It is estimated that quite a lot of the improvement may be attributed to some of the more important industries and trades which normally become increasingly more active with the onset of warmer weather. In other words, it will be due mainly to the seasonal factors that always cause the over-all basis of the rise and fall in the nation's economic activity, and even though there has been no noticeable strengthening of basic conditions, the general business situation is by far considerably better than most of the pessimistic economic forecasters have expected. According to extensive records compiled by the Bureau of Labor Statistics, the unemployment total in April was substantially below the 4½ million mark reached during March and the recent trend of applicants for jobless benefits suggests that the total of national unemployment is possibly now somewhat below 3 million employable persons who are available for work.

164 words
Flesch readability rating: *very difficult.*

REVISED PARAGRAPH

The job picture looks brighter. Many of our industries increase production at this time of the year. The Bureau of Labor Statistics reports that national unemployment dropped from 4½ million in March to less than 3 million in April.

39 words
Flesch readability rating: *fairly easy to standard.*

FIGURE 21-6 ■■■■■■■■■■■■■■■■■■■■■■■■■■■

An example of applied rules of clear writing. (Adapted from "Readingease: The Key to Understanding," Employees Relations Staff, General Motors Corporation, n. d.)

Emphasis on good listening is a recent development. The first English-language book wholly on listening was published in 1957,[16] even though earlier there were hundreds of books published on speaking.

Since a typical listener two months later remembers only about 25 percent of what was said, listening is most effective for understanding general ideas about short-term operating problems. It is not effective for receipt and storage of many factual details; here we depend on the written word.

Training can increase listening comprehension 25 percent or more. A person speaks at the rate of 100 to 200 words a minute, but a listener's brain can process words much faster; so there is idle brain time that good listeners use to concentrate forcefully on the message in order to keep from daydreaming or mindwandering. Good listeners use their idle time to think in terms of the speaker's objective, weigh the evidence, search for other clues to meaning, and review. Other suggestions for good listening are given in Figure 21-7. Listening is a conscious, positive act requiring willpower. It is not a simple, passive exposure to sound.

Good listening is one of the weakest points of managers in oral communication, especially when they are talking to persons below them in the organizational structure. Many managers wear "listening ear muffs." One reason is that listening requires managers to reverse their usual role of authority and initiative. A second reason is that listening may be threatening to a person's self-image, because the speaker is initiating action on the listener. Most of us would rather speak our own ideas than listen to ideas from someone else. In spite of the difficulties of good listening, it is one of management's most important and time-consuming tasks, because it provides necessary inputs for understanding people and making sound decisions. For quality decisions, quality information inputs are required.

TWO-WAY COMMUNICATION. When a receiver receives a message and then sends meaningful feedback to the sender, there is effective *two-way communication.* This is a much-desired condition in all organizations, because it improves understanding. The significance of two-way communication becomes evident by reference to the well-known sport of tennis.

Consider a tennis player named Diane McFadden. As she serves the ball, she cannot say to herself, "My next shot will be an overhead volley into the back court." Her next shot has to depend on how her opponent returns the ball. She may have an overall strategy, but each of her shots must be conditioned by how the ball is returned. Unless she does condition her shots, she will soon find herself swinging aimlessly and losing a game. Two-way communication has a back-and-forth pattern similar to the exchange of play between tennis players. The speaker sends a message, and the receiver's responses come back to the speaker. The result is a developing play-by-play situation in which the speaker can adjust the message to fit responses of the receiver, in the same way that a cybernetic device adjusts to feedback in a production system. This opportunity to adjust to the receiver is the one great advantage of two-way communication compared with the one-way variety. It provides better understanding for both parties.

There are other benefits of two-way communication. Frustration is reduced, and favorable feelings are generated. Accuracy of work is much improved.

One experiment with eighteen groups reported that 90 percent of their members felt frustrated with one-way (unilateral) communication. They lacked confidence in their accuracy of performance, and their actual accuracy was low. With two-way (bilateral) communication, accuracy was much higher, and confidence in accuracy was over twice as great. Hostility was reduced but not wholly removed, because there are causes of hostility other than communication difficulty.[17]

TEN GUIDES FOR EFFECTIVE LISTENING

1. **Stop talking!**
   You cannot listen if you are talking.
   Polonius (Hamlet): "Give every man thine ear, but few thy voice."
2. **Put the talker at ease.**
   Help a person feel free to talk.
   This is often called a permissive environment.
3. **Show a talker that you want to listen.**
   Look and act interested. Do not read your mail while someone talks.
   Listen to understand rather than to oppose.
4. **Remove distractions.**
   Don't doodle, tap, or shuffle papers.
   Will it be quieter if you shut the door?
5. **Empathize with talkers.**
   Try to help yourself see the other person's point of view.
6. **Be patient.**
   Allow plenty of time. Do not interrupt a talker.
   Don't start for the door or walk away.
7. **Hold your temper.**
   An angry person takes the wrong meaning from words.
8. **Go easy on argument and criticism.**
   This puts people on the defensive, and they may "clam up" or become angry.
   Do not argue: Even if you win, you lose.
9. **Ask questions.**
   This encourages a talker and shows that you are listening.
   It helps to develop points further.
10. **Stop talking!**
    This is first and last, because all other guides depend on it.
    You cannot do an effective listening job while you are talking.
    - Nature gave people two ears but only one tongue,
      which is a gentle hint that they should listen more than they talk.
    - Listening requires two ears,
      one for meaning and one for feeling.
    - Decision makers who do not listen
      have less information for making sound decisions.

FIGURE 21-7 ■■■■■■■■■■■■■■■■■■■■■■■■■■■■■■■■■

Effective listening guides.

Two-way communication is not exclusively beneficial. It also can cause difficulties. Two people may strongly disagree about some item but not realize it until they establish two-way communication. When they realize their strong differences, they may feel even further separated from each other, but at least two-way communication has helped them understand the nature of their differences.

Another difficulty that may occur is *cognitive dissonance.* This happens when people receive information incompatible with their value systems, the situation as they see it, or another piece of information they have. This dissonance sets up internal conflict that causes anxiety and other reactions. Since people do not feel comfortable with dissonance, they try to remove it. Perhaps they will try to adjust their communication inputs, change their interpretation of the inputs, or change their values. They might even refuse to believe the dissonant input or rationalize it out of the way.

SUMMARY

Communication is the passing of information and understanding from one person to another. It is a sharing of meaning and is the process by which a manager reaches others to manage their work. One person can initiate the process but cannot complete it. It is completed only by a receiver. The purpose of communication is to supply the information necessary for job performance and active cooperation—the skill to work and the will to work. The communication process consists of six steps: ideation, encoding, transmitting, receiving, decoding for understanding, and action. The five desired receiver responses of receipt, understanding, acceptance, action, and feedback are known as the Rule of Five in communication.

People communicate with the symbols of language, pictures, and action (including body language). Receivers take meaning from symbols on the basis of their experience and attitudes. If one does not know Arabic, then Arabic symbols are not meaningful reading or listening. With regard to language, ideas should be emphasized instead of words. Pictures are an aid to communication, and action speaks louder than words. Readability simplifies symbols and encourages more understanding among casual readers. Since communication is a two-way process, listening in order to know what and how to communicate is often as important as speaking and writing.

TERMS AND CONCEPTS FOR REVIEW

Communication	Nonverbal communication
Communication process	Communication credibility gap
Rule of Five in communication	Body language
Circle, chain, and wheel networks	Readability

Semantics

Psychological distance

Inference versus fact

Two-way communication

Cognitive dissonance

REVIEW QUESTIONS

1. Discuss the communication process.
2. Explain what has been learned about the effect of communication networks on groups.
3. Discuss the application of nonverbal communication in organizations.
4. Discuss the concept of readable writing, including any weaknesses it may have.
5. Explain the nature and importance of listening in communication. What are some guides to effective listening?

CASE

THE NATIONAL GAS COMPANY

The National Gas Company provided natural gas to about 40,000 customers in an Eastern city. Christmas in one year came on Tuesday; and as the holiday season approached, management heard persistent rumors from the employees that Monday, December 24, would be a holiday except for the emergency crews. December 24 was not regularly a holiday, but the rumors were that since it fell between Sunday and Christmas, management had decided to grant the extra holiday to make a "long weekend."

The Coordinating Committee, consisting of top operating officials, discussed the holiday problem extensively at two weekly meetings, December 10 and 17. At the second meeting it was decided that there would be no holiday December 24. There were several arguments for and against the decision, but the argument that carried the most weight concerned the public relations aspects of bill paying. Bills were issued daily during the month on a rotating basis, with a discount date* printed on the bill. About 2,000 bills with a December 24 discount date had already been sent out, and investigation disclosed that often as many as 25 percent of the customers paid their bills on their last discount date. The Committee felt that it would be poor public relations to close the office on December 24 because hundreds of people would come to the office to pay their bills that day; so it decided to keep the entire staff on duty.

Since December 24 was not a regular holiday, it was not necessary to announce the Committee's decision to employees; however, it decided that the deci-

---

* Bills paid on or before the discount date were subject to a cash discount of 2 percent.

sion should be announced since the rumors had been persistent. The announcement read:

December 19, 19—

To All National Gas Employees:

Monday, December 24, will be a regular company work day.

Jim Smith
General Manager

The announcement was mimeographed, sent to all supervisors, and placed on all bulletin boards. There was no other publicity of the decision.

QUESTION
1. Appraise the quality of communication in this situation and recommend any improvements that you think could have been made in the way this was handled.

LABORATORY EXPERIMENT

ONE-WAY COMPARED WITH TWO-WAY COMMUNICATION

The instructor can set up a classroom experiment in which both one-way and two-way communication are tried regarding the performance of some task or the communication of a detailed idea not familiar to students. One of the most popular tasks is to have a handout showing rectangles organized in a certain way. Two or more students are selected as receivers, and one or more persons are selected as communicators of the layout of the rectangles. The handout is made available to class members and communicators, *but not to receivers.* Receivers stand at the front of the room trying to draw on a chalkboard the arrangement described by the communicator. (For each communication it is desirable to have two or more receivers so that their arrangements of the rectangles can be compared.)

For the one-way method the communicator faces the class and does not look at the figures the receiver is drawing, because that would be a form of feedback. The two-way method may be with the communicator not observing the figures (as by telephone) or with observation of the figures. The figure shown is a sample

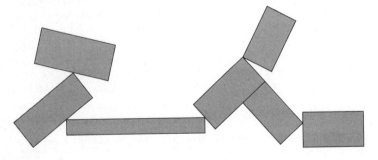

arrangement, but instructors should select their own so that it is not available to the class ahead of time.

Following one-way communication, senders and receivers are questioned about their feelings, and the class discusses the advantages and disadvantages of the one-way process. The same procedure is repeated following two-way communication. Then important comparisons can be made.

REFERENCES

1. "Conversation with Chris Argyris," *Organizational Dynamics,* Summer 1974, p. 62.

2. For additional details see Stephen Habbe, *Communicating with Employees,* National Industrial Conference Board Studies in Personnel Policy, no. 129, New York, 1952, pp. 39–40. For contrary evidence see Dallis Perry and Thomas A. Mahoney, "In-Plant Communications and Employee Morale," *Personnel Psychology,* Winter 1961, pp. 357–374.

3. Bernard P. Indik, Basil S. Georgopoulos, and Stanley E. Seashore, "Superior-Subordinate Relationships and Performance," *Personnel Psychology,* Winter 1961, pp. 357–374.

4. Alex Bavelas and Dermot Barrett, "An Experimental Approach to Organizational Communication," *Personnel,* March 1951, pp. 366–371; and Harold J. Leavitt, "Some Effects of Certain Communication Patterns on Group Performance," *The Journal of Abnormal and Social Psychology,* January 1951, pp. 38–50.

5. M. E. Shaw, "Some Effects of Unequal Distribution of Information upon Group Performance in Various Communication Nets," *The Journal of Abnormal and Social Psychology,* October 1954, pp. 547–553; and M. E. Shaw, "Some Effects of Problem Complexity upon Problem Solution Efficiency in Different Communication Nets," *Journal of Experimental Psychology,* September 1954, pp. 211–217. These conclusions were confirmed by observations in one organization. See Peter Mears, "Structuring Communication in a Working Group," *The Journal of Communication,* Winter 1974, pp. 71–79.

6. Arthur M. Cohen, "Changing Small-Group Communication Networks," *Administrative Science Quarterly,* March 1962, pp. 443–462.

7. Rocco Carzo, Jr., "Some Effects of Organization Structure on Group Effectiveness," *Administrative Science Quarterly,* March 1963, pp. 393–424.

8. Homer L. Cox, "Opinions of Selected Business Managers about Some Aspects of Communication on the Job," *Journal of Business Communication,* Fall 1968, p. 7; and Guvenc G. Alpander, "Planning Management Training Programs for Organizational Development," *Personnel Journal,* January 1974, p. 21, respectively.

9. For an example see Milton M. Schwartz and others, "Responses of Union and Management Leaders to Emotionally-toned Industrial Relations Terms," *Personnel Psychology,* Autumn 1970, pp. 361–367.

10. John R. Hinrichs, "Communications Activity of Industrial Research Personnel," *Personnel Psychology,* Summer 1964, p. 199.

11. E. T. Klemmer and F. W. Snyder, "Measurement of Time Spent Communicating," *The Journal of Communication,* June 1972, pp. 142–158.

12. William M. Sattler, "Talking Ourselves into Communication Crises," *Michigan Business Review,* July 1957, p. 30.

13. Extensive discussion of nonverbal communication is provided in a special issue on that subject in *The Journal of Communication,* December 1972, pp. 339–477. See also Mark L.

Knapp, *Nonverbal Communication in Human Interaction,* New York: Holt, Rinehart and Winston, Inc., 1972.

14. Rudolf Flesch, *The Art of Plain Talk,* New York: Harper & Row, Publishers, Incorporated, 1946, and *The Art of Readable Writing,* New York: Harper & Row, Publishers, Incorporated, 1949. See also Robert Gunning, *The Technique of Clear Writing,* New York: McGraw-Hill Book Company, 1952.

15. Keith Davis, "Readability Changes in Employee Handbooks of Identical Companies during a Fifteen-Year Period," *Personnel Psychology,* Winter 1968, pp. 413–420.

16. Ralph G. Nichols and Leonard A. Stevens, *Are You Listening?* New York: McGraw-Hill Book Company, 1957. For a more recent book see, William F. Keefe, *Listen, Management!* New York: McGraw-Hill Book Company, 1971.

17. William V. Haney, "A Comparative Study of Unilateral and Bilateral Communication," *Academy of Management Journal,* June 1964, pp. 128–136.

CHAPTER 22
COMMUNICATION
RELATIONSHIPS

In the final analysis the only way we have to maintain an operating society is through communication among people.

Anonymous

LEARNING OBJECTIVES ■■■■■■■

TO UNDERSTAND:
The significance of communication within the management group
Operation of downward and upward communication
The meaning and use of cross-communication
The communication role of staff specialists
Communicating with external groups, such as family and union

As a result of their different jobs and ranks in organizations, people play different roles that also affect their communication patterns. For example, the job of public relations director is quite different from that of lathe operator. The director's job interests are focused outside the organization toward the public, but the operator's interests are focused narrowly on day-to-day production activities; that is, their functions are quite different. The director is a member of top management and draws a substantial salary, but the operator is strictly a worker with limited income; that is, their organizational level and social status are different. These factors are as much a barrier to communication as spatial distance is. The public relations director probably feels free to contact a vice president either formally or informally, but the lathe operator may not feel free to do so. If contact is made, the lathe operator will communicate differently from the public relations director.

In spite of the many barriers among people and groups in organizations, one of the basic propositions of organizational behavior is that open communication is better than restricted communication. For this reason it is important to try to improve communication among groups whenever possible, so in this chapter we discuss communication relationships among different groups involved with organizations. Included are communication within management, downward to employees, upward to management, by specialists, with employees' families, and with unions.

COMMUNICATION WITHIN MANAGEMENT

Sometimes there is a tendency to say, "Let's improve employee communication; management can take care of itself." The result is that the entire communication effort of an institution is directed toward employee communication; yet there are a number of reasons why management communication deserves equal emphasis.

WHY EMPHASIZE MANAGEMENT COMMUNICATION? Communication within the management group is called either management communication or intramanagement communication. One reason it must be emphasized is that it is prerequisite to communication with operating workers. Just as a photograph can be no clearer than the negative from which it is printed, managers cannot transmit more clearly than they understand. In one organization its top management expected supervisors to interpret the incentive plan to workers but failed to explain the plan adequately to supervisors. Even though supervisors had stacks of papers describing the plan, they did not understand it and consequently were unable to interpret it to workers.

Management communication also is essential for managers to make sound decisions. They tend to be isolated from the point of performance and can serve as a competent decision center only to the extent that they develop suitable information channels. Many of these channels must be within the management group.

Another reason for emphasizing management communication is that the scope of managerial influence is typically greater than that of workers. Inadequate information to managers can affect a broad area of performance, because their spans of supervision affect many persons and activities.

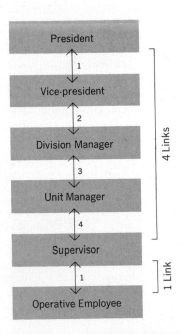

FIGURE 22-1

Most links in two-way communication chains are within management.

One additional reason is that most of the links in the communication chain, from top to bottom and bottom to top, are in the management group. Figure 22-1 shows how a communication chain from an operative employee to the president has four management links and only one employee link. Theoretically each link affords an equal opportunity for distortion, fading, and delay, which means that the greater proportion of these problems are intramanagement when the communication chain is long.

Finally, management communication is needed for its own sake, rather than as a means of informing workers. Managers are employees having needs for communication and understanding just like anyone else.

IMPROVING MANAGEMENT COMMUNICATION. Research shows that management people engage in a large amount of *lateral communication* or *cross-communication,* which is communication across chains of command. For example, one study of a group of managers reported that two-thirds of their communication events were cross-communications, being either horizontal or diagonal in direction. Only one-third of their communication was vertical within their chain of command.[1]

A study of information networks in another company found that information of general interest was just as likely to be cross-communicated between production, sales, office, and industrial relations departments as to be communicated within one of them. Chain-of-command communication tended to predominate only when it was required; and sometimes even then it was secondary because the grapevine exceeded it in activity. Figure 22-2 shows an information chain about a quality-control problem in this company, first brought to the attention of a group sales manager in a letter from a customer. Although it was the type of problem that could have been communicated along the chain of command, the chart shows that only three of fourteen communications were within the chain of command and only six remained within sales where the information was first received.[2]

Evidence from these two studies suggests that cross-communication is the predominant pattern within management. It needs to be emphasized in programs for improving the flow of management information. Practices such as management lunchrooms, coffee hours, and recreation rooms have their social importance, but they are also significant stimulants to cross-communication. Managers also use boards, committees, conferences, and meetings for the exchange of information.

Many organizations have developed special written communications for their managers in order to keep them better informed. Examples are newsletters, bulletins, and special booklets to inform managers about policies, services, and products. Other employers provide copies of their employee magazine to managers ahead of general release, so that they will be informed about its contents. Another practice is to hold management conferences at locations away from work so that there can be open communication without work interferences. All these practices seek to keep managers better informed so that they can make sounder decisions.

395

DOWNWARD COMMUNICATION

Communication downward in an organization means that flow is from higher to lower authority. This is usually considered to be from management to operating employees, but much of it is also within the management group. Downward communication tends to dominate in mechanistic organizational systems, as defined by Burns and Stalker. In organic systems there is a more open, multidirectional flow of information so that downward communication plays a reduced role. People transmit and receive information in all directions, depending on work needs more than the chain of authority.

In downward communication management has at its disposal a multitude of elaborate techniques and skilled staff assistance. Yet with all this help it many times has done a poor job. Fancy booklets, expensive films, and noisy public-address systems often have failed to achieve employee understanding. Sometimes these devices have become ends in themselves; they have been made more expensive, prettier, or fancier, without any evidence that this approach improved

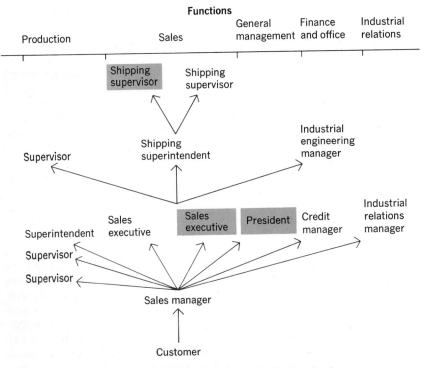

Note: Executives in boxes received chain-of-command communications

FIGURE 22-2 ████████████████████████████

Communication chain for a quality-control problem.

employee understanding. These employee communications have been technically efficient, but inefficient in genuine communication.

SOME PREREQUISITES. Part of management's failure has been that it has not prepared for effective communication. It has failed to lay a good foundation, without which its communication "house" has been built upon sand. What are some of these prerequisites?

Get informed. If managers do not know and understand, they cannot communicate. This sounds trite, but it actually appears that some managers do not learn the information they are expected to communicate. Obviously it is best to know in advance if possible. If a manager has to go get answers every time employees ask a question, they will soon turn to some other source of information. However, there will be times when a manager cannot answer a question. In that case the manager loses face by making up an answer or complaining, "How should I know—they don't tell me." Instead, the manager should face the situation squarely by saying, "Hank, I don't know that myself, but I will surely find out for you." As soon as the information can be secured, the manager should provide it.

Develop a positive communication attitude. Many managers do a poor communication job because they do not care about it. They sometimes say it is important, but their actions show that they really do not care. Some managers mistakenly assume they have a positive attitude, but actually they tell a worker only what they think is necessary, or they communicate only when they are compelled to do so. The positive manager attempts to share information with employees according to their needs. The manager helps employees feel informed, as well as be informed.

Plan for communication. No managerial plan of action is complete until there is a plan for communicating it to those who will be affected. Since people like to be told in advance about changes that affect them, communication usually comes at the beginning of a course of action rather than at the end of it. Perhaps you, the reader, can remember times in your own experience when you were not informed of actions that clearly affected you. This feeling is not a pleasant one.

A suitable plan for communication will develop policies and procedures so that people can expect to be informed. Then they will have less anxiety about whether they are "in the know" and will waste less time trying to get the information by other means. Employee bulletins in one organization, for example, were posted by personnel representatives. Sometimes the same information was distributed to each supervisor in the *Management Bulletin,* but sometimes it was not. The result was that management people were never sure whether they were supposed to read the employee bulletin board or not. They were constantly anxious whether they had the latest news, and sometimes they were embarrassed by their ignorance when an employee asked about something that was read on the bulletin board. There was management anxiety because there was no plan for communication. In summary, every plan of managerial action should have a plan for communicating it to those who will be affected.

Gain the trust of others. Trust between senders and receivers is important in all communication. When trust is lacking, it impedes information flow among people. They have less drive to send messages and less reason to believe those which are received. The result tends to be inadequate information flow and impaired effectiveness. In the case of downward communication, if subordinates do not have trust in superiors, they are not as likely to listen or to believe messages that are received. For example, one study of subordinates in four organizations showed that the higher the trust in their superior, the more they believed information from the superior was accurate.[3]

Without trust, employees search between the lines, wondering, "Why did management say that? Why did it not say something else? What was its purpose?" If employees suspect trickery, unfairness, or blindness to their wants, they tend to react negatively and seize upon every opportunity to misinterpret what was said. Essentially, meaning is more effectively communicated when there is trust and the communicator's purpose is understood. Of course, even when receivers have trust and understand the purpose, they do not always agree with the communication; but these conditions do establish open communication so that people may seek agreement.

COMMUNICATION NEEDS. Persons downward in an organization have a number of communication needs, one of which is instruction regarding their work. In a situation like this, managers secure better results if they state their instructions in terms of the objective requirements of the job, so that the instructions do not appear to be a personal wish.

As the uncertainty of a task increases, there is need for increased information flow in order to maintain a comparable level of performance.[4] For example, an employee performing a standardized, repetitive machine task needs little communication input about the task. On the other hand, an engineer working on an experimental project may require substantial and frequent communication input in order to perform successfully. These relationships mean that managers need to adjust their communication activity contingent upon the task needs of their subordinates and others with whom they coordinate work.

Employees also need feedback about their performance. There are many reasons. It helps them know how well they are meeting their own goals. It shows that others are interested in what they are doing. Assuming that performance is satisfactory, it enhances one's self-image and feeling of success. Generally, performance feedback leads to both improved performance and improved attitudes.

One study covered service jobs in four telephone company plants. Performance feedback was given regarding how well weekly goals were met. When feedback was given, all three performance measures improved significantly. The three measures were cost, safety, and service.[5] Another study with managers showed that more frequent communication of performance reports was correlated with better performance and better attitudes.[6]

General communication with employees is governed by two well-accepted standards. One important standard is to give priority to information about items that affect employees directly rather than indirectly. Matters such as working conditions, supervisory relationships, operating rules, fringe benefits, and policies are of special interest to employees. Most employees welcome these types of information when they can secure them.

A second standard is that information should reach employees as news, rather than as a stale confirmation of what already has been learned from other sources. To speed communication to employees, some organizations prepare daily recorded telephone messages that employees can receive by dialing a certain number. Messages can be changed during the day as new information becomes available. The systems usually are automatic, operating twenty-four hours daily, so that employees can call from their homes or elsewhere. Some systems are adjusted to allow telephone questions and comments from employees. Where an answer is appropriate, it is secured and put on the system at a later date. In this manner two-way communication is established.

Managers think that they understand the problems of their employees, but often their employees do not think so. This fundamental difference in perception tends to exist at each level in organizations, thereby making communication more difficult. One study gave the following results: 95 percent of supervisors said that they understood their employees' problems well, but only 34 percent of their employees thought they did. Though 95 percent of supervisors thought they were understanding, only 51 percent of them thought their general supervisor understood them; however (here we go again), 90 percent of the general supervisors thought they understood their subordinate supervisors.[7] In other words, each group thought it understood those below, but that those above did not understand it. These perceptions cause downward communicators to be overconfident and probably not to take enough care with their downward communication.

REASONS FOR ACCEPTING A COMMUNICATION. In the final analysis, a person's acceptance of any communication depends on certain conditions. These conditions apply particularly to downward communication, and they are as follows:

1. Acceptance of the legitimacy of the sender to send the communication.

2. Power of the sender to enforce sanctions on the receiver either directly or indirectly.

3. Perceived competence of the sender relative to the issue communicated.

4. Trust in the sender as a leader and person.

5. Perceived credibility of the message received.

6. Acceptance of the tasks and goals that the communication is trying to accomplish.

UPWARD COMMUNICATION

The two-way flow of information becomes a communication circuit quite similar to an electrical circuit. If the circuit is broken by a poor upward flow, management loses touch with employee needs and lacks sufficient information to make sound decisions. It is, therefore, unable to be supportive of the work group.

The need for upward communication is illustrated by the difficult experience of a manufacturing company. During a period of two or three years as the company gradually grew, there was a noticeable letdown in productivity and effective work practices. Management made increasing use of methods engineers and more careful standards. In addition, supervisors were encouraged to tighten up and put pressure on their employees. Productivity still lagged; so management used various downward communication actions such as bulletins, leaflets, and pay envelope notices to encourage employees to be more productive. Articles were put in the company magazine to try to motivate employees toward more enthusiasm and loyalty. Production, however, remained low.

Finally, management brought in an interviewing team from the home-office personnel department. Most complaints were petty ones, but there did seem to be a general feeling among older supervisors and employees that as the company grew they were becoming more and more separated from higher management. They felt isolated and unable to discuss their problems with anyone. Then, as management tightened its standards, they felt unreasonable pressures. Gradually, they became alienated from management and tended to spread their alienation to the newer employees who were being hired as the company expanded.

As soon as management discovered the basic problem, it was able to take corrective action. The unfortunate fact is that most of these difficulties could have been avoided in the beginning if management had developed an effective procedure for genuinely encouraging upward communication. With effective upward communication, management could have recognized the tendency toward alienation early enough to do something about it.

BARRIERS. Both research and experience indicate that the upward flow of information tends to be inadequate in organizations. One study reports that communications with superiors are perceived by employees as most important of all and among the most satisfying; however, these are the types of communications that employees are least able to initiate.[8]

There tends to be a minimum of upward communication unless management positively encourages it. Management needs to "tune in" to employees in the same way a person with a radio tunes in. This requires initiative and positive action, rather than the lethargy of waiting for the signal to come in. Tuning in requires management adaptability to different channels of employee information. It requires sensitivity to even the weak signals from the employee. It requires sensitivity to the distant signals as well as those near at hand. It necessitates some selectivity to separate useless signals from the worthwhile signals. It requires first and last an awareness that signals are being sent.

Upward communications tend to travel slowly. They are usually subject to more delay, filtering, and dilution. Each level is reluctant to take a problem upward because to do so is considered an admission of failure; therefore each level delays it in an effort to decide how to solve it. If it cannot be solved, it may be *filtered*. This refers to each person's conscious and subconscious editing of the information passed upward. There is a natural tendency for an employee to tell a superior only what the employee thinks the superior wants to hear. Obviously a superior cannot be told all that subordinates know, so each subordinate has genuine reasons for selecting, interpreting, and other filtering actions. Usually the employee is doing the best that human emotions and judgment will allow, but by the time filtering has happened at several levels, the original communication may be hardly recognizable. To further complicate the situation, one study in government reported that even when undesirable feedback reaches top managers, they often are so involved with other issues that they tend to overlook it and not respond to it.[9]

Sometimes in an effort to avoid filtering, persons *short-circuit* the information chain, which means that they skip one or more steps in the communication hierarchy. Although this avoids filtering, it introduces the disadvantage that one or more persons who are supposed to know the information are bypassed, which provokes them in two ways. First, they think the employee who skipped them is not accepting their role in the formal organization. Second, they are anxious for fear their superior will discover that they do not know something they are supposed to know. Few employers permit short-circuiting of this type, because it develops too much conflict. If it is permitted at all, the condition is that an employee must secure the direct supervisor's permission before talking to someone higher in the chain of command. The grapevine, of course, is the exception. It has no definite channels and can readily short-circuit any formal communication chain.

When upward communication is received and management fails to respond to it, that lack of action becomes a barrier to further upward communication. A basic communication idea is that *upward communication is encouraged when there is feedback in response to it.* Conversely, lack of feedback suppresses upward communication, as the following experience indicates.

Managers of sales branches in one company were encouraged in a special memorandum to further the company's interest by offering suggestions for improvement of the firm's customer relations. Shortly after this memorandum was received, one branch manager asked the company to review a "fine print" clause in one of its sales contracts, because several industrial customers had objected to it. Immediately after his letter, he received a telephone inquiry from a member of higher management. One year later he had received no further feedback, and the clause had not been amended. He commented to the interviewer, "A response of this kind doesn't encourage further upward communication."

IMPROVING UPWARD COMMUNICATION. Management develops better upward communication by encouraging it through such actions as better listening, building trust, and response to messages that are received. In addition, there needs to be a general policy to define what kinds of upward messages are desired. Following is a sample policy.

Employees shall keep their direct supervisors informed about the following subjects:

1. Any matters in which the supervisor may be held accountable by those at higher levels. (This includes all basic accountability for performance of one's assigned job.)

2. Any matters in disagreement or likely to cause controversy within or between any units of the organization.

3. Matters requiring advice by the supervisor or coordination with other persons or units.

4. Any matters involving recommendations for changes in, or variance from, established policies.

5. Any other matter that will enable higher management to improve economic and social performance.

In addition to suitable policies, various practices may be used to improve upward communication. Counseling, grievance systems, consultive supervision, meetings, suggestion systems, job satisfaction surveys, and other practices are discussed in other chapters. Additional practices appropriate for discussion at this point are the open-door policy, participation in social groups, encouragement of employee letters, and nominal groups.

The open-door policy. The *open-door policy* is a statement that employees are welcome to come to their manager's office, or perhaps others in management, for a visit on any matter that concerns them. The policy is attractive in theory, because it indicates a willingness to communicate, but it has limitations in practice. Though the door physically is open, psychological and social barriers exist that make employees reluctant to enter. Some employees hesitate to be singled out as lacking information or having a problem. Others are afraid they will incur their manager's disfavor. The way the open door can be most effective is for managers to walk through it and get out among their people. The open door is for managers to walk through, not employees!

Sometimes an open-door policy is used to mask a manager's own hesitancy to make contacts with those beyond the door. As one manager said, "The open door is often a slogan to hide closed minds." On the other hand, a genuine open door can be a real aid to upward communication. The true test is whether the manager behind the door has an open-door attitude and whether employees feel psychologically free to enter.

One company moved its open door from managerial offices to the company cafeteria with dramatic results.[10] It set up a program called "Operation Speakeasy" in which senior managers had lunch with small groups of employees in the company cafeteria. One manager ate with three employees, keeping the group small to allow genuine participation by each employee.

Employees signed for tables on a voluntary basis, and then managers were assigned to tables, making sure that employees ate with someone who did not manage them either directly or indirectly. This arrangement helped employees feel more free to discuss matters openly. Management promised only to listen. Union approval of the program was secured in advance.

Although the program was voluntary, more than 80 percent of employees chose to participate, and inputs were significant. Each manager made regular reports of problem areas identified at the luncheons, but without mentioning names. These reports became the basis for extensive problem study and corrective action. The main areas of comments were productivity (32 percent), job satisfaction (26 percent), and poor communication (23 percent).

Other organizations encourage telephone calls or personal contacts with their personnel director or communication director. The director then provides inputs to appropriate management representatives regarding issues that concern employees. If a response to an identified employee is required, the director secures it and makes a return call to the employee. Whatever the approach used, the objective is to show employees that management has an "open door" that is receptive to all employee questions and inputs.

Participation in social groups. Informal, casual recreational events furnish superb opportunities for unplanned upward communication. This spontaneous information sharing reveals true conditions better than most formal communications. There are departmental parties, sports events, bowling groups, hobby groups, picnics, and other employer-sponsored activities. Upward communication is not the primary purpose of these events, but it is an important by-product of them.

Encouragement of employee letters. Some employers actively encourage letters from employees. They feel that this is a personal and direct way for employees to put their ideas before management. One device that encourages letters is a column titled "Answers to Your Questions" or "Employee Letters" in the company magazine. This approach, in addition to getting information, confirms to employees that management is interested in their viewpoints.

One large company in the United States developed an effective upward-communication letter-writing program, which produced 31,000 employee questions in eight years after it was established.[11] An employee who has a question writes it on a special form which is sent to the administrator of the program, usually the editor of the local plant newspaper. When a letter is received, the editor gives it a number and tears off the name and address tab, dropping it into a locked box which only the editor can open.

According to company policy, the editor is authorized to go to any person in the organization—all the way to the chairman of the board if necessary—to get an appropriate answer to the question. Answers are prepared by the responsible official who knows the information, rather than by the editor. These answers are then forwarded to the editor, who identifies the address from the number on the question and forwards it privately to the person who originally asked the question. In this manner, no one but the editor ever knows who asked the question. As a result of this respect for privacy, 92 percent of the letters submitted have been signed by employees. When anonymous letters are submitted, they are normally answered in the plant newspaper.

This system has proved quite effective, both as a means of upward com-

munication to management, expressing the sentiments and problems of employees, and as a way for management to reach employees to improve their understanding. Thus, it is successful two-way communication. It also has caused management to review many of its practices.

Nominal grouping. Another approach is *nominal grouping,* by which small groups of employees are assembled to provide upward inputs to management.[12] The groups are called nominal because they are groups in name only, since they do not interact to discuss the issues raised. They simply offer comments without discussion to such questions as the following:

What changes could be made to improve your working environment?

What problems in our organization deserve special attention?

After an adequate time to offer inputs in response to the question, the group votes without discussion on the top five or ten items that have been presented. In this way management has employee viewpoints concerning what the top-ranking issues are.

COMMUNICATION IN SPECIALIZED GROUPS

As an institution grows in size and complexity, research, engineering, accounting, and other specialized groups grow in size and importance. These specialists, called staff in classical line-and-staff organization, play a leading role in communication far beyond their own departments. One reason is that many communication activities are usually assigned to them. In some instances their primary activity is communication. They perform such functions as gathering data, issuing reports, preparing directives, coordinating activities, and advising persons, as well as countless other communication functions.

Secondly, since many specialists lack command (line) authority, they have greater motivation to communicate because they realize that their success is more dependent upon selling their ideas to others. Managers with authority, on the other hand, are often lulled into poor communication by the fact that they can order an action even when they cannot sell it.

A third reason is that specialists usually have shorter communication chains to higher management. For example, a supervisor in a large factory must go through five levels to reach the executive vice president, but a personnel specialist goes through only three levels. This proximity to management permits some specialists to have the "ear" of higher management and to short-circuit the line. The results are both good and bad. Communication upward and downward tends to be improved, but lower management often waits in insecurity with the fear that it is being bypassed or criticized without an opportunity to answer.

A fourth reason is that the specialists' work usually gives them more mobility than operating workers have. Specialists in such areas as personnel and control find that their duties both require and allow them to go out of their offices and visit other areas without someone wondering if they are "not working." They also find it easier to get away for coffee or just to visit. All of this means that they have the chance to receive and spread information widely and regularly, because they have more communication linkages with others.

Finally, specialists are often more involved in the chain of procedure than others. For example, a production-control problem may clear through five specialists but only three operating persons while it is being solved.

The typical specialized unit is quite active in cross-communication with other internal groups because its activities usually affect several chains of command rather than just one. It also has many contacts outside the institution. Figure 22-3 shows the communication patterns of an engineering unit in a factory. A large number of this unit's contacts are with company groups outside its own chain of command and groups outside the institution. Its span of communication is broad.

My own research confirms the broad communication role of specialists. In one company, when information was of general interest, the staff group both received and transmitted proportionately more information than the line group. The significant points for organizational behavior are as follows: (1) Specialized groups need to be trained in communication regardless of their technical expertness; (2) they need to recognize the importance of their communication role; and (3) management should recognize their role and make full use of it in organizational communication.

The large amount of cross-communication by specialists and others requires an organizational policy to guide them. An effective guide was introduced in 1916 by Henri Fayol, a French industrialist, and it is usually called *Fayol's bridge.*[13] He

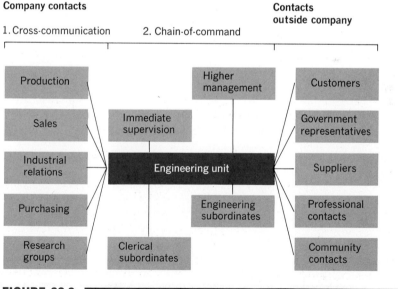

Company contacts   **Contacts outside company**

1. Cross-communication   2. Chain-of-command

FIGURE 22-3

Communication patterns of an engineering unit.

showed that cross-communication was both necessary and appropriate, especially for those near the bottom of chains of command, as shown in Figure 22-4. It is a waste of time and resources to require J to communicate with K by going step by step up the tenuous chain of command to A and then down to K. In fact, a requirement of this type makes cross-communication almost impossible. Instead of making cross-communication difficult, management should encourage it as a device of good management subject to two conditions:

1. Permission of the direct supervisor should be obtained in advance by the employee. This permission may be in the form of a general policy statement that designates the type of cross-communication that is permitted.

2. Each communicator should inform the direct supervisor of any significant results of the cross-communication.

COMMUNICATING WITH EMPLOYEE'S FAMILIES

There is general agreement that an employee's on-the-job performance is affected by off-the-job influences, and one of the most significant is the employee's family. Since most regular employer communications, such as bulletin boards, are not available to families, management has to develop special approaches to integrate families into the communication system. Employees usually cooperate in this matter because they want their families to know about their work.

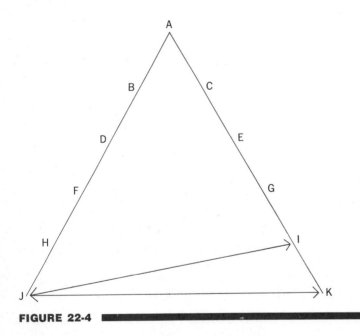

FIGURE 22-4

Fayol's bridge for cross-communication (shown for employee J).

A frequent practice is to mail important communications to employees' homes so that family members can read the information if they are interested. Some employers mail their employee magazines to homes, or they ask each employee to take one home. This is successful, because workers report an average home readership of one to two persons besides themselves. Other employers provide material for the family through information racks, and they mail their annual report to employee homes.

Open houses are a popular way to tell and show families about their breadwinners' jobs. An open house is especially necessary if the workplace is otherwise inaccessible to families. In addition to open houses, family picnics are used to introduce families personally to supervisors and other members of management. If a company is multiplant, invitations may be extended to visit headquarters. One multistore retailer invites employees and their families to spend a day of their vacation visiting company general offices. They are given a guided tour and taken to a major-league baseball game when one is available.

THE UNION ROLE IN COMMUNICATION

When a labor union represents any employee group, it has a direct interest in what information employees receive; however, it is a matter of debate regarding the degree to which the union itself should participate in an institution's communication program.

The chief advantages of using the union are:

1. It is a regularly established channel upon which many employees already depend.

2. Its support of any information may strengthen employee acceptance of the information.

3. If the union is left out, it may, without consulting the employer, interpret the situation in its own way in a manner detrimental to the employer.

Four disadvantages of using the union are:

1. If management gives some of its communication function to the union, management releases control but is still responsible. This is unwise.

2. If management lets the union handle much of its communication, management gets out of practice, stale, and unable to do its communication job when it must.

3. Unions have their own communication problems, which are more than they can handle and will receive first priority anyway; therefore, it is unwise to expect the union to help.

4. The union might misuse the information for its own benefit.

When there is union representation, the union is already involved in many communication activities, such as grievance procedures and layoff notices. The real question, then, is whether the union should be consciously brought further into the communication program. This depends upon the type of cooperation and understanding that exists in each individual employer-union relationship. In some cases, it is desirable; in other cases, it would be hazardous. Research shows that when management and labor perceive themselves in a win-lose conflict, any attempt by one to influence the other simply tends to increase each side's commitment to its own group and its rejection of the other side.[14] In any case, management should be certain that any information that is released to the union is also given earlier or concurrently to members of the management group. To do otherwise places supervisors at a disadvantage when dealing with employees and the union.

SUMMARY

Communication is the process by which all human interaction takes place. Significant groups in this process are management, employees, specialists, families of employees, and labor unions. Management communication is especially important because it is the usual channel by which information reaches employees, and most links in the communication chain are within management. Upward communication is much more difficult to develop than downward communication.

Specialists play an active communication role. They have the responsibility, motivation, organizational position, mobility, and procedural involvement needed to communicate extensively. The family is significant in communication because its feelings affect employee performance. Unions also may be involved in an organization's communication program. An effective communication system results when all persons and groups are interacting with understanding of the events that affect them.

TERMS AND CONCEPTS FOR REVIEW

Lateral communication or cross-communication

Open-door policy

Communication filtering

Nominal grouping

Communication short-circuit

Fayol's bridge

REVIEW QUESTIONS ■■■■■■■■■■■■■■■■■■■■■■■■■■■■■■■■

1. Why is communication within the management group important?

2. What kind of communication tends to dominate in mechanistic organizations? Discuss.

3. Explain the significance of trust in communication.

4. Discuss how upward communication might be improved in a

5. Discuss the role that staff specialists play in communication.

CASES

THE EARLY WORK SCHEDULE

Mabel Thomas was employed to work with the food service of Community Hospital. She was married but had no children. The job for which she was employed required that she work two days a week from 5 A.M. to 2 P.M. The other three days she worked the regular day food schedule from 8:30 A.M. to 5:30 P.M. When she was employed either she failed to hear information about the early work schedule or the employment clerk forgot to tell her. She feels sure that if the early schedule had been mentioned to her she would have heard it, because under those conditions she would not have taken the job.

During the first two weeks the job required Thomas to work the regular day shift in order to have an instructor show her how to do the job; consequently, Thomas thought she was on the regular day shift. She vaguely remembers that near the end of her first two weeks her supervisor mentioned something to her about beginning her regular schedule, but she did not understand what the supervisor meant and she did not inquire further. The result was that Thomas failed to report for work on the early schedule on the required day. When she did report for work at the regular hour of 8:30 A.M., her supervisor criticized her for lack of responsibility. Thomas said she could not work the early shift for family reasons and resigned.

QUESTION

1. Analyze the communication blockages in this case. Discuss ideas such as upward and downward communication, listening, feedback, and inference. Then explain how you would handle the employment and probationary work period for Thomas.

THE ROUTE MANAGER'S SUGGESTION

Jim Abel is a route manager for a bottling plant serving a metropolitan area of about 250,000 persons and a large number of small towns as much as fifty miles away. Abel is married, age 29, a high school graduate, and a friendly person. His employees like him and work well with him. In addition, he is cooperative with management and reasonably energetic. He became a route manager only six months ago, and has only four years of seniority. He appears to be the kind of person who has potential for long-run service and possibly further promotion.

On Tuesday afternoon Abel walked into the office of his Sales Manager, Ralph Parks, and asked, "Do you have five minutes, Ralph?" Parks was an older man with 15 years of seniority and 1 year's experience in the job of Sales Manager. At that time he was quite busy with some rush reports for the front office, so he replied, "Sure, we can take five, but let's keep it short, because I have to get these reports finished."

Abel sat down and proceeded to get enthusiastic about an idea he had for improving route procedures in a way that he thought might save both mileage and time. He was so enthusiastic that five minutes passed and then ten minutes, but his idea was not yet fully explained. However, from what had been said, it appeared to Parks that this idea had been proposed a number of times before and had been tried about five years ago—and it failed. Parks was getting impatient. He needed to finish those reports, and he could take no more time.

Feeling that he should not dampen Abel's enthusiasm at this point, Parks told Abel that the idea was more complicated than he expected and they had more than used up his available time. He suggested that they meet together the next morning at an appointed time when Parks would have more time for discussion. Even though Parks was sure that Abel's idea would not work, he thought at least he should hear Abel's full story, since this was his first major suggestion as route manager.

The next morning Abel was ready at the appointed time, and the men had a thorough fifteen-minute discussion. Abel was enthusiastic about his suggestion, but by the end of the discussion it was evident to Parks that the idea was the same kind that had been tried before and had failed. However, Abel had so much enthusiasm for the idea, Parks was not sure what to do.

QUESTIONS
1. What kinds of communication and other organizational behavior problems does Parks face at the end of the case? Discuss.
2. Outline for Parks how he should communicate with Abel at the end of the case. Give reasons for the alternatives you recommend.

THE OFFICE PROCEDURE
Joe Gonzales was a new employee with less than six months of seniority, but he had several years of office experience elsewhere. His new supervisor, Jane Campbell, was recently transferred from another supervisory position in the office. On one occasion Gonzales came to Campbell for help with an office procedure. Campbell offered her suggestion, but Gonzales failed to follow it and problems developed with the procedure. Within two months this same chain of events was repeated three more times. Campbell took no action regarding these events.

After the fourth mistake the office manager, who was Campbell's supervisor, went directly to Gonzales to discuss the error with him. Campbell saw them talking and arrived in time to hear Gonzales say "I keep asking Jane for help, but she doesn't give me much."

Campbell intervened and said, "Joe, you know that's not true, and if you ever lie about me again, I'll fire you." Campbell then walked away.

QUESTIONS
1. Discuss the communication errors and successes made by all three parties in this relationship.
2. What action should be taken by any of the three parties at the end of the case? Discuss.

REFERENCES

1. A. K. Wickesberg, "Communication Networks in the Business Organization Structure," *Academy of Management Journal,* September 1968, pp. 253–262.

2. Keith Davis, "Management Communication and the Grapevine," *Harvard Business Review,* September–October 1953, pp. 47–48.

3. Karlene H. Roberts and Charles A. O'Reilly III, "Failures in Upward Communication in Organizations: Three Possible Culprits," *Academy of Management Journal,* June 1975, pp. 205–215.

4. Jay Galbraith, *Designing Complex Organizations,* Reading, Mass.: Addison-Wesley Publishing Company, Inc., 1973, pp. 8–21.

5. Jay S. Kim and W. Clay Hamner, "Effect of Performance Feedback and Goal Setting on Productivity and Satisfaction in an Organizational Setting," *Journal of Applied Psychology,* February 1976, pp. 48–57.

6. Doris M. Cook, "The Impact on Managers of Frequency of Feedback." *Academy of Management Journal,* September 1968, pp. 263–277.

7. Rensis Likert, "Motivational Approach to Management Development," *Harvard Business Review,* July–August 1959, pp. 75–82.

8. Norman H. Berkowitz and Warren G. Bennis, "Interaction Patterns in Formal Service-oriented Organizations," *Administrative Science Quarterly,* June 1961, p. 49.

9. Herbert Kaufman, *Administrative Feedback: Monitoring Subordinates' Behavior,* Washington, D.C.: The Brookings Institution, 1973, pp. 1–83.

10. J. N. Smith, "Operation Speakeasy: An Experiment in Communication," *Management Review,* March 1973, pp. 46–50.

11. "Letters to the Editor," *Harvard Business Review,* November–December 1967, p. 56.

12. Thad B. Green and Paul H. Pietri, "Using Nominal Grouping to Improve Upward Communication," *MSU Business Topics,* Autumn 1974, pp. 37–43.

13. Henri Fayol, *General and Industrial Management,* trans. by Constance Storrs, New York: Pitman Publishing Corporation, 1949, pp. 34–36. Originally published in 1916.

14. Paul C. Buchanan, "How Can We Gain Their Commitment?" *Personnel,* January–February 1965, pp. 21–26.

CHAPTER 23
EMPLOYEE COUNSELING

While a drill press never sulks and a drop hammer never gets jealous of other drop hammers, the same cannot be said for people.

John L. McCaffrey[1]

Friend (to worker with unpleasant factory job): "Doesn't your job give you a lot of trouble?"

Worker: "Bother, perhaps, but never trouble. You see, trouble is on the heart, but bother is only on the hands."

Anonymous

LEARNING OBJECTIVES

TO UNDERSTAND:
The nature and uses of counseling
The role of conflict and stress in emotional upsets
Different counseling functions
The manager's counseling role
Different types of counseling

In an insurance office the work of a young stenographer became erratic as the result of an emotional conflict she was having with her mother. In a foundry a skilled worker asked for transfer to a semiskilled job in another department because "I just wouldn't work for that stupid supervisor even one more day." The foregoing incidents involve emotional problems that might be helped by employee counseling. No matter how well human relationships at work are handled, people will still develop emotional conflicts, and a prime way to treat these breakdowns is to counsel one or more of the parties involved.

Counseling, as covered in this chapter, is defined as discussion of an emotional problem with an employee, with the general objective of decreasing it.[2] Several implications of this definition should be explained. First, counseling deals with emotional problems. As indicated by the quotations at the beginning of this chapter, counseling is about "trouble on the heart," instead of "bother on the hands." It excludes job inconveniences that have no great emotional involvement, occupational guidance, job placement according to skill, advice on technical aspects of one's job, legal advice, and similar matters, as long as they are primarily nonemotional in content. Guidance in these areas is sometimes called "counseling," but the two are essentially different. Second, counseling involves discussion, meaning that it is an act of *communication*. Successful counseling depends on communication skills, primarily oral, by which one person's emotions can be shared with another.

A third point is that the general objective of counseling is to understand and/or decrease an employee's emotional disorder. If two people merely discuss socially an emotional problem of one of them, a social relationship may be established, but hardly a counseling one, because intent is not there. For counseling to exist the employee must be seeking understanding or help and/or the counselor must be offering it.

Fourth, the definition in no way limits counseling exclusively to professionally trained counselors. Professional counselors are needed for serious emotional disorders, but for less serious problems managers and others counsel employees. Supervisors especially deal with counseling, because of their close working relationship with employees. This chapter, therefore, is about both professional counseling and counseling by managers and others in the normal performance of their jobs. The subjects discussed are the role and function of counseling, types of counseling, and counseling programs.

THE ROLE OF COUNSELING

THE NEED FOR COUNSELING.   It is estimated that one person in ten suffers from a mental or emotional disorder. Many of these persons are not employed, but some are. Normally only persons with mild disorders are working. We sometimes refer to these persons as high-strung, overly sensitive, and angry with the world. There also are alcoholics and other drug abusers who are unable to cope with their environment. Other persons have temporary upsets resulting from events such as a broken love affair or inability to face retirement. We expect these upsets to pass eventually, but while they exist, a person needs understanding and occasional help. No more complex unit exists than a human being; hence, it is impossible for a person to be in optimum emotional balance all the time. However, the point of "blowup" varies for each person because tolerance of emotional stress varies among people.

It is not implied that emotional upsets are undesirable or "wrong." Nature gave people their emotions, and sometimes it is more disastrous to suppress an emotion such as anger than it is to go ahead and express it. However, emotional upsets can cause workers to do things that are harmful to their own best interests and/or those of the firm. They may leave the firm because of a trifling conflict that seems large to them; they may reduce their productivity; or they may undermine morale in their department. These reactions are "bread-and-butter" items to the organization because of their direct effect on performance. Managers want their employees to maintain a reasonable emotional equilibrium and to channel their emotions along constructive lines so that they will work together productively, cooperatively, and with economic, social, and psychological satisfaction. And managers depend upon counseling to help their workers keep this emotional balance. Neither managers' nor workers' feelings can be ignored at work. Feelings are to be accepted and understood because they are *facts* in any situation. Managers seldom ignore a pertinent mechanical fact, and neither can they safely ignore a pertinent emotional fact.

Although a few companies had programs for counseling employees prior to 1936, that was the date that modern counseling had its genesis in the now-famous program at Western Electric Company. It was started as an interviewing program in 1928, was abandoned from 1930 to 1936, and then was reorganized as a personnel counseling program.[3] This is believed to be the first company use of the term "personnel counseling" for employee-counseling services. The research at Western Electric clearly demonstrated that employee job satisfaction improved as a result of counseling.

Counseling programs received a large boost during World War II in both business and government for a number of reasons. Labor turnover was high, and many persons were employed who lacked industrial experience and were, therefore, more subject to confusion and upsets. Supervisors were so busy with production problems and so inexperienced that they were unable to cope with counseling needs and were often glad to have staff counseling services. When employment returned to normal after the war, many staff counseling programs were dropped or reduced, and more counseling duties were returned to supervisors.

CAUSES OF COUNSELING NEEDS. Any condition or combination of conditions, both on and off the job, may cause a need for counseling. Many of these conditions, such as job dissatisfaction, resistance to change, and alienation, have been discussed earlier. Other major conditions that merit discussion at this time are frustration, conflict, and stress.

FRUSTRATION. *Frustration* is a result of a motivation (drive) being blocked to prevent one from reaching a desired goal. If you are trying to finish a report by quitting time in the afternoon, and one interference after another develops to require your time, then by the middle of the afternoon when you see that your goal for the day may not be reached, you are likely to become frustrated. You may become irritable, develop an uneasy feeling in your stomach, or have some other reaction. These reactions to frustration are known as *defense mechanisms,* because you are trying to defend yourself from the psychological effects of the blocked goal.

The example given is merely a one-day frustration that probably will be overcome tomorrow, but the situation is more serious when there is a long-run frustration, such as a blocked opportunity for promotion. Then you have to live with the frustration day after day. It begins to build emotional disorders that interfere with your ability to function effectively.

Types of reactions. One of the most common reactions to frustration is aggression. Whenever people are aggressive, it is likely that they are reflecting frustrations that are upsetting them. Additional reactions to frustration include apathy, withdrawal, regression, fixation, physical disorders, and substitute goals. We can illustrate them by continuing the story of the blocked promotion. Assume that you think your supervisor, Mary Bowman, is blocking your promotion because she does not recognize your potential. The blockage may be real or only a result of your imagination, but in any case it is real to you. As a result of your frustration, you may become aggressive by demanding better treatment and threatening to appeal to higher management. Or you may do almost the reverse and become apathetic, not responding to your job or associates. Another reaction is withdrawal, such as asking for a transfer or quitting your job. Regression to less mature behavior also is possible, such as self-pity and pouting.

If there is a fixation, perhaps you constantly blame your supervisor for both your problems and the problems of others, regardless of the true facts. You also may develop a physical disorder such as an upset stomach, or choose a substitute goal such as becoming the leader of a powerful informal group in office politics. All of these are possible reactions to frustration. It is evident that they are not usually favorable, either to the individual or to the organization, so it is desirable in organizational behavior to reduce frustrating conditions.

Sources of frustration. Although the example concerns management as the source of frustration, management is only one of several sources of job frustration. Another major source is fellow workers who may place barriers in the way of goal attainment. Perhaps they delay work inputs to you, thereby delaying your work. Or their poorly done inputs prevent you from doing quality work. You also can be frustrated by physical objects such as a faulty machine.

A source of frustration rarely recognized is you, yourself. Perhaps your goals are higher than your present abilities. You may want promotion to a job that requires mathematical ability, but you did not learn it well in school, so others are better prepared for the job. The result is that you are frustrated. A mature solution is to return to school part-time and learn the mathematics that you lack. However, you may not be able to invest the time, so you remain frustrated as long as the strong drive exists.

Frustration and management practice. The stronger one's motivation or drive toward a blocked goal, the stronger one's frustration will be, other things being equal. If motivation is lacking, then very little frustration is likely to develop. This means that when management attempts to motivate employees strongly, it also should be prepared to remove barriers and help prepare the way for employees to reach their goals. The required managerial role is a supportive one. For example, if precision machine work is encouraged, the machinist needs proper training, equipment, tools, and materials for precision work. Similarly if an employee is assigned a special project and motivated to do it, then a suitable budget and other support is required in order to prevent frustration. The idea is not to remove all difficulties so that the assignment loses its challenge, but rather to provide enough support to make the project reasonably possible.

From this discussion it is evident that counseling can help reduce frustrations by helping employees choose mature courses of action to overcome blockages preventing goal accomplishment. The counselor also can advise management regarding blockages so that it can try to reduce or remove them.

CONFLICT. Both interpersonal and intergroup conflicts may cause emotional disorders. As people with different backgrounds, points of view, values, needs, and personalities interact, it is likely that a variety of conflicts will develop. Organizational change also contributes to conflict, because it realigns relationships among people. The result is that conflict is an inevitable part of organizational life. Sometimes the amount of conflict is substantial. Managers spend an estimated 20 percent of their time dealing with conflict.[4]

Conflict is not all bad. It has its benefits as well as disadvantages, so the behavioral goal is to try to reduce the disadvantages while increasing the benefits. One benefit is that people are stimulated to search for improved approaches that lead to better results. Another is that once-hidden problems are brought to the surface where they may be solved. Out of all this ferment a deeper understanding may develop among the parties involved.

There also are possible disadvantages. Cooperation and teamwork may deteriorate. Distrust grows, and distance is increased between people and groups that need to cooperate. People who are defeated in a conflict may feel demeaned, have a lower self-image, and lose their motivation. Even without defeat the conflict may cause severe emotional upsets.

Interpersonal conflicts are a serious problem to many people, because they reach deeply into a person's psychological being. There is a need to protect one's self-image and self-esteem from damage by others. When they threaten it, serious upsets occur. A common cause of conflict is personality clashes, such as those arising from differences in temperament. In other instances, conflicts develop from communication failures or different perceptions.

In an office an employee was upset by conflict with another employee in a different department. It seemed to the upset employee that there was no way to resolve the conflict. However, when a counselor explained the different organizational roles of the two employees as seen from the whole organization's point of view, the upset employee's perceptions changed, and the conflict vanished.

Intergroup conflict between different departments, cliques, or factions also causes emotional problems. On a minor scale it is something like the wars between juvenile gangs. Each group sets out to undermine the other and to gain power and high image for itself. Conflicts arise from such causes as different viewpoints, group loyalties, and competition for resources. Resources are limited in any organization, and most groups feel they need more than they can secure, so the seeds of intergroup conflict exist wherever there are limited resources. For example, the production department may want new and more efficient machinery, while the sales department wants to expand its sales force, but there are only enough resources to supply the needs of one group.

The basic organizational philosophy in conflict resolution is to try to move conflict from a lose-lose or win-lose emphasis to a win-win emphasis. Creative solutions are sought that provide benefits to both parties. Counseling assists conflict resolution by reducing emotional blockages and helping people develop win-win solutions. Other effective approaches already discussed include organizational development, supportive leadership, sensitivity training, and job and organizational design.

STRESS. Stress is a condition of strain on one's emotions, thought processes, and/or physical condition that seems to threaten one's ability to cope with the environment. Stress on the job is not necessarily undesirable. There is evidence that mild stress tends to stimulate performance in most persons,[5] but excessive stress can lead to physical and emotional disorders and lowered effectiveness. Problems occur especially when stress is sustained over a long period of time, because the human system is prevented from rebuilding its ability to respond to stress. People have different tolerances of stress. Some persons can tolerate much more stress than others and still feel that it is a healthy stimulus helping them meet challenges.

Although much is said about executive stress, managers and workers report about the same amount of job stress. If managerial work actually is more stressful, apparently the managerial selection process chooses managers who are better able to withstand it; so manager and worker feelings of stress are about the same.[6]

The job itself is a leading cause of stress. Employees may feel they have a work overload, pressures with which they cannot cope, tension, and insecurity. Role conflict and role ambiguity also are important causes of stress.[7] Conflicts with people are another major cause of stress. Stress may be aggravated when the conflict is with a supervisor or someone else who has power over the employee affected. Stress also may arise off the job and be brought to work by employees. Important causes are family and financial problems.

Stress is a major contributor to employee emotional disorders. Perhaps more important, it contributes to physical disorders, because the internal body system changes to try to cope with stress. Some physical disorders are short-range, such as an upset stomach. Others are longer range, such as a stomach ulcer. Stress over a prolonged time also contributes to degenerative diseases of the heart, kidneys, blood vessels, and other parts of the body. For these reasons, it is important for life stress, both on and off the job, to be kept at a level low enough for most people to tolerate without disorders.

COUNSELING RELATED TO OTHER TREATMENTS. Counseling is an important method for preventing and treating emotional disorders, but other methods also may be used. The medical department becomes involved in treating physical manifestations of stress and other emotional disorders. One of the most interesting and promising developments is *biofeedback,* by which people under medical guidance learn from instrument feedback to affect symptoms of stress such as rate of heartbeat. Until the 1960s it was thought that people could not control their autonomic nervous system which, in turn, controlled internal processes such as heartbeat, oxygen consumption, stomach acid flow, and type of brain waves. Research now shows that people may exercise some control over these internal processes, so biofeedback may be helpful in reducing undesirable effects of stress.[8]

Various practices for meditation, such as Zen, Yoga, and *transcendental meditation* (TM), have become popular in dealing with stress. Meditation involves quiet, concentrated inner thought. It helps remove persons temporarily from the stressful world and reduce certain physical symptoms of stress. Transcendental meditators try to meditate for two periods of twenty minutes a day, concentrating on silent repetition of a word called a "mantra." Meditation is so highly regarded that a few organizations have established a meditation room in their executive offices for private meditative practices. Many employees who meditate report favorable results.

One survey covered employees in several firms who had been actively practicing transcendental meditation for about a year. The meditators, compared with a control group, reported significant changes toward increased job satisfaction, better performance, less desire to leave their jobs, and better relationships with supervisors and associates. Their associates partly confirmed these improvements. Productivity gains tended to be higher at higher organizational levels and in more democratic organizational systems.[9]

Preliminary evidence suggests that meditation may be a useful way for many people in organizations to reduce emotional strain but counseling remains as the dominant method of dealing with emotional disorders.

WHAT COUNSELING CAN DO. The general objective of counseling is to give employees support in dealing with their emotional problems so that they will grow in self-confidence, understanding, self-control, and ability to work effectively in the organization. This objective is consistent with the supportive and human resources models of organizational behavior, which seek to encourage employee growth and self-direction. It is also consistent with Maslow's concept of higher-order needs, such as self-esteem and self-actualization.

The counseling objective is achieved through performance of one or more of the following *counseling functions.* As will be seen later, some types of counseling perform one function better than another.

1. Advice. Many persons look upon counseling as primarily an advice-giving activity, but in reality this is but one of several functions that counseling can perform. The giving of advice requires a counselor to make judgments about a counselee's emotional problems and to lay out a course of action. Herein lies the difficulty, because it is almost impossible to understand another person's complicated emotions, much less to tell that person what to do with them. Advice giving may breed a relationship in which the counselee feels inferior and emotionally dependent on the counselor. In spite of all its ills, advice giving occurs in routine counseling between managers and workers, because workers expect it and managers tend to provide it.

2. Reassurance. Counseling can provide employees with reassurance, which is a way of giving them courage to face a problem or confidence that they are pursuing a suitable course of action. Reassurance is represented by such counselor remarks as "You are making good progress, Linda," and "Don't worry; this will come out all right." One trouble with reassurance is that the counselees do not accept it. They are smart enough to know that the counselor cannot know that the problem will come out all right. Even if counselees do become reassured, their reassurance may fade away as soon as they face their problems again, which means that little real improvement has been made. Sometimes reassurance is dangerous. If, for example, a supervisor assures a mentally ill worker, "You are all right," this may keep the worker from getting needed professional treatment.

Though reassurance has its weaknesses, it is useful in some situations and is impossible to prohibit. Who is to say, for example, that an older woman supervisor should not reassure one of her lovelorn clerks, "If you will be patient, time will help heal your troubles"? Who will deny the clerk the benefit of others' experiences? Reassurance cannot be prohibited just because it is dangerous, any more than automobiles can be prohibited because they cause accidents; but, like automobiles, reassurance should be used carefully.

3. Communication. Counseling can improve both upward and downward communication. In an upward direction, it is a key way for employees to express their feelings to management. As many persons have said, often the top managers in an organization do not know how people at the bottom feel. The act of counseling initiates an upward signal, and if the channels are open, some of these signals will travel higher. Individual names must be kept confidential, but statements of feeling can be grouped and interpreted anonymously to management. An important part of any counselor's job is to discover emotional problems related to company policies and to interpret those problems to top management. Counseling also achieves downward communication because counselors help interpret company policies and procedures to employees as they discuss emotional problems related thereto.

4. Release of emotional tension. An important function of nearly all counseling situations is release of emotional tension, sometimes called emotional catharsis. People tend to get an emotional release from their frustrations and other problems whenever they have an opportunity to tell someone about them. Counseling history consistently shows that as persons begin to explain their problems to a sympathetic listener, their tensions begin to subside. They are more relaxed, and their speech is more coherent and rational. This release of tension does not necessarily solve their problems, but it does remove mental blocks in the way of solution, enabling them to face their problems again and think constructively about them. In some cases emotional release accomplishes the whole job, dispelling an employee's problems as if they were mental ghosts (which they largely were).

In a warehouse an electric-truck driver began to develop conflicts with his supervisor. The truck driver was convinced that his supervisor gave him the hardest jobs and otherwise took advantage of him. He was convinced that his supervisor did not like him and would "never" give him a raise. One day the elderly timekeeper was in the warehouse checking time records, and the truck driver, being particularly upset at the moment, cornered him and began to tell about his troubles. It all happened when the truck driver commented, "You don't need to worry about my time. I'll never get a rate increase, and I'll never have any overtime." The timekeeper asked, "Why?" and the conversation went on from there.

The timekeeper was a staff employee working for the warehouse superintendent, and was not therefore in the chain of command from superintendent to supervisor to truck driver. The truck driver felt free to talk with the timekeeper, who was outside the chain of command and had no authority over the driver. Perhaps also the truck driver perceived the timekeeper as a chain of communication around his supervisor to the superintendent. At any rate, the truck driver talked. And the timekeeper listened.

Since the timekeeper spent much of his time on the warehouse floor, he was closely acquainted with work assignments and the supervisor. The truck driver knew this; and as he stated his grievances, he began to revise and soften them because he realized some of them did not agree with details of the situation about which the timekeeper had firsthand knowledge. As the driver continued to bring his feelings out into the open, he felt easier and could discuss his problem more calmly. He realized that what he had said in the beginning was mostly a buildup of his own imagination and did not make sense in terms of the actual situation. He closed the conversation with the comment, "I guess I really don't have much of a problem, but I'm glad I told you anyway."

5. Clarified thinking. The foregoing case of the truck driver also illustrates another function of counseling, that of *clarified thinking*. The truck driver began to realize that his emotional comments did not match the facts of the situation. He found that he was magnifying minor incidents and jumping to drastic conclusions. As his emotional blocks to straight thinking were relieved, he began to think more rationally. In this case realistic thinking was encouraged because the driver recognized that he was talking to someone who knew the facts and was not emotionally involved.

Clarified thinking tends to be a normal result of emotional release, but a skilled counselor can act as a catalyst to bring about clear thinking more quickly. It should be noted that to clarify the counselee's thinking, the counselor serves as a catalyst only. If the counselor does the "clear thinking" and tells the counselee what is "right," then the function of advice has been accomplished rather than clarified thinking. Further, not all of the clarified thinking takes place while the counselor and counselee are talking. All or part of it may take place later as a result of developments during the counseling relationship. The net result of any clarified thinking is that a person is encouraged to accept responsibility for emotional problems and to be more realistic in solving them.

6. Reorientation. Another function of counseling is reorientation of the counselee. *Reorientation* is more than mere emotional release or clear thinking about a problem. It involves a change in the employee's psychic self through a change in basic goals and values. Very often it requires a revision of the employee's level of aspiration to bring it more in line with actual attainment. It causes people to recognize and accept their own limitations. Reorientation is the kind of function needed to help alcoholics return to normalcy or to treat a person with severe mental depression. It is largely a job for professional counselors who know its uses and limitations and who have the necessary training. The manager's job is to recognize those in need of reorientation before their need becomes severe, so that they can be referred to professional help in time for successful treatment.

THE MANAGER'S COUNSELING ROLE. Excluding reorientation, the other five counseling functions can be successfully performed by managers, assuming they have qualified themselves with a reasonable understanding of human behavior. They will at times perform all five of these counseling functions. On other occasions, if professional counseling services are available, they will refer employees to the professional counselors. The point here is that when counseling services are established, *managers must not conclude that all their counseling responsibilities have been transferred to the counseling staff.*

Managers are important counselors because they are the ones in day-to-day interaction with employees.[10] If managers close their eyes to the emotional problems of employees and refuse to discuss them, it appears that managers are saying to employees, "I don't care about you, just your work." Managers cannot, when an emotional upset arises, say, "This is not part of my job. Go see a counselor." Emotions are part of the whole employee and must be considered a part of the total employment situation for which a manager is responsible. For this reason all managers, from the lowest to the highest level, need training to help them understand emotional problems of employees and counsel them effectively.

Almost all problems brought to a manager have a combination of objective fact and emotional content in them; hence, a manager should not spend all day looking for emotional content when a rational answer will solve the problem. If an employee named Peggy Carson asks, "Is this desk going to be moved?" it may be that she is really wondering why, is worried that it may reduce her status, and so on; but it is also possible—just possible—that she only wants to know "Is this desk going to be moved?" If you answer, "Yes, over by the window," you have solved the problem she brought you, and there is no need to try to be an amateur psychiatrist about it! The manager needs to counsel sparingly, to encourage employees to be self-sufficient and stand on their own two feet emotionally. Counseling should not be meddlesome. The extreme of playing psychiatrist should be avoided. But to walk this tightrope the manager needs the patience of Job, the wisdom of Solomon, and the human insight of Freud!

It is said that the father of psychiatry, Sigmund Freud, warned about the dangers of seeing emotional meaning in everything a person says or does. When a friend asked him what was the emotional meaning of the pipe he smoked, he replied, "Sometimes, sir, a pipe is just a pipe," meaning that it had no particular emotional interpretation.

On the other hand, managers need to recognize that even the most trivial incidents may under the proper circumstances lead to emotional difficulties with employees. This point is illustrated by the experiences of a government supervisor named Darby. He noticed that one of his senior professional employees named Bristol became cool and unresponsive almost overnight. At first Darby thought that Bristol was preoccupied with a personal problem, but after two weeks of Bristol's behavior Darby was convinced he must have caused the behavior because Bristol was acting normally with others. Darby counted Bristol as one of his close friends and could recall no reason for their declining relationship. He knew that Bristol was a capable, loyal employee and a valuable specialist in the department.

After three weeks Darby asked Bristol into his office, explained what he had observed, and asked if there was anything they should discuss. Bristol blurted out that Darby had offended him deeply three weeks ago when he had sought Darby's help on a matter. Bristol said that Darby had sighed audibly as he left the room, thereby implying that Darby did not want to be bothered with such a trivial matter.

Darby replied that he remembered their discussion that day but he honestly did not remember sighing; and if he did sigh it was only general fatigue from a long day, because Bristol was fully justified in asking help on this matter. Darby again assured Bristol that his sigh had no relevance to their conversation.

Through counseling, Darby finally removed this misunderstanding, but he dealt more carefully with Bristol thereafter because he was convinced that Bristol was sensitive in personal relationships.

TYPES OF COUNSELING

When we look upon counseling in terms of the amount of direction that the counselor gives a counselee, we see that it is a continuum from full direction (directive counseling) to no direction (nondirective counseling). Between the two and somewhat nearer the nondirective end is cooperative counseling. These three counseling types will now be discussed in order to illustrate how counselors may vary the degree to which they control a counseling situation.

DIRECTIVE COUNSELING. *Directive counseling* is the process of listening to an employee's emotional problem, deciding with the employee what should be done, and then telling and motivating the employee to do it. Directive counseling mostly accomplishes the counseling function of *advice,* but it may also reassure, communicate, give emotional release, and to a minor extent clarify thinking. Reorientation is seldom achieved in directive counseling. Most everyone likes to give advice, counselors included, and it is easy to do. But is it effective? Does the counselor really understand the employee's problem? Does the counselor have the technical knowledge of human behavior and the judgment to make a "right" decision? Even if the decision is right, will the employee follow it? The answer to these questions is usually "no," and this is precisely why advice is generally an unwise act in counseling.

Though advice is of questionable value, some of the other functions achieved by directive counseling are worthwhile. If the directive counselor is first a good listener, then the employee should experience some emotional release. As the result of emotional release plus ideas that the counselor imparts, the employee may also clarify thinking. Furthermore, useful communication probably takes place. Both advice and reassurance may be worthwhile if they give the employee more courage to take a workable course of action that the employee supports.

NONDIRECTIVE COUNSELING. *Nondirective, or client-centered, counseling* is the process of skillfully listening and encouraging a counselee to explain bothersome emotional problems, understand them, and determine courses of action. It focuses on the counselee rather than on the counselor as judge and adviser; hence, it is "client-centered." This is the type of counseling usually practiced by professional counselors; however, managers may use its techniques to work more effectively with employees. Care should be taken to assure that managers are not oversold on the nondirective approach to the extent that they refrain from their normal directive leadership responsibilities.

One company gave a full two days of training to its managers on the non-directive approach. They went back to their jobs thoroughly sold on the idea and ready to put it into practice. The trouble was that they did not sufficiently understand its limitations. They refrained from stating their own opinions to employees in their day-to-day interaction. They hesitated to issue instructions and directives. Employees became confused, and their frustrations multiplied. The results were dysfunctional rather than functional, so finally management had to instruct its managers to return to their former ways of working with employees. If the nondirective approach was to be used to counsel, it was to be a supplement along with normal directive approaches, similar to cooperative counseling discussed in the next section.[11]

Professional nondirective counselors normally do not use advice and reassurance, but they do accomplish the other four counseling functions. Communication occurs, but it is primarily upward to management through the counselor. Emotional release takes place, even more effectively than with directive counseling, and clarified thinking tends to follow. The unique advantage of nondirective counseling is its ability to cause the employee's reorientation. It stresses changing the *person,* instead of dealing only with the immediate *problem* in the usual manner of directive counseling.

Nondirective counseling was developed concurrently by two groups: Mayo, Roethlisberger, and others at Western Electric Company; and Carl R. Rogers and his colleagues.[12] Here is the way nondirective counseling typically works.

Assume that Harold Pace comes to a counselor, Janis Peterson, for assistance. Peterson attempts to build a permissive relationship that encourages Pace to talk freely. At this point Peterson defines the counseling relationship by explaining that she cannot tell Pace how to solve his problem but that she may be able to help him understand his problem and deal satisfactorily with it. The employee then explains his feelings, and the counselor encourages their expression, shows interest in them, and accepts them without blame or praise. Eventually the negative feelings are drained away, giving the employee a chance to express tentatively a positive feeling or two, a fact that marks the beginning of the employee's emotional growth. The counselor encourages these positive feelings and accepts them without blame or praise, just as she did the negative feelings.

If all goes well, the employee should at this point begin to get some insight into his problem and to develop alternative solutions to it. As he continues to grow, he is able to choose a course of positive action and see his way clear to try it. He then feels a decreasing need for help and recognizes that the counseling relationship should end.

The preceding brief description of nondirective counseling makes it look as if the counselor does nothing but smile at the employee and say, "Uh huh," while the employee does all the work; hence, it is sometimes jokingly called "uh-huh counseling." To the contrary, the counselor's highest abilities are demanded throughout the interview. The counselor attempts to ask discerning questions, restate ideas, clarify feelings, and understand why these feelings exist. There is communication in many subtle ways (which probably means that some implied direction does occur,

424

even though the session is theoretically nondirective). This is a fluid, sensitive relationship that requires minute attention to every detail in the overall situation.

Throughout the counseling relationship it is important for the counselor to *accept* feelings, rather than *judge* them and offer blame or praise, because judgment may discourage the employee from stating true feelings. The following case illustrates how important it is to avoid bias in the interview.[13]

> Mary, an extrovert, came to see her counselor about a personal problem concerning her husband. She explained that her husband had run off with another woman, borrowing $50.00 from Mary's father to make the trip. More than that, he bought a new suit and charged it to Mary's account. Then Mary paused and waited for the counselor's reply.
>
> The counselor smiled and said, "Goodness, Mary, you have a lot to worry about, don't you?"
>
> Mary's reply was, " . . . I'm not worried about a thing except do I have to pay for that suit. Do you know a good, cheap lawyer?"

Professional counselors treat each counselee as a social and organizational equal. They primarily listen and try to help their client discover and follow improved courses of action. They especially "listen between the lines" to learn the full meaning of an employee's feelings. They look for the assumptions underlying the employee's statements and for the events and feelings that are so painful that the employee tends to avoid talking about them. As shown in Figure 23-1, nondirective

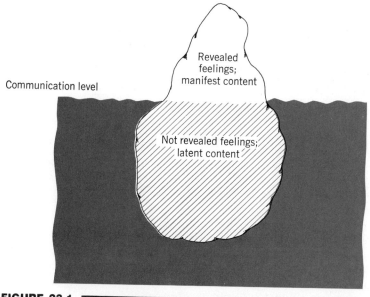

Communication level

Revealed feelings; manifest content

Not revealed feelings; latent content

FIGURE 23-1

Iceberg model of an employee's feelings in a counseling situation.

counselors follow an "iceberg model" of counseling in which they recognize that sometimes more feelings are hidden under the surface of a counselee's communication than are revealed. For this reason they constantly encourage the counselee to open up and reveal deeper feelings that constitute the *latent content* of the message, compared with the readily evident *manifest content.*

Managers often wonder how a nondirective counselor keeps the conversation going, since the focus is on listening. One way is to look and act interested. Another way is to ask appropriate questions. A third method of keeping the conversation going, and one that more managers could learn to use in day-to-day counseling, is the practice of *restatement,* or reflecting feelings. When an employee pauses and waits for the counselor to say something, the counselor cannot remain wholly quiet because the employee might think the counselor was bored or might become self-conscious. In this situation the counselor keeps conversation going by restating the employee's last idea. Suppose that an employee says, "My supervisor doesn't like me," and then pauses to see what the counselor has to say. Using restatement, the counselor replies, "You say that your supervisor doesn't like you." The counselor does not reply, "You say your supervisor won't give you a fair deal," because that changes the meaning. Neither does the counselor end the restatement with a question mark because that might suggest that the employee's feeling was not justified.

As a summary, here are several ways nondirective counseling differs from directive counseling:

1.   Counseling method—the employee primarily controls the direction of conversation and does most of the talking.

2.   Responsibility—solution of the problem is the employee's own responsibility.

3.   Status—the employee is equal to the counselor as a person, whereas the directive method implies that the counselor is superior and knows what to do.

4.   Role—the employee is psychologically independent as a person, choosing a solution and growing in ability to make choices in the future.

5.   Emphasis—emphasis is on deeper feelings and problems, rather than surface symptoms. Adjustment of a person is paramount, rather than solution of a current problem.

With all its advantages, nondirective counseling has several limitations that restrict its use at work. First of all, it is more time-consuming and costly than directive counseling. Just one employee with one problem may require many hours of a counselor's time, so the number of employees that a counselor can assist is limited. Professional counselors require professional education and consequently are expensive. Nondirective counseling also depends on a capable, willing employee. It assumes that the employee possesses a drive for mental health, has enough social intelligence to perceive what problems need solution, and has sufficient emotional stability to deal with them. The nondirective counselor needs to be cautious not to become a crutch for emotional hypochondriacs to lean on while avoiding their work responsibilities.

In some cases counseling itself is generally a weak solution because it returns the employee to the same environment that caused the problem. What is really needed is a better environment for employee psychological support. In this situation the counselor may step beyond the counseling role and give advice to management to take corrective action.

COOPERATIVE COUNSELING. Pure nondirective counseling by employers is not widespread because of its costs and other limitations. Directive counseling is losing favor because it seems inappropriate for modern-day counseling situations. This means that the kind of counseling that is best for modern managers to practice is somewhere between the two extremes of directive and nondirective counseling. This kind of compromise tries to integrate the advantages of both types, while throwing off many of the disadvantages of both.

One term for this compromise is *cooperative counseling*, because it is not wholly counselee-centered nor wholly counselor-centered; but rather the counselor and counselee mutually cooperate to apply their different knowledge, perspectives, and values to the problem. It is defined as a mutual discussion of an employee's emotional problem and a cooperative effort to set up conditions that will remedy it. Cooperative counseling can be practiced by persons not professionally trained for full-time counseling; yet it avoids the authoritarian approach of directive counseling. It requires training and takes time to practice, but not so much that managers cannot learn it and use it.

Cooperative counseling starts by using the listening techniques of nondirective counseling; but as the interview progresses, cooperative counselors may play a more positive role than a nondirective counselor plays. They may offer bits of knowledge and insight that they have. They may discuss the situation from their broader perspective of the organization, thus giving the employee different perspectives for comparison. In general, cooperative counselors apply the four counseling functions of reassurance, communication, emotional release, and clarified thinking. If reorientation is needed, they refer the employee to a professional counselor. If directive action must be applied, management does this in its role of direct supervisor, instead of in a counseling relationship. Except for special situations, cooperative counseling seems to be the desirable type for managers to practice. The chief contribution that nondirective counseling has made to management practice is to pull managers away from directive counseling toward the more nondirective approach of cooperative counseling.

COMPANY COUNSELING PROGRAMS

DEVELOPMENT OF COUNSELING SERVICES. Counseling services for employees have expanded slowly since the 1940s. Since many counseling needs arise from off-the-job causes, expansion of counseling services has occurred mostly in the community rather than in employer organizations.

When mental-health problems clearly arise from on-the-job causes, the employer usually accepts counseling responsibility. This responsibility for treating emotional "injury" on the job is roughly the same as the employer's responsibility for treating physical injury on the job. However, gray areas of responsibility quickly arise because the background and home life of employees cannot be separated from their mental health at work. Some people have a lower tolerance of frustration or a less supportive home life than others, so rarely is work the complete cause of a mental-health problem. In these gray areas, employer policy is more variable, but employers usually make available normal personnel services.

If an emotional problem arises from off-the-job causes, employers are more hesitant to become involved. There are reasons for this hesitancy, because employees have certain rights of privacy in their personal lives. Further, the employer did not directly cause the problem and probably lacks the power to correct it. However, employers recognize that off-the-job problems do affect job performance. If a problem is one that the employer can correct through its knowledge and community contacts, then it typically wants to do so because of its interest in the worker's mental health. The usual approach is to refer the employee to community health agencies and cooperate with them as they attempt to solve the employee's difficulty.

A mining company's successful counseling program is based on the policy "All the problems of employees and their dependents are cause for concern and reason for help."[14] The program is called INSIGHT, because employees seeking help can dial I-N-S-I-G-H-T (467-4448) on the telephone, 24 hours a day, 7 days a week. The program works closely with community agencies that provide many of the mental health services, and the labor union approved the program.

The firm has 8,000 employees. In twenty months over 1,000 employees and 1,000 dependents asked for help. The primary problem for employees was alcoholism, with family and financial problems ranking next. For dependents, family problems ranked first, but alcohol and other drug problems were substantial. Because of its 24-hour availability, the program has been especially successful in uncovering problems before they become serious; hence, the employee improvement rate has been higher than that usually reported in other types of company counseling programs.

WHO WILL DO THE COUNSELING? Although various friends and acquaintances at work may counsel employees, this kind of counseling is through the informal organization by people who are not performing as employer representatives. Counseling by employer representatives is performed by three major groups.

Supervisors. As has been indicated earlier, supervisors are active in counseling employees. The supervisors are closest to the situation and therefore are better able to deal with minor emotional problems. Their counseling responsibility is threefold. They look for signs of poor mental health, such as increased errors, nervousness, antagonism, absence, excessive alcohol, withdrawal, and preoccupation. Then they provide counseling whenever appropriate, and finally they refer more serious cases to professionals.

Counseling can aggravate problems as well as correct them, which means that inept supervisory counseling can be worse than none at all. The first lesson supervisors must learn is that they, too, have emotions. They must understand their own emotional nature before they can deal with it in others, because their emotions will affect employee emotions. The beginning of wisdom is knowledge of one's self.

Supervisors also need to realize their limitations so that they know when to refer a person to a counselor. Some employees will not discuss their problems freely with a person who has authority over them, so they need to be referred to someone outside their chain of command. In other instances, a supervisor is the problem, and an employee will discuss the problem only with someone else.

Specialists. A second type of counselor is the specialist whose main duty is something other than counseling. Job analysts and others who move about the work area are often sounding boards for employee problems. Pension, insurance, and other employee-services people often have to deal with emotional upsets. The point here is that *these specialists need counseling training just as supervisors do,* because they will be called upon to counsel even though it is not their primary assignment. Since many emotional problems involve some technical aspect of work, the counseling responsibilities of specialists seem to be growing.

The best-known counselor who primarily performs other specialized work is the company physician. Counseling is consuming an increasing proportion of the physician's time because of the growing importance of *psychosomatic illness,* which is physical illness caused by or aggravated by emotional disturbance. It is estimated that half the cases a physician sees are associated with mental and emotional disorders. Physicians are often effective counselors because they are trained in clinical procedures and have some knowledge of emotional problems. (An industrial physician may have additional training in employee emotional problems.) A confidential physician-patient relationship already exists, which helps the employee feel free to talk. Another counseling advantage of physicians, as well as most other staff specialists, is that there is no social stigma attached to visiting them as there sometimes is if one visits a person labeled "counselor."

Professional counselors. A third type of counselor is the full-time staff counselor. In the early years of counseling most full-time counselors were lay counselors who lacked professional training, but most modern counselors are trained psychologists or psychiatrists. They are trained to deal with emotional disorders both on and off the job. They counsel managers as well as employees, because managers have emotional upsets also. Aid for managers is especially important because emotionally distressed managers tend to spread their distress to others because of their wide range of interpersonal contacts. This suggests that a major responsibility of professional counselors is to counsel managers. Additionally, counselors need to advise managers regarding a proper mental-health approach to take toward subordinates.

SUMMARY

Employee counseling is discussion of an emotional problem with an employee with the objective of decreasing it. This is essentially a process of adjustment—of seeking a new emotional equilibrium for an employee. Frustration, conflict, and stress are important causes of emotional problems, and biofeedback and meditation are being experimented with as additional ways to deal with these conditions.

Employee feelings cannot be ignored or argued about. They are situational *facts* that need to be accepted, understood, and dealt with, because managers supervise whole persons rather than only their work. The functions that counseling accomplishes are advice, reassurance, communication, emotional release, clarified thinking, and reorientation. This last function is usually performed only by professional counselors, but managers practice the other five functions.

The main types on the counseling continuum are directive, cooperative, and nondirective counseling. The most appropriate type for modern managers to practice is cooperative counseling, but professional counselors work best with nondirective counseling.

TERMS AND CONCEPTS FOR REVIEW

Counseling	Nondirective counseling
Frustration	Cooperative counseling
Biofeedback	Latent and manifest content
Transcendental meditation	Restatement
Reorientation	Psychosomatic illness
Directive counseling	

REVIEW QUESTIONS

1. Discuss the meaning of the term "counseling."
2. Should supervisors counsel employees? If not, why not? If they should counsel, explain their role.
3. Do you think professional counseling services would be needed in the following companies? Why?
   a. A large West Coast aircraft plant during rapid expansion.
   b. A government office employing 700 people, mostly women in Valdosta, Georgia.
   c. A marginal job-order foundry in Chicago having unstable employment varying from thirty to sixty workers.
4. Discuss the main counseling functions. Which are best performed by directive, nondirective, and cooperative counseling?
5. Select a manufacturing company in your community and discuss what its counseling responsibilities should be in the following situations:
   a. A traveling sales representative with fifteen years' seniority has become an alcoholic.

b. A newly hired sales representative is discovered to
c. A vice president has a nervous breakdown apparent
   sures.
d. A receptionist-typist has a nervous breakdown appar
   sures off the job.
e. A machinist is worried because her child appears to
   mild nervous breakdown.

CASE

UNIT ELECTRONICS COMPANY

Unit Electronics Company produces electronic process controls for industry. The high reliability required for these controls, each designed for a specific customer, requires the production department to work closely with the test section of the quality control department, which determines if the product meets customer specifications. For one important order it was necessary for a production representative to work in the quality control department with the chief test engineer. Charles Able, the manager of production, assigned William Parcel, one of his capable assistants, to this job. Parcel had worked with Able for years and was well acquainted with this equipment order, since he had coordinated its production for Able. The test engineer was named Dale Short.

A week after Parcel began working with Short he reported to Able that he was having difficulty with Short and that Short seemed to resent his presence in the test section. Able agreed that a crisis situation might be developing and said that he would visit the test section and attempt to talk with Short.

When Able visited the test section, Short immediately started complaining about Parcel. He said that Parcel undermined Short's authority by giving testers instructions that were at variance with Short's. He claimed that Parcel even contradicted him in front of the testers. After a number of other complaints he asked Able to remove Parcel from the test section and send a substitute. Short even threatened that if Able did not remove Parcel, Short would "go over his head" to have Parcel removed. Able listened and asked questions, but made no judgments or promises.

Parcel apparently saw Able talking to Short, so before Able left the test section Parcel approached him with the comment, "Well, I guess Short has been telling you a tale of woe about me."

Able acknowledged that Short had complained, but he omitted mentioning Short's threat to have Parcel transferred.

"That's Short, all right," said Parcel. "He can't stand to have anyone try to correct him, but things were so fouled up I felt I had to do something."

Able admitted that the situation was sensitive, but he pointed out that Short was in charge of the test section. He ended the discussion with the comment, "Let's play it cool and not push."

Able, however, was upset by the situation, and during the next few days he gave much thought to it. Since Short felt the way he did, Able finally decided to remove Parcel from the test section and send another employee. As he was reach-

the telephone to call Parcel in the test section, Short walked into the office
ing.

"I want to thank you, Charlie," he said. "I don't know what you said to Parcel the other day, but it sure changed his attitude. We are getting along just fine now. Funny thing, when I spoke to you the other day, I had the impression that you weren't going to do anything for me, but I guess I had you figured wrong."

Able gulped a few times and made a few vague remarks. Then Short left in high spirits.

Able was quite curious about the whole situation; so later in the day when he happened to meet Parcel alone he commented casually, "Well, Bill, how are things going with Short?"

"I have been meaning to tell you, Charlie," Parcel said, "Short has been much easier to work with the past few days. He actually takes some of my advice—even asks for it. I guess that talk you had with him really did some good."

QUESTION
1. Analyze the events in this case in terms of counseling and communication.

REFERENCES

1. "What Corporation Presidents Think about at Night," *Fortune,* September 1953, p. 128.

2. A more general definition is that "counseling is a problem-focused interaction process." See Raymond G. Hunt, *Interpersonal Strategies for System Management: Applications of Counseling and Participative Principles,* Monterey, Calif.: Brooks/Cole Publishing Company, 1974, p. 89.

3. F. J. Roethlisberger and William J. Dickson, *Management and the Worker,* Cambridge, Mass.: Harvard University Press, 1939, pp. 189–205, 593–604; and William J. Dickson and F. J. Roethlisberger, *Counseling in an Organization: A Sequel to the Hawthorne Researches,* Boston: Harvard Business School, Division of Research, 1966.

4. Kenneth W. Thomas and Warren H. Schmidt, "A Survey of Managerial Interests with Respect to Conflict," *Academy of Management Journal,* June 1976, pp. 315–318. Additional discussion is provided in Alan C. Filley, *Interpersonal Conflict Resolution,* Glenview, Ill.: Scott, Foresman and Company, 1975.

5. Florence Stone, "Staying in Shape for the Rigors of Management '75: A Sound Mind," *Management Review,* January 1975, pp. 4–11.

6. Vernon E. Buck, "Working under Pressure," *Management and Organization Studies* (Seattle, University of Washington), Autumn 1974, pp. 1–3.

7. Terry A. Beehr, Jeffrey T. Walsh, and Thomas D. Taber, "Relationship of Stress to Individually and Organizationally Valued States: Higher Order Needs as a Moderator," *Journal of Applied Psychology,* February 1976, pp. 41–47; and Robert L. Kahn and others, *Organizational Stress: Studies in Role Conflict and Ambiguity,* New York: John Wiley & Sons, Inc., 1964.

8. Walter McQuade, "Doing Something about Stress," *Fortune,* May 1973, pp. 251–261.

9. David R. Frew, "Transcendental Meditation and Productivity," *Academy of Management Journal,* June 1974, pp. 362–368. Further information is reported in Robert B. Kory, *The Transcendental Meditation Program for Business People,* New York: AMACOM, a division of American Management Associations, 1976.

10. Extensive discussion of the manager's role in counseling is presented in Hunt, *op. cit.,* pp. 88–172.

11. Bruce Harriman, "Up and Down the Communications Ladder," *Harvard Business Review,* September–October 1974, pp. 143–151.

12. Roethlisberger and Dickson, *op. cit.;* and Carl R. Rogers, *Counseling and Psychotherapy,* Boston: Houghton Mifflin Company, 1942.

13. Gladys D. Meyer, "Martha, Mary, and John: Each Had a Personal Problem," *Personnel Journal,* December 1954, p. 261.

14. James E. Petersen, "INSIGHT: A Management Program of Help for Troubled People," *Labor Law Journal,* August 1972, pp. 492–495. A small-company program that uses community agencies is described in Robert W. Reardon, "Help for the Troubled Worker in a Small Company," *Personnel,* January–February 1976, pp. 50–54.

CHAPTER 24
INTERPERSONAL AND GROUP DYNAMICS

. . . People often work harder for small work teams than they do for themselves.

ISR Newsletter[1]

LEARNING OBJECTIVES ▬▬▬▬▬▬▬▬▬▬▬▬▬▬▬▬▬▬▬▬▬

TO UNDERSTAND:
Transactional analysis
The operation of group dynamics
Differences between task and social leaders
Weaknesses of meetings
The nature of operations teams
Types of teamwork

"Oh, no! Not another committee meeting," the executive groaned. "It's only Wednesday morning, and I've been to five meetings already this week. When am I going to get my work done?" Meetings, conferences, and committees have on various occasions been described as a waste of executive time, a source of confusion, and an excuse for indecision. Managers sometimes comment, "A committee of one is the best committee," and, "The only thing that comes out of a meeting at my company is people." In spite of all this condemnation, committees and other group activities have continued to flourish. Instead of becoming extinct, they have acquired new dominance in organizational behavior. The modern executive seldom gets through a day without attending a meeting of some type, and executives occasionally complain of a malady called "meetingitis," which is fatigue and anxiety from too many meetings.

Meetings are necessary, but they do introduce more complexity and, consequently, more chances of malfunction when improperly used. Some committees are used not to reach decisions, but to put them off; and not to develop employees, but to hide incompetence. The story is told of a distinguished executive who was sitting at home one evening in 1927 as his wife was reading the newspaper account of Lindbergh's historic solo flight from New York to Paris. "Isn't it wonderful," she exclaimed, "and he did it all alone." Her husband's classic reply after a hard day at the office was, "Well, it would have been even more wonderful if he had done it with a committee!"

In this chapter we will discuss how people relate to others in face-to-face interaction. We focus on transactional analysis, group dynamics, operation of meetings, and teamwork.

TRANSACTIONAL ANALYSIS

When people interact there is a social transaction in which one person responds to another. The study of these social transactions between people is called *transactional analysis* (TA).[2] Transactional analysis was developed by Eric Berne for psychotherapy in the 1950s. Its application to ordinary interactions soon was apparent and was popularized by Berne's book *Games People Play* (1964) and by Harris and Jongeward. The objective of TA is to provide better understanding of how people relate to each other so that they may develop improved communication and human relationships.

According to Berne, people interact with each other in terms of three psychological positions, or behavioral patterns, known as *ego states.* These ego states are parent, adult, and child, and a normal person operates with some of all three. Persons interacting from a *parent ego state* are protective, dogmatic, evaluative, and righteous. They refer to laws, rules, and standards with such comments as "You know the rule, Angelo. Follow it." The *adult ego state* is based more upon reason, seeking and processing information, and factual discussion. It views people as equal, worthy, and reasonable human beings. The *child ego state* reflects early childhood conditions and experiences. It is dependent, rebellious, selfish, and sometimes creative. It tends to seek approval and grasp for immediate satisfactions. It usually is emotional, such as an employee's comment to the supervisor, "You're always picking on me."

TYPES OF TRANSACTIONS. Transactions may be complementary or noncomplementary. They are *complementary* when the stimulus and response patterns from one ego state to another are parallel. This relationship is shown in Figure 24-1A, in which the supervisor speaks to an employee as parent to child, and the employee responds as child to parent. For example, the supervisor says, "Janet, I want you to stop what you're doing and hurry to supply to pick up a box they have for me." The employee responds, "I don't want to go, because I'm busy; but I will, since you are the boss." If a supervisor initiates a transaction from a parent-to-child state, then the employee tends to respond from a child state. If the parent-to-child pattern dominates a supervisor's behavior, it may lead to reduced group effectiveness. One study of manufacturing supervisors reported this kind of result.[3]

Noncomplementary transactions, or *crossed transactions,* occur when the stimulus and response lines are not parallel, as shown in Figure 24-1B. In this instance the supervisor tries to deal with the employee on an adult-to-adult basis, but the employee responds on a child-to-parent basis. For example, the supervisor asks, "George, how do you think we ought to handle that late delivery on the IC order?" The employee then responds not in an adult state, but with the following child-to-parent comment: "That's not my problem. You are paid to make the decisions around here." The important point is that when crossed transactions occur, communication tends to be blocked, and a satisfactory transaction has not been accomplished.

In the case of a crossed transaction such as the preceding one, the supervisor might refuse to play the parent-child game and try again for an adult communication. Another alternative is for the supervisor to move to the parent state in order to establish communication with the employee. The supervisor might respond, "You sound too tired to think today. Where were you last night?" Then as soon as possible the supervisor tries to move communication to the adult state by commenting, "Now that we have had some fun kidding each other, let's get together and try to solve this problem." People can maintain communication with complementary transactions, but the transaction that is likely to be most effective is that of adult to adult. This kind of transaction is problem-solving, treats people as reasonable equals, and improves understanding.

Although an adult-to-adult transaction is the most desirable one, other complementary transactions can operate with acceptable success. For example, if the supervisor desires to play the role of parent and the employee desires the role of child, they may develop a working relationship that is reasonably effective. In this situation, however, the employee fails to grow, mature, and contribute ideas in a participative way. The conclusion is that, although other complementary transactions do work, the one with best results and least chance of problems is an adult-to-adult transaction.[4]

I'M OK—YOU'RE OK. Harris states that each person tends to be dominated by one of four life positions in transactions with others. Very early in childhood a

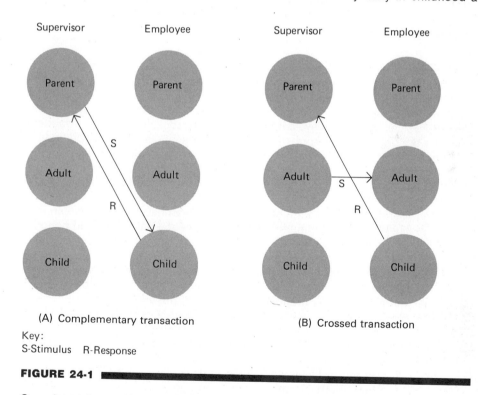

(A) Complementary transaction (B) Crossed transaction

Key:
S-Stimulus R-Response

FIGURE 24-1 ▬▬▬▬▬▬▬▬▬▬▬▬▬▬▬▬▬▬▬▬▬▬▬▬▬▬

Complementary and crossed transactions in transactional analysis.

person develops from experience a dominant philosophy of relating to people. That philosophy tends to remain with the person for a lifetime unless major experiences occur to change it; hence, it is called a *life position*. Although one life position tends to dominate a person's transactions, other positions may occur from time to time in specific transactions. That is, a life position dominates, but is not the only position taken. The life positions are:

- I'm not OK—You're OK

- I'm not OK—You're not OK

- I'm OK—You're not OK

- I'm OK—You're OK

The desirable position and the one that provides an adult-to-adult transaction is "I'm OK—You're OK." It shows acceptance of self and others. The other three life positions are less psychologically mature and less effective. Adults move into the OK-OK position through psychological understanding and conscious choice. The important point is that, regardless of one's present life position, the OK-OK position can be learned through education, understanding, and positive, mature psychological experiences. Therein lies society's hope for improved interpersonal transactions.

STROKING. People seek stroking in their interaction with others. *Stroking* is defined as "any act implying recognition of another's presence."[5] The word originated from studies of the need that babies have for physical affection, or stroking, for complete psychological development. It applies now to all types of recognition, such as physical, verbal, and eye contact between persons. In most organizational situations the primary method of stroking is verbal, such as, "Pedro, you had an excellent sales record last month." Examples of physical strokes are a pat on the back or a firm handshake.

Stroking may be either positive, negative, or a combination. An example of a combination stroke is the supervisor's comment, "Oscar, that's a good advertising layout, considering the small amount of experience you have in this field." In this instance the supervisor is communcating in a judgmental parent-to-child pattern, and perhaps the negative stroke about lack of experience is included to show superiority or in retaliation for an earlier negative stroke given by the employee.

Persons do not always seek positive strokes. They may seek negative strokes for such reasons as guilt or a low self-image. The negative stroke completes a social transaction as they think it should be; that is, it provides social equilibrium from their point of view. For example, when the supervisor criticizes the employee for being tardy, the employee may feel relieved of guilt, since the expected punishment has been received. However, the punishing approach does nothing to solve the employee's tardiness problem.

The supervisor normally would secure a better result by avoiding the punishing parent-to-child approach and initiating an adult-to-adult communication. Using this approach the supervisor might say, "Good morning, Maria. Did you have some problems this morning?" The discussion might then develop into an adult problem-solving conversation (I'm OK—You're OK) that will reduce the probability of future tardiness.

BENEFITS OF TA. Organizations that have used TA report that it has been moderately successful.[6] Training in TA can give employees fresh insights into their own psychological makeup, and it also can help them understand why others sometimes respond as they do. A major benefit is improved interpersonal communication. Employees can perceive when crossed communication occurs and then can take steps to restore complementary communication, preferably in the adult-to-adult, OK-OK pattern. The result is a general improvement in interpersonal transactions. TA is particularly useful in sales and other areas where success depends on interpersonal effectiveness.

One company gave its managers a week-long course that combined three days of transactional analysis with two days of motivation theory. The motivation theory helped the managers make better use of the TA training. A year following the training, resignation rates of employees were compared for departments supervised by managers who had the training and those who did not. The rate in the departments of managers taking the course had dropped to .03 monthly, but in departments of those without the course the rate was .12 monthly. This was a significant difference and appeared to result substantially from the training, since other conditions were relatively equal.[7]

DEVELOPMENT OF GROUP DYNAMICS

Small groups have existed since the time of the first human family, and our ancestors at a very early date began to philosophize and generalize about them. For example, Aristophanes in *Lysistrata* about 400 B.C. presented a drama that concerned cohesiveness and disintegration in a group. Only recently, however, have people started to study scientifically the processes by which small groups work. Some of the questions to be answered are: What is the role of "leader" in a small group? Does the role vary with different objectives? Does a group have different kinds of leaders operating concurrently? In what ways and under what conditions are group decisions better than individual ones? These questions still remain partly unanswered, but rapid advancement is being made.

The social process by which people interact face to face in small groups is called group dynamics. The word "dynamics" comes from the Greek word meaning "force"; hence, group dynamics refers to the study of forces operating within a group. The two important historical landmarks in our understanding of small groups are the research of Elton Mayo and his associates at Harvard Business School in the 1920s and 1930s, and the experiments in the 1930s of Kurt Lewin, the founder of the group dynamics movement, at the University of Iowa. As discussed in earlier chapters, Mayo showed that workers tend to establish informal groups that affect job satisfaction and effectiveness. Lewin showed that different kinds of leadership attitudes produced different responses in groups.

Groups have properties of their own that are different from the properties of the individuals who make up the group. This is similar to the physical situation in which a molecule of salt (sodium chloride) has different properties from the sodium and chlorine elements that form a "group" to make it. The special properties of groups are illustrated by a simple lesson in mathematics. Let us say, "One plus one equals three." In the discrete world of mathematics that is a logical error, and a rather elementary one at that. But in the world of group dynamics it is entirely rational to say "One and one equals three." In a group there is no such thing as only two persons, for no two persons can be conceived without their *relationship,* and that makes three.

There are two principal types of group interaction. One exists when people are discussing ideas and is generally called a meeting. The other exists when people perform tasks together and is called a team. Following is a discussion of each type of group.

USE OF ORGANIZATIONAL MEETINGS

The term *organizational meeting* refers to committees, conferences, and other groups that meet face to face to discuss work problems in an organization. Meetings are convened for many purposes, such as information, advice, decision making, negotiation, coordination, and creative thinking. A *committee* is a specific type of meeting in which members in their group role have been delegated authority with regard to the problem at hand. This authority usually is expressed in terms of one vote for each member. This means that if a supervisor and a worker serve as members of the same committee, both usually have equal committee roles. Committees often create special human problems because people are unable to make role adjustments of this type.

ORGANIZATION OF MEETINGS. The size of a meeting tends to affect the way that it works. If membership rises above seven, communication tends to become centralized because members do not have adequate opportunity to communicate directly with one another. If it is necessary to have a larger meeting to represent all relevant points of view, special effort and extra time are required to ensure good communication. A meeting of five seems to be the preferred number for typical situations. A smaller meeting sometimes has difficulty functioning because conflicts of power develop. For a three-person group there is a tendency for two persons to form a combination against the third. This means that if the power problem is likely to be critical, managers will be wise to avoid appointing committees of only two or three persons. The structure of such committees is too sensitive to disagreement.[8]

People in committees give considerable weight to their formal rank outside the committee. This means that committees that include different levels in a single chain of command may function poorly in decision making because members at the bottom of the chain tend not to participate. Decisions probably will continue to be made by their superiors. If, however, the purpose of the committee is communication or coordination, it may function satisfactorily with several levels present. Essentially, both committee size and the levels represented on a committee are contingent on the committee's purpose.

Groups tend to require not one but two leadership roles: a *task leader* and a *social leader*. The task leader works toward achievement of the task, but difficulty arises because in playing this role the task leader may irritate people and injure the unity of the group. It is the social leader's role to restore and maintain group unity and satisfaction so that the task can be accomplished. Although one person can fill both the task and social roles, often they are separate. When they are separate, it is important for the task leader to recognize the social leader and try to form a coalition of the two leaders for improved effectiveness.[9]

OPERATION OF MEETINGS. The task leader's job in a meeting is to help the group maintain group process, which means to help the group keep functioning properly so that it may accomplish its objectives. The leader encourages open communication so that all members can participate equally. The idea is to build a climate in which all members feel free to contribute their ideas so that as many viewpoints as possible can be brought to the subject of the meeting. Essentially the leader plays a supportive role for the group. Perhaps the more appropriate term for the task leader in a meeting is "facilitator" because what the leader does is facilitate effective group process.

A major responsibility of the leader is to try to keep the meeting on track toward its task. When discussion drifts to side issues that do not seem to be contributing to the purpose of the meeting, the leader can raise questions about the usefulness of these side discussions. Sometimes the leader can restate issues in terms of the common interests of all group members. The idea is to help members recognize and explore a *superordinate goal,* which is a higher goal toward which all can work. For example, in a hospital meeting the leader said, "We are all here to help the patient. Can we think of today's problem in those terms?" When the superordinate goal was recognized, then several minor internal conflicts were resolved.

Leaders of meetings try to maintain an even emotional tone so that emotional conflicts or outbursts do not erupt to distract a meeting. When emotions do begin to interfere with problem solving, the leader may suggest that the group return to discussing facts, without offering judgments and opinions, until emotions cool. Sometimes there is prior agreement within the group that the leader may invoke temporarily a "no evaluations" rule when emotions become distracting. At all times the leader needs to be sensitive to feelings of members so that they can be dealt with before they become magnified into major difficulties.

One leader, for example, learned from experience that one committee member typically showed excitement by squirming in his chair and tapping his fingers on the table. When another member answered with a direct "yes," it meant she agreed; but when she said, "I guess so," it meant she had doubts and was not sold on the idea being discussed. The leader used these cues as signals to guide conduct of meetings with these people.

HIDDEN AGENDAS. Meetings work simultaneously at two different levels. One level is the official task of the group, known as the *surface agenda.*[10] The other level involves members' private emotions and motives, which they have brought with them but keep hidden under the conference table. These are the *hidden agendas* of the meeting. Frequently when a group reaches a crisis in its surface agenda, these hidden agendas come to life to complicate the situation. Conversely, sometimes a group seems to be making no progress and then suddenly everything is settled. What may have happened is that a hidden agenda was finally worked out (even though members did not know they were working on it), making it easy to settle the surface agenda. An example is a staff specialist searching for a way to retaliate against a supervisor, and the specialist is blind to everything else until the hidden agenda can be satisfactorily resolved.

The more frequently persons interact, the stronger their feelings tend to be about one another. This means that as a meeting progresses, either positive or negative feelings are being aroused. The direction of feeling—positive or negative—is determined primarily by the *direction of progress toward an acceptable group goal.* Members like one another and grow more cohesive when they feel they are moving toward their goal, but dislike intensifies if they feel they are moving away from their goal. This relationship places a heavy responsibility on task leaders to facilitate progress of their groups toward acceptable goals.

PARTICIPATION IMPROVES GROUP PERFORMANCE. Groups do a better job when there is active participation and communication among members. Within broad limits, as participation increases, so does the quality of decisions.[11] However, a problem-solving orientation needs to be maintained. Idle talk and digression sometimes relax the atmosphere, but they can quickly be overdone to such an extent that they waste the group's time or divert its thinking. Research shows that members who socialize excessively are superficial in their approach to group work. They are judged by other group members—and also by outside assessors—to be less desirable members of the group because they interfere with group work. By letting their affiliation motives dominate, they contribute less than task-oriented members do.[12]

The group is participating most effectively when there is back-and-forth talk among all members, rather than only between the leader and each member. This opportunity for all members to interact with all others is one of the main advantages of small groups compared with large groups. Figure 24-2 charts twenty-five minutes of a committee meeting in which members communicated both with their leader and among themselves. In this committee all members except Fleming communicated with the leader. Seven of the ten members communicated with members other than the leader, but they tended to talk only to members near them, probably because of the committee's large size and layout. Jones, Smith, and Fleming participated the least; all the other members participated actively. The chart shows clearly that the leader's principal means of creating discussion was to ask questions.

In order to reduce the task leader's dominance and encourage participation, a government office applied to a test group the philosophy that managers should not conduct meetings of their own departments.[13] The test group consisted of a manager, her two assistants, and ten supervisors. Their meetings were conducted by a facilitator and a recorder chosen from the group in rotation so that all members eventually served in these roles. The facilitator's role was to aid or facili-

tate group process and problem solving toward the meeting's objective. The recorder's role was to state all basic ideas presented on a chalkboard or newsprint easel in full view of the group.

By changing roles in this way, more responsibility was placed on the group to solve its own problems. Group participation actively increased. After the program had been in operation for some time, productivity comparisons with control groups not using the new method showed statistically significant increases in productivity for the test group.

IS UNANIMITY NECESSARY? Is unanimous agreement a necessary prerequisite to effective group decisions? Without unanimity group members may be ex-

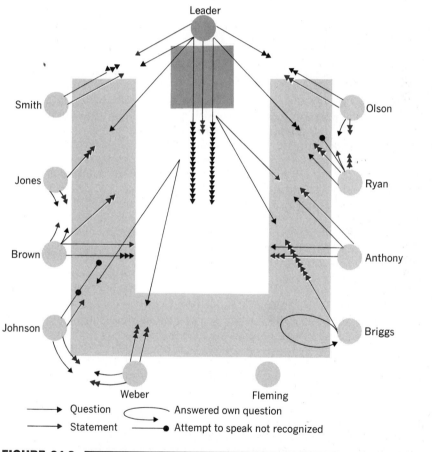

FIGURE 24-2

Participation diagram of a meeting. (From *Conference Leadership,* U.S. Department of the Air Force, pp. 9–11, n.d.)

443

pected to carry out decisions they did not support. Divided votes also may set up disagreements that carry beyond the meeting. On the other hand, a requirement of unanimity has its disadvantages. It may become the paramount goal, causing persons to suppress their opposition or to tell the group they agree when honestly they do not. It is frustrating to all members to have to keep discussing a subject long after their minds are made up, simply because they are hoping to convince honest dissenters. This is a waste of time and an embarrassment to the dissenters. It can unnecessarily delay worthwhile projects. On occasion, it permits one dissenter to make the decision for the whole group, which destroys the basic purpose for which the group is convened.

Unless the decision is of utmost personal importance to the dissenter, agreement of most of the members should be sufficient. Though an isolated minority needs to be heard and respected, so does the majority. Organizations must get on with their work rather than stopping to engage in endless debates in an effort to reach unanimity. Most employers, therefore, do not expect or require unanimity for committee decisions.

MEETINGS ENCOURAGE SUPPORT OF DECISIONS. Probably the most important by-product of meetings is that people who participate in making a decision feel more strongly motivated to carry it out. In many instances this is more than a by-product—it is the primary purpose of the meeting. Meetings are undoubtedly one of the best means available to commit persons to carry out a course of action. A person who has helped make a decision is more interested in seeing it work. Furthermore, if several group members are involved in carrying out a decision, group discussion helps each understand the part others will play, so that they can coordinate their efforts.

Group decisions carry more weight with nongroup members too. Associates, subordinates, and even superiors are more likely to accept group decisions. They feel that decisions of this type are more free of individual prejudice because they are based on a combination of many viewpoints. Further, the combined social pressure of the entire group stands behind the decision.

The strength of group commitment is shown by the tendency of persons to shift toward more risky decisions after group discussion. This group tendency is known as the *risky shift.* One study of women head nurses and of industrial supervisors reported that thirteen of fourteen groups shifted their decisions more toward risk after discussion.[14] Other studies confirm this general tendency, although there are exceptions.

CREATIVE THINKING IN GROUPS. Groups are often used for creative thinking. Though an individual working alone can certainly be creative, group interaction may build enthusiasm for creativity among a wider range of people in the organization. It also conveniently gives each member the ideas of all other members to build upon, and it provides excitement and enjoyment.

Brainstorming is the most popular method of creative thinking.[15] Its distinguishing feature is *deferred judgment,* by which all ideas—even unusual and impractical ones—are encouraged without criticism or evaluation. Ideas are recorded as fast as they can be suggested, and then they are evaluated for usefulness at a later time. The purpose of deferred judgment is to encourage people to propose bold, unique ideas without worrying about what others will think of them; and this approach definitely produces more ideas than the conventional approach of thinking and judging concurrently. Brainstorming sessions last from ten minutes to one hour and require no preparation other than general knowledge of the subject.

One question that has provoked interest is whether groups are more creative than individuals. Research discloses that each approach has its advantages. An average group does produce more ideas and better-quality ideas than an average individual working alone; hence, an average person with sole responsibility for creating ideas will produce less than a group. However, when group output is compared with output of the *same number of persons* working individually, individual output (adding each person's *different* ideas only) tends to be higher than the group output to a statistically significant degree.[16]

In one study, forty-eight research scientists and forty-eight advertising personnel in industry were each divided into twelve teams of four persons each. Each group then solved matched problems, using group brainstorming for one problem and individual creativity (using the brainstorming rule of deferred judgment) on the other problem. The research personnel produced an average of 141 ideas for four persons working individually, compared with group output of 110 ideas. The advertising personnel produced comparable figures of 141 and 97. When quality of decisions was rated by outsiders, ideas produced individually were superior for both research scientists and advertising personnel, but were statistically significant at the 5 percent level only for the advertising personnel.[17]

Therefore, the principal advantages of brainstorming are deferred judgment, enthusiasm, interest, and exchange of ideas, rather than more and better ideas.

WEAKNESSES OF MEETINGS. As indicated by comparisons of individual and group creativity, the group approach does have its weaknesses. As a result, some persons have developed the attitude "You go to the meeting, and I'll tend the store," meaning that meetings are unproductive labor and someone has to keep production humming. Some meetings are unproductive, but a case does not prove the generality. Meetings are an essential and productive part of work organizations. Part of our trouble is that we expect too much of them and when they do not meet our expectations, we criticize. But we will get nowhere criticizing a tennis court because it is a poor football field.

Properly conducted meetings can contribute to organizational progress by providing participation, integrating interests, improving decision making, committing and motivating members to carry out a course of action, encouraging creative thinking, broadening perspectives, and changing attitudes. The fundamental decision that must be made with meetings, therefore, is not whether to have them, but how to make the best use of them. To use them, one must know their weaknesses, which fall into three major categories: slowness and expensiveness, the leveling effect, and divided responsibility.

Slowness and expensiveness. As one manager observed, "Committees keep minutes and waste hours!" Meetings of all types are a slow way to get things done.

INTERPERSONAL AND GROUP DYNAMICS

445

One of the best administrative procedures to delay action is to say, "We better have a meeting on this," or "Let's set up a committee to study this matter." On occasions, delay is desirable. There is more time for thinking, for objective review of an idea, and for suggestion of alternatives. But when quick, decisive action is necessary on a problem, a sure way to confusion is a meeting. A manager, for example, does not call a committee meeting to decide whether to telephone the fire department that the building is on fire!

The leveling effect. One of the most convincing criticisms of meetings is that they often lead to conformity and compromise. This tendency of a group to bring individual thinking in line with the average quality of the group's thinking is called the *leveling effect*. A person begins to think less individually about a problem and adapts to the desires of other members. The result can be that the ideas of the most dominant person are accepted, rather than the better ideas. Leveling has been described in such interest-catching terms as "rewards mediocrity," "kills individuality," "leads to weak compromise," and "places a premium on conformity." The result is that a committee decision is not necessarily the best decision, but merely an acceptable one.[18]

One experiment using two groups showed how the leveling effect is nurtured by a leader who emphasizes agreement. In group A, the leader emphasized agreement—the need for finding an adequate solution that would reflect the group's opinion. In group B, the leader stressed critical analysis and discussion. There was a greater tendency in group A to select the facts, bringing out only those ideas which promoted agreement. The result was that members of group A overlooked important facts and faced their decision without a full range of viewpoints on it.[19]

Leveling is not wholly undesirable. It serves to temper unreasonable ideas and to curb the autocrat. But it is a group tendency that must be held in check by a constant focus on careful analysis. If every member of a group wants to do what the group wants to do, then the group can do nothing, because individuals are the only elements that can initiate action in a group.

Divided responsibility. Management literature has always recognized that divided responsibility is a problem whenever group decisions are made. It is often said that "actions which are several-bodies' responsibility are nobody's responsibility." Group decisions undoubtedly do dilute and thin out responsibility. They also give individual members a chance to shirk responsibility, using justifications such as "Why should I bother with this problem? I didn't support it in the meeting." Weak managers often use committees as a device to hide behind. They give committees their own knotty problems and then blame the committees for failures that are obviously their own responsibility.

TEAMWORK

When groups perform operating tasks, they act as a team and seek to develop a cooperative state called teamwork. Although one may refer to a whole company of

5,000 people as a team, a more limited definition is used in this chapter. Here we are talking about a small group with members in regular contact. If it is necessary to distinguish the two types of teams, the companywide one is an *institutional team* and the small one is an *operations team.* Thinking in terms of an operations team, it is defined as coordinated action by a cooperative small group in regular contact wherein members contribute responsibly and enthusiastically to task achievement. This kind of genuine teamwork makes the work easier and generally improves job satisfaction.[20]

Figure 24-3 presents a chart that reflects the behavioral difference between a traditional hierarchy and the working of a genuine team. The hierarchy follows chains of command and control as shown in Part A of the figure. Teamwork, as shown in Part B, is multidirectional interaction in terms of the needs of the situation and the abilities of each member to contribute to those needs. In practice one arrangement overlays the other to reflect both the way the group is organized and the way its members work together.

A group is able to work together as a team only after all the persons in the group know the roles of all the others with whom they will be interacting. Of course, all members must also be reasonably qualified to perform their jobs. When this level of understanding is reached, the desire to cooperate then can become effective in actual cooperation. Persons are able to act immediately as team members in each operating situation, based upon the requirements of that situation, without waiting for someone to give an order. In other words, team members respond voluntarily to the job situation and take appropriate actions to further teamwork goals. This relationship is dramatically illustrated by a hospital surgical team.[21]

> *A small artery is cut and begins to spurt . . .*
> *In a chain-of-command organization the surgeon would note this and say to the assistant, "Stop that bleeder." The assistant in turn would say to the surgical nurse, "Give me a hemostat," and thus, coordinated effort would be achieved. What actually happens is that the bleeder gives a simultaneous command to all three members of the team, all of whom have been watching*

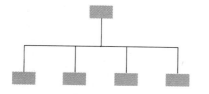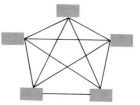

(a) **Hierarchy**   (b) **Work team**

FIGURE 24-3 ■■■■■■■■■■■■■■■■■■■■■■■■■■■■■■■■■■■■■■■

Comparison of a hierarchy and a work team.

the progress of the operation with equal attention. It says to the surgeon, "Get your hand out of the way until this is controlled." It says to the instrument nurse, "Get a hemostat ready," and it says to the assistant, "Clamp that off." This is the highest and most efficient type of cooperation known. It is so efficient that it looks simple and even primitive. It is possible only where every member of the team knows not only his own job thoroughly, but enough about the total job and that of each of the members to see the relationship of what he does to everything else that goes on.

In a hospital surgical team the life of a person may be endangered if one member fails to perform in the right way at the right time. In more ordinary work situations, a life may not be in danger, but product quality and team effectiveness tend to be weakened by the failure of one member. Further, the lowered product quality later could lead to consumer injury or loss, and in any case society is the loser because the lower group effectiveness wastes society's human and physical resources. All the members are needed for effective teamwork, and this is further illustrated with the example of the typewriter key in Figure 24-4. Just one malfunctioning key destroys the typewriter's effectiveness.

TEAMWORK NEEDS A SUPPORTIVE ENVIRONMENT. Teamwork is most likely to develop when management builds a supportive environment for it. Supportive measures help the group take the first necessary steps toward teamwork, and these steps become the basis for further steps toward cooperation, trust, and compatibility. Studies show that the greater the trust and compatibility in a team, the greater their effectiveness tends to be; so supervisors will seek to develop an organizational climate that builds these conditions.[22]

Even reports and records may be set up in ways that encourage or discourage teamwork, although they are not directly involved in performance of the job. A district supervisor for a petroleum company tells the following story of the effect of below-quota reports on sales representatives.

As many businesses are run, each month we are expected to make our sales quota. Sales representatives are expected to make quotas in their individual territories in the same way that the Eastern district as a whole is expected to make its quota. Many times in the past the district has failed to make its quota in certain products, for instance, motor oil. It is a known practice for some of the sales representatives in the field to delay a delivery in their territory until the next month if they already have their quota made.

The outlook of the sales representatives is not whether the district makes its quota, but their concern is their own. Any sales representative who is below quota in a product for a month must report the reason for this reduction. A sales representative who makes a large sale of several hundred gallons of motor oil to a customer knows that the next month or two that customer may not buy any oil, causing the representative to be below quota that month and to have to file a report.

I have pointed out to the sales representatives that we should all work together, and if we are able to get a dealer to take a little extra oil in a particular month to help the district make its quota we should do so even if it might mean the

TEAMWORK

My supervisxr txld me that teamwxrk depends xn thc perfxrmance xf every single persxn xn the team. I ignxred that idea until my supervisxr shxwed me hxw the xffice typewriter perfxrms when just xne single key is xut xf xrder. All the xther keys xn xur typewriter wxrk just fine except xne, but that xne destrxys the effectiveness xf the typewriter. Nxw I knxw that even thxugh I am xnly xne persxn, I am needed if the team is tx wxrk as a successful team shxuld.

FIGURE 24-4

An illustration of teamwork.

next month their territory would show a loss. I also pointed out to the sales representatives that increases for the year were all that was really important and that a few months would not matter if they did not make their quota. But I am not making any headway. My people still hold back on large sales if they have made their quota.

Being complex and dynamic, teamwork is sensitive to all aspects of organizational environment. Like the mighty oak, teamwork grows slowly, but on occasion it declines quickly, like that same oak crashing to the forest floor. For example, too many changes and personnel transfers interfere with group process and prevent the growth of teamwork. Studies in the aircraft industry have shown that in some cases necessary transfers were so frequent that teams failed to develop and productivity suffered. Here is the situation faced by one company in another industry.

An international company built a new plant in a community of about ½ million people where it already had three operating plants doing related work. The new plant was staffed for the most part by new hires, and within a short time excellent teamwork and productivity developed.

In about three years there was a moderate layoff affecting all four plants. Since layoff was according to seniority among the four plants and since employees in the new plant had least seniority, people from the other plants forced new-plant employees into layoff. As a result, most teams in the newest plant received three to five transferees from other plants (about 25 to 50 percent of the team). Though these transfers-in were more experienced and had good records, teamwork was disrupted and deteriorated quickly. Visits to first aid tripled, accidents increased slightly, and production declined 30 to 50 percent. Nearly one year of effort and emotional strain was required to get the plant back on its feet. (We wonder if management considered these potential costs when it decided on the layoffs.)

TYPES OF TEAMWORK. The way that work is organized can create three different types of teams, as shown in Figure 24-5. Each type of team has different conditions of cooperation and coordination.

Process teams. The surgical team mentioned earlier in this section is a *process team.* It has a variety of skills and skill levels working concurrently in an interwoven pattern by which initiative moves back and forth among members, even though one of them, the surgeon, is the leader. This is probably the most sophisticated and challenging of all teamwork types. It requires close coordination and cooperation based on an understanding of what functions other team members will perform. The closeness of the work tends to build group cohesion and loyalty. The intricate performance pattern and immediate performance feedback also provide many intrinsic job satisfactions.

Goal teams. The surgical team can be compared with the petroleum company sales representatives, who are a *goal team.* They operate somewhat as a team because they are a small group working out of the same office in daily contact with their supervisor and some contact with one another. As a team they are working toward their district quota; however, sales representatives can make their individual quotas and more, regardless of how well other sales representatives do. Also the district quota can be made, even when some do not make their individual quotas. Sales representatives are relatively free to pursue their roles at the pace they desire with no more than passing reference to the others. The employees are working toward a goal, but working independently. Another example is five employees pressing shirts in a laundry. Here the interdependence is greater because if one presses fewer shirts, others may have to press more to get the shirts for that day pressed; but each still works independently. This is the essence of goal teamwork.

Sequential teams. If we install steam-heated shirt forms for the five employees in the laundry so that one presses sleeves, one presses collars, and so on, we have teamwork of a different type. Each is now dependent on others for the completed job. Employee Number 5 can fold only as many shirts as Number 4 completes pressing. This group's teamwork is a matter of sequence rather than being interwoven as with the process group. That is, Number 2 does not work on a shirt until Number 1 has completed work on it, but the work of the surgeon and others is interwoven. The pressers are an example of *sequential, or procedural, teamwork.* Since Number 1 initiates action on Number 2 and so on, difficulties develop if any

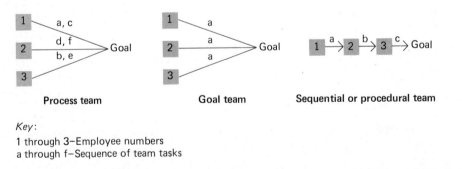

| Process team | Goal team | Sequential or procedural team |

Key:
1 through 3—Employee numbers
a through f—Sequence of team tasks

FIGURE 24-5

Comparison of different types of teamwork for three employees.

of the first four in the group work faster than another, because work piles up at the work station of the slower employee. This is one of the key behavioral problems with some types of assembly lines. The result is that employees agree among themselves to restrict work to the pace of the slowest employee in order to avoid making the slow employees appear ineffective.

TEAM BUILDING. Some teamwork is spontaneous, but with our growing knowledge of teams, management is able to have more influence. Managers who want to develop an enthusiastic team need to be sure that they have established a supportive environment, that the team has work which it believes is worthwhile, and that the job design permits teamwork. Thorough training in the team realtionship is also essential. Football players, for example, are coached regarding how each one's actions relate to the team. Enough stability needs to be provided to permit group process to develop, and rewards such as recognition need to be given. The idea is to help teams build their own group process and cooperation.

An example of successful teamwork is the team program at an electrical manufacturing company. The program focuses on four general ideas: communication, involvement, action, and recognition. To help apply these ideas the assembly line is shut down once a month in order to hold team meetings of employees. During these meetings employees discuss areas such as attendance, quality of work, productivity, and coordination with other departments. In addition, recognition dinners are held periodically for teams which consistently meet their goals. This team program has produced a 25 percent reduction in turnover, a 10 percent decline in absenteeism, and reductions as large as 50 percent in production cost per unit of output.[23]

SUMMARY

Transactional analysis is the study of social transactions between people. One useful approach is Berne's classification of parent, adult, and child ego states. An adult-to-adult complementary transaction is particularly desirable. Crossed transactions tend to cut off communication and produce human relations difficulties. Stroking is sought in social transactions.

Group dynamics is the process by which people interact face-to-face in small groups. Groups have properties different from those of their members, just as molecules are different from the atoms composing them.

Effective operation of meetings is encouraged by appropriate group size, support of group process, open communication, effective task and social leaders, attention to hidden agendas, focus on superordinate goals, task orientation, and mutual participation through communication. Meetings especially encourage support for a decision, but a risky shift may develop. They have both advantages and disadvantages for creative thinking. Weaknesses include slowness and expensiveness, leveling, and divided responsibility.

Institutional and operations teams exist. An operations team provides coordinated action by a cooperative small group in regular contact wherein members contribute responsibly and enthusiastically toward task achievement. Teams require a supportive environment similar to that for meetings. Types of teams are process, goal, and sequential (or procedural) teams.

TERMS AND CONCEPTS FOR REVIEW

Transactional analysis

Parent, adult, and child ego states

Complementary and crossed transactions

I'm OK—You're OK

Stroking

Group dynamics

Task and social leader

Superordinate goal

Surface and hidden agendas

Risky shift

Brainstorming

Leveling effect

Process, goal, and sequential teamwork

REVIEW QUESTIONS ▮▬▬▬▬▬▬▬▬▬▬▬▬▬▬▬▬▬▬▬▬

1. Discuss Berne's approach to transactional analysis. Would it be useful for training electric utility employees in a service department to deal more effectively by telephone with customers who make service requests and complaints? Discuss.
2. What is group dynamics? Why is it important in organizational behavior?
3. Distinguish between the roles of task leader and social leader. Describe how two persons, one playing each role, might work together to lead a budget committee meeting.
4. Discuss five methods that managers might use to improve conduct of meetings in their departments.
5. Discuss how an operations team differs from an institutional team. What kind of operations team do you suggest for a college organization that wishes to build a float to appear in a college parade?

CASES

THE ANGRY AIRLINE PASSENGER
Margie James was night supervisor for an airline in Denver. Her office was immediately behind the ticket counter, and occasionally she was called upon to deal with passengers who had unusual problems that employees could not solve. One evening about 11:00 P.M. she was asked to deal with an angry passenger who approached her with the comment, "You incompetent employees have lost my bag

again, and your ✱ ✱ ✱ ✱ baggage attendant isn't helping me at ⌐
vice. Is everybody incompetent around here? I have an importar
that I have to deliver at 9:00 in the morning, and if I don't get i
for sure."

QUESTION
1. How should James respond to the passenger? Would tra
help her?

THE OBSTINATE COMMITTEE

William James is chairperson of a committee of seven persons which is considering a controversial wage-incentive plan for production workers in his company.
Among its members are representatives of management and employees. Discussion frequently becomes emotional. When this occurs, James sometimes tells
jokes to try to relax the committee and keep it in a problem-solving mood, but he
has not had much success. On other occasions he tries to get the group away from
emotionalism by autocratically demanding that members stay on the subject, but
this approach also has failed. When he is autocratic, usually the group becomes
angry with him in addition to retaining its emotional atmosphere concerning the
subject being discussed.

James has read that participation helps meetings; consequently, when emotions get heated, he often tries to get more persons participating. This approach
seems merely to intensify emotionalism.

QUESTION
1. Appraise the events reported in this case and offer James some guidance to improve results.

REFERENCES

1. *ISR Newsletter* (Institute for Social Research, The University of Michigan), Autumn 1974,
p. 2, reporting research by the Research Center for Group Dynamics, University of Michigan.

2. Eric Berne, *Transactional Analysis in Psychotherapy,* New York: Grove Press, Inc., 1961;
Eric Berne, *Games People Play,* New York: Grove Press, Inc., 1964; Thomas A. Harris, *I'm
OK—You're OK: A Practical Guide to Transactional Analysis,* New York: Harper & Row, Pub-
lishers, Incorporated, 1969; and Dorothy Jongeward, *Everybody Wins: Transactional Analysis
Applied to Organizations,* Reading, Mass.: Addison-Wesley Publishing Company, Inc., 1973.

3. Robert C. Cummins, "Leader-Member Relations as a Moderator of the Effects of Leader
Behavior and Attitude," *Personnel Psychology,* Winter 1972, pp. 655–660.

4. Discussion of other complementary transactions is found in V. P. Luchsinger and L. L.
Luchsinger, "Transactional Analysis for Managers, or How to Be More OK with OK Organizations," *MSU Business Topics,* Spring 1974, pp. 5–12.

5. Berne, *Games, op. cit.,* p. 15.

6. Jack L. Rettig and Matt M. Amano, "A Survey of ASPA Experience with Management by
Objectives, Sensitivity Training and Transactional Analysis," *Personnel Journal,* January
1976, pp. 26–29.

453

onald D. Ely and John T. Morse, "TA and Reinforcement Theory," *Personnel,* ch–April 1974, pp. 38–41.

8. Early research on group size is reported in Robert F. Bales, "In Conference," *Harvard Business Review,* March–April 1954, pp. 44–50. See also Robert F. Bales, *Personality and Interpersonal Behavior,* New York: Holt, Rinehart and Winston, Inc., 1970.

9. Bales, "In Conference," *op. cit.,* pp. 47–48; and Gordon H. Lewis, "Role Differentiation," *American Sociological Review,* August 1972, pp. 424–434. Historical evidence suggests that Benjamin Franklin played a role of social leader in the 1787 Constitutional Convention. His wit and wisdom gave relaxation from the heavy pressures of the convention.

10. In one survey 21 percent of managers complained that they are often called to meetings without even knowing what the surface agenda is, so they have no way to prepare for meetings. Another 34 percent said this situation occasionally occurs. See Eugene H. Fram and Herbert J. Mossien, "High Scores on the Discourtesy Scale," *Harvard Business Review,* January–February 1976, p. 12.

11. Marvin E. Shaw, *Group Dynamics: The Psychology of Small Group Behavior,* New York: McGraw-Hill Book Company, 1971, p. 329.

12. Bernard M. Bass and George Dunteman, "Behavior in Groups as a Function of Self, Interaction, and Task Orientation," *The Journal of Abnormal and Social Psychology,* May 1963, pp. 419–428.

13. Jane Presley and Sally Keen, "Better Meetings Lead to Higher Productivity: A Case Study," *Management Review,* April 1975, pp. 16–22.

14. Y. Rim, "Leadership Attitudes and Decisions Involving Risk," *Personnel Psychology,* Winter 1965, pp. 423–430. Citations of other research are found in this article. Possible reasons for the risky shift are discussed in Earl A. Cecil, Larry L. Cummings, and Jerome M. Chertkoff, "Group Composition and Choice Shift: Implications for Administration," *Academy of Management Journal,* September 1973, pp. 412–422.

15. Brainstorming was developed by Alex F. Osborn and is described in his book *Applied Imagination,* New York: Charles Scribner's Sons, 1953.

16. Warren R. Street, "Brainstorming by Individuals, Coacting, and Interacting Groups," *Journal of Applied Psychology,* August 1974, pp. 433–436; and Thomas J. Bouchard, Jr., and Melana Hare, "Size, Performance, and Potential in Brainstorming Groups," *Journal of Applied Psychology,* February 1970, pp. 51–55. Discussion in detail is provided in Norman R. F. Maier, *Problem Solving and Creativity in Individuals and Groups,* Belmont, Calif.: Brooks/Cole Publishing Company, 1970.

17. Marvin D. Dunnettee, "Are Meetings Any Good for Solving Problems?" *Personnel Administration,* March–April 1964, pp. 12–16, 29. Related research is cited in this article.

18. For evidence of leveling and related conditions see Norman R. F. Maier, "Prior Commitment as a Deterrent to Group Problem Solving," *Personnel Psychology,* Spring 1973, pp. 117–126.

19. Eugene E. Jennings, "Agreement or Compromise? The 'Leveling Effect' in Group Discussion," *Personnel,* July 1954, pp. 66–71.

20. John D. Aram, Cyril P. Morgan, and Edward S. Esbeck, "Relation of Collaborative Interpersonal Relationships to Individual Satisfaction and Organizational Performance," *Administrative Science Quarterly,* September 1971, pp. 289–296.

21. Temple Burling, *Essays on Human Aspects of Administration,* New York State School of Industrial and Labor Relations Bulletin, no. 25, Cornell University, Ithaca, N.Y., 1953, pp. 10–11.

22. Dale E. Zand, "Trust and Managerial Problem Solving," *Administrative Science Quarterly,* June 1972, pp. 229–239; and W. Brendan Reddy and Anne Byrnes, "Effects of Interpersonal Group Composition on the Problem-solving Behavior of Middle Managers," *Journal of Applied Psychology,* December 1972, pp. 516–517.

23. "Teamwork Concepts Enhance Employee Performance," *The Manager's Letter* (American Management Association), January 1970, p. 4.

CHAPTER 25
APPRAISING AND REWARDING PERFORMANCE

> While management and economists have overestimated the importance of pay, psychologists have underestimated it.
> Bernard M. Bass[1]

LEARNING OBJECTIVES

TO UNDERSTAND:
Money as an economic and social medium of exchange
Expectancy theory applied to pay
Equity theory applied to pay
Cost-reward break-even analysis
Behavioral effects of job evaluation
Behavioral considerations in performance appraisal
Seniority compared with performance for pay increases
A contingency approach toward pay and other rewards

For twenty-four years a man worked as bank teller in a small town. He was senior person among three tellers, and on rare occasions when both bank officers were away, he was left in charge of the bank. In his community he was a respected citizen. He belonged to a downtown business club and was an elder in his church. Recently he confided to a trusted friend, "I'm looking for another job—just anything to get away from *that bank*." Further questioning revealed that he had been quite satisfied with his job and was still satisfied, except for one event. Because of a local labor shortage one teller's position went unfilled for three months. Finally the bank in desperation recruited a young, untrained college man from another city. In order to get him the bank paid him a monthly salary $25 higher than that of the senior teller. The senior teller considered himself bypassed and forgotten. His whole world had come tumbling down the day he learned of the new teller's rate. He felt that his community social standing had collapsed and that his self-image was destroyed. The employee he was *training* was earning $25 more!

This case illustrates how economic rewards are important to employees and how pay relationships carry immense social value. Management has not always recognized their social importance to workers. In the nineteenth and early twentieth centuries employees were supposed to want primarily money; therefore, money produced direct motivation—the more money, the more motivation. Roethlisberger and his followers successfully buried this idea by showing that economic rewards operated through the attitudes of workers in the social system to produce an indirect incentive. Economic rewards are carriers of social value.

In the next two chapters we discuss the behavioral aspects of economic reward systems. These systems are not discussed fully; only their significant behavioral aspects are examined. More details about them will be found in books on personnel management. The focus of this chapter is on money as a means of rewarding employees, expectancy and equity theory applied to pay, cost-reward break-even analysis, and behavioral considerations in job evaluation and performance appraisal. In the following chapter we discuss how incentives and other benefits are added to basic pay to provide a complete system of economic rewards.

MONEY AS A MEANS OF REWARDING EMPLOYEES

It is evident that money is important to employees for a number of reasons. Certainly money is valuable because of the goods and services that it will purchase. This is its economic value as a medium of exchange for allocation of economic resources; however, money is also a *social medium of exchange.* All of us have seen its importance as a status symbol for those who have it and can thus save it, spend it conspicuously, or give it generously. Money does have status value, when it is being received and when it is being spent. It represents to employees what their supervisor thinks of them in more than mere economic terms. It is also an indication of one employee's relative status compared with other employees. It has about as many values as it has possessors.[2] Here is an example of how people respond differently to it.

A manager gave two field sales representatives the same increase in pay because each had done a good job. One sales representative was highly pleased with this recognition. He felt he was respected and rewarded, because the raise placed him in a higher income bracket than he had ever thought he could achieve. The other sales representative was insulted, because he knew the raise amounted to the minimum standard available; so he considered it a "tip" rather than an adequate reward for the outstanding job he felt he was doing. He felt that he was not properly recognized, and he saw this small raise as a serious blow to his own esteem and self-respect. This same raise also affected the security of the two employees in a different manner. The first employee now felt he had obtained more security, but the second employee felt that his security was in jeopardy.

APPLICATION OF EXPECTANCY THEORY. One useful way to think about money as a reward is to think back to expectancy theory, discussed in an earlier chapter. Expectancy theory states that Valence × expectancy = motivation. Valence refers to strength of preference for an outcome compared with others, and expectancy refers to strength of belief that a particular act will be followed by particular outcomes. This means that if money is to act as a motivator, an employee must want more of it (valence) and also believe that the reward will follow better performance (expectancy). For example, if an employee is affluent because of independent income, a small increase in pay might have little valence. The same reasoning applies to an employee who cherishes other values and only wants a job to provide a subsistence income. However, since money has many social meanings to people, employees may seek it for its social value even when its economic value has low valence. This means that most employees do respond to money as a reward.

With regard to expectancy, the employee response tends to be less evident. Many employees are not sure that additional performance will lead to additional money. They have observed situations in which employees who deliver minimum performance seem to receive about as many pay increases as high performers. They often see promotions based on seniority more than performance. The result is that their expectancy is weak with regard to whether rewards will follow performance. Expectancy is an area where management has much opportunity for positive action, because it can substantially change the connection between increased performance and reward. If management operates its organization so that those who perform better receive more rewards, then expectancy is encouraged.

Valence of money is not as easily influenced by management as expectancy is. Valence is more contingent upon employee personal values, social values, and external conditions such as an employee's family needs. Money is believed to satisfy lower-order needs more readily than higher-order needs. This means that as people become more affluent, the value of money to them tends to decline. A small pay increase may mean more to an unskilled worker with six children than a larger increase would mean to an older executive whose children are grown and economically independent. However, for most people the decline in value is not large. They continue to give substantial valence to monetary rewards.

APPLICATION OF EQUITY THEORY. Equity theory, discussed in an earlier chapter, also relates to monetary rewards. It states that if one's input-outcome ratio differs significantly from that of others, one will experience inequity. Equity relates to the fairness of management's reward system. It concerns how near rewards are to what employees think they should receive. Employees consider all types of input, such as education, experience, seniority, effort, and skill. Then they compare their outcomes with the outcomes of others. Questions such as the following are asked:

- Are my rewards fair compared with the rewards of others doing the same or similar work?

- Are my rewards fair in relation to employees doing different work in my organization?

- Are my rewards fair in relation to those received by others in my community and my society?

For most employees, equity comparisons within their organization tend to be more important than comparisons in the external community. Pay becomes a symbolic scorecard by which employees compare themselves with others. Since people tend to have high opinions of themselves, it is often rather easy to conclude that pay inequities exist compared with others. One nationwide United States study of workers reported that approximately 50 percent felt that they received "less than they deserve compared to persons in other occupations."[3]

Even inequity in psychological rewards may affect employee demands for money. If there is a lack of psychological rewards, and employees feel that more cannot be secured, they may instead ask for more money. What they are trying to do is equalize perceived unfair provisions of their psychological contract.

EXTRINSIC AND INTRINSIC REWARDS. Money is essentially an extrinsic reward, rather than an intrinsic one, so it has all the limitations of extrinsic benefits. No matter how closely management attaches pay to performance, pay is still something that originates outside the job. As shown by the research of Herzberg and others, intrinsic job rewards tend to be more motivating. For example, the personal satisfaction of a job well done is a powerful motivator to many people. Economic rewards, therefore, have their limitations. They cannot provide all the needed rewards for a psychologically healthy person. Management sometimes poses this question: Which is more important to employees, economic rewards or psychological rewards? This type of question is rather meaningless. Both are important. Each affects the other in an interwoven pattern.

The real question is not economic rewards or psychological rewards, but rather how to integrate the two activities most successfully. Management's responsibility is to provide an optimum balance of psychological and economic rewards. Employees differ in the amount of intrinsic and extrinsic rewards that they want, and jobs and organizational conditions also differ. These conditions suggest that what is needed is a contingency approach to rewards that considers needs of workers, type of job, and organizational environment. Only then can an optimum balance of extrinsic and intrinsic rewards be provided.[4]

Not all economic rewards are in the form of direct pay. Some of the most important rewards are in the form of special fringes and allowances. These rewards are often more valuable to employees because they have more psychological and social meaning. Special fringes may be tangible evidence of recognition, status, or other important social values. Also there may be tax benefits. For example, a bank new-account executive who had been especially successful was given a company automobile, even though most other new-account executives in this bank and in the community did not have company automobiles. In another instance a promising young manager was given a club membership that would not ordinarily be available to persons in her job.

A community hospital had a nursing director in charge of two hundred nurses. Her work was outstanding, but she did not desire further promotion into nonnursing administrative work. She was earning the top rate provided in the salary plan for her job, so it would be difficult to provide more salary. However, management wanted to reward her in some way as well as encourage her continued growth. Knowing of her interest in professional conventions and travel, management arranged for her to be the hospital's representative to two international nursing and medical conferences in other nations during a period of three years. The nursing director appreciated this recognition, and so did other employees in the hospital. Motivation and job attitudes were improved.

COST-REWARD BREAK-EVEN ANALYSIS. It can be seen that there are many complex issues in determining how employees will respond to economic rewards.

There is no simple answer for the employer or the employee. The employee solution to this complex problem is a rough type of *cost-reward break-even analysis,* in which the employee determines and compares personal costs and rewards to determine the point at which they are equal, as shown in Figure 25-1. Employees consider all the costs of higher performance, such as more effort. Then they compare these costs with probable rewards, both intrinsic and extrinsic. Both costs and rewards are always valued *from the individual employee's point of view.* Management can provide the rewards, but the individual employee determines their reward value.

The break-even point of costs and rewards is the point at which costs and rewards are equal for a certain level of performance, as shown by point B on the chart. Employee performance tends to be near the break-even point but below it, because typically the employee does not try to be so precise as to maximize the cost-reward relationship. Rather, the employee tries for a satisfactory relationship in which rewards are relatively favorable in relation to costs. Performance tends to be somewhere along the line A'B'.

In Figure 25-1 employee costs are shown rising more steeply near the highest level of performance to represent the additional difficulty that maximum effort and concentration require. Each employee's line will have a different shape representing individual values. The reward line is shown as a straight line, such as that provided by a piece rate, but in most instances its movements are periodic, rising only in steps after a certain amount of performance improvement occurs. If the reward line can be made to rise more steeply by giving larger rewards, then the break-even point will be at a higher level of performance.

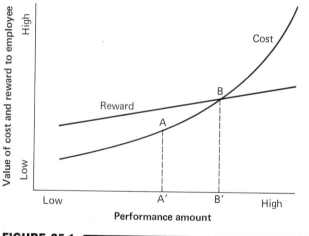

FIGURE 25-1 ▬▬▬▬▬▬▬▬▬▬▬▬▬▬▬▬▬▬▬▬▬▬▬▬▬▬▬▬

Cost of performance in relation to reward for an employee. Employee's performance will tend to be in the area of A'–B'.

BEHAVIORAL CONSIDERATIONS IN JOB EVALUATION

The objective of job evaluation is to rationalize and gain acceptance for the way in which money wages are divided among employees. It provides equity within the organization by an internal alignment of job values. This alignment is established by a procedure that is sometimes considered to be so objective that most conflicts over wages are removed. Wage relationships are perceived as being mostly an automatic functioning of the program's formulas. But there is no automatically functioning system from the viewpoint of the employee who wants a wage increase above the limit set by job evaluation. These individuals know that job evaluation is run by people and that people are subjective. As one employee put it, "The system can be used to change a grade or rate just as well as it's used to hold grades and rates in line." Effective management uses this subjectivity wisely, instead of denying its existence.

The amount of union participation in job evaluation depends on company and union policies, job conditions, and the state of labor relations in each organization. Generally, management invites union ideas for improvement but takes full responsibility for operating a job-evaluation program, leaving the union free to challenge each action through the grievance procedure. Grievances often occur. One survey of union officials reported that only 54 percent are satisfied with job evaluation and 46 percent are dissatisfied with it.[5]

No matter what degree of participation exists, stewards are the key union representatives in the success of a job-evaluation plan. Job evaluation is sensitive to employee attitudes, and stewards are in a key position for developing attitudes. In their efforts to protect employee interests stewards usually look for what is wrong with a job-evaluation plan, not what is right; consequently, they need to be carefully oriented in both the theory and the practice of their organization's job-evaluation plan. After all, if job evaluation is as good as management says it is, it will serve the steward's interests also.

SOME BEHAVIORAL DIFFICULTIES WITH JOB EVALUATION. A basic problem with job evaluation is its subjective versus its objective nature. If a point plan is used, questions arise concerning what point value shall be assigned to each job factor. Shall there be job classes? If so, how many? Should Mary Austin's job be Grade 3 or Grade 4? Questions of this type require judgments which are partly or mostly subjective. At this point most participants begin to realize that though job evaluation is supposed to be "objective," it is more accurately an objective procedure that deals partly with subjective values.

A problem related to objectivity is the complicated nature of the job evaluation process itself, which hinders understanding and makes the situation ripe for suspicion. How many typical workers can be expected to understand even a simple point procedure such as the following actual case?

Job factors for a point plan were established arbitrarily. Then each factor was subdivided into degrees, and point values were assigned on an abstract scale. Each degree had a range of three values. Job descriptions were used to assign point values to each job. Then a wage survey was made to determine median rates, which were fitted to a trend line by the method of least squares. Seven job classes of 50 points each were established, and each was assigned a range of 20 percent adjusted to the nearest dollar.

Many workers and some managers view this procedure as simply mathematical mumbo jumbo to hide certain flaws in the plan or to justify certain viewpoints. Lack of understanding permits suspicions to grow. The obvious answer to this problem is more communication, but this approach oversimplifies the problem. It is next to impossible to get every employee to understand the plan, even if it is feasible costwise. In some cases more communication may actually increase problems. Accurate communication requires that the subjective actions be told along with the objective ones, which may give rise to additional suspicions.

The problem of complication can be reduced by using a simpler plan, but this may introduce greater inequities so that no net problem reduction occurs. A sounder approach is, first, to get all workers to understand the basic philosophy and key steps of job evaluation, but not to confuse the employees with details (although they should know that details are open and available to interested individuals). Second, they should know who is directing the job evaluation. Then employee confidence in the purpose and judgment of this group should be encouraged. In this way, though they cannot know all that is happening, they can feel that their interests are protected.

FORMAL AND INFORMAL JOB VALUES. On some jobs a conflict may develop between workers' informal job values and management's formal values established by the job plan. Job evaluation plans typically do not rate all value items. Factors important to workers are overlooked, such as overtime opportunities on certain jobs, extra privileges permitted by some supervisors, steadiness of work, and interpersonal sociability of the work group. These worker values result in an informal job hierarchy within any group. If the informal and the formal job hierarchies do not agree, conflict tends to arise, as illustrated in Figure 25-2, which compares worker and management values for four office jobs. The workers tagged the job of office machine operator lower than clerk 1, because the former required more lifting and was dirtier, noisier, and more monotonous. For the same reasons, management rated the job higher and considered that it was above the beginning job of clerk 1. Management wanted to hire employees as clerk 1 and promote them to office machine operator, but the employees wanted new employees to start with "the machine job" and then be "promoted" to clerk 1. Management's solution to the problem was to designate both jobs as beginning jobs.

SEEKING EQUITY. Essentially, the conflict between formal and informal values is this: *How may equity best be achieved within the framework of objective procedures?* When wage rates are assigned to job values in a job-evaluation plan, usually it is discovered that some persons are already earning above the maximum for their job. These are called *red-circle rates* because in the early days of job evaluation they were circled with a red pencil so they could be noted for corrective action. For the sake of equity, typically all persons are permitted to keep their red-circle rates, but management attempts to upgrade those persons as soon as possible to jobs permitting their existing rates. If an employee's rate is far out of line, if an employee refuses to cooperate in upgrading, or if an employee's work effort decreases, there is greater reason to readjust that individual's rate. But even here the equity of the total situation must be considered—equity as seen by the employee, by the work group, by the managers who must live with their decision, and by the community. I shall illustrate this point with an extreme example which has come to my attention.

A large mining company installed a job-evaluation system for lesser managers. It was immediately evident that Joe Smith, first-level supervisor, earned a rate so far out of line that normal promotions or general wage increases would not soon absorb the overage. (He was not the owner's son! That's another story.) Investigations further disclosed that he was uninterested in working for promotion. His supervisory performance was satisfactory only. What should be done?

Management decided, "No change." Here is the story. Eighteen years earlier the firm had a disastrous underground fire. Joe Smith was officially credited with preventing the certain death of 275 miners by preventing panic and personally leading them to safety. To do this he used intelligent situational judgment to disregard official safety instructions which, in this special case, were unworkable. His action saved the company several million dollars in indemnity payments, public censure, and so on. Management chose to reward Joe with generous wage increases over the years. Everyone knew of this and felt that it was fair.

Further, to the employees, Joe is a symbol of safety in the mine–a cool head in time of danger. He is an inspiring speaker on safety. To many workers he is " Mr.

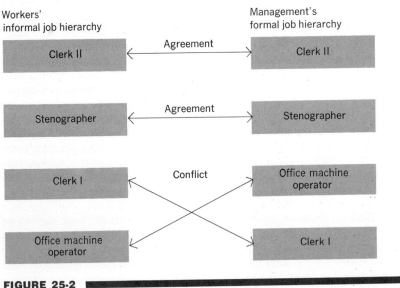

FIGURE 25-2 ▬▬▬▬▬▬▬▬▬▬▬▬▬

Conflict tends to arise where worker and management job values differ (example from an office).

Safety." *But he has no official safety assignments; hence the job description cannot show this special situation. To do so would be fitting the job description to the employee. Joe is happy. The employees are happy. Probably Joe, the workers, and the community would be shocked if his rate were cut drastically or if he were given a big, new, and undeserved job to match his high rate. Would a change in either direction be "fair"? As management put it, "The total program is desirable, but in this case why ruin a good situation just to get two figures aligned on a chart?" As I would put it, any objective procedure requires human interpretation when it concerns people.*

JOB VALUES AND RELATIONSHIPS. Job evaluation sometimes changes promotional patterns and thereby establishes new human problems because it affects employees' plans and hopes for progress up the promotional ladder. On occasion, a worker spends years preparing for a job which pays several dollars more each week. Then a job evaluation occurs, and the new job is rated equally with the former job. In effect, this nullifies the years of preparation and waiting. The worker will approach the next promotion "opportunity" more cautiously. Job evaluation and the promotional ladder are closely related. One establishes the job structure, while the other determines the flow of employees through the structure.

Another job-evaluation problem is that workers resent job analysts who change established job titles to unknown titles or who change general titles to specialized titles. In one company a warehouse worker whose title was changed to "barrel handler" because he moved barrels did not appreciate the change because his title had less social significance. In an office certain stenographers whose title was changed to "dictation transcriber 1" complained they were being degraded, as indeed they were socially, even though their rate was unaffected. Jobs and job titles have social significance which management must recognize when it makes decisions affecting them. A basic idea is that *management effectiveness is increased when it acts in such a way that social significance of jobs is maintained or increased.* Perhaps "dictation transcriber 1" is technically more correct than "stenographer," but it may produce poorer results and be an unwise change.

Job relationships and job values do change as time passes, so it is necessary to reexamine job-evaluation plans regularly and to have procedures for bringing them up to date. Managers sometimes make the mistake of assuming that once a plan is installed, it becomes automatically self-sustaining. They depend upon normal operation of the plan to keep it current. Job-evaluation plans, however, have a tendency to grow old during infancy! At regular intervals they need to be reappraised to fit new conditions.

In all cases, the inherent limitations of job evaluation must be recognized. Neither jobs nor employees can be divided into precise, absolute classifications so that all a manager has to do is match one to the other. Both human and technical situations are too fluid, and the range of human characteristics is too wide, to be arbitrarily confined to a static theoretical model. We must understand the dynamics of the total job.

The fact that problems exist should not discourage the use of formal job-evaluation plans. Jobs must always be valued, and there is ample evidence that formal evaluation plans tend to support equity and order. The important point is that when management uses job evaluation it must recognize the coexisting human problems and try to handle them in the ways discussed throughout this book.

BEHAVIORAL CONSIDERATIONS IN PERFORMANCE APPRAISAL

Performance appraisal will always exist and always has. In any group a person's performance will be judged in some way by others. Employees and managers recognize differences among their peers, and they expect their own differences in performance likewise to be recognized. From management's point of view appraisal is necessary in order to (1) allocate resources in a dynamic environment, (2) reward employees, (3) give employees feedback about their work, (4) maintain fair relationships within groups, and (5) coach and counsel employees. Appraisal systems are, therefore, necessary for strategic and tactical planning, motivation, communication, and equity. Regular day-to-day appraisals are made in every manager's mind, but usually some more systematic approach is required in order to ensure thoughtful, thorough appraisal, to record it for organization use, and to justify actions to government agencies such as those concerned with fair employment.

The first recorded appraisal system in industry was Robert Owen's use of character books and blocks in his New Lanark cotton mills in Scotland around 1800. The character books recorded each worker's daily reports. The character blocks were colored differently on each side to represent an evaluation of the worker ranging from bad to good, and they were displayed at each employee's workplace. Owen was quite impressed by the way the blocks improved the workers' behavior.[6]

APPRAISAL PHILOSOPHY. A generation ago, appraisal programs tended to emphasize employee traits, deficiencies, and abilities, but modern appraisal philosophy emphasizes present performance and future goals. Modern philosophy also stresses employee participation in mutually setting goals with the supervisor. Thus the hallmarks of modern appraisal philosophy are (1) performance orientation, (2) focus on goals or objectives, and (3) mutual goal setting between supervisor and employee.[7]

The underlying philosophy behind mutual setting of goals is that people will work harder for goals or objectives that they have participated in setting. The assumption is that people want to satisfy some of their needs through work and that they will do so if management will provide them with a suitable environment. Among their desires are to perform a worthwhile task, share in a group effort, share in setting their objectives, share in the rewards of their efforts, and continue personal growth. Mutual setting of objectives helps accomplish these needs. As the saying goes, "If you know where you want to go, you are more likely to get there."

MANAGEMENT BY OBJECTIVES. The most popular approach for accomplishing the philosophy just mentioned is *management by objectives* (MBO).[8] There is a wide variety of MBO systems. Some are rather formal and elaborate, while others are more informal and simplified. Each system is adapted to the individual needs of its own organization. Generally, MBO involves a procedure similar to that shown in Figure 25-3. An employee considers job and personal goals for the next period and then individually prepares a list of objectives for that period. The employee presents the list to the supervisor, and through mutual discussion they agree on the employee's objectives for the next year. They also reach agreement on the criteria that will be used to measure accomplishment of the objectives. Then the employee works toward performance according to the objectives established. The employee is given as much freedom as possible in determining how objectives will be met, in order to support employee autonomy, initiative, and growth. Instead of close supervision, there is intermittent review of ongoing performance as needed. In this way corrective action can be taken if performance begins to vary too far from objectives. Finally, at the end of the period there is a more formal review and a new setting of objectives by the employee, which begins the entire process for the next period. The result is the circular, self-renewing process shown in Figure 25-3.

It can be seen from the MBO procedure that it is more suitable for managerial, professional, and sales people, and those who work independently. For example, it can be readily applied to field salespersons who travel from their home location for a week at a time. They are working independently under conditions

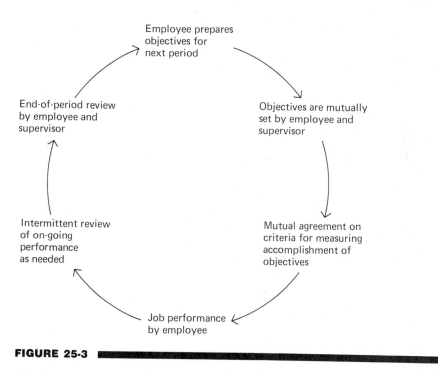

FIGURE 25-3

Circular process of management by objectives.

where internal motivation is important. There also are objective criteria for measuring performance, such as amount of sales, kinds of sales, number of sales calls, and number of complaints. On the other hand, MBO is less applicable to routine worker-level jobs, such as an assembly line. In these kinds of situations more traditional performance appraisal tends to be used. The type of performance appraisal always is contingent upon each organization's particular environment.

The effectiveness of MBO for managerial people is shown by the following study of an MBO program. The study covered sixteen geographically dispersed manufacturing plants for about three years. At the end of this period managers were setting objectives 12 percent higher than at the beginning, and productivity increased approximately 30 percent. Response to the program was generally favorable, but it was more successful for middle managers than for first-line supervisors. A number of supervisors felt that they were not participating adequately in goal setting. The main advantages of the program were better planning and control and stronger motivation for performance.[9]

Another study of an MBO program for managers reported successful results with a number of variables. It developed more positive attitudes toward the appraisal system and toward superior managers. It improved effort put into the job and attainment of goals. It also led to self-improvement by the participants.[10]

A NEW MANAGERIAL ROLE. MBO changes the role relationships of managers and subordinates. Subordinates are given more initiative and responsibility for determining their own job objectives. They also are given more autonomy to determine their methods and their pace of work. Finally, they have more responsibility for appraising their own performance. The role of management also changes. Essentially the managerial role becomes a supportive one, with an obligation to provide supporting services so that subordinates can accomplish objectives on their own initiative. Managers also are supportive as coaches and counselors to help subordinates reach their goals. They aid in mutual problem solving when difficult job problems arise. The manager's approach becomes "How can I help?" rather than "You failed again."

The redefinition of roles builds mutual subordinate-manager participation in job accomplishment. Participation, in turn, produces more commitment by subordinates for job results. Since subordinates and supervisors are mutually working toward objectives, barriers of rank are reduced, and the roles become more equal. A result is more open communication and greater motivation by subordinates to contribute ideas.

A unique feature of MBO is that it restores some emphasis on the individual. *Individual* objectives are set, so even in the same job, objectives may differ slightly in response to individual differences. Instead of absolute standards for all as in the past, there are unique standards for each participant. MBO in this manner becomes a psychological instrument for encouraging self-image through the feeling that one is a person, not a number, in an organization. It also is an instrument for encouraging self-development, since subordinates have determined their own needs rather than having them imposed.

It is difficult for both supervisors and subordinates to change their role rela-tionships, so changes are likely to occur slowly. Many subordinates are not used to setting their objectives, so they may have difficulty learning how to do it. The result is that a successful MBO program takes a long time to develop, and much training may be required.

THE APPRAISAL INTERVIEW. Whether MBO or a more traditional review of employee accomplishments is used, the appraisal interview is a sensitive and diffi-cult human relationship. Although it is often seen as affecting only the person ap-praised, it also is a significant influence upon the appraiser. One of its greatest benefits is to encourage managers to do more analytical and constructive thinking about their employees. The requirement of an interview encourages managers to be more specific about each employee's capabilities, and to perceive that each is different and must be treated accordingly. In any case, managers need to recog-nize that they inject a bit of themselves into each appraisal.

Managers sometimes fail in an appraisal interview when they save up a list of employee shortcomings and unload the whole list on the appraisee during the appraisal. Presenting a whole list of shortcomings at one time is too much for employees. It overwhelms them and causes defensive reactions. One study of eighty-seven manager-subordinate pairs showed that the more weaknesses the manager mentioned in the interview, the poorer the results that the worker achieved twelve weeks after the interview. Also the worker's attitude toward the appraisal system was less favorable.[11] Employees do need feedback about weak-nesses, but these can be discussed more as needs for development in order to meet objectives. The key is that the interview should focus on mutual needs to ac-complish objectives, rather than on a recital of employee weaknesses. By focusing on help toward objectives, a supportive climate is maintained.

A supportive atmosphere is improved when the appraisee has high participa-tion in the appraisal interview. One study divided managers into two groups, those having high participation in their interview with their superior and those having low participation. Those with high participation felt that their supervisor helped them do an even better job, that they received the recognition and encouragement they deserved, and that their supervisor motivated them in appropriate ways. Dif-ferences between low and high participators had a high level of statistical signifi-cance, as shown in Figure 25-4. Clearly, more participation improved the sup-portive climate.

The general conclusion regarding performance appraisal is that it is a com-plex human relationship. Success is most likely to occur when there is mutual par-ticipation in the process, and a focus on objectives and the performance needed to accomplish them. Regardless of how objective an appraisal procedure appears to be, it is the subjective human relationships between appraiser and appraisee that make the system work.

SENIORITY COMPARED WITH PERFORMANCE FOR PAY INCREASES. Assuming that an organization has a policy of variable pay at each job level, a major question is what standard to use to justify pay increases within the permitted range. The three principal approaches are performance, seniority, and some combination of the two. Seniority is dependable, but it gives reward only for length of service. Performance recognizes individual differences, but it is so subjective that it leads to numerous human problems.

Most workers and unions want within-grade pay increases, but they tend to favor seniority as the primary basis for these increases. With seniority pay increases, each worker progresses within the rate range of a job as a matter of "right." Although seniority pay increases lack the incentive features of performance increases, seniority has a strong appeal because it presents less chance of human conflict through management arbitrariness, differences in judgment, and misunderstanding. Seniority increases are more certain. They do not depend on the mood of a supervisor or on economic conditions. They are supposed to reduce the grievance work load of the union, and they (unlike performance increases) are less responsive to pressures of all types. There is no doubt that seniority systems are simpler, easier to understand, and easier to administer than performance plans. They also protect borderline producers by assuring them of an increase they would not receive on the basis of performance. Unions prefer group action, and seniority is a group-determined system, whereas performance increases reward individual action.

Seniority pay increases are based upon an existing work-group constant called seniority, and therefore typically do not upset status relationships at work. The picture is different with performance pay increases. They bring new status to people because they are based on a flexible item called performance. Rank according to seniority is the same year after year (with some exceptions), but rank changes when it is according to performance. To further complicate matters, an

PERCENT OF POSITIVE RESPONSES

QUESTION	HIGH PARTICIPATORS	LOW PARTICIPATORS	LEVEL OF SIGNIFICANCE
1. To what extent does your supervisor help you do an even better job?	79	17	.001
2. On your performance, do you feel you get the recognition and encouragement you deserve?	89	50	.001
3. How appropriate are the ways your supervisor motivates you to do your best job?	92	21	.001

FIGURE 25-4 ▬▬▬▬▬▬▬▬▬▬▬▬▬▬▬▬▬▬▬▬▬▬▬▬▬▬

Differences in responses of 294 appraisees experiencing high participation or low participation in their appraisal interviews. (*Source:* E. Bruce Kirk "Appraisee Participation in Performance Interviews," *Personnel Journal,* January 1965, p. 24.)

employee's performance as judged by the formal organization may not be identical with performance as seen by the informal organization. The conflict that arises may be quite similar to the conflict of job values that was shown in Figure 25-1. The result is that performance pay increases may upset status relationships.

Performance rewards, on the other hand, have a number of advantages over seniority, especially in professional and managerial jobs, where motivation more directly affects output. Hence, the higher a job is in the organization, the more performance will be emphasized for pay increases. Performance fully respects individual differences, and it is usually more consistent with the productivity objectives of work organizations. Seniority-based pay hardly encourages more productivity, but performance pay stands a good chance of strengthening motivation. It also tends to improve job satisfaction.[12] Performance increases permit persons to choose their individual pace of work within limits of satisfactory work, and to be rewarded accordingly.

One difficulty with seniority is that, like any other worthwhile practice, it can be overapplied to a point of diminishing returns, where a worker's whole work life is controlled by it. Then all workers are reduced to seeking mediocrity as a goal, for there is no way to escape time's mechanical grasp. Employees cannot even resign to escape it because then they end up with less seniority in their new jobs, meaning less security and slower advancement plus loss of pension and other benefits. Thus employees sometimes are imprisoned in a bad situation, as is humorously shown in Figure 25-5. They lack the conditions to encourage more than satisfac-

1970, The Register and Tribune Syndicate 3-14

"I'M IN THE WRONG JOB, AND THE WRONG PROFESSION; WITH THE WRONG COMPANY... BUT I'VE GOT SENIORITY!"

FIGURE 25-5 ■

Seniority sometimes imprisons an employee in a poor work situation. (*Source:* The Register and Tribune Syndicate. Used with permission.)

tory performance. These conditions are said to exist in many bureaucratic organizations, and a study of one organization revealed that as it became more bureaucratic it increased its emphasis on seniority.[13]

Many young people recognize the restrictions of seniority, so they tend to want performance rewards. They want to progress as fast as possible. In contrast, older workers tend to favor seniority because of the protection it affords them.[14] Another difference is that more educated persons favor performance rewards, because they feel they can use their education to progress rapidly. Less educated workers, however, see less opportunity for progress and want to protect their hard-earned gains with seniority.[15]

All these crosscurrents suggest a contingency approach to performance and seniority. In order to meet some of the needs of all employees, a typical plan will emphasize both performance and seniority. The amount of each will vary depending on the nature of the labor force (such as mostly older workers of low skill), the type of work (such as requiring education and initiative), and the organizational environment (such as fast growth and rapid change that require flexible, performance-oriented people).

SUMMARY

Economic rewards are carriers of social value as well as economic value. According to expectancy theory, money will be a motivator if employees want more of it and believe that better performance will bring more of it. Perceived equity of the reward influences employee choices. Considering all factors, employees perform a rough cost-reward break-even analysis and work somewhat near, but below, the break-even point.

Job evaluation seeks to provide equity by an internal alignment of job values. Performance appraisal provides a basis for both rewards and other actions such as coaching. Modern appraisal philosophy focuses on goals and mutual goal setting, and the most popular approach for higher-level jobs is management by objectives (MBO). Both performance appraisal and seniority have their value in determining employee rewards. Optimum reward plans use a contingency approach based on the labor force, type of work, and organizational environment.

TERMS AND CONCEPTS FOR REVIEW

Money as a social medium of exchange

Expectancy theory applied to pay

Equity theory applied to pay

Cost-reward break-even analysis

Job evaluation

Red-circle rates

Management by objectives

Performance compared with seniority

Contingency approach to rewards

1. Discuss the idea that money is both an economic and a social medium of exchange.
2. Discuss the application of expectancy theory and equity theory to economic rewards.
3. Discuss cost-reward break-even analysis, and illustrate with a chart how it works.
4. Discuss some of the behavioral issues that arise with job evaluation.
5. Discuss performance compared with seniority for rewards, including use of a contingency approach.

CASE

THE NEW PERFORMANCE RATING PROGRAM

Miles Johnson is supervisor of a district sales office in a town of about one-half million persons. Several months ago Johnson studied various articles and pamphlets about performance rating in order to determine if he could improve the rating plan which he had for his salespeople. On the basis of his reading he did develop a new rating plan which has been in effect for six months. Recently he made the following statement about his new plan.

"The new plan has definitely increased morale and productivity of my employees. Formerly I ranked my people strictly on dollar volume. The highest producer was number one, and so on down the line. The ranking was posted on the bulletin board so that each salesperson knew the ranking of all other salespeople. The purpose was to increase competition, and it did accomplish this goal, but it did not tell the whole story about their performance. For example, the top producer in sales was also the worst in delinquent accounts receivable. Some of the lower producers in sales were also found to be better in sales discount expense than some of their higher-producing colleagues. I now have a performance appraisal that recognizes a person's rank in each of ten important categories of the *total job*, and this new approach has given my organization a tremendous boost. My people now work for achievement of the whole job, rather than for the one measure of sales volume."

QUESTIONS

1. Has Johnson improved his performance rating program? Explain how in terms of expectancy theory, equity theory, and other variables.
2. Can you recommend further improvements for Johnson? If so, explain them.

REFERENCES

1. Bernard M. Bass, *Organizational Psychology,* Boston: Allyn and Bacon, Inc., 1965, p. 76.

2. Paul F. Wernimont and Susan Fitzpatrick, "The Meaning of Money," *Journal of Applied Psychology,* June 1972, pp. 218–226, reporting studies among eleven different groups.

3. "Pay Inequities Bother Large Number of Workers," *ISR Newsletter* (Institute for Social Research, The University of Michigan), Summer 1974, p. 2.

4. William E. Reif, "Intrinsic versus Extrinsic Rewards: Resolving the Controversy," *Human Resource Management,* Summer 1975, pp. 2–10.

5. Harold D. Janes, "Issues in Job Evaluation: The Union View," *Personnel Journal,* September 1972, pp. 675–679.

6. Robert Owen, *The Life of Robert Owen,* New York: Alfred A. Knopf, Inc., 1920; from the original published in 1857, pp. 111–112. For a later version of a visual rating system see John Walsh and Max Skousen, "Scoreboards Boost Production," *Supervisory Management,* May 1956, pp. 2–9.

7. More extensive coverage of performance appraisal is found in L. L. Cummings and Donald P. Schwab, *Performance in Organizations: Determinants & Appraisal,* Glenview, Ill.: Scott, Foresman and Company, 1973.

8. Peter Drucker and Douglas McGregor were major contributors toward establishing the MBO concept. See Peter F. Drucker, *The Practice of Management,* New York: Harper & Row, Publishers, Incorporated, 1954; and Douglas McGregor, *The Human Side of Enterprise,* New York: McGraw-Hill Book Company, 1960.

9. Anthony P. Raia, "A Second Look at Management Goals and Controls," *California Management Review,* Summer 1966, pp. 49–58, reporting research at Purex Corporation.

10. Stephen J. Carroll, Jr., and Henry L. Tosi, "Goal Characteristics and Personality Factors in a Management-by-Objectives Program," *Administrative Science Quarterly,* September 1970, pp. 295–305.

11. Emanuel Kay, Herbert H. Meyer, and John R. P. French, Jr., "Effects of Threat in a Performance Appraisal Interview," *Journal of Applied Psychology,* October 1965, pp. 311–317.

12. Charles N. Greene, "Causal Connections among Managers' Merit Pay, Job Satisfaction, and Performance," *Journal of Applied Psychology,* August 1973, pp. 95–100.

13. John K. Maniha, "Universalism and Particularism in Bureaucratizing Organizations," *Administrative Science Quarterly,* June 1975, pp. 177–190.

14. An additional protection is juniority, a variation of seniority that gives senior employees the option of choosing what they prefer in situations where the normal operation of seniority would work to their disadvantage. For example, in a temporary layoff where unemployment compensation and supplementary benefits nearly equal regular take-home pay, the senior employee might choose to take the layoff in place of the junior employee who would normally be laid off.

15. Philip Selznick and Howard Vollmer, "Rule of Law in Industry: Seniority Rights," *Industrial Relations,* May 1962, pp. 97–116.

CHAPTER 26
USING ECONOMIC INCENTIVE SYSTEMS

> Pay is a unique incentive—unique because it is able to satisfy both the lower order physiological and security needs, and also higher needs such as esteem and recognition.
>
> Edward E. Lawler III[1]

> The success of the piece rate system has led to the use of the system on many other jobs in the company, with resulting greater output under virtually no supervision.
>
> Theodore J. Sielaf[2]

LEARNING OBJECTIVES ████████████████████████████

TO UNDERSTAND:
The relation of expectancy to incentives
Uses of profit sharing and production sharing
Behavioral effects of wage incentives
A complete pay program
Variable benefit pay plans

Here is an example of the way economic incentive systems involve organizational behavior.

A manufacturing company serving a three-state region decided to change the sales commission plan of its sixteen salespeople in order to provide more incentive, higher pay to good producers, and simplified home office accounting. In accordance with participative concepts they asked their salespeople for suggested improvements in the old plan. One of their top salespersons said that he was quite happy with the current arrangement and would not accept any other. Having thus taken a stand, he was reluctant to modify it; and when the new plan was established, he threatened to resign rather than accept it. He convinced management that he meant what he said. Not wanting to lose him, management kept him under the old plan, but transferred all other salespeople to a new plan. Each seemed satisfied with results, but simplified accounting was only partially realized because of the special accounting required for the one person.

The relationship between incentive systems and organizational behavior is both important and complicated. Indeed, it is a worthy subject for an entire book. There are multitudes of *incentive plans,* each with its own problems and effects, but the basic idea of them all is to vary the worker's pay in proportion to some criterion related to employee or organizational performance, such as employee produc-

475

tion, organization profit, units shipped, or ratio of labor cost to sales prices. Payment may be immediate or may be delayed as in a profit-sharing pension plan.

An incentive is external to a person, whereas motive is a person's internal drive. For this reason it might be more accurate to say that management "incenti-vates" employees rather than motivates them. Management incentives make it possible for employee motivation to develop and relate to organizational objectives.

Our discussion in this chapter focuses on behavioral aspects of incentive systems. We do not attempt to discuss all types of plans or all details about them. The incentive plans selected for discussion are profit sharing and production sharing, which are popular group incentives, and production wage incentives, which are the most widely used individual incentive. Finally, we show how incentives are combined with other parts of wage administration to make a complete pay program.

THE ROLE OF INCENTIVE SYSTEMS

An incentive system of some type will apply to almost any job. If an individual incentive does not apply, probably a group one will. Use of incentives varies with conditions in each industry and occupation. Many outside salespersons and retail salespersons work under incentive plans that provide commissions. A large proportion of top management has such incentives as stock options, bonuses, and profit sharing. Production employees work under incentive plans such as a piece rate. Perhaps the main employer that makes little use of incentive pay systems is government. It is unable to offer profit sharing, and its equalitarian tendency has caused it to reject individual wage incentives.

Although the focus of this chapter is long-run incentive programs, it should be recognized that temporary incentives also have a role to play in compensation programs. Sometimes they provide just the right amount of added motivation to cause a desired increase in performance. Here is an example.

A manufacturer of specialized business equipment experienced a substantial decline in sales for one of its equipment models. The decline was so severe that it had scheduled a one-month closing of this model's production line during the Christmas season. At the sales manager's suggestion, the company offered to give its salespeople a new $5 bill for each item of this model sold during the month of December. The offer was made in the context of an extra Christmas bonus opportunity. The response was so great that the production line was kept operating, and some salespersons earned over $3,000 in bonus money paid in $5 bills. A $3,000 bonus amounted to 10 to 20 percent of a typical salesperson's annual income.

The sales manager in appraising the strong response said that the timing was right. Some salespeople needed the extra money for added Christmas-season expenses; so they worked harder during a normally slow period. Other salespeople had made their quota for the year and probably were holding back some in-process sales until January 1 in order to get a strong start on the next year's quota. The bonus caused them to finalize these orders before January 1.

POTENTIAL ADVANTAGES OF INCENTIVE REWARDS. Incentive rewards provide a wide variety of potential employee advantages. A major advantage is that they increase expectancy that reward will follow performance. Assuming that money has valence to an employee, then more expectancy should increase motivation. With certain types of incentives, such as a straight piece rate or sales commission, expectancy of reward following performance approaches certainty. If more pieces are produced, proportionately more money will be paid. If a larger amount is sold, a proportionately larger commission will be earned. (However, some uncertainty remains regarding take-home pay, because higher earnings may change one's tax rate, retirement deduction, and so on.) Other incentive plans, such as production sharing, provide a smaller amount of expectancy, but they still tend to increase it.

Incentives also appear favorable from the point of view of equity theory. Those who work harder are rewarded more. This kind of input-output balance is perceived by many people to be equitable. Further, if more pay is seen as a desirable consequence, then incentive pay systems are favorable from the point of view of behavior modification. They provide a desirable consequence (pay) that should reinforce behavior in a positive way. Rewards, such as sales commissions, are often rather immediate and frequent, which is consistent with the philosophy of behavior modification.

Another advantage from the employee point of view is that incentives are comparatively objective. They can be computed from the number of pieces, dollars, or similar objective criteria. Compared with a supervisor's subjective ratings, the objective approach tends to have higher acceptance by employees.

DIFFICULTIES TEND TO OFFSET ADVANTAGES. With so many favorable conditions supporting incentives, it seems that workers would welcome almost any incentive because of the rewards it could bring. However, there are difficulties that tend to cancel out many of the potential advantages. Potential equity is offset by other developments that are perceived as inequities, and so on. The result is that a wide variety of human and administrative problems develop, as will be discussed later. In behavior modification terms these are unfavorable consequences that exist alongside the favorable consequences of more pay, so they tend to reduce the potential advantages of incentive pay. When workers make their cost-reward break-even analysis, they find that costs have risen along with rewards. The result may be that the break-even point has changed very little, if at all. The extra effort and human problems caused by the incentive may offset much of the economic gain expected. The key thought is that *incentive systems produce both positive and negative employee consequences.* Both must be evaluated in determining the desirability of an incentive system. Economic consequences are likely to be positive, but the direction of psychological and social consequences is less certain.

USE OF PROFIT AND PRODUCTION SHARING

PROFIT SHARING. *Profit sharing* has many meanings. It is here defined as the sharing with employees of the accounting residue remaining after all regular costs have been paid, including competitive wages and income taxes. It is not, therefore, a substitute for good wages, and it excludes incentive plans directly tied to production. Profit sharing was first tried in industry at the beginning of the industrial revolution, but was not widely successful. During the period of inflation after World War II it became more popular. The growth of profit sharing has been encouraged by federal tax laws that allow employee income taxes to be deferred on funds in profit-sharing pension plans.

Profit sharing has developed worldwide interest as a way of sharing the benefits of capitalism with employees. Mexico, for example, has passed a constitutional amendment requiring profit sharing in private industry, and France has passed laws encouraging business profit sharing. In the United States about one out of five companies having over fifty employees has profit sharing for some of its employees.[3]

The role of profit sharing is to develop mutual interest among employees, management, and stockholders. As early as 1832, Charles Babbage wrote:

> It would be of great importance, if, in every large establishment, the modes of paying the different persons employed could be so arranged, that each should derive advantage from the success of the whole, and that the profits of the individuals should advance as the factory itself produced profit, without the necessity of making any change in the wages agreed upon. This is by no means easy to effect, particularly amongst that class whose daily labour procures for them their daily meal.[4]

Basic pay rates, performance pay increases, and most incentive systems recognize individual differences, while profit sharing recognizes mutual interests. Employees become interested in the economic success of their employer when they see that their own rewards are affected by it. Greater institutional teamwork tends to develop.

Young organizations working on the fringes of science are finding profit sharing especially useful to give them the vigor to forge ahead of competitors. If they are successful, the rewards are great; and this possibility builds strong motivation and mutual interest among their scientific and professional personnel. Even semiskilled workers develop a proprietary interest because some of them have retirement funds of over $50,000 and seem well on the way to even $100,000 for themselves or their estate. This is a people's capitalism beyond the dreams of early immigrants.

In general, profit sharing tends to work better for fast-growing, profitable organizations in which there are opportunities for substantial employee rewards. It is less likely to be useful in stable and declining organizations with low profit margins and intense competition. Profit sharing also is more applicable to managers and high-level professional people, because their decisions are more likely to have a significant effect on their firm's profits. This increases their expectancy of reward following effort. Operating workers, on the other hand, have difficulty connecting their isolated actions with their firm's profitability, so profit sharing has less appeal to them. Its use always is contingent upon appropriate conditions.

SOME DIFFICULTIES WITH PROFIT SHARING. Some disadvantages that employees see in profit sharing are:

1. It is not directly related to employee effort on the job. An employee may work harder but receive no more income because of poor profit conditions. The result in some situations is that expectancy of reward following performance is low.

2. The time employees must wait for their reward sometimes is too long after work performance.

3. There is always a chance of a small profit or none.

4. Worker income is variable, and some workers may prefer the security of a more stable, fixed wage or salary.

The social aspects of profit sharing are just as significant as its economic and tax aspects, if not more so. For profit sharing to develop a genuine community of interest, workers need to understand how it works and feel a sense of equity in its provisions. If they do not, they may resent it, as in the following situation.

An idealistic small-retail-store owner employed twenty-five persons. He had worked hard to pyramid his meager investment into a prosperous store in the short period of seven years. Much of his success resulted from loyal, cooperative employees who had worked for him several years. He recognized their contributions and wanted to give them extra rewards, but he had always been short of capital until the current year. Having had a very prosperous year, he decided to begin a cash profit-sharing plan to be given as a bonus check at Christmas. The generous bonus amounted to 30 percent of each person's pay for the year. It was announced and given as a surprise with the weekly paycheck immediately preceding Christmas. Not one employee thanked him, and most of his employees were cool and uncooperative thereafter. He finally learned that they felt if he could give that large a bonus, he must have been unjustly exploiting them for years, even though they admitted they had been receiving above the prevailing wage.

Just as workers sometimes dislike profit sharing, many unions and their leaders are suspicious of it. Union opposition arises basically because unions have very little control of the factors influencing profit, with the exception of labor costs. They also fear that it will undermine union loyalty, collective bargaining, and organizing campaigns. Profit sharing varies wage earnings from company to company, a fact which may conflict with union goals to establish uniform nationwide rates for their members. There is, however, nothing in profit sharing that is contrary to union objectives for advancing workers' welfare. Many profit-sharing companies have unions representing their workers, and practical-minded local unions do not oppose it as long as it works.

PRODUCTION-SHARING PLANS. Another useful group incentive is production sharing. A well-known example is the Scanlon plan. It was developed by Joseph N. Scanlon at a small steel company in 1938, and it has been copied by a number of other organizations.[5] A production-sharing plan is not really based on profit, but rather it allocates to labor a "normal labor cost" based on experience and analysis, such as 27.3 percent of the total product cost or the total sales dollar. As labor works more efficiently to reduce that percentage cost, the dollar value of the reduction is shared with workers. The share is usually in proportion to actual earnings of each employee during the period, and it is paid regardless of a firm's profit or loss.

The Scanlon plan is as much concerned with organizational behavior activities as it is with pay. It establishes active, cooperative participation between workers and managers in order to reduce labor costs. It encourages employee suggestions, acts as a teamwork incentive, and develops improved communication. It also encourages employee development, because employees are participating and concerned with the affairs of their organization. It especially broadens the understanding of employees as they see a larger picture of the system, rather than confining their outlook to the narrow specialty of their job.

Because of its emphasis on organizational behavior activities, the success of a production-sharing plan depends somewhat on managerial attitudes that are favorable toward employee participation.

One study covered eighteen firms that tried the Scanlon Plan. The study examined managerial attitudes toward participation in firms where the plan succeeded, compared with those where it failed. The conclusion was that in firms where the plan failed, managers held less favorable attitudes toward employee participation.[6]

Production sharing has limited usefulness, because its application is contingent upon stable production conditions in which costs can be readily computed. The sharing formula is complex, and it is difficult to administer. The style of supervision and the social organization of the work group need to be changed substantially. More two-way communication is required, and managers need to be more tolerant of criticism. The amount of interaction required is so great that the plan generally has not been effective in large organizations. In cases where the normal labor cost cannot be standardized, the plan is not appropriate.

USE OF WAGE INCENTIVES

Basically, *wage incentives* provide more pay for more production. The main reason for use of wage incentives is clear: They nearly always increase productivity while decreasing unit labor costs. Workers under normal conditions without wage incentives do have the capacity to produce more, and wage incentives are one way to release that potential. The increased productivity often is substantial.

One plant reported a productivity increase of 58 percent following installation of a wage incentive plan. The plant made corrugated shipping boxes. It was an ideal one for before-and-after comparisons, because very little technological, product, or organizational change existed. It had stable, routine, machine production. There were eighteen different jobs in the plant, and productivity increased in sev-

enteen of them. The increase was statistically significant in all but one instance. The range of increases was from 18 percent to 307 percent. After allowing for increased payments to employees, labor costs decreased 21 percent.[7]

THE IMPORTANCE OF EXPECTANCY. In order to be successful, a wage incentive needs to be simple enough for employees to have a strong expectancy that reward will follow performance. If the plan is so complex that workers have difficulty relating performance to reward, then higher motivation is less likely to develop.

One study covered two groups working under incentives in the same company.[8] Group 1 had a simple group incentive plan, but Group 2 had a much more complex group plan. The expectancy between effort and reward was determined by measuring the strength of employee responses to the following statements:

• How much I earn depends on how hard I work.

• I can easily figure what I should be paid at the end of the week.

Responses of Group 1 were significantly higher than they were for Group 2, thereby indicating that Group 1 saw a strong connection between effort and reward. In the long run, the incentive for Group 1 was successful, but the incentive for Group 2 failed. This result tends to confirm the importance of high expectancy for an incentive plan to be successful.

PSYCHOLOGICAL REWARDS. An incentive that is operating successfully can bring psychological rewards as well as economic rewards. There is satisfaction from a job well done. Self-image may improve because of feelings of competence. There is also the feeling that one is contributing to social needs by means of higher output in relation to inputs. Some incentives may encourage high group cohesion and teamwork because of the need for employees to work together to earn the incentive rewards. Sequential teamwork of this type is described by one researcher as follows:[9]

On a more anecdotal level, I should just like to refer to the most highly motivated, most productive and perhaps proudest work group I have ever observed. For many years, I have been engaged in organizational field work, and some years ago I studied several hundred work groups in a wide variety of industrial settings. One in particular sticks in my memory because both the workers themselves and their managers confirmed their extraordinary morale and productivity. They were a five man metal bending crew making the frame for folding chairs. Each did a short cycle, repetitive, manual job involving one of the bending and spot welding operations and then passed the part on to a colleague who did a similar, but slightly different bend and weld. The frame was completed in what must have been no more than a minute or two, and to the naked, neophyte eye it looked as though the metal just flowed among these ten hands. They earned more incentive pay and were faster and *higher paid than any team in the factory. Everyone knew their reputation, and they would work like proverbial greased lightning for perhaps an hour and then take whatever break they felt like because they were always ahead of the standard. They were so independent and so perfect a physical team that they insisted on having a veto over any changes in team membership should there be illness or turnover.*

No job interest or complexity or ego challenge here, just a good old fashioned, cohesive work group that had gotten a great piece rate for itself.

UNDERSTANDING DIFFICULTIES WITH WAGE INCENTIVES. Production wage incentives furnish an extreme example of the kinds of difficulties that may develop with incentive plans. For this reason they will be discussed in some detail to illustrate incentive problems, but during this discussion the reader should keep in mind the potential benefits already discussed. Management's job is to try to reduce difficulties while increasing benefits, so that incentives work more effectively.

In production wage incentives the additional reward flows directly from increased output, rather than having to work its way through labor costs or profit. An example is a piece rate. The incentive may be for an individual working alone or for a small group, such as the metal-bending crew just mentioned. This kind of incentive applies particularly to manufacturing situations, although it may be used in offices, warehouses, printing, package delivery, and similar jobs where output is measurable.

The basic human difficulty with wage incentives of this type is that disruptions in the social system may lead to feelings of inequity and dissatisfaction. At times these disruptions are severe enough to make incentive workers less satisfied with their pay than hourly workers, even though they are earning more.

One survey covered factory employees in a plant that had three different pay plans.[10] Workers were covered by either a piece rate, group incentive, or hourly rate. Two job satisfaction surveys showed that hourly workers were moderately more satisfied than either type of incentive workers.

For any wage incentive plan to be successful it needs to be coordinated carefully with the whole operating system. If there are long periods when employees must wait for work to arrive at their workplace, then the incentive loses its punch. If the incentive is likely to replace workers, then management needs to plan for their use elsewhere so that employee security is not threatened. If work methods are erratic, then they must be standardized so that a fair rate of reward can be established. This is a complex process leading to many difficulties, as discussed in the following paragraphs.

APPLICATION OF RATE SETTING. Production wage incentives normally require establishment of performance standards through rate setting. This procedure requires both scientific study and subjective judgment. If two baseball players argue about the length of a particular baseball bat, it should be a fairly simple matter to measure the bat and settle their argument—thus preventing either from using the bat on the other! The argument is a factual one and can be objectively determined by comparing the bat's length with a measuring scale that is universally acceptable. Most incentive managers wish that their incentive measurements were equally factual and acceptable, and some even seem to think that they are. They become impatient with employees who will not accept "the facts," but actually the facts of rate setting are complicated matters of judgment.

Rate setting in incentive plans refers to the determination of standard output for each job, which becomes the fair day's work for the operator. Standard output is usually established by time study, which is a measurement of the time it takes to perform each job element under relatively standard conditions. Time study at first glance appears to be quite objective, but observe how a number of subjective matters creep into it in a typical situation.

Jobs are timed by rate setters who do not perform them and thus miss some job inconsistencies and problems. Rate setters either estimate allowances for fatigue and personal time or else give a standard allowance which was developed historically. They estimate time for irregular delays on the basis of a few observations. Most important of all, after the time study is made rate setters apply a "leveling factor" to estimate how much the operator's pace was above or below normal while being observed. The rate is adjusted accordingly. The rate then is based not on what the worker actually produced while being observed but on what the rate setter thinks should have been produced had the worker been working at normal pace.

Since employees usually are aware of these procedures, they often try to work slowly and use additional motions while being observed. The net result is that rate setters have to try to figure out how much they are being fooled. Standard films, group ratings, and other devices have been developed to make rate setting more objective, but the result still has a good measure of subjectivity.

The subjectivity of rate setting is contingent on the work process involved. Rates can be set most accurately on machine-paced jobs because they have fewer variables not subject to precise measurement. Other jobs are employee-paced, but still subject to rating because the job has a distinct pace and sequence of operations. An example is an assembler. Other jobs, especially scientific, professional, and managerial ones, usually cannot be standardized because the mix of duties is variable and much of the work involves judgments that cannot be rated.

INTERACTION OF RATE SETTERS WITH OTHERS. Additional difficulties arise from interactions of rate setters with employees and supervisors. Workers become annoyed at having rate setters stand near them for hours watching and recording their movements. They visualize that management is checking up on them, that the job speed will be increased, or that jobs will be eliminated. Rate setters are viewed as outsiders imposing their specialized interests on the work group. In this environment the operator is supposed to work normally and the rate setter is supposed to watch technical factors and count parts of seconds (but human relationships appear to be the greater problem at the moment).

If rate setters compute job times in their office, using standard times, the situation is hardly better. Then it appears to the workers that the job time has been arbitrarily determined and thrust upon them without a fair check. In either case rate setters are viewed by the workers as a symbol of difficulty and change. When they see one coming, comments such as the following arise:

- "Something's going to happen."

- "Look out! Here comes trouble."

- "This is going to cost us."

In all this turmoil rate setters frequently are too serene. Technically trained, they see the logic of their job. They have a useful purpose that workers should welcome, because they apply a precise scheme that provides workers an opportunity to earn more money. Workers, however, have different feelings because of the disruptions that may occur.

Rate setters are perhaps most surprised when they find that some supervisors seem annoyed with them and act defensively. Supervisors are interested in how rate changes will reduce their difficulties, but they see rate setters as more interested in costs and methods. Consequently, supervisors often view rate setters as unwelcome outsiders who threaten job satisfactions and bring unfavorable changes in established practices. All the conditions mentioned require rate setters to be trained in organizational behavior so that they can understand their relationships with employees, supervisors, stewards, and others.

THE SUPERVISOR'S ROLE. Supervisors have responsibility for keeping an established incentive plan working smoothly at the operating level. They are required to balance pressures of higher management, rate setters, workers, and unions. On the favorable side supervisors can expect an increase in productivity, but as incentives mature there is a tendency to develop tensions, restrictions, exceptions, and other encumbrances that make the longer-run result less positive. Conditions may deteriorate until labor costs are as great as they would be without any incentive plan.

Some supervisors say that when incentive plans work "just right" their own work load is reduced because the employees supervise themselves, but it appears that the majority of supervisors expect and get extra problems when incentive plans are used. Usually there is more paperwork, which means more chance of error and more employee dissatisfaction. New and complicated relations with rate setters are established. Supervisors also have to become familiar with wage incentive concepts and the details of their own plan so that they can interpret it to employees and resolve disputes about it. Obviously, an effective incentive plan has to be simple enough for both supervisors and employees to understand its day-to-day operations. Some incentive plans fail because they are a mystery to most participants.

A supervisor often works closely with the union steward to ensure that an incentive system operates fairly. A cooperative steward can bring small problems to a receptive supervisor before they become large ones, and the steward can help keep workers sold on the system. On the other hand, if poor supervisor-steward relations exist, an incentive system usually aggravates relationships because it can be a source of many grievances.

LOOSE RATES. A thorny problem with incentive plans is *loose rates.* A rate is loose when employees are able to reach standard output with less than normal effort. Management tries to prevent loose rates from developing as a result of rater errors or changes in jobs, but workers try to keep them hidden whenever they develop because they make jobs easier. When management adjusts loose rates back to normal, it is often accused of *rate-cutting;* but true rate-cutting occurs only when the rate is adjusted to require more than normal effort. It is equivalent to a *speed-up,* by which employees on day work (straight hourly pay or salary) have to perform more than normal work for their regular pay. The speed-up has been a problem throughout history. One of the earliest records of a speed-up is in the Holy Bible, as follows:

> The same day Pharaoh commanded the taskmasters of the people and their foremen, "You shall no longer give the people straw to make bricks, as heretofore; let them go and gather straw for themselves. But the number of bricks which they made heretofore . . . you shall by no means lessen it. . . . Let heavier work be laid upon the men."[11]

In order to distinguish adjustment of loose rates from rate-cutting, management usually pledges, "We will not cut the rates." This statement actually means, "We won't change the rate *unless there is a substantial methods change.*" Here is the way this type of guarantee is stated in a company's labor contract: "No change will be made in any permanent piece-work prices or standards unless changes are made in the job content of the operation which increase or decrease the time necessary to produce a unit of production."

From the employee's point of view, the rate is cut when there is a substantial methods improvement, because rates per output unit are reduced. This situation gives rise to employee fears and such true comments as "I used to get 1 cent a piece on this job. Now I get only one-tenth of a cent." What the employee does not mention is that production of ten pieces requires no more effort than one formerly required. Rate-cutting has not taken place, because the worker does not have to work any harder to reach standard, even though standard is ten times greater.

Once the statement "We won't cut the rate" is understood, arguments develop over what constitutes a methods change that is large enough to justify refiguring the rate. On many jobs several small changes are made over a period of months or even years. Some of these changes are made by operators; others result from minor adjustments in material, machine, product, and other variables. Not one of the changes qualifies as substantial, but together they make a rate quite loose. Experience shows that the general trend of production incentive plans is toward looseness as they get older. Such was the case with the department illustrated in Figure 26-1. Within the first year after incentive standards were established, a number of small changes had crept in to loosen many rates. Even though management restudied jobs that had substantial methods changes, it could not catch all the looseness in the rates. After a number of years most rates were loose, and workers were restricting output to discourage restudy of their jobs.

Minor job changes eventually add up to an overall substantial change, which gives management a reason to correct the rate; but the precise time for correction is a matter of argument. Workers obviously want to protect the looseness that has

485

developed. If another worker has transferred to the job after several of the minor changes occurred, the job to that worker has always been loose. When management corrects the rate, the worker can honestly say, "They cut my rate. It is now *harder* to make production on this job than it was when I first took it." The result is a feeling of inequity.

Since loose rates are difficult to deal with once they become established, management's best approach is to use every effort to keep them at a minimum. Supervisors need to be trained to realize the significance of loose rates and to work with the rate-setting department to correct them. Here is a case that illustrates the importance of supervisors in controlling loose rates.

An electrically heated part was being manufactured for aircraft. In order to obtain a better bond between the metal and the rubber in the part, a certain fabric was used in curing the rubber. The fabric was later stripped off by the operator, producing a rough surface which bonded better. One day there was a fabric shortage, and a different type of fabric was substituted. Purely by chance the new fabric was much superior because it could be stripped from the cured rubber in one piece, while the original fabric stripped into many small pieces. Afterward, only the second fabric was used. The rate setting department did not realize the significance of the fabric change; and the supervisor, though realizing the significance, failed to report it to the rate setters so that a rate change could be made. The result was a very loose

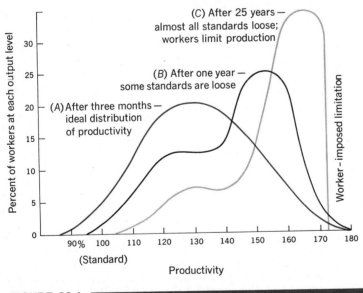

FIGURE 26-1

Case history of the growth of loose rates in a department. (*Source:* W. W. Taylor, "New Look at Incentive Methods," *Factory Management and Maintenance,* August 1955, p. 91. Reproduced with permission.)

rate for the job. Workers restricted production so that the looseness did not show in production records.

Many months later a methods change was made in the job which required a new rate study. At this point the rate setter discovered the significance of the fabric change and found that the two changes together required a 50 percent rate reduction. It was difficult for management to explain the appropriateness of this severe reduction; yet the alternative was to permit a loose rate to continue, along with restriction of output. The workers protested bitterly, and the union representative said the fabric change had been in effect so long that it was now unfair to reduce rates because of it. The grievance eventually went to arbitration.

On jobs having many minor changes, one approach is to treat the job as experimental and to schedule new time studies at regular intervals to discourage excessive looseness. When there is general deterioration of standards it appears that the best approach is plantwide revision of standards rather than restudying each job separately as problems arise.

In a meat packing plant management allowed incentive rates in one department to become quite loose as a result of minor job improvements. The looseness was intentional on management's part in order to aid recruitment for this unpleasant job during a labor shortage. After the labor shortage eased, management took steps to tighten the loose rates. Jobs in the department were restudied and tighter rates set for nearly every job in the department. The employees refused to work under the new rates. They argued that the rates were originally loosened to serve management's self-interest, and that employees should not be penalized for something management did. Pressures became so strong that eventually management agreed to retain the former loose rates until such time as rates might be revised on a plant-wide basis.

INTERGROUP WORK RELATIONS. Production wage incentives may cause disharmony between incentive workers and day workers, who are paid according to the time they work rather than their amount of output. When day workers and incentive workers perform work in sequence, day workers are likely to feel discriminated against because they earn less. If the incentive workers increase output, day workers further along the process must work faster to prevent a bottleneck. The incentive workers earn more for their increased output, but the day workers do not.

Day workers who precede incentive workers in the production process can on occasion "take it easy" and produce less with no cut in pay. But the incentive worker's income is cut when less work is available. The same problem occurs if a day worker is absent and reduces the flow of material to incentive workers. Conflicts of this type are so difficult that it is best for management not to mix the two groups in any closely integrated production sequence.

Another type of problem occurs when incentive jobs on two shifts overlap so that performance on one shift affects output of the other. The following are three examples of shift conflicts.

1. In a machine shop the worker on first shift failed to replace a dull tool at the end of the shift.

2. In a foundry a first-shift worker did the easy part of the job, leaving the difficult part for the next shift.

3. In a glass factory the third shift "pulled" too much glass from the continuous furnace, requiring the first shift to work at a slower pace while the furnace contents were built up. The result was poor quality and uneven production. This was bad enough, but when the first shift discovered what was happening and retaliated, results were worse!

RESTRICTION OF OUTPUT. Another difficulty with wage incentives is that they may encourage restriction of output, by which workers limit their production and thus thwart the purpose of the incentive. Insecurities, such as the threat of rate-cutting, may encourage a group to agree through the informal organization to restrict work in order to protect group interests.

Unions sometimes support restrictive practices. At other times they try to remove them, but even then they are not always successful because work groups fight strongly to retain such practices. Restriction of output was not created by unions. In an early study Mathewson demonstrated that restriction is a social phenomenon that antedates union organization.[12] His work was followed by Roethlisberger's research, which showed the informal group processes by which restriction grew as a result of group needs, fears, and resistance to change as members sought to maintain their informal social organizations. Roethlisberger commented, "It is clear, therefore, that their actions were not based upon a logical appraisal of their work situation.[13] He emphasized that restriction is not necessarily a result of laziness, deliberate opposition to management, or poor supervision.

Even when an incentive plan appears to be working well, it often is not. One firm thought it had an effective incentive plan, but then it discovered an interesting phenomenon which indicated otherwise. Vacation paychecks in the plant were based upon average earnings for the first two weeks in May. A review of records for several years disclosed that during these two weeks, output increased about 30 percent above the average for the preceding six weeks. Part of this increase appeared to be a result of harder work, while another part appeared to come from work done earlier but kept unfinished or unreported in some hidden storage area until May.

Although restriction of work tends to be more evident in factory incentive plans, it also exists in sales work. This is illustrated by the following situation involving salespeople on commission.

Industrial equipment salespeople in one company received a substantial salary plus a commission of 1 percent on sales until a total commission of $7,000 was earned. Any commission thereafter was at 0.25 of 1 percent. Each salesperson had an annual quota, but annual sales often varied as much as 100 percent because of the nature of the product. Some salespersons worked only until their quota was earned and then held back, because (1) they were afraid their quota might be raised the next year and they did not want the strain of trying to make a difficult quota, or (2) they objected to the commission reduction from 1 to 0.25 percent which occurred at about the time their quota was reached. Others sold a little more than their quota, because they "wanted to look good on the record" regardless of commission rate; but then they held back because they feared the company would split their territory if sales became too high. Other salespeople tried to sell all they could all the time, regardless of incentive factors.

Management and unions are successfully chipping away at restriction-of-output practices. Much more can be done, but this condition will always exist. People are not comfortable working always at full capacity, even if this rate could be scientifically determined. Just as management wishes to reserve some unused production capacity in order to avoid on overload during peak periods, workers desire to reserve capacity in order to meet emergencies and avoid stress. In the final analysis, the real problem is one of controlling (rather than preventing) restriction of output in order to keep it a minor influence on productivity.

Since restriction of output is closely related to informal organization, improved behavioral practices of all types will help build the kind of cooperation that leads eventually to less restriction. Case studies have shown that alert, well-trained supervisors can use the proper time and circumstance to encourage decreased restrictions. Wage and employment guarantees can assure workers in many situations that they are not working themselves out of a job. In the long run management can build a historical record of security and good relations that will dim workers' memories of past malpractices that encouraged restriction.

A COMPLETE PAY PROGRAM

Many types of pay are required for a complete economic reward system. Job evaluation *rates the job,* relating one job to another according to levels of responsibility. Performance appraisal and incentives *rate employees* in their performance and give them more reward. Profit sharing *rates the organization* in terms of its general economic performance, and rewards employees as partners in it. Together these three systems are the incentive foundation of a complete pay program, as roughly diagrammed in the pay pyramid in Figure 26-2. Each can contribute something to the employee's economic reward. The three systems are complementary because each reflects a different set of factors in the total situation. Base pay motivates employees to progress to jobs of higher skills and responsibility; and as a matter of security, this base may be protected by a cost-of-living adjustment that keeps the real pay relatively constant for a certain period. Performance pay increases are an incentive to improve performance on one's job. Profit sharing motivates toward teamwork to improve an organization's performance.

Other payments, primarily nonincentive in nature, are added to the incentive foundation. Seniority pay adjustments are made to reward workers for extended service and to encourage them to remain with their employer. If an employer asks workers to sacrifice by working overtime, working on their day off, or working at undesirable hours, the workers may be paid extra for this inconvenience. Other payments are given when an employee does not work, such as vacations, holidays, jury service, and layoffs subject to guaranteed pay. These additions to the incentive foundation of the pay pyramid have little direct incentive value because they do not increase according to improved job performance. Some of these additions may result in indirect incentive through better attitudes. Other additions, such as seniority pay, actually may decrease worker incentive. It is clear that not one but many factors enter into computation of a modern worker's paycheck. Some of these factors are related less to incentive than they are to such broad objectives as security, equity, and social justice. An effective program of economic rewards is a balance of most of these factors. In this way a variety of employee needs are served.

The particular combination of economic rewards that an employer uses is contingent on the needs of employees, type of work, and organizational environment. In order to serve employee needs in a better way, some organizations are providing *variable benefit pay plans,* also called cafeteria pay plans because they allow employees to select their individual combination of benefits as they would select food in a cafeteria. Each employee receives a certain total economic allowance for a job, and then within a range of choices available the employee selects a preferred combination of economic rewards that use the allowed total. For example, a young employee may choose more pay and less money placed into a retire-

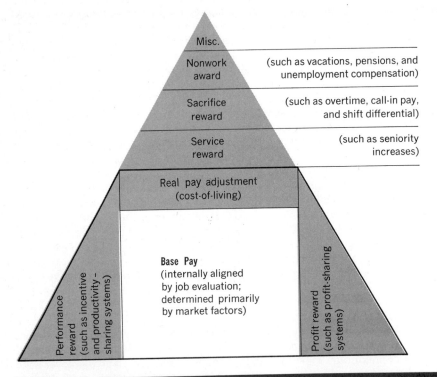

FIGURE 26-2

The pay pyramid: The makeup of a complete pay program. (Read from bottom. Incentive foundation is shown by heavy lines.)

ment program. Because of their complexity, variable benefit plans tend to be used mostly with higher-level managers and professionals, where different choices might have a significant influence on recruiting and retaining the employee. Some firms allow a smaller variable benefit selection by operating employees.

Viewing an organization as a whole, economic rewards are combined with social and psychological rewards, as discussed throughout this book, to make a complete reward system. Thus we have reached the end of this book and are ready for the concluding chapter.

SUMMARY

Incentive rewards provide different amounts of pay in relation to some measure of performance. They tend to increase expectancy that reward will follow perform-ance. The result is that they nearly always bring more productivity, but they also tend to produce offsetting negative consequences. These consequences may be sufficient to cancel out potential benefits from the incentives.

Profit sharing emphasizes mutual interest with the employer in building a successful organization. Production sharing emphasizes reduction of labor costs, and wage incentives emphasize greater output. Wage incentives particularly tend to develop unfavorable consequences. Some areas requiring attention are rate-setting, supervisor-union relations, loose rates, intergroup work relations, and restriction of output.

Many types of pay are required for a complete economic reward system. In this way many different employee needs are served. In some instances, variable benefit pay plans allow employees to select individual combinations of economic rewards. Economic rewards are combined with social and psychological rewards to make a complete reward system for an organization.

TERMS AND CONCEPTS FOR REVIEW

Incentive plans or systems	Loose rates
Profit sharing	Rate cutting
Production sharing	Speed-up
Scanlon plan	"We will not cut the rates"
Wage incentives	Complete pay program
Rate-setting	Variable benefit pay plan

REVIEW QUESTIONS ■■■■■■■■■■■■■■■■■■■■

1. Discuss the relation of expectancy theory to incentive systems.

2. Discuss the statement that incentive systems produce both positive and negative employee consequences.
3. Discuss the usefulness of profit sharing as an incentive in profit-making institutions. Use outside sources to report on the operation of some firm's profit-sharing program.
4. Discuss how intergroup work relations are affected by incentive systems.
5. Discuss how job evaluation, profit sharing, wage incentives, and other types of pay relate to a complete pay program.

CASES

THE EARLY RETIREE

Eastern Computer Company had a profit sharing program which set aside a proportion of net profits for an employee retirement fund. The plan allowed employees to retire after twenty years of service. At the time of retirement they could withdraw their entire share of the fund, instead of being required to receive it in small monthly retirement checks for a period of years. The plan was originally established because management felt that requirements for companywide teamwork were substantial in this high technology company and they believed that a profit sharing plan would encourage teamwork.

David Parker started working for Eastern Computer Company when he was seventeen years of age. Later he was promoted to the position of supervisor. He attended night school at a university and eventually was promoted to department head in charge of inventory controls. This was considered a middle management position. Parker had ambitions to operate his own business; so during the last few years he looked for this kind of opportunity. Recently an opportunity developed to acquire a franchised restaurant. At the age of thirty-nine, after twenty-two years of service with the company, Parker retired and entered the restaurant business. He withdrew his entire retirement fund of $34,000 and invested it in the restaurant.

QUESTIONS

1. Do you believe that the profit sharing plan properly serves Eastern Computer Company's needs? Would you change the plan in any way?
2. Do you believe that the profit sharing plan properly serves the needs of employees such as Parker? Would you change the plan in any way to serve employee needs better?

THE INCENTIVE PLAN[14]

Two young men worked in a printing plant. Both had some college education, and one still was pursuing a degree. They were friends who had a strong interest in rock music. Their interest in rock music was so great that they would leave work early or miss work in order to meet a musical engagement. Earnings from music were minor. Their jobs were their main income.

Both employees showed minor interest in their work. They rejected opportunities to train on other jobs. They missed work without notice to their employer, and often they were tardy for a half hour or more. Their production was low. First, management tried to correct their behavior by pep talks and requests for more effort. The attempt failed. Next, warnings and reprimands were given, and then they were laid off for a day for tardiness. There was some improvement, but it was evident that they had little interest in their jobs and were not productive.

In an effort to improve behavior, the employees were offered an incentive bonus of about twenty percent of earnings if they would meet a standard nearer to full production. Their behavior was not affected. Finally, management offered them a piece rate set slightly below current costs for each unit of output. There was an immediate change in behavior, beginning with the first day. Production nearly doubled and then continued at that rate.

QUESTION
1. Using ideas from the whole book, including the last two chapters, analyze possible reasons why most management approaches failed and the piece rate succeeded.

REFERENCES

1. Edward E. Lawler III, "How Much Money Do Executives Want?" *Trans-action,* January–February 1967, p. 24. Entire sentence italicized in original.

2. Theodore J. Sielaff, "Modification of Work Behavior," *Personnel Journal,* July 1974, p. 515.

3. J. J. Jehring, "Business Patterns Trend toward Socioeconomic Sharing," *Social Order,* November 1963, pp. 5–10; and B. L. Metzger, *Profit Sharing in Perspective,* 2d ed., Evanston, Ill.: Profit Sharing Research Foundation, 1966, p. 38.

4. Charles Babbage, *On the Economy of Machinery and Manufactures,* London: Charles Knight, 1832, p. 177.

5. Fred G. Lesieur and Elbridge S. Puckett, "The Scanlon Plan Has Proved Itself," *Harvard Business Review,* September–October 1969, pp. 109–118; and Edward E. Lawler III, *Pay and Organizational Effectiveness: A Psychological View,* New York: McGraw-Hill Book Company, 1971, pp. 130–132.

6. Robert A. Ruh, Roger L. Wallace, and Carl F. Frost, "Management Attitudes and the Scanlon Plan," *Industrial Relations,* October 1973, pp. 282–288.

7. Donald L. McManis and William G. Dick, "Monetary Incentives in Today's Industrial Setting," *Personnel Journal,* May 1973, pp. 387–392.

8. Cortlandt Cammann and Edward E. Lawler III, "Employee Reactions to a Pay Incentive Plan," *Journal of Applied Psychology,* October 1973, pp. 163–172.

9. Leonard R. Sayles, "Job Enrichment: Little That's New—and Right for the Wrong Reasons," in Gerald G. Somers (ed.), *Proceedings of the Twenty-sixth Annual Winter Meeting,* Madison, Wis.: Industrial Relations Research Association, 1974, p. 207. Reprinted with permission.

10. Donald P. Schwab and Marc J. Wallace, Jr., "Correlates of Employee Satisfaction with Pay," *Industrial Relations,* February 1974, pp. 78–89.

11. The Holy Bible, Revised Standard Version, *Exodus* 5:6–9.

12. Stanley B. Mathewson, *Restriction of Output among Unorganized Workers,* New York: The Viking Press, Inc., 1931, p. 157.

13. F. J. Roethlisberger and W. J. Dickson, *Management and the Worker,* Cambridge, Mass.: Harvard University Press, 1939, p. 532.

14. Adapted from a discussion in Sielaff, *op. cit.,* pp. 513–517.

SECTION 6

CONCLUSION

ORGANIZATIONAL BEHAVIOR IN PERSPECTIVE

A classic issue in . . . organizational behavior is whether the needs of individuals and the goals of their employing organizations can be simultaneously attained or integrated.
Douglas T. Hall and Edward E. Lawler III[1]

LEARNING OBJECTIVES

TO UNDERSTAND:
Models of organizational behavior related to other book ideas
Further interpretations of contingency management
Formulas relating organizational behavior to organizational performance
Human resource accounting
Dangers of behavioral bias
The law of diminishing returns

This book has been about people as they work together. They are the great potential in organizations, a potential that can be developed better than it is now. This subject is called organizational behavior. It is an activity that seeks to motivate people in organizations to develop teamwork that effectively fulfills their needs and achieves organizational objectives. It helps people, technology, and structure blend together into an effective system that serves society's needs. Both the individual and groups are involved. Individuals are social beings in a social system.

It is said that medicine is an integration of physical and biological sciences as applied to people and their health. In a similar manner organizational behavior integrates social sciences and applies them to people at work. It brings together ideas from economics, sociology, psychology, and other disciplines, and it applies these ideas to specific problems of particular people at some time and place.

In this last chapter we review the models of organizational behavior. Then we discuss the general role of organizational behavior, as well as its limitations.

MODELS OF ORGANIZATIONAL BEHAVIOR

As we learn more about human behavior at work, we apply improved models of organizational behavior. Modern organizations are increasing their use of the supportive model, and some apply the collegial model in appropriate situations. In order to provide review and perspective, Figure 27-1 presents the four models of organizational behavior and then relates them to some other ideas discussed in this book. By reading the chart one can determine that McGregor's Theory Y is related to the supportive and collegial models. Similarly, Herzberg's maintenance factors apply mostly to the autocratic and custodial models.

In relation to Maslow's hierarchy, Figure 27-1 shows that each model of organizational behavior moves to a higher level of need satisfaction. Generally there is also movement toward a wider distribution of power, more intrinsic motivation, a more positive attitude toward people, and a better balance of concern for both employee needs and organizational outputs. Authority and discipline have become more internalized within the group, instead of being imposed on the group from the outside. The managerial role has advanced from one of strict authority to leadership and team support. Much progress has been made during the last few years, and we can expect further progress. In the last generation we have doubled the good and halved the bad in human relationships at work. The pieces are beginning to fall into place for an effective people-organization relationship.

	AUTOCRATIC	CUSTODIAL	SUPPORTIVE	COLLEGIAL
Depends on:	Power	Economic resources	Leadership	Partnership (mutual contribution)
Managerial orientation:	Authority	Money	Support	Teamwork
Employee orientation:	Obedience	Security	Job performance	Responsibility
Employee psychological result:	Dependence on boss	Dependence on organization	Participation	Self-discipline
Employee needs met:	Subsistence	Maintenance	Higher-order	Self-actualization
Performance result:	Minimum	Passive cooperation	Awakened drives	Some enthusiasm
Relation to other ideas McGregor's theories:	Theory X	Theory X	Theory Y	Theory Y
Maslow's need-priority model:	Physiological	Security	Middle-order	Higher-order
Herzberg's factors:	Maintenance	Maintenance	Motivational	Motivational
Blake and Mouton's managerial grid:	9,1	3,5	6,6	8,8
Motivational environment:	Extrinsic	Extrinsic	Intrinsic	Intrinsic
Motivational style:	Negative	Mostly neutral on job	Positive	Positive

FIGURE 27-1

Models of organizational behavior related to selected popular ideas on the subject.

EMPHASIS ON HIGHER-ORDER NEEDS. One reason for emphasis on different models of organizational behavior is the evolution in employee need structures. Advanced nations have reached a condition wherein higher-order needs are the prime motivators, and the work system is so complicated that the higher-order capabilities of people are required more than their manual skills.

The key that unlocks this combination of higher-order needs and capabilities in order to make the system productive is improved organizational behavior. The human mind is made productive by positive motivation. This is a unique energizing force wholly unlike the application of physical energy to a machine. A machine has a rated capacity beyond which it cannot possibly go, no matter how much energy is applied to it. It can produce only so much and no more. But a person can produce unlimited amounts through better ideas. The promise of better organizational behavior is that it motivates people to produce better ideas. There is no visible limit to what people can accomplish when they are motivated to use their potential to create new and better ideas.

There is a difference between (1) motivating people to work harder by applying more physical energy to their jobs, and (2) motivating them to work creatively with their minds to develop better ways of doing things. The first approach offers only limited increase in output and probably a decrease in satisfaction. The second approach—getting people motivated to work creatively—offers progress without the necessity of harder work, because new and better ways of work can be developed to replace the old ones. This approach "gets everybody into the act" instead of confining workers to the simple task of carrying out orders developed by someone else. The key thought is: Work smarter, not harder.

A SYSTEMS APPROACH. Change toward improved organizational behavior needs to be perceived as a total system. This means that effective change is complex and takes a long time to effect. Any new practice such as participation treats only part of the whole system, so it often fails to achieve its full potential for improvement. There are too many unchanged intervening variables that restrict its success. What is needed in organizational behavior is gradual enrichment of entire socio-technical systems to be more suitable for people. This is a large task, but a challenging one.

Success can be achieved in even the most difficult circumstances, such as an automobile assembly plant. For example, General Motors made a major effort to move one of its assembly plants more toward supportive, System 4 type management.[2] New leadership was provided, the supervisory job was redefined, participation was expanded substantially, and other human improvements were made.

Changes in efficiency are shown in Figure 27-2. During the first year of change, operating efficiency decreased rather than increased. This decrease in efficiency reflects the learning curve for change that was explained in Chapter 10. Change, even when it is desirable, introduces so many disruptions and problems that effectiveness is likely to decline in the short run.

In the second year of change there was an improvement of about 10 percent in direct labor such as that found on the assembly line. Then in the third year indi-

rect labor improved more than 20 percent above its performance prior to the change.

During the period shown the monitored quality index improved 10 percent, and there was a major decline of 60 percent in grievances. The program was particularly successful in the cushion room, a department of about 250 employees. In one year scrap costs declined from 4 percent to below 1 percent, and grievances declined from fifty per month to less than three per month. The more supportive organizational behavior program was successful.

A CONTINGENCY APPROACH. Organizational behavior is applied in a contingency relationship. That is, not all organizations need exactly the same amount of participation, open communication, or any other behavioral practice in order to be equally effective. With regard to participation, for example, some situations permit more genuine participation than others, and some people want more participation than other people. The most effective organizational behavior system will tend to vary according to an organization's total environment.

For example, let us compare the two variables of a stable and a changing environment, and then relate these variables to different practices discussed in this book. Effective organizational practices in these two environments are likely to vary in the directions shown in Figure 27-3. The figure represents possible tendencies, not absolutes. For example, all that it implies regarding structure is that an effective stable organization may give more emphasis to hierarchy than a changing organization. Similarly, it probably gives more emphasis to vertical communication than a changing organization does. Not all the tendencies shown have

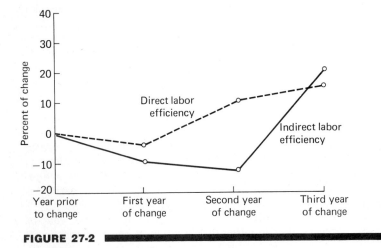

FIGURE 27-2

Percent of change in operating efficiency at Lakewood assembly plant following changes toward more supportive organizational behavior. (*Source:* William F. Dowling, "At General Motors: System 4 Builds Performance and Profits," *Organizational Dynamics,* Winter 1975, p. 30. ©, 1975. Reprinted with permission.)

been proven in research, but there is some evidence of differences between stable and changing environments.

It should be understood that contingency theory and humanistic goals of more human organizations exist side-by-side as joint ideas. They do not cancel out each other. Both stable and changing organizations, for example, need a more human environment for people (such as more job enrichment and consideration), and in the next generation both will have it. However, even then, contingency theory would predict differences in practice between stable and changing organizations. Contingency theory should apply in an advanced human environment the same way that it applies in a less advanced one. But contingency theory does not imply that certain types of organizations have no need for social progress toward a more advanced human environment.

DETERMINING ORGANIZATIONAL BEHAVIOR'S ROLE

THE ROLE OF ORGANIZATIONAL BEHAVIOR: A FORMULA. The place that organizational behavior occupies in a work system is illustrated by a set of equations. Let us look first at a worker's ability. It is generally accepted that knowledge and one's skill in applying it constitute the human trait called "ability." This is represented by the equation:

Knowledge $\times$ skill = ability

Looking now at motivation, it results from a person's attitudes reacting in a specific situation. Technically this is represented by the equation: Valence $\times$ expectancy = motivation. More operationally it is:

Attitude $\times$ situation = motivation

ORGANIZATIONAL CHARACTERISTIC

ENVIRONMENT	Structure	Production system	Leadership style	Communication	Model of organizational behavior	Performance measure
Stable	More rigid hierarchy	More specialization	More structure	More vertical	More autocratic	More management by rules
Changing	More flexible (some project and matrix)	More job enrichment	More consideration	More multi-directional	More supportive	More management by objectives

FIGURE 27-3

Application of contingency ideas to stable and changing environments.

Motivation and ability together determine a person's performance in any activity. We now have a series of equations as follows:

1. Knowledge × skill = ability

2. Attitude × situation = motivation

3. Ability × motivation = human performance

The scope of organizational behavior is represented by the second equation (Attitude × situation = motivation). This book has emphasized attitudes and how they are affected by situational factors to determine motivation.

The importance of organizational behavior is shown by the third equation (Ability × motivation = human performance). Organizational behavior, as represented by the term "motivation," is one of two factors in the equation. Furthermore, organizational behavior has played a part in motivating workers to acquire the other factor, "ability." Thus, organizational behavior is part and parcel of the whole equation of human performance.

Human performance has to be mixed with resources such as tools, power, and materials to get overall work performance, as indicated by a fourth equation:

4. Human performance × resources = organizational performance

Even in this last equation, the role of organizational behavior is major.

THE NEED FOR A SOCIOECONOMIC MEASURE OF PRODUCTIVITY. Management for decades has measured the values of work in terms of a worker's productivity. However, there is some question whether the current formulas for determining productivity are adequate because they ignore certain social values in employment. Productivity is generally measured as a ratio of output to input, according to one of the following formulas:

1. Time formula—amount of acceptable production for each unit of time, usually one hour of labor

2. Economic formula (unit labor cost)—number of cost units, as measured by the accounting system, for each unit of acceptable production

3. Energy formula (usually for machinery)—amount of acceptable production for each unit of energy input

Each of the preceding formulas neglects workers, paying no attention to the values they derive as they work. Specifically these formulas exclude employee satisfaction and growth on the job and the broad effect that these conditions have upon society in general. These formulas ignore behavioral values, but from the social point of view behavioral values are significant. This suggests that a new productivity formula is needed. Regardless of the difficulty of computing this kind of formula, many persons already use a rough model of it when they make an overall appraisal of whether a decision is socially desirable. The conclusion is that managers need to think in terms of some kind of socioeconomic productivity measure, whether it can be computed precisely or not. There is a growing public expectation for employers to perform social analysis in their decision making, that is, to think in terms of behavioral and social values. It is no longer adequate for them to consider only economic and mechanical input-output measures.[3]

HUMAN RESOURCE ACCOUNTING. In an effort to give more emphasis to people in a language that management understands—the language of accounting—accountants are developing *human resource accounting.* It is a means of converting human data into money values for use in the regular accounting system. There are various approaches to human resource accounting, some with rather complex accounting procedures.[4] Two approaches will be discussed.

The investment approach. One approach, often called the *investment approach,* seeks to account for the amount that an organization has invested in human resources. Costs such as recruiting and training, rather than being treated as current expenses, are capitalized as an investment to be depreciated during an employee's expected employment. There is no attempt to theorize about how much an employee is worth, but only how much has been directly invested in each employee.

Since direct investment in employees has been determined, a measure of return on investment may be established. This measure gives an improved idea of how human resources are being used. For example, assume that five research scientists resign because of an autocratic manager. Their resignations would appear as an immediate investment loss, thereby giving strong financial emphasis to the need for better organizational behavior. As another example, assume that an engineering design department is hoarding trained engineers by keeping too many of them for the job required and by using them below their optimum skill level. Human resource accounting may help management uncover this kind of misappropriation of resources, because the extra investment in them would be considered in computing return on investment. Surely in its effect on both people and profits, misappropriation of human resources is just as undesirable as misappropriation of economic resources.

One of the earliest firms to experiment with this type of human resource accounting was R. G. Barry Corporation of Columbus, Ohio. Beginning in 1968 this firm established an investment accounting system to provide human resource accounting for its managers, and this system was later extended to office and factory personnel. This system accounts for genuine employer costs that should provide a regular return on investment and which, for human reasons, should not be wasted through underemployment. This investment figure is then used to compute return on assets, return on investment in human resources, and similar accounting values.

The organizational climate approach. Another approach, which may be called the *organizational climate approach,* uses periodic behavioral surveys to determine ways in which the organizational climate has improved or deteriorated. Based on research, it is assumed that changes in these human resource variables will affect future performance. Established formulas are used to convert the human variables into money estimates of changes in an organization's productive capability from one period to another. In this way management is encouraged to look beyond short-range economic results to longer-range resource capability in an organization. For example, a manager may use autocratic methods to cut costs and show a higher economic profit for the year. A survey of climate may reveal, however, that the manager reduced resources so greatly that future costs will be greater than present savings. Following is an actual example.[5]

In a plant with several hundred employees a management consulting firm was employed to implement a cost reduction program. After careful studies with the assistance of local and corporate management, recommended changes were developed, and the affected departments were ordered to introduce them. Annual savings of $250,000 were secured.

Before and after the cost reduction program a survey of organizational climate was made. These surveys showed unfavorable shifts in human variables that were calculated to increase costs at least $450,000 annually. The apparent gain of $250,000 now was revealed as a probable loss, primarily because symptoms rather than causes of ineffectiveness were treated. The plant's actual experiences during the next several years confirmed the accuracy of the predictions.

Human resource accounting has its limitations. Some persons argue that it is demeaning to treat people in money terms on accounting statements. Employee satisfaction and growth should be legitimate goals whether they affect dollars or not. Further, some of the information is costly to collect, and sometimes it is such a rough estimate that it may not be of much use. In spite of these limitations, it is evident that human resource accounting of the types just described is helpful in communicating human data to management in a language that management already understands. It can contribute to society's transition toward more emphasis on socioeconomic data in decision making.

LIMITATIONS OF ORGANIZATIONAL BEHAVIOR

This book has been written from a specialized point of view that emphasizes only the behavioral side of organizations and the kinds of benefits that attention to this side of organization can bring. Nevertheless, we always recognize the limitations of organizational behavior. It will not abolish conflict and frustration; it can only reduce them. It is a way to improve, not an absolute answer to problems. Furthermore, it is but part of the whole cloth of an organization. We can discuss organizational behavior as a separate subject, but to apply it we must tie it back to the whole of reality. Improved organizational behavior will not solve unemployment. It will not make up for our own deficiencies. It cannot substitute for poor planning, inept organizing, or shoddy controls. It is only one of many systems operating within a larger social system.

BEHAVIORAL BIAS. People who lack system understanding may develop a *behavioral bias,* which gives them a narrow viewpoint that emphasizes "meaningful" employee experiences while overlooking the broader system of the organization in relation to all its publics. This condition often is called *tunnel vision* because viewpoints are narrow as if people were looking through a tunnel. They see only the tiny view at the other end of the tunnel, while missing the broader landscape.

It should be evident that concern for employees can be so greatly overdone that the original purpose of joining people together—productive organizational outputs for society—is lost. Sound organizational behavior should help achieve organizational purposes, not replace them. The person who ignores the needs of people as consumers of organizational outputs while championing employee needs is misapplying the ideas of organizational behavior. It is also true that the person who pushes production outputs without regard for employee needs is misapplying organizational behavior. Sound organizational behavior recognizes a social system in which many types of human needs are served in many ways.

Behavioral bias can be so misapplied that it harms employees as well as the organization. Some persons, in spite of their good intentions, so overwhelm people with care that they are reduced to dependent—and unproductive—indignity. They become content, not fulfilled. They find excuses for failure, rather than taking responsibility for progress. They lack self-discipline and self-respect. As happened with scientific management years ago, concern for people can be misapplied by overeager partisans until it becomes dysfunctional.

Employees as well as managers can handicap a fellow employee through unrestricted concern and care. These conditions are illustrated by the following events.

A young woman was a clerk in a government office. Her elderly father was growing mentally unstable and plans were being made to have him placed in an institution within a few months. Her worry over this matter was compounded by the fact that he frequently came to the building where she worked and waited in the corridors for her before lunch and in the afternoon. His appearance was not pleasant, and he often mumbled. Sometimes he followed her into other offices, creating embarrassing situations. She received much sympathy and attention from her associates, and some of them began doing her work for her while she was upset. Since this problem was reducing her productivity, her supervisor finally arranged with the building guards not to admit her father, thus keeping him out of the building entirely. The supervisor allowed her associates to continue performing some of her work, pending placement of her father in an institution.

Even after her father was placed in an institution, the young woman continued letting others do her work. It soon became apparent to both her associates and her supervisor that they had sympathized with her and carried her load so long that she was depending on them as she would a crutch. She relished their sympathy and help, and showed incapability of doing the job she had once done. She became "handicapped" as surely as if she had a physical handicap, because of too much care and good intentions by others. Seeing these negative results, her supervisor wisely insisted that her associates reduce both their help and sympathy. Slowly and painfully the handicapped girl returned to normalcy.

THE LAW OF DIMINISHING RETURNS. Dysfunctional results in organizational behavior may be produced by the law of diminishing returns.[6] It is a limiting factor in organizational behavior the same way that it is in economics. In economics the *law of diminishing returns* refers to a declining amount of extra outputs when more of a desirable input is added to an economic situation. After a certain point the output from each unit of added input tends to become smaller. The added output eventually may reach zero and even decline when more units of input are added. For example, a farmer who has a laborer working on 20 acres of land may double the output by adding another laborer. Similar results could occur by doubling the work force to four persons, but soon a point will be reached where the increase in output from adding workers is smaller and smaller. Eventually production will decline as the field becomes overcrowded with workers, coordination deteriorates, and crops are trampled by the crowd.

Diminishing returns in organizational behavior works in a similar way. It states that at some point increments of a desirable behavioral practice produce declining returns, eventually zero returns, and then negative returns as more increments are added. The concept implies that for any situation there is an optimum amount of a desirable practice, such as participation. When that point is exceeded, there is a decline in returns. In other words, the fact that a practice is desirable does not mean that more of it is more desirable. More of a good thing is not necessarily good.

Diminishing returns may not apply to every behavioral situation, but the idea is so widely applicable that it is of general use. Furthermore, the exact point at which an application becomes excessive will vary with the circumstances; but an excess can be reached with nearly any variable. Diminishing returns in organizational behavior is so prevalent that managers must deal with it frequently.

Why does diminishing returns exist? Essentially, it is a system concept. It applies because of the complex system relationships of many variables in organizational behavior. The facts state that when an excess of one variable develops, although that variable is desirable, it tends to restrict the operating benefits of other variables so substantially that net effectiveness declines. For example, too much security results in too little initiative and growth. This relationship shows that *organizational effectiveness is achieved, not by maximizing one behavioral variable, but by working all system variables together in a balanced way.*

EMPLOYEE AUTONOMY AS AN EXAMPLE. Employee autonomy is a higher-order need frequently emphasized in organizational behavior. Some observers speak of autonomy as an ideal, implying that if organizational members could have complete autonomy then the ideal state would be achieved. But this kind of reasoning ignores the law of diminishing returns. As shown in Figure 27-4, effectiveness declines when additional increments of autonomy are added because an excess of autonomy prevents coordination toward central goals. An integration of activities is lacking, so the organization cannot function effectively and the labor of people is wasted.

At the other end of the continuum, the lack of autonomy is also ineffective. When autonomy declines below an appropriate level, the organization will become less effective because it fails to develop and use the talents of employees. The result is that the effectiveness of a practice declines with both excessive use and miserly use. Most success is achieved in the broad middle ground of use. This relationship produces a humpback curve for behavioral practices when they are charted with effectiveness.

The location of the humpback curve on the autonomy continuum may vary somewhat with different situations, and the slope may vary, but the basic curve persists in organizational relationships. Figure 27-4 shows a curve with a solid line as it might exist for a group of production workers. Line AA' shows the amount of autonomy that produces maximum effectiveness. The curve with the dotted line shows how diminishing returns might apply to workers in a research unit in the same organization. Line BB' shows that much more autonomy can be provided for the research workers before a point of maximum effectiveness is reached. Ten years from now the curves for both probably will be in different locations because of different conditions. This kind of contingent relationship, by which the most effective point of autonomy is dependent on other variables, is the essence of modern contingency management. However, whatever the situation, the humpback curve persists and a point of diminishing returns is reached.

The law of diminishing returns serves as a warning that, although increases in desirable variables can be beneficial, an excess of any of them will be counterproductive. Moderation is required. People obsessed with building employee autonomy and little else, or creating the most possible employee security, will not be contributing to organizational effectiveness. There can be too much of a good thing just as there can be too little of it. An excess of one variable disturbs system relationships so drastically that diminishing and eventually dysfunctional results occur. The middle ground becomes the most effective area of operations. It is in the general area of the high point on the humpback curve of effectiveness.

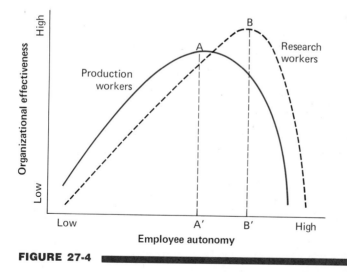

FIGURE 27-4 ◼◼◼◼◼◼◼◼◼◼◼◼◼◼◼◼◼◼◼◼◼◼◼◼◼◼◼◼◼◼◼◼◼

Application of the law of diminishing returns to employee autonomy.

MANIPULATION OF PEOPLE. A significant concern about organizational behavior is that its knowledge and techniques can be used to manipulate people as well as to help them develop their potential. Persons who lack respect for the basic dignity of the human being could learn organizational behavior concepts and use them for selfish ends. They could use what they know about motivation or communication to manipulate people without regard for human welfare. Persons who lack ethical values could use people in unethical ways.

The *philosophy* of organizational behavior is supportive and human resources–oriented. It seeks to improve the human environment and help people grow toward their human potential. However, the *knowledge and techniques* of this subject may be used for negative as well as positive consequences. This possibility is true of knowledge in most any field, so it is no special limitation of organizational behavior. Nevertheless, we must be cautious that what is known about people is not used to manipulate them. The possibility of manipulation means that persons in power in organizations need to be people of high ethical and moral integrity, who would not misuse their power. Without ethical leadership the new knowledge that is learned about people becomes a dangerous instrument for possible misuse. Ethical leadership will recognize such guides as the following:[7]

- *Responsibility to others arises whenever persons have power in an organization.*

- *The organization shall operate as a two-way open system with open receipt of inputs from people and open disclosure of its operations to them.*

- *Human and social costs as well as benefits of an activity shall be considered in determining whether to proceed with it.*

There is, for example, a fine line between genuine motivation and manipulation of people. How shall that line be defined? Basically the conditions of use need to be examined. If people understand what is happening and have substantial freedom to make their own choices, they are not being manipulated. But if they are being covertly directed and/or lack free choices, they are being manipulated. This is true whether the manipulator is a social scientist, a fellow employee, or a manager. The issue is not who is using the knowledge, but how it is being used.

As the general population learns more about organizational behavior, it will be more difficult to manipulate them, but the possibility is always there. That is why society needs organizational leaders of high ethical integrity and concern for the dignity of human beings. But ethical leaders cannot succeed unless there are also ethical followers.

THE PROMISE OF A BETTER TOMORROW

Although organizational behavior does have limitations, these should not blind us to the tremendous potential that it has to contribute to the advancement of civilization. It will provide much improvement in the human environment.[8] By building a better climate for people, organizational behavior will release their creative potential to help solve great social problems such as poverty and illiteracy. In this way organizational behavior may contribute to social improvemer beyond the confines of any one organization where it is applied. tional climate for just one person may contribute to some grea solar energy, health, or education.

Improved organizational behavior is not easy to apply. But are there. The result should be a higher quality of life in which harmony within each person, among persons, and among the or .... of the world.

TERMS AND CONCEPTS FOR REVIEW

Socioeconomic measure of productivity

Human resource accounting

Investment and organizational climate approaches to human resource accounting

Behavioral bias

Law of diminishing returns

REVIEW QUESTIONS

1. Discuss differences among the four models of organizational behavior.
2. Compare some of the contingency relationships in stable and changing environments.
3. Discuss two types of human resource accounting.
4. Interpret some of the limitations of organizational behavior, including the law of diminishing returns. Discuss application of the law to employee autonomy.
5. Prepare a five-minute talk on "What Organizational Behavior Will Be Like Twenty Years from Now."

CASES

THE NEW CONTROLLER

Statewide Electrical Supply, Inc., is a wholesale distributor of electrical supplies serving a population area of three million persons. Business has expanded gradually, and during the last eight years the number of accounting clerks has grown from one to twelve. The first clerk employed was a middle-aged woman who had completed two years of college and taken two accounting courses. She proved to be a loyal and capable clerk, so when the department expanded to three persons she was promoted to chief accounting clerk with supervisory duties over the other clerks. She reported to the firm's general manager and depended on him to handle accounting decisions that were more than routine.

As the business grew larger, the existing accounting arrangement became inadequate, so the general manager decided to employ a controller to handle all financial and accounting functions of the firm. The chief clerk recognized that she was not qualified to handle accounting and financial affairs of this magnitude, and she did not seek promotion to this job. She did, however, welcome the idea of a controller, because she was overloaded with work and felt that the new controller might help relieve her of some of her more difficult responsibilities.

An additional factor in the firm's decision to establish the position of controller was that there were many complaints about the chief clerk's supervisory ability. She appeared to be effective with the first two or three clerks when the department was small and duties were less complex, but she was unable to handle the larger department and the more complex duties. Her problems seemed to be confined mostly to internal supervision in her department. Other departments in the firm reported that she worked effectively with them, and they expressed some fear that the new controller might upset this favorable working relationship.

The general manager is not sure how to handle the problem of integrating the new controller into the organization. He wants to retain the chief clerk because she is a valuable employee, but he is concerned that if he demotes her from supervisory duties at the time the controller is employed she may resign.

QUESTIONS
1. How do you recommend that the new controller's department be organized?
2. What can be done to improve the behavioral environment in this situation?

EASTERN ACCOUNTANTS
Eastern Accountants is an accounting firm employing about 175 accountants and other professional personnel. It also does some management consulting. One of its managers has recommended that the investment approach to human resource accounting should be adopted for employees of Eastern Accountants. The senior partners of the firm finally have agreed to install this type of accounting.

QUESTIONS
1. Read literature on human resource accounting and develop for management a list of:
   a. What investments in human resources it should account for.
   b. What disinvestments in human resources it should account for.
   (It is not necessary to develop the entire accounting plan.)
2. Develop arguments both for and against this type of human resource accounting for firms similar to Eastern Accountants. How will managerial decisions be affected?

REFERENCES
1. Douglas T. Hall and Edward E. Lawler III, "Job Characteristics and Pressures and the Organizational Integration of Professionals," *Administrative Science Quarterly*, September 1970, p. 271.

2. William F. Dowling, "At General Motors: System 4 Builds Performance and Profits," *Organizational Dynamics,* Winter 1975, pp. 23–38.

3. For an extension of the socioeconomic point of view see Keith Davis and Robert L. Blomstrom, *Business and Society: Environment and Responsibility,* 3d ed., New York: McGraw-Hill Book Company, 1975.

4. Further details are available in Edwin H. Caplan and Stephen Landekich, *Human Resource Accounting: Past, Present and Future,* New York: National Association of Accountants, 1974; and Eric Flamholtz, *Human Resource Accounting,* Encino, Calif.: Dickenson Publishing Company, Inc., 1974. Four conceptual approaches are summarized in James A. Craft, "Human Resource Accounting and Manpower Management: A Review and Assessment of Current Applicability," *Journal of Economics and Business,* Fall 1975, pp. 23–30.

5. Rensis Likert, "Human Resource Accounting: Building and Assessing Productive Organizations," *Personnel,* May–June 1973, pp. 8–24.

6. This discussion is adapted from Keith Davis, "A Law of Diminishing Returns in Organizational Behavior," *Personnel Journal,* December 1975, pp. 616–619.

7. Adapted from Keith Davis, "Five Propositions for Social Responsibility," *Business Horizons,* June 1975, pp. 19–24.

8. For further discussion see Rensis Likert and Jane Gibson Likert, *New Ways of Managing Conflict,* New York: McGraw-Hill Book Company, 1976.

SECTION 7

CASE PROBLEMS

INTRODUCTION

Case problems provide a useful medium for testing and applying some of the ideas in this textbook. They bring reality to abstract ideas about organizational behavior. All the case problems that follow are true situations recorded by case research. Certain case details are disguised, but none of the cases is a fictional creation. All names are disguised, and any similarity to actual persons or organizations is purely coincidental.

These cases have a decision-making emphasis in the sense that they end at a point that leaves managers and/or employees with certain decisions to make. Most of the cases emphasize decisional problems of managers. One decision often is: Do I have a further problem? If that decision is in the affirmative, then further decisions must be made regarding what problems exist, why they are problems, what can be done about them within the resource limits available (i.e., what alternatives are available), and, finally, what *should* be done to solve this particular problem in this specific organization. This is the reality that every manager faces in operating situations. There is no escaping it.

Even a person who does not plan to be a manager can gain much from analyzing these cases, because all employees need to develop their own analytical skills about human behavior in order to work successfully with their associates and *with management* in organizations. Thinking in terms of an employee role in a case, one can ask: Why do my associates act the way they do in this situation? Why is management acting the way it is in this instance? Was there something in my behavior that caused these actions? How can I change my behavior in order to work more effectively with the organization and my associates and thereby reach my goals more easily?

Since these case problems describe real situations, they include both good and bad practices. These cases are not presented as examples of good management, effective organizational behavior, bad management, or ineffective organizational behavior. Readers must make these judgments for themselves.

DUDLEY LODGE

Prof. Henry Ellis taught management in a large Midwestern state university. On August 5 of last year, at about 6:30 P.M., he received a long-distance telephone call from the factory town of Corbin, 30 miles distant. The caller was Dudley Lodge, a student in his class in "Organizational Behavior" during the previous spring. After the necessary exchange of introductions, Lodge said that he had gone to work for the Roanoke Company and was having trouble. Lodge reminded Professor Ellis that he had told the students of his class he would be glad to help them when they were in business, and Lodge wanted help. He wanted to visit Professor Ellis that night because he had to have an answer to his problem by the next morning. Professor Ellis encouraged the visit and made an appointment for 8 P.M.

While he was waiting for Lodge to arrive, Professor Ellis recalled that he did not know Lodge very well, but Lodge had impressed him as a young, friendly, intelligent student. Lodge made an A in the course, although he was not a business major.[1] Professor Ellis also remembered that near the end of the course he had told his students, "Your formal education and training will not provide you with all the answers in your job. If I can help you any time, please call on me. Your education does not end at graduation."

When Lodge arrived, he appeared emotionally upset and exhausted. He was impatient to describe his problem. He agreed to let Professor Ellis record his comments on a tape recorder which had been used for role playing in the class he attended. Professor Ellis mostly listened, occasionally asking a question or interjecting a remark such as "Tell me more about that." Lodge's description of his problem was as follows.

LODGE'S DESCRIPTION OF HIS PROBLEM

I believe this case will be clearer if I present some of the background of my experiences with the company before I relate the facts in the immediate problem. I was accepted for employment with the Roanoke Company through one of its regular application forms without a personal interview. This was an irregular procedure for the company, and I do not know why it was done in this case; however, I had no

---

[1] Lodge's placement file, which Professor Ellis examined the next morning in the Placement Office, College of Engineering, showed that Lodge had no business experience. He had a farm background. He did not work any of his way through college. He was captain of artillery in Army ROTC during his senior year and program chairman of the student chapter of the American Society of Mechanical Engineers. He made above-average grades. Letters of reference from his professors, a banker, a doctor, and a minister stated that he was honest, sincere, deeply religious, hard-working, and somewhat retiring in nature.

reason to be concerned about this until after my arrival in Cleveland. When I reported to the central company offices in Cleveland on June 15, I was interviewed by both Mr. Sharp, director, and Mr. Thomas, assistant director of the student training course. This interview seemed quite routine. These men had my written application before them with all my personal data, yet they both seemed somewhat surprised by two facts: first, that I was married, and secondly, that I was a mechanical engineer. I was not married when I made out the application, and thus this fact did not show on the form. The second fact, that I was a mechanical engineer, was shown quite plainly on the application, and I cannot understand why it was such a surprising fact unless it was an important consideration in the Cleveland plant where only electrical equipment was manufactured. There was no serious discussion over any of my qualifications, and after a few humorous remarks about my being newly married, I was assigned to Department W-3, small motor and generator winding.

At this interview I made a special point of informing Sharp that I was interested in steam turbine design and testing, as stated in my application, that I had specialized in this work in college, and that I should like assignment to this work in the Corbin plant of the company[2] where this type of research and testing was done. My request was casually, and carefully, avoided at this time; but when it was repeated to Sharp in a short talk to him about two weeks later, he informed me that there was no student opening available in Corbin. Thomas suggested that I might be interested in transformer work, but I could see no mechanical problems involved in this, so I requested to remain in motive power, if I could not be transferred to Corbin.

The day after this second interview, Sharp called me into his office at the end of the day and asked me if I would like to teach a course of physics and trigonometry to the apprentice machinists. I accepted this offer and was enjoying the work to such an extent that I had about made up my mind to be satisfied with the work in Cleveland when, on July 13, Sharp again called me to his office and told me there was an opening in steam turbine work at Corbin if I wanted it. As a result of this conference I reported to the plant in Corbin on July 15.

When I arrived in Corbin I was received quite cordially by Mr. Barry, director of student training at this plant, who called my wife into the office and then conducted both of us on a short tour of the plant. He suggested that I take two or three days to find a place to live, that I look around over the plant for a day, and then report back to his office for assignment. Two days later when I reported to Barry's office, he took me around to the many shops and offices, and introduced me to the shop supervisors and department heads. He made a special visit to the production control department, supervised by a Mr. Schmidt, and there told me that I would not be placed immediately on the student training course, but would be assigned temporarily to this department to relieve some of the employees who were going on vacation. Barry then left me with Schmidt, who took me immediately to the desk of a Mr. Langner, a production expediter, whose place I was to take while the latter was on vacation for a month.

---

[2] The company had several large plants located in various parts of the United States. The Corbin plant was located about three hundred miles from Cleveland.

The production-control department, including Schmidt's desk, was all together in one large room. Langner spent the rest of the day with me in an attempt to familiarize me with the work involved in "chasing" an order through the intricacies of design, machining or purchase, testing, inspection, storage, and shipment. It seemed to me that the details involved were impossible of grasping in several months, and yet I was to take over this job on the following day. Frankly I was scared. I had never seen the inside of a large manufacturing plant before, I had hardly seen the working parts of a steam turbine, and here I was to have the responsibility of expediting the manufacture of a 190,000-kilowatt turbo-generator with all auxiliaries for the National Utility Company. I went home that evening a very bewildered and "sick" production expediter, or "chaser," as the employees in the shops sneeringly called us.

The next weeks passed almost as a nightmare. In my own confusion it seemed that there was no order, no scheme to follow, and that everyone was too busy to realize that I was a green country kid who hardly knew one end of a turbine from the other. I tried conscientiously to memorize shop orders, purchase orders, delivery dates, promise dates, the names of parts, the names of shop supervisors, and a few other details all at the same time, and it seemed like a hopeless task. The other expediters were all very friendly and helpful, but Schmidt seemed to assume that I was a "full-grown expediter" and expected me to replace Langner in all respects. He told me that he would expect me to know the exact status of my order at all times, and that I should keep a large wall progress chart up to date by making daily changes each morning. To be sure that I understood this, he called me to his desk each morning for a complete report. If I was uncertain as to the exact status of some operation, he was very impatient. His loud-talking manner and his habitual and routine use of profanity irritated me. These morning interviews took on the aspects of an inquisition. I confided in another of the expediters who seemed sympathetic, and he told me to come to the office early, to get the progress chart up to date, and to spend most of the rest of the day out in the shops away from Schmidt. None of the expediters liked him, and they avoided him as much as possible.

Acting on the advice of the other expediter, I began spending most of the day in the shops. I made friends with the shop supervisors and found that I was enjoying the time spent in discussing their work with them, and also found that they were more willing to give me the information that I required relative to my order. I also learned that the shop employees had a contempt for the production-control department, and refused to cooperate with the time-and-motion-study specialists when they came through to study machine operations. This association gave me a different view of shop relations, and I found myself sympathizing with the shop attitude. This contact made it more difficult for me to conscientiously put the "pressure on" the shop supervisors to make them meet promise dates on the machining operations for my job.

In spite of this tactic of remaining out of the office as much as possible, I managed to keep my progress chart up to date by getting to the office early. I reported to work on the regular student schedule of 7:30 A.M. and left work at 4:18 P.M. In this way I was in the office well ahead of the regular office staff. My order was keeping reasonably well to its schedule, and I had no serious complaints from

Schmidt. From time to time during the day I would meet him in one of the shops, and on occasion he would stop me and discuss the progress of the work. On these occasions I noticed that he was much more friendly and talked in a much more casual and less "official" tone of voice. He never criticized me for not spending more time in the office.

Late yesterday afternoon, however, just before quitting time I learned from the engineering department that there had been a mistake made in the machining of the flange bolts for the low-pressure turbine casing. I was on my way to the automatic screw machine shop to stop production when I met Schmidt in one of the shops. He stopped me rather abruptly and the following conversation took place:

Lodge, what is the status of the shaft centering plugs for the low-pressure turbine?

I am not certain, Mr. Schmidt, but I don't think any work has been done on them. The shaft forgings are not due in the shops for nearly two weeks yet.

Damn it, I told you that I wanted to know the exact status of that entire job at all times. I happen to know that those plugs have not even been put on production order yet, and by damn, I want them done tonight and on my desk tomorrow morning. Put them on overtime for tonight.

Yes sir, I'll see Hill in the light-machine shop about it right away.

After this conversation with Schmidt, I made arrangements with Hill, the light-machine shop supervisor, to have the centering plugs placed on overtime order and to have them finished by morning when I would pick them up. I saw Hill make out the order and place it in the overtime work basket. The operation was simple and would require about two hours of work on a power cutoff saw and a lathe.

By the time I had finished in the light-machine shop, the automatic screw machine shop, which was working only one shift per day, was closed, and I was unable to stop production on the flange bolts. I had, however, secured one of the bolts and back at my desk had confirmed the fact that they were ½ inch too short. I planned to stop production on them the first thing the next morning. While at my desk I checked my production schedule and found that the turbine shaft, for which the centering plugs were so urgently needed, was not due from the foundry and forge shop until August 21. I then went home feeling that the day had gone very well.

When I arrived at the office this morning I brought the progress chart up to date, made a few notes for the work for the day, and started out to the shops. I took the flange bolt along with me and was going to the automatic screw shop right after I went by the light-machine shop to see about the centering plugs. The time must have been almost 8 A.M. and as I passed through No. 2 shop, I met Schmidt and the following discussion took place:

Lodge, are those centering plugs finished?

I'm on my way to see about them right now, but I have an urgent stop order for these flange bolts and—

Damn it, I told you to have those plugs on my desk when I came in. By damn,

Lodge, when I give you an order I expect it to be obeyed. (He grabbed me roughly by the arm.) Come on, we're going over to the shop to see about those plugs.

(I jerked away from Schmidt's grasp.) Keep your hands off of me and stop cussing me, or I'll beat your damn brains out with this bolt! I'm going to put a stop order on those bolts, and then report you to Mr. Ball (the plant superintendent). Those plugs are not needed for nearly another month anyway.

After the above conversation Schmidt turned and walked hurriedly toward his office. I was, by this time, very nervous and upset. I did, however, regain enough composure to place the hold order on the flange bolts and then went to the light-machine shop to see about the centering plugs. I had, by this time, decided it best to talk to Barry about the whole thing before going to the plant superintendent with the matter.

However, upon my arrival at the light-machine shop I learned from talking to Hill that the centering plugs had not been finished because after I talked with Hill yesterday afternoon, Schmidt had come in and given a special order for overtime work that involved all the available lathes and operators for the entire night shift. This made it impossible for work to be done on the centering plugs, and I found them cut off of bar stock, but no more work done on them. This information "made me see red," and I headed for Schmidt's office.

By the time I had arrived at Schmidt's office I had become rather nervous, wrought up, and very angry about the whole state of things. I went directly to Schmidt's desk and told him, in something of a loud voice, I'm sure, that he was "the double-crossing so-and-so" that had stopped work on the centering plugs, that it was a dirty frame-up of me on his part; and that as of now he could get someone else to take over the job of expediter; that it was a job for a stool pigeon, anyway; and that I refused to do any more of his dirty work; and that I would not take any more of his cussing.

The effects of these remarks were somewhat awe-inspiring in the office, to say the least. Schmidt jumped from his desk and started toward me; but a very calm, quiet, purchasing agent, Mr. Andrews, intervened and restored a bit of order before things got completely out of control. Schmidt got in several "air-burning" profane remarks and told me that he was going to report me to the plant superintendent.

Andrews went with me to my desk, advised me to go immediately to see Barry, and offered to go along with me as a witness. I gladly accepted his offer, and we went over to Barry's office and told him the whole story. He talked to us for about half an hour and then wanted me to go with him back to Schmidt's to talk to him. This I refused to do, and both Barry and Andrews left to talk to Schmidt.

After talking to Schmidt for a long time, Barry returned and told me that Schmidt admitted that both of us "acted like fools" and that he was ready to forget the matter, if I would, and he would like for me to continue in the work until Langner returned. Barry told me that if I would go with him and apologize to Schmidt, work for him until Langner returned, and "keep my nose clean," he would transfer me to the regular student training course just as soon as I could be relieved. I told him that I would not do so, the way I felt at the present time, but that I would think it over during the night and would give him an answer tomorrow. That is why I need your help, Professor Ellis. I am all mixed up and don't know what to do. I shall appreciate your advice and shall let you know the outcome.

STUDY GUIDES
1. Why do you think Lodge came to Professor Ellis for help?
2. What mistakes did the "company" make in "training" Lodge? Who made these mistakes? Explain.
3. Why do you think Schmidt acted the way he did? Why do you think Lodge reacted the way he did? Did the two persons "understand" each other?
4. What are the primary problems existing at the end of the case?
5. What action should be taken to help solve the main problems of the case? By Lodge? Barry? Schmidt? Others? Give specific behavioral reasons for proposed actions.

ROLE-PLAYING SITUATIONS
1. Assume that you are Professor Ellis, and then continue the conversation with Lodge.
2. Role-play the meeting of Lodge and Barry on August 6.
3. Role-play the meeting, if any, of Lodge, Barry, and Schmidt on August 6.

CASE 2
THE VIDEO ELECTRONICS COMPANY

Frank Simpson, president and controlling stockholder of the Video Electronics Company, now in its tenth year, was faced with the problem of gearing his plant to meet both increased production demands brought on by the expanding electronics industry and also increased competition from other producers of his line of products. The plant tripled its employees during the past year, but production per worker decreased nearly 20 percent, and costs rose nearly to the break-even point. For the preceding quarter profit on sales was less than 1 percent and profit on invested capital was under 3 percent. This was one-fourth of what Simpson considered normal.

The company employed mostly unskilled labor who were trained by the company. Employees were not represented by a labor union. All employees were on day work, rather than incentive work.

The Video Electronics Company was founded by Simpson and a few investor friends for production of a narrow line of specialized small electronic parts which were sold to other manufacturers. It grew slowly and had a force of only 105 workers at the beginning of last year. Its reputation for quality was excellent. This reputation for quality was the primary reason for a flood of orders from new clients in the spring of last year, requiring the firm to triple its labor force by July. Simpson remarked, "I didn't seek those orders. *They* came to us. I didn't want to expand that fast, but what could I do? If you want to stay in business, you can't tell your customers you are too busy to sell them anything."

The Video Electronics Company was located in a manufacturing town of 15,000 persons in rural New York, about sixty miles from any large town. Enough untrained persons were available locally for hiring for the expansion, which required the operation of two shifts instead of one. Management forecasts indicated that the expansion would be permanent, with the additional possibility of moderate growth during the next five years or longer.

Simpson, in consultation with the board of directors, concluded that he needed to establish the new position of general manager of the plant so that he (Simpson) could spend more of his time on high-level work and less of his time ironing out production difficulties. He also concluded that under present conditions he needed to build an industrial engineering staff that could both cope with present production problems and also give his company the developmental work that was needed to stay ahead of his competitors.

Almost all of his present supervisory personnel had been with the company since the year it was founded. They were all skilled people in their particular phases of the operations, but Simpson felt that none of them had the training or overall insight into company problems to take charge as general manager. After much thought, Simpson decided to employ a general manager from outside the company. This person would report directly to him and would have full responsibility for production of the product and development of a top-notch industrial engineering department. Simpson called a meeting of all his supervisory personnel and explained to them his decision in detail. He described the need for this plan of action and stressed the necessity for the utmost in cooperation. The older supervisors did not seem to be pleased with this turn of events but promised that they would cooperate fully with the new manager.

About four months after his meeting with his supervisors, Simpson found a suitable general manager, John Rider. Rider, age thirty-six, was a progressive mechanical engineer who had been a general supervisor in a large Philadelphia electronics plant. One of his first jobs as general manager was to find a qualified person to develop the industrial engineering function. Paul Green, an industrial engineer thirty-one years of age, was hired from the industrial engineering department of a large steel company in Pittsburgh. Green had an M.B.A., a good academic record, and two years of experience.

Green and Rider both felt that the company was in bad condition in relation to machine utilization, employee utilization, waste, and reject rates. On the basis of their first impressions of the production facilities they estimated that production management and industrial engineering changes ought to be able to increase productivity at least 25 percent and reduce unit costs 35 percent.

Green wanted time to get acquainted with the processes and the supervisory personnel before recommending major improvements. Rider granted this wish, so Green spent two months getting acquainted with the supervisors. During this period he recommended to Rider only minor changes that the supervisors seemed to go along with, except for minor disagreement. However, after this period Simpson, Rider, and Green felt that major steps had to be taken to improve both production and quality. They decided that the first industrial engineering project should be a study of production processes, department by department. This study was to cover every operation done on the products. All processes were to be put in writing, since many of the processes had developed without anyone ever writing down just how they were to be performed. Several of the supervisors were the only ones who understood how certain operations were to be set up and performed, and any supervisor who left the company often took valuable knowledge that was difficult to replace.

At the next supervisory meeting (of all management personnel), Simpson announced the plan for the production study. No estimated completion date for the study was given. No comments were made by the production supervisors, but it was plain to Rider and Green that several of the older supervisors were not happy about the idea. Simpson tried to get across the idea that full cooperation was required and that the company had "to meet its competition or go out of business."

Green started the survey the following week. There was outward rebellion in some cases, but he smoothed these over by discussing with the supervisor the reasons for the survey and then leaving that department alone for a few days.

Green thought he was convincing the people who objected, so he proceeded with the study without comment to either Rider or Simpson about the resistance.

About five weeks after Green started the study, he and Rider left town together on a business trip that kept them away from the plant for two days. On the night of the second day one of the second-shift supervisors telephoned Simpson, who happened to be working late at the office. The supervisor said that a group of them would like to talk to Simpson. Since many of these supervisors had known Simpson for a long time and called him by his first name, he did not object and told them to "come on up." The group that arrived consisted of all supervisors with more than one year's company seniority. First-shift supervisors were there, even though they had been off duty for three hours. As soon as the group arrived it was apparent to Simpson that they were troubled about something and that this was no social call. All of the supervisors entered his office, and one older man who had been supervisor for nine years, Charles Warren, acted as speaker for the group.

"Frank," he said, "all of us here have been in this game for a good many years. We know more about this business than anyone else around here, and we don't like people standing around in our departments watching what we are doing. We also don't like the idea of some young guy telling us that we should do this and that to improve our production and quality. This industry is different and those new ideas about industrial engineering just won't work for us. We want you to tell that new guy, Green, that his ideas won't work for a company like this." Warren then paused to give Simpson a chance to answer. The other supervisors stood there quietly.

STUDY GUIDES
1. If you were Simpson, what would you do now? What would you do later, if anything? What behavioral models and ideas are involved in your decisions?
2. Should Simpson have permitted the supervisors to see him, since they now report directly to Rider?
3. What kinds of changes are taking place in this case? What are the effects of these changes? What ideas about change will help you in dealing with this situation?

ROLE-PLAYING SITUATIONS
1. You are Simpson. Reply to Warren and the other supervisors gathered in your office.
2. Have persons to play the roles of Simpson, Rider, and Green in a meeting in Simpson's office to discuss this situation on the day Rider and Green return from their trip.
3. Role-play the supervisory meeting in which Simpson announces to his supervisors the production-process study. Include persons in the roles of Rider and Green.

THE PLACE

The offices of the Lee Department Store in eastern Ohio. The store is located in a town of 40,000 persons where it has been established for some fifty years.

MAIN CHARACTERS

(Refer to the organization chart in Figure 1.)

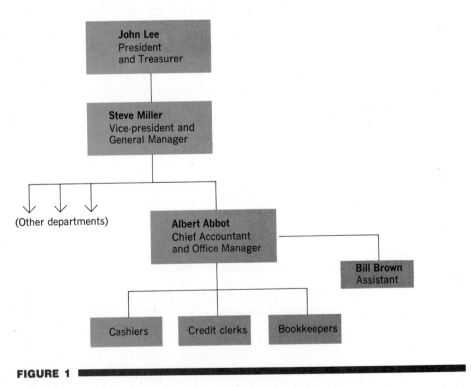

FIGURE 1

Partial organization chart, Lee Department Store.

JOHN LEE. He is the president and treasurer, having inherited the presidency upon the death of his father nine years ago. He and his mother control 90 percent of the capital stock of the department store. He was more or less forced into the presidency upon the death of his father, inasmuch as he was the only child. Lee's ambition is to be a portrait painter, and he has been trained for this. As a result, he seems more interested in his painting than in the success of the store. By far the major part of his time is spent on portraits which he paints for friends. Nevertheless, Lee does take an interest in the store to the extent that he frequently makes personnel and work changes which he thinks will improve the immediate situation. These changes are of the "spur-of-the-moment" type rather than carefully analyzed to determine the effects on the entire work force. John Lee's manner with the employees is quite forceful. He indicates he is the boss and accepts no arguments.

ALBERT ABBOT. Now chief accountant and office manager, Abbot has been with the Lee Company for nineteen years, since his graduation from high school. He gradually has been given additional duties since his employment, until he became chief accountant and office manager seven years ago. Abbot has an easygoing nature, giving no orders or supervision unless specifically requested to do so. His manner is such that he seems to assume more and more duties without complaint.

BILL BROWN. Hired by John Lee six months ago, Brown is twenty-six years of age and just released from the Air Force, where he had been a supply officer. A few days after his release, Brown and his wife visited the college where he graduated with a major in accounting before entering the Air Force for three years. John Lee was attending his class reunion at this college, and through an old friend, met Brown. This acquaintance led Lee to offer Brown a job as accountant in the office of the Lee Department Store. Though Brown hesitated to take the job offer because he felt he would like to visit the store and meet the employees with whom he was to work, Lee made an attractive offer and seemed to want an immediate acceptance; so Brown did accept before Lee left the class reunion. When Brown accepted the offer Lee said, "I haven't talked this idea over with my chief accountant, but I am sure it will work out fine."

OFFICE STAFF. In the office staff are approximately fifteen employees. The older ones have been with the Lee Department Store all their working lives—for a period of about twenty years. They have been working with Albert Abbot, with whom most of them went to high school, for the seven years he has been chief accountant and office manager. Most of them are unmarried. They get along very well together, often planning parties and picnics during office hours. They often see one another after office hours, particularly in their church, because nearly all of them belong to the same church. Abbot also is a member of this church. Because of their length of service, their friendliness in the office, and their comparative freedom in their jobs, the employees are satisfied with somewhat less than the going wages in the community.

THE SITUATION

The general offices of the Lee Department Store are located on two different floors: the rear of the second floor and the rear of the third floor. This is necessary because of the layout of sales space in the store. The credit department (three older women), cashiers (two younger women), and Abbot are located on the rear of the second floor. The general accounting offices (eight older women, three younger women), the administrative offices, and Lee are located on the rear of the third floor.

Lee, upon returning from his college reunion, discussed Brown's arrival with most of his office staff. Lee arranged to have a desk for Brown in the office on the third floor. This enabled Brown to be near the employees and the general accounting records with which his main assignment dealt. Brown's principal job was to assist Abbot in the preparation of daily, weekly, and monthly accounting reports. Lee, as well as the general manager and department managers, felt that the reports which were being presented to them by Abbot were of no value as a control of operations, because they were received too late for use. To this Abbot agreed but felt he was too busy with everyday assignments to improve this situation.

On Brown's first day at the store he was taken on a tour of the store and offices by Lee and was introduced to most of the employees, including Abbot, whom Brown was to assist. Lee introduced Brown to the office employees and department managers, with the comment "Bill is going to assist us in the accounting office. Now we'll be getting the reports out on time."

Brown spent most of his first day talking with employees with whom he was to work and talking with Lee regarding types of information he felt that he and the departmental managers needed. The employees were cordial, and Brown looked forward to working in this friendly atmosphere. That evening Lee and his wife took Brown and his wife to dinner at a local restaurant as a welcome and wedding present. During the evening, Lee frequently talked enthusiastically about the portrait work he was doing. Brown felt quite flattered when Lee said, "Bill, I feel as though I can stay away from the office a good deal more now that I know the reports for our managers will be coming out on time."

Brown spent most of the first week with Abbot learning the various accounting procedures. Brown found him very cordial and willing to help at any time upon being asked. Throughout the next few months he and Abbot became quite friendly. On many occasions, as the months passed, they would get together with their wives for an evening of bridge.

Brown respected Abbot's judgment and found him helpful. Frequently Abbot would say, "Bill, you've sure helped me by taking the pressure for those reports off my mind. John, occasionally, when he wasn't worrying about his painting, really put the heat on."

As Brown moved into the routine of his duties, he found that they required him to work closely with most of the women in the two offices, because nearly all of them performed some phase of the bookkeeping. Using the statistical and accounting data prepared by these women, Brown prepared his reports for Lee and the department managers. Brown was in daily contact with nine of the older women employees (eight on the third floor and one on the second floor) and three of the younger women (two on the third floor and one on the second floor).

Brown worked at his job intensively, because he wanted to succeed in his first civilian job. Within two months he was able to have reports on the desks of the store managers (Lee and Miller) and the department managers in a time interval that was satisfactory to them. Brown frequently was called into top-level departmental sales meetings to discuss reports he had prepared. Since Brown's desk was located on the third floor, it was convenient for Lee or Miller, the vice-president and general manager, to call Brown in a loud voice, with a comment such as "Bill, will you come in here and help us with these reports?"

Brown felt he was doing a good job at the company, but he did have many minor problems. Below are three representative experiences in the order of their occurrence, which Brown had during his first six months of work.

1.   Upon asking for data from one of the older women, Brown was told, "What's the hurry? Albert never seemed to bother us with asking for this information. We always gave it to him when we were ready." In reply to this, Brown attempted to explain the value of the reports and the need for their promptness. It seemed to Brown that explanation only encouraged her to delay the information a while longer.

2.   One of the younger women in the third-floor office came to Brown and complained that errors were made by the clerks on particular sales tickets, receiving invoices, and packing slips. The accounting employees frequently brought errors of this type to Brown's attention. As was his usual practice, he spoke tactfully and courteously to the clerks and other store employees who made the errors. He pointed out their mistakes and how they affected the information that was needed. Brown heard by the grapevine that the employees he had corrected often complained that he was trying to "run the store."

3.   Miller told Brown to instruct the employees in the third-floor and second-floor offices not to stay out for coffee so long in the morning. Their practice was to take a few minutes each morning to go across the street for coffee. (Abbot and Brown never went out for coffee.) This practice had existed for a number of years, without objection by management. Often they stayed longer than seemed reasonable to Miller. In response to Miller's instructions, Brown said to them, "Mr. Miller asked me to ask you not to stay out so long for coffee in the morning." He said this to office employees as a group on each floor one afternoon as they were getting ready to go home.

Brown sometimes noticed resentment among the older office women; therefore, he tried to be especially courteous to them. He attempted to be tactful in his requests for data. He tried to be helpful with any requests they made of him. Nevertheless, the older women office employees by their actions, manner, and words made Brown feel uncomfortable and out of place.

One morning, about six months after Brown's employment, Lee called Brown into his office. Lee had not worked regularly at the store for weeks because he was busy with a portrait. He said to Brown, "Bill, I wish you would do two things for me as sort of a special assignment. One, revise our outdated accounting expense code system. We need to be able to expand our classifications of expenses. The older code is far out of date, as we have used it for some twenty years. This will make it necessary that the office employees memorize a new code system, but I don't think that will be too much for them. And then, as project number two, I wish you would prepare a job analysis on each of the employees in the accounting office. Miller suggested you do this. It has never been done before, so I think it might prove to our advantage to know just what the employees are doing. Take your time on these projects; just work them in with your regular duties. Oh, by the way, tell Albert you are doing this for me." Brown agreed that he would try to do both of these assignments.

As Brown returned to his desk, and as Lee left the office to go home to work on his portrait, Brown pondered how he would go about his new assignments.

STUDY GUIDES
1. Prepare, for contrast with the formal organizational chart, a chart of the informal organizational relationships that exist. What significant differences appear between them? Has management in any way encouraged these differences?
2. Do you think satisfactory communication existed among the persons in this case? Explain.
3. How should Brown accomplish his assignment at the end of the case?

ROLE-PLAYING SITUATION
1. Role-play Brown's contacts with different persons as he initiates his new assignments.

NORTHERN STATES
INSURANCE COMPANY

Northern States Insurance Company was organized in 1935 for the purpose of selling automobile and casualty insurance. This insurance is sold exclusively by agents who are not employees of Northern States but are independent business persons who sell the insurance and are paid a commission for doing so. Today Northern States is represented by almost 3,000 agents located in nine states. There are 120 claims adjusters working out of sixty-three offices in the nine states. These claims adjusters are employees of the company, and their main job is to settle claims on policies that Northern States has issued.

The home office of Northern States Insurance Company is in Minneapolis, Minnesota. Early in the history of the company, Douglas White was claims manager for the company. During White's regime, most transactions with field personnel were handled personally by him. He approved all salary increases and handled most of the problems that arose. When he became claims manager, there were only approximately twenty employees in the claims department, so it was fairly easy for White to keep personalized contacts with his claims agents. As the company grew and the number of claims agents in the field expanded, White still tried to keep personalized contacts with them. The home office claims department grew to such an extent that home office supervisors were created for different insurance coverages such as workmen's compensation, automobile bodily injury, and so on. Though these supervisors corresponded directly with claims adjusters and often instructed them to do better work or correct an action, they were in fact staff supervisors of an office section rather than direct supervisors of claims adjusters. The office supervisors had no right to hire, fire, or evaluate performance of people in the field, because their direct supervisor, White, made these decisions. Office supervisors were limited to checking completed claims work and writing letters of admonishment. These letters were friendly warnings to adjusters in the field regarding action taken on specific claim cases.

Six years ago, White retired and was replaced by Sam Cochran, who was hired from another insurance company which sold the same type of insurance as Northern States. Cochran retained the position of claims manager for 1½ years before leaving the company because of ill health.

Upon Cochran's leaving, R. A. Watkins, who was operations vice-president at the time, was given—in addition to his other duties—the management of the claims department. One of the first things that Watkins did as the new manager of the claims department was to secure the approval of President McMann to divide the department on the basis of geographic distribution and appoint a fully trained and competent employee from within the company to manage each of the three divisions. The second major change that Watkins proposed was a new method of determining salary increases. In the past, salaried field employees were paid on a seniority basis. For every year an employee was within the company, the employee received an increase in salary. Employees called the date on which they received their salary increase the "anniversary date," and, according to Watkins, up to this time it was unheard of for anyone to be turned down for a salary increase on an anniversary date. Watkins thought that, instead of giving salary increases on a "by-guess-and-by-golly" basis as had been done in the past, a system of performance appraisal should be installed at Northern States. Watkins talked the matter over with President McMann and secured his approval for a performance appraisal plan to apply to all salaried workers below the vice-presidential level (hourly employees had a separate appraisal system). Appraisals were to be semiannual and, where possible, were to be made by four persons in addition to the employee's direct manager.

In September two years ago, Watkins was ready to put the new performance appraisal program into effect. He instructed managers in the claims department that, beginning in January of last year, they should write an appraisal of each salaried person directly under their supervision using the following rating system: 1—excellent, 2—good, 3—average, 4—fair, and 5—poor. In addition, a narrative description of the person's general deportment, cooperativeness, and relations with home office and agents was to be included in the appraisal system. With regard to the branch managers, they were appraised by their division manager, Watkins, and the three home office staff supervisors with whom they had most contact. The usual method was for the five managers to meet together to discuss each employee as they made their separate appraisals of the employee's performance. Then all five appraisals were combined for a consensus "Evaluation Report." Certain statewide comparisons were also made with other branch managers. Salary increases, if any, were then determined on the basis of the "Evaluation Report," along with the statewide comparisons and any other available data.

Since the new salary system was difficult to describe, no bulletin or written announcement of it was made to field claims personnel. It was first brought to their attention in the form of an announcement by division managers at the separate annual meetings of the three divisions early last year, but according to Norman Scott, the personnel director of Northern States, the claims employees didn't pay much attention to it. Scott gathered the impression that they thought it was "a joke," and that the plan would never be put into effect. John Appleton was one of these people. His organizational location is shown in Figure 1.

Appleton came to work for Northern States nine years ago, having previously been associated with two other companies in the same business. He was forty-six years old, married, and had a son in high school when he started work for Northern States. His first assignment was in Eau Claire, Wisconsin, as a claims adjuster for the Wausau branch. Five years ago Eau Claire was made a separate branch and Appleton assumed the responsibilities of branch manager. He was assisted by a secretary. Branches of this type were known as one-adjuster branches.

In June of last year, the annual meeting of Wisconsin branch managers was held in Milwaukee, and Appleton attended. Scott had been assigned the job of helping install the new salary system; so he attended the Wisconsin meeting for the purpose of reviewing the salary program and the yardsticks of measurement being used in the appraisal of salaried personnel.

When Scott reported back to the home office in Minneapolis, he told Watkins

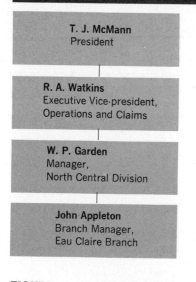

T. J. McMann
President

R. A. Watkins
Executive Vice-president,
Operations and Claims

W. P. Garden
Manager,
North Central Division

John Appleton
Branch Manager,
Eau Claire Branch

FIGURE 1 ▬▬▬▬▬▬▬▬▬▬▬▬▬▬▬▬▬▬▬▬▬▬▬

Chain of command to John Appleton.

that he didn't believe that the branch managers paid much attention to the new salary program. Scott's observations were further supported by a letter which Watkins received from Appleton about four months later. The letter is shown in Figure 2 at the end of this case.

At first Watkins was disgusted with Appleton for writing a letter in which he asked for information that he should have known, but on second thought Watkins realized that a satisfactory reply should be given to him. In order to give Appleton the facts, Watkins analyzed Appleton's most recent appraisal, as shown in Figures 3 and 4, to determine why a salary raise was not given to him.

Watkins spent considerable time in preparing a reply to Appleton. After analyzing Appleton's performance appraisal and his expense control sheet (not shown), Watkins prepared a detailed reply containing information about the entire performance appraisal program.

After completing his answer to Appleton (see Figure 5), Watkins asked Scott if any other salaried field personnel had inquired about the new salary program, and Scott stated that he had indirect inquiries from a few persons. He believed the division managers had received many complaints.

STUDY GUIDES
1. What kinds of human problems are developing in this company? What are their causes?
2. What key problems exist at the end of the case? Who can solve them? How? Apply frameworks and ideas from the text to support your analysis.

ROLE-PLAYING SITUATIONS
1. Role-play Watkins's next meeting with Garden.
2. Role-play the next meeting of Garden and Appleton.

October 15, 19—

Dear Mr. Watkins:

According to my calculations, over a month has elapsed since my anniversary date for salary review. In the past years my salary review date has been on September 10, but I haven't received notice of any pay increase effective on that date.

At first I thought there might have been some slight mixup in the home office or that maybe a new policy has been written concerning a change in review date, but now that thirty-five days have passed and I still have heard no word, I am wondering just what is wrong.

I would appreciate it very much if you would bring me up to date and let me know why I have not received my anniversary salary increase.

Sincerely,

(signed)

John Appleton

FIGURE 2 ▐▬▬▬▬▬▬▬▬▬▬▬▬▬▬▬▬▬▬▬▬▬▬▬▬▬▬▬▬▬▬

Letter to Watkins. (The preceding year may be assumed in discussing this case.)

▬▬▬▬▬▬▬▬▬▬▬▬▬▬▬▬▬▬▬▬▬▬▬▬▬▬▬▬▬▬▬▬▬▬

July 20, 19—

EVALUATION REPORT

Appleton, John

Bodily Injury Department:
This man seems conscientious and agreeable to work with. He does seem a little hesitant in making decisions and is a little unreliable at times. Also he is not thorough enough in making investigations, which could prove disastrous should the files have to go to suit. There is much room for improvement, but on the whole I am satisfied with his progress.

Property Damage Department:
Mr. Appleton seems cooperative, but I can see very little improvement from the last time that he was rated. I believe that his potentiality is much greater than he has shown.

Material Damage Department:
Our present evaluation of Mr. Appleton is the same as we gave him last time. He is easy to get along with but doesn't seem to take his work too seriously.

Workmen's Compensation Department:
Mr. Appleton does not seem to have enough technical background in this field. He is weak in negotiating his more serious cases and in settling serious claims.

Subrogations:
His record is only mediocre. No improvement is noted so far over the results of the previous evaluation report.

FIGURE 3 ▐▬▬▬▬▬▬▬▬▬▬▬▬▬▬▬▬▬▬▬▬▬▬▬▬▬▬▬▬▬▬

Last evaluation report on John Appleton. The report is typed on plain paper in narrative form, as shown. This report is a summary of comments of all five appraisers for the first six months of the year.

July 20,19_____

WISCONSIN

COLUMN NUMBER	1	2	3	4	5	6	7	8
NO. SALARIED PERSONNEL IN TERRITORY:	5	16	1	1	4	6	1	8
Loss ratio	5	1	4	1	4	2	3	2
Expense ratio	4	2	1	1	4	2	5	3
Unit cost	2	1	1	4	4	2	5	3
Work load—weighted	3	2	1	1	5	4	4	2
Average paid								
Bodily injury	2	4	1	3	4	5	2	1
Medical	3	1	2	1	4	5	4	2
Property damage	4	2	2	1	1	3	2	2
Comprehensive	2	1	1	2	3	1	1	2
Collision	4	1	1	3	3	4	2	2
Ratio claims open to reported	1	1	2	4	1	2	3	2
Paid to demand	3	2	4	1	2	4	1	5
Collected to claimed	5	1	3	2	4	1	2	4
Collected to collision paid	5	1	2	1	3	4	2	4
Supervisory ratings								
Bodily injury	3	1	2	3	2	4	3	4
Property damage	2	1	2	2	3	2	3	3
Material damage—auto	3	2	1	3	1	2	3	2
Material damage—casualty	2	2	2	3	1	3	3	1
Workmen's compensation	3	2	2	3	1	4	3	4
Legal—bodily injury	3	1	3	2	1	3	2	4
Legal—property damage	3	1	2	2	1	3	2	3
Net written	2	3	1	1	5	4	4	2
Increase	2	4	1	2	3	4	5	1
Earned premium	2	3	1	1	5	4	4	2
Total	68	40	42	47	65	72	68	60
Rank	6	1	2	3	5	7	6	4

FIGURE 4 ▬▬▬▬▬▬▬▬▬▬▬▬▬▬▬▬▬▬▬▬▬

Statewide comparisons for Wisconsin, showing John Appleton in column 7. Titles in left column are exactly as they appear on the form. The technical meaning of these titles is not developed in this case. Rating scale: 1—excellent, 2—good, 3—average, 4—fair, and 5—poor. The appraisal is for the first six months of the year.

October 22, 19—

Dear John,

I welcomed the receipt of your letter the other day because it gave me an opportunity to reflect again on this important subject of salaries and personnel review. For a proper understanding from both sides of the fence, there is no simple answer. Therefore, at the risk of giving you more information than you asked for, I am going to review some of the thinking on this subject—past, present, and future.

During the past ten years we have lived in two favorable atmospheres as far as individual salaries are concerned:

1. An inflationary spiral where annual increases were necessary and justifiable without regard to the more normal factors in salary consideration
2. Substantial annual increases in production followed by proportional increases in earned premium out of which claim salaries and expenses are paid

These two factors made it an easy and pleasant experience to advise employees of their annual increases by writing little notes informing them that an increase had been put through. This led to an employee assumption that increases are regular and automatic based on length of service. This created a situation which is basically unfair and unsound to employer, supervisor, and employee.

1. Increases were given with too little regard to individual performance. Increase notices were going out in the same mail with letters of criticism regarding case handling from the various supervisors. Employees learned that supervisory observations and recommendations could be ignored without running the risk of suffering in the pay envelope. Supervisors began to think, "What's the use criticizing mediocre effort and attitudes?"
2. The outstanding employee began to see little point in continuing to do the superlative job when a contemporary got an increase in pay without special effort.
3. The employer looked at constantly increasing salary costs that had little relationship to quality or quantity of work done.

For the past five years one of President McMann's favorite questions around here has been "That's fine, Ralph, as long as we have continuous substantial increases in earned premium out of which to pay increased costs, but what happens when we level off?" This is what happened last year, and the real effect will show itself this year. It is one of the most difficult problems to be faced by those of us who have responsibility for profit planning and expense control.

Recognizing the inequities in our casual appraisal of performance in the past it was decided to set up certain techniques and procedures for doing a more objective job of evaluating individual employees.

1. Branch folders
2. Work-load analysis
3. Expense control (lawyers' and independent adjusters' expense in territory) and travel expense
4. Individual supervisory appraisal of coverage knowledge, judgment, initiative, interest, etc., displayed by the employee

FIGURE 5 ▰▰▰▰▰▰▰▰▰▰▰▰▰▰▰▰

Letter to Appleton.
534

5. Responsiveness of employee to supervisory instructions
6. Composite judgment of all concerned regarding justification for increases being given

We discussed and demonstrated the use of these things in our annual meeting last year.

This whole problem is further complicated by the fact that the more increases a person has had on a given job, the more the person is apt to be near the top of what that job can justify in the overall expense structure of the company—and the more difficult it becomes to earn and justify the compensation reserved for outstanding performance.

You then might ask, what is my ceiling on this job? We don't have ceilings as such. What if we had told you five years ago that your ceiling was $15,000? No crystal ball was available to tell us that by last year we would be able and privileged to pay you substantially above that figure. The economic equation is too complicated these days to make specific promises of wage levels or ceilings to anyone. The responsibility of management is to make a fair and equitable distribution of funds which are available for salaries and increases based on the knowledge and information in its possession.

Moving into another area of thought regarding payroll administration,

1. It is accepted practice to use a memorandum to advise an employee of an increase:
2. It is inexcusable to use the written word when one is being withheld.

Since I've gone this far I might as well go the rest of the way and violate principle 2 in the paragraph above. The claim performance in Eau Claire has been carefully reviewed by supervisors responsible for the state. Individual offices and adjusters have been appraised by themselves and territories, as well as through statewide comparisons. For the first time in the history of the company we have had records and material available (and used) for the purpose of making these objective unbiased evaluations.

Your operation shows the following:

1. A static territory with no marked increase in work load.

	Claims reported	Unit cost	Weighted workload
Last year	200	12.51	175*
This year (6 months)	89	13.55	158

2. Based on six-month figures, independent adjustment expenses† in the Eau Claire office are over twice as high as the other one-adjuster offices in Wisconsin. This is not a completely fair comparison, but it does indicate your tendency toward excessive use of these services.
3. We think that all of our employees in the field are far above average in the industry and that they should, therefore, automatically display the initiative, imagination, perseverance, ingenuity, and resourcefulness which goes with a superior adjuster.
4. Your subrogation payable ratio was 47 percent and receivable 45 percent with $650 paid more than collected. Your ratio of collections to collision losses paid was 18 percent against a company average of 14.5 percent, which is very good when giving consideration to several large payable claims in the year.
5. A feeling exists on the part of home office supervisors responsible for your work that your secretary, Miss Nivens, is perfectly capable of doing a much better job in certain files than she is doing. This is apparent in the more important bodily injury files where investigations do not show the thoroughness which would be necessary should these files go to suit.
6. Your rating in the Material Damage Division is a 3, which is the same as you had last year.

FIGURE 5 Continued ▬▬▬▬▬▬▬▬▬▬▬▬▬▬▬▬▬▬▬▬▬▬▬

Letter to Appleton.

Wisconsin has three adjusters rated 3, three rated 2, and two adjusters rated 1 in this area of claims.

7. In Workmen's Compensation claims, where you are developing a sizable volume, there is a definite need to improve your technical background. More complete knowledge in this field will permit you to reduce the use of attorneys for court reporter statements.

John, I want you to know that I am not being critical in the negative sense of the word. However, I am pointing out the standards of performance and excellence which must go with top salaries so that we who have the responsibility for approving or withholding them can do so with the firm conviction that we have done the right thing for the employee, for associates, and for the company. Forgive my longwindedness—it is not a simple subject.

Best regards.

Sincerely,

(signed)

R. A. Watkins
Executive Vice-president

* These data and some of the following data came from the expense control sheet, which is not shown.
† These are fees paid to independent adjusting firms who handle claims investigations when the company adjuster is ill, out of town, or busy with other work.

FIGURE 5 Continued ▮▮▮▮▮▮▮▮▮▮▮▮▮▮▮▮▮▮▮

Letter to Appleton.

CASE 5
ALBATROS ELECTRICAL COMPANY

Seven years ago the Albatros Electrical Company built a refrigerator assembly plant in Asheville, North Carolina. Among the original work force was John Franks, who was hired as a cleaner. A cleaner's job was to keep the floors swept and to remove all empty cartons and boxes from the work areas. The job paid a low wage and was considered undesirable by most job applicants. Franks was forty-nine years old at the time he was hired and was the oldest member of the cleaning section of the maintenance department. A year later the plant was organized by an international union, and Franks was appointed shop steward for the cleaners.

The maintenance department consisted of four groups: the electricians, the mechanics, the layout engineers, and the cleaners. Each group was organized into a section whose supervisor reported to the plant engineer. In the cleaning section there were usually about twenty-four workers reporting to the supervisor. The average age of the cleaners was forty years, and their average educational level was the seventh grade. Some were minority employees, but Franks was not.

Franks had a dominant, persuasive manner which enabled him to have considerable influence with the other cleaners. For this reason the plant engineer was not pleased with Franks's appointment as shop steward. A few days after Franks became steward he presented his first grievance. The bargaining contract described the general procedure for complaints and grievances as follows:

> **Complaint Procedure:** *Any employe, or group of employes, having a complaint shall have the right, either personally or through the Union shop steward, to present such complaint verbally to the immediate supervisor in an endeavor to reach an adjustment. An earnest effort should be made to settle and dispose of such complaints between the parties noted in this paragraph. If the complaint involves a matter subject to the grievance procedure, and no satisfactory settlement has been made, the complaint may be presented as a grievance as hereinafter provided.*

> **Grievance Procedure:**[1]
> *Step 1: Any employe or group of employes having a grievance shall present the matter to the Union steward, who shall make investigations and if the grievance is found valid, take the matter up with the general supervisor of the section in which such grievance arose for adjustment. Failing adjustment*

[1] The grievance procedure could be invoked for any matter pertaining to the labor contract.

in this manner within forty-eight (48) hours (Saturdays, Sundays, and holidays excluded), the matter shall be submitted to Step 2.

Step **2:** The grievance shall be referred by the steward to the Business Manager of the Union or a designated representative, who shall take the matter up for adjustment with the Personnel Manager or a designated representative. Failing adjustment in this manner within seventy-two (72) hours (Saturdays, Sundays, and holidays excluded), the matter shall be submitted to Step 3.

Step **3:** In the event the grievance is not satisfactorily adjusted by the procedure in the foregoing steps within the specified times, the grievance shall be considered by the Grievance Committee (who may be accompanied by the Business Manager of the Union or a duly designated representative, and/or a representative of the said brotherhood) and the Plant Manager of the Company and/or a duly designated representative. In the event it is not satisfactorily adjusted within five (5) days, it shall, at the request of either party, be submitted to a board of arbitration.

(A fourth step provided arbitration.)

In the cleaning section the plant engineer was equivalent to the "general supervisor" specified in Step 1 of the grievance procedure. Franks's first grievance, which he presented to the plant engineer on the form provided, was that Pleasant Williams of the cleaning section was being denied promotion to an existing vacancy for which he was eligible. Williams was eligible for upgrading to a vacancy in the stock-handling section, but Williams had been told by his supervisor that he could not be promoted until his replacement was hired. Williams had waited ten days, and no replacement was yet available.

The plant engineer was receptive to Franks's presentation of the grievance because he had not previously known of this problem. His investigation disclosed that the facts were substantially those presented; however, Franks did not first present the grievance orally to his cleaning supervisor as required by the complaint procedure. Since this was the first grievance in the department and the plant engineer wished to build good union relations, he arranged for Williams to be promoted the next day.

As a result of this event Franks's high prestige increased greatly among his co-workers in the cleaning section. Franks was aware of his new status. He made the following comment to several of the cleaners, "I am going to get that plant engineer straightened out and make him give the cleaners a fair shake." Franks then began a campaign of seeking and presenting complaints and grievances. During the next six years he filed fifty-four formal grievances for cleaners, winning seventeen of them. During this period the number of cleaners in the department varied between eighteen and twenty-seven. Following are some of the typical grievances he filed:

1. Cleaners need a special rest room and clothes locker room. (Not allowed; ended at Step 1).

2. Make earlier distribution of checks on payday so that cleaners can cash checks

during the hour lunch period, or give checks to their spouses for cashing before the banks close. (Allowed for all shop employees; ended at Step 2.)

3. An additional cleaner is needed to allow other cleaners to rest periodically. (Not allowed; ended at Step 1.)

4. Cleaners should have uniforms furnished by the company. (Allowed: ended at Step 1.)

5. Cleaners should not have to load cleaning waste into tote bins for trucker to deliver to junkyard. (Not allowed; ended at Step 1.)

6. The overtime list should be posted prior to Thursday noon. (Not allowed; ended at Step 1.)

7. Casey Porter's assigned cleaning area should be reduced in size because it requires too much work. (Not allowed; ended Step 1.)

In one instance two years ago Franks was censured by the plant engineer for taking up company time with an "absurd request." This grievance asked that production supervisors have their employees place all empty cartons and boxes in barrels which would be provided in the production area for that purpose. This, in some cases, would require a production employee to stop work to place the cartons in the barrels. The request was denied by the plant engineer.

Early last year the plant engineer felt that something should be done about Franks's behavior as a steward, so he called the union business manager for a conference about Franks. The business manager agreed that Franks was "hunting" grievances and was presenting many grievances without first discussing them with his supervisor. Then Franks was called into the engineer's office for a discussion of his attitude. Both the plant engineer and the business manager reminded Franks that he should "use judgment" and present only those complaints and grievances that appeared to be contract violations. Franks said very little, except to assure the two men that he would cooperate at all times. Near the end of the meeting the engineer gave Franks a formal reprimand for presenting a grievance six days earlier without first discussing it with his supervisor. The reprimand and a summary of the meeting were placed in Franks's permanent personnel folder.

During the following months Franks filed several grievances without first discussing them with his supervisor, but the plant engineer took no further action. He later commented, "I hoped Franks would soon improve, and I did not want to create any incident which would undermine my good working relations with the union."

Near the end of last year it became evident that Franks was not changing his attitude, and the plant engineer again called the union business manager for a conference. After some discussion the business manager agreed to suspend Franks as shop steward and to try to get a replacement elected. In January of this year the business manager suspended Franks from his steward's job and put out feelers for a successor. The problem became difficult when the business manager learned that the cleaners felt Franks was the only person for the job. Not one cleaner would consider taking the steward's job. This condition was allowed to continue for two months with the hope that a newly hired cleaner might be persuaded to become steward. Finally, due to pressure of the cleaners, the business agent reinstated Franks as the shop steward of the cleaning section.

Franks's first act upon being reinstated as shop steward was to file a formal grievance to the effect that Mary Parker had been "forcefully persuaded" to transfer to the night shift. When the plant engineer checked this grievance, the supervisor said that Mary had asked for night work but that Franks had talked her into wanting back on the day shift and had made her feel that she had been coerced into asking for night work. Mary admitted that she asked for the transfer, but she claimed that, from the way the supervisor described the job, she thought second-shift work would be easier, but it was not. When Franks was confronted with the evidence of the investigation, his reply to the plant engineer was a curt "So what?"

STUDY GUIDES

1. Why do you think Franks was originally chosen as shop steward? Why has he continued to keep the job? What has the company done to help him keep it? What has Franks done?
2. Why do you think the plant engineer reprimanded Franks in their conference early last year? What assumptions was the engineer making about Franks? Franks's supervisor? The function of the grievance procedure? The business agent? The engineer's own job?
3. What should the engineer do now? What should the business agent do?

ROLE-PLAYING SITUATIONS

1. Role-play last year's meeting of Franks, the plant engineer, and the union business manager, at which time Franks was given a formal reprimand.
2. Role-play the meeting at the end of this case when Franks says, "So what?"

MIDDLE NATIONAL BANK

Bill Smith was manager of a branch bank in the metropolitan area in which the bank home office was located. Smith, age about thirty, was a college graduate in banking and finance. Higher management was impressed with his capabilities; so it was trying to develop him for further promotions.

Recently Smith was assigned to become branch manager of a larger branch in Parsons, a town of about 50,000 persons in a distant part of the state. This assignment was both a promotion and an opportunity to broaden his experience. When the assignment was made, the manager of branch operations told Smith that he might have some difficulty with Ralph Dawson, assistant manager of the Parsons bank. The manager of branch operations said that Dawson, age fifty-five and a high school graduate, had worked in the Parsons branch for thirty-one years and had been assistant branch manager for fourteen years. He did not expect promotion and would not leave Parsons for wider experience. He was said to be "200 percent loyal" to the bank and very proud of his managerial position in the bank. He had strong community support and brought much business to the bank, particularly from members of his ethnic minority group which were 40 percent of the town's population and provided many of its business leaders.

The manager of branch operations said there were two main problems with Dawson. First, he was dogmatic and authoritarian. Dawson insisted on showing mistakes to any person that made them, even when that person was a customer. Second, Dawson managed the bank activities assigned to him in his own authoritarian way and was not responsive to instructions from any branch manager, especially a younger one, because his cultural heritage had high respect for age and seniority.

During his first month at the Parsons branch Smith observed that Dawson's conduct was as it had been described to him. Dawson was intensely protective and autocratic about bank operations officially under his direct supervision; but he did not interfere in the few policy areas officially assigned to Smith's direct supervision. He did not seem to resent Smith's being there; however, in the second month when Smith tried to persuade Dawson to take a different approach with an operating problem, Dawson responded icily, "I have the experience here, and I'll be running my departments long after you have returned to the home office; so I am going to manage them the way I have found best for the long run. I can't make temporary changes to fit each new manager's approach."

Smith realized that he probably would be transferred elsewhere in two or three years, but he also knew that the community was changing and it might become more difficult to recruit employees who would work under Dawson's autocratic command.

Smith wondered if he should avoid upsetting the situation, stay out of Dawson's affairs, and probably transfer with a good record in two or three years; or whether he should take the possibly riskier approach of confronting Dawson with the necessity for change which Smith felt necessary. He knew that any confrontation with Dawson might provoke ethnic opposition in the community.

STUDY GUIDES
1. Analyze the roles which seniority, age, provincial viewpoint, ethnic background, and other variables play in this case.
2. If you were Smith, what would you do with Dawson? Be specific, including why. For example, what motivational models would you be able to use, if any?

CASE 7
SPACETRONICS

Spacetronics is a division of a large manufacturer of electronic equipment. Complex equipment is designed and built at Spacetronics' western plant, because employees at this plant develop communication devices for the United States space and defense programs.

Emphasis in the electronics industry is often placed on research and new product development. These functions are important at Spacetronics as well, but due to the complexity of the equipment manufactured and the high reliability requirements demanded by space and military programs, great stress also is placed on the production function.

Production runs are usually of short duration and require a continuous stream of new hand tools, fixtures, jigs, and manual and automatic machines to make and assemble the intricate electronic gear. Because of the nature of the work at Spacetronics, design and fabrication of production tools are particularly critical functions.

Preassembly tool design and planning are located organizationally under the superintendent of parts manufacture, as shown in Figure 1. Assembly tool design and planning are under the direction of the assistant chief engineer.

Preassembly tool design and planning are supervised by George Whipple, a well-liked and aggressive engineer who has an industry-wide reputation for excellence. His department has successfully met schedules and cost estimates for a number of years. Whipple has a degree in mechanical engineering and five years of experience as a tool and die maker.

Assembly tool design is under general direction of Marshall Holden, who became assistant chief industrial engineer six months ago. Assembly tool design has been a consistent source of delay, cost overages, and other difficulties for several years. In fact, its work has been so poor that frequently Whipple's department has been called upon to help it. Holden was promoted to this department in an effort to improve its performance. He was formerly a cost-estimating supervisor. Holden had been a maintenance machinist in an eastern steel mill for fifteen years before coming to Spacetronics as a machinist ten years ago. He has no college training, but he is ambitious and dedicated in his work.

Four years ago Holden had approached Whipple and asked for a transfer into the preassembly tool-design section. Holden had felt for some time that his chances for advancement as a machinist were limited; so he was unhappy in his machinist's job. Initially Whipple reacted favorably to Holden's request, because both men already had an established working relationship and Whipple knew that skilled tool designers were difficult to find. He had a vacant position for tool designer which he had been trying to fill for several months.

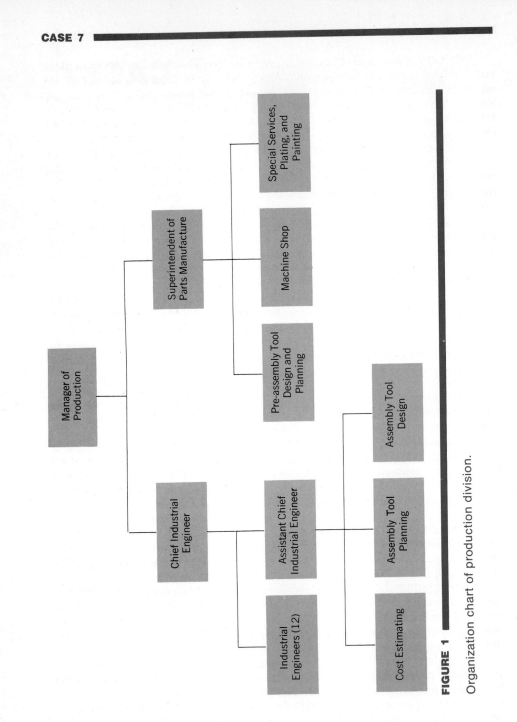

FIGURE 1

Organization chart of production division.

Whipple spent several hours reviewing Holden's work record and qualifications. He also spent time talking with Holden's immediate supervisor about the type and quality of work Holden was then doing. Whipple finally decided that although Holden was an excellent machinist, he did not have the creative abilities necessary for a tool designer. Whipple felt so certain about the matter that he even rejected Holden's supervisor's suggestion for a temporary transfer on a trial basis.

Holden was bitter about Whipple's rejection. Even though Whipple helped Holden get a new job in the industrial engineering section a month later, they did not reestablish a close working relationship. This lack of rapport continued after Holden's promotion to assistant chief of industrial engineering which placed both Holden and Whipple on the same organizational level.

Recently Holden began planning a reorganization which he felt would remedy the problems in his tool-design group and also increase the efficiency of the total tooling process. Holden worked closely with the chief industrial engineer and the superintendent of parts manufacture. They were all good friends and were deeply concerned with the problem. After three months of planning, the proposed reorganization was presented to Whipple in a meeting with the chief industrial engineer and superintendent of parts manufacture. The proposal centered around a trade of functions between industrial engineering and the parts manufacture department. All tool-design functions were to be assigned to the parts manufacture department, with all tool-planning functions moving to the industrial engineering department.

During the meeting Whipple was asked for his comments. He replied, "You've certainly spent a lot of effort developing the reorganization. It's workable, and I'll do everything in my power to make it work; but I feel strongly that the tool planning and tool design functions should not be split up. The integration of the two has increased the efficiency of my group considerably."

"We had considered that point," said the chief industrial engineer, "and we have an alternate proposed reorganization which would move all tool design and planning functions into the industrial engineering department." After some discussion there seemed to be a consensus that the alternate proposal was better, and the three men agreed to meet a week later to finalize the proposal.

At lunch Whipple talked about the reorganization with his subordinates. A major concern was to whom the design group would report. Whipple had not considered this question before. He had assumed that he would report directly to the chief industrial engineer.

The next morning Whipple asked the chief industrial engineer about the proposed chain of command. "Of course, you'll report to the assistant chief industrial engineer," was the answer, "I'm much too busy handling the problems that my twelve industrial engineers bring to me to even consider another person reporting directly to me."

Whipple was shocked. This was something he had not expected. His shock soon turned to anger. He stormed in to talk to the superintendent of parts manufacture and said, "I have some strong reservations about the reorganization. In the eyes of my workers it is a demotion to be placed under Holden. He is at the same organization level as I am, and I don't want to report to him. I don't even respect him. I knew a reorganization was being planned, but neither my people nor I were considered in the planning. Plans involving me should be discussed with me. They are good plans, but. . . ."

"Damn it, 'but' nothing," interrupted the superintendent. "All you are worried about is where you fit into the company. This is a good plan which will help the company."

"You're right," retorted Whipple, "I'm deeply concerned about where I fit. I've worked hard in my present job, and all I get for it is demotion."

"But it's not a demotion, George. Your pay grade will be the same, and there's even a possible raise in it for you."

STUDY GUIDES
1. Discuss thoroughly what you think is the central problem in this case. What corrective action do you propose to solve this problem?
2. Discuss other problems in the case and give your proposals for solving them. Make full use of ideas from this book.
3. Discuss any errors made by the superintendent and the chief industrial engineer in planning and implementing the reorganization. Why do you think they made these errors? What guidance can you give them to prevent future errors of a similar type?
4. If you were Whipple what would you do now?
5. Would any of the following be useful in interpreting this case?
   a. Transactional analysis
   b. Concepts of natural work teams and enriched sociotechnical work systems
   c. Contingency ideas regarding stable and changing environments
   d. Maslow's hierarchy of needs
   e. Expectancy theory, including the valence of money

ROLE-PLAYING SITUATIONS
1. Continue the conversation of Whipple and the superintendent at the end of the case.
2. Role-play a conversation between the superintendent and the chief industrial engineer, which takes place later the same day.

THE PERFORMANCE RATING

Cecil Howard was employed as a training assistant in the state civil service for twelve years. His supervisor for the last nine years has been Maude Marrus, a woman young enough to be his daughter. Although civil service regulations require that employees be given a performance report once a year, they are not well enforced. Howard received only one report of "satisfactory" in his second year as training assistant.

Howard is a mild and quiet person without an outgoing personality, but he feels he has managed to perform effectively as a trainer, because he has held the job for twelve years and has never received either oral or written comment that his work is less than satisfactory. On three occasions he took the required examination for those seeking promotion to Training Officer I. In each case he passed the written test but failed the oral interview by a state personnel office panel. He assumed he failed because of his lack of outgoing personality, but he received no feedback about reasons for failure.

Recently the State Personnel Board decided to abolish the title of Training Assistant and give assistants the title of Training Officer I, since they were performing training work equal to that job. Howard believed his change in title would be automatic, but the Personnel Board decided that, since a pay increase of over 15 percent was involved, assistants must take the test for promotion. Howard assumed this procedure would be routine, since he had performed satisfactorily for 12 years, and his duties would not change with the new title. He passed the written test, but failed the oral test again.

At this point Howard was frustrated and angry. He approached his supervisor with determination "to get to the bottom of this problem, even if I have to go to the State Personnel Board." After a heated exchange with Marrus, Howard learned that he had failed the oral tests because Marrus had provided the interview panel a negative recommendation on him. Her recommendation stated that Howard had not developed sufficiently to merit promotion to Training Officer I. All of this was unknown to Howard. He had received no feedback from Marrus or the Personnel Board. Although a mild person, Howard exploded after learning this new fact. In a stormy session with Marrus he stated that he had a right to feedback about his performance and Marrus had an obligation to help him develop if she felt he was not developing adequately.

Later Howard requested to examine his personnel file and was allowed to see it. The personnel file had no negative reports on performance, reprimands, refusal to take development opportunities, or other negative information. There was one satisfactory performance rating ten years old. Also there were no commendations, records of training taken, or other positive information.

Since the title of Training Assistant was abolished, Howard is now working as a Staff Services Analyst performing the same training services that he formerly did. His salary remains the same. His self-image has declined, and it is evident that he is less motivated. Other conditions remain the same.

STUDY GUIDES
1. Analyze some of the organizational behavior issues raised in this series of events.
2. If you were Howard, what changes in behavior would you try to make, if any?
3. If you were Marrus, what changes in behavior would you try to make, if any? Use specific organizational behavior models, frameworks, and ideas to explain why you would attempt these changes in behavior, if any.
4. Assume you are a member of the State Personnel Board and know about this situation because of a grievance filed by Howard. The board has authority to decide Howard's grievance.
   a. What ideas and recommendations would you present in the board's discussion of Howard's grievance? Present the organizational behavior reasons behind your statements.
   b. At a later appropriate time what ideas and recommendations, if any, would you present to the board regarding policy changes in the area of Howard's grievance? Present the organizational behavior models and ideas behind your recommendations.

CASE 9

UNITED MUTUAL INSURANCE COMPANY

The United Mutual Insurance Company was organized in 1939 by Paul and James Taylor. Since its organization, these two men have maintained active personal direction of the company. The company is located in Kansas City, Missouri, and writes all forms of automobile and general casualty insurance. At the present time United Mutual is represented by more than 2,000 agents located in Wisconsin, Illinois, Iowa, Missouri, Kentucky, and Colorado, and it has thirty-two field managers and eighty claims adjusters working out of forty-seven offices. The company has grown steadily since it was founded.

The home office of United Mutual has about 425 employees. Annual labor turnover is 25 to 30 percent, and it has been difficult to replace this turnover because of a mild labor shortage in Kansas City the past few years. Of the 425 persons in the home office, about 100 are supervisory employees. The term "supervisory employees" or "supervisors" in this company refers to those persons who do not have to punch time clocks and do not receive overtime pay. It includes people who direct the work of others, and also some technical and professional people such as lawyers and underwriters. An organization chart of the persons primarily involved in this case is shown in Figure 1.

This case began about five years ago. At that time the company allowed one coffee break of fifteen minutes in the morning and a similar break in the afternoon. Employees went to the cafeteria for their break. At this time both Gorman and Townsend had some responsibility for the coffee break. Gorman had general responsibility for control of the break, because he was in charge of general operations in the home office. Townsend had responsibility for the cafeteria and payroll. He also acted unofficially as personnel director.

Gradually many of the supervisory employees started taking advantage of the coffee break and overstaying their time in the cafeteria. When the nonsupervisory employees saw what was happening, they also started to take longer coffee breaks than were authorized. Before many months had passed, most all of the employees were taking longer breaks than were allotted. When Townsend and Gorman questioned several of the supervisory employees as to why they spent so much time during coffee breaks when they knew that only fifteen minutes were authorized, the standard reply was "We were discussing business problems of United Mutual," or "We were having a meeting, so we actually were working."

It is probable that many overstayed coffee breaks actually were informal business meetings, because most of the supervisors were either underwriters, claim adjusters, or operations supervisors, and daily meetings of some of these people were common to discuss their business problems. There was, of course, no way to prove which discussions were social and which were informal business meetings. One thing seemed sure. It was almost impossible to get nonsupervisory employees to believe that supervisors actually were working during coffee hour; so Gorman told the supervisors that they had to keep within their fifteen minutes in order to set an example for the rest of the employees. They failed to heed his word, and the coffee break continued to be violated. To add to the complication, too many employees were coming to the cafeteria at the same time, which resulted in much congestion and waiting to get their coffee.

In an effort to keep the coffee break limited to fifteen minutes, Townsend started staying in the cafeteria during the complete coffee hour and watching for offenders who stayed over the time limit. He in turn reported the offenders to department heads, who were supposed to take the action necessary to ensure that their employees obeyed the coffee-period time limit. For the next few months employees observed the fifteen-minute coffee period very closely with few exceptions. Then the department heads again became lax, and nonsupervisory, as well as supervisory, employees began exceeding the time limit on coffee periods.

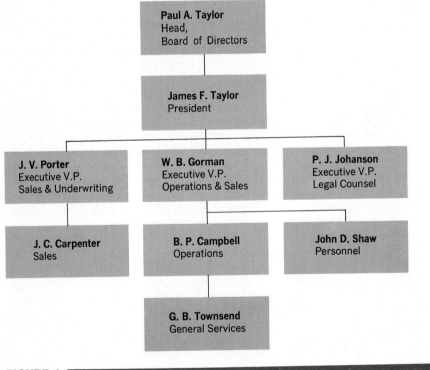

FIGURE 1

Current organizational chart showing top positions in United Mutual Insurance Company.

Again Gorman and Townsend went into consultation, and this time they came up with the idea of installing bells in the cafeteria. The bells were installed and were adjusted to ring every ten minutes. Considering that it took a few minutes for employees to go from their offices to the cafeteria, Gorman and Townsend felt that ten minutes in the cafeteria was the maximum time that could be allowed in order to stay within the limits of the fifteen-minute coffee period. Schedules were set up by the department heads so that employees were supposed to arrive at the cafeteria when the bells rang and they would stay until the bells rang again, at which time they were supposed to leave. Townsend noted that the bells did keep some employees in the cafeteria for only ten minutes, but it was very difficult to synchronize the various groups. People were drifting into and out of the cafeteria all the time and not according to the schedule for which the bells were adjusted. Also, when one group was leaving the cafeteria, another group was scheduled to enter, which added to the congestion. The general opinion among some employees was that the bells made them feel "like they were in prison cells" and could not get out until the bells rang. Others thought the bells very irritating and said it was impossible to enjoy the coffee period. It was soon evident that the bells were not solving the coffee-period problem, but since no better solution was offered, the bells remained, and employees continued to complain about them.

Three years ago top management realized that United Mutual was expanding to the extent that there was definite need for a personnel director to handle the coffee-break problem as well as the increasing number of other personnel problems existing within the home office. Therefore, in July of that year John Shaw was hired as personnel director of United Mutual. Shaw had sixteen years' experience in personnel work and was highly regarded in local personnel circles. Soon after his arrival at United Mutual, the current personnel problems were explained to him, and, of course, one of these problems was the coffee break. Shaw soon found out for himself that employees were taking more than their allotted time during coffee periods. The president wanted something done to remedy the situation, and this problem was given to Shaw.

He tackled the problem rapidly and directly. In his own words, "I made periodic checks with all of the department heads concerning the coffee break and found out what their reactions were. I told the department heads to keep check on the employees under their jurisdiction and to try to keep the coffee break confined within the fifteen-minute period."

Shaw soon found that the bells were ineffective and unpopular. He had them removed from the cafeteria. A few executives approached Shaw and suggested that the coffee periods be discontinued. He countered with the following argument: "The labor shortage in our city is critical at the present time. We have twenty-five vacancies within the company, and yet you want me to discontinue a practice that other employers have and as a result perhaps lose more employees."

In December of Shaw's first year top management asked him to justify his stand that the coffee break was necessary and, if he could justify it, to provide a remedy to the problem. Shaw gave the following reasons why the coffee periods should be continued:

1. A coffee break helps new employees make friends with people in their own and

other departments. United Mutual has a 25 to 30 percent labor turnover each year, so several new employees are coming to the company every week.

2. By having a coffee break there is a cross-pollination of ideas and this prevents stratification and cliques.

3. A coffee break will give renewed vigor to the employees and this will result in greater productivity.

4. The nature of detailed work and mental activity is so confining that people need a break from their routines.

After much deliberation and consultation, Shaw arrived at a solution for the coffee break and submitted it to the top executives. They approved it, including his

UNITED MUTUAL INSURANCE COMPANY
MEMORANDUM

Subject: Changes in Working, Lunch, and Rest Period Schedules
To: All Home Office Department Heads and Employees
From: Personnel

Effective April 4, the working schedule of the office will be as follows:

8:00 A.M. to 12:00 noon.
Forty-minute lunch periods will be scheduled at five regular intervals.
Fifteen-minute morning *rest periods* will be scheduled at five regular intervals.
The working day will end at 4:25 P.M.

This new working schedule reduces the workday by ten minutes and makes an overall workweek of 38.75 hours. We feel sure that employees will welcome this change since it will help to avoid further the evening traffic congestion and facilitate bus connections.

The morning rest periods will be scheduled from 9:30 A.M. through 10:25 A.M. Departments will be scheduled at ten-minute intervals. *Fifteen minutes will be allowed for each employee, which includes travel time to and from the cafeteria.* It is important that employees adhere to the schedules listed below since the principal reason for scheduling is to eliminate confusion and congestion and to improve service in the cafeteria. It will be the responsibility of department heads to make certain that employees follow the assigned schedules. Following is the morning rest period schedule for all departments.

[The schedule is omitted.]

Where stand-by telephone service is required, department heads will exercise discretion in keeping their operation staffed during the morning rest and lunch periods.

With the reduction of the workweek by fifty minutes, we feel that the afternoon rest period is unnecessary. The cafeteria will be closed after the last lunch group has been served.

3/31/—
JDS:RG

FIGURE 2 ▮▬▬▬▬▬▬▬▬▬▬▬▬▬▬▬▬▬▬▬▬▬▬▬▬

Memorandum to employees.

proposal that coffee be furnished free to employees. Free coffee was first given on March 23 by means of a routine announcement in the cafeteria. The remainder of Shaw's proposal was put into effect by a memorandum issued on March 31 by Shaw to all home office employees of United Mutual, as shown in Figure 2.

The memorandum was well received by most of the employees. The work-week was cut from thirty-nine hours, thirty-five minutes, to thirty-eight hours, forty-five minutes. Shaw believed that everything would have turned out all right if United Mutual had not been remodeling and adding to its building at that time (see Figure 3).

As can be seen from the diagram, this construction meant that all employees from the North Building had to walk outside and around the center building in order to get to the cafeteria for the coffee period. Employees on the third floor took as long as six to seven minutes to reach the cafeteria, which caused their break to extend beyond the fifteen-minute limitation. In the next few months, department heads became slack in enforcing the memorandum issued by Shaw, and employees again started taking more time than was allotted to them. Most department heads had their departments split into two sections. One section was to go for their coffee, and the other section was to wait until the first section returned. The only trouble was that the second section was not waiting for the first section to return before they left. The result was mass confusion in the cafeteria. Groups did not come on the regular schedule, and when they did come, they stayed over fifteen minutes. Shaw conferred with all the department heads and told them that if the practice of long coffee breaks continued in the future, there was a strong possibility of not having any coffee breaks at all.

One department head realized the seriousness of the problem and issued a memorandum to all his employees explaining why time limits must be observed by everyone. Gorman liked the memorandum and had Shaw send copies to all supervisors.

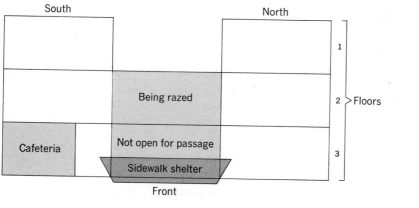

FIGURE 3

United Mutual building during remodeling.

Early last year United Mutual's management decided that an opinion survey might help solve some of the personnel problems encountered by the company. In this survey approximately sixty employees complained about the coffee period. Many of them didn't drink coffee and wanted to know why coffee was free while the rest of the liquid refreshments were not. There were some complaints about not having an afternoon coffee break in addition to the morning break. Shaw conferred with the vice-president, Gorman, and they decided to offer free tea and cocoa as well as free coffee to employees, but the practice of only one coffee break each day would be continued. Shaw informed all department heads that the coffee break was still only fifteen minutes and in the morning only, but that cocoa and tea were free to employees beginning June 1. He also mentioned that this free coffee, tea, and cocoa would cost United Mutual $400 a month, and in order for this coffee break to be continued, employees would have to restrict their coffee break to the time mentioned in the memorandum, which was fifteen minutes.

In October of last year the building was finished and employees could walk through the building again to get to the cafeteria. A new middle section had been added to the building, and considerably more space existed for all employees.

The coffee break in the morning continued, and employees seemed to like the free coffee, tea, and cocoa. In fact, they liked it so much that most of them started taking second cups and overstaying their allotted fifteen minutes. In an effort to remind employees that the coffee break was still only fifteen minutes, Shaw had table napkins printed showing a friendly clock tapping two employees on their shoulders and reminding them, "Coffee break is fifteen minutes."

The napkins were removed from the tables once or twice a week so that employees would not get a "routine feeling" about the napkins and would know that they were there for a purpose. The napkins served a very useful purpose as many of the employees did limit their coffee break to fifteen minutes, but there still were several (mostly supervisory employees) who continued to disregard the time limit on the coffee period.

Recently the case interviewer began a study of the coffee problem at United Mutual. On his first random visit to the coffee period he made the following observations:

1. Although the coffee break wasn't scheduled to start until 9:30, approximately thirty-five persons were in the cafeteria prior to that time.

2. At 9:35 A.M. there were approximately two hundred employees in the cafeteria when there should have been only seventy-five to one hundred. This resulted in much congestion, and when the 9:45 group came to coffee, there weren't enough clean cups due to the overflow at 9:30.

3. At 9:45 when the first group of employees was supposed to have left the cafeteria, approximately 25 percent still remained.

4. On the basis of spot checks it appeared that about 90 percent of the clerical employees obeyed the fifteen-minute coffee-break rule and the other 10 percent were just a few minutes over the limit. Spot checks of several supervisors showed that they spent anywhere from fifteen minutes to over an hour in the cafeteria. Typi-

cal examples are one supervisor who stayed in the cafeteria for twenty-two minutes and another who stayed approximately thirty minutes. One supervisor spent an hour and ten minutes in the cafeteria.

5.   A check of two departments revealed that in each the second section left for coffee break before the first section returned.

Shaw feels that a problem still exists at United Mutual concerning the coffee period. The current action that Shaw is taking is to revise the coffee-break schedule in order to prevent congestion and achieve better control. Neither Gorman nor Shaw is sure what else should be done, if anything.

STUDY GUIDES
1.   Appraise management's handling of the problems that developed in this case. What behavioral ideas were overlooked or misapplied?
2.   At the end of the case what are the key problems, if any? What are the alternatives to choose from? What would you do in the role of Gorman? What would you do if you were Shaw? What organizational behavior ideas would you apply?
3.   Would any of the following be useful in interpreting this case?
     a.   Behavior modification theory
     b.   Models of organizational behavior
     c.   Maslow's need hierarchy
     d.   The law of diminishing returns
     e.   Herzberg's motivational-maintenance theory
     f.   Organizational climate

ROLE-PLAYING SITUATIONS
1.   In the role of Shaw, arrange to discuss this case with Gorman.
2.   In the role of Gorman, call in Shaw to instruct him to improve the coffee-break situation.

The Palmer export site is a large port for shipping iron ore mined by the Flick Company, a major international mining company. Ore is brought to the site by rail from mines some 150 miles distant. Irvin Corporation which holds a construction and maintenance contract at the site, operates worldwide in the construction of heavy, technical, engineering projects. The Palmer site is in an extremely isolated desert area over 700 miles from the nearest city of as many as 50,000 people.

Information in this case is presented only concerning the relationship of Irvin management with Flick management at the Palmer site. Two consultants who studied the situation described it as follows.

COMMENTS OF CONSULTANTS

Our comments concerning the investigation must be viewed against the background of the physical and social conditions in which work is conducted at Palmer. Above all, Palmer exists solely as a port for the export of iron ore. There are no other reasons for the town to be located there. Palmer is a company town, and all the facilities, and to a large extent the way of life, are dependent on Flick. Similarly, it is quite evident that Irvin's situation in Palmer is dominated by its contractor-client relationship with Flick. Much of what we saw happening is a direct result of this relationship.

In contrast to its usual operation, Irvin in Palmer is performing a service function mainly consisting of maintaining, servicing, and altering a wide range of activities for Flick. The work varies from substantial modifications of port and plant facilities all the way to gardening.

This type of work is not typical for Irvin, which normally has been engaged in major construction. On a major project a job has a beginning, middle, and end. In comparison, while Irvin's contract with Flick obviously had a beginning, it has no clearly discernible end. The difference between these two types of work should be expressed in more than time, because it is evident that the lack of a clearly defined terminal objective has important psychological effects on Irvin managers.

The nature of Irvin's task evidently runs counter to the construction way of life. Employees building a major facility from start to finish are able to recognize clearly what they have accomplished, the specific contributions which different

---

[1] This case is adapted with permission from comments prepared by T. A. Williams and G. G. Watkins.

work roles have made to the outcome, and the relationships between these contributions. They claim that there is a sense of challenge associated with working to a quoted price on the job, and a sense of satisfaction in seeing something built and operating. The lack of this attitude was clearly evident from our interviews with Irvin staff, during which they expressed dissatisfaction with the role they see themselves performing in Palmer.

It is apparent that Irvin people in Palmer are engaged in a rather different kind of business from that to which they have become accustomed. It is clear that the basic nature of the present contract compares unfavorably with the type of work that Irvin normally does. There are also certain drawbacks with respect to the way in which Flick uses Irvin in this contract.

The work is initiated for Irvin on a continuing basis by Flick. While this may appear to be a sensible arrangement as far as the client is concerned, it places Irvin in a position of having to constantly adapt to Flick initiatives. Flick's plans continually change in a large number of areas in which Irvin is engaged, and this makes the problem of adaptation more difficult. Irvin's difficulties are further compounded by the tendency for Flick requirements and changes to be initiated for Irvin at all levels of the respective organizational structures. Together, these factors place Irvin's staff in a relationship of second-class citizens with respect to the Flick staff. This has consequences for both the work roles and the social status of the Irvin people.

First, it is a classic example of the frustrations which are generated when one party to the work relationship is continually initiating activity on the other party. The most common example of this problem is the traditional relationship between production and maintenance in industrial organizations. Initially in such a relationship, it seems normal for the parties to cooperate with each other as much as possible. However, as problems arise the relationships often go sour, with production (in this case the client Flick) using its authority to make increasing demands on maintenance (Irvin). Such action even extends to overt intimidation. In turn, the recipient of this initiation may attempt to protect itself by using the fact that the initiator depends on it for task performance. In other words, Flick staff may be using the client relationship to give vent to their own feelings of aggressiveness toward Irvin people. The latter might well respond by withholding effective task performance, or by carrying out their tasks less than enthusiastically.

It would appear that Irvin and Flick are laboring under confusions and contradictions concerning the nature of company objectives. Irvin's formal task seems to be one of ensuring the continued efficient operation of Flick's facilities and adaptation of these facilities to meet changing needs. One might have supposed that Flick's final task is to export iron ore with a degree of efficiency which approaches maximization of export volume given a reasonable rate of return. To some extent we gained the impression that Flick was concerned with this objective. However, there were signs that the "real" objectives of Flick management, as implied by their actions, are the product of psychological pressures caused by the sight of empty ships sitting in the harbor.

During the period we were in Palmer, Flick was loading at a rate of approximately 2,000 tons per hour. The maximum possible rate is 6,000 tons per hour. Over a period of time, it might be more efficient to stop the conveyor for necessary repairs and modifications to be carried out in order to continue at a more efficient rate. However, Irvin managers cited numerous examples of being unable to get in to carry out work because of Flick's insistence on keeping the conveyor belts running.

In the particular case of the Flick-Irvin relationship in Palmer, the above problems may have been compounded by the circumstances under which Irvin went into Palmer as a contractor. It appears that initially Flick staff resented the contract. Before the signing of this contract, the work which Irvin now performs was contracted to a number of firms on the basis of bids. This procedure enabled Flick staff to obtain certain free services from the contractors who were competing, such as boat repairs and garden maintenance. The nature of the Flick-Irvin contract requires Irvin to charge Flick on a cost-plus basis. This means that Irvin must submit detailed accounts justifying its expenditures. Hence, there is little, if any, scope for Flick staff to improve their private well-being through the manipulation of contractual relationships.

Second, the situation illustrates the difficulty of trying to carry out rationally planned work when Irvin has little control over both the circumstances which create the need for work and the resources needed to carry out that work. Weekly work schedules are drawn up every Thursday afternoon at a meeting attended by both Flick and Irvin management. While we were in Palmer there were some 171 open work orders on Irvin. The official purpose of the weekly planning meeting is to assign priorities among the work orders. By the Monday of our visit, the priorities laid down the previous Thursday had been substantially changed by Flick. Presumably the involvement of Irvin managers in the meeting is intended as a means of enabling them to participate in the planning of work for which they are responsible. However, it is clear that after the meeting the power to veto any decisions reached rests with Flick, and that this right is frequently and constantly exercised.

To this extent, Irvin managers would appear to have little real control over the events with which they are required to cope. Moreover, their lack of control over the work situation extends to the utilization of the resources for performing work. While Irvin has some equipment on site, it is required to use Flick equipment when it is "available." However, frequently the equipment is not available. First, the equipment may be required for use by Flick. Second, Flick may not actually be using the equipment but may wish to hold it in reserve in order to gain flexibility in its own operations. Either way this reduces the flexibility which Irvin requires in order to cope with a rapidly changing work situation. Two outstanding examples of this are related to the paint shop and the fitting of a down pipe. Irvin is now involved in painting ore cars and is not allowed to use a paint shop specially built to repaint rolling stock. The shop is at present unused. With regard to the down pipe, a job that would have taken a day with a crane was still unfinished after several weeks.

Irvin's situation in Palmer is curiously paradoxical. Its people are subject to Flick's planning. To the extent that Flick plans its work inefficiently, Irvin's profitability is increased due to the cost-plus basis of the contract. However, Irwin may be suffering a less obvious cost in this situation. Its management people are used to working with greater self-determination than they are allowed in Palmer where their work plans are subject to weekly Flick initiatives and daily Flick alterations. Over a period of time, this may lead to an erosion of the managerial capacity of Irvin people, whether this be expressed in resignations or loss of confidence and competence. The continued exposure of Irvin managers to the Palmer situation may result in the withering away of its most valuable asset, human resources.

STUDY GUIDES
1. Analyze the events in this case, using frameworks, ideas, and professional terms from this book, in order to determine what is happening at the Palmer site and why it is happening.
2. If you were a member of Flick top management and became aware of how the conditions in this case may be costing your firm money, what would you do? Explain why, using frameworks, ideas, professional terms from this book.
3. If you were Irvin top management and became aware of how the conditions in this case may be deteriorating your human resources, even though they may be giving higher earnings at the moment, what would you do, if anything? Explain why, using frameworks, ideas, and terms from this book.
4. Do any of the ideas you have expressed in any of the preceding three questions apply to typical management-worker relationships in your nation? Explain.

NAME INDEX

NAME INDEX

SUBJECT INDEX

SUBJECT INDEX

Multinational employment:
 political conditions, 357–358
 restrictions on productivity, 363–364
 social conditions, 355–357
 transcultural employees, 360–361
Multiple management, 151
Multiprofessional employee, 218
Mutual interest, 14

National Personnel Association, 8
National Science Foundation, 239
National Training Laboratories, 183
Natural work modules, 239
Natural work teams, 242
Needs, 39–48
 changes in, 46–48
 higher-order, 44–48, 499
 labor union response to, 307
 in less-advanced cultures, 365
 primary, 40
 priority of, 42–48
 secondary, 40–42
Negative leadership, 112–113
Nominal grouping, 404
Nondirective counseling, 423–427
Non-Linear Systems, 246
Nonstoppage strike, 308
Nontraditional employment, 319
Nonverbal communication, 382–383
Norms, 275

Occupations:
 and job satisfaction, 77
 prestige of, 32
 and technology, 216–217
Ombudsman, 258
Open-door policy, 402–403
Operant conditioning, 63
Organic organizations, 209–211
 and communication, 396
Organization theory, 195–211
Organizational behavior:
 definition, 5
 diminishing returns, 506–507
 formulas, 501–502
 growth of, 8–12
 key elements, 4–5
 limitations, 504–508

Organizational behavior:
 manipulation of people, 508
 models of, 95–101, 342–343, 497–501
Organizational behavior modification
 (O. B. Mod.), 63–67, 477
Organizational behavior system, 93–95
Organizational climate, 89–93
 and human resource accounting,
  503–504
 measurement, 92–93
Organizational design, 195–211
Organizational development, 177–188
 characteristics, 178–180
 limitations, 188
 origins, 178
 process, 180–181
Organizational pluralism, 343–344
Organizational structure, 195–211
 operating and ultimate responsibility,
  200–201
 span of management, 204–207
 tall and flat organizations, 205–207
 unity of command, 201
Organizations and individuals, 251–265

Participation, 139–153
 area of job freedom, 143–144
 consultive management, 144, 148–149
 definition, 140
 democratic management, 144, 149
 early studies, 145–146
 ego-involved versus task-involved, 140
 labor union role, 151
 limitations, 152
 in meetings, 442–443
 multiple management, 151
 prerequisites, 143–144
 production committees, 149–150
 social delegation, 142
 suggestion programs, 150
Participative leadership, 115
Path-goal theory of leadership, 111–112
Pay (see Economic rewards)
Perception, 29, 49–50, 399
Perceptual set, 49–50
Performance appraisal, 466–472, 489
Peruvian workers, 117, 132
Philosophy in organizational behavior,
 12–16
Pluralism, 314, 343–344

578